ROYAL HORTICULTURAL SOCIETY

GARDEN PLANTS AND FLOWERS IN AUSTRALIA

ROYAL HORTICULTURAL SOCIETY

GARDEN PLANTS AND FLOWERS IN AUSTRALIA

IAN SPENCE

AUSTRALIAN CONSULTANT
KEVIN WALSH

A DORLING KINDERSLEY BOOK

LONDON, NEW YORK,
MUNICH, MELBOURNE, DELHI

Senior Editor Annelise Evans
Senior Art Editor Alison Donovan
Project Art Editor Murdo Culver
Designers Gillian Andrews, Vanessa Hamilton, Rachael Smith
Editor Letitia Luff
Additional Editors Louise Abbott, Pamela Brown, Candida Frith-Macdonald
Managing Editor Anna Kruger
Managing Art Editor Lee Griffiths
DTP Designer Louise Waller
Media Resources Lucy Claxton, Richard Dabb
Picture Research Samantha Nunn
Production Controller Mandy Inness

Australian Consultant Kevin Walsh
Australian Managing Editor Rosie Adams
Australian Editorial Assistant Kate McLeod

DK India Pankaj Sharma, Sunil Sharma

This edition first published in Australia in 2004 by
Dorling Kindersley Pty Ltd
250 Camberwell Road, Camberwell, Victoria 3124
A Division of Pearson Australia Group Pty Ltd.

National Library of Australia Cataloguing-in-Publication data:
Spence, Ian.
Royal Horticultural Society garden plants and flowers in Australia.
Includes index.
ISBN 1 74033 399 3.
1. Plants - Encyclopedias. 2. Flowers - Encyclopedias.
I. Royal Horticultural Society (Great Britain). II. Title.
635.903

Colour reproduction by Colourscan, Singapore
Printed and bound by Mohndruck GmbH, Germany

Contents

Key to symbols used in the text

♕	RHS Award of Garden Merit
↕	Height of mature plant
↔	Spread of mature plant
✲✲✲	Fully frost-hardy: plant can withstand temperatures down to -15°C (5°F)
✲✲	Frost-hardy: plant can withstand temperatures down to -5°C (23°F)
✲	Frost-tender: plant can withstand temperatures down to 0°C (32°F)
❀	Very frost-tender: plant may be damaged by temperatures below 5°C (41°F)

introduction

Gardening has never been more popular than it is today. It has become a huge industry, supplying everything from garden ornaments and gadgets to hard landscaping materials, with a proliferation of expert advice in the media on all aspects of gardening from design to topiary.

In the midst of this, we sometimes forget that the real stars of the show are the plants. There is an astonishing diversity and a huge number of garden plants available to the gardener, from tiny alpines to large trees. Plant breeders also introduce more and more new cultivated varieties, or cultivars, each year. Some of these new plants go just as quickly out of fashion, but others go on to become firm favourites. It can therefore seem daunting and confusing, especially to those new to gardening, to have to select from this vast array of plants and mass of information. This is where I hope this book will help.

RHS Garden Plants and Flowers includes a selection of plants that have proved to be reliable performers in the garden. Most are robust, hardy, and not difficult to grow. Some may need a little tender loving care to see them through harsh conditions, but the results are well worth the effort. There are also a few more unusual plants.

To make your choice as easy as possible, every entry is illustrated so that you can judge the plant's appeal for yourself. The entries have been divided into several chapters, dealing with different types of plant, and within chapters, are arranged alphabetically by botanical name. This is because not all plants have a common name, and some common names are shared by more than one plant; where they exist, common names are listed too.

As well as basic information on each featured plant, there is practical advice on caring for plants as well as quick-reference lists of plants for different sites and uses in the garden. Once you start growing plants, like me, you may be hooked for life.

Happy gardening!

IAN SPENCE

A–Z of GARDEN PLANTS

In this plant catalogue, more than 2,500 plants are illustrated, and information given on many more, to enable you to create your own collection of star plants for the garden. To make it easier to choose, the catalogue is divided into chapters covering different groups of plants, from trees and shrubs to climbing plants, flowering plants, bamboos and grasses, and ferns. Within each chapter, plant entries are ordered alphabetically by their botanical names, so that you can quickly look up a particular plant. Familiar common names are included in each entry.

Trees and Shrubs

using trees and shrubs

Trees and shrubs are essential to the garden, providing a framework within which other, less permanent plants can be displayed. They also have a tremendous range of habits, shapes, flowers, and foliage. By wisely selecting different trees and shrubs, you can have flowers every month of the year as well as spectacular autumn colour. Even after the leaves drop, many trees and shrubs have distinctive bark that looks stunning throughout the winter. Evergreen trees and shrubs also provide that vital element – year-round privacy – and a constant foil to the changing highlights of other plants.

How to place trees and shrubs in the garden

Trees and shrubs, once planted, will be in your garden for a long time, and will form the main structure of the design, so choose them carefully and plant them before other types of plants such as bulbs and border perennials. Think about what role they are to play in the garden.

Many trees and shrubs are handsome enough to be grown on their own, as a focal point to draw the eye to a particular point in your garden or simply as a specimen to be admired in solitary splendour. Pick a tree or a shrub that will achieve a suitable size when mature: it must be large enough to impress, but not so huge that it will overshadow other plantings.

One of the best ways of using trees and shrubs is in mixed borders, when combined with more seasonal or showy plants. You can also use them to create microclimates within the border, for example birches (*Betula*) gives light, dappled shade ideal for woodland plants such as anemones.

Trees and shrubs can be grown as hedging, either as boundaries or to subdivide the garden. Hedges are much more pleasing than fencing and are invaluable for attracting wildlife, such as birds, which then help to control pests without you having to reach for the sprayer.

You can plant a living screen to hide unsightly views or objects like compost bins, and to provide privacy or shade. Trees and shrubs also make more effective windbreaks than solid barriers, because they diffuse wind without creating the turbulence found in the lee of a fence or wall. A delightful use of trees and shrubs is to frame a view of the surrounding landscape, creating a seamless transition from your garden to the countryside.

You can even grow dwarf trees and shrubs in containers, making it easier to enjoy them close up.

Variations on a theme This mixed border includes trees and shrubs and some perennials with a wide variety of forms, heights, and textures, yet the restrained palette of colours, in shades of green, white, and gold, pulls the planting together for a harmonious display.

Year-round interest

One of the great joys of gardening is watching trees and shrubs changing throughout the year. Many are very decorative in more than one season. Among the first signs of spring is the bursting of trees into blossom, and with a mix of plants, you can maintain a continuous display of flower from spring all through summer. Some trees and shrubs also produce fruits that add a splash of vivid colour and will entice birds into the garden.

Autumn is the time for foliage to impress with brilliant hues of gold, purple, and crimson. The new leaves of some trees and shrubs, including conifers, may also be tipped with colour in spring. In winter, some trees and shrubs reveal attractively textured and coloured bark or bright stems.

When choosing trees and shrubs, remember to consider these features and how they will complement other plantings through the seasons.

Spring blossom Ornamental cherries, like this Fuji Cherry (*Prunus incisa*), make lovely specimen trees.

Summer fruits Viburnums produce masses of berries – in blue, black, or scarlet (here 'Compactum').

Autumn leaves Some deciduous trees, such as this Vine Maple (*Acer circinatum*) glow with colour at leaf fall.

Winter bark The spectacular bark of trees like this Birch, *Betula papifera*, is best appreciated in winter.

Growth habits of trees and shrubs

Before selecting trees or shrubs for your garden, consider their ultimate shapes. There are many habits and forms available, such as prostrate, conical, pyramidal, and globular, as well as those shown (*see right*). The type you choose will depend on the amount of space in, and the style of, your garden. A columnar tree, for example, would be a better choice for a limited space than a tree with a broad, spreading canopy. Be aware also of the eventual height of the mature tree or shrub. A very large specimen tree could cast shade over most or all of the garden.

The growth habit of a tree or shrub also contributes to the style of your garden. Columnar trees, such as the Italian Cypress (*Cupressus*), commonly evoke a formal atmosphere, while weeping trees, for example willows (*Salix*), look especially graceful when stirred by a breeze. Shrubs such as cotoneaster can be grown as a free-standing plant or trained up against a wall. The shape and size of a tree can be modified by pruning (*see below*).

Columnar tree This type of tree has a narrow, upright shape, with thin, upward branches from top to bottom. The main stem often forks into two or three higher up.

Standard tree These trees have a single clear trunk, or stem, and a rounded canopy, or head, of branches.

Mounding shrub These shrubs form a dense, rounded outline.

Weeping tree The branches of this type of tree cascade outwards to form a mushroom shape or fall straight down towards the ground.

Multi-stemmed shrub These shrubs possess many dense and twiggy, upright, or arching stems.

What is the difference between trees and shrubs and other perennials?

Trees and shrubs are all woody, perennial plants, and are much longer-lived than herbaceous perennials. Trees generally have one main stem or trunk with a head of branches above. A shrub has many branches arising near the base of the plant and lacks a central trunk. Some trees do however have a shrubby habit, naturally growing with more than one stem.

It is generally easy to distinguish a woody plant from an herbaceous one. Trees and many shrubs have rigid stems with a protective outer layer of bark, which is quite distinct from the soft, green stems of herbaceous perennials (*see pp.160–161*). In some shrubs, called subshrubs, the stems may be more flexible and similar in appearance to herbaceous shoots – except for the stem bases, which in subshrubs are distinctly woody.

Woody stems heal over, or callus, when cut so most trees and shrubs can be pruned (*see pp.382–384*). This can be done to keep the plant healthy, to train it into a different shape (*see right*), or to keep it to the desired size.

The power of pruning
If left to its own devices, this form of the Monterey Cypress, *Cupressus macrocarpa* 'Goldcrest', becomes a stately columnar tree of up to 5m (15ft) in height (*see left*). With regular pruning, however, it can assume a quite different character, such as a picturesque piece of topiary (*see right*), but this does require frequent clipping to keep a neat shape.

You could also try less radical degrees of pruning trees and shrubs, for example removing the lower branches of a shrub to make a clear trunk, or shaping several into a screen or hedge.

Abelia

THESE DECIDUOUS AND EVERGREEN shrubs are grown for their profuse clusters of white, pink, or cerise flowers and glossy, rounded foliage. The flowers are borne on slender, arching stems during summer and autumn, and in some species, such as *Abelia chinensis* and *A. schumannii*, they are scented. The sizes of different cultivars can vary dramatically, from 1.5m (5ft) to 5m (15ft) in height, and between 2m (6ft) and 4m (12ft) in width. Abelias are generally trouble-free and ideal for sunny border sites. If you have room, they make attractive planting partners for escallonia (*see p.54*) and berberis (*see p.27*). In areas prone to frost, plant less hardy species against a warm, north- or west-facing wall.

Hardiness Frost-hardy ❄❄ to frost-tender ❄.

Cultivation Grow in any fertile, well-drained soil in full sun and shelter from hot, drying winds. **Prune** deciduous species in late winter or early spring, removing misplaced or crossing shoots to maintain a good shape. For evergreen species, lightly trim back after flowering any flowered shoots that would spoil the symmetry. **Take** softwood cuttings in early summer, or semi-ripe cuttings in late summer (*see p.394*).

Abelia × grandiflora ♀

↕3m (10ft) ↔ 4m (12ft), semi-evergreen, fragrant flowers in midsummer to autumn ❄❄

Abelia schumannii ♀

↕2m (6ft) ↔ 3m (10ft), deciduous, lightly scented flowers in late summer to autumn ❄❄

Abelia floribunda ♀

↕3m (10ft) ↔ 4m (12ft), evergreen, flowers early summer, may spread further when grown against a wall ❄

Abeliophyllum distichum

White Forsythia

↕↔ 1.5m (5ft)

CLUSTERS OF FLOWERS borne on the bare wood of this deciduous shrub open from late winter to perfume the garden with a delicate scent. Matt green leaves follow, and turn purple before falling in autumn. This open, spreading shrub is related to the Forsythia (*see p.58*) and just as versatile. You can grow it as a freestanding shrub in a sunny garden, but train it against a sheltered, north- or west-facing wall and it will reward you by bursting into flower earlier and more profusely. It makes a fine companion for other early-flowering shrubs such as mahonias (*see p.87*), forsythias, and viburnums (*see pp.126–127*).

Hardiness Fully frost-hardy ❄❄❄, provided that the wood was well ripened by a good summer. Early flowers may be damaged by frosts.

Cultivation Grow in fertile, well-drained soil in full sun. **Prune** after flowering; if freestanding, cut back flowered shoots to strong buds or shoots close to the base. If wall-trained, cut back all flowered shoots to within 2–4 buds of a permanent framework. **Take** semi-ripe cuttings, or layer low-growing shoots, in summer (*see pp.394–395*).

Abeliophyllum distichum

Taller if grown against a wall, white flowers sometimes tinged with pink

Abies

Firs

LONG, SWEEPING BRANCHES are a typical feature of these stately, evergreen conifers. They make excellent specimen trees, and can also be used to provide shelter from wind or as a screen. The needles usually range in colour from mid-green to bluish-green, with silvery undersides. In late spring and early summer, some plants produce decorative cones; erect, purplish-blue ones on the upper branches will be female, while the pendent cones lower down are male, usually green maturing to brown or purplish-blue. For small gardens there are several small and even dwarf firs, such as *Abies balsamea* 'Nana' which grows to just 1m (3ft), ideal for a rock garden. For the largest spaces, *A. grandis* attains a majestic stature of up to 45m (150ft).

Hardiness Fully frost-hardy ***, but frost may damage young foliage.
Cultivation Grow in any fertile, moist but well-drained, neutral to slightly acid soil in sun. Tolerate a little shade. Like most conifers, needs no pruning. **Sow** seed (*see pp.391–392*) in containers when ripe or in winter; expose seed to cold for three weeks before sowing.

***Abies lasiocarpa* 'Arizonica Compacta'** 🏆
↕3–5m (10–15ft) ↔ 2–3m (6–10ft), small, slow-growing type of corkbark fir, with a neat conical shape

Abies procera 🏆 (Noble Fir)
↕25–45m (80–150ft) ↔ 6–9m (20–28ft), silvery grey bark, bears large green or brown, 15–25cm (6–10in) long female cones

Abies koreana (Korean Fir)
↕10m (30ft) ↔ 6m (20ft), produces decorative female cones that are 5–8cm (2–3in) long, from a young age

***Abies nordmanniana* 'Golden Spreader'** 🏆
↕1m (3ft) ↔ 1.5m (5ft), slow-growing, shrubby dwarf conifer with spreading branches and greenish-brown cones

Abutilon

Chinese Lantern

A LONG FLOWERING SEASON, often continuously from spring until autumn, is a key attraction of these rather spindly-stemmed shrubs, most of which benefit from some support. They flower in shades of red, orange, pink, and white; some even have bicoloured blooms. There are also several that have variegated leaves. Tender and half-hardy types can be planted out with summer annuals, staked with canes if necessary; hardier species can be trained against a sunny, sheltered wall, or in warmer areas are excellent for adding height to a garden.

Hardiness Frost-hardy ✲✲ to very frost-tender ❀.

Cultivation Grow in any fertile, well-drained soil or loam-based compost in a container. Position in full sun; in frost-prone areas grow abutilons in pots in sheltered sites. Bring plants under frost-free cover during winter. **Prune** in late winter or early spring;, cut back flowered shoots to a permanent framework of main stems (*see p.383*), and remove misplaced or crossing shoots. **Sow** seed (*see pp.391–392*) in heat in spring; take softwood cuttings in spring, or semi-ripe cuttings in summer (*see p.394*). If whiteflies or red spider mite infest plants under cover, biological controls may be effective (*see p.397*).

Abutilon vitifolium* var. *album
↕5m (15ft) ↔ 2.5m (8ft), fast-growing, deciduous shrub, sometimes tree-like, flowering in early summer ✲✲

Abutilon megapotamicum ♀ (Trailing Abutilon)
↕↔ 2m (6ft), semi-evergreen or evergreen, ideal against a wall; flowers borne from summer to autumn ✲✲

***Abutilon* 'Boule de Neige'**
↕to 4m (12ft) ↔ to 3m (10ft), vigorous evergreen, erect to spreading habit, flowers from spring to autumn ✲

WHITEFLY ON LEAVES can be a problem, but are relatively easy to control.

***Abutilon vitifolium* 'Veronica Tennant'** ♀
↕5m (15ft) ↔ 2.5m (8ft), fast-growing, deciduous, upright – sometimes tree-like shrub, flowers in early summer ✲✲

ACACIA
Wattle

↕to 30m (100ft)
↔to 10m (30ft)

CLUSTERS OF TINY, often sweetly fragrant, bright yellow flowers clothe these evergreen trees and shrubs, mostly in winter or spring. Most species are very fast-growing, and are useful where a quick screen is required. In frost-prone climates, choose the hardier species. Grow them with other winter-flowering evergreens, such as mahonias (*see p.87*) and viburnums (*see pp.126–127*), for an uplifting winter display.

Hardiness Fully frost-hardy ❄❄❄ to very frost-tender ❀.

Cultivation Grow in reasonably fertile, neutral to acid (lime-free) soil. **Position** in full sun. **Prune** after flowering, removing any crossing or misshapen branches to maintain a good framework, and lightly trimming shoots that spoil the shape of the tree. **Sow** seed (*see pp.391–393*) at 18°C (64°F) in spring after soaking in warm water until the seeds are swollen. **Take** semi-ripe cuttings (*see p.394*) in summer. Trees are generally trouble-free.

Acacia fimbriata (Fringed Wattle)
↕6m (18ft) ↔ 4m (12ft), bushy small tree flowering in late winter and well into spring ❄❄

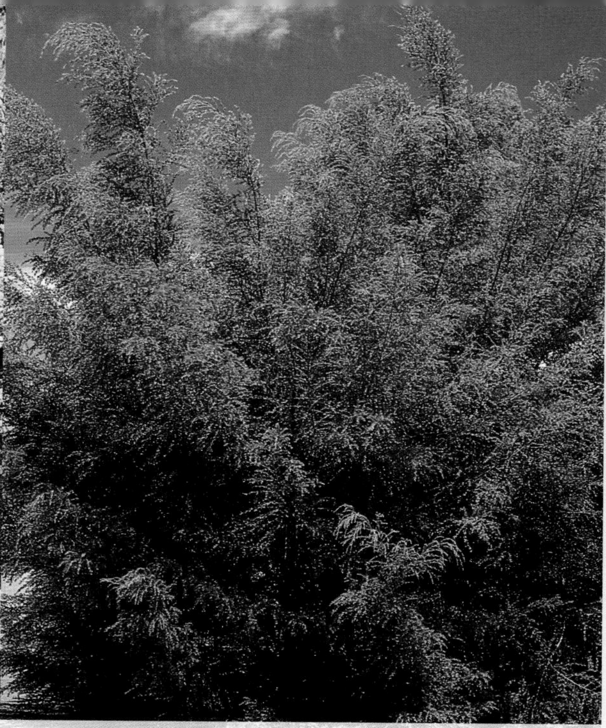

Acacia howittii (Sticky Wattle)
↕6m (18ft) ↔ 3m (9ft), very quick growing shrub with spring flowers ❄❄

Acacia baileyana 🏆 (Cootamundra Wattle)
↕5–8m (15–25ft) ↔ 3–6m (10–20ft), small tree or large shrub, evergeen, abundant flowers from winter to spring ❄❄

Acacia pravissima (Ovens Wattle)
↕6m (18ft) ↔ 3m (9ft), dense spring flowering shrub, often with an arching or pendulous habit ❄❄

Acacia pycnantha
↕5–10m (15–30ft) ↔ 2–5m (6–15ft), Australia's floral emblem has showy flowers in late winter and spring ❄❄

ACER

Maple

MAPLES ARE PRIZED FOR THEIR DELICATE FOLIAGE, which is particularly fine and fern-like in some cultivars of Japanese Maple (*Acer palmatum*). There is enough variety in the group to provide interest at any time of the year. Some have brightly coloured leaves in spring, others have variegated grey-green, white, or pink foliage, and many give a brilliant display of intense reds, yellows, and oranges in autumn. Nearly all maples are deciduous. Several also have handsome bark, which helps to enliven the winter months; on *Acer griseum* it peels attractively, while on *A. davidii* it is striped and streaked in green and white. The inconspicuous spring flowers are followed by winged fruits. Maples include both trees and shrubs, with a type to suit most gardens. The largest trees make striking specimens if you have the space, while smaller trees and those of shrubby habit can be grown in gardens of any size. Many cultivars are excellent grown in containers; the restricted root space will keep them compact, and less hardy varieties can also be moved to a sheltered position close to the house during the coldest months.

Hardiness Most fully frost-hardy ❄❄❄, some frost-hardy ❄❄.

Cultivation Maples prefer well-cultivated soil in sun or partial shade. **Plant** container-grown trees at any time of the year, but bare-root trees only when dormant, from late autumn to late winter. Water trees well before and after planting, and continue watering regularly. **Shelter** those with delicate foliage from hot winds and late frosts that can scorch the young leaves. **Stake** taller maples and those grown in exposed gardens. **Prune** young plants to form the basic framework for the tree or shrub; after this maples need minimal pruning. Remove any badly placed and crossing shoots to maintain a well-balanced shape (*see p.382*), and cut out any dead or diseased wood from late autumn to midwinter, or in spring for plants in containers. **Sow** seed outside as soon as it is ripe (*see pp.391–392*) and take softwood cuttings of cultivars in early summer (*see p.394*).

Looking after maples in containers

Maples grown in containers require more care than those planted in open ground, because the roots cannot grow deep down in search of water and nutrients. A thick mulch (*see p.388 and below*) will help retain moisture, but you will still need to water regularly – probably daily during dry spells. Top-dress the container annually (*see below*) in early spring to remove weeds and algal growths in the surface layer and ensure that the plant has the nutrients it requires for the growing season. Every three to five years, repot your maple, either back into the same container with fresh potting mix, or into a slightly larger one. Remove the plant from its pot, then gently tease out the roots and cut back any large, coarse ones. Put the tree in the new container, then fill in with fresh potting mix so the root ball sits at the same level as before. Water in well and mulch.

❶ *Using a trowel or a small hand fork, scrape away the top 5cm (2in) of old potting mix and mulch, here bark chippings, and discard.*

❷ *Top up the container with fresh potting mix mixed with some slow-release fertilizer. Water well and top with a fresh mulch to suppress weeds.*

① *Acer cappadocicum* ↕20m (70ft) ↔ 15m (50ft) ② *circinatum* ↕5m (15ft) ↔ 6m (20ft)
③ *griseum* 🏆 ↕↔ 10m (30ft), attractive bark ④ *japonicum* 'Aconitifolium' 🏆 ↕5m (15ft) ↔ 6m (20ft)
⑤ *negundo* 'Flamingo' ↕15m (50ft) ↔ 10m (30ft) ⑥ *negundo* 'Variegatum' ↕15m (50ft) ↔ 10m (30ft)
⑦ *palmatum* f. *atropurpureum* ↕8m (25ft) ↔ 10m (30ft) ⑧ *palmatum* 'Bloodgood' 🏆 ↕↔ 5m (15ft)

⑨ *palmatum* 'Butterfly' ↕3m (10ft) ↔ 1.5m (5ft) ⑩ *palmatum* 'Corallinum' ↕1.2m (4ft) ↔ 1m (3ft) ⑪ *palmatum* Dissectum Atropurpureum Group ↕2m (6ft) ↔ 3m (10ft) ⑫ *palmatum* 'Linearilobum' ↕5m (15ft) ↔ 4m (12ft) ⑬ *palmatum* 'Red Pygmy' 🏆 ↕↔ 1.5m (5ft) ⑭ *palmatum* 'Sango-kaku' 🏆 ↕6m (20ft) ↔ 5m (15ft) ⑮ *platanoides* 'Crimson King' 🏆 ↕25m (80ft) ↔ 15m (50ft) ⑯ *pseudoplatanus* 'Brilliantissimum' 🏆 ↕6m (20ft) ↔ 8m (25ft) ⑰ *rubrum* 'October Glory' 🏆 ↕20m (70ft) ↔ 10m (30ft) ⑱ *saccharinum* ↕20m (70ft) ↔ 12m (40ft) ⑲ *shirasawanum* 'Aureum' 🏆 ↕↔ 6m (20ft)

Acmena

THESE EVERGREEN TREES ARE GROWN principally for their glossy evergreen foliage of small oval leaves. Generally tall trees, they have small white or creamy flowers in spring followed by showy edible white, red, purple, or pinkish berries in the late autumn and into winter. They naturally occur in moist places such as rainforests and creek sides. The common Lilly Pilly, *Acmena smithii*, is the one most often seen in gardens and is useful for tall screens and windbreaks, or even as a specimen in a lawn. Grow as a background to winter flowering plants such as wattles (*Acacia, see p.17*) and banksias (*Banksia, see p.27*).

Hardiness Frost-hardy ❄❄ to very frost-tender ❄.

Cultivation Grow in full sun or partial shade in any well-drained soil, provided it can be kept moist. **Prune** minimally; remove any shoots that spoil the shape of young trees to encourage a good form (*see pp.382–384*). Plants grown as a hedge should be clipped with shears in spring and again in summer. **Sow** seed as soon as it is ripe in a cold frame (*see p.391*). **Take** semi-hardwood cuttings, preferably with a heel, in summer (*see p.394*).

Acmena smithii
↕20m (65ft) ↔ 15m (50ft), glossy, dark green foliage offsets the showy, pink berries seen in autumn and winter ❄

Aeonium

PRIZED FOR THEIR EXOTIC FORMS, aeoniums bear tight rosettes of fleshy leaves in shades of light green to a striking black-purple. From spring to summer, they send up clusters of small starry flowers in pale to bright yellow, white, pink, or copper-red. With some species, the flowering stem dies back once the seed is set. Aeoniums look stunning in containers, especially grouped with other succulents, or with the dark leaves of cultivars such as 'Zwartkop' contrasted with silvery-blue or grey foliage. Grow them in pots on a patio or in a well-drained border in sun or partial shade. Some are tender, so will have to be brought into frost-free conditions for the winter.

Hardiness Very frost-tender ❄; they can withstand short periods of frost in dry conditions.

Cultivation Grow in fertile, very well-drained soil or gritty potting mix, in sun or partial shade. **Keep** the plants fairly dry during their dormant period in winter. **Sow** seed (*see pp.391–392*) in heat in spring. **Take** cuttings (*see p.394*) in early summer, waiting until the cut surface of the cuttings calluses, or heals over, before inserting them in gritty potting mix. Place them in good light and keep warm and on the dry side until rooted.

***Aeonium* 'Zwartkop'** 🏆
↕↔ to 1m (3ft), pyramid-shaped spikes of yellow flowers appear in late summer, superb architectural plant for summer display

Aesculus

Horse Chestnut

HORSE CHESTNUTS ARE HANDSOME trees with fingered leaves that turn golden yellow or glowing orange in autumn. In spring and early summer, they are covered in large spikes or "candles" of white or pink flowers. In autumn, their smooth- or prickly-coated, rounded fruits split to reveal shiny, brown seeds or conkers; they can cause stomach upsets if eaten. Because of their size – up to 25m (80ft) – most horse chestnuts can be grown only in large gardens. Their spreading branches and large leaves cast a deep shade.

Hardiness Most garden species are fully frost-hardy ❄❄❄.

Cultivation Grow in any fertile soil in sun or partial shade. **Prune** young trees to remove any misplaced or crossing shoots (*see p.382*) in late winter or early spring to maintain a healthy framework of branches and good symmetry. **Sow** seed (*see pp.391–393*) in a seedbed outdoors as soon as it is ripe.

Aesculus hippocastanum 🏆
↕25m (80ft) ↔ 20m (70ft), vigorous tree with a rounded, spreading shape, bears the familiar, spiky-shelled conker

AGATHIS
Kauri Pine

THESE VERY LARGE EVERGREEN TREES are found naturally growing in rainforests. They have broad crowns of dense, leathery, linear to lance-shaped, dark green leaves. The trunk is often clear of branches for many, many metres, showing off the bark, which is generally a feature of these trees. This is grey, brown, or pink and often has rounded flakes. Although first impressions may not suggest it, this tree is a conifer, bearing cones that are globular to slightly barrel-shaped. Too big for most gardens, the straight, coloured trunk makes it an interesting tree for specimen or avenue planting.

Hardiness Frost-hardy ✻✻ to very frost-tender ❁.

Cultivation Grow in full sun in any well-drained soil that is reasonably fertile. They do best in tropical areas, although *A. robusta* succeeds in temperate areas with light frosts only. **Prune** only to shape the tree when young and to establish one main central trunk (*see pp.382–384*). **Sow** seed in spring in a cold frame (*see p.391*).

Agathis robusta (Queensland Kauri)
↕ 50m (150ft) ↔ 20m (60ft), a famous timber tree, this is best suited for parks or very large gardens only ✻✻ (borderline)

AGAVE
Agave, Century Plant

NATIVE TO DESERTS AND MOUNTAINS, these bold, structural succulents have fleshy, spiked leaves up to 2m (6ft) long, in wide-spreading rosettes. In summer, mature plants may produce funnel-shaped flowers on leafless stems that soar up to 8m (25ft). With most species, the main rosette dies after flowering and fruiting, but leaves a number of offsets – smaller rosettes that develop around it – to mature in later years. These can be split off to make new plants. In frost-prone areas, grow agaves in containers that can be moved into frost-free conditions over winter. If frost is not a problem, grow them as specimen plants in gardens protected from excessive winter wet. The spiked leaves are very sharp, so avoid planting them close to seating and play areas.

Hardiness Frost-hardy ✻✻ to very frost-tender ❁.

Cultivation Grow in slightly acid, fertile, very well-drained soil or gritty potting mix in full sun. **Sow** seed (*see pp.391–392*) in heat in early spring. **Remove offsets** in autumn or spring. Insert unrooted offsets in pots containing free-draining potting mix. Rooted offsets can be treated like mature plants.

Agave americana 'Mediopicta' 🏆
↕ 2m (6ft) ↔ 3m (10ft), impressive specimen plant when mature, in warm regions flowers in summer on stems up to 8m (25ft) tall ❁

AGONIS

THESE ARE EVERGREEN TREES AND SHRUBS, usually much-branched and densely foliaged, although some species have a beautiful weeping habit. The leaves can be short or quite long, and are usually lance-shaped. They have small, white, five-petalled flowers in spring. These are grouped together along the stems of smaller branches or at the tips, and are followed by a cluster of woody seed capsules. The bark is often fissured on older specimens. Agonis are good in a mixed garden and also make worthwhile screens or windbreaks. Many will tolerate extreme coastal conditions and some will tolerate waterlogged soils. Stems of *Agonis parviceps* make long-lasting cut flowers.

Hardiness Frost-hardy ✻✻ to frost-tender ✻.

Cultivation Grow in most soils that are well drained, in full sun or partial shade. **Tip** prune after flowering those plants that have flowers at the ends of growing tips. Little other pruning is needed; remove any shoots that spoil the shape of young plants to encourage a good form (*see pp.382–384*). **Sow** seed from year-old capsules in a cold frame (*see p.391*). **Take** semi-hardwood cuttings in summer (*see p.394*).

Agonis flexuosa (Willow Myrtle)
↕ 12m (40ft) ↔ 10m (33ft), its graceful weeping habit belies its ability to withstand tough coastal conditions ✻

ALLOCASUARINA

She-oak

THESE EVERGREEN TREES ARE GENERALLY UPRIGHT to conical in outline and broaden out with age. The leaves are tiny and the green foliage visible is actually the slender branchlets. These feature regularly spaced nodes and are often grey-green, although some, particularly on *Allocasuarina torulosa*, can be bronze. Male flowers appear on the ends of the branchlets, while the female cones are on short stems on older wood. The cones are small, round, spherical, or slightly elongated, often with sharply pointed valves holding the seeds. The trees can make good specimens as well as being useful for windbreaks, especially in tough conditions.

Hardiness Frost-hardy ✲✲.

Cultivation Best grown in full sun on soil that is free-draining, although some species can withstand wet conditions. **Prune** minimally; remove any shoots that spoil the shape of young plants to encourage a good form (*see pp.382–384*). **Sow** seed collected from cones that are about one year old in a cold frame (*see p.391*).

Allocasuarina verticillata (Drooping She-oak)
↕8m (25ft) ↔ 8m (25ft), extremely tough weeping tree withstanding a range of harsh conditions ✲

ALNUS

Alder

↕to 25m (80ft)
↔to 10m (30ft)

FAST-GROWING AND TOLERANT of poor soils, alders are useful trees and shrubs. They are mostly deciduous, and broadly conical in shape, with toothed leaves, and delicate catkins that appear in late winter to spring. The catkins, usually yellow, are followed by green fruits that turn brown in autumn and look like tiny pine cones. Alders, especially those with ornamental foliage such as *Alnus rubra*, *A. glutinosa* and *A. incana,* make attractively light, slender specimen trees. They do not mind wet feet, so they are a sound choice for a damp site or by a creek or pond. As they are quick-growing, they make ideal screens or windbreaks.

Hardiness Fully frost-hardy ✲✲✲.

Cultivation Grow in fertile, moist, but well-drained soil in full sun; *A. cordata* and *A. incana* will tolerate dry soils. **Pruning** is rarely necessary; remove branches that cross or spoil the shape of the tree between the time of leaf-fall and midwinter to avoid sap bleeding. **Sow** seed (*see pp.391–392*) in a seedbed as soon as it is ripe. **Take** hardwood cuttings in winter (*see p.394*).

Alnus cordata 🏆
↕25m (80ft) ↔ 6m (20ft), originates from the Mediterranean and tolerates dry soil, catkins appear in late winter before the leaves

ALYOGYNE

THESE FAST-GROWING SHRUBS ARE GROWN for their showy, hibiscus-like flowers, which occur from spring through the summer. These are up to 20cm (4in) across and white to mauve in colour, although yellow flowered forms of *Alyogyne hakeifolia* are occasionally available. They are small to medium evergreen shrubs, with rough stems and branches, and an erect habit, tending to open up with age. Leaves are most often deeply lobed, coarse to the touch and dark green. Most are tough enough to withstand harsh growing conditions such as dry periods and indifferent soils, although they cannot take heavy frosts.

Hardiness Frost-hardy ✲✲ to frost-tender ✲.

Cultivation Grow in a sunny spot on a free-draining soil enriched with well-rotted organic matter. **Prune** to encourage a bushy form by constant tip pruning and occasional removal of older shoots altogether (*see pp.382–384*). **Sow** seed in a cold frame in spring and summer (*see p.391*). **Take** semi-hardwood cuttings in summer (*see p.394*).

Alyogyne huegelii (Blue Hibiscus)
↕2m (6ft) ↔ 1.5m (5ft), summer flowering over a long period ✲✲ (borderline)

Angophora

Apple Gum

THESE ARE MOSTLY TALL AND BROAD TREES, although some only reach the stature of tall shrubs. They are evergreen and look very much like many eucalypts in habit, flower, and foliage. The leaves are leathery, dark green and heart-shaped to lanceolate, with a distinctive mid-rib. The flowers are in large clusters at the growing tips and are petal-less, being made up of the stamens. Colours range from white to red, although cream is the most common colour. The bark is an attractive feature on some species, notably *Angophora costata*, which has smooth, red bark that peels, revealing pinkish-orange new bark underneath. Use as specimens or for windbreaks where there is plenty of space.

Hardiness Frost-hardy ❄❄ to frost-tender ❄.

Cultivation Grow in full sun in any well-drained soil. Full sun is best. **Prune** minimally; remove any shoots that spoil the shape of young trees to encourage a good form (*see pp.382–384*). **Sow** seed in a cold frame at any time of the year (*see pp.391–392*).

Angophora costata
↕30m (90ft) ↔ 15m (45ft), the bark is a feature as are the profuse summer flowers ❄

Araucaria

ONE OF THE MOST ANCIENT TREES, the Monkey Puzzle is so-called because its branches are clad in sharp, scale-like leaves that make them uncomfortable, if not impossible, to climb. Although hailing from the tropical rainforest, this araucaria *Araucaria araucania* is fully hardy, and has long been a garden favourite for its novelty value. Many, unfortunately, are planted in gardens that are far too small (especially since they are deceptively slow-growing when young), necessitating unsightly lopping that completely ruins their shape. They need plenty of room for their forms to develop – at first conical, then losing the lower branches to form a graceful, rounded head atop a tall, clear trunk. Male and female cones tend to be borne on different trees; female cones are more rounded than the male ones.

Hardiness Fully frost-hardy ❄❄❄ to frost-tender ❄.

Cultivation Grow in any fertile, well-drained soil in an open site. **Sow** seed (*see pp.391–392*) in a seedbed as soon as it is ripe. **Take** cuttings (*see p.394*), from vertical shoot tips only, in midsummer and root in a cold frame. Cuttings from horizontal branches will never make upright trees.

Araucaria heterophylla (Norfold Island Pine)
↕30m (90ft) ↔ 10m (30ft), stately symmetrical conifer that is often planted near the coast ❄

Arbutus

Strawberry Tree

ARBUTUS ARE BROAD, sometimes bushy trees with attractive, peeling, red-brown bark and dark, glossy leaves. Clusters of tiny white or pink flowers are produced from autumn to spring. These are followed by bright orange to red, strawberry-like fruits (hence the common name) which are edible, if rather tasteless. Although they can reach up to 15m (50ft), they are slow-growing and many will remain small shrubs for several years. Arbutus are excellent for a large shrub border or as specimens, where their handsome, coloured barks can be admired.

Hardiness Fully frost-hardy ❄❄❄ when mature (young trees not so) to frost-hardy ❄❄.

Cultivation Grow in fertile soil, enriched with plenty of bulky, well-rotted organic matter, in a sheltered site in full sun. Both *A.* × *andrachnoides* and *A. unedo* will tolerate alkaline (limy) soils; other species, such as *A. menziesii*, need acid soils. **Prune out** any misplaced shoots to maintain a good shape in winter or late spring when the tree is dormant, but keep pruning to a minimum. **Sow** seed (*see pp.391–392*) in containers as soon as it is ripe and place in a cold frame. **Take** semi-ripe (stem-tip) cuttings in summer (*see p.394*).

Arbutus unedo ♈ (Irish Strawberry Tree)
↕↔ 8m (25ft), fruits appear with pendent flowers in autumn, but take a year to ripen fully ❄❄❄

Archontophoenix

THESE TALL PALMS HAVE a single straight trunk that is grey and often marked with horizontal lines, which are scars where old leaves have been shed. The arching leaves occur at the top of stems and are up to 3m (9ft) long. The flowers appear in summer and are creamy-white, occurring in large bunches that hang just below the foliage. These are followed by bunches of round, red fruit, each one containing a single seed. These palms do best in warmer areas and add a tropical look and feel to a garden. Small plants are often grown in pots as glasshouse or conservatory plants.

Hardiness Very frost-tender ❀.

Cultivation Grow in any frost-free spot in well-drained soil that is reasonably fertile and preferably enriched with well-rotted organic matter. They do best in warmer climates and must be kept moist at all times. **Sow** seed as soon as it is ripe in a cold frame, but germination may take up to a year (*see p.391*).

Archonotophoenix alexandrae (Alexandra Palm)
↕20m (60ft) ↔ 12m (35ft), a palm suited to warmer areas

Argyranthemum

Marguerite Daisy

ARGYRANTHEMUMS ARE HARD-WORKING shrubs that produce a succession of cheery, daisy blooms from early summer through to autumn. There are single- and double-flowered types, in hues of white, soft yellow to apricot, and pale pink to deep cerise. Formerly classed as chrysanthemums, they have similar foliage: almost fern-like, and either green or greyish-green. They are invaluable in pots or in mixed gardens, where they inject a light and breezy feel. Some make elegant specimens or are trained as standards (in a "lollipop" shape with a single, bare stem and a bushy head).

Hardiness Frost-hardy ❄❄ (in mild areas) to very frost-tender ❀.

Cultivation Grow in well-drained fertile soil in full sun. Most species will tolerate salt-laden winds in coastal areas. **Pinch** out the growing tips of young plants to encourage a bushy habit. **Prune** back the flowered shoots to within 2.5cm (1in) of their base after flowering or in early spring. **Take** softwood cuttings in spring or semi-ripe cuttings in summer (*see p.394*).

Argyranthemum frutescens (Daisy Bush, Marguerite Daisy)
↕1m (3ft) ↔ 1m (3ft), quick growing and long flowering in spring and summer

Argyranthemum frutescens **'Summer Angel'**
↕1m (3ft) ↔ 1m (3ft), flowers are up to 8cm (3in) across

Argyranthemum frutescens **'Summer Pink'**
↕1m (3ft) ↔ 1m (3ft), showy pink flowers in summer

Artemisia

Wormwood

↕5cm–1.5m (2in–5ft)
↔15cm–1.5m (6in–5ft)

Artemisias have ferny, aromatic, grey or silver foliage that gives year-round interest and acts as a foil for flowering plants or those with bolder leaves. There are evergreen and deciduous types, all bearing tiny, unimpressive flowers – the leaves are the chief draw. Artemisias look good in herb gardens (French tarragon is a form of *Artemisia dracunculus*), rock gardens, and shrub or flower borders. They are often featured in drought-tolerant, Mediterranean-style gardens, although a few, notably *A. lactiflora*, need moist soil.

Hardiness Fully frost-hardy ❄❄❄ to frost-hardy ❄❄.

Cultivation Grow in fertile, well-drained soil in a sunny position. *A. arborescens* needs a little protection in frost-prone areas. In heavy clay soil, dig in plenty of gypsum and organic matter to improve drainage; plants can be short-lived in wet conditions. **Prune** plants that have grown over-large and leggy to the ground, in autumn or spring, to encourage a compact habit. **Sow** seed (*see pp.391–392*) in containers in a cold frame in autumn or spring. **Take** heel cuttings in early summer (*see p.394*).

① ***Artemisia abrotanum*** 🏆 ↕↔ 1m (3ft), semi-evergreen, flowers in late summer ❄❄❄ ② ***Artemisia arborescens*** ↕1m (3ft) ↔ 1.5m (5ft), evergreen with silky leaves ❄❄❄

Aucuba

Aucubas are useful, evergreen shrubs grown for their bold, glossy foliage and large fruits. They hardly ever suffer from pests and diseases, and tolerate all sorts of difficult growing conditions, including full shade, dry soils, pollution, and salt-laden winds. This makes them a popular choice for town gardens. Aucubas can be used in mixed and shrub gardens, or as informal hedging (if trimmed, they do not fruit as well). The variegated and spotted cultivars (such as 'Sulphurea Marginata' and 'Crotonifolia') make a bright splash in dark corners where little will grow.

Hardiness Fully frost-hardy ❄❄❄.

Cultivation Grow in any fertile soil except waterlogged conditions, in full sun or full shade; variegated species prefer partial shade. In areas with hot summers, grow in full shade. Use soil-based potting mix if growing in a container. Feed plants in pots once a month with a liquid fertilizer, and water freely when in full growth, but sparingly in winter. **Trim** aucubas in spring to shape and cut back hard if they are growing too large. Prune wayward shoots by cutting them well back into the centre of the bush. **Sow** seed (*see pp.391–392*) in containers in autumn. **Take** semi-ripe cuttings (*see p.394*) in summer.

Aucuba japonica
↕↔ 3m (10ft), female plants will produce bright red berries (*see inset*) if a male is grown nearby

Austromyrtus

These evergreen shrubs and trees are related, as the name implies, to the *Myrtus* genus. Naturally occurring in moist environments, they have glossy, generally dark green leaves, sometimes paler on the undersides. Some have bright pink new growth and silver hairs on the leaves. Spreading and densely foliaged, they make worthwhile screeners. The spring and summer flowers are small and white but generally very numerous. The fruit is a small, round berry that is white, mauve, or black. Some of the paler-coloured ones can feature black dots on the surface. The fruit of *Austromyrtus dulcis* is edible and sweet. The smooth, green bark with orange splotches of some species is also a feature.

Hardiness Frost-hardy ❄❄ to very frost-tender ❅.

Cultivation Grow in any well-drained soil that is kept relatively moist. Full sun or partial shade is best, along with some protection from the extremes of the weather. **Prune** minimally; remove any shoots that spoil the shape of young plants to encourage a good form (*see pp.382–384*). **Sow** seed as soon as it is ripe in a cold frame (*see p.391*). **Take** stem cuttings in summer (*see p.394*).

Austromyrtus tenuifolia
↕1–3m (3–9ft) ↔ 1–2m (3–6ft),everygreen shrub with small edible berries ❄❄

Azara

Strongly vanilla-scented flowers are the main attraction of this group of evergreen shrubs and small trees. The flowers are produced in tight clusters or spikes carried on the undersides of the branches, with different species flowering at times ranging from midwinter to midsummer. The flowers have no petals, but showy stamens give them a decorative, fluffy appearance. Berries may follow after hot summers. These trouble-free shrubs need a sunny and sheltered position, ideally against a warm wall. The green leaves vary in size and are sometimes in distinctive unequal pairs, with a small leaf opposite a much larger one.

Hardiness Fully frost-hardy ❄❄❄ to frost-tender ❄.

Cultivation Grow in moist soil enriched with plenty of well-rotted organic matter. **Site** in sun or partial shade, sheltered from hot winds, which will scorch the leaves and cause them to drop. In colder areas, grow and train azaras against warm, sunny walls. **Prune out** shoots that spoil the shape of the shrub after flowering.

Azara microphylla 🏆 **(inset: *microphylla* 'Variegata')**
↕10m (30ft) ↔4m (12ft), hardiest of the species, will also tolerate full shade ❄❄❄

Backhousia

Evergreen trees and shrubs from rainforests, the leaves of these plants give off a sweet aroma when crushed. Generally densely foliaged, the leaves are bright to dark green and shiny. As well as the aromatic leaves, these plants are grown for their flowers, for although these are individually small, they are borne in large, showy clusters at the tips of the plant. They are white and cream, and feature four petals and many conspicuous stamens. Depending on the species, these occur in spring, summer or autumn. Use as specimen trees, to give shade and shelter, and the smaller ones as flowering screens.

Hardiness Frost-hardy ❄❄ to very frost-tender ⌂.

Cultivation Grow plants in full sun or partial shade in well-drained soil that is kept continually moist. **Prune** minimally; remove shoots that spoil the shape of young plants to encourage a good form (*see pp.382-384*). **Sow** seed in spring in a cold frame (*see pp.391-392*). **Take** semi-hardwood cuttings in summer.

Backhousia myrtifolia (Ironwood)
↕7m (20ft) ↔4m (12ft), flowers in late spring into summer ❄❄

Baeckia

These evergreen shrubs range from small groundcovers up to tall shrubs. Their natural habitat also varies considerably, from sandy, dry country to sub-alpine and even coastal conditions. They are grown principally for their flowers, which are five-petalled and white to pink. These are small, but very ornamental and occur singly on short stems and, in some species, in clusters. The majority flower in spring, with a few having sporadic flowers at other times of the year. The foliage is fine and on thin, wispy stems, giving the plant a delicate appearance. Taller specimens are used as screens, while the majority make interesting additions to shrub gardens.

Hardiness Fully frost-hardy ❄❄❄ to frost-tender ❄.

Cultivation Grow in full sun or partial shade, in soil that is free-draining. **Trim** lightly after flowering to promote bushiness and additional flowers. **Sow** seed in a cold frame (*see pp.391-392*). Seed is difficult to collect, as it is ejected from the seed pods when ripe. **Take** semi-hardwood cuttings in spring and summer (*see p.394*).

Baeckia linifolia (Weeping Baeckia)
↕3m (10ft) ↔1.5m (5ft), a graceful, medium shrub with a few flowers through the year, but particularly abundant in summer ❄❄

Banksia

These are evergreen, variable shrubs and trees from small, ground-hugging clumps to large, open trees. The leaves are often white underneath, stiff and linear, and heavily toothed, with saw-like edges or even triangular lobes. Some have fine foliage that is soft and like that of the Heaths. The petal-less flowers are balls or cylinders, sometimes held at the growing tips, and sometimes among the foliage. These can be quite small or as long as 30cm (1ft) and in colours ranging from yellow to red. Many are popular cut flowers. Flowering times vary and cover all times of the year; some species have flowers throughout the year. The seeds are held in woody cones.

Hardiness Frost-hardy ❄❄ to very frost-tender ❄.

Cultivation Grow in full sun or partial shade and in an area that is particularly free-draining. **Prune** minimally; remove shoots spoiling the shape of young plants to encourage a good form (*see pp.382-384*). **Sow** seed (*see p.391*) in containers and keep moist and warm.

Banksia serrata (Saw Banksia)
↕10-15m (30-45ft) ↔ 5-10m (15-30ft), tolerates coastal and ccol mountain conditions provided drainage is good ❄❄

Banksia ericifolia (Heath Banksia)
↕6m (18ft) ↔ 5m (15ft), autumn or winter flowering, making it particularly useful for attracting birds ❄❄

Banksia integrifolia (Coast Banksia)
↕10-20m (30-60ft) ↔ 5-10m (15-30ft), this plant will withstand the toughest coastal conditions ❄❄

Berberis

Barberry

Barberries are grown for their ornamental foliage and their glowing, yellow to dark orange flowers. The flowers are produced in spring and summer, usually in small clusters, and are often followed by colourful fruits in autumn. There are evergreen and deciduous barberries, many of the latter showing fiery autumn colours. All have spiny stems, making an excellent choice for an impenetrable hedge, but with a wide range of species and cultivars to choose from, you can find a barberry for almost any aspect in the garden. They range from large specimens for hedging or borders to dwarf shrubs suitable for rock gardens.

Hardiness Fully frost-hardy ❄❄❄ to frost-hardy ❄❄.

Cultivation Grow in any moist but well-drained soil. Position in full sun or partial shade: autumn colours and fruiting are best in full sun. **Prune** after flowering: lightly trim or prune any shoots that spoil the shape of evergreens and cut back flowered shoots of deciduous types to strong buds or shoots. Trim hedges after flowering. **Take** semi-ripe cuttings of both types or softwood cuttings of deciduous types in summer (*see p.394*).

Berberis darwinii
↕↔ 3m (10ft), upright, evergreen, flowering in spring, sometimes again in autumn, with blue-black fruit in autumn ❄❄❄

Betula

Birch

THESE GRACEFUL, DECIDUOUS trees provide a display in every season: the textured bark, often peeling and silvery-white or coppery-brown, looks stunning in winter when there is little else to see; male and female flowers are borne in separate catkins on the same tree during spring, and the small, toothed, mid- to dark green leaves generally turn a soft yellow in autumn. This is a large group, with several species suitable for small gardens. The slender forms of many species look particularly attractive if room can be found for a small group of trees. The popular weeping birches are among the most beautiful and elegant of specimen trees for a garden.

Hardiness Fully frost-hardy ✲✲✲.

Cultivation Grow in reasonably fertile, well-drained soil. Site in sun or light, dappled shade; most will tolerate exposed positions. **Prune** out any misplaced or crossing branches during winter, when the trees are dormant, to maintain a healthy framework of branches. **Sow** seed (*see pp.391–393*) in a seedbed outdoors in autumn. **Take** softwood cuttings (*see p.394*) in summer.

Betula papyrifera (Canoe Birch, Paper Birch)
↕20m (70ft) ↔ 10m (30ft), newly exposed bark is pale orange-brown, paling with age, and autumn leaves are yellow to orange

***Betula pendula* 'Youngii'** (Young's Weeping Birch)
↕8m (25ft) ↔ 10m (30ft), a domed form of the usually upright silver birch, suitable for small gardens

Betula nigra (Black Birch, River Birch)
↕18m (60ft) ↔ 12m (40ft), conical to spreading in habit, the bark becoming fissured and grey-white or blackish on old trees

Boronia

DELICIOUS PERFUME IS ONE OF THE KEY ATTRACTIONS of these plants. They are evergreen shrubs, mostly small in stature, although there are a few larger ones. Plants are generally open in appearance and lightly foliaged. The leaves are small, fine and narrow or slightly oval, and many give off a strong aroma when crushed. The four-petalled flowers are mostly pink through to mauve, small and starry or bell-shaped. Some readily display their flowers, while others have them hanging on short stems along the undersides of the stems. The majority of species flower in the spring. Grow where the scent of the foliage and flowers can be enjoyed.

Hardiness Frost-hardy ✲✲ to very frost-tender ❀.

Cultivation Excellent drainage is essential for success, although the ground should not be allowed to dry out. Dappled light or partial shade and shelter from hot, drying winds is best, along with soil that is slightly alkaline. **Tip prune** lightly to promote bushy growth (*see pp.382–384*). **Sow** seed (*see p.391*) that has been soaked in boiling water in containers. **Take** cuttings of firm, young wood in spring or summer (*see p.394*).

Boronia megastigma
↕1.5m (5ft) ↔ 60cm (2ft), highly fragrant flowers in spring ✲✲

Brachychiton

THESE TREES ARE MOSTLY EVERGREEN, although some can be partially deciduous. Small to large trees, many develop stout to bottle-shaped trunks with age. The leaves are extremely variable and can be so even on the one tree. Oval, kidney-shaped or lobed, they are light to dark green and often shiny on the upper surface. Many trees shed a large number of leaves at flowering or in response to drought. The flowers occur in spring or summer. They are bell-shaped to tubular, and are cream, yellow, pink or red. Leathery, brown, boat-shaped seed pods hold rows of seeds surrounded by small hairs that are known to cause irritation to the skin.

Hardiness Frost-hardy ❄❄ to frost-tender ❄.

Cultivation Grow in any well-drained soil in full sun, preferably in a hot climate. **Prune** minimally; remove any shoots that spoil the shape of young plants and to encourage a straight central trunk (*see p.382*). **Sow** seed (*see p.391*) while fresh straight into containers.

Brachychiton acerifolius (Flame Tree)
↕20m (60ft) ↔ 15m (45ft), the tree often sheds many or all of its leaves when it flowers in spring or summer ❄

Buckinghamia

AN EVERGREEN TREE OF THE RAINFORESTS, it can be very tall when conditions are right. However, in cooler climates it tends to stay bushy and only reach the size of a small tree or even a large shrub. The leaves are light green and shiny, and are oval or lobed. The flowers are small and sweetly scented, and occur in summer through to autumn. They appear in long, pendulous cylinders that are very showy. Grow as a specimen tree or at the back of a garden as a screen and where its foliage can act as a foil to colourful shrubs and perennials in front.

Hardiness Very frost-tender ❅.

Cultivation Grow in any well-drained soil that is reasonably fertile and enriched with well-rotted organic matter. An acid (lime-free) soil is best, as is full sun or partial shade. **Keep** moist during dry periods. **Prune** minimally; remove any shoots that spoil the shape of young plants (*see pp.382–384*)). **Sow** seed (*see p.391*) when ripe in containers in a cold frame. **Take** hardwood cuttings in summer and autumn (*see p.394*).

Buckinghamia celcissima
↕20m (65ft) ↔ 10m (30ft), an impressive sight when covered in catkin-like, drooping clusters of scented, cream-white flowers

Buddleja

Butterfly Bush, Orange Ball Tree

↕↔ to 5m (15ft)

The fragrant flowers of buddlejas are wonderful for attracting hordes of butterflies. Most widely grown is the hardy *Buddleja davidii* and its cultivars, most growing to 2.5–3m (8–10ft) tall in a single season, with pink, purple, lilac, or white flowers in conical spikes on tall, arching shoots from late summer to early autumn. *B. globosa*, the orange ball tree, is a larger, rounded shrub, also hardy, that flowers in early summer. Buddlejas may be deciduous, semi-evergreen, or evergreen. They make an effective backdrop to other summer-flowering shrubs such as St. John's Wort (*Hypericum, see p.74*) or potentillas (*see p.99*).

Hardiness Fully frost-hardy ❄❄❄ to frost-tender ❄.

Cultivation Grow in fertile, well-drained soil in full sun; poorer soils are tolerated. **Prune** *B. davidii* and its cultivars by cutting old stems back to the base, in early spring (*see p.383*). Trim other buddlejas after flowering, only to keep them neat and within bounds. **Take** semi-ripe cuttings (*see p.394*) in summer or hardwood cuttings of *B. davidii* in autumn. If caterpillars are troublesome, pick them off by hand.

① ***davidii* 'Royal Red'** 🏆 ↕3m (10ft) ❄❄❄ ② ***davidii* 'White Profusion'** 🏆 ↕3m (10ft) ❄❄ ③ ***globosa*** 🏆 ↕↔ 5m (15ft) ❄❄ ④ **'Lochinch'** 🏆 ↕2.5m (8ft) ↔ 3m (10ft) ❄❄❄

BUXUS

Box, Boxwood

EVERGREEN BOX IS ONE OF the garden's most versatile plants. Although many varieties are naturally large and shrubby, all respond well to regular trimming, making them equally at home in formal and informal settings. Tiny, yellow-green flowers appear in spring, but it is the neat, leathery foliage that generally steals the show. Used in hedges or screens, it furnishes a constant backdrop for seasonal action in the garden. You can clip box into ornamental topiary shapes; simple forms need trimming only once or twice a year. Dwarf boxes were traditionally used to create knot gardens and parterres; they are also excellent for edging paths and borders. There are many types of box, some of them variegated.

Hardiness Fully frost-hardy ❄❄❄ to frost-hardy ❄❄.

Cultivation Box needs fertile, well-drained soil, ideally in partial shade. **Trim** shrubs and hedges in spring and summer; box tolerates hard pruning in spring if fed and well watered after. **Take** semi-ripe cuttings in summer (*see p.394*).

① *sempervirens* 'Elegantissima' 🏆 ↕↔ 1.5m (5ft)
② *sempervirens* 'Suffruticosa' 🏆 ↕1m (3ft) ↔ 1.5m (5ft)

CALLICARPA

Beauty Berry

↕1–3m (3–10ft)
↔1–2.5m (3–8ft)

APTLY NAMED, THE BEAUTY BERRY is valued for its vibrantly coloured, bead-like, autumn berries. These remain on bare stems of deciduous species after the leaves fall, bringing colour to a winter garden. Berries may be violet, lilac, white, or dusky purple and are most abundant after a long, hot summer. If you have space, plant groups of three or more to maximize fruiting. These shrubs are deciduous or evergreen with deep green or bronze leaves and varied habits. They bear clusters of small, white, red, purple, or pink flowers in summer. Other berrying shrubs and trees, such as viburnums (*see p.126*) and sorbus (*see p.118*), make good companions.

Hardiness Fully frost-hardy ❄❄❄ to frost-tender ❀.

Cultivation Fertile, well-drained soil in full sun or light, dappled shade is suitable. If drastic pruning is required, cut back flowered shoots close to the base. **Sow** seed (*see pp.391–393*) in pots in a cold frame in autumn or spring. **Take** softwood cuttings in spring or semi-ripe cuttings in summer (*see p.394*).

Callicarpa bodinieri* var. *giraldii
↕3m (10ft) ↔ 2.5m (8ft), deciduous, upright bush, clusters of small pink flowers in midsummer ❄❄❄

CALLISTEMON

Bottlebrush

↕1–15m (3–50ft)
↔1–8m (3–25ft)

THESE PLANTS ARE GROWN for their impressive bottlebrush-like flowers. Mostly shrubs, there are a few that will reach the size of small to medium trees. They are generally bushy and erect in appearance, although there are a number that have a delightful weeping habit. All are evergreen and feature stiff, leathery, linear to lance-shaped leaves, some of which give off a scent when crushed. Flower colours range from white through cream to pink, mauve, and red. Bushy forms can make excellent screens, while weepers make attractive specimen plants. All are renowned for attracting birds to the garden.

Hardiness Fully frost-hardy ❄❄❄ (borderline) to very frost-tender ❀.

Cultivation Grow in well-drained soil in full sun or partial shade. Some withstand dry while others will need additional water in dry times. **Trim** off spent flowers just behind the flower. This will promote bushiness, but will also result in a lot more flowers being produced (*see p.384*). **Sow** seed (*see p.392*) from year-old seed capsules. **Take** semi-hardwood cuttings from growing tips in mid to late summer and place in a cold frame (*see p.394*).

Callistemon pallidus (Lemon Bottlebrush)
↕↔ 2–4m (6–12ft), erect to spreading shrub, downy shoots, dark to grey-green leaves, 10cm (4in) flowers in summer and autumn ❄

Callistemon citrinus (Crimson Bottlebrush)
↕4m (12ft) ↔ 4m (12ft), spring flowering, bushiness can be promoted by removing the spent flowers ❄❄

Callistemon viminalis (Weeping Bottlebrush)
↕6m (18ft) ↔ 4m (12ft), graceful weeping habit and showy summer flowers ❄❄

CALLITRIS

Cypress Pine

THESE EVERGREEN CONIFERS ARE MOSTLY small to medium-sized trees or large shrubs. They generally have a narrow and columnar habit, making them useful where a formal look is required. The leaves are small scales and are bright green. Male cones are very small and occur at the growing tips, either singly or in groups. The female cones are mostly made up of six segments, holding winged seeds. These cones are woody, small and globular, and remain on the tree for several years. The timber of taller species is favoured for its durability.

Hardiness Fully frost-hardy ❄❄❄ to frost-tender ❄.

Cultivation Soil should be well-drained. Grow in full sun or partial shade. **Prune** minimally; remove any shoots that spoil the shape of young plants to encourage a good form (*see p.384*). **Sow** seed (*see p.392*) in a cold frame at any time of year. **Take** hardwood cuttings in summer, but these are slow to form roots (*see p.394*).

Callitris rhomboidea (Port Jackson Pine)
↕6–10m (18–30ft) ↔ 2–4m (6–12ft), dense, formal looking tree for screening or use as a specimen ❄❄

CALOTHAMNUS

SHOWY PINK OR RED FLOWERS are the main reason these evergreen shrubs are grown. The bird-attracting flowers occur in spring and summer, although some have a few flowers at all times of the year. These are bunches of long, red stamens, often occurring on one side of the stem, resulting in one of the common names being One-sided Bottlebrush. They occur on one-year-old wood, so pruning should be restricted to light trims only. The leaves are narrow, linear to needle-like and green or grey-green. Most are open shrubs of similar height to spread, and generally under 2m (6ft).

Hardiness Frost-tender ❄ to very frost-tender ❅.

Cultivation Grow in full sun or very light shade on a free-draining soil. **Trim** lightly after flowering to promote bushiness (*see pp.390*). **Sow** seed (*see p.392*) collected from seed capsules that are at least one year old in a cold frame. **Take** semi-hardwood cuttings in late spring or summer (*see p.394*).

Calothamnus quadrificus (Common Net Bush)
↕2m (6ft) ↔ 2m (6ft), flowers over a long period from spring through summer into autumn ❄

Camellia

↕1–20m (3–70ft)
↔60cm–8m (2–25ft)

THESE ELEGANT, EVERGREEN SHRUBS suit a range of uses from borders to woodland settings. They are also excellent container plants, and this is an ideal way of growing them if your soil is alkaline (high lime content), since camellias prefer a neutral to acid soil. There are over 250 species, and the largest are very tall, but there are many smaller cultivars that are more suited to most gardens. The exquisite flowers in shades of pink, scarlet, and white appear in spring and last for several weeks. Borne singly or in clusters, they last well as cut flowers and some are slightly fragrant. Flowers may be single or double, and vary considerably in size, the largest measuring 13cm (5in) or more across, but the average bloom is about half that size. Most commonly grown camellias are hardy, although *Camellia reticulata* and its cultivars are half-hardy and need a sheltered site. Dark green, glossy foliage ensures that camellias stay handsome all year.

Hardiness Fully frost-hardy ❄❄❄ to very frost-tender ❀.

Cultivation Grow in moist but well-drained, humus-rich, acid soil (pH 5.5–5.6). **Shelter** from hot winds and position in partial shade, since early sun may damage the buds and flowers on frosty mornings. **Plant** with the top of the root ball just below the surface of the soil. Mulch in spring with 5–8cm (2–3in) leafmould or shredded bark. **Feed** with a balanced fertilizer in mid-spring and again in early summer, and keep well watered during dry spells to prevent bud drop. **Prune** lightly to shape in late spring or early summer after flowering, and deadhead. **Take** semi-ripe cuttings from late summer until early winter (*see p.394*).

Pruning young camellias

Young camellias develop a variety of habits. Careful pruning of young plants can help produce a well-balanced shape and encourage new, bushy growth. Reduce any thin, weak growth by cutting back to two or three buds or pruning it out entirely. Established plants require very little pruning. If plants have outgrown their space they can be cut back hard in early spring.

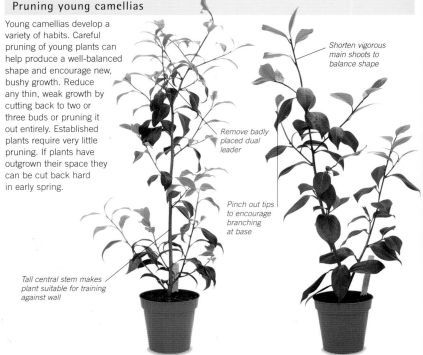

Shorten vigorous main shoots to balance shape
Remove badly placed dual leader
Pinch out tips to encourage branching at base
Tall central stem makes plant suitable for training against wall

1
5
10
11
15

① × *williamsii* 'Debbie' ↕2m (6ft) ↔1.5m (5ft) ② *japonica* 'Desire' ↕3m (10ft) ↔2m (6ft) ③ *sasanqua* 'Plantation Pink' ↕5m (15ft) ↔3m (10ft) ④ 'Queen Diana' ↕3m (10ft) ↔2m (6ft) ⑤ *sasanqua* 'Setsugekka' ↕4m (12ft) ↔2.5m (8ft) ⑥ *japonica* 'Ave Maria' 🏆 ↕9m (28ft) ↔8m (25ft) ⑦ *japonica* 'Betty Sheffield Supreme' ↕2–4m (6–12ft) ↔1.5–3m (5–10ft) ⑧ *japonica*

'Elegans' 🏆 ↕4m (12ft) ↔ 3m (9ft) ⑨ *japonica* 'Guilio Nuccio' 🏆 ↕4m (12ft) ↔ 3m (9ft) ⑩ *japonica* 'Hagoromo' 🏆 ↕4m (12ft) ↔ 3m (9ft) ⑪ *japonica* 'Mrs D.W. Davis' ↕4m (12ft) ↔ 3m (9ft) ⑫ *japonica* 'R.L. Wheeler' 🏆 ↕4m (12ft) ↔ 3m (9ft) ⑬ *japonica* 'Rubescens Major' 🏆 ↕4m (12ft) ↔ 3m (9ft) ⑭ *reticulata* 'Arch of Triumph' ↕3m (10ft) ↔ 5m (15ft)

⑮ *reticulata* 'William Hertrich' ↕5m (15ft) ↔ 3m (9ft) ⑯ *tsaii* ↕4m (12ft) ↔ 2m (6ft) ⑰ × *williamsii* 'Anticipation' 🏆 ↕4m (12ft) ↔ 2m (6ft) ⑱ × *williamsii* 'Donation' 🏆 ↕5m (15ft) ↔ 2.5m (8ft)

CARPINUS

Hornbeam

THERE ARE 35–40 SPECIES of these deciduous, woodland trees, several of which make good garden trees and can also be grown as handsome hedges. Grown as trees, they have an elegant habit, ranging from columnar and pyramid-shaped – the flame-like *Carpinus betulus* 'Fastigiata' being particularly popular – to rounded and spreading. Their beech-like foliage is mid- to dark green and often glossy; smooth, fluted grey bark is another pleasing feature. In spring, they produce yellow-green catkins, followed by drooping, hop-like, green fruits, maturing to brown or yellow. Autumn foliage colour is striking, too, the leaves turning to gold and amber.

Hardiness Fully frost-hardy ✲✲✲.

Cultivation Grow in reasonably fertile, well-drained soil in sun or partial shade. **Prune** young trees to remove any misplaced or crossing branches in late winter or early spring; trim hedges in mid- to late summer. Hornbeams can withstand severe pruning if they outgrow their space. **Sow** seed in a seedbed outdoors in autumn (*see pp.391–393*). **Take** greenwood cuttings in early summer (*see p.394*).

Carpinus betulus ♀

↕25m (80ft) ↔ 20m (70ft), as a tree pyramid-shaped, rounded when mature; as hedge (*see above*) retains brown leaves over winter

CARYOPTERIS

SMALL, DAINTY SHRUBS with a mound-forming habit, caryopteris bear masses of small, fluffy flowers in shades of blue. The group includes both these deciduous shrubs and some perennials, found in a variety of habitats from dry, hot slopes to woodland. They flower from late summer until autumn; most have grey- or silvery-green foliage, giving a cool look, although 'Worcester Gold' has warm yellow foliage. Caryopteris are elegant front-of-garden shrubs, especially planted in groups; they make a striking contrast with yellow-flowered potentillas (*see p.99*) or St. John's Wort (*Hypericum, see p.74*).

Hardiness Fully frost-hardy ✲✲✲ to frost-tender ✲.

Cultivation Grow in light but moderately fertile soil, in full sun. Plant against a warm wall in very cold areas, especially if summers are also cool. **Prune** the previous year's flowered shoots in early spring, cutting them back to only three or four good buds, so that a permanent stubby framework of shoots develops. If necessary, caryopteris can be cut down almost to soil level. **Sow** seed in autumn in a cold frame (*see pp.391–392*). **Take** softwood cuttings in late spring, or semi-ripe cuttings in early summer (*see p.394*).

Caryopteris × clandonensis 'Kew Blue'

↕1m (3ft) ↔ 1.5m (5ft), excellent on chalky soils, leaves silver-grey underneath, attractive seedheads ✲✲✲

CASUARINA

THESE ARE LARGE TREES AND SHRUBS that have minute leaves which are hardly visible and occur at regularly spaced nodes along the stems and branchlets. It is the green and grey-green of the stems and branchlets that give these plants their colour. Pollen is released from male flowers at the very tips of the branches. The female cones are woody and spherical or barrel-shaped, and often prickly on the surface. They remain on the plant for a number of years. They are often erect as young plants and become more spreading and weeping with age. Most are adapted to very harsh growing conditions.

Hardiness Frost-hardy ✲✲.

Cultivation Grow in well-drained soil, although some can withstand long periods of wet soil. Full sun is best or light shade only. **Prune** minimally; remove any shoots that spoil the shape of (young) plants to encourage a good form (*see pp.382–384*). **Sow** seed (*see p.391*) collected from year-old capsules in a cold frame.

Casuarina cunninghamiana (River She-oak)

↕20m (60ft) ↔ 10m (30ft), fast growing and tolerant of dry and moist conditions

Casuarina glauca (Swamp She-oak)
↕ 20m (60ft) ↔ 10m (30ft), grows well in wet areas

Catalpa

Catalpas are deciduous trees with year-round appeal, with their showy, often beautifully coloured foliage, large flowers, and distinctive seed pods. The bell-shaped flowers are borne in upright clusters in mid- and late summer. They are followed in autumn by bean-like seed pods, usually more than 30cm (1ft) long. Catalpas have a wide, spreading habit and are best admired when grown as specimen trees in a lawn. They will thrive in sheltered town gardens, provided they are given plenty of space.

Hardiness Fully frost-hardy ✲✲✲, although soft, young shoots can be prone to frost damage.

Cultivation Grow in fertile, moist but well-drained soil in full sun, with shelter from strong winds. In gardens that are cold, protect young plants from severe frosts. **Prune** in late winter or early spring, only if necessary to maintain a healthy branch framework. **Sow** seed in pots in autumn (*see pp.391–392*). **Take** softwood cuttings in late spring or summer (*see p.394*).

Catalpa bignonioides 🏆 (Indian Bean Tree)
↕↔ 15m (50ft), broad heart-shaped leaves, fragrant flowers, pencil-thin seed pods to 40cm (16in) long (*see inset*)

Casuarina equisetifolia subsp *incana* (Coastal She-oak)
↕ 10m (30ft) ↔ 5m (15ft), graceful weeping habit for warmer areas including coastal exposure

Catalpa bignonioides 'Aurea' 🏆
↕↔ 10m (30ft), slow-growing, leaves bronze when young and unfold in early summer

Catalpa speciosa
↕↔ 15m (50ft), spreading habit, flowers larger and showier than most other catalpas, seed pods to 50cm (20in) long

Ceanothus

California Lilac

VIGOROUS, SPREADING SHRUBS, California Lilacs are grown for their masses of usually blue, but sometimes white or pink flowers. They flower abundantly, in small, fluffy clusters at the tips of stems or on small sideshoots. Most ceanothus are best suited to growing in full sun. Prostrate or low-growing species make superb ground-cover plants and are ideal for providing colour on sloping banks. Most survive dry conditions very well. California Lilacs are not very long-lived, and dislike being transplanted.

Hardiness Fully frost-hardy *** to frost-hardy **.

Cultivation Grow in any reasonably fertile soil in full sun. They are tolerant of limy soils. **Prune** in early spring, lightly trimming evergreens to maintain a good shape. **Take** semi-ripe cuttings of all types in late summer (*see p.394*).

Ceanothus 'Concha'
↕2–3m (6–9ft) ↔ 2–3m (6–9ft), dense mounding shrub with spring flowers **

Cedrus

Cedar

↕to 40m (130ft)
↔to 10m (30ft)

THESE LARGE, EVERGREEN conifers make impressive specimen trees, needing plenty of space if their stature is to be fully appreciated (although there are some dwarf cultivars). Conical when young, they later develop spreading, horizontal branches. Cedars are best grown on their own, or with other large trees where space allows; they are very long-lived. Their needles are arranged in clusters on short shoots; there are cedars with either bright golden or glaucous blue foliage, as well as plain green. Male cones are cylindrical and light brown; female cones are oblong or barrel-shaped, and green when they first appear, ripening and turning brown over two years.

Hardiness Fully frost-hardy ***.

Cultivation Grow in any reasonably fertile soil in an open, sunny position. **Prune** only if the trees happen to produce two leading shoots, cutting out the weaker shoot in autumn. **Sow** seed (*see pp.391–393*) in spring after keeping them moist and in a refrigerator at 0–5°C (32–41°F) for three weeks.

Ceanothus 'Blue Cushion'
↕45–75cm (18–30in) ↔ 1–2m (3–6ft), spreading but dense and tidy evergreen, ideal as a ground-cover plant, flowering profusely in summer 18m (60ft)

Cedrus deodora 'Aurea' 🏆
↕5m (15ft), a slow-growing cultivar with golden-yellow spring foliage that becomes greener in summer

Celtis

Evergreen, deciduous and semi-deciduous trees, celtis grow on all continents except Antarctica. The leaves are broadly lance-shaped, and are usually lightly toothed along the margins and asymmetrical at the leaf base, two characteristics they share with their relatives the elms (*Ulmus*, *see p.125*). The flowers are inconspicuous, but are followed in summer by small, brown to black berries. These have a thin outer flesh but are mostly full of the hard, central stone or pip. They are broad-crowned trees, with a central trunk, making them useful as specimens and shade trees. They are often also found planted as street trees, sometimes as a substitute for elms.

Hardiness Fully frost-hardy ✽✽✽ to very frost-tender ❀.

Cultivation Grow in full sun in any well-drained soil that is reasonably fertile. **Prune** minimally; remove any shoots that spoil the shape of young plants and to encourage a good form (*see p.384*). **Sow** seed (*see pp.391–393*) in spring in a cold frame.

Celtis australis
↕18m (60ft) ↔ 10m (30ft), deciduous shade tree used as a specimen or for street planting 18m (60ft)

Ceratostigma

Chinese Plumbago

True blue, late-summer flowers, from pale Wedgwood to deep indigo, distinguish these small shrubs, all growing to about 1m (3ft) tall. The group also includes the woody-based perennial *Ceratostigma plumbaginoides*, which is half the height and perfect for the front of a garden bed. There are deciduous, evergreen and semi-evergreen species, the leaves of all turning red in autumn to provide a brilliant foil for late flowers. Their colouring is particularly dramatic in a mixed garden next to yellow daylilies (*Hemerocallis*, *see p.258*) or St John's Wort (*Hypericum*, *see p.74*). Growth often dies back in very cold winters, but usually regrows in spring.

Hardiness Fully frost-hardy ✽✽✽ to frost-tender ✽.

Cultivation Grow in light, reasonably fertile soil, in full sun. **Prune back** to within 2.5cm (1in) of a permanent framework after flowering or in early spring. **Remove** any growth that has been damaged during winter in spring; new shoots will appear from the base. **Take** softwood cuttings in spring or semi-ripe cuttings in summer (*see p.394*). Shoots can be layered (*see p.395*) in autumn.

Ceratostigma willmottianum ♀
↕1m (3ft) ↔ 1m (3ft), bushy deciduous shrub with purple-edged leaves, turning red in autumn

Cercidiphyllum

Katsura Tree

Fiery autumn displays of yellow, orange, and red leaves that smell of burnt sugar when crushed are the chief attraction of this tree. The mid-green, oval to rounded leaves are also bronze when young. The best autumn colour is produced on acid (lime-free) soils. All katsuras belong to one species, *Cercidiphyllum japonicum*. There is a weeping form, and also a variety that is a smaller tree, despite being called *magnificum*. Planted as a specimen tree, the katsura can show off its form, pyramidal when young and becoming more rounded with age. Open woodland settings are also attractive if space allows.

Hardiness Fully frost-hardy ✽✽✽, although the young leaves may be damaged by late frosts. New foliage should grow again.

Cultivation Grow in good, fertile soil enriched with plenty of well-rotted organic matter in sun or partial shade, sheltered from hot, drying winds. **Prune out** any crossing branches or those that spoil the shape of the tree in late winter or early spring. Plants often develop several main stems, but these can be reduced to one if desired, provided that the tree is still young. **Take** semi-ripe cuttings in midsummer (*see p.394*).

Cercidiphyllum japonicum ♀ (Katsura Tree)
↕20m (70ft) ↔ 15m (50ft), eventual size is affected by climate, and the tree tends to remain smaller in cooler areas

CERCIS

Redbud

↔ to 10m (30ft)

DECIDUOUS TREES from woodland edges, these make excellent specimen plants in a lawn or in a large mixed garden. They are grown for their foliage and their clusters of pink or purple flowers, borne in profusion in spring before the leaves. The flowers of the Judas Tree, *Cercis siliquastrum*, appear directly on the branches and even the trunk. This is the largest species; choose *C. chinensis* or *C. canadensis* for a smaller garden. The leaves of all species are heart-shaped, and turn yellow, orange, or red in autumn.

Hardiness Fully frost-hardy ✽✽✽; frosts may damage young growth.

Cultivation Grow in fertile, moist but well-drained soil in full sun or partial shade. Plant while the trees are young; older plants resent root disturbance. **Prune out** crossing branches in late winter or early spring to maintain a healthy, well-shaped framework. **Sow** seed (*see pp.391–392*) in containers in a cold frame in autumn. **Take** semi-ripe cuttings (*see p.394*) in summer.

***Cercis canadensis* 'Forest Pansy'** (Eastern Redbud)
↕↔ 5m (15ft), may not flower in all locations, but the purple foliage gives a reliable display

CHAENOMELES

Flowering Quince, Japanese Quince, Japonica

↕ to 2.5m (8ft)
↔ to 5cm (15ft)

THESE VERSATILE SHRUBS, flowering in late winter, are usually grown in mixed gardens, but also make a useful informal hedge, even in shade. Deciduous and spiny-branched, they flower in shades of white, red, and pink. The flowers, single or double, are borne all along the stems, appearing before and with the leaves. They are followed in autumn by an occasional apple-like, yellow to green fruit, which is edible after being cooked, although the true edible quince is a different tree, *Cydonia* (*see p.47*).

Hardiness Fully frost-hardy ✽✽✽.

Cultivation Grow in reasonably fertile soil: they are best not planted in very limy (alkaline) soil, where the leaves may yellow (chlorotic). Position in full sun or partial shade. Withstands dry conditions. **Cut back** flowered shoots after flowering: cut to strong buds lower down. **Sow** seed (*see pp.391–393*) in containers in a cold frame or outdoors in a seedbed. **Take** semi-ripe cuttings (*see p.394*) in summer or layer shoots (*see p.395*) in autumn.

***Chaenomeles speciosa* 'Moerloosei'** 🏆
↕ 2.5m (8ft) ↔ 5m (15ft), particularly early-flowering, with fragrant fruits (*see inset*) in autumn

CHAMAECYPARIS

False Cypress

IDEAL FOR HEDGING, these evergreen, coniferous trees are fairly vigorous and tolerate some clipping; their attractive growth habit also makes many of them handsome specimen plants. Grow them with other conifers such as *Cupressus* (*see p.46*), or with large rhododendrons (*see pp.104–107*). There are also many dwarf or slow-growing cultivars, and these can be used in smaller gardens or even in large rock gardens. The leaves are scale-like and flattened; contact with the foliage may aggravate some skin allergies. False cypresses bear round or oval male cones in spring, which are followed in summer by round or angular female cones that ripen in autumn.

Hardiness Fully frost-hardy ✽✽✽.

Cultivation Grow in moist but well-drained, preferably neutral to acid (lime-free) soil, although these trees will tolerate deep, chalky soils. Position in full sun. **Trim** trees used for hedging from late spring to autumn, but do not cut into older wood. **Sow** seed (*see pp.391–393*) in a seedbed outdoors in spring or take semi-ripe cuttings (*see p.394*) in late summer.

① ***lawsoniana* 'Pembury Blue'** 🏆 ↕ 15m (50ft) ② ***nootkatensis* 'Pendula'** 🏆 ↕ 30m (100ft) ③ ***obtusa* 'Nana Aurea'** 🏆 ↕ 2m (6ft) ④ ***pisifera* 'Filifera Aurea'** 🏆 ↕ 12m (40ft)

Chamaelaucium

Evergreen shrubs, these plants are grown for their showy, five-petalled flowers. At least one species, *Chamelaucium uncinatum*, is grown commercially for its cut flowers. These appear from late winter into early summer, are white, pink, or red, and have a waxy look and feel to the petals. The foliage gives off a pleasant aroma when crushed, and the leaves are fine and needle-like. The bushes are open and upright, but thicken up with regular pruning, particularly as a result of flower picking.

Hardiness Frost-hardy ❄❄ to frost-tender ❄.

Cultivation It is important that the soil be free-draining and sandy soils are preferred. Full sun is best also. **Prune** to remove flowers to enjoy inside, or give a light overall clip after flowering has finished (*see p.384*). **Take** semi-hardwood cuttings in late spring and place in a cold frame (*see p.394*).

Chamaelaucium uncinatum (Geraldton Wax)
↕3–4m (9–12ft) ↔ 3–4m (9–12ft), flower colours vary in nature and there are a number of named cultivars

Chimonanthus praecox

Wintersweet

Powerfully fragrant, waxy flowers hang from the bare shoots of *Chimonanthus praecox* throughout winter. This deciduous shrub has flowers that are pale sulphur-yellow, stained brown or purple inside. Young plants take a few years to reach flowering age. Although the shrub is not unattractive in leaf, winter is its real season of interest, so plant it near a doorway or where you will come across it and its extraordinary scent on winter walks.

Hardiness Fully frost-hardy ❄❄❄.

Cultivation Grow in any fertile, well-drained soil in full sun. **Prune** only mature shrubs that flower regularly in late winter, when dormant, or in early spring. Cut out any crossing or misshapen branches to maintain a healthy framework and good shape. **Sow** seed (*see pp.391–392*) in containers in a cold frame as soon as it is ripe. **Take** softwood cuttings (*see p.394*) in summer.

Chimonanthus praecox
↕4m (12ft) ↔ 3m (10ft), flowers that are both larger and a deeper yellow than the species

Chionanthus

Fringe Tree

Large, attractive shrubs, fringe trees are grown for their long, narrow leaves and their fragrant, white flowers, which are borne in clusters during summer. Two spreading, deciduous shrubs from this large and varied genus are grown in gardens: *Chionanthus retusus* has upright flower clusters and peeling bark, while *C. virginicus* has hanging flower clusters and larger leaves that have bright, golden-yellow autumn colour. In autumn, the flowers of both are followed by blue-black fruits. Fringe trees make excellent specimen plants; they also work well grown in a shrub garden along with plants such as abelias (*see p.14*), choisyas (*see p.40*), or camellias (*see pp.32–33*).

Hardiness Fully frost-hardy ❄❄❄.

Cultivation Grow in reasonably fertile soil in full sun: *C. retusus* tolerates limy (alkaline) soil, but *C. virginicus* needs an acid soil. Flowering and fruiting are best in climates with hot summers. **Prune out** crossing or badly placed branches in winter or early spring, to prevent growth becoming unhealthily crowded. **Sow** seed (*see pp.391–392*) in containers in a cold frame in autumn; germination may take as long as 18 months.

Chionanthus virginicus
↕3m (10ft) ↔ 3m (10ft) or more, the lower branches can be pruned back to the trunk to encourage a more tree-like form

Choisya

Mexican Orange Blossom

THE GLOSSY, AROMATIC FOLIAGE of these evergreen shrubs ensures that they have year-round appeal in any garden, quite apart from the fact that most give a superb, spring show of abundant, starry, sweetly fragrant flowers. Of the commonly available Mexican orange blossoms, 'Aztec Pearl' and *Choisya ternata* are particularly good value, since they also produce a flush of blooms in late spring and more flowering throughout the warmer months. Although *C. ternata* SUNDANCE rarely flowers, this is more than made up for by its spring foliage, which can light up the dullest garden with a ray of sunshine.

Hardiness Fully frost-hardy ❄❄❄ to frost-hardy ❄❄.

Cultivation Choisyas prefer a fertile, well-drained soil in full sun, but tolerate partial shade. **Trim** any shoots that spoil the shape of the shrub after flowering. **Take** semi-ripe cuttings in summer (*see p.394*). Snails and slugs have a liking for these shrubs; while the plant is small and vulnerable, it is well worth discouraging them (*see p.260*).

Choisya ternata SUNDANCE ♀ ('Lich')
↕↔ 2.5m (8ft), the buttery young foliage of this cultivar is best in bright sun, achieving only a greenish-yellow in shade ❄❄

Cistus

Rock Rose

↕↔ most to 1m (3ft), some to 2m (6ft)

ROCK ROSES ARE EVERGREENS, grown for their profuse, saucer-shaped flowers in white to purplish-pink. They appear from early to late summer; each bloom lasts only one day but is quickly replaced to keep the display going. Rock roses thrive in sunny spots in a garden bed, at the base of a wall, around a patio, or spilling over the side of a raised bed. Usefully, they appreciate dry conditions and poor soil, and so grow very well as low-maintenance container plants and alongside demanding plants such as shrub roses that take a lot out of the soil. They can be short-lived; it is worth taking cuttings to make replacement plants.

Hardiness Frost-hardy ❄❄.

Cultivation Grow rock roses in full sun, in poor to reasonably fertile, well-drained soil. **Pinch out** the growing tips of young plants to encourage a bushy habit; lightly trim shoots that spoil the shape of the shrub in spring, or after flowering. Old, woody plants are best replaced. **Sow** seed (*see pp.391–392*) in a cold frame when it is ripe, or in spring. **Take** softwood cuttings in summer (*see p.394*).

Cistus × purpureus **'Brilliancy'**
↕ 1.5m (5ft) ↔ 2m (6ft), summer flowering over a long period and good for dry conditions

Clerodendrum

THIS IS A LARGE GROUP OF TROPICAL and subtropical plants, although some of the elegant, shrubby species are robust enough to be grown outdoors in cooler, temperate climates. The hardy, deciduous shrubs include *Clerodendrum trichotomum*, a large shrub for a large garden or woodland glade, and the Glory Flower (*C. bungei*), smaller but still up to 2m (6ft) tall. This species is only frost-hardy and will be happiest in a warm, sheltered garden. Both are valued for their large clusters of often fragrant flowers, usually produced from late summer to autumn.

Hardiness Fully frost-hardy ❄❄❄ to very frost-tender ❅.

Cultivation Grow in soil enriched with well-rotted organic matter to make sure it is fertile and moist but well-drained, in full sun. **Pruning** is rarely needed; wayward branches can be removed, or shoots trimmed, in late winter or early spring. **Sow** seed (*see pp.391–392*) at 13–18°C (55–64°F) in spring. **Take** semi-ripe cuttings in summer (*see p.394*), rooting them in a heated propagator. *C. bungei* tends to produce suckers (a new shoot growing from below ground) that can make new plants: scrape back the soil to find one that has developed some roots in autumn or spring; carefully cut it away from the parent plant; and pot it up.

Clerodendrum ugandense (Blue Butterfly Bush)
↕ 3m (9ft) ↔ 2m (6ft), an upright shrub with a loosely open habit and purple-blue flowers in summer

Clethra

Lily-of-the-valley Tree

These evergreen and deciduous shrubs and trees are grown for their handsome foliage and spikes of white flowers. The blooms are very fragrant and are borne from mid- to late summer; sited beneath the canopy of a woodland garden, they will perfume the still air wonderfully. Lily-of-the-valley Tree can also be grown in a shady corner of a shrubbery, or close to a seating area where their scent can be enjoyed.

Hardiness Fully frost-hardy ✲✲✲ to frost-tender ✲.

Cultivation Grow in dappled shade in acid (lime-free), fertile, moist, well-drained soil. **Prune out** wayward branches in late winter. *C. arborea* need only be deadheaded, although it can be pruned to fit the available space. **Sow** seed (*see pp.391–392*) at 6–12°C (43–54°F) in spring or autumn. **Take** semi-ripe cuttings of deciduous species in mid- or late summer (*see p.394*).

Clethra arborea (Lily-of-the-valley Tree)

↕8m (25ft) ↔ 6m (20ft), young shoots are red, the spikes of flowers may be up to 15cm (6in) long ✲✲

Coleonema

These are evergreen, small to medium shrubs with scented, aromatic foliage. The leaves are small and narrow, and the overall impression is of a heath-like plant. Most are upright, green shrubs, although a number of golden-leafed and spreading forms are available. The flowers are white or pink and starry. Although small, they are borne in large enough numbers on most species to be quite a feature. They occur in spring, and are good, quick fillers for new gardens. The golden, leaf-spreading form 'Sunset Gold' is a reliable and tough ground cover.

Hardiness Frost-hardy ✲✲.

Cultivation Grow in full sun in any well-drained soil that is reasonably fertile and enriched with well-rotted organic matter. Plant away from strong winds that may be able to dislodge young plants. **Trim** young plants lightly after flowering to promote a bushy plant (*see p.384*). **Take** cuttings of softer tip growth in late summer or autumn (*see p.394*).

Coleonema pulchrum (Diosma)

↕1.5m (5ft) ↔ 1.5m (5ft), scented foliage and starry spring flowers are features of this evergreen shrub

Cordyline

Cabbage Palm, Cabbage Tree

The palm-like cordylines are architectural shrubs that can bring a touch of the exotic to a garden. Use them as focal points; given the time and space, most species will become tree-like in stature. Cordylines make handsome container plants in a conservatory, greenhouse or on a paved area. These plants are mainly valued for their spiky, leathery leaves, which are often variegated or brightly coloured. An occasional bonus in summer are tall, heavy stems of white, perfumed flowers, followed by bead-like berries in white, red, or purple.

Hardiness Frost-hardy ✲✲ to very frost-tender ❀; some cultivars can withstand freezing, but the top-growth may be damaged.

Cultivation Grow in fertile, well-drained soil in full sun or semi-shade; the cultivars with coloured foliage prefer some shade. In containers, use any good potting mix and top-dress annually in spring (*see p.386*). **Sow** seed (*see pp.391–392*) in spring at 16°C (61°F) or, for an instant result, cut well-rooted suckers (small plantlets growing up around the central crown) away from the parent plant in spring and pot them up individually.

Cordyline australis (Cabbage Palm)

↕12m (36ft) ↔ 4m (12ft), eventually tree-like, this New Zealand native flowers in early summer ✲✲

CORNUS

Dogwood

BEAUTIFUL FLOWERHEADS, DECORATIVE BARK, and vibrant autumn leaves make these outstanding garden plants. Dogwoods include deciduous shrubs, small trees, and woody-based perennials. Some, such as *Cornus alternifolia*, have an airy, tiered shape, and make graceful specimen trees. Many of the shrubby types, such as *C. alba* and *C. sanguinea* and their cultivars, are grown principally for their bright red, yellow, or green bark. These dogwoods are especially welcome in winter, when the thickets of stems seem to glow with colour, at its most intense if the plants are regularly coppiced. Creeping *C. canadensis* can be used in woodland or as ground cover in a shrub garden. The small, starry flowers are borne in clusters at the tips of the shoots, and in dogwoods grown for their flowering displays, for example *C. capitata*, *C. florida*, *C. kousa* and *C. nuttallii*, and many hybrids, they are surrounded by prominent petal-like bracts (modified leaves), which may be cream, white, or pink. In some plants, the berries or strawberry-like fruits that follow the flowers in autumn could cause mild stomach upset if eaten.

Hardiness Fully frost-hardy ❄❄❄ to frost-hardy ❄❄.

Cultivation Dogwoods can be grown in sun or partial shade. **Plant** flowering dogwoods (those with large bracts) in fertile, neutral to acid soil with plenty of well-rotted organic matter added to it. All other types tolerate a wide range of conditions. Those that are grown for their winter stem colour are best positioned in full sun. **Prune** those grown for stem colour hard (coppice) every spring to produce young shoots, which have the brightest colour (*see below*). Other dogwoods require little pruning except to keep them within bounds or to maintain the shape of the shrub. **Renovate** neglected plants by cutting out old wood at the centre of the shrub. **Sow** seed in a seedbed in autumn, or expose it to a period of cold weather and sow in spring (*see pp.391–393*). **Take** hardwood cuttings (*see p.394*) of dogwoods grown for stem colour in autumn.

How to coppice dogwoods

Allow a full year after planting for the shrub to develop, then cut back hard before growth starts in spring. Afterwards apply a general organic fertilizer around the shrub to encourage strong new growth and mulch with a thick layer of well-rotted organic matter.

▷ ***Pruning for coloured stems*** *In the first year after planting, cut back all the stems to 5–8cm (2–3in) from the base. After this the stems can be cut back each spring to just above two buds of the previous year's growth; this allows the plant to develop into a larger shrub.*

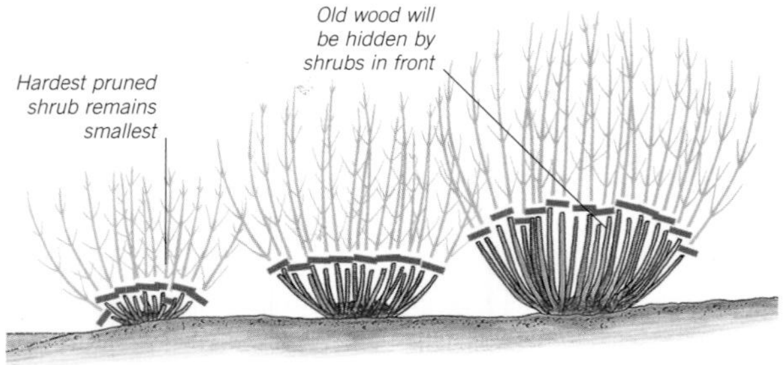
Hardest pruned shrub remains smallest
Old wood will be hidden by shrubs in front

◁ ***Staggered pruning*** *Where shrubby dogwoods are planted in a group, coppicing to varying levels creates a sloping effect rather than a dense mass of stems of uniform height. This is particularly useful for breaking up a border and making it look more interesting.*

① ***Cornus alba*** 'Elegantissima' ♀ ↕↔ 3m (10ft), stems, leaves ② ***alba*** 'Sibirica' ♀ ↕↔ 3m (10ft), stems ③ ***alba*** 'Spaethii' ♀ ↕↔ 3m (10ft), stems, leaves ④ ***alternifolia*** 'Argentea' ♀ ↕ 3m (10ft) ↔ 2.5m (8ft), leaves ⑤ ***capitata*** ↕↔ 12m (40ft), flowers, fruits ⑥ ***controversa*** 'Variegata' ♀

↕↔ 8m (25ft), flowers, leaves ⑦ **'Eddie's White Wonder'** ↕ 6m (20ft) ↔ 5m (15ft), flowers, autumn leaves ⑧ ***florida* 'Cherokee Chief'** ↕ 6m (20ft) ↔ 8m (25ft), flowers, autumn leaves ⑨ ***florida* 'Welchii'** ↕ 6m (20ft) ↔ 8m (25ft), flowers, autumn leaves ⑩ ***kousa* var. *chinensis*** ♀ ↕ 7m (22ft) ↔ 5m (15ft), bark, flowers, autumn leaves ⑪ ***mas*** ↕↔ 5m (15ft), flowers, fruits, autumn leaves ⑫ **'Norman Hadden'** ♀ ↕↔ 8m (25ft), flowers, fruits ⑬ ***nuttallii*** ↕ 12m (40ft) ↔ 8m (25ft), flowers, fruits

CORREA

THESE ARE GREAT BIRD-ATTRACTING PLANTS for the garden, particularly as most flower over a long period in the winter months, offering nectar when it may otherwise be in short supply. The flowers are pendulous tubes, although those of *Correa alba* are split to appear like four-petalled stars, and those of *C. decumbens* are upright. The colours vary considerably, and include shades of cream, green, red, and pink, as well as forms that start in red and are green or cream at the ends. Leaves are small and oval to linear, and are slightly coarse to the touch. They range from very densely foliaged medium shrubs down to sprawling groundcovers.

Hardiness Frost-hardy ✲✲.

Cultivation Grow in any well-drained soil in full sun or partial shade. **Trim** lightly after flowering to keep plants bushy (*see p.384*). **Take** semi-hardwood cuttings, preferably with a heel. They strike more readily with bottom heat (*see p.394*).

Correa reflexa
↕1.5m (3ft) ↔ 1.5m (3ft), a good bird attracting shrub that flowers late winter and into spring

CORYLUS

Hazel

LONG CATKINS AND ATTRACTIVE FOLIAGE and habits make hazels worthy garden plants. These small to medium-sized, deciduous shrubs and trees begin the season in late winter or spring by producing yellow, occasionally purple, male catkins. Broadly heart-shaped, toothed leaves follow that may be coloured. Some foliage displays autumnal tints. *Corylus avellana* 'Contorta', also called Twisted Filbert, has strikingly twisted stems that enhance the winter garden and are favourites with flower arrangers. Edible hazelnuts and filberts are produced by *C. avellana* and *C. maxima* in autumn. Larger hazels look good as specimens; use smaller species in a garden with shrubs such as hamamelis (*see p.68*) or mahonias (*see p.87*).

Hardiness Fully frost-hardy ✲✲✲.

Cultivation Hazels grow well in fertile, well-drained, preferably limy soil, in sun or partial shade. **Remove** suckers (strong, straight growths from the base of the plant) as soon as you see them. **Layer** shoots (*see p.395*) in autumn. **Prune** if needed, only to keep them in shape, in winter or early spring (*see p.383*).

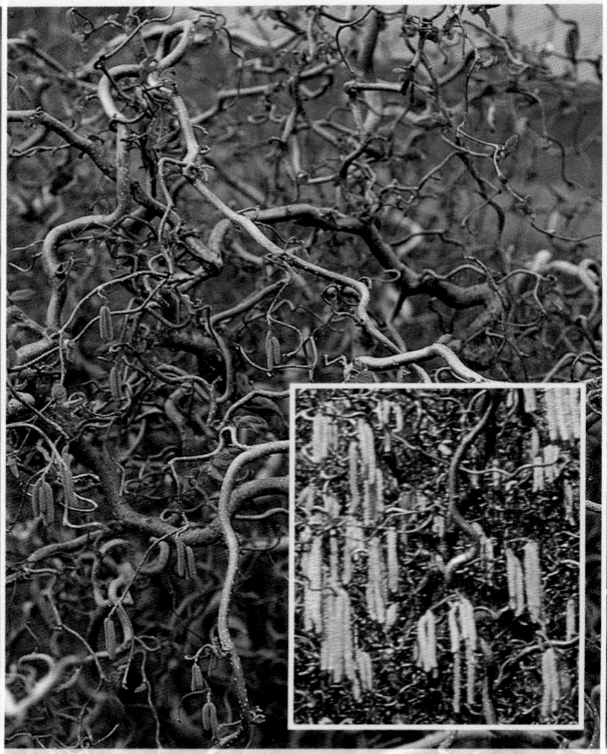

***Corylus avellana* 'Contorta'** (Corkscrew Hazel)
↕↔ 3m (9ft), upright shrub with mid-green leaves, 6cm (2½in) catkins in late winter and early spring (*see inset*)

CORYMBIA

THESE ARE EVERGREEN TREES that all formerly belonged in the *Eucalyptus* genus. Most are smooth-barked, including some, such as *Corymbia citriodora*, where the bark is particularly attractive. A number have fibrous bark. The flowers are petal-less bunches of showy stamens that are cream, yellow, pink, or red. Flower season depends on species. Some are short, stocky trees with dense canopies, while others are taller and more open-branched. All feature trunks that are clear of branches. The leaves are leathery and lance-shaped, and give off a delightful aroma when crushed. This genus includes *C. ficifolia*, probably the best known of the flowering gums.

Hardiness Frost-hardy ✲✲ to very frost-tender ❀.

Cultivation Full sun and plenty of room to grow is essential. **Prune** minimally; remove any shoots that spoil the shape of young plants to encourage a good form (*see p.384*. **Sow** seed (*see pp.391-392*) in spring and summer.

Corymbia ficifolia (Red Flowering Gum)
↕7m (20ft) ↔ 5m (15ft), a popular and not over large gum with showy flowers, suited to frost-free gardens ✲

Corymbia maculata (Spotted Gum)
↕33m (100ft) ↔ 15m (45ft), the trunk is covered in smooth grey bark with darker splotches and spots

Corymbia citriodora (Lemon-scented Gum)
↕20m (60ft) ↔ 10m (30ft), smooth grey bark peels annually to reveal young pink bark underneath

COTINUS

Smoke Bush

↕5–10m (15–30ft)
↔5–8m (15–25ft)

THIS SMALL GROUP OF deciduous shrubs and small, bushy trees are prized for their ornamental, colourful foliage and unusual flowers. These are tiny, but mass in great plumes above the foliage in summer. These resemble puffs of smoke from a distance – hence the common name. The flowers are followed by tiny fruits lasting into autumn, when the foliage usually changes colour. That of *Cotinus coggygria* 'Royal Purple' turns from dark red-purple to red; that of *C.* 'Grace' from purple to a bright, translucent scarlet. They look particularly good in autumn as specimens or planted in groups.

Hardiness Fully frost-hardy ❄❄❄.

Cultivation Cotinus prefer reasonably fertile, well-drained soil, in sun or partial shade. Purple-leaved types have the best-coloured foliage in full sun. **Cut** out misplaced or crossing shoots to maintain a well-shaped flowering shrub, in late winter or early spring (*see p.382*). **Take** softwood cuttings (*see p.394*) in summer or layer shoots (*see p.395*) in spring.

1

2

① ***coggygria* 'Royal Purple'** ↕↔ 5m (15ft), flowers green, turning grey in autumn ② **'Grace'** ↕6m (20ft) ↔ 5m (15ft), vigorous, flowers purple-pink

COTONEASTER

DENSE BUT DAINTY FOLIAGE, a variety of ornamental forms, and autumn berries ensure this plant a place in many gardens. There is a variety of deciduous, semi-evergreen, and evergreen shrubs to choose from. Tiny, pink or white flowers in summer are followed by masses of berries in vivid reds and yellows. The wide range of growth habits make cotoneasters suitable for many sites. They can be grown as freestanding shrubs, weeping trees or hedging, trained against walls, or used as ground cover. You can also use dwarf species in a rock garden. Do not grow close to natural bushland.

Hardiness Fully frost-hardy ❄❄❄.

Cultivation Reasonably fertile, well-drained soil in sun or partial shade is best, but most cotoneasters tolerate dry conditions. Dwarf evergreens fruit better if they are sheltered. Most cotoneasters require little pruning, but will tolerate hard renovation pruning (*see p.384*) if required. **Trim** formal hedges in mid or late summer. **Take** greenwood cuttings of deciduous species in early summer and semi-ripe cuttings of evergreens in late summer (*see p.394*).

Cotoneaster horizontalis 🏆 (Fishbone cotoneaster)
↕1m (3ft) ↔ 5m (15ft), deciduous shrub, spreads in herringbone pattern, red autumn leaves (*inset*), pinky-white flowers in late spring

CRATAEGUS

Hawthorn

THESE EXTREMELY HARDY TREES and shrubs are particularly valuable in exposed gardens. They are usually spiny, deciduous, and medium-sized, with a rounded or spreading habit. Their mid- to dark green foliage often has attractive tints in autumn. Hawthorns produce flat clusters of white or pink blossoms at the ends of the branches. Birds enjoy the berries that follow in autumn, which are mostly scarlet, but sometimes are coloured black, orange, yellow, or blue-green. The berries may cause stomach upsets if eaten. Some species are weeds in certain areas.

Hardiness Fully frost-hardy ***.

Cultivation Hawthorns will grow in any soil, except waterlogged ground, in full sun or partial shade. **Prune out** any crossing or misshapen branches in winter or early spring, to maintain a good shape and healthy framework of branches. **Trim** hedges after flowering or in autumn. **Remove** seed from the berries as soon as they are ripe and sow in a seedbed or in containers (*see pp.391–393*). Germination may take up to eighteen months. Cherry slug and powdery mildew may attack the foliage; pick off the insects or affected leaves if possible.

***Crataegus laevigata* 'Paul's Scarlet'** 🏆
↕↔ to 5m (15ft), thorny, deciduous tree, lobed leaves, abundant flower clusters in late spring are occasionally followed by red berries

CRYPTOMERIA JAPONICA

Japanese Cedar

THIS CONIFEROUS TREE FROM THE FORESTS of China and Japan is grown for its neat, conical or columnar habit and evergreen foliage. This is produced in cloud-like clumps of soft, glossy, dark green needles. Large, round, female cones are borne singly and the smaller, male cones cluster at the shoot tips. The red-brown bark is rugged and fibrous. This is a large tree, reaching up to 25m (80ft), but there are also several smaller cultivars that have pleasingly tinted foliage. Japanese cedars make handsome specimen trees, and the smaller types also blend well in a border with rhododendrons and azaleas (*see pp.104–107*). Try dwarf forms in a large rock garden with heaths (*Erica, see pp.52–53*) and heathers (*Calluna, see p.31*).

Hardiness Fully frost-hardy ***.

Cultivation The Japanese Cedar tolerates most well-drained soils, including limy soils, in full sun or partial shade. It grows best in deep, fertile, moist but well-drained soil that has been enriched with organic matter. This shrub requires no formal pruning.

***Cryptomeria japonica* 'Elegans Compacta'** 🏆
↕2–4m (6–12ft) ↔ 6m (20ft), conical shrub, leaves are dark green when new, turning bronze in autumn, as shown here

x CUPRESSOCYPARIS LEYLANDII

Leyland Cypress

↕35m (120ft)
↔5m (15ft)

THIS WIDELY GROWN CONIFEROUS TREE is most often used as a hedging or screening plant. It has a tapering habit and smooth bark that becomes stringy as it ages. The dense sprays of scale-like foliage are dark green with grey tints. Its dark brown female cones are larger than its yellow male cones. Cultivars with tinted foliage are available, in tones of gold, grey-green, blue-grey, bronze, and lime-green. The Leyland Cypress is a fast-growing tree – if well maintained from a young plant, it forms a fine hedge, windbreak, or specimen tree. If it grows too big, it is better to take it out and start again: you cannot cut it back into old wood because it will not regrow.

Hardiness Fully frost-hardy ***.

Cultivation Any deep, fertile, well-drained soil in full sun will suit this vigorous tree. When grown as a specimen, it needs no formal pruning. **Trim** hedging plants, two to three times a year (without cutting into the old wood), finishing in early autumn (*see p.384*). **Take** semi-ripe cuttings (*see p.394*) in late summer.

× Cupressocyparis leylandii 🏆
Often grown as a hedge, which must be trimmed several times a year to keep it under control

Cupressus

Cypress

From the slender silhouette of the Italian cypress (*Cupressus sempervirens* 'Stricta') to the more stately Monterey Cypress (*C. macrocarpa*), these evergreen, coniferous trees have attractive columnar or conical habits. There are also a few weeping cypresses. Cypresses have scale-like, sometimes glaucous foliage in dark, grey- or blue-green. The bark sometimes peels; the Smooth Cypress (*C. arizonica* var. *glabra*) has reddish-purple bark. Female cones are small and round, and remain for several years; male cones are green, and are found on the shoot tips. Large cypresses are excellent specimen trees; smaller ones can be grouped with other conifers or shrubs. *C. macrocarpa* is good for hedging.

Hardiness Fully frost-hardy ❄❄❄ to frost-tender ❄.

Cultivation Since they come from dry, hillside forests, cypresses tolerate dry soils and grow in any well-drained soil in full sun. **Trim** hedges in late spring (*see p.384*), but do not cut back into old wood because it will not regrow. **Take** semi-ripe cuttings (*see p.394*) in late summer. **Canker** may cause bark to recede, killing twigs and then the tree; cut affected branches back to healthy wood to stop it spreading.

Cupressus macrocarpa 'Goldcrest' 🏆
↕ to 5m (15ft) ↔ 1m (3ft), narrow and upright growing conifer with golden foliage

Cupressus macrocarpa
↕ 25m (75ft) ↔ 15m (45ft), trees often start out columnar but broaden out as they mature ❄❄

Cupressus sempervirens 'Swane's Golden'
↕ to 5m (15ft) ↔ 1m (3ft), a golden form of the common Pencil Pine that originated in Australia

Cytisus

Broom

Abundant, pea-like flowers are produced by these deciduous to evergreen shrubs in spring and summer. The flowers are often fragrant and are borne singly or in clusters, in a variety of shades from white and crimson to yellow. Long, flat, often downy seed pods follow. The usually small, palm-like leaves are mostly mid-green, but the shrubs often become leafless as they mature. Brooms vary in habit from prostrate or spreading to upright, arching or bushy. Smaller species and cultivars suit a rock garden and larger species a shrub or mixed garden. The splendid, tree-like *Cytisus battandieri* (*below*) can be trained against a north-facing wall or fence, where it benefits from the shelter and its silvery leaves reflect the sun.

Hardiness Fully frost-hardy ❄❄❄ to very frost-tender ❄.

Cultivation Grow brooms in reasonably fertile soil in full sun. Brooms thrive in poor, acid soils, but some may become chlorotic (show yellowing leaves) on shallow, alkaline soils. **Plant** young, container-grown shrubs because older plants resent root disturbance. Some species are weedy.

Cytisus battandieri 🏆 (Pineapple Broom)
↕↔ 5m (15ft), deciduous, upright shrub, silvery leaves, pineapple scented flowers from mid- to late summer, needs shelter ❄❄

Daboecia cantabrica

Cantabrican Heath, St. Dabeoc's Heath

THIS EVERGREEN, HEATHER-LIKE SHRUB has given rise to a large number of garden plants. They are grown for their spikes of urn-shaped flowers, appearing from early summer to mid-autumn, in white and purple-crimson, and are typically larger than those of other heaths and heathers. The leaves are small, thin, and dark green. The species is 25–40cm (10–16in) high and spreads to 65cm (26in), but the cultivars vary in size. These shrubs make useful ground-cover plants, around taller heathers or other acid-loving shrubs such as rhododendrons (*see pp.104–107*). If your soil is alkaline, grow them in large pots or a raised bed of potting mix for acid-loving plants.

Hardiness Fully frost-hardy ❄❄❄ to frost-tender ❄.

Cultivation These shrubs need well-drained, acid (lime-free) soil in full sun; they will tolerate neutral soil in part shade. Daboecias are susceptible to root rot, particularly on heavy, wet soils, so on clay soil dig in some gypsum and organic matter to improve drainage. **Prune back** flowered growth in early or mid-spring each year to keep the plant shapely; the easiest way to do this is by clipping it over with shears. **Take** semi-ripe cuttings (*see p.394*) in midsummer.

Daboecia cantabrica 'William Buchanan' ♀
↕35cm (14in) ↔ 55cm (22in) ❄❄

Daphne

DELICIOUSLY FRAGRANT FLOWERS are borne in winter or early spring on these shrubs, so plant them where the wonderful scent can be fully appreciated. The flowers, in shades of red-purple, pink, white, and yellow, may be followed by round, white, pink, red, orange, or purple fruits. Mostly slow-growing, daphnes are generally compact enough for even small gardens. They may be upright, bushy, or prostrate in habit, and there are deciduous, semi-evergreen, and evergreen species, all with neat, usually dark but sometimes variegated leaves. All parts of these plants are toxic, and the sap may irritate skin.

Hardiness Fully frost-hardy ❄❄❄ to frost-hardy ❄❄.

Cultivation Grow in reasonably fertile soil that is well-drained but does not dry out, and is preferably neutral (neither acid nor alkaline). Position in part shade; all resent root disturbance, so choose the site carefully. **Mulch** annually with organic matter around the base (*see p.388*) to keep the roots cool and moist. **Prune** only if absolutely necessary, in late winter or early spring. **Sow** seed in a cold frame as soon as it is ripe (*see pp.391–392*). **Take** softwood cuttings in early and midsummer, and semi-ripe cuttings in late summer (*see p.394*).

Daphne cneorum (Garland Flower)
↕15cm (6in) or more ↔ to 2m (6ft), trailing evergreen with pink or occasionally white, very fragrant flowers in late spring ❄❄❄

Daphne bholua 'Jacqueline Postill' ♀
↕2–4m (6–12ft) ↔ 1.5m (5ft), upright evergreen, fragrant flowers in winter or early spring, black-purple fruits ❄❄❄ (borderline)

Daphne odora 'Aureo-marginata'
↕1.2m (4ft) ↔ 1.2m (4ft), highly perfumed late winter flowers on an evergreen shrub with creamy leaf margins

Daphne × ***burkwoodii*** (Burkwood's Daphne)
↕ 1m (3ft) ↔ 1m (3ft), semi-deciduous small shrub with scented flowers in early to mid spring ✻✻

Daphne mezereum (Mezereon)
↕ 1.2m (4ft) ↔ 1m (3ft), upright, deciduous cottage-garden classic, flowers in late winter or early spring, fleshy red fruits ✻✻✻

Davidia involucrata

Dove Tree, Ghost Tree, Handkerchief Tree

THIS EXTRAORDINARILY BEAUTIFUL tree is festooned with pure white bracts (modified leaves) along the branches in spring. Its unique appearance is reflected in the variety of common names. The leaves are up to 15cm (6in) long, oval in shape with heart-shaped bases and sharply pointed tips. Mid-green and strongly veined, they have reddish stalks and soft hairs underneath. The bracts surround small flowerheads, which are followed by greenish-brown fruits in autumn. Davidia is a large tree; it is related to the dogwoods (*Cornus, see pp.42–43*), which include more compact, but less dramatic, species suited to smaller gardens.

Hardiness Fully frost-hardy ✻✻✻.

Cultivation Grow in fertile, well-drained but moisture-retentive soil, in sun or partial shade. Position where there is shelter from strong, hot winds. **Trim out** any crossing or misplaced branches on young trees in late winter or early spring. **Sow** whole fruits in a container as soon as ripe (*see pp.391–392*): germination will take at least two winters outdoors. Seed-raised trees may take up to ten years to reach flowering size. **Take** hardwood cuttings in winter (*see p.394*).

Davidia involucrata
↕ 15m (50ft) ↔ 10m (30ft), this tree needs plenty of space to develop its shape and be seen at its best

Deutzia

↕↔ to 3m (10ft)

CLUSTERS OF STARRY, white or pink flowers, fragrant on *Deutzia gracilis* and *D. scabra*, almost smother these deciduous shrubs from mid-spring to midsummer. Most have oval leaves, although some are prettily willow-like. All are easy to grow. The larger ones make good specimen plants, often developing attractively peeling bark as they mature, although in colder regions it is best to grow the less hardy types among other trees and shrubs, or in the shelter of a warm wall. Try them alongside shrubs such as Mock Orange (*Philadelphus, see p.93*) and weigelas (*see p.128*) for a harmonious early-summer show.

Hardiness Fully frost-hardy ✻✻✻ to frost-hardy ✻✻.

Cultivation Grow in fertile soil that is not too dry, ideally in full sun; some tolerate part shade. **Cut back** flowered stems to strong buds or young shoots lower down. Encourage new growth on mature plants by cutting one in three or four of the old branches to the base. **Sow** seed in containers in a cold frame in autumn (*see pp.391–392*). **Take** softwood cuttings in summer or hardwood cuttings in autumn (*see p.394*).

① ***Deutzia gracilis*** ↕↔ 1m (3ft) ✻✻✻
② ***D. scabra*** ↕ 3m (10ft) ↔ 2m (6ft) ✻✻✻

Dodonaea

THESE ARE EVERGREEN SHRUBS OR SMALL TREES. The flowers are insignificant, but result in interesting seed capsules, which is one of the main reasons for growing these plants. The seed capsules are small and spherical, and feature three to five papery and wavy wings running down the sides of the capsule. Colours vary, but include yellow, green, or red, and a few have both red and pale green on them. Most stand out brightly against the foliage. The leaves vary and can be oval to linear and even pinnate. They are usually pale to dark green, but forms with purplish foliage are available. The leaves are often sticky with oil, and aromatic when they are crushed.

Hardiness Frost-hardy ❄❄ to frost-tender ❄.

Cultivation Grow in full sun or dappled shade in a well-drained soil. **Prune** minimally; remove any shoots that spoil the shape of (young) plants to encourage a good form (*see p.384*). **Sow** seed (*see p.392*) in a cold frame as soon as it is ripe. **Take** tip cuttings of wood that is just getting hard in spring and summer (*see p.394*). Watch out for scale insects and control them as soon as they are seen (*see p.398*).

Dodonaea viscosa 'Purpurea' (Purple Hop Bush)
↕3–5m (9–15ft) ↔ 2m (6ft), evergreen shrub with bronze foliage and papery seed capsules ❄❄

Dryandra

These are mostly small shrubs that are evergreen and have amazing foliage. This is generally very long and linear, and saw-toothed along the margins, like those of banksias (*see p.27*). Some are holly-like. The flowers are similar to those of the proteas (*see p.99*), to which this plant is related. They have no petals, but some have petal-like coloured foliage, or bracts, at the base. Flowering time is mostly spring, although some flower in summer. The yellow to orange flowers last well as freshly cut flowers and dried. The plants naturally occur on sandy soils so good drainage is essential.

Hardiness Frost-hardy ❄❄ to frost-tender ❄.

Cultivation Full sun is best and the soil must be well-drained. **Tip prune** when young to promote a bushy plant (*see p.390*). **Sow** seed (*see p.391*) in autumn or spring and pot up soon after germination.

Dryandra praemorsa
↕3m (9ft) ↔ 3m (9ft), evergreen shrub with long lasting cut flowers in late winter and into spring

Echium

EVERGREEN SHRUBS THAT ARE NOTED for their vibrant purple-blue flowers. These are in erect cones at the growing tips of the plant in spring and into summer, and are notable bee attractors. The leaves are grey-green, and long and lance-shaped. The plants make rounded shrubs with foliage right to the ground. Fairly fast-growing, they make quick, useful fillers. Grow along with other blue-flowering plants such as ceanothus (*see p.36*) and lavender (*Lavandula, see p.80*), or with yellow-flowered plants such as phlomis (*see p.94*) for contrast. There are also a number of annual and biennial species.

Hardiness Frost-tender ❄ to very frost-tender ❄.

Cultivation Grow in full sun in any well-drained soil that has been enriched with well-rotted organic matter. **Remove** spent flowers to keep the plants bushy and to encourage a good form (*see p.390*). **Sow** seed (*see p.393*) in seedbeds in spring and transplant to permanent positions as soon as possible.

Echium candicans
↕1.8m (6ft) ↔ 1.8m (6ft), bee and butterfly attracting purple-blue flowers in late spring

Elaeagnus

Tough, fast-growing, and resistant to coastal winds, these are immensely useful shrubs and trees. Evergreen or deciduous, they have ornamental, lance-shaped to oval leaves. These may be plain green or silvery, and there are also many with silver or gold variegation. Evergreen elaeagnus make good hedging plants, and the variegated types are great for brightening up a dull garden when used as specimen plants. As a bonus, small clusters of bell-shaped, sometimes very fragrant flowers are borne in summer or autumn, and these are occasionally followed by quite small berries.

Hardiness Fully frost-hardy ❄❄❄.

Cultivation Grow in fertile, well-drained soil; dry soils are tolerated, but the leaves may become yellow on shallow, alkaline soils. Position ideally in full sun; evergreens tolerate partial shade. **Prune** deciduous plants in late winter or early spring, evergreens in mid- or late spring, removing any crossing branches and those that spoil the shape (*see p.382*). **Trim** hedges in late summer. **Cut out** any shoots that revert to plain green leaves on variegated types. **Take** greenwood cuttings in late spring or early summer, or semi-ripe cuttings of deciduous species in late summer (*see p.394*).

Elaeagnus pungens 'Maculata'
↕4m (12ft) ↔ 5m (15ft), dense, slightly spiny evergreen, pendent silvery-white flowers in autumn, brown berries ripening to red

Embothrium coccineum

Chilean Fire Bush, Flame Flower

Spectacular when in flower, this evergreen tree or shrub and its cultivars have an upright, but freely branching or suckering habit, and are capable of very rapid growth in mild conditions. The glowing scarlet flowers are carried in dense clusters in late spring and early summer. The narrowly lance-shaped leaves are up to 13cm (5in) long. In cool climates, the plant is happiest against a warm wall or in a sheltered spot, such as a woodland garden, in a sunny position; in areas where there are few frosts, it will tolerate a more open aspect and make a good specimen tree.

Hardiness Fully frost-hardy ❄❄❄ (borderline) to frost-hardy ❄❄.

Cultivation Grow in fertile, neutral to acid (lime-free) soil enriched with well-rotted organic matter, in full sun or part shade. **Trim off** any crossing shoots and those that spoil the shape in late winter or early spring. **Sow** seed (*see pp.391–392*) at 13–16°C (55–61°F) in spring. **Take** greenwood cuttings in early summer, or semi-ripe cuttings in mid or late summer (*see p.394*). Take root cuttings, or dig up rooted shoots (suckers) growing up around the main plant, in winter.

Embothrium coccineum
↕10m (30ft) ↔ 5m (15ft) or more, ❄❄

Enkianthus

Pendent flower clusters and rich autumnal foliage tints give these plants two seasons of interest. A small group, they are for the most part deciduous shrubs, sometimes trees. The small, delicate flowers are borne at the branch tips from mid-spring to early summer. They are urn- to bell-shaped, in shades from cream or pure white to pink and deep purple-red, with contrasting veins. The autumn display is if anything more distinctive and varies according to the species. *Enkianthus campanulatus* passes through every shade from yellow to red; *E. perulatus* turns brilliant scarlet; and *E. cernuus* f. *rubens* is flushed reddish-purple. They make ideal specimens in a woodland garden.

Hardiness Fully frost-hardy ❄❄❄.

Cultivation Grow in acid (lime-free), moist but well-drained soil enriched with well-rotted organic matter. Position in an open site in full sun or partial shade. **Prune** in late winter or early spring, only to remove misplaced or crossing branches. **Sow** seed at 18–21°C (64–70°F) in late winter or early spring (*see pp.391–393*). **Take** semi-ripe cuttings in summer (*see p.394*) or layer in autumn (*see p.395*).

① *campanulatus* 🏆 ↕↔ 4–5m (12–15ft) ② *cernuus* f. *rubens* 🏆 ↕↔ 2.5m (8ft) ③ *deflexus* ↕2.5–4m (8–12ft) ↔ 3m (10ft) ④ *perulatus* 🏆 ↕↔ to 2m (6ft)

Epacris

These heath-like evergreens are mostly small or even dwarf shrubs, although a few will reach a couple of metres. They have fine, small leaves that are often sharply pointed, and are arranged on the stems directly or with very short leaf stems. The flowers are either starry or small tubes that are starry at the ends. The majority flower in winter or spring. They are white, pink, or red, or even a combination of these colours, and can be quite showy. Dappled shade that mimics their natural habitat is best. Most will also do very well as container plants.

Hardiness Frost-hardy ❄❄.

Cultivation Grow in any well-drained soil that is in part shade and kept reasonably moist. **Tip prune** from a young age to help keep plants bushy. Hard pruning after flowering will encourage new growth. **Take** cuttings of soft wood in spring (*see p.394*).

Epacris impressa 'Spring Pink'
↕60cm (2ft) ↔ 60cm (2ft), has light pink flowers over a couple of months in early and mid spring

Eremophila

Emu Bush

This is a diverse and variable range of plants, from low, squat groundcovers to tall shrubs and small trees. All are evergreen, with foliage that can be dark green through to almost pure silver. Leaves are oval to linear and often hairy. Flowers appear predominantly in spring, although they can occur at other times of the year. These are tubes with a curled lip at the top and bottom of the opening. Flowers can be blue, mauve, red, orange, yellow, or white, and often feature spots on both the exterior and interior of the tube. Most plants grow well in containers where excellent drainage can be ensured.

Hardiness Frost-hardy ❄❄ to very frost-tender ❁.

Cultivation Excellent drainage is the key, along with full sun and a neutral to alkaline soil. **Prune** minimally; tip pruning of plants will encourage bushiness and a good form (*see p.390*). **Take** semi-hardwood or hardwood cuttings (*see p.394*). Many forms are propagated by grafting.

Eremophila glabra
↕1.5m (5ft) ↔ 1.5m (5ft), form and flower colour are variable in this plant

Eremophila maculata 'Aurea'
↕1–2m (3–6ft) ↔ 3m (10ft), bright yellow flowers occur on this form of the Emu Bush

Eremophila maculata 'Nivea'
↕2m (6ft) ↔ 1m (3ft), silvery foliage and lilac-mauve flowers in spring

Erica

Heath

Heaths are evergreens with masses of tiny, usually bell-shaped flowers ranging from shades of red and pink to white, with some bicolours. In some cultivars, the small, tightly curled leaves are tinted with red or gold, or colour in cold weather, so the right choice of cultivars can ensure interest all through the year. Hardy, prostrate species make colourful ground cover, while the taller, upright types, such as *Erica arborea*, can make excellent specimen plants in gardens. Heaths are mainly found in wet areas, but will grow in a variety of conditions.

Hardiness Fully frost-hardy ❄❄❄ to frost-hardy ❄❄.

Cultivation Grow in well-drained, acid soil in an open site in full sun. A few winter- and spring-flowering types, such as *E.* × *darleyensis*, will tolerate a slightly alkaline (limy) soil. **Trim** plants after flowering only as necessary to keep them bushy. **Take** semi-ripe cuttings in mid- or late summer (*see p.394*).

Erica* × *darleyensis (Darley Heath)
↕60–90cm (2–3ft) ↔60cm (2ft), evergreen shrub flowering in late autumn and winter

Erica cerinthoides
↕1m (3ft) ↔ 1m (3ft), flowers in late winter and into spring

Erica melanthera
↕60cm (2ft) ↔ 60cm (2ft), evergreen shrub smothered in flowers in spring

Erythrina

Coral Tree

Large and showy clusters of bright scarlet-red tubular to pea-shaped flowers stand out on these plants, especially as they often appear while the plant is without leaves. Late winter is usually when this happens, although some flower in spring. Tropical trees and shrubs, they can be fully deciduous, semi-deciduous or evergreen. Many also feature sharp prickles or spines. Leaves are variable, but are usually made up of three large, round to heart-shaped leaflets. The seeds are often red and are held in a long, drooping seed pod. These plants do best in warm, dry climates.

Hardiness Frost-tender ❄ to very frost-tender ❀.

Cultivation Grow in full sun in well-drained soil that is kept moist. **Prune** minimally; remove shoots that spoil the shape of young plants to encourage a good form (*see p.384*). **Sow** ripe seed (*see p.391*) in containers after nicking or lightly sandpapering the outer coating.

Erythrina crista-galli
↕6m (20ft) ↔ 3m (10ft), often pruned hard after flowering as the shoots die off after setting seed

Escallonia

Glossy, evergreen foliage and a profusion of flowers are the attractions of these excellent shrubs. Borne over a long period, mainly in summer, the flowers are tubular or saucer-shaped, in shades of white, pink, or red. Escallonias are undemanding plants, being fairly fast-growing and drought-tolerant. Widely grown as tough, wind-resistant hedging, they also make fine, freestanding shrubs in a garden. They are particularly good in coastal areas, where the tough leaves stand up to salt-laden winds. Try them with other robust shrubs, such as cotinus (*see p.44*), lilacs (*Syringa, see p.121*) and abelia (*see p.14*).

Hardiness Fully frost-hardy ❄❄❄ to frost-tender ❄.

Cultivation Grow in fertile, well-drained soil. Position in full sun. **Trim** back shoots that spoil the shape of the shrub lightly in mid- or late spring. **Clip** hedges after flowering. **Take** softwood cuttings in early summer or semi-ripe cuttings in late summer; or try hardwood cuttings from late autumn to winter (*see p.394*).

Escallonia 'Apple Blossom' 🏆
↕↔ 2.5m (8ft), compact bush, slow-growing, flowers in early and mid-summer, suitable for hedging ❄❄

Escallonia rubra 'Woodside'
↕75cm (30in) ↔ 1.5m (5ft), dwarf form, flowers from summer to early autumn, cut out any overly vigorous shoots promptly ❄❄❄

Eucalyptus

Gum

These distinctive trees and shrubs are grown for their handsome, often aromatic, evergreen foliage, and their ornamental bark. The foliage is usually mid- or grey-green and leathery. The young, or juvenile, leaves of many species are most attractive, and look rather like silvery circles. These are replaced by the familiar sickle-shaped leaves as the plant matures. Small clusters of petal-less flowers open in summer, and may be white, creamy yellow, or red. The bark is smooth and white in some species, flaking or striped in shades of green or tawny brown in others, or black, thick and deeply furrowed. As specimen trees they grow quickly and need quite a bit of space.

Hardiness Fully frost-hardy ❄❄❄ to very frost-tender ❄.

Cultivation Grow in most soils in full sun. **Prune** crossing or misplaced branches in late winter or early spring. **Sow** seed at 13–18°C (55–64°F) in spring or summer (*see pp.391–392*).

Eucalyptus gunnii 🏆 (Cider Gum)
↕10–25m (30–80ft) ↔ 6–15m (20–50ft), flowers in summer or autumn (*see inset*), bark shed in late summer ❄❄❄ (borderline)

Eucalyptus caesia subsp. *magna*
↕10m (30ft) ↔ 5m (15ft), weeping habit, showy flowers and attractive bark ❄❄

Eucalyptus dalrympleana 🏆 (Mountain Gum)
↕20m (70ft) ↔ 8m (25ft), vigorous tree, blue-green new leaves, flowers late summer to autumn, tolerates chalk soil ❄❄❄ (borderline)

EUCRYPHIA

Leatherwood

↕to 15m (50ft)
↔to 8m (25ft)

VALUED FOR THEIR late flowering, this is a small group of mostly evergreen, columnar trees and shrubs. Their beautiful, often fragrant flowers are white, occasionally pink or with pink edges to the petals, and have a fluffy mass of stamens at the centre. They are borne from summer to early autumn, once the plants are a few years old. The leaves are leathery, usually oval but sometimes made up of narrow leaflets along a central stalk. Eucryphias make glorious specimen plants or flowering hedges in a sheltered spot.

Hardiness Fully frost-hardy ❄❄❄ to frost-hardy ❄❄.

Cultivation Grow in fertile, moist but well-drained soil that is neutral to acid (lime-free). *E.* x *nymanensis* tolerates alkaline soil. Position with the roots in shade and the crown in full sun. Needs shelter from hot, drying winds in all but mild areas. **Remove** fading flowers if the plant is small enough to make this practical. **Prune out** any crossing or dead wood in late winter or early spring, or lightly trim shoots that spoil the shape in mid- or late spring (or for *E. lucida*, after flowering). Do not overprune, or you will lose the flowers. **Take** semi-ripe cuttings (*see p.394*) in summer, and overwinter new plants in frost-free conditions.

Eucalyptus leucoxylon 'Rosea'
↕8m (20ft) ↔ 8m (20ft), a smaller growing gum tree with bird attracting flowers in autumn, winter or spring

Eucalyptus pauciflora (Snow Gum)
↕6m (20ft) ↔ 6–15m (20–50ft), slow-growing, flowers late spring to summer, bark sheds late summer to autumn ❄❄❄

Eucryphia glutinosa 🏆
↕10m (30ft) ↔ 6m (20ft), deciduous or semi-evergreen tree or shrub, flowers in mid- to late summer, tolerates exposed sites ❄❄❄

Euonymus

Spindle Tree

COLOURFUL FOLIAGE IS the main feature of this large group of shrubs and trees. Deciduous types have fiery autumn foliage and decorative fruits, while most of the evergreens have bright variegation that brings colour to the garden all year. The leaves are variable, but usually broadly oval, and small clusters of purple-red or red-brown flowers appear in late spring or summer. The evergreens can be used as specimen shrubs in gardens, or as hedging or ground cover. Some *Euonymus fortunei* types will climb if planted by a wall. Young plants are useful in winter window boxes and containers. All parts may cause mild stomach upset if eaten.

Hardiness Fully frost-hardy ❄❄❄ to frost-hardy ❄❄.

Cultivation Grow in any well-drained soil; deciduous species are more drought-tolerant. Site in full sun (especially variegated types) or partial shade; in full sun they need moist soil. **Prune** deciduous types in late winter or early spring if needed and evergreens if necessary after flowering (*see p.383*). **Sow** seed (*see pp.391–392*) in a container in a cold frame as soon as it is ripe. **Take** softwood cuttings of deciduous species, and semi-ripe cuttings of evergreens in summer (*see p.394*). Ensure good air circulation to prevent attack of mildew.

NON-VARIEGATED SHOOTS should be removed as soon as they are seen to stop the plant reverting. Green shoots in particular are vigorous and will take over the plant.

***Euonymus fortunei* 'Emerald 'n' Gold'** 🏆
↕60cm (24in) ↔ 90cm (36in), dense, bushy, evergreen shrub, gold leaf edges turn pink in winter, white fruits and orange seeds ❄❄❄

Euphorbia

Milkweed, Spurge

see also pp.242–243

IN THIS LARGE AND WIDELY VARIED group of plants, there are a few evergreen shrubs and trees. They are grown for their impressive foliage and distinctive flowerheads. The leaves are mostly narrow and lance-shaped; in *Euphorbia characias* they are blue-green and very architectural. *E.* × *martini* has leaves that are flushed purple when young, on red-tinged stems; its flowerheads are long-lasting and borne in spring and summer. The flowers are brown and honey-scented in *E. mellifera*, the honey spurge, and yellow-green with dark-red nectar glands in *E.* × *martini*. Spurges are suitable for coastal gardens. All parts of euphorbias can cause severe discomfort if eaten, and contact with the milky sap may irritate skin.

Hardiness Fully frost-hardy ❄❄❄ to frost-hardy ❄❄.

Cultivation Grow in well-drained soil in full sun. Dig in plenty of gypsum and organic matter on heavy clay soils to improve drainage. **Take** softwood cuttings (*see p.394*) in spring or early summer, wearing gloves, and dipping the ends in lukewarm water to stem the bleeding of sap. Aphids (*see p.398*) may need treatment in severe cases.

Euonymus alatus 🏆 (Winged Spindle)
↕2m (6ft) ↔ 3m (10ft), dense, deciduous shrub, red-purple fruits with orange seeds, dark green leaves until autumn ❄❄❄

Euphorbia characias
↕1.5m (5ft) ↔ 1.5m (5ft), drought tolerant spring flowering shrub

Euryops

CHEERFUL, YELLOW DAISY FLOWERS are the hallmark of these plants. These often occur in winter, brightening up an otherwise dull garden. Some flower in spring or summer and can even provide a few flowers throughout the year if conditions are right. The leaves are sometimes bright green, but mostly they are grey-green and fern-like. They are small to medium, evergreen shrubs that are fairly quick-growing. All enjoy full sun and many withstand very dry conditions. Grow with other winter-flowering plants such as wattles (*Acacia*, *see p.17*) and japonica (*Chaenomeles*, *see p.38*).

Hardiness Frost-hardy ❄❄ to frost-tender ❄.

Cultivation Grow in full sun in any well-drained soil that is enriched with well-rotted organic matter. **Trim** all over with hedge shears after flowering to remove the spent flowers and to keep the plant bushy (*see p.384*). **Take** heeled cuttings in late summer and early autumn and place in a cold frame (*see p.394*).

Euryops pectinatus
↕1.8m (6ft) ↔ 1.2m (4ft), a compact daisy with bright flowers in winter

Exochorda

Pearl Bush

↕↔ 2–4m (6–12ft)

SHOWY, PURE WHITE blooms wreath the branches of these shrubs in spring to summer; not for nothing is the most popular variety named 'The Bride'. All are deciduous, with an attractive, arching habit, and are equally impressive grown with other shrubs in a garden or as isolated specimen plants. They flower at around the same time or a little later than the spring-flowering magnolias (*see p.86*) and their flowers are more resistant to heavy frost, which makes them an excellent alternative for a blossom display in frost-prone areas where magnolia flowers might be spoiled.

Hardiness Fully frost-hardy ❄❄❄.

Cultivation Grow in fertile, moist, but well-drained soil; these shrubs will tolerate all but the shallowest, alkaline soils, where the leaves may become yellow (chlorotic). Position in full sun or partial shade. **Encourage** fresh growth on mature plants by cutting one in three or four older branches back to the base every few years. **Take** softwood cuttings (*see p.394*) in summer.

***Exochorda* × *macrantha* 'The Bride'** 🏆
↕2m (6ft) ↔ 3m (10ft), forms a compact, arching mound with fragrant flowers in late spring and early summer

Fagus

Beech

THESE STATELY, DECIDUOUS TREES are grown for their fine forms and handsome foliage. They are large and spreading, with wavy edged or toothed, oval leaves. In most, these are pale green when they first open in spring, maturing to dark green and then taking on soft yellow or russet-brown tones in autumn, but there are several beeches with dramatic, dark, purple or coppery foliage. All make fine specimen trees in a large garden; the common beech, *Fagus sylvatica,* is also used as a hedge; when clipped, it retains its brown leaves all winter. For smaller gardens, look for narrow or compact forms, such as 'Purpurea Pendula', with branches that often trail to the ground.

Hardiness Fully frost-hardy ❄❄❄.

Cultivation Grow in any well-drained soil. Position in sun or part shade; purple-leaved types have the best foliage colour in full sun. **Prune out** crossing branches and any that spoil the shape of the tree in late winter or early spring. **Trim** hedges of *F. sylvatica* in mid- to late summer. **Sow** seed in a seedbed in autumn or spring (*see pp.391–392*).

***Fagus sylvatica* 'Dawyck Purple'** 🏆
↕20m (70ft) ↔ 5m (15ft), particularly good purple-leaved type, also one of the narrowest columnar forms

Fatsia japonica

Fatsia, Japanese Aralia

THE LARGE, GLOSSY GREEN LEAVES of these evergreen, spreading shrubs are ideal for creating a jungly garden, and make a dramatic contrast to feathery foliage plants such as ferns (*see pp.356–365*). An excellent architectural plant for a shady garden, it tolerates pollution and thrives in city gardens, but is also a good choice for coastal areas, where the tough leaves will withstand salt-laden winds and sea spray. Broad, upright clusters of rounded, creamy white flowerheads are produced in autumn, followed by small, round, black berries that are inedible. There are also some variegated cultivars, but they tend to be less hardy.

Hardiness Fully frost-hardy ❄❄❄ to frost-tender ❄.

Cultivation This shrub will thrive in any fertile, moist but well-drained soil in full sun or partial shade. **Trim** lightly or prune shoots that spoil the shape in mid- or late spring. **Remove** the fading flowers unless seed is wanted. **Sow** seed (*see pp.391–393*) at 15–21°C (59–70°F) in autumn or spring. **Take** greenwood cuttings (*see p.394*) in early or mid-summer.

Fatsia japonica ♀

↕↔ 1.5–4m (5–12ft), leaves are 15–40cm (6–16in) across ❄❄❄

Ficus carica

Common Fig

↕3m (10ft)
↔4m (12ft)

UNLIKE MOST FIGS, *Ficus carica* is hardy. It can be grown as a free-standing tree, but will quickly spread to cover a large area if trained against a wall. The handsome, deciduous foliage is its main attraction, along with its edible figs. In summer, these pear-shaped "fruits" appear with true flowers inside. The fruits are green when young and mature after a second, long, hot summer into dark green, purple, or dark brown figs. The leaves can cause skin rashes in sunlight (photodermatitis).

Hardiness Fully frost-hardy ❄❄❄.

Cultivation Figs prefer moist but well-drained soil, enriched with plenty of well-rotted organic matter, in full sun or partial shade. **Prune out** misplaced or crossing shoots that spoil the shape in late winter or early spring.

Ficus carica

The leathery leaves can reach 24cm (10in) across and are fairly tolerant of salty air

Forsythia

THESE SUPERBLY RELIABLE, deciduous shrubs will be covered in flowers every spring and sometimes in late winter, no matter what the weather throws at them. The bright yellow blooms appear in profusion all along the length of the stems, singly or in small clusters, before the leaves open. Most forsythias are medium-sized, bushy or upright shrubs; a few are semi-evergreen. These versatile shrubs can be grown freestanding, and also make good informal hedging plants. A classic spring planting combination involves forsythias along with red-flowering currants (*Ribes, see p.109*).

Hardiness Fully frost-hardy ❄❄❄.

Cultivation Reasonably fertile, moist but well-drained soil is needed. **Position** in full sun or partial shade. **Prune back** flowered shoots to strong shoots lower down after flowering. Cut about one-third to a quarter of old stems on mature plants to the base every 4–5 years: cut back hard neglected, leggy plants over two years to rejuvenate (*see p.384*). **Trim** hedges in summer. **Take** greenwood cuttings in early summer or semi-ripe cuttings in late summer (*see p.394*).

Forsythia suspensa

↕↔ 3m (10ft), upright or arching, leaves mid- to dark green, flowers in early and mid-spring, tolerates south- or east-facing wall

Forsythia × *intermedia* 'Lynwood' ♡
↕↔ 3m (10ft), bushy habit, sharply toothed leaves, flowers are 2.5–3.5cm (1¼–1½in) across and borne in early and mid-spring

FOTHERGILLA

THERE ARE JUST TWO SPECIES of these deciduous, low-growing shrubs from woodlands and swamps. They are grown for their bottlebrush-like clusters of scented flowers which are produced before the leaves unfold. Fothergillas also have attractive, dark green foliage, which has toothed edges and turns brilliant shades of red, orange, and golden yellow in autumn. The witch alder (*Fothergilla gardenii*) is the smaller of the two, forming a dense bush with a height and spread of 1m (3ft); it flowers in spring. The slow-growing *F. major* is an upright shrub and has more glossy leaves; its flowers are occasionally tinged with pink.

Hardiness Fully frost-hardy ❄❄❄.

Cultivation Grow fothergillas in moist but well-drained, acid (lime-free) soil that has been enriched with well-rotted organic matter. **Position** in full sun or partial shade; full sun encourages more flowers and better autumn colour. **Prune off** crossing or misshapen shoots that spoil the shape of the shrub in late winter or early spring, only if necessary (*see p.382*). **Sow** seed (*see pp.391–393*) in a container in autumn or winter; it will take two years to germinate. **Take** softwood cuttings (*see p.394*).

Fothergilla major ♡
↕2.5m (8ft) ↔ 2m (6ft), found naturally in drier habitats than *F. gardenii*, including dry woods and rocky riverbanks

FRAXINUS

Ash

THESE DECIDUOUS TREES ARE TOUGH as well as decorative. They tolerate pollution and wind, and have fine foliage. The leaves are made up of small leaflets along central stalks up to 50cm (20in) long. Fast-growing, ash trees have attractive habits, ranging from narrow or columnar to round or spreading. Ash trees have tiny flowers, but those of *Fraxinus ornus* are decorative. Most are suitable only for large gardens, being 15–30m (50–100ft) tall: the weeping *F. excelsior* 'Pendula' is smaller than many. Ashes seed themselves about quite prolifically, so be vigilant in rooting out any seedlings. They look good with trees such as birches (*Betula*, *see p.28*), beeches (*Fagus*, *see p.57*), and oaks (*Quercus*, *see p.103*).

Hardiness Fully frost-hardy ❄❄❄ to frost-hardy ❄❄.

Cultivation Ash trees need fertile, moist soil that is well-drained and neutral to acid (lime-free); *F. angustifolius* and *F. ornus* tolerate fairly dry soils from acid to alkaline (limy). **Position** in full sun. **Sow** seed (*see pp.391–393*) in autumn or spring in an open cold frame; the seed requires 2–3 months of cold before it will germinate.

Fraxinus excelsior 'Jaspidea' ♡
↕30m (100ft) ↔ 20m (70ft), yellow shoots and leaves in winter and spring, leaves dark green in summer, sold as *F. excelsior* 'Aurea'

FUCHSIA

THE BRIGHTLY COLOURED, PENDULOUS FLOWERS of fuchsias are unmistakeable. They vary from elegant, single and semi-double forms to frilly, fully double blooms, and appear from summer until late autumn. Deciduous or evergreen shrubs, fuchsias are very versatile. They can be planted in mixed gardens and as hedging, some can be trained against walls or grown as standards or pillars (*see below*), and cultivars with a trailing habit are ideal in raised containers and hanging baskets, where the flowers spill over the edges to great effect. Fuchsias can be divided into two groups, very frost-hardy to frost-hardy, and frost-tender to very frost-tender. The former may lose all their leaves in harsh winters, but will reshoot in the spring if they have been well planted and mulched. The latter, with a wide range of extravagant flowers, can be grown outdoors in the summer, making showy plants either in gardens or in containers underplanted with annuals, but need protection during severe winters: keep frost-tender types in a frost-free greenhouse, shed, or garage, and very frost-tender plants in a slightly warmer place.

Hardiness Fully frost-hardy ✻✻✻ to very frost-tender ❀.

Cultivation Grow in fertile, moist but well-drained soil in full sun or partial shade, with shelter from hot, drying winds. **Water** well in summer and feed with a balanced liquid fertilizer every two weeks. **Cut** the old stems of hardy fuchsias to the ground in spring. **Lift** tender cultivars in autumn, keeping them in a frost-free place during winter and spring, watering sufficiently to keep them just moist. **Take** softwood cuttings in spring (*see pp.394*). Treat grey mould (botrytis) with fungicide, and rust (tiny orange pustules) by removing affected leaves.

Pruning and training

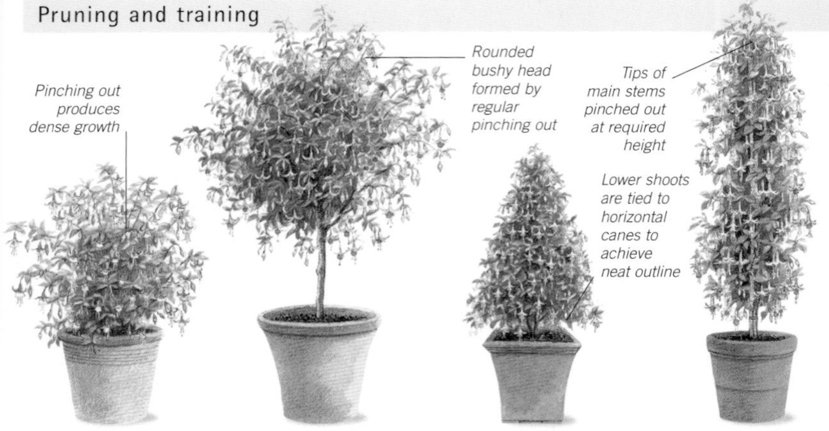
Pinching out produces dense growth
Rounded bushy head formed by regular pinching out
Tips of main stems pinched out at required height
Lower shoots are tied to horizontal canes to achieve neat outline

Bush *When each shoot has made about three pairs of leaves, pinch out the tip. This encourages the plant to produce sideshoots. Continue to do this three or four times and then allow the plant to flower.*

Standard *This shape is achieved by training a shoot up a cane, removing sideshoots. When the main stem reaches the required height, pinch out the tip and treat the top as for a bush. Training takes 2–3 years.*

Pyramid *Allow the main stem to grow to 23cm (9in). Pinch out the tip, keeping one shoot to continue as a new leader. Pinch out all sideshoots at three pairs of leaves. Repeat until the right height and shape is reached.*

Column *Allow two shoots to develop as central stems, and stop them at the desired height. Pinch the sideshoots regularly to create dense, bushy growth. As with a standard, this takes 2–3 years.*

1

2

5

6

11

① 'Annabel' 🏆 ↕↔ 30–60cm (12–24in) ✻ ② ***arborescens*** ↕ 2m (6ft) ↔ 1.7m (5½ft) ❀
③ 'Bicentennial' 🏆 ↕ 30–45cm (12–18in) ↔ 45–60cm (18–24in) ✻ ④ 'Billy Green' 🏆 ↕ 45–60cm (18–24in) ↔ 30–45cm (12–18in) ✻ ⑤ 'Celia Smedley' 🏆 ↕↔ 45–75cm (18–30in) ✻

⑥ 'Checkerboard' 🏆 ↕75–90cm (30–36in) ↔ 45–75cm (18–30in) ❄ ⑦ 'Coralle' ↕45–90cm (18–36in) ↔ 45–60cm (18–24in) ❀ ⑧ 'Dark Eyes' 🏆 ↕45–60cm (18–24in) ↔ 60–75cm (24–30in) ❄ ⑨ 'Display' 🏆 ↕60–75cm (24–30in) ↔ 45–60cm (18–24in) ❄❄ ⑩ 'Dollar Princess' 🏆 ↕45cm (18in) ↔ 45–60cm (18–24in) ❄❄ ⑪ 'Flirtation Waltz' ↕45–60cm (18–24in) ↔ 30–45cm (12–18in) ❄ ⑫ *fulgens* 🏆 ↕1.5m (5ft) ↔ to 80cm (32in) ❀ ⑬ 'Genii' 🏆 ↕↔ 75–90cm (30–36in) ❄❄ ⑭ 'Golden Marinka' 🏆 ↕15–30cm (6–12in) ↔ 30–45cm (12–18in) ❄

15

16

17

21

22

23

24

26

27

32

31

⑮ **'La Campanella'** 🏆 ↕15–30cm (6–12in) ↔ 30–45cm (12–18in) ✻ ⑯ **'Lady Thumb'** 🏆 ↕15–30cm (6–12in) ↔ 30–45cm (12–18in) ✻✻ ⑰ **'Leonora'** ↕60–75cm (24–30in) ↔ 30–60cm (12–24in) ✻ ⑱ **'Lye's Unique'** 🏆 ↕45–60cm (18–24in) ↔ 30–45cm (12–18in) ✻

⑲ **'Machu Picchu'** ↕↔ 30–60cm (12–24in) ✻ ⑳ ***magellanica*** ↕↔ 2–3m (6–10ft) ✻✻ ㉑ **'Marinka'** 🏆 ↕15–30cm (6–12in) ↔ 45–60cm (18–24in) ✻ ㉒ **'Mary'** 🏆 ↕↔ 30–60cm (12–24in) ❀ ㉓ **'Mieke Meursing'** 🏆 ↕↔ 30–60cm (12–24in) ✻ ㉔ **'Mrs Popple'** 🏆 ↕↔ 1–1.1m (3–3½ft) ✻✻✻

18

19

20

25

29

30

28

33

34

㉕ **'Peppermint Stick'** ↕↔ 45–75cm (18–30in) ❄ ㉖ **'Phyllis'** 🏆 ↕ 1–1.5m (3–5ft) ↔ 75–90cm (30–36in) ❄❄ ㉗ ***procumbens*** ↕ 10–15cm (4–6in) ↔ 1–1.2m (3–4ft) ❄❄ ㉘ **'Red Spider'** ↕ 15–30cm (6–12in) ↔ 30–60cm (12–24in) ❄ ㉙ **'Royal Velvet'** 🏆 ↕ 45–75cm (18–30in) ↔ 30–60cm (12–24in) ❄

㉚ **'Rufus'** 🏆 ↕ 45–75cm (18–30in) ↔ 30–60cm (12–24in) ❄❄ ㉛ **'Swingtime'** 🏆 ↕ 30–60cm (12–24in) ↔ 45–75cm (18–30in) ❄ ㉜ **'Thalia'** 🏆 ↕↔ 45–90cm (18–36in) ❀ ㉝ **'Tom Thumb'** 🏆 ↕↔ 15–30cm (6–12in) ❄❄ ㉞ **'Winston Churchill'** 🏆 ↕↔ 45–75cm (18–30in) ❄

Gardenia

Delicious perfume is the principal reason these evergreen shrubs and trees are grown. The scent comes in summer from creamy to white flowers that are spiral in the bud before they unfurl. Various flower forms are available, and doubles are particularly popular. The foliage is dense and made up of glossy, dark green leaves, often indented along the veins. They are gross feeders, and a watch should be kept for yellowing of foliage, which indicates lack of nutrients, particularly nitrogen. They make particularly good container plants, which means their perfume can be enjoyed in courtyards, patios, and even on balconies.

Hardiness Frost-tender ❄ to very frost-tender ❄.

Cultivation Grow in any well-drained soil that is fertile, enriched with well-rotted organic matter and on the acidic (lime-free) side. Keep moist and grow in full sun or partial shade. **Prune** minimally; remove any shoots that spoil the shape of young plants to encourage a good form (*see p.384*). **Take** semi-hardwood tip cuttings from autumn to spring and place in a cold frame (*see p.394*).

Gardenia augusta 'Florida'
↕1m (3ft) ↔ to 1m (3ft), beautifully scented summer flowers❄

Garrya

Long catkins adorn these tough, large, evergreen shrubs from mid- to late winter. Male and female flowers are borne on separate plants, the male catkins being more dramatic. Most widely grown is the silk-tassel bush, *Garrya elliptica*. Garryas are versatile: they can be grown in a garden, trained against a wall, or even used as hedging. They tolerate urban pollution, and the leathery, wavy-edged leaves stand up to salt-laden winds and sea spray in coastal areas. Grow with other winter-flowering shrubs like *Jasminum nudiflorum* (*see p.76*), trained against a wall, and mahonias (*see p.87*).

Hardiness Fully frost-hardy ❄❄❄ (borderline) to frost-tender ❄.

Cultivation Grow in reasonably fertile, well-drained soil, in full sun or partial shade. **Prune** lightly after flowering, cutting out shoots that spoil the shape. Garryas tolerate hard renovation pruning (*see p.384*). **Take** semi-ripe cuttings (*see p.394*) in summer.

Garrya elliptica 'James Roof' 🏆
↕↔4m (12ft), vigorous shrub, male plants noted for particularly long catkins up to 20cm (8in) ❄❄❄

Gaultheria

Pernettya

Colourful autumn fruits are the main attraction of these trouble-free, evergreen shrubs. They bear small flowers just 7mm (¼in) long, usually in small clusters, in spring or summer. These are followed in autumn by berries in dusky shades of red, purple, and pink to white. These are edible; all other parts cause stomach upsets if eaten. Small to medium-sized, these shrubs have neat, dark green, leathery leaves and varied habits. Gaultherias can be grown in mixed gardens, rock gardens, or woodland settings, and they make excellent companions for rhododendrons (*see pp.104–107*). Some have been subject to name changes, and they are often sold simply as pernettyas.

Hardiness Fully frost-hardy ❄❄❄ to frost-tender ❄.

Cultivation Gaultherias need acid (lime-free), moist soil, ideally in partial shade, although they will tolerate full sun where the soil is permanently moist. **Prune** lightly after flowering, cutting back shoots that spoil the shape of the shrub. Restrict the spread of plants by removing suckering growths. **Sow** seed (*see pp.391–393*) in containers outdoors in a cold frame in autumn. **Take** semi-ripe cuttings (*see p.394*) in summer or remove rooted suckers in spring and replant.

Gaultheria hispida
↕1m (3ft) ↔ to 1m (3ft), needs a cool and moist root run to do well

GENISTA

Broom

THESE ELEGANT SHRUBS are grown for their pretty, pea-like yellow flowers, borne in small clusters from spring to summer. They are related to the other brooms, cytisus (*see p.47*) and spartiums (*see p.118*). The leaves are small. Although some species are almost leafless and almost all are deciduous, the green stems give some colour to a garden even in winter. Habits vary from upright to arching, tree-like forms. Brooms contrast well with broader-leaved plants such as ceanothus (*see p.36*) and fatsias (*see p.58*). The Mount Etna Broom makes a graceful specimen in a lawn or shrub border, while dwarfer species, like the dense, spiny *Genista hispanca*, suit rock gardens. Some are environmental weeds so check before planting any.

Hardiness Fully frost-hardy ❄❄❄ to frost-tender ❄.

Cultivation Genistas like light, poor to reasonably fertile, well-drained soil, in full sun. **Prune** minimally; remove misplaced or crossing shoots that spoil the shape, in late winter or early spring. Avoid cutting into old wood, because it will not produce new shoots. **Sow** seed (*see pp.391–393*) in a cold frame in autumn or take semi-ripe cuttings (*see p.394*) in summer.

Genista lydia 🏆
↕ to 60cm (24in) ↔ to 1m (3ft), domed shrub with spine-tipped, blue-green shoots, flowers in early summer ❄❄❄

Genista aetnensis 🏆 (Mount Etna Broom)
↕↔ 8m (25ft), weeping shrub or small tree, leaves produced only on the younger shoots, fragrant flowers borne in profusion at ends of shoots in mid- to late summer ❄❄

GINKGO BILOBA

Maidenhair Tree

PERHAPS THE MOST ANCIENT OF ALL LIVING TREES, the ginkgo is an upright or columnar tree when young and becomes spreading as it ages. The deciduous foliage, which is similar to that of maidenhair ferns (*Adiantum, see p.360*) and gives the tree its common name, turns a soft, golden yellow in autumn. Catkin-like, yellow male flowers and tiny female flowers are produced on separate trees. Given warm summers, female flowers produce plum-like, yellow-green fruits in autumn that smell unpleasant but contain large, edible nuts that are traditionally roasted. Trouble-free and easy, if a little slow, to grow, ginkgos will tolerate atmospheric pollution and are excellent as landscape trees, especially as specimens.

Hardiness Fully frost-hardy ❄❄❄.

Cultivation Any fertile, well-drained soil, in full sun will suit ginkgos. **Prune out** any crossing or misshapen branches that spoil the shape of the tree, in late winter or early spring, to maintain a healthy framework (*see p.382*). **Sow** seed (*see pp.391–393*) in a cold frame as soon as it is ripe. **Take** semi-ripe cuttings (*see p.394*) in summer.

Gingko biloba 🏆
↕ to 30m (100ft) ↔ to 8m (25ft), extinct in the wild, the ginkgo has long been grown in temples and as a street tree in China and Japan

Gleditsia

Honey Locust

DECORATIVE FOLIAGE AND SEED PODS, and an elegant, spreading habit, make these deciduous trees beautiful specimen plants. The glossy, ferny leaves are divided into as many as 24 smaller, pale to dark green leaflets. In autumn, long, curved and twisted, pendent seed pods and foliage in yellow tints give further interest. The widely grown honey locust, *Gleditsia triacanthos*, usually has spiny trunks and shoots. 'Elegantissima' is a much smaller and thornless form of this tree, while 'Rubylace' has dark bronze-red young leaves that turn to dark bronze-green by mid-summer, and is also thornless. To highlight the autumn foliage of these trees, grow them alongside dark-leaved shrubs like cotinus (*see p.44*).

Hardiness Fully frost-hardy ❄❄❄.

Cultivation Grow gleditsias in any fertile, well-drained soil, in sun. **Pruning** is rarely necessary. **Sow** seed (*see pp.391–393*) in an open frame in autumn. **Prepare** the seed by chipping each seed coat with a knife or rubbing it with sandpaper to allow moisture in. Gall midges may cause swellings on the leaves.

Gleditsia triacanthos **'Sunburst'** (Golden Honey Locust) 🏆
↕12m (40ft) ↔ 10m (30ft), fast-growing and thornless

Gordonia

THE FLOWERS ARE BEAUTIFUL, single and white with prominent central stamens, and look like those of a single-flowered camellia (*see p.32*), to which these plants are related. The flowers appear in autumn and winter, which is a decided attraction about this plant. The leaves are glossy, dark green and oval to lance-shaped. They are mostly shrubs or small trees, and all are evergreen. Grow as a background plant where its flowers will still be visible. Grow with camellias, azaleas (*see p.104*) and rhododendrons (*see p.104*), which enjoy the same conditions.

Hardiness Very frost-tender ❅.

Cultivation Grow in dappled light in any well-drained soil that is reasonably fertile and enriched with well-rotted organic matter that is acid (lime-free). **Prune** minimally; remove any shoots that spoil the shape of plants to encourage a good form (*see p.384*). **Take** heeled semi-hardwood cuttings in late summer to autumn (*see p.394*).

Gordonia axillaris
↕5m (15ft) ↔ 3m (9ft), late winter and spring flowers on a dense evergreen shrub

Grevillea

AN INCREDIBLY DIVERSE AND VARIABLE RANGE of evergreen plants, from large, upright trees down to scrambling groundcovers. The majority are medium shrubs. The leaves can be large or small, range from needle-like through to broad, and can be heavily lobed. Many have sharp tips. They are mostly mid-green, and paler underneath, although some are grey. The flowers are spider-like and often appear in long, toothbrush-like clusters. The colours are mostly orange to red, although white, yellow, and green are not uncommon. Flowering time varies and every time of the year would be covered by one form or another. These plants are justifiably famous for attracting birds to the garden.

Hardiness Fully frost-hardy ❄❄❄ to very frost-tender ❅.

Cultivation Grow in any well-drained soil in full sun or partial shade. **Trim** young plants to encourage a good form and bushiness (*see p.384*). **Sow** fresh, ripe seed (*see pp.391–392*) in a cold frame after nicking the outer coating or lightly rubbing with sandpaper. **Take** semi-hardwood cuttings in spring and summer (*see p.394*).

Grevillea **'Robyn Gordon'**
↕1.5m (5ft) ↔ 1.5m (5ft), free flowering throughout the year, but unfortunately known to cause skin rashes ❄❄ (borderline)

Grevillea 'Poorinda Peter'
↕3m (9ft) ↔ 3m (9ft), flowers late winter and into spring ❄❄ (borderline)

Grevillea 'Bronze Rambler'
↕30cm (1ft) ↔ 4m (12ft), spreading groundcover sometimes grafted on tall rootstock to become a weeping standard ❄❄ (borderline)

Grevillea robusta
↕20m (60ft) ↔ 10m (30ft), the large orange flowers on this tree appear in midsummer ❄❄

Hakea

A variable group of evergreen shrubs and small trees, some are grown for their showy flowers and others for their bold foliage. The flowers are spidery and although hidden on some plants, on many they are very conspicuous and occur in balls or bottlebrush or toothbrush arrangements. White, cream, and red are the most common colours. The rigid leaves can be needle-like, oval, or broad, and edged with lobes and short spines. Some, such as *Hakea victoria*, feature leaf variegations, such as green, orange, and red. The seed pod is a hard, rough, woody nut, often with a sharp beak and holding only one or two seeds.

Hardiness Frost-hardy ❄❄ to very frost-tender ❄.

Cultivation Grow in any well-drained soil, although some will tolerate poor conditions. Full sun is best. **Prune** minimally; remove any shoots that spoil the shape of young plants to encourage a good form (*see p.384*). **Sow** seed (*see pp.391–392)* in containers soon after it has been collected.

Hakea laurina
↕4–8m (13–25ft) ↔ 3–10m (10–30ft)

Hamamelis

Witch Hazel

FRAGRANT, SPIDERY BLOOMS and autumn colour make these medium-sized to large, deciduous shrubs important in the winter garden. The striking flowers, with four narrow, twisting, ribbon-like petals, cluster thickly on bare stems from winter to early spring. Frost does not damage them. The broad, oval leaves turn yellow in autumn. Try witch hazels as specimen plants in gardens, or grow them in groups for high impact in winter.

Hardiness Fully frost-hardy ✻✻✻.

Cultivation Witch hazels prefer reasonably fertile, moist but well-drained, ideally neutral to acid (lime-free) soil. Position them in sun or partial shade, in an open but not exposed spot. **Prune** any crossing shoots in late winter or early spring, after flowering, to maintain a good shape. Named witch hazels are grafted and are best bought from a nursery or garden centre.

SUCKERS should be removed, otherwise they will spoil the shrub. Pull them off, or cut them off, at the base. Watch for buds sprouting and rub off.

Hamamelis 'Brevipetala'
↕↔ 4m (12ft), upright shrub, soft, hairy, blue-green leaves turn rich yellow in autumn, very fragrant flowers in mid- and late winter

Harpullia

EVERGREEN TREES AND SHRUBS of the warmer areas and tropics, these are grown as shade trees and for their showy fruit. These are round, yellow, orange, or red, averaging about 25mm (1in) across, and mostly appear in autumn and winter. The leaves are made up of up to 14 dark green leaflets on either side of a central stem. The flowers are small, white to pink and lightly perfumed. They occur in pendulous clusters up to 30cm (1ft) long in the spring and summer. Some, such as *Harpullia pendula*, are often seen growing as street trees.

Hardiness Frost-tender ✻ to very frost-tender ❁.

Cultivation Grow in any well-drained soil that is reasonably fertile and is kept moist. **Prune** minimally, except to establish a straight trunk on young trees. **Sow** seed (*see pp.191–192*) into individual containers as soon as it is collected.

Harpullia pendula
↕ 15m (50ft) ↔ 12m (40ft), summer flowering evergreen tree ✻

Hebe

VARIED AND ATTRACTIVE, EVERGREEN FOLIAGE and pretty flowers, in a huge range of shrubs from low, sprawling plants to large domed bushes, means that there is a hebe for almost any situation. Hebes have neat, matt, or glossy foliage in tones of grey-, blue- or true green, sometimes with coloured edges. Spikes up to 30cm (12in) long or clusters of small flowers are usually borne from early to mid-summer. They vary in hue from white to pinks, blues, purples, or red. Hebes provide year-round interest in mixed or shrub gardens, rock gardens, gravel gardens, or even in pots on the patio. In mild areas, particularly coastal ones, they can be used as hedging or as groundcovers.

Hardiness Fully frost-hardy ✻✻✻ to frost-tender ✻.

Cultivation Hebes grow in poor to reasonably fertile, moist but well-drained, preferably neutral to slightly alkaline (limy) soil. Sun or partial shade is best. **Remove** any misplaced growths that spoil the shape in late winter or early spring, but little pruning is needed. **Take** semi-ripe cuttings (*see p.394*) in summer or autumn.

Hebe albicans ♕
↕ 60cm (24in) ↔ 90cm (36in), dense, mound-forming or spreading shrub, flowers from early to mid-summer ✻✻

Hebe 'Inspiration'
↕ 1m (3ft) ↔ 1.5m (5ft), summer flowering evergreen tree ✲

Hebe 'Wiri Image'
↕ 1m (3ft) ↔ 1m (3ft), early summer violet flowers on a vigorous evergreen shrub

Hebe 'Wiri Cloud'
↕ 15m (50ft) ↔ 12m (40ft), summer flowering evergreen tree ✲

Hebe 'Wiri Grace'
↕ 1.5m (5ft) ↔ 1.5m (5ft), pale purple flowers in summer on an erect showy spike

Hebe 'Wiri Charm'
↕ 75cm (30in) ↔ 75cm (30in), purple flowers in summer

Helianthemum

Sun Rose

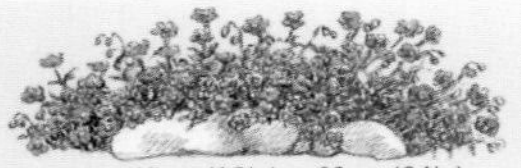
↕to 45cm (18in) ↔ 60cm (24in)

The pretty, papery, saucer-shaped flowers of these little evergreen shrubs have ensured that they remain a firm favourite of many gardeners. Most grow to only 15–30cm (6–12in) tall. A profusion of blooms, in a wide range of vivid and pale colours, are borne over a long period from late spring to mid-summer against a background of silver to grey- or mid-green foliage. They love to bask in sunshine and, with their compact habit, thrive in dry conditions, such as a rock garden or a raised bed, or at the front of a garden. A gravel mulch suits them very well, both looking good and giving them a dry, warm, free-draining surface over which to spread.

Hardiness Fully frost-hardy ❄❄❄ to frost-hardy ❄❄.

Cultivation Sun roses enjoy well-drained, neutral to alkaline (limy) soil, in full sun. **Pruning** is very easy; after flowering use garden shears to trim the plant lightly all over. **Take** softwood cuttings (*see p.394*) in late spring or early summer.

Helianthemum **'Rhodanthe Carneum'** 🏆
↕30cm (12in) ↔ 45cm (18in), sometimes sold as 'Wisley Pink', with an especially long flowering season ❄❄❄

Heliotropium

Heliotrope, Cherry Pie

↕↔60cm (24in)

Heliotrope is a treasured cottage-garden plant, loved for its dense, sweetly-scented flowerheads. Most heliotropes on sale are related to *Heliotropium arborescens*, the only commonly grown species, which although it is a woody shrub is quite tender – hence heliotropes are most often used in frost-prone climates as container plants, for summer display. They can be overwintered under cover, but new plants grown over winter from cuttings taken from the parent often make more successful, bushier plants to set out the following year. The wrinkled leaves are sometimes tinged purple, complementing the tiny blue or purple flowers borne in large clusters throughout summer.

Hardiness Very frost-tender ❄.

Cultivation Grow heliotropes in any fertile, moist but well-drained soil, in full sun. In containers such as pots, tubs, and windowboxes, use any good-quality potting mix. **Sow** seed (*see pp.391–393*) at 16–18°C (61–64°F) in spring. **Take** softwood or semi-ripe cuttings (*see p.394*) in summer.

Heliotropium arborescens **'Marine'**
↕45cm (18in) ↔ 30–45cm (12–18in), flowerheads to 15cm (6in) across

Hibbertia

see also p.142

Sunny, bright yellow flowers are the main attraction of these plants. These are five-petalled, and open wide to show off the central stamens. The petals can be wavy-edged and occasionally heart-shaped. They occur in spring and summer, with some offering the odd flower at other times of the year as well. Leaves are oval to linear and glossy dark green. They are often leathery or even fleshy, and some are covered in fine hairs. Most are small to medium shrubs of various shapes, sizes, and habits. A number are climbers or groundcovers.

Hardiness Frost-hardy ❄❄ to frost-tender ❄.

Cultivation Grow in any well-drained soil, in full sun or partial shade and shelter from hot, drying winds. **Tip prune** regularly to promote bushy plants and avoid hard pruning, which can result in dieback. **Take** cuttings of firm young growth in spring and summer (*see p.394*).

Hibbertia dentata
↕30cm (1ft) ↔ 2m (6ft), trailing shrub or groundcover flowering in spring and summer ❄

Hibiscus

Famous for their spectacular flowers from spring until autumn, hibiscus are available in a rainbow of bright hues. The blooms are carried against glossy-green, occasionally variegated foliage. Although the group includes many annuals and perennials, as well as shrubs, the woody, deciduous *Hibiscus syriacus* and its cultivars are probably the most commonly grown in cool climates because they are fully hardy. Hibiscus are a welcome addition to a garden, and thrive in large pots. This is particularly useful if you want to grow the Chinese hibiscus (*H. rosa-sinensis*) or other tender species, since the container can be moved under cover in winter.

Hardiness Fully frost-hardy ✲✲✲ to very frost-tender ❀.

Cultivation Grow in moist, well-drained, preferably slightly alkaline (limy) soil, in full sun. The longer and hotter the summer, the more flowers are produced, so give hibiscus a warm, sheltered position in cooler areas, and apply a mulch (*see p.388*). Little pruning is needed other than to remove wayward branches and any dead or damaged wood. **Sow** seed (*see pp.391–392*) at 13–18°C (55–64°F) in spring. **Take** semi-ripe cuttings in summer (*see p.394*), or layer shoots (*see p.395*) in late spring.

***Hibiscus rosa-sinensis* 'Kinchen's Yellow'**
↕3m (10ft) ↔ 3m (10ft), bright yellow flowers through summer and autumn ❀

***Hibiscus rosa-sinensis* 'Agnes Galt'**
↕3m (10ft) ↔ 3m (10ft), an old favourite among the evergreen hibiscus ❀

***Hibiscus syriacus* 'Woodbridge'** 🏆
↕3m (10ft) ↔ 2m (6ft), with flatter, more mallow-like, but intensely coloured blooms ✲✲✲

Hoheria

Grown for their showy flowers and lovely foliage, these trees are evergreen, deciduous, or semi-deciduous. The white flowers appear in late summer and into autumn, and are open, single, and five-petalled. They are held on long, thin stalks that can be softly pendulous. Leaves are lance-shaped and serrated or toothed along the margins. They are mostly mid- to dark green, but variegated forms with cream and gold variegation are also available. Trees are generally densely foliaged and upright, often tall but very narrow. Evergreen forms make good windbreaks and screeners.

Hardiness Fully frost-hardy ✲✲✲ to frost-hardy ✲✲.

Cultivation Grow in well-drained soil that is reasonably fertile, in full sun or partial shade, and keep moist in drier periods. **Prune** minimally. **Sow** seed (*see p.391*) in a cold frame in autumn. **Take** semi-hardwood cuttings in late spring (*see p.394*).

Hoheria sexstylosa
↕7m (20ft) ↔ 4m (12ft), upright evergreen tree with drooping branches and fragrant flowers in autumn ✲✲

HYDRANGEA

see also p.143

↕↔ 1m (3ft) to 7m (22ft)

THESE SHRUBS HAVE LONG BEEN GARDEN favourites for their large, stately flowerheads. These may be flat or domed and are made up of clusters of tiny, fertile flowers and larger, sterile flowers with petal-like sepals. The many cultivars of the most common species, *Hydrangea macrophylla*, include two types: hortensias have round "mopheads" of sterile flowers, whereas lacecaps have flat flowerheads of fertile flowers edged with sterile ones. Flower colour is affected by the acidity or alkalinity of the soil. Hydrangea blooms of certain cultivars are blue on acid soils and pink on alkaline (limy) soils; on neutral soils, the hues can be mixed, often being bluish-pink. The white-flowered cultivars are not affected. Most garden hydrangeas are deciduous. Some hydrangeas also have flaky, peeling bark and handsome foliage, which has good autumn colour. These excellent plants can be used in many sites, especially as specimen plants or in gardens. The flowers dry to parchment shades and are useful in arrangements.

Hardiness Fully frost-hardy ❄❄❄ to frost-hardy ❄❄.

Cultivation Hydrangeas thrive in moist, well-drained, fertile soil in filtered sun or shade, if sheltered from hot, drying winds. **Pruning,** for most cultivars except those mentioned below, consists of cutting out misplaced or crossing shoots in late winter or early spring. **Sow** seed (*see pp.391–393*) in containers in spring. **Root** soft stem-tip cuttings in early summer or take hardwood cuttings in winter (*see p.394*). Hydrangea blooms may be spoiled by grey mould (botrytis) in very wet summers.

How to prune hydrangeas

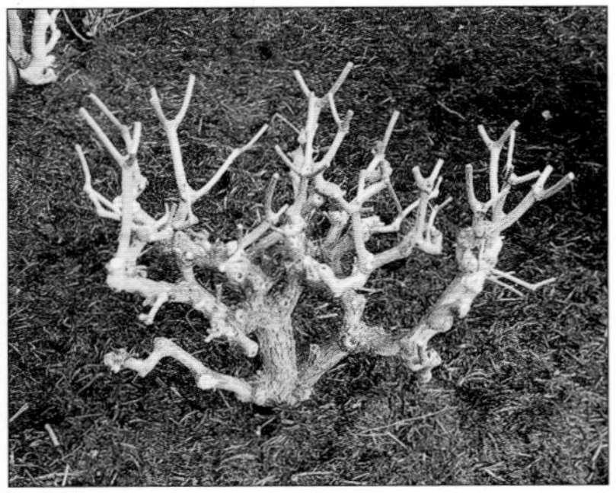

Hard pruning (see left) *of* H. paniculata *in early spring – before it produces its flowering shoots – results in a much better show of flower. If not pruned, the plants, which normally put on a lot of growth, become very tall and the flowers appear only at the tips where they are difficult to see.*

Hard pruning involves cutting off all the previous year's flowering wood to leave a base of woody stems, as low as 25cm (10in) in exposed gardens or 60cm (24in) at the back of a border. Cut each stem back to a pair of healthy buds at the required height. Neglected plants also respond well to this type of hard pruning.

Light pruning *is advisable for hortensias (also called mophead hydrangeas), all other* H. macrophylla *cultivars,* H. serrata *and its cultivars, and 'Preziosa'. These hydrangeas all flower on stems formed in the previous year. On the whole, they manage this without much attention, but a little annual pruning enhances flowering and keeps the shrubs healthy.*

Leave old flowerheads over winter to protect the new buds. Then, in late winter, prune the previous year's flowered shoots by up to 30cm (12in) to just above two strong buds (see inset). *Cut out weak and thin shoots and prune one or two of the oldest stems to the base.*

1

5

9

12

13

① *Hydrangea arborescens* 'Annabelle' ♀ ↕↔ 2.5m (8ft) ❄❄❄ ② *arborescens* 'Grandiflora' ♀ ↕↔ 2.5m (8ft) ❄❄❄ ③ *aspera* Villosa Group ♀ ↕↔ 1–4m (4–12ft) ❄❄❄ ④ *involucrata* 'Hortensis' ♀ ↕ 1m (3ft) ↔ 2m (6ft) ❄❄ ⑤ *macrophylla* 'Ayesha' (hortensia) ↕ 1.5m (5ft) ↔ 2m (6ft) ❄❄❄ ⑥ *macrophylla* 'Hamburg' (hortensia) ↕ 1.5m (4ft6in) ↔ 2m (6ft) ❄❄❄ ⑦

2

3

7

4

6

8

10

15

11

17

14

16

macrophylla 'Lanarth White' ♀ (lacecap) ↕↔ 1.5m (5ft) ❄❄❄ ⑧ *macrophylla* 'Mariesii Perfecta' ♀ (lacecap) ↕ 1.5m (4ft6in) ↔ 2m (6ft) ❄❄❄ ⑨ *macrophylla* 'Veitchii' ♀ (lacecap) ↕ 1.5m (4ft6in) ↔ 2m (6ft) ❄❄❄ ⑩ *paniculata* 'Floribunda' ↕ 3m (10ft) ↔ 2.5m (8ft) ❄❄❄ ⑪ *paniculata* 'Grandiflora' ♀ ↕ 3m (10ft) ↔ 2.5m (8ft) ❄❄❄ ⑫ *paniculata* 'Pink Diamond' ♀ ↕ 3m (10ft) ↔ 2.5m (8ft) ❄❄❄ ⑬ *paniculata* 'Praecox' ↕ 3m (10ft) ↔ 2.5m (8ft) ❄❄❄ ⑭ *paniculata* 'Unique' ♀ ↕ 3m (10ft) ↔ 2.5m (8ft) ❄❄❄ ⑮ 'Preziosa' ♀ ↕↔ 1.5m (5ft) ❄❄ ⑯ *quercifolia* ♀ ↕ 2m (6ft) ↔ 2.5m (8ft) ❄❄❄ ⑰ *serrata* 'Bluebird' ♀ (lacecap) ↕↔ 1.2m (4ft) ❄❄

Hymenosporum

Native Frangipani

THERE IS A SINGLE SPECIES in this Australian genus and it eventually grows into a tall tree. Evergreen, it is often only half as wide as it is tall. The leaves are lance-shaped, dark green and glossy on the upper surface, and a little lighter and duller underneath. The flowers start out cream and fade to an orangey-yellow colour before dropping from the tree. Individually they are small tubes, but they appear in large, conspicuous clusters at the growing tips of the tree in spring to summer. These are highly scented, even from a distance, which is the main reason this tree is grown and gives rise to its common name.

Hardiness Frost-tender ✲ to very frost-tender ❁.

Cultivation Grow in any well-drained soil that is enriched with well-rotted organic matter. Keep moist and grow in full sun or partial shade. **Prune** minimally; remove any shoots that spoil the shape of young plants to encourage a good form (*see p.384*). **Sow** seed (*see p.391*) in containers when ripe. **Take** cuttings of firm young growth in spring (*see p.394*).

Hymenosporum flavum
↕10–20m (30–65ft) ↔ 5–7m (15–22ft), superb perfume, even at a distance, is the main reason for growing this tree ✲✲ (borderline)

Hypericum

St John's Wort

↔ 1–2m (3–6ft)

THIS DIVERSE GROUP ranges from large shrubs to small annuals and perennials, but in summer all bear similar, distinctive, bright yellow flowers with a central boss of golden stamens. Some are decorated with berries through autumn. The shrubs are most commonly cultivated, both evergreens and deciduous species that provide lovely autumn colour. There is a hypericum for most situations: the larger species are good for a border, smaller ones for a rock garden. The spreading Rose of Sharon (*Hypericum calycinum*) makes ideal ground cover, although it can become invasive so is not recommended for mixed garden beds.

Hardiness Fully frost-hardy ✲✲✲ to frost-hardy ✲✲.

Cultivation Larger shrubs prefer moist but well drained soil in sun or partial shade, the small rock-garden types full sun and good drainage. *H. androsaemum* and *H. calycinum* tolerate even deep shade. **Trim** in spring to keep them neat; larger deciduous species can be cut back hard to a permanent framework in early spring to keep them smaller. **Take** semi-ripe cuttings in summer (*see p.394*).

PRUNING GROUND COVER
Encourage fresh growth by cutting *H. calycinum* back to the ground in spring, either with shears or a nylon-line trimmer.

Hypericum calycinum (Aaron's Beard, Rose of Sharon)
↕60cm (24in) ↔ indefinite, evergreen or semi-evergreen with creeping, rooting stems, flowers from summer to autumn ✲✲✲

Hypocalymma

THESE ARE EVERGREEN SHRUBS, mostly small in size. Rounded in outline, they are made up of many erect, rigid branches. They have stiff, needle-like, linear or short oval leaves that are sometimes hairy when young. The flowers appear along the stems and branchlets at the spot where the leaves meet. These have five petals and prominent stamens. They are white, cream, yellow, or pink and are quite showy, and a number of them are used as cut flowers. Naturally occurring on sandy and gravelly soils, they need well-drained soils to do well.

Hardiness Frost-hardy ✲✲ to frost-tender ✲.

Cultivation Grow in full sun or partial shade in any soil as long as it is well-drained. **Prune** minimally; remove any shoots that spoil the shape of young plants to encourage a good form (*see p.384*). **Take** stem cuttings from new growth after flowering (*see p.394*).

Hypocalymma angustifolium
↕1m (3ft) ↔ 1.5m (5ft), evergreen shrub smothered in flowers late winter and spring ✲✲

ILEX
Holly

HOLLIES ARE BEST KNOWN for winter berries and stiff, prickly, evergreen foliage, but not all are spiny. Their glossy leaves may be plain dark or mid-green, or may be edged, splashed, or striped with silver or gold. The flowers are tiny, the berries usually red or black; they can cause a stomach upset if eaten. Grow hollies in mixed gardens, with winter-flowering shrubs like mahonias (*see p.87*), or as specimens, so that their dense, shapely forms and pale grey bark can be appreciated. *Ilex* × *altaclerensis* and *I. aquifolium* cultivars can be used as formal hedging, but frequent trimming can mean fewer berries.

Hardiness Fully frost-hardy ❄❄❄ to frost-hardy ❄❄.

Cultivation Best planted in late winter or early spring. Full sun encourages bright colour in variegated hollies, but otherwise site in sun or shade in moist, well-drained soil. **Prune** free-standing specimens only if needed to maintain a well-balanced shape; trim hedges in late summer. Topiary may need an extra trim in spring. **Take** semi-ripe cuttings in late summer or autumn (*see p.394*).

***Ilex* × *altaclerensis* 'Golden King'** ♕
↕6m (20ft) ↔4m (12ft), compact, female shrub, good conical form (*see inset*) but berries can be sparse in some years ❄❄

INDIGOFERA

↕↔ 2–3m (6–10ft)

THE EVERGREEN AND DECIDUOUS shrubby indigoferas are the most commonly cultivated in this varied group. They need space to grow and show off their elegant habits, and they look particularly good in raised garden beds. Indigoferas bear masses of pea-like flowers from early summer until early autumn, against a background of soft-green leaves. *Indigofera australis* is the most commonly grown.

Hardiness Fully frost-hardy ❄❄❄ to frost-hardy ❄❄.

Cultivation Grow in moist but well-drained soil, in full sun or dappled shade. **Trim** lightly each year after flowering to keep the plant bushy. **Take** semi-ripe cuttings in early or mid-summer (*see p.394*).

Indigofera australis
↕2m (6ft) ↔2m (6ft), drooping clusters of pink flowers in spring on a lightly suckering evergreen shrub ❄❄

ISOPOGON

THESE ARE SMALL AND DWARF EVERGREEN SHRUBS, most of which flower in the spring or summer. The flowers are variable although all are without petals. They are spidery globes, often at the growing tips of the plant, in colours of pink, mauve, and yellow. The buds are very tight, round balls and the subsequent seed cones are also globular, giving rise to one of the plant's common names, Drumsticks. The leaves are variable and are often strongly divided or deeply lobed. This foliage is an added attraction of the plant.

Hardiness Frost-hardy ❄❄ to frost-tender ❄.

Cultivation Grow in any well-drained soil, in full sun or partial shade. **Prune** minimally; remove any shoots that spoil the shape of young plants to encourage a good form (*see p.384*). **Take** tip cuttings of firm, young shoots in summer (*see p.394*).

Isopogon anemonifolius (Broad Leaf Drumsticks)
↕1–2m (3–6ft) ↔1–2m (3–6ft), the spring flowers are long lasting as cut flowers ❄❄

JACARANDA

A SPECTACULAR SHOW OF MAUVE FLOWERS all over its broad canopy is the reason this tree is grown. The flowers are tubular and appear at the growing tips in late spring and early summer. Most of the tree's foliage has been shed by this time, adding further to the drama of the display. The leaves are fern-like, and mid-green in colour. In mid-spring they turn a rich yellow, and fall just before the flowers appear. New leaves emerge towards the end of flowering. The seed pods are flat, round discs holding numerous small seeds. These are great as specimen trees, particularly in warmer areas.

Hardiness Frost-tender ✻.

Cultivation Grow in full sun in any well-drained soil that is reasonably fertile, and shelter from cold, winter winds in cooler districts. **Prune** minimally, except to establish a strong, straight central trunk on young trees (*see p.384*). **Sow** seed (*see p.392*) in a warm glasshouse. **Take** heeled semi-hardwood cuttings in mid-summer (*see p.394*).

Jacaranda mimosifolia
↕↔ 12m (40ft), covered in deep mauve flowers in late spring, a blossoming jacaranda is an unforgettable sight

JASMINUM NUDIFLORUM

Winter Jasmine

see also p.144

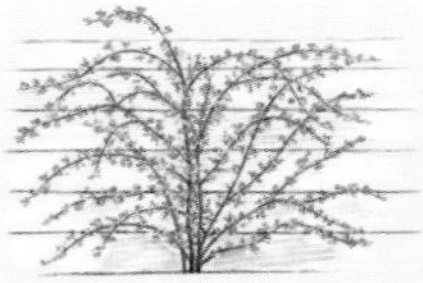

↕↔ 3m (10ft)

MOST COMMONLY GROWN jasmines are climbers, but this one is a shrub, albeit a rather lanky one. The Winter Jasmine may not be quite as intensely perfumed as its spring- and summer-flowering cousins, but is highly valued nevertheless for its golden flowers through the barest months of the year. This slender-stemmed, arching, often quite untidy plant can be clipped into a hedge. Cut sprigs and bring them indoors while the buds are still closed; the warmth of a room should force them into flower early for a touch of winter cheer and delicate scent.

Hardiness Fully frost-hardy ✻✻✻.

Cultivation Grow in fertile, well-drained soil in full sun or partial shade. **Prune** flowered shoots back to strong buds, and once plants are older, after flowering, remove up to one in four of the main stems at the base to encourage fresh growth (*see p.383*). **Take** semi-ripe cuttings in summer or autumn (*see p.394*); alternatively shoots can be layered (*see p.395*) in autumn.

Jasminum nudiflorum 🏆
↕↔ 3m (10ft), deciduous shrub with fragrant flowers in winter, leaves are dark green and appear after flowering

JUNIPERUS

Juniper

THESE EVERGREEN, CONIFEROUS TREES and shrubs are grown for their sculptural habits and colourful foliage. They come in all shapes and sizes; large trees, dwarf cultivars, and spreading shrubs, and their leaves, or needles, can be dark green, golden yellow or even blue. A fantastic tapestry of shapes, colours and textures can be built up by growing a collection of junipers together, or with other conifers. The females bear round, fleshy cones, rather like berries; these are used in cooking and also as one of the flavourings of gin. Junipers will tolerate a wide range of conditions: larger trees can be used as specimens as well as windbreaks and hedges, small shrubs in a rock garden with alpines, and prostrate cultivars as ground cover.

Hardiness Fully frost-hardy ✻✻✻ to frost-hardy ✻✻.

Cultivation Junipers are unfussy and will grow in any well-drained soil, in sun or partial shade. **Pruning** is generally unnecessary, although if prostrate species spread too far you can remove selected stems carefully to keep them within bounds. **Propagation** is tricky, and seed may take up to five years to germinate, so new plants are probably best bought from a nursery.

***Juniperus squamata* 'Blue Star'** 🏆
↕ 40cm (16in) ↔ to 1m (3ft), a compact, spreading bush forming wave-like, cascading shapes ✻✻✻

***Juniperus scopulorum* 'Skyrocket'**
↕6m (20ft) ↔ 50–60cm (20–24in), pencil-thin, columnar tree that provides a spectacular focal point ✻✻✻

***Juniperus* × *pfitzeriana* 'Pfitzeriana Aurea'**
↕90cm (36in) ↔ 2m (6ft), spreading shrub, the golden yellow needles become greenish-yellow over winter ✻✻✻

***Juniperus chinensis* 'Pyramidalis' 🏆**
↕2m (6ft) ↔ 60cm (24in), small cultivar with a neat, compact shape ✻✻✻

***Juniperus communis* 'Compressa' 🏆**
↕80cm (32in) ↔ 45cm (18in), dwarf and very slow-growing, suitable for combining with alpine plants in a rock garden ✻✻✻

KALMIA

KALMIAS ARE ACID-LOVING, evergreen shrubs with clusters of pretty, pink, bowl-shaped flowers in mid-spring and early summer. Throughout the year, the branches are clothed with glossy, leathery leaves. The larger kalmias, such as *Kalmia latifolia* and its cultivars, are spectacular in gardens or among groves of trees.

Hardiness Fully frost-hardy ✻✻✻.

Cultivation Grow in moist, acid (lime-free) soil, preferably in partial shade unless the ground remains continually damp; a layer of leaf mould or compost around the plants in spring will help retain moisture. If you live in an area with limy soil, grow kalmias in pots filled with lime-free potting mix. **Prune** after flowering only if necessary to trim shoots that spoil the shape of the shrub. If you have a leggy specimen, then renovate it over several seasons (*see p.384*), unless it is *K. angustifolia,* which can be cut back hard in a single year, and will regrow well. **Take** semi-ripe cuttings in mid-summer (*see p.394*), or layer low-growing shoots in late summer (*see p.395*).

***Kalmia angustifolia* 🏆 (Sheep Laurel)**
↕60cm (24in) ↔ 1.5m (5ft), mound-forming shrub, flowers are occasionally white

KERRIA JAPONICA

Japanese Rose

↔ to 3m (9ft)

KERRIA AND ITS CULTIVARS are vigorous, lightly suckering shrubs that are good value all year round. In mid- and late spring, they bear single or double, golden yellow flowers. The deciduous foliage is bright green. When the leaves fall, winter interest is then provided by the dense clumps of arching, light green stems. Grow kerrias in a border where they have room to spread out among other shrubs.

Hardiness Fully frost-hardy ✻✻✻.

Cultivation Grow kerrias in fertile, well-drained soil in full sun or partial shade. **Prune** the stems when they have flowered to sideshoots or strong buds lower down on the shrub (*see p.383*). **Propagate** from suckers (stems growing up from the roots) in spring. Find a sucker and dig down to check it has developed some roots of its own. Cut it away from its parent, cut back its stem by a half, and replant it.

Kerria japonica (Japanese Rose)
↕ 1.8m (6ft) ↔ 1.5m (8ft), bright yellow flowers stand out against the emerging light green foliage in spring

KOELREUTERIA

Golden Rain Tree

↔ 10m (30ft)

THESE MAKE FINE SPECIMEN trees throughout the year. They have a spreading shape, elegant, deciduous leaves, large clusters of yellow flowers in summer, and unusual, bladder-like fruits in the autumn. The Golden Rain Tree (*Koelreuteria paniculata*) is the most widely available, and also perhaps the most impressive, of the three species. Its leaves emerge reddish-pink in spring, mature to mid-green, and give a lovely show of butter-yellow and orange tints in autumn. In summer, it bears sprays of small, golden flowers, up to 30cm (12in) long, followed by pink- or red-flushed fruit capsules. The flowers are more abundant in areas with long, hot summers.

Hardiness Fully frost-hardy ✻✻✻ to frost-hardy ✻✻.

Cultivation Grow in fertile, well-drained soil in full sun. **Prune out** any damaged or dead wood (*see p.382*) when dormant in winter, but no further pruning is necessary. **Sow** seed (*see pp.391–392*) in autumn, in a container, and place in a cold frame.

FRUIT CAPSULES

Koelreuteria paniculata ♀ (Golden Rain Tree, Pride of China)
↕↔ 10m (30ft), leaves to 45cm (18in) long ✻✻✻

KUNZEA

THESE ARE EVERGREEN SHRUBS and small trees that have flowers very similar to those of the bottlebrushes (*Callistemon, see p.30*), with which they are sometimes confused. The flowers are indeed like bottlebrushes, although they tend to be at the growing tips of the plant, shorter than those of *Callistemon* and almost round. They are red, pink, white, cream, or pale yellow. The majority flower in spring, although one or two do so in summer or winter. The leaves are small, linear and have a pleasant aroma when crushed. These plants are particularly good for attracting nectar-feeding birds.

Hardiness Frost-hardy ✻✻ to frost-tender ✻.

Cultivation Grow in any moist but well-drained soil that is neutral to acid (lime-free), in full sun or partial shade. **Tip prune** young plants regularly after flowering to promote a dense bushy habit (*see p.390*). Most tolerate hard pruning if this is carried out while they are growing actively (*see p.383*). **Sow** seed (*see p.391*) in spring or early autumn. **Take** semi-hardwood cuttings in spring or summer (*see p.394*).

Kunzea ambigua
↕ 2–3m (6–9ft) ↔ 2–3m (6–9ft), spring flowering evergreen shrub that tolerates extreme coastal exposure ✻✻

Lagerstroemia

Crepe Myrtle

EVERGREEN OR DECIDUOUS, these are mostly small to medium trees that are grown for their showy flowers. The flowers are arranged in loose cones at the tips of the new season's growth in summer. Flower colours vary and can be white, pink, mauve, or even red. The leaves are oval, light to mid-green and glossy. On deciduous trees they turn bright yellow before falling in autumn. Most have smooth trunks and branches covered in pinky-grey bark that is lightly rippled, looking a little like the muscles of arms or legs, and adding year-round interest to these relatively trouble-free plants.

Hardiness Frost-tender ✲.

Cultivation Grow in any well-drained soil that is reasonably fertile and enriched with well-rotted organic matter. An open sunny spot will help prevent powdery mildew. **Prune** minimally; remove any shoots that spoil the shape of young plants to encourage a good form (*see p.384*. **Take** hardwood cuttings in winter and set them in rows in the garden (*see p.394*). **Watch** for powdery mildew and treat as required (*see p.398*).

Lagerstroemia indica (Pride of India)
↕7m (21ft) ↔ 4m (12ft), in summer the flowers appear at the growing tips of this small deciduous tree

Lagunaria patersonii

Norfolk Island Hibiscus

THIS IS A TALL, NARROW EVERGREEN TREE with a roughly conical shape. The leaves are oval, grey-green and are covered in a white bloom underneath. The flowers are the main reason this plant is grown, along with its ability to withstand harsh conditions such as coastal exposure, air pollution and the like. The flowers are hibiscus-like, although a little smaller. They are pale pink and carried quite profusely, mostly in summer. A rough, round seed capsule follows. Inside this the seeds are surrounded by fine hairs that can cause skin irritation, and explain one of the common names of this plant, Cow Itch Tree.

Hardiness Frost-tender ✲.

Cultivation Grow in any well-drained soil in full sun or partial shade. **Prune** minimally; remove any shoots that spoil the shape of young plants to encourage a good form (*see p.384*). **Sow** seed (*see pp.391–392*) when ripe, in containers in a cold frame.

Lagunaria patersonii
↕10m (30ft) ↔ 7m (22ft), a tough tree for harsh conditions, but watch for the irritating hairs around the seeds

Laurus nobilis

Bay, Sweet Bay, Bay Laurel

THE BAY FORMS a large shrub or small, conical tree with evergreen, aromatic foliage that is used as a culinary flavouring. Cultivars with golden leaves are also available. Both male and female flowers are greenish-yellow, but are borne on separate plants in spring; if grown together, then black berries may follow on the female tree. Bay is often clipped and looks elegant with other formal topiary, such as box (*Buxus, see p.30*), or in a pot as a handsome patio plant. Neat bushes or standards in containers have the bonus of being easily moved if necessary. Bay can also be grown in its natural form as a specimen, in gardens or as a tall screen.

Hardiness Frost-hardy ✲✲; foliage may be damaged by cold winds.

Cultivation Grow in moist, well-drained soil, in sun or partial shade, with some shelter. **Remove** wayward or crossing shoots of naturally shaped bay (*see p.382*). **Clip** topiary once or twice in summer to keep it neat. **Sow** seed (*see pp.391–392*) in pots in a cold frame in autumn. **Take** semi-ripe cuttings (*see p.394*) in summer. Round, brown scale insects may be a problem on plants growing under cover; remove any shoots with mildew (*see p.398*).

Laurus nobilis ♀
↕12m (40ft) ↔ 10m (30ft), widely available, contact with foliage may inflame skin allergies

LAVANDULA

Lavender

LAVENDERS ARE DESERVEDLY POPULAR PLANTS, grown for their evergreen, aromatic foliage, and scented flowers in mid- to late summer. There are many types, some more strongly perfumed than others, most with silvery foliage and nectar-rich blooms that are irresistible to pollinating bees. To dry the flowers so you can enjoy their summery aroma in winter, cut them before they are fully open and hang them upside down in bunches in a dry place. Lavenders can be used in borders and are classic partners for roses; they are wonderful grown as low edging for a bed, sending up great wafts of scent as you brush past. Some species are not fully hardy but can be easily grown in pots and taken into a protected spot over winter.

Hardiness Fully frost-hardy ❄❄❄ to frost-tender ❄.

Cultivation Lavenders are undemanding, provided that they have well-drained soil in full sun. **Trim** in early or mid-spring: use shears to create a neat, rounded mound, taking off shoot tips but never cutting into old, bare wood. Trim lightly again to remove faded flower stalks (see right). **Sow** seed in a container in a cold frame in spring (*see pp.391–392*). **Take** semi-ripe cuttings in summer (*see p.394*) for quicker results.

DEADHEADING LAVENDER
Neaten up lavender bushes when the flowers have faded, by trimming them over with a pair of garden shears, back to within 2.5cm (1in) of the old growth.

Lavandula angustifolia 'Munstead'
↕45cm (18in) ↔ 60cm (24in), more compact than the species ❄❄❄

Lavandula angustifolia 'Hidcote' ♀
↕60cm (24in) ↔ 75cm (30in), compact lavender whose vivid flowers contrast spectacularly with the grey leaves ❄❄❄

Lavandula angustifolia 'Nana Alba'
↕↔ 30cm (12in), forms a very compact, neat bush, good for containers and edging ❄❄❄

Lavandula 'Marshwood'
↕↔ 60cm (24in), bushy plant with similar flowers to the French lavenders ❄❄❄ (borderline)

Lavatera

Mallow see also p.270

↔2m (6ft)

THERE ARE LOTS OF MALLOWS; the shrubby ones need space to grow as they get quite large, but they respond well to hard pruning. They are valued for their profusion of ice-cream-coloured flowers in summer and autumn. The foliage of both deciduous and evergreen types is soft green, with downy hairs, rather coarse in appearance, so these shrubs are best used to provide a substantial backdrop for smaller ornamental plants; put them near the back of the garden, preferably against a wall in areas with very cold winters. Mallows are ideal for coastal gardens, enjoying the sandy soil and often mild, frost-free conditions.

Hardiness: Fully frost-hardy ✲✲✲ to frost-hardy ✲✲.

Cultivation Mallows prefer light, sandy soil in full sun, but tolerate heavier ground. **Prune** lightly in early spring to keep the shrub compact. **Take** softwood cuttings (*see p.394*) in early summer; lavateras can be short-lived and it is wise to grow replacements.

Lavatera maritima
↕1.8m (6ft) ↔ 1.2m (4ft), flowering over many months from spring through to autumn

Leptospermum

Tea-tree

FIVE-PETALLED FLOWERS are one of the attractions of this group of evergreen trees and shrubs. Mostly the flowers are small, single, and white, but there are also cream, pink, and mauve ones, as well as double flowered forms. Flowering generally occurs in spring, although some flower in summer, with the flowers occurring along the stems among the leaves. The grey-green leaves are small and oval, and often quite stiff, ending with a sharp point. Overall the plants are dense and bushy, with foliage down to the ground unless pruned to be otherwise. A number make good windbreaks and several can be trimmed into hedges.

Hardiness Frost-hardy ✲✲ to frost-tender ✲.

Cultivation Full sun is best, although some will tolerate partial shade. Soil should be well-drained. **Prune** minimally. **Sow** seed (*see pp.391–392*) in a cold frame as soon as it is ripe. **Take** heeled cuttings in late summer and autumn (*see p.394*).

Leptospermum scoparium 'Pink Cascade'
↕60cm (2ft) ↔ 1.5m (5ft), broad spreading, low growing evergreen shrub flowering on arching stems in spring and summer

Leucadendron

THESE EVERGREEN TREES AND SHRUBS look very similar in many ways to proteas (*see p.99*), to which they are closely related. The leaves are long and linear, and arranged in whorls around the stems. The late-winter and spring flowers are small cones held at the growing tips of the plant and surrounded by modified leaves known as bracts. These are often coloured red, yellow, and orange. They have a long vase life and are popular cut flowers. Bushes are stiff, upright plants with erect branches. They do well in dry conditions and could be grown with proteas, bottlebrush (*Callistemon, see p.30*) and banksias (*see p.27*).

Hardiness Frost-hardy ✲✲ to frost-tender ✲.

Cultivation Grow in full sun in any well-drained soil that is reasonably fertile, enriched with well-rotted organic matter and acidic (lime-free). Cutting flowers to enjoy inside will also help to keep the plant bushy. **Sow** seed (*see pp.391–392*) in autumn in a cold frame. **Take** semi-hardwood cuttings in summer and autumn (*see p.394*).

Leucadendron 'Safari Sunset'
↕2m (6ft) ↔ 3m (9ft), upright growing evergreen commercially grown for its cut flowers

LEUCOPHYTA BROWNII

Cushion Bush

THIS DWARF SHRUB IS GROWN for its almost white appearance. It makes a mound up to 1m (3ft) high of silvery-white branches, branchlets, and stems. On these are the tiny white leaves growing flat against the stems. The flowers appear in spring or summer, and are small balls at the growing tips of the plant. These start out white and end up pale yellow. Naturally occurring in the harshest of coastal environments, this is suitable for seaside gardens. Its interesting form and light colour make it a useful highlight against darker-foliaged plants such as hebes (*see p.69*) or bronze-foliaged ones like Bronze Fennel (*Foeniculum vulgare* 'Purpureum', *see p.245*).

Hardiness Frost-hardy ❄❄.

Cultivation Grow in any well-drained soil, in full sun or partial shade. It does not like humid conditions. **Trim** regularly to maintain the nice mounded shape and to keep bushy (*see p.384*). **Sow** seed (*see pp.391–392*) in spring in a cold frame. **Take** semi-hardwood cuttings in late summer and autumn (*see p.394*).

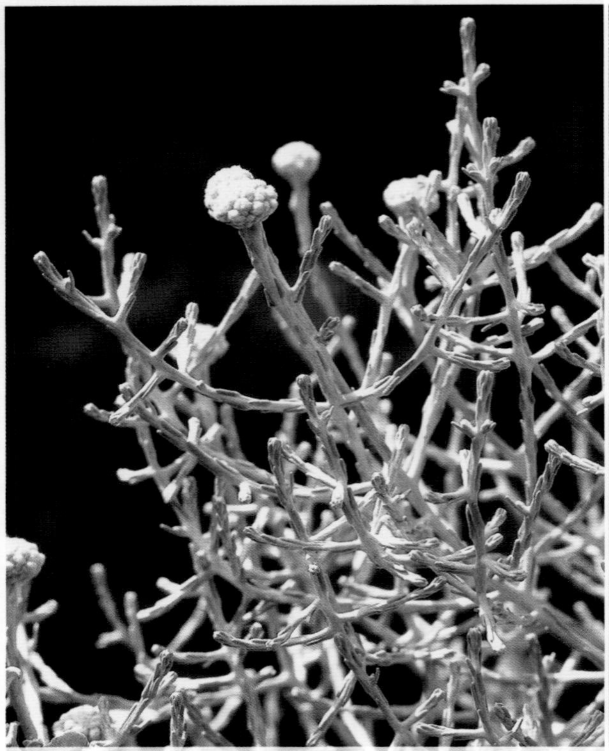

Leucophyta brownii
↕↔ 1m (3ft), adds interesting form and light with a mound of silvery foliage

LEUCOTHOE

THESE DECIDUOUS, EVERGREEN and semi-evergreen shrubs resemble pieris (*see p.97*) in many ways, with an upright habit, arching branches, and attractive, bell-like, white flowers that appear in spring. The leaves of all are handsome, but novel foliage colour is an added attraction in cultivars of *Leucothoe fontanesiana* such as 'Rainbow'. Leucothoes grow best in a shady position, accompanying shrubs such as rhododendrons (*see pp.104–107*), ericas (*see pp.52–53*) and pieris, which all like similar soil conditions. Most are good choices for a woodland garden; the small *L. keiskei* is suitable for a rock garden.

Hardiness Fully frost-hardy ❄❄❄ to frost-hardy ❄❄.

Cultivation Grow in partial or deep shade, in soil that is acid (lime-free) and reliably moist; add plenty of well-rotted organic matter. **Prune** in late winter or early spring, only to take out any crossing or badly placed branches. **Sow** seed in containers in a cold frame in spring (*see pp.391–392*). **Take** semi-ripe cuttings (*see p.394*) in summer.

***Leucothoe fontanesiana* 'Rainbow'**
↕1.5m (5ft) ↔ 2m (6ft), clump-forming variety that makes good underplanting for a woodland garden, flowers in late spring ❄❄❄

LIGUSTRUM

Privet

MOST COMMONLY USED AS HEDGING, privets are evergreen or semi-evergreen shrubs found in many an urban garden, since they happily withstand shade and pollution. Easy to grow, they thrive in most garden soils and situations. White flowers with a musty scent appear in spring or summer, followed by black fruits, but the dense, neat foliage is the main feature. The habit can be upright or conical, rounded or spreading. Some species, such as *Ligustrum japonicum*, with large, glossy leaves, can be used as specimen shrubs or in a mixed garden. Others, such as the Golden Privet (*L. ovalifolium* 'Aureum') and *L. undulatum*, make the best hedges. Some are serious environmental weeds.

Hardiness Fully frost-hardy ❄❄❄ to frost-hardy ❄❄.

Cultivation Grow in any well-drained soil in full sun or partial shade; variegated cultivars produce the best-coloured foliage in full sun. **Prune** shrubs in late winter or early spring, cutting out any overcrowded or crossing branches. **Clip** hedges at least twice a year. **Sow** seed in containers in a cold frame in autumn or spring (*see pp.391–392*). **Take** semi-ripe cuttings in summer, or hardwood cuttings in winter (*see p.394*).

***Ligustrum ovalifolium* 'Aureum'** (Golden Privet)
↕3m (10ft) ↔ 1.8m (6ft), popular for hedging and topiary

Liquidambar

↕to 25m (80ft)
↔to 12m (40ft)

THESE DECIDUOUS TREES BEAR maple-like leaves that turn to stunning shades of purple, crimson, orange, and gold in autumn. In late spring, tiny, yellow-green flowers are produced, followed by spiky, round fruit clusters. Liquidambars have an upright, open habit and look attractive either in a woodland setting or as specimens, isolated from other trees. The common liquidambar (*Liquidambar styraciflua*) is excellent value as a garden tree, pyramid-shaped with glossy, dark-green leaves and grey, deeply grooved bark. In autumn, its leaves are a blaze of fiery colour for up to four weeks. Its shallow roots can be a problem in lawns.

Hardiness Fully frost-hardy ❄❄❄ to frost-hardy ❄❄.

Cultivation Grow in reasonably fertile, preferably acid (lime-free), moist but well-drained soil. The best autumn colour is produced in full sun, but they will tolerate partial shade. **Prune** young trees to remove any crossing or misplaced branches, in late winter or early spring (*see p.382*). **Sow** seed in containers in a cold frame in autumn (*see pp.391–392*). **Take** soft stem-tip cuttings (*see p.394*) in summer.

Liquidambar styraciflua
↕25m (80ft) ↔ 12m (40ft), brilliant autumn colour is a feature of this old favourite

Liquidambar formosana
↕20m (60ft) ↔ 10m (30ft), three-lobed leaves and bright autumn colours

① ***styraciflua* 'Golden Treasure'** ↕10m (30ft) ↔ 6m (20ft)
② ***styraciflua* 'Worplesdon'** 🏆 ↕25m (80ft) ↔ 12m (40ft), in autumn, leaves turn purple

Liriodendron

Tulip Tree

↕to 20m (70ft)
↔to 12m (40ft)

EXCELLENT AS A SPECIMEN, the tulip tree has distinctive leaves that turn from dark green to butter-yellow in autumn. The trees are deciduous, with a stately, broadly columnar habit. In summer, mature trees produce curiously tulip-shaped, pale green flowers, although these are not really visible from a distance. It is only after quite a few years that the tree is likely to flower well. It is well worth growing for the foliage alone, but only if you have plenty of space. For a smaller garden, choose the more compact *Liriodendron tulipifera* 'Aureomarginatum'.

Hardiness Fully frost-hardy ❄❄❄.

Cultivation Grow in reasonably fertile soil that is moist but well-drained, and preferably slightly acid (lime-free). Will grow in full sun or partial shade. **Prune out** any crossing or misshapen branches while trees are young, in late winter or early spring, to create a healthy, well-shaped framework of branches (*see p.382*). **Sow** seed in containers in a cold frame in autumn (*see pp.391–392*). Leaf spot (*see p.399*) may affect trees, but is generally worth treating only if they are young.

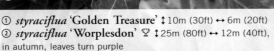

Liriodendron tulipifera 🏆
↕30m (100ft) ↔ 15m (50ft), vigorous, broadly columnar to conical tree, leaves to 15cm (6in) long, flowers 6cm (2½in) long

LIVISTONA

THESE TALL PALMS HAVE CLEAR GREY TRUNKS holding a head of bright green fronds. These are large fans held on metre-long stalks that are lined with solid thorns. The flowers are yellow and appear in large, drooping bunches in summer. The fruit is round and very dark, often black. Most grow into very large specimens suitable for avenue and specimen planting. Many, however, can be excellent container plants for quite a few years. All prefer to grow in warmer areas.

Hardiness Frost-hardy ✻✻ to very frost-tender ❅.

Cultivation Grow in well-drained soil that is enriched with well-rotted organic matter, in full sun or partial shade. **Prune** minimally. **Sow** seed (*see pp.391–392*) in containers as soon as collected, as it loses viability quickly.

Livistona australis
↕20–30m (60–90ft) ↔ 7m (20ft), stately palm trees for larger gardens

LONICERA

Honeysuckle

see also p.146

THESE HONEYSUCKLES ARE SHRUBS, not the climbers that are most commonly grown. There are two distinct types: deciduous species grown for their powerfully perfumed flowers (the most popular species, such as *Lonicera fragrantissima*, bearing these in the depths of winter), and small-leaved evergreens such as *L. nitida* and *L. pileata*, which have tiny flowers but a dense, neat habit, and are valuable for hedging and ground cover respectively. All tolerate a wide range of conditions and need little maintenance. Their berries can cause mild stomach upset if eaten.

Hardiness Fully frost-hardy ✻✻✻.

Cultivation Grow in any well-drained soil in full sun or partial shade. **Trim** deciduous shrubs after flowering if needed to restrict size, cutting back flowered shoots to strong sideshoots lower down. When plants grow old and growth is crowded, take out a main branch at the base. Evergreens can be trimmed as necessary. If *L. nitida* is grown as a hedge, it will need trimming at least twice, in summer. **Sow** seed (*see pp.391–392*) in a container when ripe, placing it in a cold frame. **Take** semi-ripe cuttings of evergreens in summer, and hardwood cuttings of deciduous types in autumn (*see p.394*).

Lonicera fragrantissima
↕2m (6ft) ↔ 3m (10ft), arching habit, deciduous or semi-evergreen, fragrant winter flowers best in full sun and shelter, dull red berries

LOPHOSTEMON

SMALL TO MEDIUM EVERGREEN TREES, these have very bushy and dense heads of foliage carried on stout trunks. The leaves are leathery, dark green, lance-shaped and look similar to those of some gums (*Eucalyptus, see p.54*). White flowers appear in summer and, although small, are held in conspicuous clusters, which are followed by woody seed capsules. The trunks are often very attractive, with a smooth texture and brown to pink colouring. Successfully grown as a street tree, they can also make good windbreaks. Variegated forms are also available.

Hardiness Frost-hardy ✻✻ to frost-tender ✻.

Cultivation Grow in full sun or part shade, in any soil, provided it is well-drained. **Prune** minimally; remove any shoots that spoil the shape of (young) plants to encourage a good form and a straight central trunk (*see p.384*). **Sow** seed (*see pp.391–392*) in spring and summer in a cold frame. Variegated forms must be grafted.

Lophostemon confertus (Brush Box)
↕15–30m (50–100ft) ↔ 10–20m (30–65ft), large evergreen tree

LUCULIA

EVERGREEN OR SEMI-DECIDUOUS SHRUBS and small trees, these are grown for the remarkable perfume of their flowers. On some species these occur in summer, while in others it is in winter, adding further to their attraction. The flowers are held in round clusters at the growing tips, and are slender tubes with starry petals at the opening. Colours range from white to pink. The leaves are lance-shaped and glossy mid-green, with indented veins. Plants tend to have many erect or lightly arching branches from the ground up, and can need staking in wind-prone areas.

Hardiness Frost-tender ❄ to very frost-tender ❅.

Cultivation Grow in any well-drained soil that is reasonably fertile and enriched with well-rotted organic matter. Partial shade is best, or full sun if adequate water can be kept up. Shelter from hot, drying winds. **Prune** minimally; remove any shoots that spoil the shape of young plants to encourage a good form (*see p.384*). **Sow** seed (*see pp.391–392*) in a cold frame in spring. **Take** semi-hardwood cuttings in summer (*see p.394*).

Luculia gratissima
↕3m (9ft) ↔ 2m (6ft), highly perfumed flowers in the middle of winter make this a most desirable evergreen shrub

LUMA

↕6–15m (15–20ft)
↔5–15m (15–50ft)

THESE SOUTH AMERICAN evergreen shrubs and small trees have aromatic, leathery leaves and cup-shaped, white flowers, blooming in summer and autumn. *Luma apiculata* is also prized for its striking peeling bark. The oval leaves are usually dark green, though *L. apiculata* 'Glanleam Gold' has foliage with creamy yellow margins. The flowers are followed by purple or black berries. Grow lumas in small groups, or as specimens in a lawn. *L. apiculata* can also be used as a screening or hedging plant.

Hardiness Frost-hardy ❄❄.

Cultivation Grow in fertile soil, enriched with well-rotted organic matter, in full sun or partial shade. **Prune out** any crossing or misshapen branches (*see p.382*) in late winter or early spring to maintain a good shape and a healthy framework of branches, and clip regularly to keep it neat. **Trim** hedges in spring. **Sow** seed in containers in a cold frame in spring (*see pp.391–392*); lumas may also self-seed in the garden. **Take** semi-ripe cuttings in late summer (*see p.394*).

Luma apiculata 🏆
↕↔ 5m (15ft), upright, vigorous, cinnamon-brown and cream peeling bark, flowers from mid-summer to mid-autumn, purple berries

MACADAMIA

THESE RAINFOREST TREES produce the edible nuts that many people would be familiar with. Tall and evergreen, they are densely clothed in dark green, oblong leaves that may have toothed edges, sometimes with short sharp spines. The spring flowers are bottlebrush-like, pendulous clusters that are white or pink. The nuts that follow are brown and shiny. These plants do best in warmer areas but can be grown further south provided they are kept frost-free, out of harsh winds and moist. The macadamias that are grown commercially for their nuts are *Macadamia integrifolia* and *M. tetraphylla.*

Hardiness Very frost-tender ❅.

Cultivation Grow in any well-drained soil that is fertile and enriched with well-rotted organic matter. Keep moist and grow in full sun, sheltered from strong winds. **Prune** minimally, other than to establish a straight trunk while trees are young (*see p.384*). **Sow** seed (*see pp.391–392*) in a cold frame when ripe.

Macadamia integrifolia
↕15m (45ft) ↔ 10m (30ft), native to Australia, this tree is the source of Macadamia nuts

Maclura

THE MACLURAS GROWN IN GARDENS are large, deciduous shrubs or small trees, prized for their elegant foliage and unusual fruits. Both a male and a female need to be planted to obtain fruits, or you can buy a female plant with a male branch grafted on to it. They need long, hot summers to grow well and fruit. *Maclura pomifera* has a rounded habit and is thorny when young. It has tiny, cup-shaped, yellow-green flowers and dark green leaves that turn yellow in autumn, surrounding the fruits. Grow macluras among shrubs or as specimens; *M. pomifera* can also be used for hedging.

Hardiness Fully frost-hardy ✲✲✲. Unripened shoots on young plants may be damaged by spring frosts.

Cultivation Grow in reasonably fertile soil in full sun. **Prune** young trees in late winter or early spring to remove any misplaced or crossing shoots; cut frost-damaged growth back to a strong bud. **Sow** ripe seed in pots in a sheltered spot outside (*see pp.391–392*). **Take** semi-ripe cuttings in summer, or take root cuttings in winter (*see p.394*).

Maclura pomifera (Osage Orange)
↕15m (50ft) ↔ 12m (40ft), flowers in early summer, fruits (*see inset*) up to 13cm (5in) across

Magnolia

↕to 20m (70ft)
↔ to 15m (50ft)

SPLENDID, SOLITARY, often fragrant, cup- or saucer-shaped flowers distinguish these stately, slow-growing, deciduous and evergreen trees and shrubs. A magnolia in full flower is a sight never to be forgotten. The range of flower colours includes pure white, pink, rich purple, and shades of creamy and greenish-yellow. Most flower between early spring and early summer, many before the tough, but handsome leaves unfurl. Some produce cone-like pods studded with red-coated seeds in autumn. Magnolias make fine specimens.

Hardiness Fully frost-hardy ✲✲✲ to very frost-tender ❀.

Cultivation Grow in moist but well-drained, fertile soil in sun or partial shade. They prefer neutral to acid (lime-free) soil, but some tolerate alkaline soil. **Prune** only if absolutely necessary, in late winter or early spring. **Take** softwood cuttings of deciduous species in early summer; take semi-ripe cuttings of evergreens in late summer or early autumn (*see p.394*).

Magnolia* × *soulangeana
↕↔ 6m (20ft), deciduous shrub or tree, may be wall-trained, flowers open in mid- and late spring, on bare branches ✲✲✲

Magnolia wilsonii 🏆
↕↔ 6m (20ft), deciduous shrub or tree, red-purple shoots, leaves felted red-brown underneath, flowers in late spring ✲✲✲

***Magnolia* 'Elizabeth'** 🏆
↕10m (30ft) ↔ 6m (20ft), deciduous tree, leaves bronze when young, then dark green, flowers mid- to late spring ✲✲✲

Mahonia

↕60cm–5m (2–15ft)
↔1–4m (3–12ft)

THESE EVERGREEN SHRUBS are valued for their honey-scented, winter (occasionally spring) flowers and bold foliage. The large, leathery leaves are divided into spiny leaflets. Most have either rounded clusters or star-burst spikes of usually yellow flowers that last for many weeks over winter, followed by purple to black berries. Although mahonias are mostly upright, some have a low-growing, spreading habit and make good ground cover. Taller ones are ideal at the back of a garden or as specimen plants. Use with other winter-interest plants such as holly (*see Ilex, pp.74–75*) and *Viburnum × bodnantense* (*see pp.126–127*).

Hardiness Fully frost-hardy *** to frost-hardy **.

Cultivation Mahonias prefer reasonably fertile soil enriched with well-rotted organic matter. Most prefer full or partial shade, but tolerate full sun where the soil is moist at all times. **Prune** after flowering, lightly cutting back shoots that spoil the shape. Mahonias regrow well from hard pruning if necessary (*see p.384*). **Take** semi-ripe cuttings (*see p.394*) from late summer until autumn.

Mahonia lomariifolia
↕3m (10ft) ↔2m (6ft), upright growing evergreen with yellow flowers from autumn followed by purple berries **

Malus

Crab Apple

AMONG THE MOST POPULAR flowering trees, especially since so many are ideally sized for the smaller garden, crab apples are renowned for their pink or white spring blossom. Golden or scarlet fruits follow in the autumn; inedible raw, they can be made into wine and jellies. The fruits attract birds, and the autumn foliage colour of these trees is often brilliant too, making them a real focus of interest late in the year. All crab apples are deciduous; some form a rounded crown, while others (such as *Malus floribunda*) have long, arching branches that are particularly graceful. They look equally good as specimens or with other small trees, such as hawthorns (*Crataegus, see p.46*), birches (*Betula, p.42*), and rowans (*Sorbus, p.118*).

Hardiness Fully frost-hardy ***.

Cultivation Grow in reasonably fertile soil that is moist but well-drained, in full sun; most tolerate partial shade. **Prune** young trees to remove any shoots that spoil a good branch framework in late winter or early spring (*see p.382*).

***Malus* 'John Downie'** 🏆
↕↔6m (20ft), narrow habit, conical when mature, reliable and heavy cropper, fruit to 3cm (1¼in) long, good for jelly

Melaleuca

Paperbark

THIS LARGE GROUP OF EVERGREEN TREES and shrubs ranges from low groundcovers up to tall trees. They occur naturally over a wide range of growing conditions; there is a melaleuca for every situation. Many have cream-coloured, peeling, papery bark that gives rise to one of the common names, paperbark. Leaves are small to medium, lance-shaped and often finish in a small but sharp point. Mostly green, a few have grey foliage. The flowers are bottlebrush-like balls or cylinders, and can be white, cream, yellow, green, pink, mauve, or red. Most flower in spring or summer, with some flowering at other times.

Hardiness Frost-hardy ** to frost-tender *.

Cultivation Grow in full sun in any well-drained soil, although a few can withstand wet conditions. **Prune** minimally; remove any shoots that spoil the shape of plants and prune while young to encourage a good form (*see p.384*). **Sow** seed (*see pp.391–392*) collected from year-old capsules in spring and summer. Germination is quick if the temperature is maintained between 18 and 28°C (64 and 82°F). **Take** cuttings of firm young growth in spring and summer (*see p.394*).

Melaleuca armillaris (Bracelet Honey Myrtle)
↕5m (15ft) ↔5m (15ft), quick growing, tough and dense evergreen shrub **

MELIA

DECIDUOUS SHRUBS AND SMALL TREES, only one, *Melia azedarach*, is common in gardens. It is a short yet broad tree, with clusters of pale purple flowers in late spring and summer. These are showy and have a sweet perfume to them. Pendulous groups of small, round, yellow-brown fruits follow in late summer, but these should be avoided as they are poisonous. The leaves are similar to those of ash trees (*Fraxinus, see p.59)*, being large but made up of many pairs of leaflets. Often seen as a street tree, this is a good shade tree provided the woody fruits do not pose a problem.

Hardiness Frost-hardy ✻✻.

Cultivation Grow in full sun in any well-drained soil that is reasonably fertile. **Prune** minimally, other than to establish a strong central trunk when young. **Sow** seed (*see p.391*) in a cold frame in spring and summer. **Take** hardwood cuttings in winter (*see p.394*). **Watch** for caterpillars, especially in warmer districts. (*see p.399*).

Melia azedarach (White Cedar)
↕10–25m (30–80ft) ↔ 5–15m (15–50ft), open-crowned deciduous treee

MESPILUS GERMANICA

Medlar

↕6m (20ft)
↔8m (25ft)

THE MEDLAR IS A DECIDUOUS TREE or large shrub that originates in mountainous regions of southern Europe and Asia. It makes an interesting specimen tree, with a pleasing, spreading habit, bowl-shaped, white (occasionally pink-tinged) flowers that appear from late spring to early summer, and round, fleshy fruits that follow in autumn. The fruits can be made into jelly. Raw fruits are an acquired taste; they are edible, but only when well ripened or partly rotted ("bletted"). The medlar is lovely in autumn with other fruiting trees, such as hawthorns (*Crataegus, see p.46*) or crab apples (*Malus, see p.87*).

Hardiness Fully frost-hardy ✻✻✻.

Cultivation Grow in reasonably fertile, moist but well-drained soil in full sun or partial shade. **Pruning** is unnecessary except to remove any shoots that are crossing, dead or misshapen in late winter or early spring (*see p.382*). **Sow** seed in a seedbed in autumn (*see pp.391–393*).

Mespilus germanica
↕↔ 4m (12ft), flowering (see inset) in spring, the foliage turns yellow-brown in autumn as the fruits ripen

METROSIDEROS

New Zealand Christmas Tree, Pohutukawa

DENSELY FOLIAGED EVERGREEN SHRUBS and small trees, these are particularly useful in tough coastal conditions, which they withstand with ease. The leaves are broadly oval and dark green above, and white and felty underneath. Variegated forms are also available. The flowers are very showy, bright red, round bottlebrushes covering the growing tips of the plant in summer. When grown as specimen trees, they tend to be upright and fairly narrow compared to their height. These also make good windbreaks, and cope with regular pruning to form a hedge, although flowering may suffer if pruning is carried out too late in spring.

Hardiness Frost-tender ✻.

Cultivation Grow in full sun in any well-drained soil that is reasonably fertile. **Prune** minimally; remove any shoots that spoil the shape of young plants to encourage a good form (*see p.384*). As plants flower at the tips of new wood, avoid clipping after late winter and begin again after flowering. **Sow** seed (*see pp.391–392*) in spring in a cold frame. **Take** semi-hardwood cuttings in late summer and autumn. These will strike better with bottom heat (*see p.394*).

Metrosideros excelsus (New Zealand Christmas Bush)
↕10m (30ft) ↔ 7m (20ft), flowers in summer at Christmas

Morus

Mulberry

The black, white, and red mulberries, native to China, South-western Asia, and the Americas respectively, were first cultivated to provide leaves for the silkworm industry. All have raspberry-shaped, edible fruits, first white or green, then ripening to dark purple, yellow, or red among attractive, rounded or heart-shaped leaves that turn yellow in autumn. Orange, scaly bark provides winter interest. Mulberries become beautifully shaped trees with age, so grow them as specimens – the small, weeping, White Mulberry (*Morus alba* 'Pendula') is an excellent choice for small gardens. Do not site mulberries overhanging paving, or the fruits will stain it badly.

Hardiness Fully frost-hardy ✻✻✻.

Cultivation Grow in reasonably fertile soil enriched with well-rotted organic matter, in full sun, with shelter from hot, drying winds. **Prune** only in late autumn or early winter, if necessary. If pruned at any other time, the cuts will "bleed" sap badly. **Sow** seed in containers in a cold frame in autumn (*see pp.391–392*). **Take** semi-ripe cuttings in summer, or hardwood cuttings in autumn (*see p.394*).

Morus nigra ♀ (Black Mulberry)

↕↔ 10m (30ft), fruits pleasant if a little dull eaten raw, but good for jam and wine

Murraya

Evergreen shrubs, these are justifiably famous for their strong and sweet perfume. This arises from creamy white, citrus-blossom-type flowers that are held in loose balls at the ends of the growing tips. The main flowering is in spring, but there is generally another crop in late summer or autumn, as well as sporadic flowering throughout the year. Leaves are glossy, rich, dark green and are made up of pointed oval leaflets. Overall the plant is a broad yet dense shrub that is multi-stemmed from the ground. As well as the perfume, these can be grown for screens or as backdrops to smaller flowering plants.

Hardiness Frost-tender ✻ to very frost-tender ❁.

Cultivation Grow in any well-drained soil that is reasonably fertile and enriched with well-rotted organic matter. It does best in warmer areas where it will grow in full sun or partial shade. **Prune** lightly overall after the autumn flowers to help promote future flowers and keep the plant dense (*see p.384*). **Take** heeled semi-hardwood cuttings in winter (*see p.394*). Bottom heat will increase strike rates.

Murraya paniculata (Orange Jessamine)

↕3m (9ft) ↔ 3m (9ft), a perfumed evergreen that grows well in containers

Myrtus communis

Common Myrtle

↕↔ to 3m (10ft)

Grown for its rich, delicate scent, myrtle is a bushy, upright, evergreen shrub or tree with glossy, dark-green, aromatic leaves. It produces white, sweet-smelling, bowl-shaped flowers in abundance from spring to autumn. Both the flowers and the purple-black berries that follow in autumn are dependent on long, hot summers. Myrtles only thrive in a warm, sheltered position. They look well in shrub and mixed gardens, or as an informal hedge. They can also be trained against a wall, or grown in containers for a patio where their scent can be best appreciated.

Hardiness Frost-hardy ✻✻.

Cultivation Grow in reasonably fertile, moist but well-drained soil or quality potting mix, in full sun with shelter. **Lightly trim** or prune shoots that spoil the shape in mid- or late spring. Trim hedges in spring (*see p.384*). **Sow** seed in containers in a cold frame in autumn (*see pp.391–392*). **Take** semi-ripe cuttings in late summer (*see p.394*).

Myrtus communis ♀

↕↔ 3m (10ft), of Mediterranean origin, upright but branches arching with age, thrives in town and seaside gardens

NANDINA DOMESTICA
Sacred Bamboo

↕to 2m (6ft)
↔to 1.5m (5ft)

GROWING WILD in the mountain valleys of India, China, and Japan, Sacred Bamboo is an elegant, upright shrub, grown for its flowers, fruits, and handsome foliage. The leaves are red to reddish-purple when young, mature to green, and turn crimson again in autumn in colder areas. In mid-summer, small clusters of star-shaped, white flowers with yellow centres appear, followed, in warmer climates or after hot summers, by bright red fruits. Nandinas are evergreen or semi-evergreen, but may not survive extremely cold winters. Grow them with other shrubs with good autumn colour. The low-growing Dwarf Sacred Bamboo, *Nandina domestica* 'Nana', makes an excellent low, informal hedge.

Hardiness Frost-hardy ✻✻.

Cultivation Grow in moist but well-drained soil, in full sun, but tolerates dry conditions. **Prune back** hard after planting, then prune in mid-spring to keep the plant tidy and maintain a good shape (*see p.383*). **Sow** seed in containers in a cold frame as soon as it is ripe (*see pp.391–392*). **Take** semi-ripe cuttings in summer (*see p.394*).

Nandina domestica ♀
↕2m (6ft) ↔ 1.5m (5ft), can be slightly invasive in hot climates, but behaves well in temperate gardens

NERIUM
Oleander

EXTREMELY TOUGH, the downside of these plants is that all parts are poisonous. They are bushy, evergreen shrubs with a multitude of erect stems rising from ground level to make a tall, vase-shaped bush. The leaves are long and narrowly lance-shaped. Generally dark green, there are also variegated leaf forms. Flowers come in a range of colours and are sweetly scented. They are small, slender tubes that flare out to flat at the opening. They appear over a long period from late spring until the end of summer, and are white, pink, or crimson, with some double forms also available.

Hardiness Frost-hardy ✻✻.

Cultivation Grow in full sun in just about any soil, provided it is well-drained. **Prune** minimally; old plants can benefit from staggered renovation pruning if they become straggly (*see p.384*). **Take** semi-hardwood cuttings in autumn (*see p.394*).

Nerium oleander
↕4m (12ft) ↔ 3m (9ft), perfumed flowers in spring and summer

NYSSA
Tupelo

THE TUPELO IS A DECIDUOUS TREE prized for its outstanding foliage, which is bronze when young, matures to dark green, then turns to brilliant hues of amber, ruby, and gold in autumn. It does produce tiny green flowers, followed by small, blue fruits. However, the autumn foliage tints are the main attraction. Tupelo makes an ideal specimen tree, and looks effective planted near water (it thrives in wet, swampy areas). Try *Nyssa sinensis* with birches (*Betula, see p.28*) as the golden autumn foliage of the birch will contrast brilliantly with the tupelo's scarlet leaves.

Hardiness Fully frost-hardy ✻✻✻, but best in areas with mild summers.

Cultivation Grow in fertile, moist but well-drained, neutral to acid soil, in sun or partial shade with shelter from hot, drying winds. **Choose** young, container-grown specimens, since they resent root disturbance more and more as they get older. **Trim** shoots that are crossing or misplaced in late winter or early spring to maintain a good shape and healthy framework (*see p.382*). **Sow** seed in a seedbed in autumn (*see pp.391–393*). **Take** greenwood cuttings in early summer, or semi-ripe cuttings in midsummer (*see p.394*).

Nyssa sinensis ♀
↕↔ 10m (30ft), broadly conical, often multi-stemmed habit, usually with sweeping lower branches, green leaves turn fiery in autumn

Olea
Olive

Most people are familiar with the common olive tree, from which the edible fruits are harvested. This is a broad, evergreen tree, much-branched from a short, stocky trunk. With age, the trunks and branches become interestingly twisted and gnarled, and a flared buttress grows at ground level. The leaves are narrowly lance-shaped, grey-green above, and silvery underneath. The creamy summer flowers are very small and not significant. The fruit is oval and starts out green, ripening to purple-black. These need to be prepared before eating. There are also olea species that naturally occur in South Africa (*Olea capensis*) and Australia (*Olea paniculata*).

Hardiness Frost-hardy ❄❄.

Cultivation Grow in any well-drained soil that is in full sun. **Prune** minimally; remove any shoots that spoil the shape of the young plants and encourage a good form (*see p.382*). **Sow** seed (*see pp.391–392*) into containers as soon as it is collected. **Take** semi-hardwood cuttings in mid-summer (*see p.394*). The varieties that are grown for their fruit are budded or grafted.

Olea europea
↕8m (25ft) ↔ 6m (20ft), this is the tree from which the common olive is harvested

Origanum
Marjoram, Oregano

see also p.295

Aromatic plants from the Mediterranean, marjorams may be shrubs, subshrubs (shrubs that are woody only at the base), or herbaceous perennials. All are very similar: small, with an upright to spreading habit and tiny, pink to mauve flowers borne through summer amid more conspicuous, often brightly coloured bracts (modified leaves). The flowers are magnets for bees and other pollinating insects. Larger species are suited to a herb bed, raised bed, or in containers near the house, where the fragrant leaves can be rubbed to release their scent. They also look good as edging plants for borders or paths, where they will sprawl contentedly.

Hardiness Fully frost-hardy ❄❄❄ to frost-hardy ❄❄.

Cultivation Grow in full sun, in poor to reasonably fertile soil. Very rich soil encourages leafy growth at the expense of flowers. Marjorams prefer a free-draining, alkaline (limy) soil. **Cut back** old flowered stems in early spring (*see p.383*). **Take** cuttings of new shoots growing from the base in late spring and treat as softwood cuttings (*see p.394*).

Origanum 'Kent Beauty'
↕10cm (4in) ↔ 20cm (8in), prostrate, with trailing stems, semi-evergreen, named for its hop-like flowers ❄❄❄

Osmanthus

Useful for a shrub garden or woodland feel, this group of evergreen shrubs is grown for its glossy, dark green foliage, and white, occasionally yellow or orange flowers, which are scented like jasmine. These are produced in early and mid-spring, and are followed by round, blue-black fruits. *Osmanthus heterophyllus* and *O.* × *fortunei* have spiky, holly-like foliage. Osmanthus has a dense, neat habit, and is an effective foil to showier shrubs in the garden. *O. delavayi* and *O. burkwoodii* are good for hedging, while *O. heterophyllus* 'Aureomarginatus' will liven up a dull corner with its yellow-margined leaves.

Hardiness Fully hardy ❄❄❄ to frost-tender ❅.

Cultivation Grow in fertile, well-drained soil, in sun or partial shade, and shelter from hot, drying winds. **Trim** lightly or prune back shoots after flowering, taking out any that spoil the shape of the shrub (*see p.382*). Trim hedges in summer. All species tolerate hard pruning if necessary (*see p.384*). **Sow** seed in a container in a cold frame as soon as it is ripe (*see pp.391–392*). **Take** semi-ripe cuttings (*see p.394*) in summer and put in a propagator with bottom heat, or layer low-growing shoots in autumn or spring (*see p.395*).

① ***O.* × *burkwoodii*** 🏆 ↕↔ 3m (10ft), rounded habit, good for topiary ❄❄❄ ② ***O. delavayi*** 🏆 ↕2–6m (6–20ft) ↔ 4m (12ft), rounded habit ❄❄❄

OXYDENDRUM ARBOREUM

Sorrel Tree, Sourwood

↕15m (50ft) ↔8m (25ft)

THE SORREL TREE IS A deciduous tree or large shrub with a conical or columnar habit. It is a dual-season tree for interest, with white flowers in the summer and boldly coloured foliage in the autumn. Its flowers, produced in late summer and early autumn, are tiny, about 6mm (¼in) long, but gain impact by being borne in large, airy plumes, up to 25cm (10in) long, at the ends of the shoots. The leaves are glossy, toothed, and dark green through summer, turning brilliant shades of red, yellow, and purple in autumn. Grow it as a specimen tree or in a mixed garden bed.

Hardiness Fully frost-hardy ❄❄❄.

Cultivation Grow a sorrel tree in fertile, moist but well-drained soil, preferably acid (lime-free), avoiding exposed sites. **Prune** young trees in late winter or early spring to remove any crossing or misplaced branches. **Sow** seed in a container in a cold frame in autumn (*see pp.391–392*). **Take** semi-ripe cuttings in summer (*see p.394*).

Oxydendrum arboreum
↕15m (50ft) ↔8m (25ft), lightly perfumed summer flowers and good autumn colour

PAEONIA

Tree Peony

see also p.298

↕↔ to 2.2m (7ft)

SHRUBBY PEONIES, as opposed to the herbaceous kinds that die down each year, are commonly known as tree peonies. These peonies also have the characteristically voluptuous flowers in a wide range of colour, occasionally scented, borne from spring to early summer, with the bonus of permanent stature in a mixed garden. Flowers can be single or double, cup- or saucer-shaped, and up to 30cm (12in) across. The stamens in the centre are often in a contrasting colour. Leaves are usually mid- to dark green, often feathery. Grow these peonies in a shrub, or mixed, garden.

Hardiness Fully frost-hardy ❄❄❄ to frost-hardy ❄❄. Severe late frosts may damage young growth and flower buds.

Cultivation Grow in deep, fertile soil enriched with well-rotted organic matter, in full sun or partial shade. Peonies prefer shelter from hot, drying winds. **Prune out** flowered shoots (*see inset*). **Take** semi-ripe cuttings in summer (*see p.394*).

PRUNING SPENT WOOD
Once shoots have flowered and set seed, they die back to new growth. Prune spent shoots back to a new leaf in autumn.

Paeonia delavayi 🏆
↕↔ 1.2m (4ft), flowers up to 10cm (4in) across in early summer, leaves dark green and blue-green underneath ❄❄❄

Paeonia delavayi* var. *ludlowii 🏆
↕2m (6ft) ↔ 1.2m (4ft), flowers up to 13cm (5in) across in late spring, new leaves deep maroon (*see inset*), then bright green ❄❄❄

Paulownia

Princess Tree

↕to 12m (40ft)
↔to 10m (30ft)

THESE VIGOROUS, DECIDUOUS trees make striking additions to the garden. They grow and flower best in areas with long, hot summers. The fast-growing Foxglove or Princess Tree (*Paulownia tomentosa*) is tolerant of air pollution. *P. fortunei* is smaller, to 8m (25ft) tall. Both bear their fragrant flowers in late spring, often on near-bare branches. They make fine specimen trees in a lawn.

Hardiness Frost-hardy ❄❄. Young trees may be damaged by frosts unless protected in their early years.

Cultivation Grow in fertile, well-drained soil in full sun. Shelter from hot, drying winds. **Prune** paulownias grown as trees only if necessary. **Sow** seed in containers in a cold frame in spring or autumn (*see pp.391–392*). **Take** root cuttings in winter (*see p.394*). Young plants benefit from being grown on in pots and overwintered under glass.

Paulownia tomentosa 🏆 (Princess Tree, Foxglove Tree)
↕12m (40ft) ↔ 10m (30ft), flowers well (*inset*) the year after a hot summer

Perovskia

Russian Sage

A GRACEFUL SHRUB, perovskia has tall, wand-like stems of tiny, violet-blue flowers in late summer or early autumn. Both stems and leaves are usually grey-white or grey-green, and the foliage is aromatic, with a pleasantly sharp, lemony scent. The stems can reach a height of up to 1.2m (4ft) in a single season, bearing their small flowers along about half their length. Perovskias add height and a cloud of hazy blue in a massed herbaceous planting, and like perennials, are best cut back hard in early spring, or they will become leggy and bare. They also look striking against a grey or white-painted wall.

Hardiness Fully frost-hardy ❄❄❄.

Cultivation Grow in well-drained soil that is poor or reasonably fertile in full sun. Perovskias will grow in dry, chalky soils and in coastal areas. **Prune** hard in spring, cutting back the previous season's growth to within 5–10cm (2–4in); gradually, a permanent, stubby, woody framework will develop (*see inset, below*). **Take** softwood cuttings in late spring, or semi-ripe cuttings in summer (*see p.394*).

PRUNING PEROVSKIAS
Before new growth starts, cut away old stubby parts of the plant that did not shoot the previous year.

***Perovskia* 'Blue Spire'** 🏆
↕1.2m (4ft) ↔ 1m (3ft), leaves slender and silver-grey, hugging the stems, the flowers resemble those of lavender

Philadelphus

Mock Orange

DELICIOUSLY FRAGRANT FLOWERS are a feature of this group of mainly deciduous shrubs. The flowers are cup or bowl-shaped, single, semi-double, and double, and usually white, often with yellowish stamens. They are produced either singly or in clusters. The leaves are mid-green; *Philadelphus coronarius* has white-variegated and golden-leaved forms. There is no missing a mock orange in flower, since the scent drifts in the air for a considerable distance. Grow them in a shrub garden, with other early and midsummer-flowering shrubs like weigelas (*see p.128*), or as specimen plants.

Hardiness Fully frost-hardy ❄❄❄ to frost-tender ❄.

Cultivation Grow in any reasonably fertile, well-drained soil, in full sun or partial shade. *P. microphyllus* needs full sun, but its golden-leaved form 'Aureus' must have some shade. **Prune** after flowering, cutting back flowered stems to strong buds or new shoots lower down. On mature plants, cut one or two old branches to the base each year to encourage new growth. **Take** softwood cuttings in summer, or hardwood cuttings in autumn or winter (*see p.394*).

① **'Belle Etoile'** 🏆 ↕1.2m (4ft) ↔ 2.5m (8ft) ② ***coronarius* 'Aureus'** 🏆 ↕2.5m (8ft) ↔ 1.5m (5ft) ③ **'Virginal'** ↕3m (10ft) or more ↔ 2.5m (8ft)

Phebalium

Ranging from dwarf shrubs up to small trees, these evergreens occur naturally over a wide range of growing conditions. The spring flowers appear at the growing tips and are small and starry. They are mostly white, cream, yellow, and pink, although some have green flashed with red. In some species they arise out of attractive buds. Leaves are small and linear or oval, and often have a gentle aroma when crushed. The plants are rounded in form and usually have fairly erect branches, although some have a spreading form.

Hardiness Frost-hardy ❄❄.

Cultivation Grow in any well-drained soil, in light shade, with mulch helping to keep the root area cool. **Prune** minimally; remove any shoots that spoil the shape of plants to encourage a good form (*see p.382*). **Take** cuttings of firm, but young wood in summer (*see p.394*).

Phebalium squamulosum (Forest Phebalium)
↕1–3m (3–9ft) ↔ 1–3m (3–9ft), variable shrub flowering in spring

Philotheca

These evergreen native shrubs have starry flowers at the ends of the growing tips. They are usually white, often with pale pink to the underside, although greenish-yellow flowers also occur. Flowering time is usually late winter and into spring. The leaves are short and linear, and often are a little rough to the touch. These plants are generally small shrubs, and form round, ball shapes as wide as they are tall. Grow with other Australian native plants such as banksias (*see p.27*), bottlebrushes (*Callistemon, see p.30*) and the similar-looking *Chamelaucium* (*see p.39*).

Hardiness Frost-hardy ❄❄ to frost-tender ❄.

Cultivation Grow in well-drained soil, in full sun or partial shade. **Prune** minimally; remove any shoots that spoil the shape of young plants to encourage a good form (*see p.382*). **Take** heeled cuttings in late summer and place in a cold frame (*see p.394*).

Philotheca myoporoides
↕↔ 1.5–3m (5–10ft), a profusion of starry white flowers in spring

Phlomis

see also p.306

These attractive and undemanding evergreen shrubs are grown for their sage-like foliage and their unusual, often hooded, flowers. The leaves are variable in shape: narrow and lance-shaped to more oval. In colour, they range from light green to grey-green, and are often hairy. The flowers are produced in early and mid-summer in shades of golden yellow, lilac-pink, purple to pink, and occasionally white, and are borne in dense tiers, or clusters, on tall, erect stems. These small to medium-sized shrubs have an upright or rounded habit. Phlomis look particularly at home among herbs such as sage and lavender (*see p.80*), but they can also be grown in mixed gardens. There are also some herbaceous perennial phlomis.

Hardiness Fully frost-hardy ❄❄❄ to frost-hardy ❄❄.

Cultivation Grow these shrubs in any fertile, well-drained soil in full sun. **Deadhead** for a longer flowering display and lightly trim any shoots that spoil the overall shape of the shrubs when flowering has finished. **Sow** seed (*see pp.391–393*) in spring, or take softwood cuttings (*see p.394*) in summer.

Phlomis fruticosa 🏆 (Jerusalem Sage)
↕1m (3ft) ↔ 1.5m (5ft), mound-forming ❄❄❄ (borderline)

Phormium

New Zealand Flax

With striking, sword-like foliage and exotic-looking flowers, these architectural plants develop into large, handsome clumps that can act as focal points in a garden, in gravel or against a building. Their versatility is enhanced by the range of leaf colours available, from bronze-green with rose-pink margins to dark green with red, orange, or pink stripes. In summer, they produce tall, leafless spikes bearing abundant tubular flowers in erect clusters. These may not flower in colder areas. With their thick, tough leaves they are also ideal for coastal gardens where they often flower well. Plant a phormium in a large pot to add a touch of drama to a patio or terrace.

Hardiness Frost-hardy ✻✻ to frost-tender ✻.

Cultivation Grow phormiums in fertile, moist but free-draining soil where they receive full sun. Although these plants are not completely hardy, in frost-prone areas they may survive winter temperatures as low as -12°C (10°F) if they are given a deep mulch (*see p.388*) around their roots. **Sow** seed (*see pp.391–393*) in spring. **Divide** the woody crowns of large, established clumps, also in spring, to increase stocks (*see p.395*); you may need a large knife to cut through the crown.

Phormium tenax 𝕐
↕4m (12ft) ↔ 2m (6ft), dull red flower spikes are up to 4m (12ft) tall ✻✻

Photinia

These evergreen or deciduous shrubs and trees are grown for their attractive foliage and varied habits. Some are spreading trees, but many are upright or rounded shrubs, ranging in height from 3m (10ft) to 12m (40ft). They produce small clusters of tiny, white flowers in summer, although the deciduous species are mainly prized for their autumn leaf colours and fruits. Evergreen types often have striking, reddish new leaves in spring before they turn glossy dark or mid-green. Photinias look good in a shrub garden or as specimen plants. They are most often used as hedging plants, where regular trimming encourages new, coloured foliage.

Hardiness Fully frost-hardy ✻✻✻ to frost-hardy ✻✻; young growth may be damaged by late spring frosts.

Cultivation Grow in fertile, moist but well-drained soil, in full sun or partial shade with protection from cold winds. **Trim** any crossing or misshapen shoots in winter or early spring, to maintain a good shape and a healthy framework of shoots. Trim hedges in summer when the colour of the young growth has faded. **Propagate** all types by semi-ripe cuttings in summer; sow seed of deciduous types in autumn (*see pp.391–393*).

Photinia × *fraseri* 'Red Robin' 𝕐
↕↔ 5m (15ft) upright evergreen shrub or small tree, bronze to scarlet young foliage, flowers in mid- to late spring ✻✻

Phygelius

↕1–1.2m (3–4ft)
↔1–1.5m (3–5ft)

Hanging clusters of flowers produced over a long period in summer, and often into autumn, are the main reason for growing these evergreen or semi-evergreen shrubs. They have oval- to lance-shaped leaves, and flowers in several shades of yellow, orange-red, creamy yellow, and orange. Phygelius will thrive in a garden in a sunny spot, and spread by means of suckers. Where temperatures often fall below freezing, treat them as herbaceous perennials – although the top-growth may be killed off, they should grow away again in spring.

Hardiness Frost-hardy ✻✻.

Cultivation Phygelius like fertile, moist, well-drained soil in full sun. **Deadhead** to encourage more flowers. **Protect** the roots, in frost-prone areas, with a dry winter mulch of straw. Overwinter young plants in frost-free conditions. **Cut back** the stems in spring of plants being treated as herbaceous perennials; otherwise lightly trim any shoots that spoil the shape. **Take** softwood cuttings (*see p.394*) in late spring or remove rooted suckers for replanting in spring.

① ***aequalis* 'Yellow Trumpet'** 𝕐 ↕1m (3ft) ② × ***rectus* 'African Queen'** 𝕐 ↕1m (3ft) ③ × ***rectus* 'Moonraker'** ↕to 1m (3ft) ④ × ***rectus* 'Salmon Leap'** 𝕐 ↕1.2m (4ft)

PICEA

Spruce

SPRUCES ARE EVERGREEN, coniferous trees grown mainly for their dense foliage and attractive shapes. The most familiar is the Norwegian Spruce or "Christmas tree", *Picea abies*. The needles, which vary in colour from dark green to the silvery blue of *P. pungens* 'Koster', make a good textural contrast to plants with bolder leaves. In summer and autumn, older trees produce cones, which emerge green or red then mature to purple or brown. The larger spruces are useful on their own, to show off their handsome forms, or in groups, especially to create shelter. Like all evergreen conifers, they provide a year-round backdrop and add structure to the garden. The dwarf or slow-growing spruces are suitable for small spaces and rock gardens.

Hardiness Fully frost-hardy ❄❄❄ to frost-hardy ❄❄.

Cultivation Grow in any deep, moist, but well-drained soil, ideally neutral to acid (lime-free), in full sun. No pruning required. **Sow** seed in containers in a cold frame in spring (*see pp.391–392*). **Take** stem-tip cuttings (*see p.394*) of dwarf forms in late summer. May attract aphids (*see pp.398–399*); treat only badly affected young or dwarf plants.

① ***abies*** 🏆 ↕to 40m (130ft) ↔ 6m (20ft) ② ***glauca* 'Conica'** 🏆 ↕2–6m (6–20ft) ↔ 1–2.5m (3–8ft) ③ ***mariana* 'Nana'** 🏆 ↕↔ to 50cm (20in) ④ ***pungens* 'Koster'** 🏆 ↕15m (50ft) ↔ to 5m (15ft)

PICRASMA QUASSIOIDES

Quassia

THIS ELEGANT, UPRIGHT TREE is grown mainly for its attractive foliage, which fades to lovely shades of yellow, orange, and scarlet before the leaves drop in autumn. Oriental in origin, *P. quassioides* bears a passing resemblance to the Tree of Heaven, *Ailanthus altissima*, to which it is related. Each glossy, mid-green leaf is divided into several leaflets. In early summer, minute, bowl-shaped green flowers are borne in clusters, but they have little ornamental value. Site this fine tree in an open position.

Hardiness Fully frost-hardy ❄❄❄.

Cultivation Grow in fertile, well-drained soil in full sun or partial shade. **Prune out** any crossing branches and those that spoil the shape of the tree in late winter or early spring. **Sow** seed in containers in a cold frame in autumn (*see pp.391–392*).

Picrasma quassioides
↕↔ 8m (25ft), an elegant tree, with glossy mid-green leaves before autumn foliage (*shown here*) develops

PIERIS

↕to 5m (15ft)
↔ to 4m (12ft)

THESE COLOURFUL EVERGREEN shrubs are valued for their glossy, leathery foliage and delightful flowers. They are best placed in a shrub or woodland garden, or in a container. Not all are large, and some are useful for small gardens or containers. The young leaves are often brilliantly coloured, and, in spring, clusters of small, white, or pink flowers almost cover the shrub. Rhododendrons, azaleas and camellias make good companions, as all require similar soil.

Hardiness Fully frost-hardy ❄❄❄ to frost-hardy ❄❄; the young growth may be damaged by late frosts in spring.

Cultivation Grow in reasonably fertile, moist but well-drained, acid (lime-free) soil, or potting mix for acid-loving plants, in full sun or partial shade. **Trim back** any shoots that spoil the shape after flowering, and remove faded flowers if the shrubs are not too large. **Sow** seed in containers in a cold frame in spring or autumn (*see pp.391–392*). **Take** softwood cuttings in early summer, or semi-ripe cuttings from mid- to late summer (*see p.394*).

***Pieris japonica* 'Flamingo'**
↕4m (12ft) ↔ 3m (10ft), compact, rounded shrub, dark red buds, dark pink flowers in late winter and spring ❄❄❄

PIMELEA

THESE ARE MOSTLY SMALL SHRUBS, but there are a few that are more or less herbaceous. Evergreen, the shrubs are densely-foliaged plants that can be round or sprawling in shape. The leaves, which are small, linear to narrowly oval, and bright green, run in four rows up the stems. The small, starry flowers can be quite showy. Generally they are held in tight, round clusters at the very tips of the stems. Some species have clusters of flowers in the leaf axils. Colours vary from white through cream and yellow, to pink and even deep red; flowers occur in spring and summer.

Hardiness Frost-hardy ✲✲ to frost-tender ✲.

Cultivation Grow in full sun or partial shade, in a free-draining soil that is acid (lime-free). **Prune** minimally; remove any shoots that spoil the shape of young plants to encourage a good form (*see p.382*). **Take** cuttings of firm, yet fresh, young wood in late winter or early spring (*see p.394*).

Pimelea ferruginea
↕1m (3ft) ↔ 2m (6ft), flowers occur at the very tips of the growth in spring and summer

PINUS

Pine

THE PINES COMPRISE a large and varied group of evergreens, both trees and shrubs, with distinctive, needles, ornamental cones, and attractive, scaly bark. The larger species are very tall trees with striking, often sparsely branched silhouettes compared with other conifers. Habits vary, from slender giants such as the Scots pine (*Pinus sylvestris*) to the umbrella-shaped stone pine (*P. pinea*). Where a spacious garden allows, they make grand specimen trees, either individually or in groups, and also excellent windbreaks; *P. radiata* and *P. nigra* tolerate coastal exposure. There are medium-sized and dwarf pines, often very slow-growing, for the smaller garden and for rock gardens; look especially among the cultivars of *P. sylvestris*, *P. densiflora* and *P. mugo*.

Hardiness Fully frost-hardy ✲✲✲ to frost-hardy ✲✲.

Cultivation Grow in any well-drained soil in full sun. No pruning required. **Sow** seed in a cold frame in spring (*see pp.391–393*).

***Pinus mugo* 'Mops'** ♀ (Dwarf Mountain Pine)
↕to 3.5m (11ft) ↔ to 5m (15ft), often much smaller; dense, near-spherical bush; very resinous, scaly, grey bark ✲✲✲

Pinus patula ♀ (Mexican Weeping Pine)
↕15–20m (50–70ft) ↔ 6–10m (20–30ft), spreading or rounded tree, reddish-brown bark, thrives in mild areas ✲✲

Pinus nigra ♀ (Austrian Pine, European Black Pine)
↕to 30m (100ft) ↔ 6–8m (20–25ft), domed tree, brown or black bark that becomes deeply fissured with age (*see inset*) ✲✲✲

Pittosporum

↕to 20m (70ft) ↔to 6m (20ft)

GLOSSY, LEATHERY LEAVES, often with wavy edges and sometimes variegated, are the main attraction of these evergreen shrubs. They have a naturally dense, neat habit but also respond well to pruning. The lower branches may be removed to produce a more tree-like shape, allowing for some underplanting. In mild areas, they make handsome specimen plants or windbreak hedges for coastal gardens. Dark-leaved forms form an excellent contrast to bright-leaved or variegated shrubs such as elaeagnus (*see p.50*) and euonymus (*see p.56*). In spring and early summer, they bear small, five-petalled flowers.

Hardiness Frost-hardy ❄❄ to very frost-tender ❀.

Cultivation Grow in fertile, moist but well-drained soil, in full sun or partial shade; site those with variegated or purple foliage in sun for the best colour. **Trim** hedges in spring and late summer. **Sow** seed (*see pp.391–392*) as soon as it is ripe, or, in spring, in containers in a cold frame. **Take** semi-ripe cuttings (*see p.394*) in summer.

① ***tenuifolium*** 🏆 ↕to 10m (30ft) ❄❄ ② ***tenuifolium*** **'Irene Paterson'** 🏆 ↕1.2m (4ft) ❄❄ ③ ***tenuifolium*** **'Tom Thumb'** 🏆 ↕1m (3ft) ❄❄ ④ ***tobira*** 🏆 ↕2–10m (6–30ft) ❄

Platanus

Plane Tree

THESE ARE VERY LARGE, DECIDUOUS TREES with a strong central trunk and a broad, shade-giving crown. The mid-green leaves are large and maple-like, and can be deeply lobed in some species and forms. Autumn colour is not remarkable. Trunks on mature plants often show interesting bark with splotches of cream, grey, and brown. Flowers are insignificant, but the globular seed pods are about 2.5cm (1in) across and held on pendulous stems. These are frequently grown as street trees because of their ability to withstand air pollution and heavily compacted soil. Probably only suitable for larger gardens.

Hardiness Frost-hardy ❄❄.

Cultivation Full sun and plenty of space are the main requirements of these trees. Grow in any well-drained soil, but they will tolerate compacted soils. **Prune** young plants to encourage a good form and a strong, straight central trunk (*see p.384*). **Sow** seed (*see pp.391–392*) in late winter or early spring from seed balls collected straight from trees. **Take** hardwood cuttings in winter (*see p.394*).

Platanus orientalis (Oriental Plane Tree)
↕30m (90ft) ↔20m (60ft), large deciduous shade tree often grown as a street tree

Populus

Poplar, Cottonwood

THE LEAVES OF THESE VIGOROUS, deciduous trees are perhaps their prettiest feature, usually showing silvery undersides when ruffled by the wind. Some are also balsam-scented. In a large garden, these make fine specimen trees or windbreaks, and look good with birches (*Betula, see p.28*), beeches (*Fagus, see p.57*), or oaks (*Quercus, see p.103*), but plant them well away from buildings and drains; they have invasive roots. Shapes vary, from the spreading Silver Poplar (*Populus alba*), with triangular leaves, to the conical Canadian poplar (*P. × canadensis*) and the classic columnar Lombardy poplar (*P. nigra* var. *italica*). Poplars bear catkins in early spring, usually with male and female flowers on separate trees.

Hardiness Fully frost-hardy ❄❄❄.

Cultivation Poplars tolerate all but dry soils, but grow best in fertile, moist but well-drained soil. Position in full sun. **Prune out** any crossing, dead or misplaced branches that spoil the shape of young trees in late winter or early spring. Remove any suckers growing up from the ground around the tree in autumn or winter. **Take** hardwood cuttings (*see p.394*) in winter.

Populus nigra **'Italica'** (Lombardy Poplar)
↕40m (120ft) ↔3m (10ft), upright deciduous tree with bright yellow autumn colour

Potentilla

Cinquefoil

see also p.311

↕1m (3ft)
↔1.5m (5ft)

BEARING BRIGHT FLOWERS for many weeks over summer and autumn, these reliable shrubs are excellent value for a garden. There are also many non-woody potentillas, with very similar flowers – most shrubby types are cultivars of *Potentilla fruticosa*. Their flowers are cup- to saucer-shaped, borne singly or in small clusters, and produced in colours from purest white to shades of pink, red, orange, and yellow. Because they flower over such a long period, they make good foils for other plants with a briefer flowering display. Wider than they are tall, they also make good low edging.

Hardiness Fully frost-hardy ✻✻✻.

Cultivation Grow in poor to reasonably fertile soil that is well drained. Position most in full sun, red-flowered types in light shade. **Cut back** flowered shoots to within 2.5cm (1in) of old growth after flowering or in early spring; the easiest way to do this is with shears. **Sow** seed (*see pp.391–392*) in containers in a cold frame in autumn or spring. **Take** softwood cuttings (*see p.394*) in early summer.

Potentilla nepalensis 'Miss Willmott'
↕30cm (1ft) ↔60m (2ft), summer flowering sub-shrub

Protea

ALL THE PROTEAS ORIGINATE in South Africa, but they are now grown in many parts of the world, and are valued in floristry as both fresh and dried flowers that are long-lasting. They are evergreen trees and shrubs, usually much branched from down low, and with erect, woody branches. On the top of these, the flowers appear in autumn, winter, or spring. These are cylindrical or cup-shaped, and feature white, cream, or red flowers surrounded by colourful modified leaves known as bracts, again in various colours, and some with a feathery appearance. The leaves are stiff, leathery and linear to oval in shape, and occur in pairs opposite each other along the stems.

Hardiness Frost-hardy ✻✻ to frost-tender ✻.

Cultivation Grow in full sun, in just about any soil, although it must be free-draining. Most prefer soil that is acid (lime-free). **Tip prune** young plants to encourage a bushy framework (*see p.390*). Plants benefit from picking flower stems too, as this will also promote bushiness. **Take** cuttings of firm wood in summer and place in a cold frame (*see p.394*.

Protea cyanaroides (King Protea, Giant Protea)
↕2m (6ft) ↔2m (6ft), long lasting cut flower and floral emblem of South Africa ✻

Prostanthera

Mint Bush

THESE EVERGREEN SHRUBS are grown for their aromatic leaves and clusters of bell-shaped flowers. Bushy or spreading, they have mid- to dark green or grey-green leaves that smell of mint, and flower from late spring until summer. In frost-prone areas, the purple- to pink-flowered *Prostanthera ovalifolia* and *P. rotundifolia* need protection in winter. In milder areas, they thrive in the shelter of a warm wall; the hardier, white-flowered *P. cuneata* may be grown in sheltered garden beds. Position it towards the back or centre of a grouping with lower plants in front, because it often becomes bare at the base, and hard pruning to correct this is not possible.

Hardiness Frost-hardy ✻✻ to very frost-tender ❀.

Cultivation Grow in reasonably fertile, well-drained soil, and site in full sun. **Trim** or lightly prune back shoots that spoil the shape of the shrub after flowering. Avoid hard pruning, which can be detrimental. **Sow** seed (*see pp.391–392*) indoors in spring. **Take** semi-ripe cuttings (*see p.394*) in summer.

Prostanthera cuneata (Alpine Mint Bush)
↕↔30–90cm (1–3ft), has small, very aromatic, glossy leaves, and flowers profusely in late spring ✻✻

Prunus

Ornamental Prunus and Laurels

THIS GROUP CONTAINS TWO VERY DIFFERENT types of plant: ornamental or flowering prunus and laurels. In spring, ornamental prunus billow with blossom in shades of pink, white, and sometimes red. *Prunus* × *subhirtella* produces its delicate flurries of flowers in mild spells from autumn to spring. Some, such as *P. serrula*, are also grown for their rich cinnamon-coloured bark, and others, like *P. cerasifera* 'Nigra', have leaves that are in shades of purple. Laurels, on the other hand, are dense, bushy evergreens, such as *P. laurocerasus* and *P. lusitanica*, with much less showy flowers but handsome, glossy leaves. Prunus also includes many trees grown especially for fruit, including plum, peach, and cherry, but the fruits of laurels and most ornamental cherries can cause severe discomfort if eaten and should be left for the birds. Ornamental prunus are upright, rounded, or spreading trees or shrubs; many are suitable for smaller gardens, and make excellent specimen plants. Laurels are classic and reliable hedging plants.

Hardiness Fully frost-hardy ❄❄❄ to frost-hardy ❄❄.

Cultivation Grow in any moist, well-drained soil in full sun or partial shade. **Water** young trees well until they are properly established. **Prune** each of the types slightly differently. For most deciduous shrubs and trees, simply remove any misplaced shoots to maintain a good shape. This can be done at any time of the year. For *P. glandulosa* and *P. triloba*, prune hard after flowering. **Trim** evergreen hedges in early to mid-spring and again in summer if necessary. If possible, use secateurs to achieve the neatest possible finish on laurel hedges. **Sow** seed of species in containers outside in autumn (*see pp.391–392*), or propagate deciduous cultivars by greenwood cuttings, which are taken slightly later than softwood cuttings when the stem is a little firmer and darker (*see p.394*). Budding and grafting is the best technique. Ornamental prunus are sometimes attacked by pear and cherry slug; pick them off or spray with a suitable insecticide. Birds occasionally strip the flower buds.

Using ornamental prunus in the garden

Specimen tree *Most of the flowering prunus make excellent specimen trees for their remarkable displays of spring blossom. Being small to medium trees, there is one to suit even the smallest garden. They can be used within a garden bed or as isolated specimens in a lawn. Ones with purplish foliage, such a* P. cerasifera *'Nigra' and* P. x blireana*, add another dimension to the garden and can be used as a backdrop or foil for other plants.*

Ornamental hedging *Several prunus are suitable for growing as hedging. Evergreen shrubs such as* P. laurocerasus *and* P. lusitanica *make dense screens. When planting, prepare the soil by adding plenty of well-rotted organic matter. Make sure the top of the root ball is just above soil level and firm in gently. The usual planting distance for hedging is 60–75cm (24–30in). Water well after planting and, in exposed situations, erect a wind barrier until the plants become established.*

① ***cerasifera*** **'Nigra'** 🏆 ↕↔ 5m (15ft), early spring, followed by plum-like, edible fruit ② ***glandulosa*** **'Alba Plena'** ↕↔ 1.5m (5ft), late spring ③ **'Kanzan'** 🏆 ↕↔ 10m (30ft), mid- and late spring ④ **'Kiku-shidare-zakura'** 🏆 ↕↔ 3m (10ft), mid- and late spring ⑤ **'Okame'** 🏆 ↕2m (6ft) ↔ 8m (25ft), early spring ⑥ ***padus*** **'Watereri'** 🏆 ↕10m (30ft) ↔ 8m (25ft), late spring

2

7

3

4

10

8

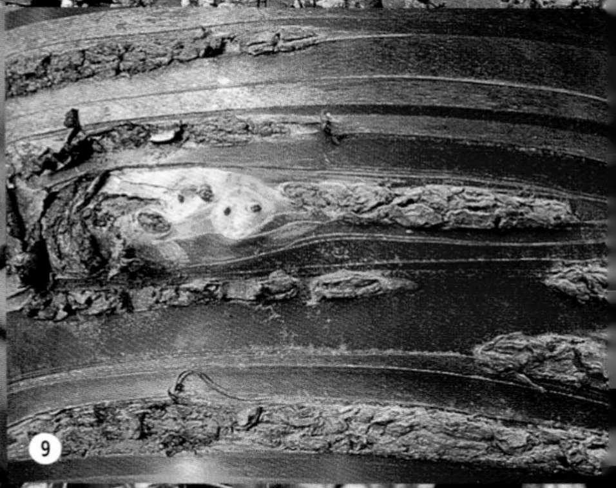
9

11

15

13

14

⑦ **'Pink Perfection'** 🏆 ↕↔ 4m (12ft), late spring ⑧ ***sargentii*** 🏆 ↕ 6m (20ft) ↔ 5m (15ft), mid-spring ⑨ ***serrula*** 🏆 ↕↔ 5m (15ft), late spring ⑩ **'Shirofugen'** 🏆 ↕ 5m (15ft) ↔ 6m (20ft), late spring ⑪ ***spinosa*** ↕ 5m (15ft) ↔ 4m (12ft), early to mid-spring, followed by blue-black fruit (sloes) used to flavour alcohol ⑫ × ***subhirtella*** **'Autumnalis Rosea'** 🏆 ↕↔ 5m (15ft), autumn to spring ⑬ **'Taihaku'** 🏆 ↕ 6m (20ft) ↔ 5m (15ft), mid-spring ⑭ ***triloba*** 🏆 ↕↔ 2m (6ft), early and mid-spring ⑮ **'Ukon'** 🏆 ↕ 6m (20ft) ↔ 5m (15ft), mid-spring

Pultenaea

THESE EVERGREEN SHRUBS range from low, prostrate groundcovers to upright, bushy shrubs, most of which do not reach much more than a metre in height. Showy, pea-like flowers in yellow with orange markings are the most common, although other colours and combinations occur. Flowers generally appear in spring or summer and last for quite some time. The leaves are small and often finish in a short, sharp point. Most species are relatively fast-growing. Grow them in a mixed garden bed with other plants that like free-draining soils, such as *Chamelaucium*, (*see p.39*), *Pimelea* (*see p.97*) and Sturt's Desert Pea (*Swainsona, see p.153*).

Hardiness Frost-hardy ❄❄ to frost-tender ❄.

Cultivation Grow in full sun or partial shade, in a well-drained soil that is enriched with well-rotted organic matter. **Prune** minimally; remove any shoots that spoil the shape of young plants to encourage a good form (*see pp.382–384*). **Sow** pre-soaked seed in spring (*see p.391*). **Take** young, yet firm, cuttings in summer (*see p.394*).

Pultenaea pedunculata (Matted Bush-pea)
↕10cm (4in) ↔ 2–3m (6–9ft), a ground covering shrub with sunny yellow and orange flowers in spring

Punica

Pomegranate

THESE DECIDUOUS TREES HAVE AN UPRIGHT HABIT, generally with quite a few trunks from ground level, unless pruned to be otherwise. The leaves are light green and oval to lance-shaped, and turn yellow before falling in autumn. Small thorns occur occasionally on the stems. In summer it has orange-red flowers that are like starry funnels. Double forms are also available. The fruit is tennis-ball sized and orange, and when ripe, splits to reveal a crimson pulp inside holding the myriad seeds. Fruit can often be seen hanging on trees in winter after all the leaves have fallen. A dwarf form (*Punica granatum* 'Nana'), reaching only about one metre, is also popular.

Hardiness Frost-hardy ❄❄.

Cultivation Full sun and adequate drainage are the main requirements. This plant can withstand periods of dry. **Prune** minimally; remove any shoots that spoil the shape of young plants to encourage a good form (*see pp.382–384*). **Take** hardwood cuttings in late autumn (*see p.394*).

Punica granatum (Pomegranate)
↕4m (12ft) ↔ 3m (9ft), the summer flowers are followed in autumn by an interesting orange fruit

Pyrus

Pear

PEARS ARE VALUED NOT ONLY for their sometimes edible fruits, but also for their flowers, and in some cases, their attractive habits exemplified by the silvery Weeping Pear. The trees are usually deciduous, and some have excellent autumn colour. The flowers, which appear in spring, are white or pink. Fruit shapes vary from the typical pear shape to round; many varieties have been developed over the centuries for their fine-flavoured fruits. Ornamental varieties include *Pyrus calleryana*, which is thorny and develops red foliage and small, round, brown fruits in autumn, and the snow pear (*P. nivalis*), which has silvery grey leaves – both have conical habits and flower in spring. The more compact ornamental pears are ideal for a small garden as specimens in a lawn.

Hardiness Fully frost-hardy ❄❄❄.

Cultivation Grow pears in fertile, well-drained soil in full sun. **Prune out** any shoots that spoil the shape of the tree in late winter or early spring. **Watch** for attacks by pear and cherry slug. Remove by hand or spray with a suitable insecticide.

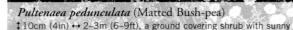

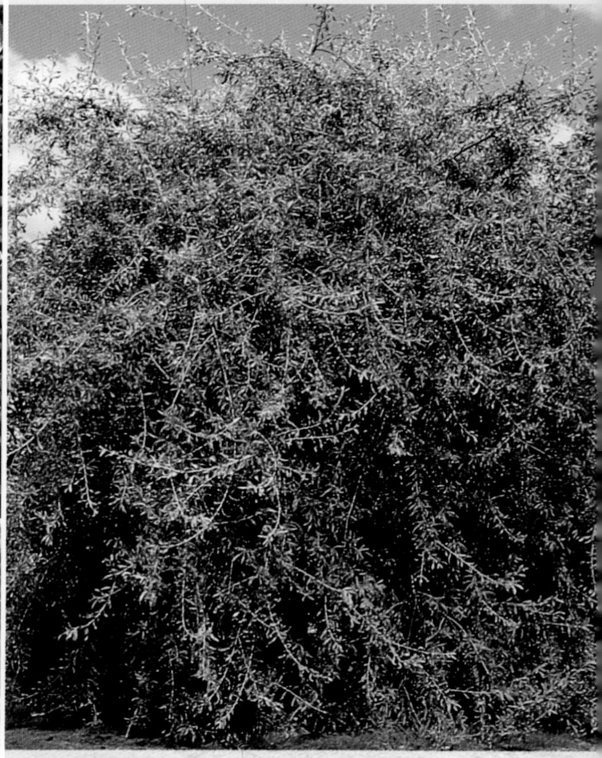

Pyrus salicifolia **'Pendula'** 🏆 (Weeping Pear)
↕↔ 4m (12ft), ideal for smaller gardens; willowy, silvery, felted leaves; pear-shaped, green fruits 3cm (1¼in) long

Pyrus calleryana 'Chanticleer'
↕12m (35ft) ↔ 6m (18ft), autumn colour is bright red on a tree that is conical in form

Pyrus communis
↕4–10m (12–30ft) ↔ 3–6m (9–18ft), the common edible pear is available in hundreds of forms

Quercus

Oak

OAKS ARE LARGE, STATELY TREES, known for their longevity, with attractive foliage and fissured bark. They form a large group of deciduous and evergreen trees with a great range of leaf shapes, colours, and growth habits. Acorns 1–3cm (½–1¼in) long are borne in autumn. Many deciduous oaks are excellent for autumn colour, with foliage in a variety of brilliant shades. The classic common or English Oak (*Quercus robur*) with the typical oak leaf is a huge, spreading tree so is suited only to parks or rural properties, but if you have a large garden, there are smaller – although still large – oaks that are well worth growing as specimen trees. Plant the sapling in its permanent position because it may not survive later transplanting.

Hardiness Fully frost-hardy ❄❄❄ to frost-hardy ❄❄.

Cultivation Oaks need deep, fertile, well-drained soil in full sun. **Prune** out any shoots that spoil the shape of the tree on planting; mature oaks need little pruning except the removal of dead wood (*see p.382*). **Sow** acorns in a seedbed or cold frame as soon as they fall (*see p.393*).

Quercus ilex 🏆 (Holm Oak)
↕25m (80ft) ↔ 20m (70ft), evergreen with smooth, dark grey bark, variable leaves silvery grey when young, thrives in coastal sites ❄❄

Quercus coccinea (Scarlet Oak)
↕20m (70ft) ↔ 15m (50ft), rounded canopy, pale grey-brown bark, dark green leaves turn red in autumn, needs lime-free soil ❄❄❄

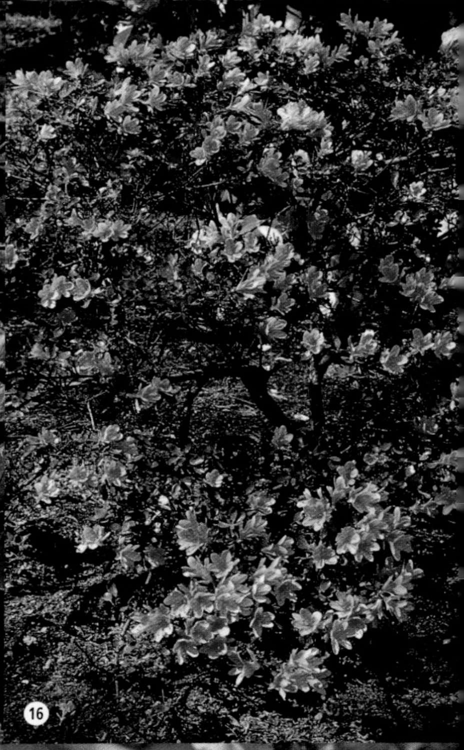

⑫ **'Hatsugiri'** ↕↔ 60cm (24in), dwarf evergreen azalea ✻✻✻ ⑬ **'Hinode-giri'** ↕↔ 60cm (24in), dwarf evergreen azalea ✻✻✻ ⑭ **'Hinomayo'** 🏆 ↕↔ 60cm (24in), dwarf evergreen azalea ✻✻✻ ⑮ **'Homebush'** 🏆 ↕↔ 1.5m (5ft), deciduous azalea ✻✻✻ ⑯ **'Kirin'** ↕↔ 1.2m (4ft), evergreen azalea ✻✻✻ ⑰ **'Kure-no-yuki'** ↕↔ 1m (3ft), evergreen azalea ✻✻✻ ⑱ **'Lavender Girl'** 🏆 ↕↔ 2m (6ft), evergreen shrub ✻✻✻ ⑲ ***occidentale*** 🏆 ↕↔ 3m (10ft), deciduous shrub ✻✻✻ ⑳ **'Pink Pearl'** ↕↔ 3m (10ft), evergreen shrub ✻✻✻ ㉑ **'President Roosevelt'** ↕↔ 2m (6ft),

17

18

19

20

24

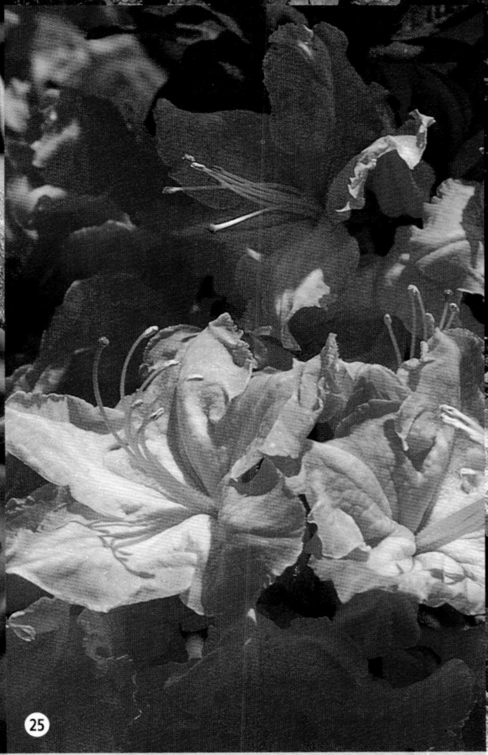
25

26

evergreen shrub ❄❄❄ ㉒ **'Ptarmigan'** 🏆 ↕↔ 90cm (36in), dwarf evergreen shrub ❄❄❄ ㉓ **'Purple Splendour'** 🏆 ↕↔ 2m (6ft), evergreen shrub ❄❄❄ ㉔ **'Saint Valentine'** ↕ 1.5m (5ft) ↔ 2m (6ft), evergreen shrub ❄ ㉕ **'Strawberry Ice'** 🏆 ↕↔ 2m (6ft), deciduous azalea ❄❄❄

㉖ ***yakushimanum*** ↕↔ 2m (6ft), evergreen shrub ❄❄❄

Rhagodia

Grey foliage is the outstanding feature of these plants, along with the ability to withstand tough conditions. The leaves are small, yet often smother the whole bush. The flowers are insignificant and followed by a small, red berry. Plants are sprawling, lax, evergreen shrubs, with generally as much spread as height. Most are drought-hardy and are successfully grown on salt-affected land. They are also fire-resistant. They make great plants to grow on steep, hot embankments, where they will thrive unwatered once established.

Hardiness Frost-hardy ❄❄.

Cultivation Grow in full sun on any well-drained soil. Trimming is rarely necessary. **Take** cuttings of firm young wood at any time of the year (*see p.394*).

Rhagodia spinescens (Hedge Saltbush)
↕0.6–1.5m (2–5ft) ↔ 1.5–4m (5–12ft), drought and salt tolerant sprawling shrub that responds well to regular clipping

Rhaphiolepis

These are evergreen shrubs with glossy, dark-green foliage and fragrant flowers that look similar to apple-blossom. The white or pink flowers appear among the leaves in small clusters in spring or summer, making an eye-catching display. They are good companions to small flowering trees such as Crab Apple (*Malus, see p.88*) and hawthorn (*Crataegus, see p.46*). Rhaphiolepis generally grow into dense, compact shapes, around 2m (6ft) tall and wide, although there are one or two much smaller varieties. Grow the smaller types in containers, and take them under frost-free cover for the winter.

Hardiness Frost-hardy ❄❄ to frost-tender ❄.

Cultivation Grow outdoors in moist but well-drained soil in full sun. If growing them in pots, use a good quality potting mix and water moderately in summer, giving monthly feeds of a balanced fertilizer. **Trim** lightly after flowering, removing stems that spoil the shape of the shrub. **Take** semi-ripe cuttings in late summer (*see p.394*), or layer shoots in autumn (*see p.395*).

Rhaphiolepis umbellata 🏆
↕↔ 1.5m (5ft), slow-growing, bushy, rounded habit, flowers (*inset*) in early summer, berries only after long, hot summers ❄❄

Rhapis

These are slender, clump-forming palms. The dark green leaves are fan-like, although very heavily divided. These are held at the tops of erect or slightly arching stems. A multitude of these stems grow close to one another, giving rise to the common name of Bamboo Palm. They are best grown in tropical and sub-tropical areas, or situations that simulate these with high humidity and ample soil moisture. They can be grown as tub specimens both indoors and outside. Grow them in large enough containers to allow for expansion of the clump and re-pot once the container is taken up.

Hardiness Frost-tender ❄ to very frost-tender ❅.

Cultivation Grow in well-drained soil that is reasonably fertile and enriched with well-rotted organic matter. Rhapis do best in partial or even deep shade; full sun should be avoided. **Trim** out untidy stems or brown leaves. **Propagate** by dividing established clumps (*see p.394*).

Rhapis excelsa
↕4.5m (12ft) ↔ indefinite, gracious, clump-forming palms for warm, humid spots

Ribes

Flowering Currant

CLOSELY RELATED TO EDIBLE CURRANT BUSHES, most ornamental ribes have a blackcurrant- or even cat-like scent, both in flower and when the leaves are crushed. These are old-fashioned, cottage-garden-style, mainly deciduous shrubs, grown for their cheering spring flowers ; pink-flowered *Ribes sanguineum* is a traditional partner for yellow forsythias (*see p.58*). It is also often seen as a flowering hedge. There are ribes that flower in cerise, pale pink, white, or greenish-yellow. They do bear fruits, although these are usually inedible. Most make quite large shrubs, although there are compact varieties, including one or two with bright golden foliage.

Hardiness Fully frost-hardy ❄❄❄ to frost-hardy ❄❄.

Cultivation Grow in reasonably fertile, well-drained soil, in full sun. **Prune** after flowering, cutting back flowered shoots to strong buds or shoots lower down the stem. **Prune out** one or two old main branches on mature plants every three or four years. **Trim** hedges after flowering. **Take** hardwood cuttings of deciduous ribes in winter and semi-ripe cuttings of evergreens in summer (*see p.394*).

Robinia

ROBINIAS ARE TREES AND SHRUBS found in woodland and thickets in North America. They are usually thorny and have bright, graceful, long leaves, and, in late spring and early summer, sprays of white or pink, pea-like flowers. These are followed by large, dark brown seedpods. Grow the trees as specimens in a lawn, and the shrubby species in a large shrub garden, especially among darker-leaved trees or shrubs. *Robinia pseudoacacia* 'Frisia' and *Acer palmatum* 'Rubrum', with its dark red-purple leaves, (*see pp.18–19*), make striking companions.

Hardiness Fully frost-hardy ❄❄❄.

Cultivation Robinias like full sun in reasonably fertile soil, ideally moist but well-drained, but will tolerate dry, poor soils. Shelter from strong winds; the branches are rather brittle and break easily. **Prune out** any misplaced or crossing branches that spoil the shape of young trees in late summer or early autumn (*see p.382*). Remove any suckers (shoots growing up from the ground around the tree). **Sow** seed in a container in a cold frame in autumn (*see pp.391–392*). **Take** root cuttings (*see p.394*) in autumn.

***Robinia* x *pseudoacacia* 'Umbraculifera'** (Mop Top)
↕3m (9ft) ↔ 4m (12ft), deciduous tree often used to bring a formal element to a garden

Ribes sanguinem (Red Flowering Currant)
↕3m (9ft) ↔ 2m (6ft), deciduous shrub, early spring flowering, just before new leaves emerge

***Robinia pseudoacacia* 'Frisia'** 🏆 (Golden Robinia)
↕15m (50ft) ↔ 8m (25ft), fast-growing, suckering tree, fragrant flowers, foliage turns orange-yellow (*see inset*) in autumn

***Robinia* x *ambigua* 'Decaisneana'** (Pink Wisteria Tree)
↕15m (50ft) ↔ 8m (25ft), late srping flowering deciduous tree

ROSA

Rose

see also pp.150–151

SUPERB, OFTEN HIGHLY SCENTED FLOWERS in summer and autumn make roses enduring garden favourites. They are mostly deciduous shrubs, and with hundreds of colourful varieties to choose from, there is one suitable for almost any situation. Shrub roses look best mixed with other plants; the miniature varieties can be grown in rock gardens and in large pots. The flowers, borne in clusters at the tips of upright, sometimes arching or trailing, thorny stems, are excellent for cutting. They vary enormously in form and size, from small single or double blooms to immense, rounded doubles. Colours range from purest white through yellows and pinks to deep blackish-crimson. The red autumn fruits (hips) of some roses also make a striking display.

Hardiness Fully hardy ❄❄❄.

Cultivation Grow in an open, sunny position, in fertile soil with plenty of well-rotted organic matter. **Plant** bare-root roses when dormant, from late autumn to early spring, container-grown plants at any time. **Feed** with a balanced fertilizer in spring and mulch with organic matter. **Prune** in late winter; deadhead to encourage more flowers. **Take** hardwood cuttings (*see p.394*) in autumn. Blackspot, powdery mildew, or rust may affect roses. Choose disease-resistant cultivars if possible. Control aphids.

Modern bush roses

↕to 1m (3ft)
↔to 1m (3ft)

***These upright shrubs** are useful in garden beds, being compact and repeat-flowering with single or double flowers. They bear large flowers singly or in small clusters (hybrid tea) or small flowers in large clusters (floribunda). Prune hard, cutting the main stems of hybrid tea roses to 50–60cm (20–24in) and those of cluster-flowered roses to 60–90cm (24–36in) above the ground, and reducing sideshoots to two or three buds.*

Dwarf patio roses

↕60cm (24in)
↔60cm (24in)

***Compact shrubs** with a bushy habit, these roses are ideal for growing at the front of gardens, in containers or even in a rock garden. They produce abundant clusters of single to double, sometimes scented flowers in a wide range of colours throughout summer. Grow them in fertile soil in full sun. Only light pruning is needed: cut down the main stems and sideshoots by no more than one-third to half their length.*

Ground-cover roses

↕to 60cm (24in)
↔to 1m (3ft)

***Spreading in habit,** these roses have numerous stems bearing clusters of small flowers, usually double or semi-double and lightly scented. They are ideal for ground cover and also for edging paths or growing in large pots. Prune to keep plants to the desired size, cutting to an outward-facing bud. If sideshoots are overcrowded, prune to two to four buds. Every three or four years cut out the oldest wood to encourage new growth; if neglected, they can be cut back hard.*

Standard roses

↕to 2m (6ft)
↔to 1.5m (5ft)

***Ideal for pots,** formal schemes, or to add height in gardens, these are modern bush roses top-grafted onto clear stems of rootstocks; ramblers (see pp.150–151) can be used to make weeping or trailing standards. There are two types of standards; half-standards have a stem of 75cm (2½ft) and full-standards a stem of 1.1m (3½ft). Both need permanent staking. Prune the head according to the rose type used.*

Modern shrub roses

↕1.2–2m (4–6ft)
↔to 2m (6ft)

***A diverse group** of roses, varying in size, habit, and flower type. Most are upright with flowers similar to modern bush roses, and make impressive specimen plants. Some have only one flush of blooms while others repeat-flower through the summer. Heavy pruning can spoil their character: remove dead or diseased wood and shorten main stems by up to one-third, sideshoots by half. Cut one in three old stems to the base each year.*

Old garden roses

↕1.2–2m (4–6ft)
↔to 2m (6ft)

***A varied group,** upright or arching, most flowering once but some are repeat-flowering, most with semi-double or double flowers, often fragrant. Position arching types so they do not crowd plants, and give them only a light annual pruning, removing some of the older wood to encourage new shoots from the base of the shrub. Upright types require only the occasional removal of thin, weak, or dead shoots.*

① *Rosa* AMBER QUEEN ('Harroony') ♀ ↕↔ 60cm (24in), floribunda ② ANGELA RIPPON ('Ocaru') ↕45cm (18in) ↔ 30cm (12in), miniature modern bush ③ 'Belle de Crécy' ♀ ↕1.2m (4ft) ↔ 1m (3ft), old rose ④ 'Boule de Neige' ↕1.5m (5ft) ↔ 1.2m (4ft), old rose ⑤ 'Bourbon Queen' ↕2.5m (8ft) ↔ 1.5m (5ft), old rose ⑥ 'Buff Beauty' ♀ ↕↔ 1.2m (4ft), modern shrub ⑦ 'Cécile Brünner' ♀ ↕75cm (30in) ↔ 60cm (24in), old rose ⑧ 'Ballerina' ♀ ↕1.5m (5ft) ↔ 1.2m (4ft),

7

8

3

4

9

10

12

13

14

15

18

19

20

21

modern shrub ⑨ **'Charles de Mills'** ♀ ↕↔ 1.2m (4ft), old rose ⑩ **'Chinatown'** ♀ ↕ 1.2m (4ft) ↔ 1m (3ft), modern shrub ⑪ **'Cornelia'** ♀ ↕↔ 1.5m (5ft), modern shrub ⑫ **'Crimson Glory'** ↕↔ 60cm (24in), hybrid tea ⑬ **'Doris Tysterman'** ↕ 1.2m (4ft) ↔ 75cm (30in), hybrid tea ⑭ **'Elizabeth Harkness'** ↕ 80cm (32in) ↔ 60cm (24in), hybrid tea ⑮ ENGLISH GARDEN **('Ausbuff')** ↕ 1m (3ft) ↔ 75cm (30in), modern shrub ⑯ **'English Miss'** ♀ ↕ 75cm (30in) ↔ 60cm (24in), floribunda ⑰ ESCAPADE **('Harpade')** ♀ ↕ 75cm (30in) ↔ 60cm (24in), floribunda ⑱ **'Fantin-Latour'** ♀ ↕ 1.5m (5ft) ↔ 1.2m (4ft), old rose ⑲ **'Felicia'** ♀ ↕ 1.5m (5ft) ↔ 2.2m (7ft), modern shrub ⑳ FRAGRANT CLOUD **('Tanellis')** ↕ 75cm (30in) ↔ 60cm (24in), hybrid tea ㉑ **'Fru Dagmar Hastrup'** ♀ ↕ 1m (3ft) ↔ 1.2m (4ft), old rose

㉒ *gallica* 'Versicolor' 🏆 ↕80cm (32in) ↔ 1m (3ft), old rose ㉓ **'Geranium'** 🏆 ↕2.5m (8ft) ↔ 1.5m (5ft), old rose ㉔ **'Glenfiddich'** ↕80cm (32in) ↔ 60cm (24in), floribunda ㉕ GRAHAM THOMAS (**'Ausmas'**) 🏆 ↕↔ 1.2–1.5m (4–5ft), modern shrub ㉖ **'Great Maiden's Blush'** ↕2m (6ft) ↔ 1.35m (4½ft), old rose ㉗ HANNAH GORDON (**'Korweiso'**) ↕80cm (32in) ↔ 60cm (24in), floribunda ㉘ ICEBERG (**'Korbin'**) 🏆 ↕80cm (32in) ↔ 65cm (26in), floribunda

㉙ *Rosa* 'Frühlingsmorgen' ↕2m (6ft) ↔ 1.5m (5ft), modern shrub ㉚ **'Ispahan'** 🏆 ↕1.5m (5ft) ↔ 1.2m (4ft), old rose ㉛ **'Julia's Rose'** ↕75cm (30in) ↔ 45cm (18in), hybrid tea ㉜ **'Just Joey'** 🏆 ↕↔ 75cm (30in), hybrid tea ㉝ **'Madame Isaac Pereire'** 🏆 ↕2.2m (7ft) ↔ 2m (6ft), old rose ㉞ **'Maiden's Blush'** 🏆 ↕1.2m (4ft) ↔ 90cm (36in), old rose ㉟ MARGARET MERRIL (**'Harkuly'**) 🏆 ↕80cm (32in) ↔ 60cm (24in), floribunda ㊱ MOUNTBATTEN (**'Harmantelle'**) 🏆 ↕1.2m (4ft) ↔ 75cm

25

26

27

28

31

38

32

40

37

39

45

46

47

48

(30in), floribunda ㊲ **'National Trust'** ↕↔ 60cm (24in) hybrid tea ㊳ **'Nevada'** 🏆 ↕↔ 2.2m (7ft), modern shrub ㊴ **PEACE ('Madame A. Meilland')** 🏆 ↕ 1.2m (4ft) ↔ 1m (3ft), hybrid tea ㊵ **'Perle d'Or'** 🏆 ↕ 1.2m (4ft) ↔ 1m (3ft), old rose ㊶ **POLAR STAR ('Tanlarpost')** ↕ 1m (3ft) ↔ 70cm (28in), hybrid tea ㊷ **PRETTY POLLY ('Meitonje')** 🏆 ↕↔ 45cm (18in), patio ㊸ ***rugosa*** ↕↔ 1–2.5m (3–8ft), species ㊹ **'Silver Jubilee'** 🏆 ↕ 1.1m (3½ft) ↔ 60cm (24in), hybrid tea

㊺ **'Souvenir de la Malmaison'** ↕↔ 1.5m (5ft), old rose ㊻ **'The Fairy'** 🏆 ↕↔ 60–90cm (24–36in), floribunda ㊼ **'The Queen Elizabeth'** ↕ 2.2m (7ft) ↔ 1m (3ft), modern bush ㊽ **TRUMPETER ('Mactru')** 🏆 ↕↔ 60cm (24in), floribunda

ROSMARINUS

Rosemary

AROMATIC AND EVERGREEN, these rather angular shrubs add height and structure to a herb garden, and they also grow well in pots. Native to Mediterranean regions, they prefer sun and free-draining soils. Use the prostrate forms to cascade over a stony bank or a retaining wall. Rosemary leaves are dark green, while the stems often have a greyish bloom. From late winter to early summer, they bear clusters of blue, mauve, or white, tubular flowers towards the shoot tips.

Hardiness Fully frost-hardy ❄❄❄.

Cultivation Grow in well-drained to dry, relatively poor soil, in full sun. **Trim** lightly but regularly to keep plants bushy and to encourage the soft, succulent young shoots that are best for cooking. **Sow** seed (*see pp.391–392*) in a container in a cold frame in spring. **Take** semi-ripe cuttings (*see p.394*) in summer.

Rosmarinus officinalis **Prostratus Group** (Prostrate Rosemary)
↕15cm (6in) ↔ 1.5m (5ft), prostrate and trailing form of the herb

Rosmarinus officinalis (Rosemary)
↕1.5m (5ft) ↔ 1.5m (5ft), popular and well known culinary herb

Rosmarinus officinalis **'Roseus'** (Pink Rosemary)
↕1.5m (5ft) ↔ 1.5m (5ft), pink flowered version of the evergreen shrub

SALIX

Willow

THIS IS A LARGE AND VARIED group of deciduous trees and shrubs. Spring catkins are one of the striking features, but they also have attractive habits, and in some cases decorative stems. The weeping *Salix caprea* 'Kilmarnock' is a favourite centrepiece for a small lawn or garden. Some of the larger species, generally too vigorous for most gardens, can be grown as shrubs, cut back annually to make them compact and encourage brightly coloured stems. *S. alba* 'Britzensis', for example, makes a fine display with mahonias (*see p.87*) and dogwoods (*Cornus, see pp.42–43*). Willows can be invasive in creeks and rivers, so use them with caution in rural areas.

Hardiness Fully frost-hardy ❄❄❄.

Cultivation Grow in any deep, moist but well-drained soil, in full sun. **Pruning** is rarely necessary except for those grown for winter stems; in early spring, cut these stems back to within three or four buds of the base or to a permanent stubby framework (*see right, and p.383*). **Take** greenwood cuttings in early summer, or hardwood cuttings in winter (*see p.394*). Willow cuttings root easily.

COPPICING WILLOWS
Several species of willow can be cut back to the base in spring; this will produce the most brightly coloured winter stems.

Salix alba **'Britzensis'** 🏆
↕25m (80ft) ↔ 10m (30ft), naturally a large tree, annual coppicing will keep it in bounds, dull-green leaves, catkins in spring

Salix caprea **'Kilmarnock'** (Kilmarnock Willow)
↕ 1.5–2m (5–6ft) ↔ 2m (6ft), weeping stems are grafted on to upright rootstock, catkins in mid- and late spring, dark green leaves

SALVIA

Sage

see also p.318

THE SAGES ARE A VERY LARGE GROUP of plants that include annuals and perennials as well as evergreen shrubs. The best-known of these is the common sage (*Salvia officinalis*) that is a culinary herb, but there are a number of others that make worthwhile garden plants. The leaves are green to grey-green, and give off an aroma when crushed. They are lance-shaped to oval, and have indented veins. The flowers are tubes of red, blue, mauve, white, or purple, and appear in spring or summer, although many have flowers at other times of the year. Most are small, round to upright, evergreen bushes.

Hardiness Frost-hardy ✱✱ to frost-tender ✱.

Cultivation Grow in any well-drained soil, in full sun. **Tip prune** young plants to promote bushiness and give older plants an all-over trim after flowering to keep them bushy. **Take** softwood cuttings in spring and summer (*see p.394*).

Salvia leucantha (Mexican Bush Sage)
↕ 1m (3ft) ↔ 1m (3ft), soft fluffy flowers in autumn make this a great plant for children's gardens ✱

SAMBUCUS

Elder

THESE DECIDUOUS SHRUBS AND TREES are grown for their flowers and ornamental foliage. From spring to early summer, they produce dense, flat clusters of white or creamy yellow flowers, followed by black or glossy red fruits. The leaves may be variegated, dark green, or golden yellow, and are made up of small leaflets, deeply fringed in some cultivars. Elders are suitable for mixed gardens or as specimens. The yellow-leaved types provide a good contrast with *Photinia* × *fraseri* 'Red Robin' (*see p.94*), with its red young foliage.

Hardiness Fully frost-hardy ✱✱✱.

Cultivation Grow in reasonably fertile soil that is moist but well-drained. Position in full sun or partial shade: leaves colour most strongly in full sun, but retain colour better in dappled shade. **Prune** only to remove crossing or misplaced shoots, in winter or early spring. Prune hard to restrict size if necessary. **Sow** seed (*see pp.391–392*) in a container in a cold frame in autumn. **Take** hardwood cuttings in winter, or softwood cuttings in early summer (*see p.394*). Aphids (*see pp.398–399*) may infest young growth, but can be treated.

Sambucus racemosa **'Plumosa Aurea'** (Red-berried Elder)
↕↔ 3m (10ft), bushy shrub, leaves are bronze when new (*see inset*) and can scorch in full sun, flowers in mid-spring

Santolina

Cotton Lavender

↕15–75cm (6–30in)
↔20cm–1m (8–36in)

COMPACT, ROUNDED, EVERGREEN – or rather, "evergrey" – shrubs, these can be used as low hedges or to edge borders, and are ideal for rock gardens, being naturally found in dry sites. They are grown principally for their fine, aromatic foliage. The long-stemmed flowerheads are button-like, yellow or creamy-yellow, surrounded by broad rings of similarly coloured bracts (modified leaves) that make them more conspicuous. The plants spread to cover the ground, and effectively suppress weeds. For a heady mix of scents, grow with other aromatic herbs, such as lavenders (*Lavandula, see p.80*) and rosemary (*Rosmarinus, see p.114*).

Hardiness Frost-hardy ✻✻.

Cultivation Grow in poor to reasonably fertile soil that is well-drained and in full sun. **Cut back** flowered shoots to within 2.5cm (1in) of old growth in spring. **Sow** seed (*see pp.391–392*) in containers in a cold frame in autumn or spring. **Take** semi-ripe cuttings (*see p.394*) in late summer and root in a propagator with bottom heat.

PRUNING SANTOLINAS
Never cut santolinas back beyond the point where you can see fresh growth shooting from old wood.

Santolina chamaecyparissus (Lavender Cotton)
↕15–75cm (6–30in) ↔ 20cm–1m (8–36in), fine, grey aromatic foliage and yellow flowers in summer

Scaevola

Fan Flowers

THESE ARE SMALL EVERGREEN PLANTS, and while some are obviously shrubby, most are somewhere between shrubs and evergreen, herbaceous perennials, forming permanent, but not woody, stems. They have small but distinctive fan-shaped flowers. These smother the plants in spring and summer in the most commonly grown forms, although flowering times differ with other species. Flowers are generally mauve, but blue, white and pink are also found. The leaves are small and oval to linear, and these and the stems are often covered in very fine hairs. Many species and forms make excellent, showy groundcovers for sunny spots.

Hardiness Frost-hardy ✻✻ to very frost-tender ❁.

Cultivation Grow in a well-drained soil in full sun. **Tip prune** young plants to encourage side shoots (*see p.382*). **Take** cuttings at any time of the year from firm, young, non-flowering shoots (*see p.394*).

Scaevola 'Mauve Clusters'
↕15cm (6in) ↔ 1–2m (3–6ft), summer flowering suckering sub-shrub

Senecio cineraria

Cineraria

see also p.325

↕↔ to 60cm (24in)

THESE MOUNDING, evergreen shrubs are grown chiefly for their leaves, soft like felt, in a range of delicate shapes and shades of silvery green and grey. Yellow flowerheads are produced, but the flowers are not particularly attractive. The foliage is at its pristine best when plants are young. They can be grown in shrub gardens, but are mainly used as dot plants or edging, where their foliage acts as a foil for flowering plants. A classic combination is cinerarias with red salvias (*see pp.318–319*); for a more subdued effect, pair them with purple heliotropes (*Heliotropium, see p.70*).

Hardiness Frost-hardy ✻✻.

Cultivation Grow in reasonably fertile soil, in full sun. **Trim** plants if necessary to improve the shape. **Sow** seed (*see pp.391–393*) in spring at 19–24°C (66–75°F). **Take** semi-ripe cuttings (*see p.394*) in mid- or late summer.

Senecio cineraria 'Silver Dust' ♀
↕↔ 30cm (12in), particularly bright foliage

SENNA

THESE ARE EVERGREEN PLANTS, ranging from low to medium-sized shrubs. A feature of many of them is the silvery foliage. In some species the leaves are almost needle-like, and in others they are oval. Flowers are small yet showy, and have five yellow to yellow-brown petals. Not all varieties open right out, some staying in a cup shape. Flowering times vary widely, and quite a number of species have sporadic flowering throughout the year. Grow with other plants that enjoy drier conditions, with the yellow being a good foil for the blue of the flowers of Californian Lilac (*Ceanothus, see p.36*) and agapanthus (*see p.170*).

Hardiness Frost-hardy ❄❄ to frost-tender ❄.

Cultivation Grow in any free-draining soil, in full sun or partial shade. **Prune** minimally; remove any shoots that spoil the shape of plants to encourage a good form (*see pp.382–384*). **Sow** seed after soaking, in containers in a cold frame (*see p.391*). **Take** cuttings of firm, young growth at any time of year (*see p.394*).

Senna artemisiodes
↕2m (6ft) ↔ 3m (10ft), fine foliage and spring and summer flowers on a shrub that particularly enjoys sandy soils ❄

SEQUOIA SEMPERVIRENS

Californian Redwood

GIANT EVERGREEN CONIFERS, wild specimens of sequoia are amongst the oldest and tallest plants in the world. The trunks are bulky and tend to flare out at the base, and are covered in a thick, spongy, furrowed, reddish-brown bark. The leaves are small, ferny and dark green, and are carried on long, drooping branches. Cones occur towards the ends of the branch tips, and are brown and barrel-shaped, but only 2.5cm (1in) long. The size of this tree means these are probably only for parks and large gardens. They prefer cool yet humid areas away from hot, drying winds and air pollution. The closely related and equally large Giant Redwood (*Sequoiadendron giganteum*) occurs only in California.

Hardiness Frost-hardy ❄❄.

Cultivation Grow in any well-drained soil that is reasonably fertile and preferably enriched with well-rotted organic matter. Full sun and plenty of space are needed, along with shelter from hot, drying winds. **Prune** minimally except to establish a straight central trunk when young. **Sow** seed (*see p.391*) in a seedbed in spring.

Sequoia sempervirens
↕100m (330ft) ↔ 50m (165ft), reaches massive proportions in its native habitat, and will need plenty of space if grown in a garden

SOPHORA

GROWN FOR THEIR FINE FOLIAGE and their clusters of bright flowers, these trees and shrubs need long, hot spells to flower well, but are worth growing for the leaves alone. These are composed of small leaflets arranged along a central leaf stalk, and have a very elegant appearance. There are both deciduous and evergreen sophoras. The pea-like flowers are carried in clusters at the ends of the branches, in colours that include purple-blue to white and golden-yellow. Grow in a mixed garden bed in full sun in a frost-free area to encourage flowering.

Hardiness Fully frost-hardy ❄❄❄ to frost-hardy ❄❄.

Cultivation Grow in reasonably fertile, well-drained soil, in full sun. **Prune out** any misplaced or crossing shoots that spoil the shape of young trees in late winter or early spring, to create a healthy framework of branches. **Sow** seed (*see pp.391–392*) in a container in a cold frame as soon as they are ripe.

Sophora davidii
↕2.5m (8ft) ↔ 3m (10ft), bushy or spreading, deciduous shrub or tree, flowering in late summer or early autumn when mature

SORBUS

Rowan, Whitebeam, Mountain Ash

UPRIGHT, COLUMNAR, OR SPREADING trees and shrubs, sorbus have an attractive branch structure and flower in spring or summer. Their foliage is ornamental, with leaves in a range of shapes, often colouring well in autumn, and the bark is textured when mature, but the main highlight is the autumn show of berries, which are attractive to birds. These are mostly in shades of red, orange, and yellow, but some have white berries, often tinted pink, as in the tree *Sorbus cashmiriana*. The thicket-forming shrub *S. reducta* has crimson berries that become white as the leaves turn red and purple in autumn. Use sorbus as specimens or grow in a garden with hawthorns (*Crataegus*, *see p.46*) or amelanchiers (*Amelanchier*, *see p.22*) for a richly coloured autumn display.

Hardiness Fully frost-hardy ✻✻✻.

Cultivation Grow in any reasonably fertile, moist but well-drained soil, in full sun or dappled shade. **Prune out** crossing or misplaced shoots in late winter or early spring, but only if necessary. **Sow** seed (*see pp.391–392*) in a container in a cold frame in autumn.

Sorbus aucuparia (Rowan)
↕10m (30ft) ↔ 4m (12ft), the fruits occur in late summer and into autumn

Sorbus aria **'Lutescens'** 🏆
↕10m (30ft) ↔ 5m (15ft), silvery foliage is one of the main attractions of this deciduous tree

'Joseph Rock'
↕10m (30ft) ↔ 4m (12ft), a form with pale fruit

SPIRAEA

THERE IS A SPIRAEA FOR ALMOST any position in the garden. This varied group of evergreen, semi-evergreen and deciduous shrubs contains many elegant and easily cultivated plants, in various sizes. They are grown mainly for their dense clusters of small, saucer-shaped or bowl-shaped flowers, carried at the branch tips in spring and summer. These range from white, pink, and yellow, to purple. Some spiraeas have coloured leaves, like *Spiraea japonica* 'Goldflame', which has bronze-red young leaves that turn to bright yellow, then to mid-green; its flowers are dark pink.

Hardiness Fully frost-hardy ✻✻✻, although new growth may be damaged by frosts.

Cultivation Grow in fertile, moist but well-drained soil in full sun. **Encourage** new growth from the base of mature plants by cutting out about one in every three or four old stems each year. **Prune** *S. japonica* and its cultivars, which flower on the current year's growth, differently, cutting them back to a permanent low framework of shoots in early spring. **Take** greenwood cuttings in summer (*see p.394*).

A LOW HEDGE
'Snowmound' is, as its name suggests, dense in habit, so makes a good compact hedge. Prune immediately after flowering.

Spiraea nipponica **'Snowmound'** 🏆
↕↔ 1.2–2.5m (4–8ft), fast-growing, deciduous, smothered with white flowers in early summer

Spiraea japonica 'Anthony Waterer'
↕to 1.5m (5ft) ↔ 1.5m (5ft), deciduous, leaves are bronze when young and often edged pink or white, flowers in mid- and late summer

Stachyurus

A SMALL GROUP OF SPREADING, deciduous and semi-evergreen shrubs, these are grown for their late winter and early spring flowers, which are small, bell-shaped, and pale yellow. The yellow buds are produced in clusters along the bare stems in autumn, opening in spring before the leaves appear. Only *Stachyurus chinensis* and *S. praecox* are reliably grown; *S. chinensis* is the smaller of the two, while *S. praecox* has a popular variegated cultivar, 'Magpie'. Both have pointed, dark green leaves on arching, slender, glossy shoots, which are red-brown in *S. praecox* and purplish in *S. chinensis*. Grow them in a mixed garden.

Hardiness Fully frost-hardy ❄❄❄.

Cultivation Grow in light, moist but well-drained, acid (lime-free) soil, in full sun or partial shade. Position in a spot sheltered from hot, drying winds. **Prune** out any crossing or misplaced shoots after flowering. Mature plants may be rejuvenated, when necessary, by cutting them to the base after flowering. **Sow** seed (*see pp.391–392*) in a cold frame in autumn. **Take** semi-ripe cuttings (*see p.394*) consisting of a side shoot with a sliver of older stem (a "heel") attached in summer.

Stachyurus praecox 🏆
↕ 1–4m (3–12ft) ↔ to 3m (10ft), deciduous shrub, one of the first to flower in late winter and early spring

Stenocarpus

LARGE, EVERGREEN TREES of warm rainforests, these are most often seen as specimen and street trees. The leaves are long and shiny on the upper surface, and duller underneath. Trees are often quite tall and although not columnar, they are not very broad. The bark is a quite attractive grey or brown. The remarkable feature, however, and the main reason these are grown, is their unusual flowers. These consist of up to twenty individual flowers arranged radiating out from a central point like the spokes of a wheel. Depending on the species, they appear in late autumn and into winter, or in summer, and are either red or greenish-cream.

Hardiness Frost-tender ❄ to very frost-tender ❀.

Cultivation Grow in full sun, in any well-drained soil that is reasonably fertile and enriched with well-rotted organic matter. **Prune** minimally except to establish a straight central trunk while young (*see pp.382–384*). **Sow** seed (*see p.391*) in winter in a cold frame.

Stenocarpus sinuatus
↕30m (100 ft) ↔ 15m (50ft), grown for its interesting wheel-shaped, red flowers; does best in warmer districts

Stewartia

↕6–25m (20–80ft) ↔3–8m (10–25ft)

A SUCCESSION OF FLOWERS in the summer, fine autumn colour, and beautifully textured bark on older specimens all make these large, evergreen or deciduous trees and shrubs worth growing. The rose-like, white flowers have creamy yellow stamens in the centre and are produced singly or in pairs. Stewartias are related to camellias (*see pp.32–33*) and prefer broadly similar conditions, making excellent specimen trees in a woodland setting or shady garden. Try them with eucryphias (*see p.55*) which bear similar open, white flowers at different times of the year, depending on the species.

Hardiness Fully frost-hardy ❄❄❄ to frost-hardy ❄❄.

Cultivation Grow in moist but well-drained, reasonably fertile, neutral to acid (lime-free) soil. Position in full sun or partial shade, with shelter from strong, cold winds. Buy container-grown plants and choose the right spot first time; they resent root disturbance. **Sow** seed (*see pp.391–392*) in a cold frame in autumn. **Take** greenwood cuttings in early summer or semi-ripe cuttings from mid- to late summer (*see p.394*), or layer low-growing shoots in autumn (*see p.395*).

Stewartia pseudocamellia ♀
↕20m (70ft) ↔ 8m (25ft), peeling bark (see inset), leaves turn yellow, then orange and red, flowers in mid-summer ❄❄❄

Styrax

BELL-SHAPED, PURE WHITE or pink-tinged flowers give these plants a graceful look. A large group of deciduous or evergreen shrubs and small trees, most are compact enough to be included in almost any garden. The dainty, fragrant flowers are produced in summer on short branches formed in the previous year. The leaves are variable in shape, and some colour well in autumn. Shrubby forms are ideal for a garden with mock oranges (*Philadelphus, see p.93*), *Weigela* (*see p.128*), and potentillas (*see p.99*); plant trees where the flowers can be seen from below.

Hardiness Fully frost-hardy ❄❄❄.

Cultivation Grow in moist but well-drained soil that has been enriched with well-rotted organic matter, and is preferably neutral to acid (lime-free). Position in full sun or partial shade, with protection from hot, drying winds. **Prune out** any misplaced or crossing shoots that spoil the shape of shrubs or young trees in late winter or early spring. **Sow** seed (*see pp.391–392*) as soon as ripe; this needs some care, maintaining 15°C (59°F) for three months and then keeping the seedlings frost-free until they are established. **Take** greenwood cuttings (*see p.394*) in summer.

Styrax obassia ♀ (Fragrant Snowbell)
↕12m (40ft) ↔ 7m (22ft), broadly columnar tree, downy leaves that turn yellow and red in autumn, flowers in early and mid-summer

Symphoricarpos

Snowberry

THESE DECIDUOUS SHRUBS are grown for their autumn and winter show of berries, which are usually white or rose-tinted, but are dark blue or purple in some species. In summer, they bear clusters of small, bell-shaped flowers which, although too small to be decorative, are rich in nectar and attract bees and other beneficial insects into the garden. The berries last well into winter as they are not eaten by wildlife; they may irritate the skin. Often forming thickets, these are very hardy plants and tolerant of a wide range of conditions including poor soil and pollution. They are best grown in a wild garden along a boundary with other shrubs, such as hawthorn (*Crataegus, see p.46*), to form a screen or mixed informal hedge.

Hardiness Fully frost-hardy ❄❄❄.

Cultivation Grow in any reasonably fertile, well-drained soil, and position in full sun or partial shade. **Prune out** misplaced or crossing shoots that spoil the shape of the shrub in late winter or early spring (*see p.382*); reduce size by cutting back flowered stems to strong shoots lower down, after flowering. **Divide** large, clumping plants in autumn (*see p.395*). **Take** greenwood cuttings in summer, or hardwood cuttings in autumn (*see p.394*).

Symphoricarpos albus (Snowberry)
↕1.2m (4ft) ↔ 1.2m (4ft), white berries hang on the deciduous shrub well after the leaves have dropped in autumn

Syringa

Lilac

Renowned for their beautiful and exquisitely scented flowers in early summer, these deciduous shrubs, traditionally mauve-flowered, are also available in white, cream, pale yellow, pink, magenta, and wine red. Most lilacs in gardens are the familiar cultivars of *Syringa vulgaris*, with a relatively short but always eagerly anticipated season in bloom, their flowers borne in distinctive conical clusters. These can grow quite large, and suit the back of a garden or a wild garden area well, or can be pruned to a more shapely form. However, there are others, such as *S. meyeri* 'Palibin', that fit into any small garden and can even be trained as standards.

Hardiness Fully frost-hardy ✻✻✻; late frosts may damage new growth.

Cultivation Grow in fertile soil enriched with well-rotted organic matter, preferably neutral to alkaline. Site in full sun. **Deadhead** young lilacs to prevent the plant's energy going into setting seed. **Prune out** any crossing or misshapen branches in late winter or early spring (*see p.382*). *S. vulgaris* and its cultivars can be renovated by pruning hard. **Sow** seed (*see pp.391–392*) in a cold frame, as soon as ripe or in spring. **Layer** low-growing shoots (*see p.395*) in early summer.

Syringa meyeri 'Palibin' 🏆
↕1.5–2m (5–6ft) ↔ 1.2m (4ft), slow-growing, rounded shrub, smaller but profuse flower clusters in late spring and early summer

Syringa vulgaris 'Katherine Havemeyer'
↕3m (9ft) ↔ 2m (6ft), large dense clusters of strongly perfumed flowers in mid-spring

Syringa vulgaris 'Primrose'
↕3m (9ft) ↔ 2m (6ft), spreading shrub or small tree, small clusters of flowers, in unusual colour for lilacs, in late spring to early summer

Syzygium

Lilly Pilly

This is a very large genus of evergreen trees and shrubs. They are closely related to lilly pillies (*Acmena, see p.20*), which they resemble in many ways, and with which they share a common name. The leaves are small, oval to linear and very shiny, often with young shoots that are creamy-pink or red. The flowers are showy bunches of white, cream, pink, or even red stamens. These are followed a few months later by attractive and conspicuous clusters of small, round berries that may be white, cream, pink, red purple, or black. Larger plants make good specimens or informal hedges and windbreaks. There are a number of smaller forms available for use as hedges and topiary work, including standards.

Hardiness Frost-tender ✻ to very frost-tender ❁.

Cultivation Grow in any well-drained soil that is enriched with well-rotted organic matter and can be kept relatively moist. **Prune** minimally; remove any shoots that spoil the shape of young plants to encourage a good form (*see p.382*). **Sow** seed as soon as it is ripe, first removing the flesh from the fruit (*see p.391*). **Take** heeled cuttings in mid-summer and place in a cold frame (*see p.394*).

Syzygium australe (Brush Cherry)
↕8m (25ft) ↔ 5m (15ft), purplish-red round berries are a feature of this tree in late summer and autumn ✻

Tamarix

Tamarisk

Invaluable in seaside gardens, these are graceful deciduous shrubs or small trees with red-brown, arching stems. Their flowers are pink and carried in dense, plume-like sprays. Naturally found in coastal sites, tamarisks happily withstand salt-laden winds and sea spray. They have tiny, tough, feathery leaves from which little water evaporates; this makes them ideal for a windbreak hedge or screen where winds are not cold. In a sheltered site, they do grow leggy if not checked by regular pruning. Most widely seen are *Tamarix parviflora*, flowering in mid- to late spring, and *T. ramosissima*, which flowers from late summer.

Hardiness Fully frost-hardy ***.

Cultivation Grow in full sun, in well-drained soil in coastal or inland areas. **Prune** young plants almost to ground level after planting and trim regularly to stop the plants from becoming top-heavy (*see p.383*). Cut the flowered stems of spring-flowering types back to strong new shoots; prune autumn-flowering types slightly harder, in early spring; all tolerate renovation pruning, almost to the base. **Sow** seed (*see pp.391–392*) as soon as it is ripe in containers in a cold frame. **Take** hardwood cuttings in winter or semi-ripe cuttings in summer (*see p.394*).

Tamarix ramosissima
↕↔ 5m (15ft), flowers in dense clusters on the new year's shoots in late summer and early autumn

Taxus

Yew

Uncommon conifers, yews are grown for their handsome evergreen foliage and sculptural forms. They have reddish-brown, often peeling bark and narrow, very dark green leaves (there are also golden forms). Female plants bear red berries in autumn. Yews can be grown as freestanding trees or clipped into topiary shapes, and make great formal hedges in cold districts; prostrate ones make good ground cover. Unlike most conifers, they can be pruned hard into old wood, so are quite easy to renovate if they are overgrown or damaged. All parts except the flesh of the red fruits are poisonous.

Hardiness Fully frost-hardy ***.

Cultivation Grow in any except wet soil, and in any site, from full sun to full shade. **Trim** hedges and clipped shapes in summer and early autumn. Renovate in autumn to early winter. **Sow** seed (*see pp.391–393*) as soon as ripe in a cold frame or seedbed; they may take two years or more to germinate. **Take** semi-ripe cuttings (*see p.394*) in late summer, choosing upright shoots (except for prostrate forms), otherwise they may not form a central upright stem.

Taxus baccata 'Fastigiata' (Irish Yew)
↕ 10m (30ft) ↔ 6m (20ft), female, particularly narrow as a young plant, forms a striking, smoke-like column (see inset) when mature

Telopea

Waratah

Waratahs are evergreen shrubs or small trees that are densely foliaged, often right down to the ground. The leaves are stiff and leathery, and occur all the way up the long, erect stems. The red flowers are large and conspicuous, and are amongst Australia's best-known wildflowers. They appear at the tips of the growing stems in spring, and are semi-spherical globes, surrounded at the base by matching red bracts. These make excellent cut flowers. Grow as specimen plants or in a mixed garden with other shrubs that also enjoy free-draining soils, such as banksias (*see p.27*), dryandras (*see p.50*) and proteas (*see p.99*).

Hardiness Frost-hardy ** to frost-tender *.

Cultivation Grow in any well-drained acid (lime-free) soil, in full sun or partial shade. **Tip prune** when young to promote bushiness. **Cut** flower stems to enjoy indoors as this will help promote additional flowers in the future. **Sow** seed in spring (*see p.391*).

Telopea speciosissima
↕ 3m (10ft) ↔ 2m (6ft), the floral emblem of New South Wales, spectacular when in flower

TEUCRIUM

Germander

GROWN FOR THEIR AROMATIC FOLIAGE and attractive summer flowers, these evergreen and deciduous shrubs are part of a large group that also includes non-woody plants. The leaves are often grey-green with silvery undersides, and the flowers are tubular or bell-shaped, in shades of pink, yellow, or blue, and are borne in clusters in summer. A sunny spot in a sheltered garden will be necessary in colder areas, but wall germanders (*Teucrium chamaedrys*) make good hedging and edging plants in milder regions. Grow with other summer-flowering shrubs that enjoy the same conditions, such as lavenders (*Lavandula, see p.80*), artemisias (*see p.25*), and rosemary (*Rosmarinus, see p.114*) for an aromatic mix.

Hardiness Fully frost-hardy ✽✽✽ to frost-hardy ✽✽.

Cultivation Grow in well-drained soil that is slightly alkaline (limy); the smaller species require very sharply drained soil. Position in full sun. **Trim back** growth to maintain a good shape in spring or late summer, after flowering. **Take** softwood cuttings in early summer, or semi-ripe cuttings in late summer, rooting both in a heated propagator (*see p.394*). Overwinter young plants in frost-free conditions.

Teucrium fruticans (Shrubby Germander)
↕2m (6ft) ↔ 2m (6ft), summer flowers on a bushy shrub with grey foliage

THUJA

Cedar, Arborvitae

THESE CONIFERS, BOTH LARGE AND SMALL, make handsome specimen trees, and also hedges because they stand up well to clipping. They have flattened sprays of scaly foliage, usually aromatic. The White Cedar, *Thuja occidentalis,* is a rounded tree that can reach 20m (70ft), with billowing branches, peeling, orange-brown bark, and apple-scented leaves. It has many different forms, and widely varying colours and sizes. 'Caespitosa', for example, is cushion-like and slow-growing, reaching only 30cm (12in) high, suitable for a rock garden. *T. plicata* is a popular hedge, but otherwise only suitable for large gardens. It also has a range of smaller forms, like blue-green 'Hillieri', growing to just 2m (6ft).

Hardiness Fully frost-hardy ✽✽✽.

Cultivation Grow in deep, moist but well-drained soil. Position in full sun. **Trim** hedging in spring and late summer. **Sow** seed (*see pp.391–392*) in late winter in containers in a cold frame or take semi-ripe cuttings (*see p.394*) in late summer. **Watch** for aphids (*see pp.398–399*) and small, limpet-like pests known as scale insects: if these become a problem, control with insecticide.

① ***occidentalis*** **'Rheingold'** 🏆 ↕1–2m (3–6ft) ↔ to 1–1.2m (3–4ft), yellow leaves are tinted pink when young ② ***plicata*** (Western Red Cedar) ↕20–35m (70–120ft) ↔ 6–9m (20–30ft)

THYMUS

Thyme

↕to 30cm (1ft)
↔to 60cm (2ft)

LOW-GROWING EVERGREEN shrubs with small, aromatic leaves and pretty flowers, thymes will attract bees and other beneficial insects into the garden. During summer, they produce clusters of tiny flowers, usually in pink, purple, or white. Provided that they do not sit in the wet, thymes can be grown in a wide range of situations, with other decorative herbs such as lavenders (*Lavandula, see p.80*) and with chives. They are ideal for the front or edges of a bed, and mat-forming types can be planted in crevices between paving, where stepping on them will release the scent from the foliage. In containers, perhaps with other herbs, they will trail over the edge attractively.

Hardiness Fully frost-hardy ✽✽✽ to frost-hardy ✽✽.

Cultivation Grow in neutral to alkaline (limy) soil that is well-drained. Position in full sun. **Trim back** after flowering to keep the plants compact. **Sow** seed (*see pp.391–392*) in a container in a cold frame in spring, or divide plants (*see p.395*) in spring. **Take** softwood cuttings (*see p.394*) in mid- to late summer.

Thymus vulgaris 'Silver Posie'
↕to 30cm (1ft) ↔ to 60cm (2ft), has slightly larger and showier flowers than the common thyme

Tibouchina

Lasiandra

A FAVOURITE IN WARMER CLIMATES, where it thrives without too much attention apart from water in dry times, lasiandra has vibrant purple, five-petalled flowers over a long period in summer. The plants are upright-growing, evergreen shrubs or small trees. They are clothed in lance-shaped leaves that feature indented veins and are a beautiful velvet to the touch. Grow as a tall screen or specimen in a wind-protected spot. In garden beds it will combine nicely with Native Frangipani (*Hymenosporum flavum, see p.74*), bougainvillea (*see p.135*) and hibiscus (*see p.71*).

Hardiness Frost-tender ❄ to very frost-tender ❀.

Cultivation Grow in any well-drained soil that is fertile and enriched with well-rotted organic matter. Full sun in warmer districts is best, and shelter from hot, drying winds. **Cut back** flowered shoots by about one quarter to keep the plant neat (*see p.382*). **Take** semi-hardwood cuttings in summer or early autumn, or hardwood cuttings in early winter, and row them out in seedbeds (*see p.394*).

Tibouchina urvilleana 'Grandiflora'

↕3m (9ft) ↔ 2m (6ft), a popular plant in frost free areas, this form has flowers up to 12cm (5in) across ❄

Tilia

Linden, Lime

LARGE, STATELY, DECIDUOUS trees, lindens are grown for their habit, foliage and scented flowers. All have broadly oval to rounded, bright or dark green leaves that turn yellow in autumn. From mid-summer, they produce hanging clusters of creamy-white or pale yellow flowers. These attract pollinating insects, bees in particular, into the garden. They are followed by dry fruits that are nut-like in appearance, but not edible. As the trees age, the silver-grey bark becomes fissured. Lindens can be used as specimen trees, but you must have a spacious garden to accommodate one.

Hardiness Fully frost-hardy ❄❄❄.

Cultivation Grow in moist, but well-drained soil; lindens prefer alkaline (limy) or neutral soil, but will tolerate acid soils. Avoid wet sites or very dry conditions, and sites exposed to strong, cold winds. Position in full sun or partial shade. **Prune** in late winter or early spring, cutting out any crossing or misplaced shoots that spoil the shape of young trees. **Keep** seed in cold conditions for 3–5 months before sowing in containers in a cold frame in spring (*see pp.391–392*). **Aphids** attack, but cannot harm, lindens; however, the sticky honeydew they excrete can be a nuisance as it rains from the tree in summer: do not plant lindens where they will overhang paths or parked cars.

Tilia platyphyllos (Large-leaved Linden)

↕30m (100ft) ↔ 20m (70ft), a broad column of a tree, with leaves up to 15cm (6in) long, flowers in mid-summer

Toona

THESE ARE LARGE, EVERGREEN and deciduous trees, although the two grown in Australia – *Toona ciliata* and *T. sinensis* – are both deciduous. The leaves are pinnate, that is, they occur as leaflets opposite each other on a long, central stem. They are often pinkish when just emerging, and turn orange-yellow in autumn. The flowers are very small and almost insignificant, yet have a light perfume. The most commonly grown is the Red Cedar (*T. ciliata*, syn *T. australis*), which makes a valuable shade tree for parks and very large gardens. Valued for its beautiful timber, over-logging has made it rare in the wild.

Hardiness Frost-tender ❄ to very frost-tender ❀.

Cultivation Grow in any well-drained soil that is fertile and receives plenty of moisture. **Prune** minimally; remove any shoots that spoil the shape of young plants to encourage a good form (*see pp.382–384*). **Sow** seed as soon as it is collected (*see p.391*).

Toona ciliata (Red Cedar)

↕35m (115 ft) ↔ 20m (65ft), a large deciduous tree famous for its timber

TRACHYCARPUS

THESE EVERGREEN PALMS have dark green leaves made up of many pointed segments joined in a fan shape. They usually form a strong single main stem, as in *Trachycarpus fortunei*, which is the most widely seen in gardens. Small, yellow flowers are borne in summer in large, hanging clusters, which emerge close to the base of the leaves. Male and female flowers are borne on separate plants in early summer; if they are grown together, female plants produce round, blue-black fruits. Superb feature plants, these palms can be grown in large pots while young. Grow among bamboos and ornamental grasses (*see pp.340–355*) or with ferns (*see pp.356–365*) for a jungle look in a sheltered courtyard.

Hardiness Frost-hardy ❄❄.

Cultivation Grow in well-drained, fertile soil. Position in full sun or partial shade. **Pruning** is unnecessary, but trim off dead leaves (do not cut close to the trunk). **Sow** seed (*see pp.391–393*) in spring or autumn at 24°C (75°F).

Trachycarpus fortunei ♀ (Chinese Windmill Palm)
↕to 15m (50ft) ↔ 2.5m (8ft), drought- and frost-tolerant, unlike many palms

TRISTANIOPSIS

THESE ARE EVERGREEN TREES AND SHRUBS that are generally from moist, forested areas. Most have a broad, dense canopy carried on solid branches arising from a stout trunk. The leaves are narrowly lance-shaped, with a prominent mid-rib. Flowers occur in summer, and are yellow, cream, or white. They have five petals and many stamens, and appear in a globular cluster towards the ends of the branches. These plants can be used as street trees, or as specimens in parks and gardens. They are also often used as screen plants. In all situations, though, they must have ample water.

Hardiness Frost-hardy ❄❄ to frost-tender ❄.

Cultivation Grow in full sun or even deep shade, but ensure ample water is kept up at all times. **Prune** minimally, except to establish a healthy framework (*see pp.382–384*). **Sow** seed as soon as it is collected, in a cold frame (*see p.391*).

Tristaniopsis laurina (Water Gum)
↕15m (50 ft) ↔ 10m (30ft), as its common name implies, this tree needs adequate water ❄❄

ULMUS

Elm

THESE MOSTLY DECIDUOUS TREES have appealing foliage, which turns golden-yellow in autumn, and an attractive habit. They also produce clusters of tiny, red-tinted, bell-shaped flowers, usually in spring but sometimes in autumn. These are followed by winged, green fruits. Larger elms, such as *Ulmus glabra* 'Lutescens' are suitable as specimen trees in larger gardens. *U. glabra* 'Camperdownii' is a weeping elm, useful where a formal touch is needed. The Chinese Elm (*U. parvifolia*) is evergreen.

Hardiness Fully frost-hardy ❄❄❄.

Cultivation Grow in any well-drained soil, in full sun or partial shade. **Prune out** any crossing or misplaced branches that spoil the shape of the tree in late winter or early spring. **Sow** seed (*see pp.391–392*) in containers outdoors in spring or autumn, or take softwood cuttings (*see p.394*) in summer. **Watch** out for Elm Leaf Beetle; if it is seen, ask your council for assistance with control.

Ulmus glabra **'Exoniensis'** (Exeter Elm)
↕20m (60ft) ↔ 15m (45ft), a less common elm with upward growing branches and bright autumn colour

Viburnum

FLOWERS, FRUITS, AND FOLIAGE are all valued in this large and widely varying group of evergreen, semi-evergreen, and deciduous shrubs. The flowers are pink, or pink-flushed white or cream, and in some plants intensely fragrant. They are borne in winter, spring, or summer, often in rounded clusters at the ends of the branches. The red or black berries that follow may also be ornamental; if space allows, grow several plants of the same species together to ensure good pollination and a more generous show of berries. The foliage also provides interest. On some viburnums, the leaves are rough-textured, on others smooth and glossy, while many have striking, prominent veins. Most deciduous types colour brilliantly in autumn. Viburnums are usually grown in shrub or mixed gardens or in woodland settings. Some are used as hedges.

Hardiness Fully frost-hardy *** to frost-hardy **.

Cultivation Grow in any good soil that is moist but well-drained. Position in full sun or partial shade. **Prune** deciduous species after flowering, lightly trimming shoots that spoil the shape of the shrub. Most deciduous types and *V. tinus* will tolerate hard pruning. Remove misplaced branches or crossing shoots from evergreens in late winter or early spring to maintain a good framework. **Sow** seed in containers in a cold frame in autumn (*see pp.391–392*), or propagate deciduous species by greenwood cuttings, which are taken slightly later than softwood cuttings when the stem is a little firmer and darker (*see p.394*). Sooty moulds may form on the foliage of *V. tinus* if colonized by whiteflies: control with a suitable insecticide if necessary.

Using viburnums in the garden

In the border *Viburnums are ideal shrubs for hedging or for a mixed garden, since many, such as* V. opulus, *have an attractive, naturally rounded habit that requires little or no pruning; 'Compactum' is especially neat. Others are more architectural, for instance the tiered* V. plicatum *'Mariesii'.* V. davidii *is a useful evergreen for shade.*

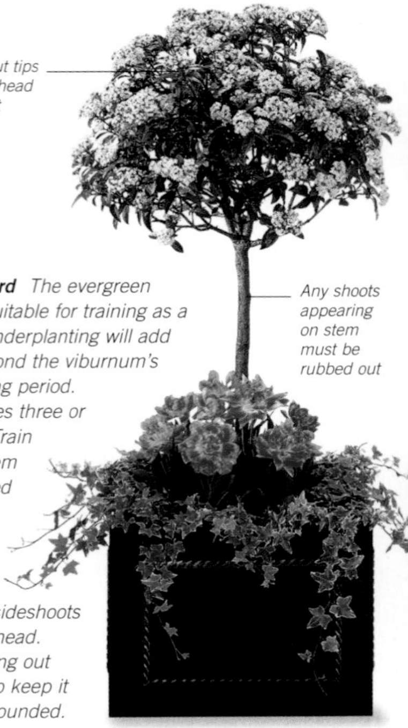
Pinch out tips to keep head compact
Any shoots appearing on stem must be rubbed out

As a standard *The evergreen* V. tinus *is suitable for training as a standard; underplanting will add interest beyond the viburnum's own flowering period. Training takes three or four years. Train the main stem to the desired height and pinch out the tip to encourage lots of new sideshoots to form the head. Keep pinching out sideshoots to keep it dense and rounded.*

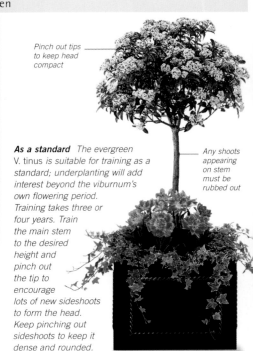

1

2

5

6

11

15

14

① × ***bodnantense*** 'Dawn' 🏆 ↕↔ 2m (6ft), deciduous ② × ***burkwoodii*** ↕↔ 2.5m (8ft), evergreen ③ × ***burkwoodii*** 'Anne Russell' 🏆 ↕ 2m (6ft) ↔ 1.5m (5ft), evergreen ④ × ***carlcephalum*** 🏆 ↕↔ 3m (10ft), deciduous ⑤ 'Chesapeake' ↕ 2m (6ft) ↔ 3m (10ft) , semi-evergreen ⑥ ***davidii*** 🏆 ↕↔ 1–1.5m (3–5ft), evergreen ⑦ ***dentatum*** 🏆 ↕↔ 3m (10ft), deciduous

3

8

9

4

7

10

16

12

13

17

⑧ ***farreri*** 🏆 ↕2m (6ft) ↔ 2.5m (8ft), deciduous ⑨ × ***juddii*** 🏆 ↕1.2m (4ft) ↔ 1.5m (5ft), deciduous ⑩ ***macrocephalum*** ↕↔ 4m (12ft), evergreen ⑪ ***opulus*** **'Compactum'** 🏆 ↕↔ 1.5m (5ft), deciduous ⑫ ***plicatum*** **'Mariesii'** 🏆 ↕3m (10ft) ↔ 4m (12ft), deciduous ⑬ ***plicatum*** **'Pink Beauty'** 🏆 ↕3m (10ft) ↔ 4m (12ft), deciduous ⑭ ***rhytidophyllum*** ↕5m (15ft) ↔ 4m (12ft), semi-evergreen ⑮ ***sargentii*** ↕↔ 3m (10ft), deciduous ⑯ ***opulus*** **'Xanthocarpum'** 🏆 ↕3m (10ft) ↔ 4m (12ft), deciduous ⑰ ***tinus*** **'Variegatum'** ↕↔ 3m (10ft), evergreen

Weigela

For a showy display of flowers in spring or summer, few shrubs are more reliable than weigelas. The flowers, bell- or funnel-shaped, come in shades of ice-cream pink to ruby red and occasionally pure white or yellow. Weigelas are deciduous, and most grow to around 1.5m (5ft), making them suitable for even small backyards. They do well in almost any reasonable garden soil and can withstand neglect. If space allows, plant them with other shrubs that flower around the same time, such as potentillas (*see p.99*) or mock oranges (*Philadelphus, see p.93*). Just make sure they have room to show off their arching stems.

Hardiness Fully frost-hardy ***.

Cultivation Grow in any fertile, well-drained soil in full sun or partial shade. Variegated types produce the best-coloured foliage in full sun, golden-leaved forms in partial shade. **Cut back** flowered stems after flowering to strong buds or shoots lower down the shrub. Once plants are mature and growth is crowded, cut out an entire old branch or two, to encourage new growth from the base. **Take** greenwood cuttings in early summer or semi-ripe cuttings in mid-summer, or try hardwood cuttings from autumn until winter (*see p.394*).

Weigela florida 'Foliis Purpureis' ♀
↕1m (3ft) ↔ 1.5m (5ft), low, spreading habit, tolerant of pollution, likes a warm, sunny site, flowers in late spring and early summer

Weigela 'Looymansii Aurea'
↕↔ 1.5m (5ft), slow-growing, spreading, arching habit, leaf colour is best in partial shade, flowers in late spring and early summer

Westringia

These evergreen shrubs are dense and bushy to the ground, making them popular choices for screens and hedges. They are also valued for their general toughness, as most will withstand frost, dry and coastal exposure. The fine, narrow leaves are grey-green, and even paler underneath. Most species tend to have a few flowers year-round, with a main flowering in spring or summer. The flowers are white to pale purple, often with darker purple spots around the centre.

Hardiness Frost-hardy ** to frost-tender *.

Cultivation Grow in any well-drained soil in full sun or partial shade. **Trim** all over regularly with hedge shears to help keep the plant bushy (*see pp.382–384*). **Take** semi-hardwood cuttings in late summer and early autumn (*see p.394*).

Westringia fruticosa
↕2m (6ft) ↔ 2m (6ft), a tough shrub for screening that can be clipped into a hedge **

YUCCA

ERHAPS BEST KNOWN AS A POTPLANT, the yucca is a pectacular architectural plant for the garden. Yuccas nclude around 40 evergreen shrubs and trees, all of vhich come from hot, dry deserts and plains. They usually have a stout, upright stem; with maturity, some pread and become branched. Their sword-like leaves are produced in shades of mid- to dark green or blue-green. A few have cream or yellow edges. Towering pikes of bell-shaped, usually white flowers rise above he leaves in summer and autumn. Use yuccas as dramatic focal points in a garden, or in pots on the patio. They grow and flower particularly well in mild coastal areas. Many have sharp spines at the ends of he leaves, so keep them away from pedestrian traffic.

Hardiness Fully frost-hardy ✽✽✽ to very frost-tender ❁.

Cultivation Grow in any well-drained soil, in full sun. If growing hem in pots, use a quality potting mix; water occasionally during summer and feed annually with a balanced fertilizer. **Sow** seed in spring at 13–18°C (55–64°F) (*see pp.391–392*). **Take** root cuttings in vinter (*see p.394*), or remove rooted suckers (plantlets around the nain crown) in spring and replant.

Yucca gloriosa ♡ (Spanish Dagger)
↕↔ 2m (6ft), long, blue-green leaves mature to dark green, mature plants flower in late summer ✽✽

ZAUSCHNERIA

Californian Fuchsia

THIS EXOTIC-LOOKING SHRUB offers spectacular colour late in the season when most other plants are past their peak. Evergreen in its native California, it may die back in temperate regions, but should recover. It bears show-stopping, narrow, scarlet trumpets on the tips of shoots, which appear over a long period in late summer and autumn. Californian Fuchsias thrive in hot, sunny sites with sharp drainage. Rock gardens or dry stone walls are perfect. They can also be planted in a mixed or herbaceous garden alongside other late-flowering shrubs and perennials, such as hardy fuchsias (*see pp.60–63*), rudbeckias (*see p.317*), asters (*see pp.192–193*), and sedums (*see p.324*).

Hardiness Fully frost-hardy ✽✽✽ to frost-hardy ✽✽.

Cultivation Grow in reasonably fertile, well-drained soil in full sun. **Protect** in winter in the coldest areas by spreading a layer of organic matter around the crown of the plant to shield from severe frosts. **Sow** seed in a container in a cold frame in spring (*see pp.391–392*). **Take** cuttings of strong, young shoots from the base in spring; treat these as softwood cuttings (*see p.394*), and root in a propagator. Young growth may need protection from slugs (*see p.398*).

Zauschneria californica
↕ to 30cm (12in) ↔ 50cm (20in), evergreen or semi-evergreen, clump-forming ✽✽✽ (borderline)

ZELKOVA

THESE STATELY TREES COMBINE a distinctive, upright, then spreading habit with dark green leaves that turn to fiery shades of yellow, orange, and red in autumn. There are about six species in the group; all are deciduous and are often confused with their close relatives, the elms (*Ulmus, see p.125*). They have tiny, green flowers in spring followed by small, green fruits. Zelkovas make handsome specimens for large gardens or open spaces, or to flank wide avenues. They are often used as alternatives to elms in areas where Elm Leaf Beetles occur. Good companions include lindens (*Tilia, see p.124*) and birches (*Betula, see p.28*).

Hardiness Fully frost-hardy ✽✽✽.

Cultivation Grow in deep, fertile soil that is moist but well-drained, in full sun or partial shade. **Prune** young trees in late winter or early spring, removing any branches that are crossing or misplaced, and that spoil the shape of the tree (*see p.382*). **Sow** seed in containers outdoors in autumn (*see pp.391–392*). **Take** softwood cuttings in summer (*see p.394*).

Zelkova serrata ♡
↕ to 30m (100ft) ↔ 18m (60ft), spreading habit, smooth grey bark peels to show orange patches beneath, rich autumn colour (*above*)

Climbing Plants

using climbers in the garden

When planning what to plant in a bed or other area of the garden, do not forget to include some climbers. They add height to a bed if grown up a freestanding support or through a tree or shrub. In a small garden where there is little space to grow trees or large shrubs, climbers may be the only way to introduce some height or provide some privacy. Against a wall or fence, they extend the area of foliage and flowers on display and provide a feature or a backdrop that changes with the seasons.

Ways of using climbing plants

Climbers are perfect for covering and adding interest to bare or unsightly features in the garden, such as walls, fences, tree stumps, or outhouses. Their bright flowers and varied foliage can provide tremendous visual impact, helping to draw the eye upwards, and making full use of all the space in the garden while making it appear larger.

Clematis (*see pp.136–139*) and roses (*see pp.150–151*) offer a huge range of flower colours and sizes. Combine two or more climbers for a longer season of interest. For example, evergreen *Clematis cirrhosa* will provide cover all year round but flowers in early spring, so it works well with the pink summer blooms of *Rosa* 'New Dawn'. For scent, grow a honeysuckle (*Lonicera, see p.146*) or for really vibrant autumn foliage, try one of the Virginia creepers (*Parthenocissus, see p.148*). If you want an evergreen covering, then go for ivies (*Hedera, see p.142*), which are available in a myriad of leaf shapes and colours.

A pergola covered with climbing plants in flower becomes an enticing spot in any garden, and an arbour surrounded by scented plants will be a relaxing haven. Make sure you choose a plant that will suit the size of the structure. Climbing roses are a classic choice – rambling roses are usually too large – but vines (*Vitis, see p.154*) also look good on a large pergola.

A frame of wisteria Climbers can be used to emphasize a view, or to lead the eye to a focal point in the garden, such as a statue or an urn. This metal screen is clothed with *Wisteria sinensis*, which produces masses of flowers in early summer that hang down, releasing their scent. The pendent flowers frame the statue on the bench beyond.

If you do not have the space for a pergola or arbour, you could train a climber up a pillar, obelisk, or a tripod in a bed or border or even in a large container to change the pace of the planting and to create a focal point. Again, check the mature size of the climber so that it does not outgrow the support; small or medium-sized climbers, like sweet peas (*Lathyrus odoratus, see p.145*) work well.

Climbers look natural scrambling through large trees or shrubs, perhaps adding colour to a conifer. This is a good way of using a climber with a straggly habit, such as any of the *Clematis viticella* cultivars.

If you need a screen for privacy, training a climber up a fence or trellis is a decorative and speedy solution.

For all climbers, aim to grow a plant with a well-balanced shape by pruning and training it (*see p.384*). Some woody climbers, especially, bear more blooms if new stems are trained along horizontal supports each year, because this encourages flowering sideshoots.

What is a climbing plant?

'he term "climber" refers to plants that ı nature grow through host plants by arious means to reach the light. Most limbers are perennials: some are woody nd are part of the permanent structure f the garden; others are herbaceous, ying down in winter. Some are annuals nd must be grown from seed each year. 'here are also a few evergreen climbers. 'limbing plants can be self-clinging, wining, scrambling, or trailing.

Self-clinging climbers have aerial roots, or adhesive pads on their shoots, that attach themselves to the surface against which they are growing. Some cling by tendril tips. These climbers do not need training into supports.

Twining climbers twine stems or coil tendrils around the support. Some, such as clematis and tropaeolums (*see p.154*), attach themselves by curling leaf stalks. Scrambling and trailing plants are usually very vigorous with long stems that need tying into supports to assist them to climb. Alternatively, they can be left to ramble over walls or banks.

After planting, all climbing plants need encouragement to start climbing. Insert a cane beside the plant, angling it towards the support, and tie the shoots to the cane. Remove the cane once the plant has become established on the support (*see p.390*).

erial roots grow out from the stems (here of n ivy) and cling to walls, fences, and trees. If ou are growing self-clinging climbers up old valls, make sure that the mortar is sound.

Tendrils Plants such as these passion flowers (*Passiflora*) and sweet peas use tendrils to enable them to climb. These quickly coil around anything they come into contact with.

Twining leaf stalks Twining leaf stalks (here on a clematis) spiral around the support, in a similar way to tendrils. Climbers with a twining habit prefer a permanent structure to grow through.

Planting sites and aspects

Dressing a tree Climbers with aerial roots or a twining habit, like this clematis, are ideal for clothing the trunks of large, mature trees. They provide extra flower power and, as they mature, may twine attractively around the branches.

When planning where to plant a climber, you will need to assess the soil and aspect. The soil at the base of a tall wall or fence can often be extremely dry because it shelters the ground from most of the rain, an area known as a rain shadow. The same is true at the base of a tree or large shrub. In these situations, incorporate plenty of well-rotted organic matter into the soil (*see p.377*) to retain moisture before planting. Then position the climber 30–45cm (12–18in) from the wall, or at the edge of a tree canopy, where the soil should be less dry.

Many hardy climbers will perform well without any protection at all, withstanding very cold conditions. A brick or stone wall, however, will give protection from several degrees of frost. This helps tender plants, which thrive in a north-facing aspect. Avoid placing early-flowering plants where they will catch the morning sun; if there is frost when they are in flower, the rapid thawing may damage both buds and flowers.

If the site is cast into shade for much of the day, your choice will be more limited, especially if it is also cold and south-facing, but many ivies and climbing hydrangea (*see p.143*) thrive in such conditions.

Containers

Many climbers, especially herbaceous and smaller, woody types, are happy growing in containers. You could use a container to grow a climber on a patio and train it into a trellis in the same way as for climbers growing in open ground. Alternatively, you could use a freestanding support such as a tripod of canes, or an obelisk, in the container so that it can be moved around the garden. Containers are ideal for less hardy plants, such as some jasmines, since they can be taken into a heated greenhouse or conservatory for the winter.

Be prepared to feed and water (*see pp.386–387*) climbers in containers regularly. You may have to water once or even twice daily in dry weather.

Quick topiary Make an interesting feature by training a small climber, such as a passion flower or ivy, onto a wire frame inserted into a container – there are ready-made shapes available or you could fashion your own.

AKEBIA

Chocolate Vine

THE COCOA-COLOURED FLOWERS of this small group of twining, woody climbers give them their common name. They hang from the branches in long clusters through early spring and, if the summer is long and hot, are followed by impressive, sausage-shaped fruits that ripen from green to purple. In milder areas, the dark green leaves of the semi-evergreen *Akebia quinata* do not fall in winter and become tinged purple in the cool weather. Chocolate vines are splendid plants for a pergola or archway, where the spicy fragrance of the flowers can be enjoyed fully. They can grow quite large, so provide a sturdy support.

Hardiness Fully frost-hardy ***, but late frosts may damage flowers.

Cultivation Chocolate vines are not very demanding and can be grown in any moist but well-drained soil, in sun or partial shade. **Pruning** is minimal – simply trim back after flowering to keep it under control (*see p.384*). **Sow** seed (*see pp.391–392*) in containers in a cold frame, or on the windowsill, as soon as it is ripe, or take semi-ripe cuttings (*see p.394*) in summer.

Akebia quinata

↕10m (30ft), the undersides of the leaves are blue-green and are evergreen in milder climates ***

AMPELOPSIS

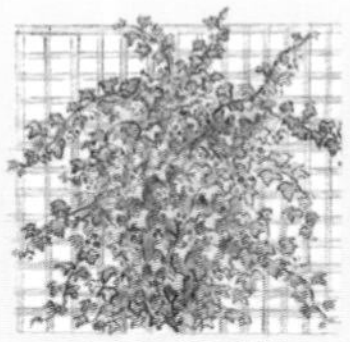

↕5–12m (15–40ft)

USING TWISTING TENDRILS, these handsome, deciduous climbers can cling to walls or fences or can be trained over pergolas or old trees. They are grown for their large leaves, which give a fiery display of colour in autumn. Variegated cultivars, such as *Ampelopsis glandulosa* 'Elegans' are less vigorous than the species, so suit smaller spaces, and the white and pink mottling is a welcome splash of colour on a dull wall. In warm areas, following the tiny, late-summer flowers, you may get masses of ornamental pink, blue, black, or orange berries.

Hardiness Fully frost-hardy ***, although *A. glandulosa* 'Elegans' benefits from the shelter of a warm wall.

Cultivation Grow in any moist but well-drained soil in sun or partial shade. Fruits are more abundant in sun or if the roots are restricted in a container. **Trim** vigorous plants in spring (*see p.384*), making sure that tendrils are kept clear of roof tiles and gutters. **Sow** seed (*see pp.391–392*) in a cold frame in autumn, or take softwood cuttings (*see p.394*) in summer.

Ampelopsis glandulosa var. *brevipedunculata*

↕5m (15ft), the pink or purple berries change colour to a clear sky-blue as they ripen ***

BERBERIDOPSIS CORALLINA

Coral Plant

THIS IS A TWINING, WOODY perennial. It has long, heart-shaped leaves with tiny spines around the edges, but it is mainly grown for its fuchsia-like flowers that hang from the shoots like baubles through summer to early autumn. It is excellent scrambling through a tree, which will provide it with the ideal conditions of some shelter and partial shade. The snowy mespilus (*Amelanchier, see p.22*) or rowan (*Sorbus, see p.118*) make good supports since the red flowers of the coral plant bridge the gap between the spring flowers and autumn colour of the tree. Alternatively, train it against a shaded, sheltered wall.

Hardiness Frost-hardy **.

Cultivation Plant in neutral or acid (lime-free) soil and dig in plenty of well-rotted organic matter. Choose a shady area with shelter from cold winds and protect roots in winter with a thick mulch (*see p.388*). **Tie in** young shoots to their support (*see p.380*). **Trim** in late winter or early spring if it becomes too big (*see p.384*). **Sow** seed (*see pp.391–392*) in a cold frame in spring; root semi-ripe cuttings (*see p.394*) in late summer; or layer shoots (*see p.395*) in autumn.

Berberidopsis corallina

↕5m (15ft), a rare, but interesting, climber

BOUGAINVILLEA

THESE ARE SCRAMBLING EVERGREENS, climbing by hrowing out long, lax canes which hook on by way of curved thorns. The leaves are mid-green and lance-haped. The flowers are actually tiny tubes, often ellow at the mouth. The "flowers" that give the plant ts colour are actually coloured, modified leaves known as bracts. These vary enormously in range and nclude virtually every shade of pink, red, and purple. Double-flowered forms are also available, as well as one that is variegated. Give them a sturdy north-facing structure to climb on, preferably away from pedestrian traffic to avoid scratches by the thorns.

Hardiness Frost-tender ❄ to very frost-tender ❀.

Cultivation Grow in warmer frost-free areas in full sun on any well-drained soil that is fertile and enriched with well-rotted organic matter. **Trim out** any wayward canes whenever they appear. (*see p.382*). **Take** heeled cuttings in summer or early autumn (*see p.394*).

***Bouganvillea* 'Miss Manilla'**
↕to 5m (15ft), showy, coloured leaves known as 'bracts' make up the flowers over a long period in summer ❀

CAMPSIS

Trumpet Creeper, Trumpet Vine

↕10m (30ft)

THERE ARE ONLY TWO CAMPSIS, *Campsis radicans* and *C. grandiflora*, used in gardens. From late summer until autumn, they produce exotic flowers, usually in shades of yellow, orange, or red, in small clusters amongst dark green leaves. These woody-stemmed climbers cling with aerial roots, although they will need some extra support. They are impressive growing up a wall, fence, or pergola, or through a large tree.

Hardiness Fully frost-hardy ❄❄❄ to frost-hardy ❄❄.

Cultivation Grow in moist but well-drained soil. In areas with sharp frosts, they are best grown against a warm, sunny wall. **Fan out** the young stems to provide good coverage of the support and cut away misplaced shoots; it may take 2–3 years to establish a main framework of branches. You will need to tie in young shoots until the aerial roots take firm hold (*see p.380*). Once the framework is in place, prune sideshoots back to two or three buds every year, after flowering. Keep clear of roofs and gutters. **Sow** seed (*see pp.391–392*) in containers in autumn or root semi-ripe cuttings in summer (*see p.394*).

Campsis grandiflora
↕to 10m (30ft), late summer and autumn flowers on a large climber that clings with aerial roots ❄❄

CISSUS

THIS IS A LARGE GROUP OF EVERGREEN, woody climbing plants. The leaves are oval, pointed-oval, to rhomboid and often softly toothed along the edges. They are mid- to dark green and paler underneath, often with indented veins. *Cissus discolor* features silvery colouring between the veins. The stems are thin and wiry, and plants benefit from being tied to a pole or frame to get them going vertically. Many will be ground covers if grown in the open without something to climb upon. They tolerate shade and need to be grown in warmer moist climates. Many make excellent indoor and glasshouse plants.

Hardiness Frost-tender❄ to very frost-tender ❀.

Cultivation Grow in warmer districts in any well-drained soil that is enriched with well-rotted organic matter **Grow** in full sun or shade and maintain soil moisture in drier times. **Prune** as needed to keep it within bounds (*see p.382*). **Take** stem cuttings at any time of year (*see p.394*).

Cissus antarctica
↕to 5m (15ft), a moderately quick growing evergreen climber for a shady spot ❀

CLEMATIS

Old Man's Beard, Traveller's Joy, Virgin's Bower

see also p.214

OFTEN KNOWN AS THE QUEEN OF CLIMBERS, the climbing clematis have been favourites of gardeners for many years because of their beautiful blooms. There are hundreds to choose from with varied habits, from clump-forming herbaceous plants to evergreen scramblers up to 15m (45ft) or more. These climbers will clothe large trees. Many more are less vigorous and perfectly suited to growing on fences or through shrubs. The flowers vary widely in size, shape, and hue – from large, flat blooms to small nodding bells in soft and bold shades of white, gold, orange, and blue to pinks and scarlets, often with a contrasting boss of anthers. The foliage also varies, but it is delicately shaped. Some, such as *Clematis tangutica,* have attractive, silky seedheads.

Hardiness Fully frost-hardy ❄❄❄ to frost-tender ❄.

Cultivation Clematis are divided into groups for pruning (*see below*), but other cultivation needs are similar for all types. **Grow** clematis in well-cultivated soil with plenty of organic matter, in sun or partial shade. They prefer a cool root run. **Tie in** a newly planted clematis to a cane and angle it towards the permanent support to encourage the plant to cling to it. **Sow** seed of species when they are ripe in autumn (*see pp.391–393*) and place them in a cold frame. **Take** softwood cuttings in spring or semi-ripe cuttings in summer (*see p.395*).

Pruning group 1

This group produces *flowers in spring from the previous year's growth. The flowers are usually bell-shaped or single and 2–5cm (¾–2in) long or saucer-shaped and 4–5cm (1½–2in) across. Prune after flowering to remove dead or damaged shoots; shorten others to the allotted space. This encourages new growth in summer that will bear flowers in the following spring. Once established, vigorous montana types need regular pruning only to stop them outgrowing their space. Cut back overgrown plants hard, then leave for at least three years.*

Pruning group 2

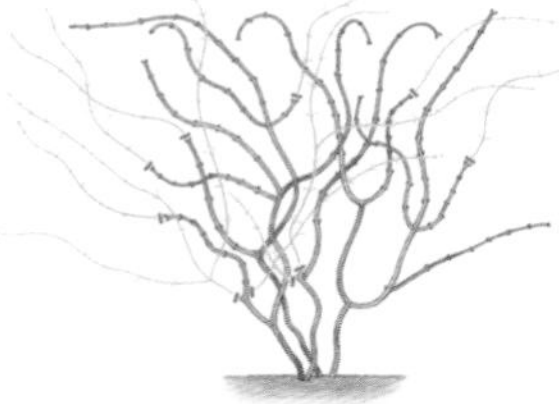

These large-flowered *hybrids flower in late spring and early summer on sideshoots produced in the previous year. They are deciduous. The flowers are held upright and may be single, semi-double, or fully double, 10–20cm (4–8in) across, and are mostly saucer-shaped. In late winter or early spring, prune out any weak or damaged shoots back to their point of growth or cut out entire shoots if they are damaged. It may be easier on a large plant to cut the sideshoots back by going over the plant with a pair of garden shears, but make sure that all the dead wood has been removed.*

Pruning group 3

All the clematis *in this group bear flowers on the current year's wood. The large-flowered hybrids are deciduous with single, saucer-shaped flowers, 8–15cm (3–6in) across, in summer and early autumn. Species and small-flowered hybrids flower from summer to late autumn. Their blooms may be single or double, star- or bell-shaped, or tubular and 1–10cm (½–4in) across. Prune this group in late winter or early spring by cutting all the stems back to about 30cm (12in) above the ground, just above a pair of healthy buds. Make sure that any dead growth is completely cut out.*

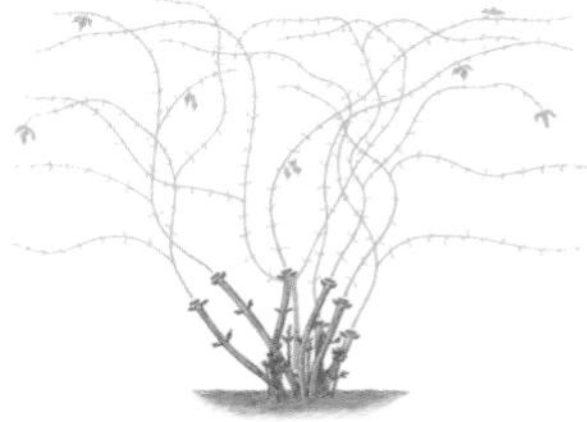

① *Clematis* **'Abundance'** 🏆 ↕3m (10ft) ↔ 1m (3ft), group 3 ② **'Alba Luxurians'** 🏆 ↕1.5m (5ft) ↔ 1m (3ft), group 3 ③ ***armandii*** ↕3–5m (10–15ft) ↔ 2–3m (6–10ft), group 1, evergreen ❄❄ ④ ***cirrhosa*** ↕2.5–3m (8–10ft) ↔ 1.5m (5ft), group 1, evergreen, silky seedheads ❄❄ ⑤ **'Doctor Ruppel'** ↕2.5m (8ft) ↔ 1m (3ft), group 2 ⑥ **'Duchess of Albany'** ↕2.5m (8ft) ↔ 1m

5

6

3

4

9

10

13

14

15

16

(3ft), group 3 ⑦ **'Elsa Späth'** ↕2–3m (6–10ft) ↔ 1m (3ft), group 2 ⑧ **'Etoile Rose'** ↕2.5m (8ft) ↔ 1m (3ft), group 3 ⑨ **'Etoile Violette'** 🏆 ↕3–5m (10–15ft) ↔ 1.5m (5ft), group 3 ⑩ ***flammula*** ↕6m (20ft) ↔ 1m (3ft), group 3, prefers sheltered sun ❄❄ ⑪ ***florida* var. *sieboldiana*** ↕2.5m (8ft) ↔ good for containers, group 2 ⑫ **'Gravetye Beauty'** ↕2.5m (8ft) ↔ 1m (3ft), group 3 ⑬ **'Hagley Hybrid'** ↕2m (6ft) ↔ 1m (3ft), group 3, fades in sun ⑭ **'Henryi'** 🏆 ↕3m (10ft) ↔ 1m (3ft), group 2 ⑮ **'H.F. Young'** ↕2.5m (8ft) ↔ 1m (3ft), group 2 ⑯ **'Huldine'** 🏆 ↕5m (15ft) ↔ 2m (6ft), group 3

⑰ *Clematis* **'Hybrida Sieboldii'** ↕3m (10ft), group 2, prefers full sun ⑱ **'Kathleen Dunford'** ↕2.5m (8ft), group 2 ⑲ **'Lasurstern'** 🏆 ↕2.5m (8ft), group 2 ⑳ **'Lincoln Star'** ↕2.5m (8ft), group 2, flowers fade in full sun ㉑ ***macropetala*** ↕3m (10ft), group 1, decorative seedheads ㉒ ***macropetala*** **'Markham's Pink'** 🏆 ↕3m (10ft), group 1, decorative seedheads

㉓ **'Madame Edouard André'** ↕2.5m (8ft), group 2 ㉔ **'Madame Julia Correvon'** 🏆 ↕3m (10ft), group 3 ㉕ **'Minuet'** 🏆 ↕3m (10ft), group 3 ㉖ ***montana*** ↕5–14m (15–46ft), group 1 ㉗ ***montana*** **var.** ***rubens*** ↕10m (30ft), group 1 ㉘ ***montana*** **'Tetrarose'** 🏆 ↕5m (15ft), group 1 ㉙ **'Mrs George Jackman'** 🏆 ↕2.5m (8ft), group 2 ㉚ **'Niobe'** ↕2–3m (6–10ft), group 2, fades in full sun

19

20

21

22

32

27

28

29

33

41

34

39

40

42

(31) **'Perle d'Azur'** ↕3m (10ft), group 3 (32) **'Proteus'** ↕3m (10ft), group 2 (33) **'Pruinina'** ↕2–3m (6–10ft), group 1, decorative seedheads (34) **'Richard Pennell'** 🏆 ↕3m (10ft), group 2 (35) **'Nelly Moser'** 🏆 ↕3m (10ft), group 2, fades in full sun (36) ***tangutica*** ↕6m (20ft), group 3, decorative seedheads (37) **'The President'** 🏆 ↕3m (10ft), group 2 (38) **'Venosa Violacea'** 🏆 ↕3m (10ft), group 3

(39) **'Ville de Lyon'** ↕3m (10ft), group 3, best grown through an evergreen shrub, because lower foliage may become scorched (40) ***viticella* 'Purpurea Plena Elegans'** 🏆 ↕3m (10ft), group 3 (41) ***rehederiana*** ↕7m (22ft), group 3 (42) **'Vyvyan Pennell'** ↕3m (10ft), group 2

Clerodendrum

Members of this genus are mostly from the tropics and sub-tropics and include trees and shrubs as well as climbers. These are evergreen twiners with lance- or heart-shaped leaves, often with slightly indented veins and a coarse texture. The flowers are tubular and usually red with protruding stamens. In the commonly grown *Clerodendrum thomsoniae* only the tip of the flower peeps out from a round, showy white calyx. The flowers occur in clusters beyond the foliage on the end of thin stems. These should be grown in warm humid areas and can be used as glasshouse and indoor plants if the conditions are too cold outside.

Hardiness Very frost-tender ❀.

Cultivation Grow in any well-drained soil that is fertile and enriched with well-rotted organic matter in full sun or partial shade with ample moisture. **Cut** back in the spring and summer to kerb excessive top growth and keep bushy. *(see p.382)*. **Take** firm tip cuttings in spring or plant up rooted suckers at any time *(see p.394)*.

Clerodendrum thomsoniae
↕ to 3m (10ft), summer flowering, this climber is only for the warmest districts or a heated glasshouse ❀

Clytostoma

These evergreen woody-stemmed climbers cling by the use of tendrils. They are very fast growing, and have shiny, oblong to oval leaflets. The flowers smother the plant in spring and summer. These are lavender-pink trumpets that have purple veins on them and are up to 10cm (4in) across. Interest is added by the fact that the flowers fade to pale pink, giving a range of hues to a flowering specimen. Provide a solid yet open frame that the tendrils can cling to and grow in frost-free areas only.

Hardiness Very frost-tender ❄.

Cultivation Grow in full sun or partial shade in any well-drained soil that is enriched with well-rotted organic matter and water in summer. Little pruning is needed; remove any shoots that spoil the shape of young plants to encourage a good form *(see p.382)*. **Take** semi-ripe cuttings in summer *(see p.394)*.

Clytostoma callistegiodes
↕ 3m (10ft) ↔ 5m (15ft), grow in frost-free areas and enjoy the profuse spring and summer flowering

Cobaea

Only the cup and saucer vine (*Cobaea scandens*) is commonly cultivated. Although a perennial climber, it is tender, so in frost-prone climates it is best used as an annual. It has rich green leaves and creamy-white, fragrant blooms that become purple as they age. Grow this lovely plant over an arbour or an archway, where the perfume of the flowers can easily be enjoyed, or train it on a sunny wall. In colder areas, a good option is to grow a cobaea through a tree or shrub so that there is no ugly, bare support left at the end of the season. Alternatively, use it in containers and hanging baskets and let the shoots trail over the rim.

Hardiness Very frost-tender ❄, although *C. scandens* can survive cold snaps close to 0°C (32°F).

Cultivation Grow in well-drained soil, in a sheltered spot with full sun. **Sow** seed *(see pp.391–392)* at 18°C (64°F) in spring, and plant out when the threat of frost has passed, or root softwood cuttings *(see p.394)* in summer.

Cobaea scandens ♆ (Cathedral Bells, Cup and Saucer Vine)
↕ to 5m (15ft), much less if grown as an annual

Dicentra

see also p.229

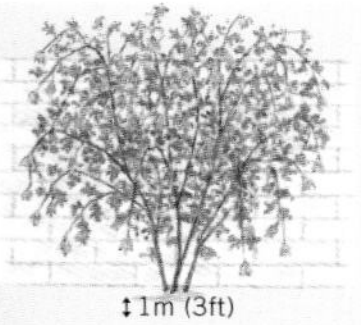

↕1m (3ft)

These climbing perennials have unusual flowers that appear on the scrambling, slender stems throughout summer. In common with the non-climbing, spreading or clump-forming dicentras, the flowers look as if they have been gently inflated. There are two available climbing species: *Dicentra macrocapnos*, which has ferny foliage and yellow flowers into late autumn, and *D. scandens*, which has deeply lobed, mid-green leaves. They are excellent plants for walls or fences at the back of a garden, or for training through a shrub or a hedge.

Hardiness Fully frost-hardy ❄❄❄, but frost may damage early growth.

Cultivation Dicentras prefer moist, slightly alkaline (limy), humus-rich soil and partial shade. They are perfect for a woodland garden or other shady spot, but will tolerate more sun in reliably damp soil. **Sow** seed (*see pp.391–392*) in containers in a cold frame as soon as it is ripe, or wait until spring. **Slugs** (*see p.398*) may leave large holes in the leaves, so it is worth protecting young plants against them.

Dicentra scandens
↕1m (3ft), flowers may also be white or tipped with pink ❄❄❄

Eccremocarpus scaber

Chilean Glory Flower

The only available plants from this small group of fast-growing, evergreen climbers are *Eccremocarpus scaber* and its cultivars. From late spring until autumn, spectacular clusters of exotic, brightly-coloured flowers appear. They are eye-catching clambering up a fence or wall, through a large shrub, or over an arch. The light green, or grey-tinted foliage is composed of neat leaflets. In colder areas, Chilean glory flowers are best used as annuals or as container plants, but in warm climates they can be grown as short-lived perennials.

Hardiness Fully frost-hardy ❄❄❄ to very frost-tender ❁.

Cultivation Grow in fertile, well-drained soil in a sunny position, or in a container of loam-based potting mix to be moved under cover in winter. **Tie in** to its support regularly (*see p.380*) until the tendrils get a firm grip. **Trim** plants grown as a perennials in early spring to fit the available space (*see p.384*). **Sow** seed (*see pp.391–392*) at 13-16°C (55-61°F) in late winter or early spring or root softwood cuttings (*see p.394*) in spring or summer in a propagator.

Eccremocarpus scaber
↕to 3m (10ft), somewhat rare, but worth growing for the long flowering period ❄

Gelsemium sempervirens

Carolina Jasmine, Evening Trumpet, False Yellow Jasmine

↕3–6m (10–20ft)

Of these twining perennials, *Gelsemium sempervirens* is the only common ornamental. It has handsome, glossy leaves and from spring to late summer clear-yellow, perfumed flowers. In places prone to frost, it needs the protection of a warm wall, or it can be grown in a container and brought under cover in winter. In warmer areas, it is lovely climbing over a pergola or arch, beneath which you can linger to enjoy the sweet fragrance of the flowers. All parts of the plant are toxic and have been used historically as a poison.

Hardiness Frost-tender ❄; will survive a short spell at 0°C (32°F).

Cultivation Grow in well-drained soil, in full sun or semi-shade, with shelter from hot, drying winds. **Plant** in containers in frost-prone areas so it is easy to move under cover in winter. Use a quality potting mix and repot or top-dress annually. **Thin out** the flowered stems when they have faded. **Sow** seed (*see pp.391–392*) at 13–18°C (55–64°F) in spring, or take semi-ripe cuttings (*see p.394*) in summer.

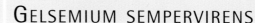

Gelsemium sempervirens (Carolina Jasmine)
↕to 3m (10ft) or more, late spring to summer, beautifully fragrant flowers

HARDENBERGIA

THERE ARE ONLY THREE SPECIES IN THIS GENUS. They are climbers, or ground covers if there is nothing around for them to cling to. They climb by twining around objects, including nearby plants, so provide a trellis or other frame for them. However, make sure it is very solid as the vigorous growth of hardenbergias is known to crush timber trellises after a few years. Leaves are leathery, deep green, long and lance-shaped. The flowers appear in late winter and into spring and are small and pea-shaped, but occur in profusion. They are usually purple, but a number of other colours are also available.

Hardiness Frost-hardy ❄❄ to frost-tender ❄.

Cultivation Grow in any well-drained soil in full sun or partial shade. Hard pruning can be used to rejuvenate older plants (*see p.382). **Sow*** seed after soaking (*see p.391*). **Take** cuttings of firm young wood in summer and place in a cold frame (*see p.394*).

Hardenbergia violacea 'Happy Wanderer'
↕3m (10ft), is a particularly vigorous and floriferous form of this native climber ❄

HEDERA

Ivy

see also p.69

IVY LEAVES COME IN MANY SHAPES and shades of green, some with bright gold or silver variegation that will cheer up a dull corner. Young ivies creep flat against surfaces using aerial roots, but at maturity they become tree-like, with large, bushy growths and the foliage loses its familiar shape. These woody, evergreen climbers vary hugely in size, hardiness, and shade tolerance. Grow them up a wall or tree, or let them scramble as ground cover. Keep trimmed to prevent flowering. Seed pods should be removed to prevent seed spread.

Hardiness Fully frost-hardy ❄❄❄ to frost-tender ❄.

Cultivation Ivies tolerate most soils, especially alkaline (limy), and most positions, but all grow best in fertile soil enriched with well-rotted organic matter. Green-leaved types thrive in shade; variegated cultivars prefer more light and some shelter from cold winds. **Prune** to fit the available space at any time of year (*see p.384*); keep clear of roofs and gutters. **Root** semi-ripe cuttings in summer (*see p.394*).

Hedera helix 'Buttercup'
↕2m (6ft), compact ivy, butter-yellow in sun – a good contrast for coppery bark (*see inset*), leaves 6cm (2½in) or more across ❄❄❄

HIBBERTIA

see also p.70

THE VAST MAJORITY OF THE PLANTS IN THIS GENUS are shrubs *(see p.70)*, with a couple being scrambling climbers with reddish-brown stems. These tend to be light twining plants that can also be groundcovers. The leaves are very glossy, dark green and oblong to oval. Flowers appear in spring and sporadically throughout the year and are golden yellow. They open flat and are five-petalled, with a conspicuous boss of central stamens and sometimes heart-shaped petals. Both will grow in filtered light or full sun and *Hibbertia dentata* will also do well in containers, including hanging baskets. *H. scandens* makes an excellent plant for coastal gardens and is more vigorous than its sibling.

Hardiness Frost-hardy ❄❄ to frost-tender ❄.

Cultivation Grow in any soil as long as it is well drained, in full sun or partial shade. **Provide** a frame for climbing if not using as a ground cover. **Tip prune** when young to encourage bushy plants (*see p.383*). **Take** cuttings of firm young growth any time of the year (*see p.394*).

Hibbertia scandens
↕ to 5m (15ft), showy yellow flowers in spring, with a few at other times of the year as well

HOYA

Wax Flower

THESE ARE EVERGREEN TWINING PLANTS with thin wiry stems. The leaves are pointed ovals and pale to mid-green. They are very thick and shiny and almost look as if made of plastic. The flowers generally occur in summer and are waxy, pale pink, small and starry but held in conspicuous spheres. These balls are held on a slightly pendulous thin stem and are beautifully perfumed. Flowers appear on the same stem year after year, so it is important to retain these. They are very well adapted to growing in containers and do not mind being pot-bound. This, and their scent, have made them favourite patio plants for decades.

Hardiness Frost-tender ❄ to very frost-tender ❅.

Cultivation Grow in any well-drained soil or good quality potting mix that is reasonably fertile. Partial shade or early morning sun only is best, along with shelter from hot, drying winds. **Provide** a frame to climb on. Little pruning is needed. **Propagate** by stem cuttings or by single leaves, which have a little stem on them, similar to heeled cuttings (*see pp.394*).

Hoya carnosa
↕3m (10ft), bears balls of starry flowers from the same stems year after year

HUMULUS

Hop

HOPS ARE TWINING, PERENNIAL climbers, with soft, hairy shoots that die down in winter. They are admired for their large, ornamental leaves, which are often patterned with white or yellow. In summer, male and female flowers are borne on separate plants; males in clusters and females in unusual spikes that resemble papery, green pine-cones. The female hop flowers are used in brewing beer, and also in fresh or dried flower arrangements. Hops are vigorous but not rampant, perfect for any area if provided with trellis, wires, or mesh to wind around, or for growing through a large shrub or small tree.

Hardiness Fully frost-hardy ❄❄❄.

Cultivation Grow in moist, well-drained soil in sun or partial shade. **Root** softwood cuttings in spring (*see p.394*). **Cut back** dead stems in winter, or in spring in cold areas.

***Humulus lupulus* 'Aureus'** 🏆 (Golden Hop)
↕6m (20ft), the golden leaves are brightest in full sun, fragrant flowers

HYDRANGEA

Climbing hydrangea

see also pp.72–73

↕15m (50ft)

THE CLIMBING HYDRANGEAS are popular for their abundance of huge, frothy white flowers in summer. Evergreen species such as *Hydrangea seemannii* and *H. serratifolia* are only frost-hardy, but are great year-round plants, with large, leathery leaves. The deciduous *H. anomala* subsp. *petiolaris* is commonly grown in cooler areas and has the bonus of leaves that turn golden-yellow in autumn. These sturdy plants will cling, using aerial roots, to large areas of wall, fence, or even old tree stumps. Once established, they grow quickly to provide invaluable cover, particularly on a shady, south- or east-facing wall where little else can thrive.

Hardiness Fully frost-hardy ❄❄❄ to frost-hardy ❄❄.

Cultivation Grow in any moist, well-drained soil in sun or shade. **Prune** to fit space after flowering (*see p.384*). **Root** softwood cuttings in early summer or hardwood cuttings in autumn (*see p.394*) or layer in spring (*see p.395*).

LAYERING SHOOTS Peg a shoot to the ground, aerial roots downwards, and lightly cover 15cm (6in) of the stem with soil. When rooted, cut from the parent and plant in its new position.

Hydrangea anomala* subsp. *petiolaris 🏆
↕15m (50ft), flowerheads may reach an impressive 25cm (10in) across ❄❄❄

JASMINUM

Jasmine, Jessamine

see also p.76

↕2–12m (6–40ft)

MANY OF THE TWINING, climbing jasmines are tender, but are worth growing because of their honeyed, fragrant, usually yellow or white flowers. They are lovely in any situation, although in frost-prone areas some species need the shelter of a sunny wall. The Poet's Jasmine (*Jasminum officinale*), *J. beesianum* and *J.* × *stephanense,* are quite hardy and bear heavily perfumed flowers in summer. Common jasmine (*Jasminum polyanthum*) is vigorous and may smother a small arch or trellis.

Hardiness Frost-hardy ✲✲ to very frost-tender ❀.

Cultivation Grow jasmines in fertile, well-drained soil in full sun. **Thin out** the old and flowered shoots from *J. officinale*; thin other jasmines after flowering (*see p.384*). **Root** semi-ripe cuttings in summer (*see p.394*).

Jasminum mesnyi (Primrose Jasmine)
↕3m (10ft) ↔ 1–2m (3–6ft), habit is naturally that of an open shrub, but it is usually trained as a climber ✲

KENNEDIA

EVERGREEN SPRAWLING GROUND COVERS and climbers, these vigorous and fast-growing plants make quick screens. The leaves are leathery, and made up of one, three or five oval leaflets. Flowers occur mostly in spring and are pea-shaped. They are most often in shades of red, from pale through to scarlet, but mauve, violet, and even black are also part of the range. They climb by twining, so will need an open frame, wire or trellis to twine around. They are sometimes used as groundcovers, but will climb over nearby plants if allowed. Most do very well in coastal conditions.

Hardiness Frost-tender* to very frost-tender ❀

Cultivation Grow in any well-drained soil in full sun or partial shade. **Prune** minimally, only to remove wayward growth. **Sow** seed in a cold frame after placing in hot water and soaking for 24 hours (*see p.391*) Take cuttings of firm young growth in summer (*see p.394*).

Kennedia rubicunda (Dusky Coral Pea)
↕3m (10ft), spring flowering climber, sometimes also used as a groundcover ✲

Kennedia nigricans (Black Coral Pea)
↕3m (10ft), a large and very vigorous climber needing a strong support frame ✲

Kennedia coccinea
↕2–3m (6–10ft), spring flowering climber or groundcover if it has nothing to climb on ✲

LAPAGERIA ROSEA

Chilean Bellflower

↕5m (15ft)

THE CHILEAN BELLFLOWER is a woody, twining climber, with leathery, dark green leaves. It is prized for its exotic, fleshy, raspberry-red flowers, borne in summer and late autumn. There are also luscious white and pink cultivars available. It is native to dense forest and in cultivation prefers a similarly still, shady environment. A sheltered site, close to the house for extra warmth, but away from full sun, is perfect. In cold areas, the Chilean Bellflower is best grown in a container and moved under cover in winter.

Hardiness Frost-hardy ❄❄ (borderline).

Cultivation Grow in well-drained, slightly acid soil improved with plenty of well-rotted organic matter. In containers, use good quality potting mix. **Mulch** thickly over the rooting area through the winter (*see p.388*). **Trim** over-long stems to fit the available space (*see p.384*) if needed, but leave unpruned if at all possible. **Sow** seed (*see pp.391–392*) at 13–18°C (55–64°F) in spring, or root semi-ripe cuttings (*see p.394*) in summer.

Lapageria rosea ♀ (Chilean Bellflower)
↕2–3m (6–10ft), summer flowering evergreen ❄❄ (borderliine)

LATHYRUS ODORATUS

Sweet Pea

see also p.269

↕2–2.5m (6–8ft)

SWEET PEAS ARE THE MOST FAMILIAR CLIMBERS in this group, prized for their showy, usually fragrant flowers in opulent shades of red, pink, mauve, blue, and white. If they are regularly deadheaded, and have the nutrients from rich soil or regular feeding, they will bloom from winter well into spring, even summer in some districts. The climbers of this group are very versatile: they cling with tendrils that corkscrew tightly around almost any support. Train them on trellis, netting, wires, obelisks, through shrubs, or up an arch. There are other perennial peas, also with richly coloured, sweet-smelling flowers, such as *Lathyrus latifolius.*

Hardiness Fully frost-hardy ❄❄❄ to frost-hardy ❄❄.

Cultivation Grow in fertile soil in full sun or dappled shade. Dig lots of well-rotted organic matter into the ground. Feed plants fortnightly (*see p.386*). **Sow** seed (*see pp.391–393*) in deep pots or sweet peas tubes in a cold frame, or in situ in late summer or autumn in armer districts or winter to early spring in cold areas. For earlier flowers, sow in a cold frame in autumn. **Deadhead** regularly (*see p.390*) or flowering will cease. **Slugs,** snails, and aphids (*see p.398*) are common.

Lathyrus 'Bijou'
↕45cm (18in) ↔ 45cm (18in), a smaller growing annual sweet pea useful for containers, including hanging baskets

Lathyrus odoratus
↕2m (6ft) ↔ 45cm (18in), delightfully perfumed, tall annual needing a support to climb up

Lonicera

Honeysuckle

see also p.84

A CLASSIC COTTAGE-GARDEN FAVOURITE, honeysuckles are valued for their delicate flowers that are often fragrant enough to perfume the entire garden. The twining climbers are especially popular. They are very adaptable and can be trained on walls, through large shrubs or trees, or over arches. They are particularly lovely around a seating area where the scent can be enjoyed while you relax. There are many available that produce flowers in many shades. Snowy-white and double-cream are traditional, but there are exotic coral and gold honeysuckles available. The red or black berries can cause a slight stomach upset if they are eaten. There are also shrubby species.

Hardiness Fully frost-hardy *** to frost-tender *.

Cultivation Grow in any moist but well-drained soil, in full sun or partial shade, ideally with the roots in shade. **Prune** to fit the available space in early spring or after flowering. The easiest way to tidy up larger specimens is to cut them with a hedgetrimmer (*see p.384*). **Sow** seed (*see pp.391–392*) in a cold frame as soon as it is ripe.

Lonicera japonica 'Halliana' ♀
↕10m (30ft), vigorous evergreen or semi-evergreen, very fragrant flowers from late spring to late summer, red berries in autumn ***

Lonicera × americana
↕7m (22ft), deciduous, very fragrant flowers in summer and early autumn, red berries in autumn ***

TRAINING HONEYSUCKLE
Encourage the soft new shoots to climb by winding them around their support, here wires stretched up a wooden pergola post.

Macfadyena

THESE VIGOROUS CLIMBERS CLING to just about any surface by means of claw-like tendrils. The leaves are glossy and occur in pairs. Yellow flowers appear in late spring and into summer. These are trumpet-shaped, with a flared, petal-like opening, and feint stripes in the flower tube. Evergreen and fast, these can cover a very large area quickly and are useful for disguising bigger objects, such as sheds. Used in this way Macfadyena can be a useful screener as well as a backdrop to other yellow- or blue-flowered plants such as euryops (*Euryops, see p57*), phlomis (*Phlomis, see p.306*), ceanothus (*Ceanothus, see p.36*) and agapanthus (*Agapanthus, see p.170*).

Hardiness Frost-hardy ** to frost-tender *.

Cultivation Grow in full sun in a well-drained soil. **Prune** minimally. **Sow** seed when ripe straight into containers (*see pp.391). **Take** cuttings of firm young wood in summer. These root better if in a heated glasshouse (*see p.394).*

Macfadyena unguis-cati
↕4m (12ft), will cover a large, unsightly area quickly and provide yellow flowers in spring

MANDEVILLA

A VARIABLE GENUS which includes evergreen, semi-evergreen and deciduous members, all of which climb by twining, so it is important to provide an open frame for the purpose. Leaves are lance-shaped and soft, often with indented veins. Flower buds are slightly twisted, like corkscrews, and open to reveal a trumpet-shaped flower with ruffled or wavy-edged petals. A delightful fragrance fills the air around these spring- or summer-flowering plants. Flower colours range from pure white through pink to red. Grow this climber close to the house where the fragrance can be enjoyed and where the building can offer protection for these frost-sensitive beauties.

Hardiness Frost-tender* to very frost tender ❄.

Cultivation Grow in any well-drained soil that is enriched with well-rotted organic matter. Full sun is best, along with shelter from hot, drying winds. **Prune** minimally. **Sow** seed in spring in a cold frame (*see p.391*). **Take** semi-hardwood cuttings in summer (*see p.394*).

Mandevilla x amabilis 'Alice Du Pont' 🏆
↕3m (10ft), fragrant pink flowers in summer

MAURANDELLA ANTIRRHINIFLORA

Violet Twining Snapdragon

↕1–2m (3–6ft)

DELICATE AND SLENDER-STEMMED, this twining climber is a herbaceous perennial with lush, bright green leaves that provide a splendid backdrop for the main attraction: the flowers. They are borne in abundance throughout the summer and autumn and are usually violet. Plant it so it can wind its way through trellis, taut wires, or netting attached to any vertical surface. It is grown as an annual in cool climates, but the shorter season means it does not grow to full size; combine it with other climbers to cover a larger area and prolong the display.

Hardiness Frost-tender *.

Cultivation Grow in moist but well-drained soil in light shade, or in morning sun. Protect from hot,drying winds. **Deadhead** regularly (*see p.390*), and if growing it as a perennial, remove the dead top-growth at the end of the season. **Sow** seed (*see pp.391–393*) at 13–18ºC (55–64ºF) in spring. **Take** softwood cuttings (*see p.394*) in spring and root in a propagator.

Maurandella antirrhiniflora
Flowers have violet, purple, or sometimes pink lobes

MUEHLENBECKIA

THESE PLANTS ARE EVERGREEN CLIMBERS that often form a thick, almost impenetrable mat. The stems are thin and wiry, but are also very strong. The leaves are small and round and cover the plant densely. The yellowish flowers are quite small and not of any consequence. Muehlenbeckia make vigorous climbers once established. They take well to clipping and if grown on a suitable frame can be clipped regularly so that they appear as a hedge. These can be maintained at one metre up to several metres tall. The most commonly grown is *Muehlenbeckia complexa*, which can withstand a range of conditions from snow to periods of dry.

Hardiness Fully frost-hardy *** to frost-tender *.

Cultivation Grow in any well-drained soil in full sun or partial shade. **Trim** regularly to keep within limits (*see p.384*). **Sow** seed in spring (*see p.391*). **Take** cuttings of firm young growth in spring or summer (*see p.394*).

Muehlenbeckia complexa
↕2m (6ft), is often used more as a thick hedge than a climber

Pandorea

SHOWY TUBULAR FLOWERS are the main reason these vigorous climbers are grown. These appear at the ends of the growing tips in spring and summer. Colours vary from white to cream, through to pink, and most feature pronounced splotching or darker colours within the flower tube. The evergreen leaves are made up of mid-green leaflets opposite each other on a central stem. These plants do not have clinging tendrils but grow by twining and may need to be tied to their climbing frame occasionally to encourage growth where it is wanted. This is especially the case when they are young.

Hardiness Frost-tender ✻ to very frost-tender ❁.

Cultivation Grow in a well-drained soil in full sun or partial shade, provided it is out of frosts. Trim out older shoots if needed to promote more vigour (*see p.384*). Sow seed as soon as collected (*see p.391*). Take semi-hardwood cuttings from sideshoots in summer. Alternatively, layering is a successful means of propagation (*see p.394*).

Pandorea pandorana (Wonga Wonga Vine)
↕4m (12ft), fast growing, twining climber for frost free areas ✻

Parthenocissus

Virginia Creeper

VIRGINIA CREEPERS CAN CLING strongly to almost any surface using tiny suckers at the end of their tendrils. These deciduous, woody climbers are grown for their attractive leaves that give an amazing, bonfire-like show of colour in autumn. The dense foliage has the added bonus of providing a home for a variety of beneficial wildlife. Tiny, summer flowers may be followed by toxic black berries. These are vigorous vines that can be trained to cover walls, fences, and any ugly garden structures. Virginia Creepers are easily controlled, but take care where they climb because the suckers can leave unsightly marks on walls and fences.

Hardiness Fully frost-hardy ✻✻✻; *Parthenocissus henryana* is frost-hardy ✻✻ unless grown against a wall.

Cultivation Grow in fertile, well-drained soil in sun or shade; grow *P. henryana* in partial shade. **Support** young plants until they firmly attach themselves (*see p.380*). **Trim** in winter and summer to keep within bounds (*see p.384*) and clear of gutters and roofs. **Sow** seed (*see pp.391–392*) in pots in a cold frame in autumn, or take softwood cuttings in summer or hardwood cuttings in winter (*see p.394*).

① ***henryana*** ♀ ↕10m (30ft) ② ***tricuspidata*** ♀ (Boston Ivy) ↕20m (70ft) ③ ***tricuspidata*** **'Lowii'** ↕20m (70ft) ④ ***tricuspidata*** **'Veitchii'** ↕20m (70ft)

Passiflora

Passion Flower, Passionfruit

DESPITE THEIR TROPICAL APPEARANCE, some of these mostly evergreen climbers, notably the Blue Passion Flower (*Passiflora caerulea*), can be grown outdoors in cool climates. They climb using tendrils, so need the support of stretched wires, netting, trellis, or a large shrub. They are good all-round plants, with pleasing foliage, and unusual and exotic flowers through summer and autumn that are followed by edible, but not always tasty, fruits. In warm climates, they can be used in almost any situation, but in cold areas the tender species are best grown in containers and moved under cover in autumn, well before the first frosts.

Hardiness Frost-hardy ✻✻ to frost-tender ✻, *P. manicata* may survive a frost if well-ripened.

Cultivation Grow in soil that is moist but well-drained, in full sun or partial shade, or in tubs of good quality potting mix. Give shelter from hot winds and apply a mulch (*see p.388*) if grown outside in cold areas. **Root** semi-ripe cuttings (*see p.394*) in summer or layer (*see p.395*) in spring or autumn.

Passiflora caerulea **'Constance Elliot'**
↕to 8m (24ft), fragrant flowers from summer to autumn, orange-yellow fruits ✻✻

Phaseolus caracalla

Snail Flower

An unusual snail-like flower is one of the principal reasons for growing this climber. The fact that it flowers over a relatively long period from summer into autumn and that the flowers are perfumed is also part of its attraction. The flowers are pea-like, except they tend to be twisted and contorted. They are white with pink to dark purple and fade to cream before dropping. Leaves are made up of three oval leaflets and look similar to those of beans, to which the plant is related. This is supported by the appearance of bean-type pods in autumn. Originally from tropical America, it does not like frosts and does best in warmer districts.

Hardiness Very frost-tender ❅.

Cultivation Grow in well-drained soil that is enriched with well-rotted organic matter, in full sun or partial shade. **Prune** minimally. Sow seed into containers as soon as collected (*see pp.391*).

Phaseolus caracalla
↕3m (10ft), features unusual and beautifully scented flowers

Plumbago

Leadwort

Plumbago is grown for its large clusters of simple, flat flowers. There are annuals, perennials, and shrubs in the group, but the evergeen climbers are most commonly cultivated. Their bright, matt-green leaves provide the perfect foil for the sky-blue or pure white flowers. In mild climates, grow plumbago over a pergola or arch, or against a wall. In cool areas, where temperatures fall below 7°C (45°F), it is best grown in a sheltered, sunny spot, away from frosts.

Hardiness Frost-tender ✲ to very frost-tender ❅.

Cultivation Grow in fertile, well-drained soil in full sun. **Tie** shoots of young plants (*see p.380*) into the support as they grow to create a permanant framework of well-spaced stems. **Prune** lightly with hedge clippers after flowering, to promote bushiness. **Sow** seed (*see pp.391–392*) at 13–18°C (55–64°F) in spring or take semi-ripe cuttings (*see p.394*) in midsummer.

Plumbago auriculata 🏆 (Cape Leadwort)
↕3–6m (10–20ft) ↔ 1–3m (3–10ft), flower clusters from summer to late autumn are up to 15cm (6in) across ✲

Pyrostegia

This is an extremely vigorous climber, especially in warmer districts, to which it is particularly suited and where it is justifiably popular. In spring it is smothered with slender, bright orange, tubular flowers in clusters. It is densely covered in mid green, oval to oblong leaflets year round. The plant climbs by means of tendrils and so it will need wires or a frame of thin timber or metal strips which the tendrils can wrap around. In this way it will quickly cover a wall or fence.

Hardiness Frost-hardy ✲✲ to frost-tender ✲.

Cultivation Grow in full sun, although it will tolerate some shade. A moist, well-drained soil is ideal, particularly if enriched with well-rotted organic matter. **Prune** minimally; remove any wayward shoots that spoil the shape of the plant (*see p.383*). **Take** semi-hardwood cuttings in late summer and early autumn. (*see p.394*).

Pyrostegia venusta
↕8m (25ft), valuable for its vigorous growth and prolific spring flowering

Rosa (climbing and rambling)

Rose

see also pp.110–113

The glorious displays produced by climbing and rambling roses are one of the delights of the summer garden, but the thorny, arching stems will need some form of support and, in most cases, regular tying in. Climbers tend to have stiff stems, with the flowers, often scented, carried singly or in clusters. Some have one main show of blooms on wood produced the previous year, while others flower in succession on the current season's growth. Ramblers are generally more rampant and have more flexible stems. The sometimes scented flowers are usually borne in clusters in one main flush on the previous year's growth. Both types can be trained against walls and fences or over pergolas and other ornamental structures (*see below*).

Hardiness Fully frost-hardy ✲✲✲ to frost-hardy ✲✲.

Cultivation Roses tolerate a wide range of conditions, but prefer fertile soil in a sunny site. Plant bare-root roses while dormant, from late autumn to early spring. Container-grown roses can be planted at any time. **Water** well after planting and keep watered until established. **Prune** sideshoots of climbers back to two or three buds in autumn or spring once the basic framework is established; cut one or two old stems to the base every three or four years to encourage new growth. Ramblers produce shoots from the base, so cut out one in three main stems after flowering each year. **Take** hardwood cuttings (*see p.394*) in autumn. Plants may be affected by mildew, blackspot, or rust. If possible choose a disease-resistant variety, improve air circulation around the plant, or spray with a suitable fungicide.

Covering an arch with a rose

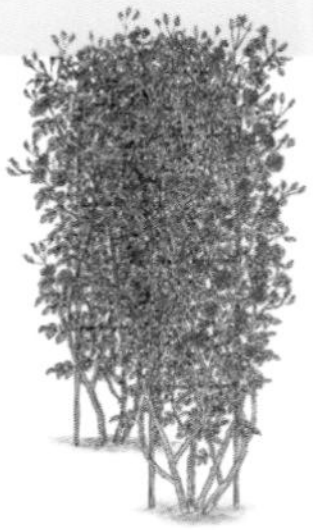

***Climbing or rambling** roses look particularly good when trained over an arch, an arrangement that also makes it easy to enjoy the scent of the flowers. The arch must be strong enough to bear the weight of the numerous shoots and flowers in summer. Check, too, that it is securely anchored into the ground. Tie in the stems as they grow, spreading them evenly over the frame. This is much easier done while the shoots are still young and flexible, especially on climbers. Deadhead faded blooms regularly to encourage more flowers on those varieties that produce a succession.*

Training a rambler into a tree

***Ramblers with** pliant, far-reaching stems will scramble into trees to provide a spectacular display. Check first that the tree can support the mass of growth, especially if choosing a vigorous rose. Plant the rose at least 1–1.2m (3–4ft) away from the trunk, and add plenty of organic matter to the planting hole to aid moisture retention. Site the rose on the windward side so that shoots are blown towards the tree, and train it into the tree up a length of rope leading from a stake at the rose's roots to a low branch. Protect the bark with a piece of rubber hose. No further training should be needed.*

Growing a climber up a pillar or tripod

***Roses trained** up structures such as pillars, tripods, or obelisks add useful height to a bed or border. Choose one of the less vigorous climbers to reduce the need for pruning. Keeping stems close to the horizontal encourages the development of flowering sideshoots so, where possible, train stems in a spiral fashion around the pillar or tripod. Tie in stems regularly as they grow, while they are still young and flexible. Once they start to stiffen up, they are liable to break rather easily. Prune out any unwanted or over-long stems as necessary.*

1

7

6

11

12

17

18

① ***Rosa* 'Albertine'** 🏆 ↕5m (15ft) ↔4m (12ft), rambler ② **'Aloha'** 🏆 ↕3m (10ft) ↔2.5m (8ft), climber ③ **'American Pillar'** ↕5m (15ft) ↔4m (12ft), rambler ④ ***banksiae* 'Lutea'** 🏆 ↕↔6m (20ft), rambler ✲✲ ⑤ **Breath of Life ('Harquanne')** ↕2.5m (8ft) ↔2.2m (7ft), climber ⑥ **'Chaplin's Pink Climber'** ↕5m (15ft) ↔2.5m (8ft), climber ⑦ **'Climbing Iceberg'** 🏆 ↕↔3m (10ft), climber ⑧ **'Compassion'** 🏆 ↕3m (10ft) ↔2.5m (8ft), climber

2

3

4

5

8

14

9

10

13

15

16

19

20

21

22

⑨ **'Dortmund'** 🏆 ↕3m (10ft) ↔ 2m (6ft), climber ⑩ **DUBLIN BAY ('Macdub')** 🏆 ↕↔ 2.2m (7ft), climber ⑪ **'Félicité Perpétue'** 🏆 ↕5m (15ft) ↔ 4m (12ft), rambler ⑫ ***filipes* 'Kiftsgate'** 🏆 ↕10m (30ft) ↔ 6m (20ft), rambler ⑬ **'Gloire de Dijon'** ↕5m (15ft) ↔ 4m (12ft), climber ⑭ **'Golden Showers'** 🏆 ↕3m (10ft) ↔ 2m (6ft), climber ⑮ **HANDEL ('Macha')** 🏆 ↕3m (10ft) ↔ 2.2m (7ft), climber ⑯ **'Madame Grégoire Staechelin'** 🏆 ↕6m (20ft) ↔ 4m (12ft), climber ⑰ **'New Dawn'** 🏆 ↕3m (10ft) ↔ 2.5m (8ft), climber ⑱ **'Paul's Lemon Pillar'** ↕4m (12ft) ↔ 3m (10ft), climber ⑲ **'Pink Perpétué'** ↕3m (10ft) ↔ 2.5m (8ft), climber ⑳ **'Rosy Mantle'** ↕2.5m (8ft) ↔ 2m (6ft), climber ㉑ **'Sander's White Rambler'** 🏆 ↕↔ 4m (12ft), rambler ㉒ **'Zéphirine Drouhin'** 🏆 ↕3m (10ft) ↔ 2m (6ft), thornless climber

Schizophragma

These woody, deciduous climbers are in the same family as hydrangeas (*see p.143*). The resemblance can be clearly seen in their huge, flat clusters of creamy-white, subtly fragrant flowers. They are borne in abundance in midsummer, against a background of dark green leaves. These plants provide unusual ground cover when grown without support in the dappled shade beneath deciduous trees and shrubs. Train schizophragmas up walls to which they cling strongly using aerial roots. These large climbers are very heavy when mature, so choose a suitably robust support that will not collapse under the weight.

Hardiness Fully frost-hardy ❄❄❄ to frost-hardy ❄❄.

Cultivation Grow in moist, well-drained, humus-rich soil in sun or partial shade. **Tie** in the shoots of young plants to their support until the aerial roots take hold (*see p.380*). **Trim** them in spring if they outgrow their space (*see p.384*). **Root** semi-ripe cuttings (*see p.394*) in late summer.

Schizophragma integrifolium 🏆
↕12m (40ft) ❄❄

Solanum

This huge group of plants contains varieties that are annuals, perennials, shrubs, and trees, but the climbing solanums are quite uncommon, apart from the well-known Potato Vine (*Solanum jasminoides*). They are grown for their bell- or trumpet-shaped flowers in regal blues and purples, or pure white, from spring right through to autumn. In some years, shiny, round berries may follow. Although solanums count potatoes and aubergines among their number, most of the ornamental species are toxic if eaten, and can cause severe discomfort. Some care should be taken as the fruits can be very appealing to children. Solanums need a warm, sunny wall to thrive in temperate climates. Grow them with other sun-worshippers such as jasmines (*see p.144*) and roses (*see pp.150–151*).

Hardiness Frost-hardy ❄❄ to frost-tender ❄.

Cultivation Grow in well-drained soil in full sun. **Tie** in shoots regularly (*see p.380*). **Sow** seed (*see pp.391–392*) at 18–20°C (64–68°F) in spring or root semi-ripe cuttings (*see p.394*) in summer in a propagator.

***Solanum rantonnetii* 'Royal Robe'**
↕1–2m (3–6ft) ❄❄ – flowers from summer to autumn

Solanum jasminoides
↕3–5m (10–15ft), fast growing late spring and summer flowering climber, useful as a quick screen

SOLLYA

3luebell Creeper

THIS IS A MEDIUM-SIZED, evergreen twining climber hat can sometimes appear almost like a shrub. The lowers are blue to purple-blue, giving rise to the ommon name of Bluebell Creeper. There is also a orm with pink flowers. These occur in spring and ummer and are small and pendulous and hang ndividually on thin stems. A small purple-black berry ollows that is also pendulous. The stems are thin and viry and hold the narrow deep green leaves. Provide frame for them to twine around. This plant can e an environmental weed in some areas, so plant vith caution.

lardiness Frost-hardy ❄❄ to frost-tender ❄.

:ultivation Grow in any well-drained soil in full sun, although part hade is probably best. Little pruning is needed, except to remove any hoots that spoil the shape of the plant (*see p.383*). **Sow** seed in utumn in a cold frame (*see p.391*). **Take** heeled tip cuttings in mid- late summer and place in a glasshouse, preferably with bottom heat see p.394).

Sollya heterophylla
3m (9ft), is covered in dainty blue flowers in spring and summer

SWAINSONA

Sturt's Desert Pea

GROWN FOR THEIR SUMMER FLOWERS, these trailing plants are easily encouraged to climb if they are tied in regularly to their supports. Sturt's Desert Pea (*Swainsonia formosus*) is a perennial in warm climates, but is tender and so best grown as an annual in cold gardens. It is a good plant for hanging baskets.

Hardiness Frost-tender ❄.

Cultivation Grow in a container of gritty, loam-based potting mix and move under cover in winter, or outdoors in well-drained, fertile soil. Sturt's Desert Peas need full sun, shelter from cold winds, and a deep, dry, winter mulch (*see p.388*). **Prune** minimally: trim shoots by no more than one-third, after flowering, only if it becomes necessary. **Sow** seed (*see pp.391–392*) at 18°C (64°F) in spring.

Swainsonia formosus (Sturt's Desert Pea)
↕20cm (8in) ↔ 1m (3ft)

TECOMARIA

BRIGHT ORANGE-RED FLOWERS BRING ATTENTION to this South African climber. These are slender tubes grouped together in clusters at the end of the new growth. They are most prolific in late summer and last well into autumn. The glossy, mid-green leaves are made up of many leaflets. An evergreen, this plant can be quite shrub-like or can climb to as much as 4m (12ft) tall if given the right conditions. It has a very sprawling habit and tends to throw out long, cane-like shoots. It will tolerate light frosts only.

Hardiness Frost-hardy ❄❄ to frost-tender ❄.

Cultivation A sunny spot away from frosts is best, along with a well-drained soil that is enriched with well-rotted organic matter. **Prune** regularly to keep in check by removing wayward shoots as they appear. **Take** semi-hardwood cuttings in late summer and early autumn (*see p.394*).

Tecomaria capensis 'Aurea'
↕4m (12ft) ↔ 2m (3ft), is a vigorous, evergreen, shrubby climber, popular in old-fashioned gardens

THUNBERGIA

VALUED FOR THEIR ABUNDANCE of exotic, brightly coloured flowers, these tropical, perennial climbers are usually grown as annuals in cool areas, or in pots. The blooms come in shades of gold, orange, or blue, and are borne against a background of soft green leaves. Their slender, twining stems can wind round a freestanding arch or obelisk, or through a shrub. Otherwise attach trellis, wires, or netting to a fence or wall to provide a support that they can scramble up. Create a fabulous, jewel-like display through summer by growing thunbergias with other annual climbers, such as sweet peas (*Lathyrus, see p.145*), on a single support.

Hardiness Frost-tender ✲ to very frost-tender ❀.

Cultivation Grow in a reasonably sheltered site in moist, well-drained soil and full sun. **Train** the young plants towards their support (*see p.380*). **Trim** thunbergias grown as perennials in early spring if they are taking up too much room (*see p.384*). **Sow** seed (*see pp.391–392*) at 16–18°C (61–64°F) or take semi-ripe cuttings (*see p.394*) in summer.

① ***grandiflora*** 🏆 ↕5–10m (15–30ft) ✲
② ***alata*** (Black-Eyed Susan) ↕1.5–2m (5–6ft) as an annual, 2.5m (8ft) as a perennial ✲

TRACHELOSPERMUM

↕6–9m (20–28ft)

THESE WOODY, EVERGREEN climbers are widely available. They are grown for their glossy, dark green leaves and immaculate white, perfumed flowers in mid- and late summer, which, on *Trachelospermum asiaticum,* age to yellow. Train them against a warm wall in frost-prone areas: trellis or taut, horizontal wires, fixed 5cm (2in) away from the wall, provide perfect support for twining stems. In very cold areas, grow in a container and move under cover in winter. The mature plants can be used to support spring- and summer-flowering annuals, such as tropaeolums (*see right*), to create a stunning mass of colour.

Hardiness Frost-hardy ✲✲.

Cultivation Choose a spot with fertile, well-drained soil, in sun or partial shade, with shelter from cold, drying winds. For containers use a good quality potting mix. **Trim** back long shoots in spring if you find the plant is outgrowing its support (*see p.384*). **Root** semi-ripe cuttings in summer (*see p.394*).

Trachelospermum jasminoides 🏆 (Confederate Jasmine, Star Jasmine)
↕9m (28ft), aging flowers remain pure white, bronze winter foliage

TROPAEOLUM

see a p.3

CLIMBING TROPAEOLUMS use long, twining leaf-stalks to scale fences, trellises, or pergolas. They can also scramble through shrubs, or without support grow as ground cover. In summer, they are decorated with masses of flamboyant flowers, often in glowing shades of red and yellow. Many species are tender, but even the perennials can be grown successfully as annuals in cold climates. The climbing nasturtiums (*Tropaeolum majus* and some cultivars) flower best on poor soil and are a useful stop-gap in neglected plots. The leaves and flowers of annual species are edible and can be used as a peppery addition to salads.

Hardiness Frost-hardy ✲✲ to frost-tender ✲.

Cultivation Grow these plants in moist but well-drained soil in full sun. **Tie in** young stems to their support (*see p.380*) to encourage them in the right direction. **Sow** seed of perennials in containers in a cold frame when ripe. Annual seed needs temperatures of 13–16°C (55–61°F) in early spring, or can be sown in situ in mid-spring (*see pp.391–393*).

Tropaeolum speciosum 🏆 (Flame Nasturtium)
↕3m (10ft), perennial, prefers acid (lime-free) soil, flowers are follow by blue berries in red, papery jackets, mulch in winter ✲✲

/ITIS

'ine

↕7m (22ft) to 15m (50ft)

THE ORNAMENTAL VINES in this group, unlike those grown for grapes or to make wine, are valued for their large leaves, which turn brilliant shades of bright red or plum-purple in autumn. They generally do not bear fruit. Strong endrils fasten these vigorous, woody, deciduous limbers to the nearest support. Train against a wall or ence. A vine makes a handsome cover for an arbour r pergola, especially over an eating area, because the afy growth provides cool shade in summer but llows the sun through in winter.

ardiness Fully frost-hardy ❄❄❄.

ultivation Grow vines in well-drained, neutral or slightly alkaline imy) soil, in full sun or semi-shade. **Prune** in winter and again in ummer if growth needs to be restrained (*see p.384*). If your vine is ore formally trained against a wall, prune sideshoots to two or three uds from the main framework in winter. **Sow** seed (*see pp.391–392*) a cold frame in autumn or spring or take hardwood cuttings (*see .394*) in winter. **Caterpillars** can be troublesome, so spray them if ey appear.

Vitis coignetiae ♕
15m (50ft), widely available, dark green leaves are up to 30cm 12in) long (shown here with autumn colour)

WISTERIA

THE ORIENTAL ELEGANCE of wisterias ensures that they remain very popular. The flowers are very fragrant and borne in long clusters in spring and are followed by green, bean-like pods. These woody, deciduous, twining climbers can be trained over a sturdy arch or pergola so you can enjoy the perfume as you walk beneath, or against a wall or verandah. Wisterias are long-lived and can grow very large if they are on rich soil. Prune plants twice a year to keep them within bounds and maximize flowering. A low-maintenance option is to scramble wisteria through a large tree where it will need no pruning.

Hardiness Fully frost-hardy ❄❄❄; buds may be damaged by late frost.

Cultivation Grow in moist but well-drained soil, in sun or semi-shade. **Tie in** shoots (*see p.380*) to form a permanent framework. Keep the main stems horizontal. If necessary trim sideshoots in late summer to 4–6 leaves, or about 15cm (6in), from the main branches. Shorten again in winter, to 2–3 buds.

Wisteria floribunda 'Alba'
↕9m (28ft) or more, flower clusters up to 60cm (24in) long open from base to tip, followed by velvety, green pods

Wisteria floribunda 'Multijuga' ♕
↕9m (28ft) or more, flower clusters up to 30cm (12in) long open from base to tip, followed by velvety, green pods

Wisteria brachybotrys 'Shiro-kapitan'
↕9m (28ft) or more, foliage is softly hairy, flowers clusters to 15cm (6in) long, occasionally produces double flowers

Flowering Plants

using flowering plants

Flowering plants are the mainstay of the garden, providing the "understorey" of planting in gardens and a varied complement to more permanent trees and shrubs. This chapter covers the huge range of non-woody, or herbaceous, plants, apart from grasses (*see pp.340–355*) and ferns (*see pp.356–365*). Herbaceous perennials, annuals, biennials, and bulbs – including alpines, some succulents, garden orchids, and herbs – provide a great deal of colour in the garden.

A plant for every place

There is a huge variety of flowering plants and you can find some to furnish any part of the garden. Before selecting plants, think about your soil and conditions in different parts of the garden – whether the soil is dry or moist, alkaline or acid, and how much sun or shade each area receives. It is easier to grow plants that are suited to the particular spot or container in your garden than to try to alter the conditions to suit the plants.

Most flowering plants will tolerate a fairly wide range of soil conditions, but some have specific requirements that, if not met, will result in poor growth. For instance, rhododendrons require an acid soil (one that is lime-free), otherwise the leaves will turn yellow and the plant will eventually die.

The amount of sun and shade in different parts of your garden will determine which plants you can grow where. Shade may be cast by existing buildings, or by trees and shrubs that are already established. Most perennials and annuals need full sun to flower well, whereas foliage plants such as hostas and lungworts (*Pulmonaria*) and many bulbs tolerate shady conditions.

How wet or dry your soil is will also influence the plants that can be grown. You can fill shady areas with moist soil by a pond or stream with moisture-loving plants like primulas, whereas plants such as lavender need dry soil in an open, sunny position.

Spring is the peak for most flowering plants, but quite a few provide welcome colour in summer, autumn and winter. With careful choices you can have something in flower for twelve months of the year.

Plants in a shady site Many people regard shady sites as problem areas, but there is a wide choice of flowering plants available that can be grown in shady sites to create a charmingly natural planting effect. Here, the bold foliage of *Hosta sieboldiana* contrasts well with the narrower leaves and white flowers of *Primula pulverulenta* growing under trees by a pool. These plants both thrive in the moist soil beside water.

Designing a planting scheme

The best way to plan a planting scheme is to decide on the plants you would like to grow and then choose cultivars in colours you wish to predominate. Colour is always important (*see right*), but consider also the texture and the shapes of leaves and stems. You can evoke different moods with the types of plants that you choose. For example, lots of bright colours and small leaves could create a cottage-garden effect whereas large-leaved plants and pale shades look more contemporary.

Find out the mature height and spread of each plant before planting it. To determine the distance you should leave between any two plants, add the spreads of both plants and divide by two. Generally taller plants are best at the back of the garden and shorter ones at the front, but placing some taller ones near the middle or front gives an undulating effect and can prevent the planting scheme from looking too flat. They will also partly obscure other plants, creating an element of mystery.

Don't forget to mix in some early-spring bulbs and autumn-flowering plants such as asters and rudbeckias to prolong the flowering display.

Architectural plants Architectural plants with strong outlines are ideal as specimen plants or massed for bold effects. Here a modern, formal water cascade mirrors the clean shapes of the leaves and flowers of *Zantedeschia aethiopica*.

Planting in groups For the greatest impact, particularly in borders, plant in groups of three, five, or seven. This creates bold drifts of colour that are much more effective than the piecemeal effect of combining single plants of each variety.

Form and texture Selecting the right planting combinations can create wonderful contrasts in colour, form, and texture. Here the upright, sword-like foliage and orange flowers of montbretia (*Crocosmia*) stand above and contrast well with the rounded, softer foliage and lime-yellow flowers of *Alchemilla mollis*. Planting combinations like this can often happen by happy accident.

Painting with plants

The subject of colour in the garden is a very personal one and you should not be dogmatic about it. Experiment with different colour combinations between adjacent plants and in a garden as a whole and don't be afraid to move plants if the colours do not work together. You could create very harmonious effects by using tones of the same or similar colours, or make exciting contrasts with different hues, but aim for an overall balance.

Reds, yellows, and oranges are vibrant, hot colours that liven up the garden; for a cool, reflective mood choose shades of white, blue, and purple. The apparent size of a garden can be affected by colour. Hot hues draw the eye so distances appear shorter. Cool shades seem to recede into the distance, making a garden look larger.

Light, the season, and time of day alter the effect of colour. Often white and pastel shades look lost among bright colours and appear washed out in intense sunlight, but become almost luminous in evening twilight.

Subtle hues The complementary shades of *Eryngium bourgatii* and stachys in tones of blue and lilac bring a cooling and restful atmosphere to the border. The spiky foliage of the eryngium contrasts well with the softer foliage of the stachys.

Clashing contrast For a lively planting, grow large swathes of hot-coloured plants. Here red salvias shout out above a contrasting clump of *Heliotropium*.

Flowers with fragrance

Scent gives many flowering plants an added dimension. Flower scents vary from deliciously fresh sweet peas (*Lathyrus odorata*) to the musky aroma of phlox. Some plants have scented leaves; try artemisias, mint, and some pelargoniums. The perfume of many flowers is stronger in the cool of the evening and can be more intense in a corner or an enclosed area; place a seat there to catch the full fragrance or plant below a window so that the balmy air can float indoors.

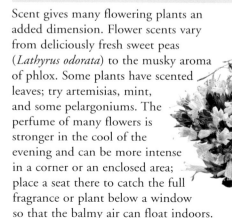

Added attraction The scent of many plants attracts butterflies (here on marjoram flowers), bees, and other insects to the flowers and to your garden. Many of them help to pollinate the plants. Other scented plants that attract insects include red valerian (*Centranthus ruber*), heliotropes, *Iris graminea*, evening primrose (*Oenothera biennis*), stocks (*Matthiola*), and tobacco plant (*Nicotiana*).

perennials

What is an herbaceous perennial?

An herbaceous perennial, commonly called a perennial, is a non-woody plant that grows and flowers over several years. Some perennials are evergreen, but in most, the top-growth dies down in winter while the roots remain alive. In spring, new growth starts up again from the base, or crown. The majority of perennials are long-lived plants that will thrive for years, but some are short-lived, lasting only three or four years. These short-lived plants often tend to seed themselves quite freely around the garden, so there is often no need to buy replacements for plants that are growing older.

Perennials demonstrate an immense variety of sizes, shapes, colours, scents, textures, and habits and are among the most versatile of garden plants. They range from tall plants, like *Cephalaria gigantea*, which reach up to 2m (6ft) in one season to small plants, for example some hardy geraniums, which are no more than 15cm (6in) tall and make good ground-cover plants.

Perennials encompass not only traditional garden plants, but also alpines and rock-garden plants, water-garden plants, and succulents.

Large perennial Some perennials, like these lupins, make a tremendous amount of growth in a season, forming large architectural plants and bringing a touch of height and drama to the garden. Large-flowered cultivars can be top-heavy, so will need staking to prevent them from flopping over or their brittle stems being broken in the wind.

Tiny perennial Some perennials, such as this *Pulsatilla halleri*, are very small. They are best grown in containers where they can be fully enjoyed without being swamped by larger plants.

Choosing perennials for the garden

Since they are so versatile, you should be able to find a perennial for any purpose or site you require, with an appropriate height and spread for the amount of space you have available.

You can create pleasing planting schemes by using plants with different growth habits. A spreading perennial contrasts well with one of strong, upright growth, while mound-forming plants lend a softer, gentler feel to the garden. Dense clumps of bright colour combine well with airy flower sprays of plants such as gypsophila. There are carpeting perennials that can be used as ground cover beneath other perennials or under shrubs such as roses.

Most perennials are rightly valued for their flowers: these vary as much as the habits and provide much of the seasonal colour in the garden, from the elegant blooms of lilies and blowsy poppies to the daintiness of pinks (*Dianthus*). Choose flowers that fit in with your preferred planting style. In general, flowers of species are more delicate in appearance, whereas cultivars are larger and more showy.

Some perennials are chosen mainly for their foliage. It usually lasts longer than the flowers, so consider the potential of leaf shape, size, and texture in your planting scheme, since it will extend the period of interest. This is especially important in a small garden.

Try cultivars with variegated leaves, and look for contrasts of glossy or matt and hairy or waxy textures. Use small-leaved plants with those that have large or strongly shaped leaves, or try strappy iris leaves with the star-shaped leaves of astrantias. Bear in mind that some perennials have foliage in hues other than green, such as heucheras.

Handsome foliage Here hostas form a bold combination of foliage, the variegated forms highlighted by the plain greens. Hostas have attractive flowers held above the foliage in summer.

Trailing habit Use trailing perennials, such as this *Aurinia saxatilis*, to add an air of informality, and to soften the hard edges of raised beds, low walls, or steps.

In garden beds

The way herbaceous perennials are used in garden beds has changed over time as well as with fashions in gardening. Traditionally, they were grown on their own in long, formal gardens, each backed by a hedge or fence. This worked well if you had a large garden with plenty of room to grow perennials, trees, and shrubs in separate gardens. Now, with gardens getting smaller, there is not often the space to grow plants separately in this way and we tend to create mixed gardens, incorporating the perennials with trees, shrubs, and perhaps some climbers and annuals, too.

Formal herbaceous borders usually have straight edges and the planting is graded, with lower plants at the front and taller ones at the back. In mixed gardens, a more informal approach to planting works well. In this situation, perennials are often used to fill the gaps between the shrubs while they are still young, and the gradation of plant height is less strictly followed.

Island beds are a modern way of growing perennials. They are plots surrounded by lawn, paving, or gravel, so they can be viewed from all sides. They are usually planted with the taller plants in the middle, tapering to shorter ones at the edges of the bed. Plants tend to grow better in island beds because they are in a more open situation. Include a couple of striking specimen plants, such as cannas or yuccas, to give the bed a focal point.

Herbaceous border This traditional herbaceous border contains euphorbias, daylilies (*Hemerocallis*), phloxes, and lilies and is designed to be at its glorious flowering peak in midsummer. All these plants are easily grown and are planted in bold groups of three to five plants. Some taller plants are grown at the front of the border to add a little variation in pace.

Cottage planting This style of planting is relaxed and informal, and features annuals and perennials that are allowed to seed themselves freely. This bed includes traditional cottage-garden plants such as aquilegias, euphorbias, fennel (*Foeniculum*), irises, and scabious. There is little need to worry about the relative heights and spreads of plants since spontaneity is all part of the charm.

Seasonal interest

While we rely on perennials to fill the garden with colour throughout summer, they can also provide a lot of interest even when not in flower in spring, autumn, and even in winter.

Fresh foliage emerging from barren soil and unfurling after winter is a welcome sight and a promise of things to come. At the other end of summer, many perennials have interesting seedheads and some have berries. Don't be in a hurry to cut down the old growth in autumn – birds will appreciate the seeds and the old stems can look very attractive, especially when covered with frost. Beneficial insects may also make a home among the old stems in winter.

Summer beauty Anise hyssop (*Agastache foeniculum*) is upright and aniseed-scented with purple flowers from midsummer.

Mellow autumn In autumn, the seedheads, held on tall stems, turn a parchment brown, and give some structure to the border.

Winter frost In the depths of winter, shimmering frost encrusts the seedheads, altering their appearance once again.

Naturalistic plantings

Some perennials, especially those that are species rather than cultivars, look very good in naturalistic settings, appearing to grow as they would in the wild. You might create a woodland feel under some trees, or a meadow in grass, or a naturalistic planting in a border. Such plantings require a lot of planning to achieve the desired effect. Make beds in informal, irregular shapes to blend in with the surroundings.

Plant drifts that intermingle or create substantial clumps of some plants to imitate how plants grow naturally. As the planting style is fairly loose, you can add new plants from time to time, but avoid creating a fussy effect with a lot of different, single plants.

Woodland display Here the huge leaves of *Gunnera manicata* form a dramatic backdrop for the dark, purple-black foliage and deep scarlet flowers of *Lobelia* 'Queen Victoria'.

annuals and biennials

What are annuals and biennials?

Annuals are plants that complete their life cycle of germination, flowering, seed production, and death within one year. Hardy annuals can withstand frost. Those that are damaged or killed by frost and low temperatures are known as half-hardy annuals and are raised after frosts have ended in spring or under glass, then planted out when all danger of frost has passed.

Biennials need two growing seasons to complete their life cycle. In the first, they produce leafy growth, then flower in the following year. Tender perennials, which need frost protection in winter, are often treated as annuals in cooler climates to avoid overwintering them.

As annuals and biennials grow and flower in one season, they are perfect for providing colour very quickly and cheaply. They also offer a huge range of flower forms and growth habits. As fillers among young shrubs or creating a colourful display in an empty garden, they are unrivalled. Hardy annuals are the easiest of all because they can be sown outdoors where they are to flower.

Annual poppies (*Papaver*) fill the garden with colour all summer long and are available in delightful shades of scarlet, orange, pink, and white. Sow seeds in shallow drills or just scatter them in a patch and cover them lightly. Thin the seedlings when they are 2.5cm (1in) tall. If you leave the seedheads on, they will seed themselves over the garden.

Biennial foxgloves (*Digitalis*) require two seasons to reach flowering size. The long spikes of flowers come in a wide variety of colours and are ideal for giving a cottage-garden feel to a border.

Planning annual beds

Informal bedding An informal bedding scheme is a great addition to a garden in the right setting. Either raise your own plants or buy young plants from the garden centre. This bold, flowing scheme is made up of *Celosia* 'New Look' among petunias. To keep the display at its peak and to encourage more new blooms, remove the fading flowers regularly so that the plants do not set seed.

A garden bed devoted to annuals and biennials, whether informal or formal, is usually a mass of flower, and since it lasts for only one season, you can experiment with confidence. For an informal bed, you could choose a limited palette of colours, such as reds and oranges, or pinks, purples, and blues, and sow in broad drifts that intermingle. Alternatively, mix up the seed before you sow it to obtain a completely random riot of colour.

Formal bedding schemes tend to consist of half-hardy annuals and biennials planted in symmetrical or stylized patterns. These are most often seen in public parks, but on a smaller scale they can look very striking in your own garden. Think about what design you want to achieve before getting the seed or the plants. Select one or two colours and a simple pattern, such as a crescent, an undulating curve, or a chequerboard, and either plot it out on some graph paper or trace it out on the soil with some sand. Formal bedding schemes do need more maintenance to keep them neat and tidy and looking good, but the rewards are worthwhile.

Whatever sort of annual bed or border you would like, plan it carefully before sowing so that the flowering periods of the different plants overlap and provide interest over a long season. Half-hardy annuals past their peak can be replaced with home-grown or bought plants to create different effects.

Although foliage is not the most prominent feature of annuals, don't forget to mix leaf shapes and textures.

Using annuals and biennials around the garden

Annuals are excellent in mixed gardens among perennials, trees, and shrubs. Because they have few special soil needs and such a brief life span, they will not interfere with the growth of surrounding plants.

Take advantage of trailing annuals such as nasturtiums, and biennials such as the spring-flowering wallflowers (*Erysimum*), to provide speedy ground cover and add variety to the established garden. You could also try leaving space in a mixed or herbaceous border and plant a different selection of annual and biennials each year.

If you have just moved into a new house with a sparsely planted garden, growing a selection of annuals is a cheap way of filling the garden with colour, while you plan the more permanent features and planting. New trees, shrubs, and perennials will take several seasons to fill out and fill the borders, so use annuals and biennials in-between them to provide temporary colour and to keep the weeds down.

Informal planting With informal planting schemes you are aiming to create a mixture of plants growing happily together in an apparently naturalistic fashion. Take care in positioning your informal area – it might look odd alongside a formal water feature, for example. The mixture of old-fashioned annuals and biennials here includes sunflowers, foxgloves, and poppies.

Annual edging These pot marigolds (*Calendula officinalis*) are low enough to be used as an edging around a vegetable plot. The bright flowers attract beneficial insects to the garden and these help with pollination and controlling pests.

Annuals for cutting

Almost all annual flowers can be cut and arranged indoors. If you have a vegetable garden or an out-of-the-way plot, sow an area with annuals so that you can cut them without spoiling the display in the main garden. Keep them in water in a cool place and they will last for days, or even weeks. Some, such as statice (*Limonium*) and helichrysum, can be cut and hung up in an airy spot for use in dried arrangements.

Cutting flowers *Zinnia elegans* is a flamboyant flower borne on a tall stem, so is ideal for cutting. Cut the flowers just as they are opening so that they last longer once put in water. Trim off any leaves below the water line.

Annuals and biennials in containers

With their short growing season, annuals and biennials, and tender perennials, are ideal for temporary containers, either on their own or mixed with other plants. The planted containers can form a focal point, be moved around so that the plants are seen to their best advantage, and are perfect for filling gaps in a border.

Any container is suitable, from a pot or a tub to a windowbox or a hanging basket, providing that it has drainage holes in the base. Assess how sunny the site is going to be in order to decide which plants to grow. Then select a container that looks good in the site, and that complements the plants you want to grow. Containers in hot, sunny places or exposed windy sites will dry out quickly. They need to be watered every day in hot weather, so take this into account when choosing a position. If necessary, use cultivars with compact growth so that they are not blown about in windy conditions.

Hanging baskets and windowboxes are perfect for trailing plants. Good choices are pelargoniums (upright and trailing), fuchsias, and busy lizzies (*Impatiens*). Others to try include petunias, marigolds (*Tagetes*), lobelia, and alyssum. Heliotropes mixed with showier plants, especially near the house, will give off a delightful scent.

Potful of charm This pot is overflowing with *Viola tricolor*. This delightful annual will flower for many weeks over summer and may be kept over winter if you have frost-free conditions.

Hanging basket A riot of different shades of pink, and both bold and delicate flowers, this hanging basket includes diascias, lobelia, pelargoniums, phloxes, and verbenas.

bulbs

What are bulbous plants?

A bulbous plant is a perennial that has a food storage organ – a swollen part of the stem or root – that enables the plant to remain dormant until conditions are favourable for growth. The term bulbous plants is commonly used to describe true bulbs, corms, tubers, and rhizomes – all different types of food-storage organs.

A true bulb consists of tightly packed modified leaves on a reduced stem; you can see the "leaves" when you slice open an onion. Corms are enlarged underground stems; tubers are formed from swollen roots or underground stems.

Other bulbous plants store food in creeping, underground stems, called rhizomes; these may be thick and stubby, as in bearded irises, or long and thin, as with lily-of-the-valley (*Convallaria*).

Stem (here of tulip) grows from bud in centre of bulb

Simple bulb (daffodil)

Scaly bulb (lily)

True bulb There are two types of true bulb: a simple bulb has tightly packed leaves and a papery skin, or tunic; a scaly bulb has loosely packed leaves, or scales, and dries out more quickly.

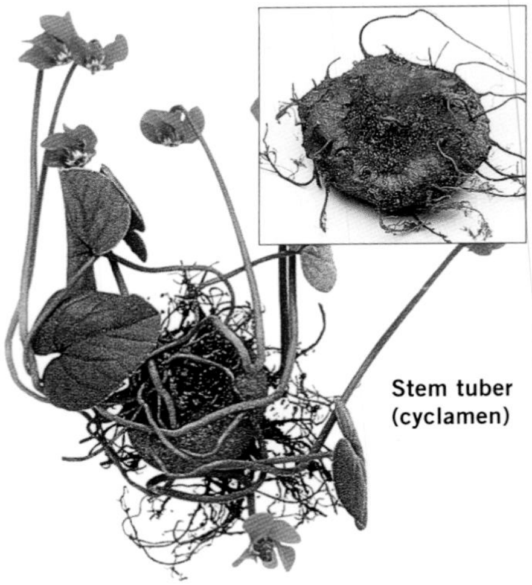

Stem tuber (cyclamen)

Tuber Shoots emerge from buds at the top of the tuber; stem tubers have more buds than root tubers. Root tubers are replaced by fresh ones each year, but stem tubers get bigger each season.

Corm (colchicum)

Corms and cormlets (gladiolus)

Corm One or two buds arise on the corm surface. Usually, a new corm forms at the base of the stem each year. Small cormlets may also develop around the old corm and can be removed to grow on.

Where to grow bulbs

Summer highlights Many summer-flowering bulbs, including lilies and montbretias (*Crocosmia*), are tall plants with striking flowers that are ideal for use in mixed borders with herbaceous perennials. This border in high summer has a touch of drama provided by the bold, showy flowerheads of alliums. They contrast well with the more delicate blooms of columbines (*Aquilegia*) and catmint (*Nepeta*).

Bulbous plants are generally not too fussy about soil conditions, as long as they have well-drained soil, and many are very hardy. You can grow bulbs in any aspect except deep shade. Many bulbs prefer hot, sunny sites, but those from woodland habitats thrive in light, dappled shade; the hardy cyclamens tolerate even dry shade. Some bulbs are delicate enough for the rock garden.

Bulbs look good if planted in large groups. For maximum impact, plant up a formal bed with spring bulbs in different colours. Once they die down, lift and store them in a cool, dark place to make way for summer bedding.

For a more informal display, use the bulbs among other perennials, so that the dying foliage will be hidden by the perennials. Don't think of bulbs as plants only for spring; choose bulbs with different flowering periods and you can have a beautiful display from the earliest snowdrops (*Galanthus*) to richly coloured cyclamens in winter.

Formal bedding Plant spring bulbs, like these tulips, in large blocks to bring a splash of colour to the garden. They also look good with wallflowers (*Erysimum*) and forget-me-nots (*Myosotis*).

Naturalizing bulbs in the garden

If left undisturbed in the ground in a site that suits them, many bulbs will naturally increase to form large clumps, and then drifts, of colour. Making use of this natural method of reproduction is a simple way to bring seasonal colour to new areas of the garden. Once they are planted, the bulbs will come up year after year with very little attention.

The easiest way to naturalize bulbs is to grow them in grass. After flowering, the grass needs to be left uncut for about eight weeks to allow the foliage to die down. In this way, the bulbs draw energy from the foliage and build up food reserves, and flower buds, for the following year. Think first about how often you wish to mow an area of lawn.

Sea of daffodils Here, bright yellow daffodils flower beneath an ornamental cherry tree (*Prunus* × *yedoensis*) in full blossom to create a pretty spring garden. The showy blooms of bulb cultivars look spectacular under specimen trees in the garden, while the more delicate flowers of species bulbs are a more appropriate choice in native woodland, small copses, or in containers.

Early-flowering bulbs, like snowdrops, are suitable for a lawn that will be cut from spring. Later-flowering bulbs such as some daffodils may suit an area that can be left unmown for longer, perhaps around the edge of a lawn or on a grassy bank. Some bulbs, such as the snake's head fritillary (*Fritillaria meleagris*), thrive when planted in a wildflower meadow that is not cut until late summer or early autumn.

Choose vigorous bulbs since they will have to put up with competition from the grass roots. The best way to achieve a natural effect is to scatter the bulbs and plant them where they fall. As long as the bulbs are at least 20cm (4in) apart, they should flower well.

Spring- and autumn-flowering bulbs also thrive under deciduous trees where they can flower either before or after the leaf canopy is at its most dense. Plant them under individual specimen trees in the garden, or in loose drifts in a woodland setting.

In woodland Some bulbs look most at home in a natural woodland setting; this effect could be achieved in a small area with just a few trees and shrubs. Carpet the ground with low-growing bulbs, punctuated with larger ones, like this giant lily (*Cardiocrinum*) which likes moist shade.

Using bulbs in containers

Most bulbs grow well in windowboxes and other containers because they enjoy the free drainage. Aim to choose a container that suits the size of the bulbs. A lily, for example, will need a deep pot to balance its height when fully grown, while small bulbs such as crocuses look appealing grown in wide, shallow bowls or pans.

Planting one species of bulb to each container provides dense clumps of flower; you can place containers of different bulbs together as they come into flower. If you wish to plant a mixture of bulbs in one container, plant them in layers with larger bulbs at the bottom and smaller ones at the top for a succession of bloom. Spring bulbs are likely to be among the earliest flowers in the garden, so place them where you can see them easily, perhaps by the front door, outside a window, or to form a focal point. Have pots of fragrant bulbs such as hyacinths close to the house where the scent can be easily enjoyed.

Once the flowers are over, move the pots to a less prominent area, or remove the bulbs and temporarily plant them in a corner of a bed, while the foliage dies down. This frees up the pots to use for other plants. When the foliage is dead, lift the bulbs to store them or plant them in a border.

Classic beauty Some bulbs have elegant blooms and foliage that work well in a traditional or formal style. This terracotta urn, backed by a hornbeam (*Carpinus*) hedge, is simply planted with tulips.

Forcing bulbs

The best way to bring colour and fragrance into the home in the dark days of winter is to force bulbs in pots (*see also p.288*). Growing them in relatively warm conditions indoors makes them flower earlier than usual. Hippeastrums, with their giant, exotic blooms, scented hyacinths, and daffodils are all suitable for forcing.

Plant the bulbs in autumn in a soilless potting mix. Keep them watered until just moist in a cool, dark place for a few weeks until a good root system has formed. Check the bulbs regularly and bring them into the light when they have made about 2.5cm (1in) of growth.

ACAENA

New Zealand Burr

THESE LOW, CREEPING herbaceous perennials form dense mats of evergreen foliage by virtue of their rooting stems. This makes for good ground cover in a rock garden or at the front of a flower garden, but plants can be invasive. In summer, the plant is covered with round flowerheads, which later develop into the characteristic, spiny, red burrs for which these plants are known. New Zealand Burrs are valued for their colourful grey-blue leaves. Other plants that combine well with them include erect perennials such as irises (*see pp.264–267*) and flax (*Phormium, see p.95*).

Hardiness Fully frost-hardy ❄❄❄.

Cultivation Grow in reasonably fertile soil in full sun or part shade. If necessary, curb a spreading plant by pulling out unwanted rooted stems. **Sow** seed (*see pp.391–392*) in containers in a cold frame in autumn. **Make** new plants by digging up rooted stems and transplanting them to a new position, in autumn or early spring.

Acaena novae-zelandiae
↕10–15cm (4–6in) ↔ 1m (3ft), forms a tight mat of interesting foliage, while the creeping stems are useful for holding soil together

ACANTHUS

Bear's Breeches

WITH THEIR TALL SPIKES of unusual flowers above the striking spiny, dark green foliage, acanthus make valuable architectural plants for the herbaceous or mixed border. The individual tubular flowers, each up to 5cm (2in) long, come in combinations of white, pink, and purple, and are borne on spikes up to 1.2m (4ft) tall. These are produced from late spring to midsummer, and can be cut and dried for indoor display. Leave a few spikes on the plant over winter, however, since they look good when covered in frost. Acanthus are vigorous herbaceous perennials and associate well with other perennials such as hardy geraniums (*see pp.250–251*) and phloxes (*see p.306*).

Hardiness Fully frost-hardy ❄❄❄ to very frost-tender ❀.

Cultivation Grow in any reasonably fertile soil in sun or partial shade, although they do best in deep, fertile, well-drained loam. **Remove** dead foliage and old flower spikes in late winter or early spring. **Sow** seed in pots in a cold frame (*see pp.391–392*) in spring, or divide clumps in spring or autumn (*see p.395*). **Take** root cuttings in winter (*see p.394*).

Acanthus hungaricus ↕60–120cm (2–4ft), deep purple flowers in summer

Acanthus mollis ↕1.5m (5ft), can be used to rapidly fill even a dark spot in a garden, while the late spring to summer flowers will provide added interest

Acanthus spinosus 🏆 ↕1.5m (5ft), deeply divided foliage adds interest to a mixed garden bed, summer flowers

ACHILLEA

arrow

'HE FERNY, GREY-GREEN FOLIAGE and flat-topped owerheads of yarrows are mainstays of the cottage arden or herbaceous border. Low-growing types are leal for rock gardens. Herbaceous perennials, yarrows uickly form spreading, drought-resistant clumps that re suited to most soil types, including gravelly soils. 'heir summer flowerheads, in a wide range of olours, attract bees, butterflies, and other beneficial isects, making them a good choice for wildflower ardens. The flowerheads can be dried for indoor ecoration. Grow with other herbaceous perennials ıch as lythrums (*see p.283*), phloxes (*see p.306*), and dalceas (*see p.325*). Contact with the foliage may ggravate some skin allergies.

ardiness Fully frost-hardy ✲✲✲.

ultivation Grow in moist, but well-drained soil in an open site full sun, although most yarrows tolerate a wide range of soils ıd conditions. **Remove** faded flowers to encourage more to follow. **ow** seed outdoors (*see pp.391–393*) in situ, or divide clumps every -3 years in spring (*see p.395*) to increase stock and maintain vigour. humid, overcrowded conditions, powdery mildew may spoil foliage.

***Achillea filipendulina* 'Gold Plate'** ♀
↕90cm (3ft) ↔ 45cm (18in), this classic variety, with golden yellow flowerheads throughout summer, is also one of the tallest

chillea 'Moonshine' ♀
→ 60cm (24in), once the bright yellow flowers start to open in ımmer, 'Moonshine' puts on a fine display well into autumn

***Achillea* 'Fanal'**
↕75cm (30in) ↔ 60cm (24in), the bold crimson flowerheads are ideal cutting material; a good contrast to grey or silvery plants

Aconitum

Aconite, Monkshood

MONKSHOODS ARE NAMED for their hooded flowers, which come in shades of lilac, blue, and pale yellow. These are arranged on tall spires held well above the clumps of divided green foliage. The flowers, which appear from early summer to autumn depending on variety, attract bees and butterflies into the garden. Monkshoods are spreading herbaceous perennials, at their best in reasonably moist beds and borders where they associate well with other perennials such as achilleas (*see p.167*), phloxes (*see p.306*), and delphiniums (*see p.224*). The flowers are good for cutting, but take care when handling this plant because all parts are toxic if eaten and contact with the foliage may aggravate some skin allergies.

Hardiness Fully frost-hardy ❄❄❄.

Cultivation Monkshoods prefer cool, moist, fertile soil in partial shade, but most soils are tolerated, as is sun if the site is damp enough. **Stake** taller monkshoods to prevent them keeling over. **Cut down** the previous year's growth in late winter or early spring. **Sow** seed (*see pp.391–392*) in pots in a cold frame in spring. Divide clumps every three years in autumn or late winter to maintain vigour (*see p.395*).

Aconitum carmichaelii 'Arendsii'
↕to 90cm (3ft) ↔ 30cm (12in), flowers in early and mid-autumn

Aconitum 'Ivorine'
↕90cm (36in) ↔ 45cm (18in), a choice variety for a cool, moist site, flowers in early summer

Aconitum nepallus
↕1m (3ft) ↔ 1m (3ft), late summer flowers, grown best in dappled shade with plenty of moisture

Aconitum carmichaelii
↕1m (3ft) ↔ 1m (3ft), late summer into autumn

Actaea

Baneberry, Bugbane

THIS GROUP OF PLANTS, which now includes those formerly known as *Cimicifugas*, comprises a range of clump-forming perennials for woodland gardens, shady borders, or streamsides. All have attractive foliage and flowers, and in some cases fruits. Plumes or spires of small, white or pink-tinged flowers appear above the foliage from mid-spring to late summer and autumn. Varieties such as *Actaea rubra* also develop clusters of shiny red or black berries, which are highly poisonous. The divided leaves are usually green. Bugbanes combine well with other perennials such as sidalceas (*see p.325*), goldenrods (*Solidago, see p.327*), and rudbeckias (*see p.317*).

Hardiness Fully frost-hardy ❄❄❄.

Cultivation Grow in moist, fertile soil, enriched with well-rotted organic matter, in partial shade. Keep well watered in dry spells. **Sow** seed in containers in a cold frame in autumn (*see pp.391–393*); divide plants in spring (*see p.395*).

Actaea rubra 🏆
↕45cm (18in) ↔ 30cm (12in), the white flowers, as well as the red berries that follow, will enliven areas of light shade in woodland

Actaea simplex (syn. *Cimicifuga simplex*)
↕1–1.2m (3–4ft) ↔ 60cm (24in), feathery spires of flowers appear in late summer and autumn

Aeonium

These are evergreen succulents which have oval, lance- or spade-shaped leaves. These are thick and fleshy and are mid-green, although purple and almost black forms are available. They are arranged in a tight rosette. In some species the rosettes are virtually stemless, sitting on the soil surface. In others they are held at the top of many branched stems. These rosettes can be flat, cup-shaped or open. The flowers are small, yellow stars arranged in showy cones above the foliage in spring. They are adapted to extremely dry conditions and all do very well when grown in containers.

Hardiness Frost-tender ❄ to very frost-tender ❅.

Cultivation Grow in full sun or in partial shade in the hottest districts. The soil or potting mix must be free-draining. **Pruning** is generally unnecessary. **Sow** seed in summer (*see p.391*). **Take** stem cuttings in late summer for the shrub-like forms and leaf cuttings from the others (*see p.394*).

Aeonium 'Zwartkop'
↕60cm (2ft) ↔ 1m (3ft), has remarkable rosettes of purple-black foliage for adding contrast to a garden bed of waterwise plants

Aethionema

Stone Cress

Clusters of dainty flowers, in cheerful shades of red, pink, creamy-white, and pure white, are the main reason for growing these annuals and evergreen or semi-evergreen, woody-based perennials. The flowers are produced on short stems from spring to early summer. The leaves are small, usually stalkless, and rather fleshy. They tend to be short-lived plants and it is best to increase them from cuttings every two or three years to make sure they perform well. As petite plants, they are obvious candidates for the front of an herbaceous border or as part of a rock garden. Try growing them with dicentras (*see p.228*), *Euphorbia polychroma* (*see p.242*), and doronicums (*see p.231*).

Hardiness Fully frost-hardy ❄❄❄ (given good drainage).

Cultivation These plants grow best in fertile, well-drained, alkaline (limy) soil in full sun, but they also tolerate poor, acid (lime-free) soils. **Sow** seed (*see pp.391–393*) in containers in a cold frame in spring; sow seed of annuals in autumn directly where they are to grow. **Take** softwood cuttings (*see p.394*) in late spring or early summer.

Aethionema grandiflorum 🏆
↕20–30cm (8–12in), perennial, flowers in late spring and early summer

Agapanthus

African Blue Lily

Vigorous and clump-forming, these large perennials bear round or pendent heads of bell-shaped flowers in deep shades of blue and violet-blue, or in white, from midsummer to early autumn. They generally have handsome, long, strappy leaves. A number of cultivars are deciduous, while some species are evergreen. The blooms make excellent cut-flower displays. These late-flowering perennials also look particularly good in containers. Remove seedheads to prevent self-sowing.

Hardiness Fully frost-hardy ❄❄❄ to frost-tender ❄.

Cultivation Agapanthus prefer fertile, well-drained soil, in full sun, but will grow on poor soils in dry conditions. **Container-grown** plants are best in quality potting mix. Water them sparingly during summer; and even less in winter. During summer, feed the plants with a balanced liquid fertilizer until flowering commences. **Sow** seed (*see pp.391–393*) when they are ripe or in spring. Keep the seedlings in a frost-free cold frame for their first winter. Most seedlings do not come true to type. **Divide** large clumps (*see below and p.395*) in spring.

DIVIDING A ROOTSTOCK
Use a clean, sharp knife to trim off damaged root tissue and old stems. Dust the cuts with fungicide to avoid rot.

Agapanthus campanulatus
↕60–120cm (24–48in) ↔ 45cm (18in), deciduous, grey-green leaves, flowers – sometimes white – in mid- and late summer ❄❄❄

Agapanthus 'Blue Giant'
1.2m (4ft) ↔ 60cm (24in), flowers in mid- to late summer ***

Agapanthus 'Bressingham White'
↕ 90cm (36in) ↔ 60cm (24in), flowers in mid- and late summer ***

Agastache

THESE PERENNIALS ARE GROWN for their long-lasting, loose spikes of small, tubular flowers, which are up to 30cm (12in) long and borne from midsummer until autumn. These are erect, bushy plants, with lance-shaped to oval, aromatic leaves. Suitable for herbaceous and mixed borders, agastaches associate well with perennials such as yarrows (*see p.167*) and phloxes (*see p.306*).

Hardiness Fully frost-hardy *** to frost-tender *.

Cultivation Grow these plants in fertile, well-drained soil in full sun. In warm areas, the less hardy species will survive winter conditions outside if they are planted in a sheltered site. **Sow** seed (*see pp.391–393*) in early spring. **Take** semi-ripe cuttings (*see p.394*) in late summer. **Powdery mildew** may be a problem on the leaves in dry summers; keep the soil thoroughly watered, but avoid splashing the foliage.

Agastache foeniculum (Anise Hyssop)
↕ 90–150cm (3–5ft) ↔ 30cm (12in), flowers from midsummer to early autumn **

Ageratum

Floss Flower

THESE DELIGHTFUL FLOWERING PLANTS are either annuals or biennials, although most that are grown are treated as annuals. They are small and tightly foliaged in pointed-oval leaves. The flowers cover the top of the plant from summer into autumn. These are small and fluffy and are most often blue, particularly in a pale mauve hue. However, it is possible to obtain a range of pastel colours, including white, pale pink, mauve and lavender-blue. They are useful for adding summer colour to a garden and are good as low edgers. They will also grow quite well in containers.

Hardiness Frost-tender ✻ to very frost-tender ❀.

Cultivation Grow in well-drained soil that is reasonably fertile and enriched with well-rotted organic matter. Full sun is best, although they tolerate light shade. **Deadheading** will promote a longer flowering period (*see p.390*). **Sow** seed year round in warm areas and in late spring in cooler districts. Sow directly into the garden and thin out seedlings to about 15cm (6in) apart. (*see p.393*).

Ageratum houstonianum
↕15–30cm (6–12in) ↔ 15–30cm (6–12in), has fluffy pastel blue flowers to bring cool colour to the summer garden

Ajuga

Carpet Bugle

CARPET BUGLES MAKE EXCELLENT GROUND COVER in shade or partial shade, particularly in moist ground. They have a dense, spreading habit and can carpet large areas quickly, yet are easy to pull up if they start to grow into other plants. A few are annuals but, for the most part, those grown in gardens are evergreen perennials. The leaves of some bugles have a metallic sheen, but for added colour, choose those that are tinted bronze or purple-red, or splashed with cream and pink. From late spring until early summer, the mats of foliage are studded with short spikes of usually blue or mauve flowers. Undemanding and easy to grow, carpet bugles are a good choice for the edge of a shady border or for growing under shrubs.

Hardiness Fully frost-hardy ✻✻✻.

Cultivation Grow in any moist but well-drained soil in partial shade or, for good leaf colour, some sun. *Ajuga reptans* and its cultivars tolerate poor soils and full shade. **Separate** rooted stems to make new plants, or take softwood cuttings in early summer (*see p.394*). In overcrowded, humid conditions, powdery mildew may spoil leaves. After flowering, remove old flower stems and excess growth to avoid it.

***Ajuga reptans* 'Multicolor'**
↕15cm (6in) ↔ 60–90cm (24–36in), evergreen, will tolerate full shade but needs sun to bring out the lovely colours in its leaves

***Ajuga reptans* 'Catlin's Giant'** 🏆
↕15cm (6in) ↔ 60–90cm (24–36in), the dark blue flowerheads are up to 20cm (8in) tall on this large-leaved evergreen

***Ajuga reptans* 'Atropurpurea'**
↕15cm (6in) ↔ 60–90cm (24–36in), the lustrous evergreen leaves look particularly effective with shade-loving Primroses (*Primula*)

Alcea

Hollyhock

An old-fashioned, cottage garden favourite, hollyhocks are short-lived perennials or biennials. The tall, showy spires of flowers, up to 2.5m (8ft) tall, come in a variety of shades including shell pink, apricot, lemon, cerise, white, and purplish-black. The flowers, especially if single, are attractive to butterflies and bees. At their most impressive when grown at the back of a garden or along a wall or fence, hollyhocks associate well with cottage garden favourites with soft colours and billowing outlines, such as rambling roses (*see pp.150–151*) and lilacs (*Syringa, see p.121*). Mingle the brightest types with delphiniums (*see p.224*).

Hardiness Fully frost-hardy ❄❄❄.

Cultivation Grow in reasonably fertile, well-drained soil in full sun. In exposed places, stems may require staking. **Treat** as annuals or biennials (sow one year to flower the next year) to limit the spread of hollyhock rust, the most common disease, which causes orange-brown pustules on the leaves. Rust-resistant varieties are available. **Sow** seed (*see pp.391–393*) of annuals at 13ºC (55ºF) in late winter or where it is to grow in spring. For biennials, sow in midsummer where plants are to flower and thin out or transplant small seedlings, as necessary, in autumn.

① *rosea* **Chater's Double Group** ↕2–2.5m (6–8ft) ↔ to 60cm (24in), vigorous, flowers in many bright or pale shades
② *rosea* **'Nigra'** ↕to 2m (6ft) ↔ to 60cm (24in)

Alchemilla

Lady's Mantle

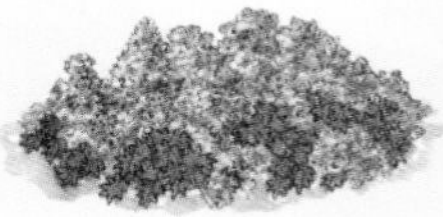

↕5–60cm (2–24in)
↔20–75cm (8–30in)

The most widely grown plant in this group of perennials, all with greyish-green leaves and frothy, luminous yellow flowers, is *Alchemilla mollis*. Clump-forming, it makes excellent ground cover. The flowers appear for long periods from early summer and are good for cutting, and for drying. Most other alchemillas, such as *A. erythropoda*, are smaller. Lady's Mantle self-seeds prolifically unless fading flowers are removed before they set seed. Grow it in beds and borders or along paths to soften hard lines. It associates well with shrub roses (*see pp.110–111*) and penstemons (*see p.304*), and contrasts beautifully with blue flowers.

Hardiness Fully frost-hardy ❄❄❄ to frost-hardy ❄❄.

Cultivation Grow in any reasonably fertile soil in sun or partial shade. **Deadhead** *A. mollis* and cut back foliage after flowering for fresh leaves. **Sow** seed (*see pp.391–393*) in pots in a cold frame in spring, or divide plants (*see p.395*) in early spring or autumn.

Alchemilla alpina (Alpine Lady's Mantle)
↕8–13cm (3–5in) ↔ to 50cm (20in), mat-forming, leaves with silvery undersides, flowers in summer, good for a rock garden ❄❄❄

CRYSTAL DROPS The downy leaves retain beads of sparkling dew and raindrops.

Alchemilla mollis 🏆
↕60cm (24in) ↔ 75cm (30in), velvety grey-green leaves and yellow-green flowers from early summer to early autumn ❄❄❄

Althaea

↕1.5m (5ft)
↔45cm (18in)

THESE WOODY-BASED PERENNIALS and annuals are similar to hollyhocks (*see Alcea, p.173*), but they have smaller flowers which, unlike hollyhocks, are on stalks. The blooms appear from midsummer until early autumn in shades of lilac, deep pink, or rose-pink, sometimes with darker eyes. Althaeas have dark green leaves with lobed or toothed edges and pale undersides. The stems are strong and wiry and rarely need supporting. These are pretty plants for a mixed or herbaceous border as well as a wildflower garden. Grow them with other summer-flowering perennials, like daylilies (*see Hemerocallis, p.258*) and loosestrife (*see Lysimachia, p.283*).

Hardiness Fully frost-hardy ❄❄❄.

Cultivation These plants tolerate a range of conditions, but do best in fertile, moist but well-drained soil. **Sow** seed of perennials in rows outdoors (*see pp.391–393*) in midsummer and transplant seedlings in early autumn; for annuals, sow seed in pots in late winter, or directly in the ground in mid-spring. **Rust**, orange-brown pustules, may afflict the leaves; pick them off and destroy them. *A. rosea* is less susceptible.

Althaea officinalis
↕1m (3ft) ↔45cm (18in), upright perennial with summer flowers

Amaranthus

↕30cm–1.5m (1–5ft)
↔30–75cm (12–30in)

THESE ERECT OR PROSTRATE, bushy annuals or short-lived perennials have red, purple, or green stems and large, shapely leaves – some in bright hues of purple, maroon, bronze, gold, and red. From summer until early autumn, they produce hanging clusters up to 60cm (24in) long of crimson-purple, red, maroon, or rose-pink flowers that look like woolly tassels. In autumn, coloured seedheads follow. They are commonly grown as annuals in summer bedding schemes and, for truly dramatic effects, try them next to plants with large leaves or flowers of strongly contrasting colours. Some can be grown in containers and hanging baskets.

Hardiness Frost-tender ❄.

Cultivation Grow them in moist, reasonably fertile, well-drained soil, in full sun. **Keep** well watered in dry spells during summer to prolong flowering. **Sow** seed (*see pp.391–393*) in mid-spring in containers or, in milder areas, directly in the garden where plants are to grow. Thin the seedlings to 60cm (24in) apart.

COLLECTING SEED
When the flowers begin to change colour, gently run your fingers down the tassels to dislodge the seed.

Amaranthus caudatus (Love-Lies-Bleeding, Tassel Flower)
↕1–1.5m (3–5ft) ↔45–75cm (18–30in), annual or perennial, leaves up to 15cm (6in), tolerates poor soil

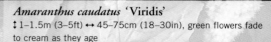

***Amaranthus caudatus* 'Viridis'**
↕1–1.5m (3–5ft) ↔45–75cm (18–30in), green flowers fade to cream as they age

< Amarygia parkeri

↕90cm (3ft)
↔30cm (12in)

The parents of this hybrid are *Amaryllis belladonna* (*see right*) and *Brunsvigia*. Opening on bare, stout stems before the leaves appear, its large, pink flowers make an eye-catching addition to the summer garden. The leaves, which are up to an impressive 45cm (18in) long and grow from the base of the plant, are semi-rect and strappy. In colder areas, the plant benefits rom the shelter at the foot of a warm wall, or in an erbaceous or mixed border. Grow it with other ulbous perennials, such as crinums (*see p.218*), and erennials such as achilleas (*see p.167*).

lardiness Frost-hardy ❄❄.

:ultivation Plant bulbs from early to late summer with the necks ıst above soil level, in full sun in sandy soil that has been enriched vith well-rotted organic matter. **Water** freely during summer and feed ıonthly with a well-balanced fertilizer. **Remove** offsets to replant (*see .395*) from congested plants just before they come into growth in ummer. The leaves are prone to scorch.

< *Amarygia parkeri*
90cm (3ft) ↔ 30cm (1ft), an unusual inter-generic hybrid with cented flowers in summer

Amaryllis belladonna

Belladonna Lilies, Naked Ladies

Stately, scented, and showy, the clusters of flowers of this bulbous perennial open on stout stems in the summer. It has strappy, fleshy leaves, up to 40cm (16in) long, which are produced after the flowers open. It looks attractive partnered with other summer-flowering plants, such as coneflowers (*see Rudbeckia, p.317*). These plants are sometimes referred to as "Naked Ladies" as the summer flowers are produced straight from bare ground while the bulbs have no foliage.

Hardiness Frost-hardy ❄❄.

Cultivation Plant the bulbs just below soil level when they are dormant, in late summer. **Remove** offsets (*see p.395*) in late spring and plant in their permanent position straight away.

Amaryllis belladonna 'Hathor'
↕90cm (3ft) ↔ 30cm (1ft), this white flowered form flowers in summer

Amaryllis belladonna
↕60cm (24in) ↔ 10cm (4in), each flower is up to 10cm across

Anacyclus

↕↔ 30cm (12in)

APPEALING, DAISY FLOWERS and feathery foliage are the attractions of these creeping, low-growing annuals and herbaceous perennials. The flowers, which are usually white with yellow centres, are borne on short stems in summer, held just above a low mound of foliage; the leaves are finely cut and attractive in their own right. Anacyclus hate cold, wet conditions, and are most suited to growing in a rock garden, raised bed, or alpine trough; a top-dressing of grit over the soil will help keep their stems dry, and also enhances their sun-loving, Mediterranean look.

Hardiness Frost-hardy ❄❄, but can withstand to –5°C (23°F) if protected from winter wet.

Cultivation Grow in gritty, sharply drained soil in full sun, with shelter from the worst winter rains if possible. If growing in containers, use a quality potting mix with a little sand added. **Sow** seed in an open frame in autumn (*see pp.391–393*). **Take** softwood cuttings in spring or early summer (*see p.394*).

Anacyclus pyrethrum var. *depressus*
↕2.5–5cm (1–2in) or more ↔ 10cm (4in), perennial, leaves grey-green, solitary flowers on short, slender stems, petals red on reverse

Anaphalis

Pearl Everlasting

THESE MEDIUM-HEIGHT, SPREADING or upright perennials have woolly, grey foliage, and clusters of papery, "everlasting" white flowers, produced from midsummer until autumn and very popular for cutting and drying. The smaller varieties suit a rock garden; grow the more upright varieties in a herbaceous or mixed border. They are ideal plants for a white-themed scheme, since the flowers and silvery foliage provide several months of colour. Pearl Everlasting is also especially useful in locations that are too moist for growing other grey- or silver-leaved foliage plants that prefer better-drained soils. To dry the flowers, cut them soon after they are open and hang upside down in bunches in a light, airy place.

Hardiness Fully frost-hardy ❄❄❄.

Cultivation Grow in reasonably fertile soil that is fairly well-drained, but does not dry out during hot spells in summer. They prefer full sun, but will tolerate partial shade. **Divide** plants in early spring (*see p.395*). **Sow** seed in a container in a cold frame in spring (*see pp.391–392*). **Take** stem-tip cuttings in early summer (*see p.394*).

Anaphalis triplinervis 🏆
↕80–90cm (32–36in) or more ↔ 45–60cm (18–24in), flowers in mid- and late summer

Anaphalis margaritacea
↕↔ 60cm (24in), flowers midsummer to early autumn

ʼNCHUSA

,lkanet

,LKANET FLOWERS HAVE A DEPTH OF BLUE that is not ften seen in other plants. The small, but numerous owers are produced in spring and early summer n branching stems, that are upright in taller cultivars r prostrate in the dwarf, mound-forming types, in nades of indigo, clear gentian blue, or ultramarine, ome with a white centre. Bees love them. The leaves re long and thin, coarse, and often bristly. Alkanets nay be annual, biennial, or perennial. The taller ones ive a vivid accent to a herbaceous or mixed garden.)warf types, such as *Anchusa cespitosa*, bring jewel-ke brilliance to a rock garden or alpine trough.

ardiness Fully frost-hardy ❄❄❄ to frost-hardy ❄❄.

ultivation Grow in any moist but well-drained soil that is oderately fertile, in full sun. Most alkanets resent excessive winter et. Dwarf types in particular must have free-draining soil, or gritty otting mix. **Stake** taller anchusas if necessary as they grow (*see .390*). **Deadhead** after the first flush of flowers to encourage more ter on. **Cut back** top-growth after flowering to encourage new growth iat will overwinter. **Sow** seed in a container in a cold frame in spring see *pp.391–392*). **Take** basal cuttings in spring, or root cuttings in inter (*see p.394*). May suffer from mildew (*see pp.398–399*).

***Anchusa capensis* 'Blue Angel'**
↕20cm (8in) ↔ 15cm (6in), biennial often grown as an annual, leaves bristly, flowers in summer ❄❄

Anchusa officinalis
30–60cm (1–2ft) ↕30cm (1ft), late summer flowering biennial

ANDROSACE

Rock Jasmine

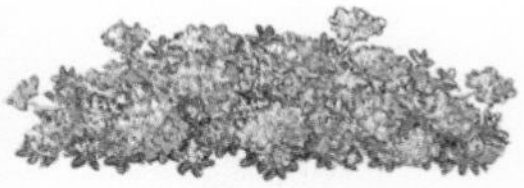

↕25cm (10in)
↔30cm (12in)

THESE PRETTY PERENNIALS make dense cushions or mats of evergreen foliage that is smothered in small pink or white flowers. The flowers are tubular and appear singly or in clusters from late spring to late summer. The cushion-forming species from high mountainous regions are ideal for an alpine house (an unheated, well-ventilated greenhouse) where they are easily protected from winter wet. The rest, however, are suitable for rock gardens, dry-stone walls, and alpine troughs, and look good with other cushion-forming plants such as saxifrages (*see pp.320–321*).

Hardiness Fully frost-hardy ❄❄❄.

Cultivation Grow in vertical crevices in walls in moist, well-drained soil in full sun. In containers, use a quality potting mix with extra sand, and add sand at the base of planting holes to improve drainage. **Top-dress** the soil surface with grit or fine gravel (*see p.386*) to protect plants from wet, which causes fungal disease. **Sow** seed in a cold frame when ripe or in autumn (*see pp.391–393*). **Take** single rosettes as cuttings in early to midsummer; water from below to avoid wetting the rosettes.

Androsace lanuginosa 🏆
↕ to 10cm (4in), clusters of light pink flowers in the summer months

ANEMONE

Windflower

THIS LARGE AND VERSATILE GROUP of perennials has delightful flowers from spring to autumn, and displays a wide range of habits, sizes, and tolerance for different situations. The flowers vary from pink, blue, and violet to red and yellow. They are usually saucer- to cup-shaped with a central boss of stamens and are either solitary or in clusters. Leaves are mid- to dark green with toothed edges. Anemones are divided into three main groups: spring-flowering types, growing in woodland and pastures, some with tubers or rhizomes; tuberous Mediterranean species, flowering in spring or early summer; and larger, tall herbaceous perennials, flowering in late summer and autumn.

Hardiness Fully frost-hardy *** to frost-tender *.

Cultivation Grow in moist, well-drained soil in sun or partial shade. Plant in autumn or spring and mulch with well-rotted organic matter (*see p.388*). **Sow** seed (*see pp.391–393*) in containers in a cold frame when ripe; germination may be slow and erratic. **Divide** (*see p.395*) autumn-flowering anemones in winter or spring. Separate tubers of tuberous species in summer when they are dormant. Foliage may be eaten by slugs (*see p.398*).

Anemone blanda **'White Splendour'** ♀
↕↔ 15cm (6in), like 'Radar' (*see left*) in every respect, apart from its white flowers, which can be breathtaking if planted *en masse* ***

STAKING TALL PLANT
Tall anemones are easily blown over. Stake them e in the season, pushing th supports well into the gr and raising them as the p grows and fills out.

Anemone* × *hybrida (Japanese Anemone)
↕ 1.2m (4ft) ↔ indefinite, prefers moist, humus-rich soil, in shade, and will flower from late summer to mid-autumn

Anemone blanda **'Radar'** ♀
↕↔ 15cm (6in), grows from knobbly tubers and prefers sun or partial shade and well-drained soil; it flowers in spring ***

Anemone nemorosa ♀ (Windflower, Wood Anemone)
↕ 8–15cm (3–6in) ↔ 30cm (12in) or more, this creeping, spring-flowering Anemone is at home under hedges or deciduous trees ***

ANETHUM GRAVEOLENS

ill

HE AROMATIC GREEN AND BLUE-GREEN FOLIAGE f dill is its distinctive feature, complemented in idsummer by its flattened clusters of greenish-yellow r yellow flowers. Dill is annual or biennial and has ollow, ridged stems and aniseed-scented leaves that e finely divided into thread-like leaflets. The seeds d leaves have many culinary and medicinal uses. ill looks at its best grown with other herbs in a herb r vegetable garden, but the fine, ferny foliage also ts as a wonderful contrast to perennials with bolder aves such as hostas *(see pp.260–261).*

ardiness Fully frost-hardy ✻✻✻.

ultivation Grow in fertile, well-drained soil in full sun with shelter om strong, hot winds. **Water** freely during dry spells in summer to event it running to seed. **Sow** seed (*see pp.391–393*) from spring midsummer for a succession of fresh foliage. Young plants do not ansplant well so thin seedlings to 10cm (4in) apart. If you have little ace, sow a pinch of seed in a large pot and grow on the patio.

nethum graveolens

60cm (24in) or more ↔ 30cm (12in)

ANGELICA

ARCHITECTURAL ANGELICAS bring height and drama to a garden. Clump-forming perennials and biennials, their majestic stems are topped with umbrella-shaped flower clusters, followed by attractive seedheads. The flowers are lime-yellow on *Angelica archangelica* and open in early summer; those of *A. gigas* appear in late summer and, like the stems, are a striking red-purple. Grow them in gardens, or as specimens in a woodland setting. They also thrive in damp soil along streams or pond edges.

Hardiness Fully frost-hardy ✻✻✻.

Cultivation Grow in deep, moist, fertile soil in full sun or partial shade. *A. archangelica* dies after flowering, but if the fading flowers are cut off before the seedheads form it may survive and flower for a second year. It may also self-seed freely. **Sow** seed (*see pp.391–393*) in a container in a cold frame as soon as it is ripe; do not cover with potting mix or compost, as it needs light to germinate. **Transplant** the seedlings while small since larger plants resent root disturbance. They will take around two years to flower from seed. Slugs and snails may be troublesome (*see p.398*).

Angelica archangelica

↕2m (6ft) ↔ 1.2m (4ft), the leaf stalks of this aromatic herb can be candied for use in sweets and cake decoration

ANIGOZANTHOS

Kangaroo Paw

UNUSUAL, BIRD-ATTRACTING FLOWERS are the hallmark of these popular Australian plants. The flowers are long, flattened tubes covered completely in very fine hairs that have the look and feel of short fur. They are held above the foliage in spring or summer on stems that are also covered in fine hairs. They come in a broad range of colours including pale yellow, green, reds and black. Single colours occur, but combinations such as red and black, and red and green are common. There is a large range of cultivars available. Plants are evergreen perennials or occasionally can be deciduous. They have very narrow, erect sword-like green foliage.

Hardiness Frost-hardy ✻✻ to frost-tender ✻.

Cultivation A free-draining, even sandy, soil is important, as is full sun. **Pruning** is unnecessary, although spent flower stems can be removed for neatness (*see p.385*). **Sow** seed as soon as collected into individual pots (*see p.391*). **Divide** rhizomes in autumn or spring (*see p.395*). Plants can suffer from 'ink disease', particularly in cooler and moister areas, which results in spots on the foliage and can kill less vigorous plants. Spray with copper oxychloride.

Anigozanthos manglesii

↕1.2m (4ft) ↔ 1m (3ft), flowers spring to summer and should be divided and replanted every couple of years ✻

ANOMATHECA

↕15–30cm (6–12in)
↔ 5cm (2in)

CLOSELY RELATED TO FREESIAS, this small group of perennials bears delicate flowers in shades of red, green, and pure white. These appear in late spring and early summer and are followed by brown seedheads containing scarlet seeds. Anomathecas grow from corms and, like freesias, in climates subject to severe winter frosts, are best grown in a container away from the worst frosts. In light frost regions, plant them at the front of a sheltered border; they make splendid companions for late-flowering tulips.

Hardiness Frost-tender ❄, but will withstand occasional temperatures down to –5°C (23°F).

Cultivation Plant corms in spring 5cm (2in) deep in free-draining, sandy, reasonably fertile soil, in full sun. If growing in containers, use a good potting mix. **Water** well and feed with a balanced fertilizer at monthly intervals during the growing season. Keep the corms completely dry while dormant. **Divide** clumps in spring, as necessary (*see p.395*). **Sow** seed (*see pp.391–393*) at 13–16°C (55–61°F) in spring, but allow up to two years for the seedlings to flower.

Anomatheca laxa ♀
↕15–30cm (6–12in) ↔ 5m (2in), each corm produces up to six flowers in early summer

ANTHEMIS

AROMATIC FOLIAGE AND DAISY FLOWERS are the chief attributes of these clump-forming and mat-forming perennials. The golden-eyed, yellow or white flowers are produced in succession from early spring until late summer and are often excellent for cutting. Anthemis enjoy sunny, well-drained conditions, the smaller types such as *Anthemis punctata* making valuable plants for the rock garden. In borders, their finely cut foliage, sometimes silver-grey, can look effective next to other filigree-leaved plants such as artemisias (*see p.25 and pp.188–189*) and argyranthemums (*see p.24*). Alternatively, contrast anthemis with bold, sword-leaved plants such as irises (*see pp.264–267*) and yuccas (*see p.129*).

Hardiness Fully hardy ❄❄❄ to frost-hardy ❄❄.

Cultivation Grow in reasonably fertile, well-drained soil in full sun. *A. sancti-johannis* and *A. tinctoria* can be short-lived plants. **Cut back** hard, to the new shoots at the base, after flowering to encourage new growth and increase longevity. **Sow** seed (*see pp.391–392*) in pots in a cold frame in spring. **Divide** in spring (*see p.395*) to make new plants or take basal cuttings in spring or late summer (*see p.394*). Some species grow from layers (*see p.395*).

Anthemis tinctoria 'E.C. Buxton'
↕45–70cm (18–28in) ↔ 60–90m (24–36in), flowers are produced in abundance all summer, if deadheaded regularly ❄❄❄

Anthemis sancti-johannis
↕60–90cm (24–36in) ↔ 60m (24in), a short-lived but free-flowering plant, best supported with twiggy sticks in exposed sites ❄❄❄

ANTHERICUM

WITH GRACEFUL, NARROW LEAVES to 40cm (16in) ong, these rhizomatous perennials are ideal for naturalizing. In late spring and early summer, the clumps of mid- or grey-green leaves produce delicate, ily-like, white flowers in small clusters on slender tems. The flowers are at their largest, up to 3cm 1¼in) across, in *Anthericum liliago* var. *major.* n autumn, these are followed by decorative brown eedheads. Anthericums are excellent naturalized with other wild flowers, or in a herbaceous border or mixed garden. They look good alongside early summer-flowering Oriental Poppies (*Papaver, see p.299*). The flowers are also good for cutting.

Hardiness Fully frost-hardy ✲✲✲ to frost-hardy ✲✲.

Cultivation Grow in any fertile, well-drained soil in full sun. **Sow** seed (*see pp.391–393*) in a container in a cold frame in autumn or spring. Seedlings may take up to three years to flower. Alternatively, ncrease stock by dividing (*see p.395*) in spring as growth begins, although the new plants may not flower until the following year.

Anthericum liliago (St Bernard's Lily)
↕60–90cm (24–36in) ↔ 30m (12in), this is a versatile plant for naturalistic and sophisticated schemes ✲✲✲

ANTHRISCUS

THE DAINTY FLOWERHEADS AND LACY FOLIAGE of *Anthriscus sylvestris* introduce an airy, natural charm into the garden from mid-spring until early summer. This is the most commonly grown ornamental of the various annual, biennial, and perennial types of Anthriscus, although *A. cerefolium*, Chervil, is an invaluable aniseed-flavoured herb. The tiny, white or creamy-white flowers are followed by flat seedheads. The delightful, dark-leaved *A. sylvestris* 'Ravenswing' has flowerheads with a tinge of pink. Usually biennial, but sometimes a short-lived perennial, it is particularly at home in meadow-style plantings. In the herbaceous border, team it with spiky-flowered stachys (*see p.328*), veronicas (*see p.337*), or salvias (*see p.318*).

Hardiness Fully frost-hardy ✲✲✲.

Cultivation Grow in any moist but well-drained soil, in full sun or partial shade. It self-seeds prolifically. Sow seed (*see pp.391–392*) in a container in a cold frame in spring or autumn. If grown well away from other Anthriscus, 'Ravenswing' produces dark-leaved seedlings.

***Anthriscus sylvestris* 'Ravenswing'**
↕1m (3ft) ↔ 30cm (12in), like all Cow Parsleys, this will produce self-seedlings but select only those with dark, purple-brown foliage

ANTIRRHINUM

Snapdragons

APPEALINGLY SHAPED FLOWERS, usually in a riot of bright colours, make snapdragons hugely cheering. They belong to a group of annuals and perennials that flower from early summer until autumn. The most popular are those grown as annuals in bedding or cottage-garden schemes. Although technically short-lived perennials, the best flowers are usually obtained in their first year, so new plants should be bought, or raised from seed, each spring. The dark green leaves will be almost entirely hidden by the flowers when plants are grown closely together, in blocks or with other summer-bedding plants. There are trailing types especially bred for hanging baskets too. If you have a rock garden, try growing some of the lesser-known, more delicate, shrubby snapdragons.

Hardiness Fully frost-hardy *** to frost-tender *.

Cultivation Grow in fertile, well-drained soil in full sun. Shrubby species require very well-drained soil and shelter from strong, hot winds. **Remove** fading flowers to prolong the flowering display. **Sow** seed of *A. majus* cultivars at 16–18°C (61–64°F) in early spring, and of shrubby species in a container in autumn or spring (*see pp.391–393*).

Antirrhinum hispanicum
↕20cm (8in) ↔ 45cm (18in), subshrubby, compact plant, good for small rock gardens or an alpine trough, dislikes winter wet ***

Antirrhinum majus **Madame Butterfly Series**
↕60–75cm (24–30in) ↔ 45cm (18in), perennial grown as annual, good as cut flowers, long-lasting with tall stems *

Antirrhinum braun-blanquetii
↕↔ 45cm (18in), a bedding type, very densely packed flowers, ideal for containers ***

\QUILEGIA

:olumbine

:HE NODDING, BONNET-LIKE FLOWERS of columbines re invaluable in informal planting schemes, from a unny cottage garden to a lightly shaded woodland rea. From late spring, and in some cases until late ummer, mostly bell-shaped flowers with spurred etals are borne singly or in small clusters on long talks. Columbines are upright, vigorous perennials nd the larger species, including *Aquilegia vulgaris,* are t home in dappled shade or massed in a garden with pright flowering plants such as Lupins (*see p.280*), lelphiniums (*see p.224*) and other perennials. The \lpine Columbine is best grown in a rock garden in harply drained soil.

Iardiness Fully frost-hardy ***.

:ultivation Grow the larger types in fertile, moist but well-drained oil in full sun or light shade. Grow alpine species in well-drained soil ı full sun and mulch (*see p.388*) with grit. **Sow** seed in a container ı a cold frame as soon as it is ripe (*see pp.391–392*). Seed of alpine species may take two years to germinate. Columbines do self-seed reely if seed is allowed to ripen on the plants, so do not be hasty ı cutting back stems in autumn.

***Aquilegia* McKana Group**
↕75cm (30in) ↔ 60cm (24in), flowers from late spring to midsummer, vigorous but short-lived

Aquilegia fragrans
↕15–40cm (6–16in) ↔ 15–20cm (6–8in), fragrant flowers may be tinged blue in early summer, needs rich soil, tolerates light shade

***Aquilegia vulgaris* 'Nivea'** ♀
↕90cm (36in) ↔ 45cm (18in), grey-green foliage, flowers in late spring and early summer

***Aquilegia vulgaris* 'Nora Barlow'** ♀
↕90cm (36in) ↔ 45cm (18in), vigorous, with uncharacteristic spurless, double pompon flowers, good in a cottage garden

***Aquilegia alpina* (Alpine Aquilegia)**
↕45cm (18in) sometimes more ↔ to 30cm (12in), flowers in late spring, prefers rich soil in sun or partial shade

Arabis

Rock Cress

THESE SMALL, MAT-FORMING, evergreen or semi-evergreen perennials can bring colour to poor or dry sites where many other plants would not survive. Loose clusters of cross-shaped flowers are borne on slender stems during late spring and early summer. The leaves are often hairy, and on some cultivars are variegated white or yellow. Rock Cress is very easy to grow and *Arabis alpina* subsp. *caucasica* is a good ground-cover option for dry soils. It is often used as a spreading plant in a rock garden, at the edge of a border, or in crevices in a wall.

Hardiness Fully frost-hardy ❄❄❄.

Cultivation Grow Rock Cress in any well-drained soil in full sun. It will tolerate poor, infertile soils, even in very hot or dry conditions. **Site** vigorous species, such as *A. alpina* subsp. *caucasica,* with care as they may swamp small neighbours. **Trim** with shears, after flowering, to keep plants dense and neat. **Sow** seed (*see pp.391–392*) in a container in autumn and give seedlings the protection of a cold frame. Alternatively, take softwood cuttings (*see p.394*) in summer.

Arabis procurrens **'Variegata'** 🏆
↕5–8cm (2–3in) ↔ 30–40cm (12–16in), evergreen or semi-evergreen, remove any stems with non-variegated leaves

Arctotis

African Daisy

SILVERY LEAVES AND A SOUTH AFRICAN origin mark out these annuals and perennials as heat-loving plants. Long, sturdy stems support the daisies from midsummer until autumn. They are brightly coloured orange, white, or creamy yellow; the petals are often marked near the base with a contrasting shade. The flowers have a tendency to close on dull days or in mid-afternoon, although modern varieties have been bred to stay open longer. African Daisies are often used in summer bedding displays, and are wonderful in gravel gardens or in containers. In cool climates, the perennials are often grown as annuals.

Hardiness Frost-hardy ❄❄ to very frost-tender ❁.

Cultivation Grow in sharply drained soil in full sun. **Sow** seed (*see pp.391–393*) at 16–18ºC (61–64ºF) in early spring or autumn. After gemination, prick seedlings out into individual 10cm (4in) pots to minimize root disturbance before planting out. **Root** stem cuttings (*see p.394*) at any time – it is the best method for propagating plants with especially fine flowers, because seed may not come true.

Arctotis* x *hybrida **'Red Magic'**
↕20cm (8in) ↔ 1m (3ft), flowers in summer through to winter ❄

Arctotis* x *hybrida **'Flame'**
↕30cm (1ft) ↔ 1m (3ft), flowers in spring and autumn with occasional flowers at other times ❄

ARENARIA

Sandwort

MOST OF THE SANDWORTS are low-growing or spreading perennials; some of them are evergreen, although there are a few annual species. All have narrow, greyish-green leaves, borne on wiry stems that can form loose mats or dense cushions. From late spring until early summer, they bear a profusion of small, cup-shaped, usually white flowers. Sandworts, which come from mountainous regions, thrive in a rock garden or the crevices of dry stone walls. They are excellent, too, for planting between paving slabs to soften the hard edges and will transform a bare patio if grown in this way with other mat-forming plants such as aubrietas (*see p.195*) and arabis (*see p.186*).

Hardiness Fully frost-hardy ❄❄❄.

Cultivation Grow in moist, but well-drained, sandy or poor soil, in full sun. *Arenaria balearica* grows well in partial shade; *A. tetraquetra* needs very well-drained soil. **Divide** plants (*see p.395*) in early spring. **Sow** seed (*see pp.391–392*) in a cold frame in autumn, or take new shoots from the base and treat as softwood cuttings (*see p.394*) in early summer.

① *balearica* (Corsican Sandwort) ↕1cm (½in) ↔ 30cm (12in) or more ② *montana* 🏆 ↕2–5cm (1–2in) ↔ 30cm (12in), flowers only in early summer

ARISAEMA

A GROUP OF SMALL TUBEROUS PERENNIALS closely related to the Arum Lily (*Arum, see p.190*). They have dissected leaves made up of between three and 17 small leaflets on the top of arching fleshy stems. Flowers usually appear in spring or early summer amongst the foliage. These are tiny and are arranged on a thin pencil-like rod known as a spadix. What appears to be the "flower" is actually a coloured and modified leaf called a spathe. These are curled into a tube around the spadix and are white, often striped with brown or purple. They are open at the top and often hooded, sometimes featuring a long curly "tail". Plants die down in autumn and emerge again with new flowers and foliage in spring.

Hardiness Frost-hardy ❄❄ to frost tender ❄.

Cultivation Grow in a moist, well-drained soil that is enriched with well-rotted organic matter. Grow in partial shade and shelter from hot, drying winds. **Sow** seed in winter in a cold frame (*see p.391*). **Take** offsets from existing tubers in autumn (*see p.394*). Most can be grown successfully in containers.

Arisaema flavum
↕15–30cm (6–12in) ↔ 15–30cm (6–12in), flowers in summer ❄

ARISARUM

ONLY TWO OF THIS GENUS ARE CULTIVATED in gardens and even they are far from common. They have heart- or arrowhead-shaped leaves that are mid-green. Amongst these in spring are seen the 'flowers', which are actually modified leaves. *Arisarum vulgare* has ones that are like upright tubes that have a flared hood over the opening at the top. This, and the colouring of chocolate brown with white stripes in the lower section, has given rise to the common name of Cobra Lily. Its sibling, *A. proboscoideum*, has a similar flower but it features a thin, curved 'tail' up to 15cm (6in) long, giving rise to the common name of Mouse Lily. Both plants are deciduous tuberous perennials.

Hardiness Frost-hardy ❄❄ to frost-tender ❄.

Cultivation Grow in shade in well-drained soil enriched with well-rotted organic matter. **Propagate** by divisions of the tuber in autumn (*see p.395*).

Arisarum vulgare
↕5–10cm (2–4in) ↔ 5–10cm (2–4in) is a useful colonizer of moist shady spots and has cobra-like flowers

Aristea

Evergreen, fibrous-rooted, evergreen perennials that form clumps of upright, narrow, sword-like, grey-green leaves. The flowers adorn the top of a straight flower spike just above the foliage. Individual flowers are small, open and purple-blue to sky-blue. The size and arrangement of these summer flowers is similar to the *Sisyrinchium*, to which it is related. Use as an erect focus amongst lower-growing summer flowering plants, such as snow in summer (*Cerastium, see p.210*) and anthemis (*Anthemis, see p.182*), and ground-covering forms of wormwood (*Artemisia, see right*).

Hardiness Frost-hardy ✻✻.

Cultivation Grow in full sun in a spot that can be watered in summer yet drains well. **Pruning** is not needed, except to remove spent flower stems in autumn or winter (*see p.385*). **Propagate** by division of established clumps in autumn.

Aristea ecklonii
↕1m (3 ft) ↔ 60cm (2 ft), has striking blue flowers in summer

Armeria

Sea Pink, Thrift

Thrifts are a delightful group of clump-forming perennials, useful as seaside plants. They are loved for their small and fluffy, rounded flowerheads in late spring to summer, borne at the tips of slender stems above the rather grassy foliage. Flower colours range from white to pale and dark pink. Whether you garden inland or by the coast, these are ideal plants for growing in a rock garden or at the front of a mixed garden. They also make a decorative edging plant alongside a path, and thrive between cracks in paving. Try growing them in a trough with other small rock-garden plants like *Rhodohypoxis.*

Hardiness Fully frost-hardy ✻✻✻.

Cultivation Grow in well-drained, poor to reasonably fertile soil in an open spot in full sun. **Sow** seed in a pot or tray (*see pp.391–393*) in a cold frame in spring or autumn. **Divide** plants in early spring (*see p.395*).

Armeria pseudarmeria
↕to 50cm (20in) ↔ 30cm (12in), a tufting perennial flowering in spring and summer, and into autumn

Artemisia

Mugwort, Sagebrush, Wormwood

see also p.25

Gardeners are attracted by artemisias' silvery and aromatic, ferny foliage, which is shown to advantage when set beside plants with bold or plain leaves. Most artemisias have a bushy habit, but there are some creeping or spreading forms, such as *Artemisia pedemontana*, which make good ground-cover plants. The majority are perennial, and a few are classed as shrubs (*see p.25*). If the small and insignificant flowers spoil the overall appearance, snip these off as they appear in summer. Artemisias make splendid partners for many plants, including silver-leaved shrubs such as lavenders (*see p.80*), and plants with purple, pink, or red flowers. They also look good at the base of roses (*see pp.110–113 and 150–151*).

Hardiness Fully frost-hardy ✻✻✻ to frost-hardy ✻✻.

Cultivation Grow in well-drained, fertile soil in full sun. Improve heavy soils before planting by digging in plenty of coarse grit. **Cut back** in spring to maintain a compact habit. **Divide** plants in spring or autumn (*see p.395*). **Sow** seed in containers in a cold frame in spring (*see pp.391–392*). **Take** greenwood or heel cuttings in summer, slightly later than softwood cuttings when the stem is a little firmer (*see p.394*).

Artemisia schmidtiana 'Nana' 🏆
↕8cm (3in) ↔ 30cm (12in), low, compact plant with silky, silvery foliage that is ideal for rock gardens and troughs ✻✻✻

Artemisia 'Powis Castle' ♀
‡60cm (24in) ↔ 90cm (36in), this silvery artemisia forms a fine, billowing clump of foliage but may not survive severe winters ❄❄

Artemisia pontica
‡40–80cm (16–32in) ↔ 90cm (36in), forms dense, all-year ground cover, but it can be too vigorous for small areas ❄❄❄

ARTHROPODIUM

THE GRASSY, BLUE- OR GREY-GREEN leaves and small, starry flowers in midsummer are the main points of interest of this little-known group of evergreen and deciduous perennials. Relatives of the lily, arthropodiums grow from short rhizomes, producing leaves that are up to 25cm (10in) long. The pendulous, white, pale violet, or blue flowers are borne in loose clusters, and have a wiry delicacy. *Arthropodium candidum* and *A. milleflorum* are the two most commonly grown plants in this group, suiting sunny rock gardens or sheltered herbaceous and mixed gardens, where they mix well with foliage plants such as tradescantias (*see p.331*).

Hardiness Frost-hardy ❄❄; will withstand temperatures down to –10ºC (14ºF) if given good drainage.

Cultivation Grow in fertile, well-drained, gritty soil in full sun. In frosty areas, grow at the base of a warm, sheltered wall, or in a cold or cool greenhouse or conservatory. **Sow** seed in containers in a cold frame in autumn or early spring (*see pp.391–392*). **Divide** plants in early spring (*see p.395*). Young plants are best overwintered in frost-free conditions. New growth is vulnerable to slugs (*see p.398*).

Arthropodium milleflorum
‡to 50cm (20in) ↔ to 20cm (8in), the bluish- or greyish-green foliage is spangled with flowers in midsummer

ARUM

Lords and Ladies

↕15–50cm (6–20in)
↔15cm (6in)

WITH THEIR ARROW-SHAPED LEAVES emerging in late autumn and winter, these tuberous perennials make good foliage plants at a time of year when fresh growth is particularly welcomed. Reaching 35cm (14in) long, the leaves can be glossy green and have pale green or cream marbling. Between late spring and summer, leaf-like flowers are produced in pale green, white, or yellow. Enclosed within is a prominent spike, which bears persistent, bright orange-red berries later in the year. The best and largest leaves are produced in light shade, but a sunny, open site is needed for the plant to flower well. All parts of the plant are toxic.

Hardiness Fully frost-hardy ❄❄❄ to frost-tender ❄.

Cultivation Grow in a sheltered site in well-drained soil enriched with organic matter. **Plant** tubers up to 15cm (6in) deep in autumn or spring. **Divide** after flowering to make new plants (*see p.395*).

Arum italicum 'Marmoratum' 🏆
↕30cm (12in) ↔15cm (6in), marbled leaves are striking from winter to late spring, flowers in early summer, berries last to autumn ❄❄❄

ARUNCUS

Goatsbeard

↕to 2m (6ft)
↔to 1.2m (4ft)

FEATHERY PLUMES OF FLOWERS are borne above mounds of handsome, heavily veined leaves from early to midsummer. Goatsbeards belong to a small genus, related to filipendulas (*see p.244*) and spiraeas (*see p.119*), containing just a few species, all perennial. The tiny cream or white flowers that form the plumes may be either male or female, with the females subsequently producing small, green seedpods that will scatter seed freely if they are not deadheaded. Both seedheads and flowerheads are popular for indoor arrangements. In the garden, this clump-forming plant thrives in moist soil and suits being grown at the edge of a pond or in damp woodland. *Aruncus aethusifolius* is a small, very compact form.

Hardiness Fully frost-hardy ❄❄❄.

Cultivation Grow in moist, fertile soil, in partial shade. **Plant out** in autumn or early spring. **Sow** seed in containers (*see pp.391–393*) placed in a cold frame. **Lift and divide** in spring or autumn every two or three years to make new plants and maintain vigour (*see p.395*).

Aruncus dioicus 🏆
↕2m (6ft) ↔1.2m (4ft), will tolerate drier conditions than other types, but much prefers a fairly damp site

ASARINA PROCUMBENS

Creeping Snapdragon

↕5cm (2in) ↔to 60cm (24in)

THE DELICATE, PALE YELLOW flowers of this trailing, evergreen perennial closely resemble those of the snapdragon (*see Antirrhinum, p.184*), giving rise to its common name. Appearing from early summer until early autumn, the flowers have deep yellow throats with light purple veining and reach 3.5cm (1½in) long. They are borne above grey-green leaves that are soft, hairy, and slightly sticky. Asarina's trailing habit makes it a favourite for growing as a ground cover over the edge of a shady wall, a raised bed, or the stony slopes of a rock garden. The plant tends to be short-lived, but does seed itself freely about the garden.

Hardiness Fully frost-hardy to –10°C (14°F) ❄❄❄.

Cultivation Grow in well-drained soil enriched with well-rotted organic matter. **Plant** in partial shade for best results. **Sow** seed in early spring (*see pp.391–392*) at a temperature of 16°C (61°F).

Asarina procumbens
↕5cm (2in) ↔ 60cm (24in), a useful plant for ground cover in shade with a prolonged flowering season

ʌSCLEPIAS

ilkweed, Milkweed

:OLOURFUL CLUSTERS OF FLOWERS are produced by ɿis large group of perennials (and a few shrubs) in ɿch abundance that they attract great numbers of utterflies and bees, especially the Butterfly Weed, *sclepias tuberosa*. The flowers range in colour from urple-pink, deep pink, and orange-red to yellow nd appear from midsummer until autumn. They are ɔllowed by fruits which split when ripe to reveal rows f seeds with long, silky hairs, hence the common ame of silkweed. The leaves and tips of the stems ontain a milky sap, which can irritate skin. Silkweeds ke a variety of sites from sunny borders to pondsides; ɿany are suited to wildflower plantings.

ardiness Fully frost-hardy ❄❄❄ to very frost-tender ❁.

:ultivation Most grow well in fertile, well-drained soil in full sun, lthough *A. incarnata* prefers fairly moist conditions. In frost-prone reas, grow frost-tender types in a cool greenhouse or conservatory. **ow** seed in spring in containers in a cold frame (*see pp.391–392*). **ivide** in spring to make new plants (*see p.395*) and, if necessary, eep clumps under control. Some, especially *A. hallii* and *A. syriacus*, pread quickly by underground suckers and can be invasive.

Asclepias incarnata (Swamp Milkweed)
↕1.2m (4ft) ↔ 60cm (24in), likes a moist site and grows well near streams and pools ❄❄❄

ASPHODELINE

Jacob's Rod

↕1–1.5m (3–5ft)
↔30cm (12in)

STRIKING SPIRES OF YELLOW OR WHITE starry flowers emerge in spring and summer, rising above the clumps of blue-green, grassy leaves. These herbaceous biennial and perennial plants, natives of the Mediterranean, grow from swollen, fleshy roots (rhizomes), which allow them to withstand dry conditions. They thrive in dry, sunny sites such as banks and well-drained garden beds. Good companions include many annuals, such as the Corn Marigold (*Chrysanthemum segetum*), eryngiums (*see p.238*), and other Mediterranean plants like rosemary (*see p.114*) and phlomis (*see p.306*).

Hardiness Fully frost-hardy ❄❄❄.

Cultivation Grow in reasonably fertile, well-drained soil in full sun. **Sow** seed in a container (*see pp.391–393*) in a cold frame in spring. **Divide** plants (*see p.395*) in late summer or early autumn, taking care not to damage the roots.

Asphodeline lutea (Yellow Asphodel, King's Spear)
↕1.5m (5ft) ↔ 30cm (12in), fragrant flowers in late spring, the spires of seedpods are also attractive

ASPHODELUS

Asphodel

GROWN FOR THEIR SLENDER SPIKES of delicate flowers in shades of white or pink, asphodels, like their close cousins asphodelines (*see left*), are excellent plants for a dry, sunny border. Those grown in gardens are mostly perennial, but there are also some annuals. The flowers open in late spring and early summer and often have attractive, contrasting markings on the petals. The tall flower stems rise up from dense tufts of grassy foliage. Natives of warm, well-drained, sometimes quite barren places, asphodels need a sheltered site and free-draining soil in cool climates where winters tend to be wet. A beautifully bold plant for naturalistic plantings.

Hardiness Fully frost-hardy ❄❄❄.

Cultivation Grow in well-drained soil in full sun. **Sow** seed in a container (*see pp.391–393*) in a cold frame in spring. *Asphodelus fistulosis* is generally grown as an annual and needs to be raised from seed each year. **Divide** plants (*see p.395*) in late summer or early autumn, taking care not to damage the roots.

Asphodelus albus
↕90cm (36in) ↔ 30cm (12in), clumping perennial, flowers in mid- or late spring

Aster

Asters bring cheer to the late-summer and autumn garden with masses of daisy flowers, which give *Aster novi-belgii* types the name Michaelmas Daisy. Varying in hue from sky blue to white, scarlet, pink, and lavender, all with bright golden centres, flowers are carried at the tips of the stems, either singly or in clusters. Asters are mostly perennial, but also include a few annuals, biennials, and shrubby types; they range from tiny alpines no more than 15cm (6in) tall to upright, clumps of 1.2m (4ft) or more. There are asters for many positions in a garden, since they grow naturally in both moist woodland and mountainous areas. Try smaller asters at the front of gardens or in rock gardens; taller ones look best in a mixed border. Flowering times vary slightly. Some, such as *A.* × *frikartii*, put on a particularly long display.

Hardiness Perennials are mostly fully frost-hardy ✻✻✻, shrubby types are very frost-tender ❀.

Cultivation Asters grow in a variety of sites from open sun to partial shade. Plant them according to which of the three cultivation groups they fall into. **Group 1** needs moist, fertile, well-cultivated soil in sun or partial shade. **Group 2** needs open, well-drained, moderately fertile soil, and a position in full sun. **Group 3** needs moist, moderately fertile soil in partial shade. **Support** taller Asters to prevent them from keeling over (*see below*); this is best done in early spring. **Cut down** old stems in autumn, making it easier to give plants a winter mulch, or if preferred leave and cut down in winter or early spring. **Divide** clumps (*see p.395*) every three to four years, both to give more plants and to maintain vigorous growth, especially for *A. novae-angliae* and *A. novi-belgii* cultivars. **Sow** seed (*see pp.391–393*) in spring or autumn in a cold frame. Grey mould (botrytis) and powdery mildew can affect plants, particularly in cultivars of *A. novi-belgii*; remove infected parts and spray with fungicide. *A. amellus* and *A.* × *frikartii* types are generally trouble-free.

How to stake Asters

Canes and twine *This is the most inexpensive method of staking. Space the canes evenly around the plants and among clumps and weave the twine around them, keeping it taut, to provide support. This may look unsightly at first, but both canes and twine will soon be completely hidden by the foliage and flowers. Put a cap on all canes to prevent accidental damage to your eyes. L-shaped linking stakes are a proprietary alternative, adaptable to any size of clump and easy to store.*

Sticks *Use branching, twiggy sticks as a most versatile method of staking. The garden may look a little like a forest immediately after they are put in, but they are soon hidden once the plants grow and cover them. The tops of the sticks can be bent over, providing additional support for the plants to grow through. The sticks should last for several seasons. If you don't have any sticks, try stems from tall shrubs like Buddleja (*see p.29*) that are pruned in early spring, just when staking is needed.*

Grow-through supports *These consist of a mesh or grid of rigid plastic across a hoop supported by four legs. The support is simply pushed into place over the plant, which grows through the mesh. Grow-through supports can gradually be raised as plants become taller. It is essential to get this type of support in place over the aster early in the season, when the plant has made about 30cm (12in) of growth. Grow-through supports are easily removed when the old stems are cut back in autumn.*

① ***Aster alpinus*** ♀ ↕25cm (10in) ↔45cm (18in), Gp 2 ② **'Barr's Pink'** ↕1m (3ft) ↔60cm (2ft), Gp 2 ③ ***novae-angliae*** **'Harrington's Pink'** ♀ ↕1.2m (4ft) ↔60cm (2ft), Gp 1 ④ × ***frikartii*** **'Mönch'** ♀ ↕70cm (28in) ↔35–40cm (14–16in), Gp 2 ⑤ ***lateriflorus*** **'Horizontalis'** ♀ ↕60cm (2ft) ↔30cm (1ft), Gp 3 ⑥ ***cordifolius*** **'Silver Spray'** ↕1.2m (4ft) ↔45cm (18in), Gp 3 ⑦ ***novi-belgii*** **'Snowsprite'** ↕25–30cm (10–12in) ↔45cm (18in), Gp 3 ⑧ **'Winston Churchill'** ↕60cm (2ft) ↔30cm (1ft), Gp 2

2

3

4

7

8

Astilbe

WITH THEIR PLUMES OF TINY, STARRY flowers, astilbes bring both elegance and texture to the garden. The flowerheads, in shades of white, cream, pink, and red, are produced in summer and, if left on the plant to fade, turn a rich russet brown, extending the period of interest into autumn. The cut flowers also last well in water in arrangements. Handsome, mid- to dark green, divided leaves add to the attractions of these clump-forming perennials. They particularly suit damp sites close to ponds and streams, or in bog gardens, and combine well with ferns (*see pp.356–365*) and grasses (*see pp.340–355*).

Hardiness Fully frost-hardy ❄❄❄.

Cultivation Grow in moist soil enriched with plenty of well-rotted organic matter in sun or partial shade. Astilbes will not thrive in soils that dry out in summer. **Divide** plants in late winter or early spring every three or four years to maintain vigour (*see p.395*). The flowers and young leaves can, occasionally, be damaged by late frosts. Foliage may also be marred by a greyish-white coating of powdery mildew, mainly if plants are in too humid a site.

***Astilbe* × *arendsii* 'Fanal'** 🏆
↕60cm (24in) ↔45cm (18in), the crimson flower plumes appear in early summer

***Astilbe chinensis* 'Purpurlanze'**
↕1.2m (4ft) ↔90cm (36in), vigorous, flowers in late summer and early autumn; tolerates drier conditions than most

***Astilbe* × *arendsii* 'Irrlicht'**
↕↔ 50cm (18in), flowers in late spring and early summer, somewhat smaller than many astilbes

ASTRANTIA

Hattie's Pincushion, Masterwort

THE DELICATE AND DISTINCTIVE FLOWERHEADS that grace these clump-forming perennials are in fact composed of an outer circle of papery bracts (modified leaves) and a central cluster of pinhead-like true flowers. In early and midsummer, strong stems hold the blooms of white, pink, or red well above the foliage. *Astrantia* 'Sunningdale Variegated' has leaves with creamy yellow margins, at their most striking early in the season. The flowers look attractive in dried flower arrangements. Astrantias make good companions for many other herbaceous perennials, including asters (*see pp.192–193*), astilbes (*see left*), and rudbeckias (*see p.317*).

Hardiness Fully frost-hardy ❄❄❄.

Cultivation Grow in moist, fertile soil, enriched with well-rotted organic matter, in sun or partial shade. 'Sunningdale Variegated' needs full sun for the best foliage colour. **Remove** faded flowers if you do not want plants to self-seed. **Divide** plants in spring (*see p.395*) to maintain vigour and make new plants. **Sow** seed in a container in a cold frame as soon as it is ripe (*see pp.391–392*). **Powdery mildew** may spoil the leaves in humid or overcrowded sites (*see p.399*).

Astrantia major 'Rubra'
↕60cm (24in) ↔45cm (18in), will tolerate slightly drier conditions

Astrantia 'Hadspen Blood'
↕60cm (24in) ↔45cm (18in), one of the darkest of all Astrantias and useful for adding depth of colour to planting schemes

Astrantia major 'Alba'
↕60cm (24in) ↔45cm (18in), the delicate white flowers will enliven a shady corner

AUBRIETA

↕5cm (2in)
↔60cm (24in)

MATS OR LOW HUMMOCKS of pink, magenta, mauve, and purple flowers, make aubretia a useful addition to the spring rock garden and border edge. It is a useful plant, too, for growing in crevices in walls. When in bloom, the small, cross-shaped flowers, which may be single or double, obscure the evergreen foliage. This spreading perennial is most popularly combined with rock-garden plants of a similar habit, such as soapworts (*Saponaria, see p.319*) or saxifrages (*see pp.320–321*).

Hardiness Fully frost-hardy ❄❄❄.

Cultivation Grow in reasonably fertile, well-drained soil, preferably neutral to alkaline (limy), in full sun. **Cut back** hard after flowering to maintain a compact habit and prevent the centre from becoming straggly and bare. **Sow** seed (*see pp.391–393*) in a cold frame in spring or autumn; named cultivars rarely come true to type. **Take** softwood cuttings in early summer (*see p.394*).

Aubrieta 'Royal Red'
↕5cm (2in) ↔40cm (16in), spring flowers and tight matting foliage make this a good rockery plant

Babiana

Baboon Flower

THESE SPRING FLOWERING BULBS make a dense clump of erect, narrow, sword-like leaves up to 20cm (8in) tall. The leaves are ribbed and slightly hairy. Above these are held the flowers on a stocky yet hairy stem. Flowers are starry and six-petalled and are most commonly in forms of dark purple, blue and wine red, although there is a pure white form also available occasionally. In winter rainfall areas these are relatively easy to grow and can remain in the ground for years. In summer rainfall areas the soil must be well drained or bulbs will be lost. If in doubt lift them when the foliage has died down and replant the following autumn.

Hardiness Frost-hardy ❄❄.

Cultivation Grow in full sun in well-drained soil that is reasonably fertile. **Sow** seed in autumn or spring in a cold frame (*see p.391*). **Propagation** is usually from bulblets, which form readily and can be separated in autumn (*see p.395*).

Babiana rubrocynea (Wine cup Babiana)
↕15cm (6in) ↔ 10cm (4in), early spring flowers on spikes holding about six flowers

Baptisia

False Indigo, Wild Indigo

FALSE INDIGO IS A VIGOROUS, clump-forming perennial that sends up tall, lupin-like spires of royal blue, purple, or white, pea-like flowers in early summer, followed by large, puffy seedpods that last into the autumn months. Informal in form, it can be used to add height to a wildflower garden, but also thrives when grown among other clump-forming plants of medium height, benefiting from their support. Grow it towards the centre of a traditional border with other robust perennials such as lupins (*see p.280*), eryngiums (*see p.238*) and Oriental Poppies (*see Papaver, p.299*), or mix with tall grasses such as calamagrostis (*see p.344*), *Stipa gigantea* (*see p.355*), and miscanthus (*see p.350*) for a prairie-like effect.

Hardiness Fully frost-hardy ❄❄❄.

Cultivation Grow in full sun in a well-drained soil. Take care to choose the right site, because the plants resent root disturbance once established. Plants grown in open or windy sites usually benefit from staking. **Sow** seed (*see pp.391–392*) in pots in a cold frame as soon as it is ripe. **Divide** (*see p.395*) in early spring, keeping the sections of rootball as intact and large as possible.

Baptisia australis 🏆 (False Indigo)
↕1.5m (5ft) ↔ 60cm (24in), erect to spreading, flowers in early summer followed by pods, at both stages good for cutting

Begonia

MOST BEGONIAS USED IN THE GARDEN produce spectacular flowers – great either in individual size or their sheer number – in whites, yellows, apricots, and pinks, through to bright orange, cerise, and rich reds. There are also types grown chiefly for their heavily patterned foliage. The most familiar are the small, fibrous-rooted *Begonia semperflorens* plants, so widely used for bedding and containers. Larger types make useful dot plants for summer accents in borders and in patio containers; use trailing begonias for hanging baskets. Overwinter in frost-free conditions.

Hardiness Frost-tender ❄ to very frost-tender ❀.

Cultivation Grow in fertile, well-drained soil in full sun or partial shade. In pots, use a multipurpose potting mix; keep well watered, and feed weekly with tomato feed. **Deadhead** to prolong the flowering period. **Cut back** semperflorens kinds in autumn; lift and pot them up if necessary; and bring them into a conservatory or cool room; place in good light and water moderately until spring. **Lift tubers** before first frosts, and store them, clean and dry, over winter; in spring, pot them up, and start into growth by watering. **Sow** seed (*see pp.391–392*) in late winter or early spring at 21°C (70°F). **Take** stem-tip cuttings (*see p.394*) in spring or summer.

***Begonia* 'Crystal Brook'**
↕15cm (6in) ↔ 1m (3ft), fibrous-rooted perennial, small and spreading, overwinter under cover in pots ❀

Begonia 'City of Ballarat'
↕60cm (2ft) ↔ 30cm (1ft) tuberous large flowers in late summer ❄

Bellis

Daisy, Double Daisy

ALTHOUGH BELLIS ARE IN FACT PERENNIALS, they are very often grown as biennials. Their small, perky flowerheads, to 8cm (3in) across, in white tinged with maroon, pink, or red, are borne from late winter until late summer. These highly bred varieties of the lawn-type daisy make great cottage-garden plants, and are also good for containers. Those with tight, pompom flowerheads can also have a formal, old-fashioned charm; use them in blocks to fill beds in a potager, herb, or knot garden, before summer salads, herbs, or bedding plants go in.

Hardiness Fully frost-hardy ***.

Cultivation Grow in well-drained soil, in full sun or partial shade. **Deadhead** to prolong the flowering display of bedding plants, or to prevent plants grown as perennials from self-seeding. **Sow** seed (*see pp.391–393*) in containers in early spring, or outdoors in early summer where the plants are to grow – or, if raising bedding for the next year, in a nursery bed. **Divide** plants grown as perennials just after flowering (*see p.395*).

Begonia 'Can-Can'
↕90cm (36in) ↔ 45cm (18in), tuberous, upright habit, flowers to 18cm (7in) across in summer, ❄ (min. 10°C/50°F)

Bellis perennis Tasso Series
↕↔ 5–20cm (2–8in), flowers to 6cm (2½in) across, raise plants in early summer or buy in late summer to flower early the next spring

Bergenia

Elephant's Ears, Elephant-Eared Saxifrage

As their common name so aptly describes, bergenias have large, glossy or leathery, tough leaves, and the plant spreads to make excellent ground cover. Bergenias are evergreen perennials that produce clusters of creamy-pink to purple-pink flowers on sturdy stems in winter to early spring. The rounded leaves are usually mid- to dark green but in some such as 'Ballawley', they turn bronze-red in winter. Bergenias can be grown at the front of a garden, but may need cutting back if they spread too far. They are, however, particularly useful for covering dry and shady areas in the shadows of walls or shrubs and trees.

Hardiness Fully frost-hardy *** to frost-hardy **.

Cultivation Grow in well-drained soil enriched with well-rotted organic matter, in partial shade. **Slice down** with a spade to remove growth exceeding the allotted space. **Divide** old, leggy-looking clumps every three to five years after flowering or in autumn (*see p.395*), replanting healthy sections of rhizome with roots and one or more leaves. Pick off any foliage that develops dark leaf spots (*see p.399*).

Bergenia 'Ballawley' ♀ ↕60cm (24in) ↔ indefinite, pink flowers on upright stems in winter

Blandfordia

Christmas Bells

Upright, clump-forming, herbaceous perennial with grass-like foliage that is triangular in section if cut through. In December tall, straight, flower spikes rise from the foliage. At the top of these hang the large and conspicuous tubular to bell-shaped flowers that are red with yellow at the opening. These open over a couple of months and are generally in flower by Christmas as the common name suggests. They need a moist – even damp – soil to really succeed, along with dappled light. They grow quite successfully in containers, and the flower stems can be picked to enjoy indoors in a vase.

Hardiness Frost-hardy ** to frost-tender *.

Cultivation Grow in a moist, acid (lime-free) soil that is enriched with well-rotted organic matter. **Seed** should be collected in late summer and sown straight away or in spring (*see p.391*). **Divide** clumps of mature plants in late winter (*see p.395*).

Blandfordia punicea
↕30–80cm (12–32in) ↔ 20–40cm (8-16in) showy clusters of red and yellow flowers around Christmas **

Bletilla

↕30–60cm (12–24in)
↔ 60cm (24in)

These orchids are native to temperate regions of China and Japan. They have delicate, bell-shaped, magenta flowers that are arranged in upright clusters, with up to 12 flowers on each cluster. The narrow, mid-green leaves that spring up from the bulbous, fleshy rootstock die back in winter. Bletillas look charming in a sheltered woodland setting with other small, spring-flowering plants, such as *Anemone blanda* (*see p.180*). They can also be grown in a raised bed, bringing their exquisite flowers nearer the eye. In frost-prone areas they need winter protection, either in situ with a thick mulch or cold frame, or potted up under cover.

Hardiness Frost-tender * to very frost-tender ❁.

Cultivation Grow in partial shade, in moist but well-drained soil enriched with well-rotted organic matter, or in soil-based potting mix with added leafmould. **Mulch** in autumn with a layer of organic matter at least 5cm (2in) thick to protect from frost. Alternatively, lift and overwinter in a frost-free place. **Divide** in early spring (*see p.395*).

Bletilla striata
↕↔ 30–60cm (12–24in), fleshy underground storage organs known as pseudobulbs; flowers from spring to early summer *

3OLTONIA

↕to 2m (6ft)
↔60cm (24in)

THERE ARE AROUND EIGHT SPECIES of these perennials, all of which thrive in moist, sunny sites. They have masses of daisy flowers in shades of white, lilac, or pinkish-purple with canary-yellow centres. The flowers are set off by blue-reen or mid-green, sometimes finely toothed foliage. 'heir loose, relaxed appearance is ideal for a wild arden, or they can add a light, airy feel to a border. 'he flowers are also good for cutting. Boltonias are olerant of most garden soils and will put up with ›artly shaded conditions. Plant alongside other tall ›erennial daisies, such as Michaelmas Daisies (*see Aster,* ›*p.192–193*) and rudbeckias (*p.317*). Stonecrops (*see* *ìedum, p.324*) are also good companions.

Iardiness Fully frost-hardy ✲✲✲.

:ultivation Grow in any reasonably fertile, moist, well-drained soil, ı full sun or partial shade. **Divide** plants in spring every two or three ears to maintain their vigour (*see p.395*). **Sow** seed in containers ı a cold frame in autumn (*see pp.391–392*). Can be susceptible to ›owdery mildew (*see pp.398–399*) in humid conditions.

Boltonia asteroides
↕2m (6ft) ↔ 1m (3ft), glaucous, blue-green leaves become greener with age, flowers in late summer to mid-autumn

BORAGO

Borage

BORAGE GROWS WILD IN ROCKY PLACES in western and southern Europe. They are robust plants with hairy stems and leaves, and flower for long periods over summer, producing nodding heads of intensely blue, or occasionally white, starry flowers. The annual, common borage, *Borago officinalis*, needs sun and tolerates dry places. It has cucumber-flavoured leaves that are often added to fruit cups, alcoholic drinks, and salads, and the flowers make a pretty garnish. It looks attractive growing with mint, sage, and feverfew, but may be too thuggish for a small, neat herb garden; if so, it looks fine in a garden bed. All species self-seed freely.

Hardiness Fully frost-hardy ✲✲✲ to frost-hardy ✲✲.

Cultivation Grow in any reasonably well-drained soil, in full sun or partial shade. **Sow** seed of *B. officinalis* where you want it to grow in spring (*see pp.391–393*).

Borago officinalis (Borage)
↕60cm (24in) ↔ 45cm (18in), freely branching annual, with a long flowering time, attractive to bees ✲✲✲

BOYKINIA

ORIGINATING IN MOIST WOODLAND and mountain regions, boykinias are clump-forming perennials with dark green foliage that is occasionally tinted bronze when young. The mounds of round- to kidney-shaped leaves that develop around the base of the plants make good ground cover. In spring or summer, lax clusters of crimson or white, bell-shaped flowers rise above the leaves on long stalks. Boykinias thrive in cool, moist soil in partial shade. In the garden, they are best suited to a shady garden or rock garden, or woodland edge. Pair them with violas (*see p.338*), or grow in clumps among other low, informal perennials that are not too vigorous and enjoy similar conditions, such as heucheras (*see p.259*) and dicentras (*p.228*). Small species also grow well in troughs and sinks.

Hardiness Fully frost-hardy ✲✲✲.

Cultivation Grow in lime-free (acid) soil, or potting mix for acid-loving plants, in partial shade. **Divide** in spring (*see p.395*). **Sow** seed in containers in a cold frame as soon as it is ripe (*see pp.391–392*).

Boykinia jamesii
↕↔ 15cm (6in), flowering in mid- and late spring, the frilled flowers have green centres

Brachyscome

Swan River Daisy

THESE DROUGHT-TOLERANT PLANTS, often also called Brachycome, without the "s", are grown for their cheerful, scented daisies. Borne in summer, these may be white, pinkish-purple, or blue, with bright golden-yellow centres. The soft foliage is green or downy-grey, often very finely divided and feathery. Grow these annuals or short-lived perennials in a summer garden scheme, or let them spill over the edges of retaining walls or containers such as windowboxes and large pots.

Hardiness Frost-hardy ❄❄ to frost-tender ❄.

Cultivation Grow in fertile, well-drained soil and position in a sheltered spot in full sun. Use a loam-based compost if growing them in containers, watering freely during summer and feeding weekly with a balanced fertilizer. **Pinch out** the tips of young plants to encourage a bushy habit and plenty of flowers. **Sow** seed (*see pp.391–393*) at 18°C (64°F) in spring and plant out in early summer when any threat of frost has passed.

Brachyscome multifida
↕30cm (1ft) ↔ 30cm (1ft), late spring through summer flowering
❄❄

Brodiaea

THESE PLANTS ARE PERENNIALS, growing from corms (*see p.164*), that in early summer produce funnel-shaped flowers in shades of violet, lilac, deep purple, or pink. The flowers are carried in large, open clusters, with each flower on its own short stalk, at the top of tall stems, and are excellent for cutting. Strappy, blue-green or mid-green leaves grow from the base of the plant, often dying back before the flowers emerge. Altogether they look similar to agapanthus (*see p.170–171*), but smaller. Grow brodiaeas at the front of a garden, or in a rock garden or raised bed, or in shallow pots and bowls.

Hardiness Frost-hardy ❄❄.

Cultivation Grow in light, well-drained soil in full sun or partial shade. **Plant** corms 8cm (3in) deep in autumn. **Water** freely when plants are in full growth, but keep warm and dry after they die down in summer. **Sow** seed (*see pp.391–392*) at 13–16°C (55–61°F) as soon as ripe. Remove offsets (*see p.365*) when the corms are dormant.

Brodiaea californica
↕50cm (20in) ↔ 8cm (3in), the flowers may be violet, lilac, pink or white in this species

Browallia

Amethyst Violet

GROWN FOR THEIR MASS of deep blue and pure white flowers, these are woody-based perennials that flower profusely in their first year, and are more often grown as annuals. Each flower is a tube opening to a flat face, up to 8cm (3in) across in some selections. They are produced during summer either singly or in small clusters where the leaves join the stems. The leaves are narrow and pointed, and feel slightly sticky. Outdoors, these plants combine well with other summer bedding plants such as heliotropes (*see p.70*), pelargoniums (*see pp.300–303*) or marigolds (*Tagetes, see p.329*). They make fine container plants, and are also popular as winter pot plants indoors.

Hardiness Very frost-tender ❁.

Cultivation Grow in fertile, well-drained soil, in full sun or partial shade. Use a good quality potting mix if growing them in containers; water freely during summer; feed with a balanced fertilizer at monthly intervals. **Sow** seed (*see pp.391–393*) at 18°C (64°F) in early spring for summer flowering or in late summer for winter-flowering pot plants. Aphids and whiteflies may be a problem (*see pp.398–399*).

Browallia speciosa
↕to 25cm (10in) ↔ 25cm (10in), flowers are usually purple, but white flowers are occasionally available

›RUNNERA MACROPHYLLA

↕45cm (18in)
↔60cm (24in)

THIS CLUMP-FORMING perennial and its cultivars have both delicate flowers and attractive foliage. In mid- and late spring, they produce clusters of small, usually bright blue flowers similar to those of ›rget-me-nots (*Myosotis, see p.287*). The softly hairy ›aves on the stems are broadly lance-shaped, those at ›e base larger and more heart-shaped. Excellent for ›oodland areas beneath deciduous trees and shrubs, ›runneras also make good ground cover in gardens – ›pecially those with patterned foliage that remains ›tractive once flowering is over. Grow them with ›her spring-flowering perennials such as Leopard's ›ane (*see Doronicum, p.231*).

›ardiness Fully frost-hardy ❄❄❄.

›ltivation Grow in reasonably fertile soil that is moist but well-›ained, preferably in a cool site in part shade. Dig in well-rotted ›ganic matter when planting. **Divide** established plants (*see p.395*) ›early spring. **Sow** seeds (*see pp.391–392*) in a container in a cold ›me in early spring. Take root cuttings in winter (*see p.394*).

Brunnera macrophylla **('Langtrees')**
This spotted form is easy to grow, tolerating moderate variation in soil moisture and some morning sun

BULBINE BULBOSA

Bulbine Lily

THIS NATIVE BULBOUS PLANT is evergreen. It has thin upright leaves forming a clump. These are slightly succulent or fleshy, and about 40cm (16in) long. In spring a central flower stem or two arises that is eventually taller than the foliage. The top of this is clothed with starry yellow flowers that open from the bottom up to the top. Not a well-known plant, but one that is relatively easy to grow, and one that will grow happily in containers. Otherwise, grow in a rockery or with cottage-garden plants in full sun or the dappled shade of taller plants.

Hardiness Frost-hardy ❄❄.

Cultivation Grow in a well-drained soil that is enriched with well-rotted organic matter. Full sun or partial shade with ample moisture is important. It will withstand wet periods. **Sow** seed in spring (*see p.391*). **Propagation** by division is probably a more convenient method. This should be done in autumn.

›runnera macrophylla **'Dawson's White'**
›e wide creamy edges of the leaves help to brighten the light shade that this plant needs to thrive, but ›s plant needs richer soil than other forms and is slightly less easy to grow

Bulbine bulbosa
↕60cm (2ft) ↔ 30cm (1ft), is an attractive small spring-flowering bulb native to Australia

Bulbinella

THE FLOWERS OF THIS SOUTH AFRICAN rhizomatous perennial resemble another South African perennial – the Red Hot Poker (*Kniphofia, see p.268*). The flowers are grouped at the top of a straight fleshy stem. They open from the bottom to the top in a conical arrangement and are starry. They are buttery yellow and appear in winter to early spring. The leaves are long and very thin and tend to arch and flop over. Although evergreen, this plant tends to have a dormant period in the summer and autumn, making it an excellent choice for waterwise gardens.

Hardiness Frost-hardy ❄❄.

Cultivation Grow in well-drained soil in full sun and do not over-water in summer. Deadheading can be carried out for neatness, but this will remove potential seeds (*see p.390*). **Sow** seed in autumn in a seedbed (*see p.391*). Root cuttings can also be successful (*see p.394*). **Divide** mature clumps in late summer or early autumn (*see p.395*).

Bulbinella floribunda
↕60cm (2ft) ↔ 45cm (18in), is particularly useful for bringing bright yellow flowers to the late winter garden

Caladium

FOR MOST PEOPLE, THESE FOLIAGE PLANTS will be grown in a warm, humid glasshouse, or even as a short-lived indoor pot plant to be disposed of. However, if you live in the tropics or areas of high humidity, these plants can add drama. They have very large heart- or arrowhead-shaped leaves. These come in a remarkable array of colours and include variegations of white, pink, and yellow, often with all colours on the same leaf. The flowers are like those of the arum lily (*Arum, see p.190*), to which it is related. The tubers go dormant for several months over autumn, winter and into spring, when they can be re-potted if necessary.

Hardiness Very frost-tender ❀.

Cultivation Grow in any well-drained soil or potting mix that is reasonably fertile and enriched with well-rotted organic matter. Shade is important, as is protection from hot, drying winds. **Remove** small tubers from parent bulbs in the dormant period and pot up individually (*see p.395*).

Caladium bicolor
↕↔ 60cm (2ft) a fine foliage plant only in gardens of the warmest areas. Indoor or glasshouse plant elsewhere

Calaminthe

THIS IS A GENUS OF MOSTLY HERBACEOUS PERENNIALS although many can appear shrub-like. The foliage is lance-shaped and gives off a pleasant aroma when crushed. The summer flowers are similar to those of catmint (*Nepeta, see p.290*) or thyme (*Thymus, see p.123*) to which it closely related. Some are blue-flowered, although pink flowers are found on *Calamintha grandiflora*, which also has the largest flowers of the genus as the name suggests. They are sprawling plants, useful for covering rocky embankments.

Hardiness Frost-hardy ❄❄ to frost-tender ❄.

Cultivation Grow in any well-drained soil in full sun or very light shade. **Cut back** flowered stems in autumn (*see p.382*). **Take** semi-hardwood cuttings in late summer or autumn (*see p.394*). **Division** is the most convenient method of propagation and should be carried ou in autumn (*see p.395*).

Calaminthe nepeta
↕40–60cm (16–24in) ↔ 40cm (16in), pale lilac flowers in late summer which are very attactive to bees ❄❄

ALATHEA

HIS IS A LARGE GENUS OF TROPICAL PLANTS grown r their brightly coloured foliage. This is sometimes lvety to the touch and often features a regular ttern of striping in cream, light green or white ainst a darker green. Some have large splotches of lver on them and others can be purplish underneath. he leaves are broadly oval and held on strong right stems. The plant makes a thick clump and is tually considered to be an evergreen perennial. Most ten seen as a pot plant, these can be grown in the ound in warmer districts.

ardiness Very frost-tender ❀.

ultivation Grow in any well-drained soil that is enriched with well-tted organic matter. Shade, humidity and plenty of moisture are eded if growing in the ground. **Trim out** any dead or damaged leaves keep the plant tidy (*see p.382*). **Division** of established clumps can ke place in late spring (*see p.395*).

Calathea makoyana (Peacock Plant)
↕60cm (2ft)↔ 60cm (2ft), also known as Cathedral Windows as the light is seen through the foliage

alathea zebrina
↔ 45cm (18in), grown for its remarkable foliage rather than its owers

CALCEOLARIA

Pouch Flower, Slipper Flower, Slipperwort

THE CURIOUS FLOWERS of calceolarias always arouse interest, with their vivid colours and strange balloon or pouch shapes. They are a group of annuals and perennials that generally flower throughout spring and summer, depending on when the seeds are sown. On flowering, they form massed or loose clusters of red, orange to yellow, even rich brown blooms, which are often spotted. The bedding forms are short-lived and can be prone to frost damage, but they make striking spring and summer container plants. The hardier perennial and alpine species are ideal for a rock garden or trough.

Hardiness Fully frost-hardy ✻✻✻ to very frost-tender ❀.

Cultivation Grow in light, reasonably fertile soil in sun or partial shade. They require cool, moist conditions to flower freely. Grow alpine species like *C. arachnoidea* in moist, gritty soil and protect from winter wet. **Sow** seed of annual and biennial types at 18°C (64°F) in late summer or spring. Do not cover these tiny seeds with potting mix; cover the pots with plastic instead to prevent drying out.

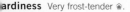

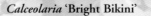

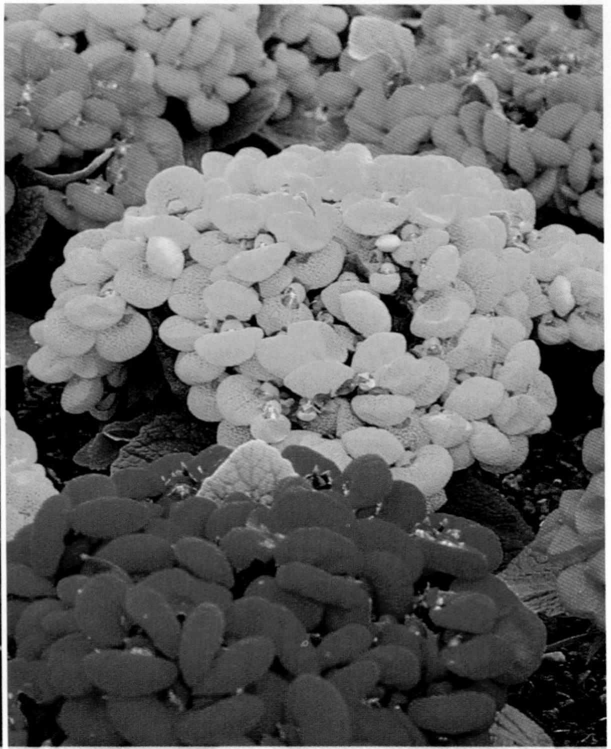

***Calceolaria* 'Bright Bikini'**
↕20–45cm (8–18in) ↔ 15–30cm (6–12in), bedding biennial with compact growth and dense flower clusters in summer, perfect for a patio pot or windowbox ✻

Calendula officinalis

Pot Marigold, English Marigold, Marigold

THIS ANNUAL CALENDULA is the one most widely grown in gardens: they are exceptionally easy, fast-growing plants that bear a succession of vibrant orange, yellow, soft cream, or apricot, daisy-like flowers from summer to autumn. The wide range of cultivars includes many with double or "pompom" flowers, varying from compact, dwarf plants to taller forms. All make good cut flowers. Pot Marigolds continue flowering into winter if unchecked by frost and, although annual, can survive into the following year. They make excellent, robust plants for hardy annual borders, and are equally useful in bedding schemes or in containers. Plants self-seed prolifically so they can be enjoyed year after year.

Hardiness Fully frost-hardy ❄❄❄.

Cultivation Sow seed outdoors in spring or autumn where plants are to grow (*see pp.391–393*), in sun or partial shade. Thin out seedlings to 15cm (6in) apart. Autumn-sown seedlings will benefit from some protection to keep off the worst of the winter weather. **Deadhead** flowers regularly to prolong flowering (*see p.390*).

Calendula officinalis

↕30–75cm (12–30in) ↔ 30–45cm (12–18in), softly hairy, aromatic leaves, flowers 10cm (4in) across

Calendula officinalis 'Fiesta Gitana' 🏆

↕30cm (12in) ↔ 30–45cm (12–18in), dwarf annual, double flowers in a variety of warm shades, sometimes bicoloured

Calla palustris

Bog Arum

↕20–25cm (8–10in)
↔15–50cm (6–20in)

THIS EASY-TO-GROW PERENNIAL is an excellent marginal aquatic plant and looks particularly attractive growing along slow-moving stream edges. It spreads through shallow water – no more than 25cm (10in) deep – by means of creeping underground stems (rhizomes) below the soil. In midsummer, large white "hoods" appear that surround the cone-like flower clusters, which in autumn develop into spikes of scarlet berries. The leaves remain on the plant during mild winters. Contact with the foliage may cause skin allergies, so wear gloves when handling the plant.

Hardiness Fully frost-hardy ❄❄❄.

Cultivation Grow Bog Arums in very moist soil at the edge of a stream or pond. **Plant** in aquatic planting baskets using garden soil, or directly into mud in shallow water, which should be still or slow-moving. Position the plants in full sun to encourage more flowers. **Divide** (*see p.395*) in spring, severing the underground stems carefully. **Sow** seed (*see pp.391–392*) in late summer in containers submerged in shallow water.

Calla palustris

ʼALOCHORTUS

ʼat's Ears, Fairy Lantern, Mariposa Tulip

to 70cm (28in)

SHYLY NODDING, BUT EYE-CATCHING, cup-shaped flowers, produced in spring and summer, are the key attraction of these bulbous perennials. The flower colours range from shades of white to pale pink or yellow, all bearing distinctive, ontrasting markings on the insides of the petals. The eaves are long and strappy and mid- to grey-green n colour. Calochortus look good in herbaceous or nixed borders with other bulbs such as late-flowering ʼulips (*see pp.334–335*).

ardiness Frost-hardy ❄❄.

ultivation Plant bulbs 10–15cm (4–6in) deep in autumn, in full un, in free-draining soil. In areas of heavy rainfall or on heavy soils, is better to grow them in pots and place them in a cold frame to eep dry because the bulbs may rot in winter wet. In pots, use a uality potting mix with added grit for good drainage. **Water** bulbs in ots freely when growing, but keep dry when the bulbs are dormant ı winter. **Sow** seed in a cold frame as soon as it is ripe (*see p.391–392*). Some species produce bulbils in the joints between tems and leaves, as Lilies do (*see p.274*), and these can be grown n in late spring or early summer.

Calochortus splendens
↕45cm (18in) ↔ 30cm (12in), flowers in late summer

CALTHA PALUSTRIS

Kingcup, Marsh Marigold

THIS MOISTURE-LOVING PERENNIAL and its cultivars display striking yellow or white flowers in spring and early summer, which are followed by architectural, heart-shaped leaves up to 15cm (6in) in diameter. The plants spread by means of underground stems (rhizomes), and prefer a moist soil at the edge of water, although they will thrive in non-aquatic garden sites provided that the soil remains reliably moist. *Caltha palustris* will tolerate being grown in water up to 23cm (9in) deep, but prefers more shallow water or a boggy soil. Grow them with other moisture-loving plants such as mimulus (*see p.286*) and calla (*see p.204*).

Hardiness Fully frost-hardy ❄❄❄.

Cultivation Marsh marigolds prefer an open site with constantly moist soil in full sun. When planting in water, use an aquatic planting basket and top with gravel. **Divide** plants (*see p.395*) in late summer or early spring. Marsh Marigolds are prone to powdery mildew (*see pp.398–399*) when conditions are hot and dry, especially when they are growing in soil rather than water.

1

2

① *Caltha palustris* 🏆 ↕10–40cm (4–16in) ↔ 45cm (18in)
② *Caltha palustris* 'Flore Pleno' 🏆 ↕60cm (24in) ↔ 70–75cm (28–30in)

CAMASSIA

Quamash

THESE BULBOUS PERENNIALS are grown for their tall spikes of large flowers, in sky-blue or creamy white. These are borne in late spring and early summer amid clumps of strappy, prominently veined, grey-green leaves. There are many types to choose from, but all are very similar. Grow them near the front or in the middle of a garden or in containers. The frilly flower spikes would contrast well with the drumstick flowers of alliums (*see p.174*), perhaps underplanted with soft yellow cowslips (*Primula veris, see pp.312–313*). The flowers are ideal for cutting, lasting well in indoor arrangements.

Hardiness Fully frost-hardy ❄❄❄ to frost-hardy ❄❄.

Cultivation Plant bulbs 10cm (4in) deep in autumn, in moist but well-drained soil enriched with well-rotted organic matter, in full sun or partial shade. In heavy clay soils, fork in gypsum before planting to improve drainage. **Protect** with a winter mulch in very cold areas (*see p.388*). **Sow** seed (*see pp.391–392*) in a container in a cold frame as soon as it is ripe, or remove bulb offsets (*see p.395*) in summer when the bulbs are dormant.

Camassia leichtlinii 🏆
↕60–130cm (2–4½ft), flowers in late spring ❄❄

Campanula

Bellflower

CAMPANULAS ARE OLD FAVOURITES in cottage gardens for their pretty tubular, bell- or star-shaped flowers. They are borne in clusters, or occasionally singly, in a range of shades from white to lavender, sky-blue, and soft lilac-pink. Campanulas form a large group of perennial, biennial, or annual plants and vary greatly in habit from spreading mats no more than 5cm (2in) tall, and clump-forming or trailing plants, to upright giants 1.5m (5ft) tall. Smaller species are best for rock gardens or raised beds. Tall campanulas can punctuate mixed gardens or be naturalized.

Hardiness Fully frost-hardy ❄❄❄ to very frost-tender ❀.

Cultivation To make cultivation easy, Campanulas are divided into groups. **Group 1** need fertile, well-drained, slightly alkaline soil, in sun or partial shade. Taller species require staking. Cut back after flowering to encourage more flowers later. **Group 2** are rock-garden species that need well-drained soil in sun or partial shade. **Groups 3 and 4** are specialist alpine or tender plants that are not often grown in temperate gardens. **Rust**, a fungal disease that causes orange or brown patches to develop on leaves or stems, may afflict some Campanulas. Remove affected foliage and thin out congested growth of affected plants. Use an appropriate fungicide if necessary.

Campanula alliariifolia (Ivory Bells)
↕30–60cm (12–24in) ↔ 45cm (18in), clump-forming perennial, flowers from midsummer to early autumn, cultivation group 1 ❄❄❄

Campanula lactiflora 'Loddon Anna' ♡
↕1.2–1.5m (4–5ft) ↔ 60cm (24in), upright perennial, flowers from early summer to early autumn, cultivation group 1 ❄❄❄

Campanula glomerata 'Superba' ♡ (Clustered Bellflower)
↕60cm (24in) ↔ indefinite, perennial, spreading clumps of upright stems, flowers throughout summer, cultivation group 1 ❄❄❄

Campanula persicifolia 'Telham Beauty'
↕↔ 90cm (36in), rosette-forming perennial with upright stems, flowers in early and midsummer, cultivation group 1 ❄❄❄

͏CANNA

ndian Shot Plant

↕to 2.2m (7ft)
↔50cm (20in)

THESE STRIKING PERENNIALS bring a touch of the exotic to any garden and height to otherwise low plantings. They have dramatic foliage, with large leaves in shades of purple-brown to mid-green, sometimes with attractive veining, as well as showy, gladioli-like flowers. The lowers appear in pairs from midsummer to early autumn, in bright shades of scarlet to golden yellow. Cannas have underground stems (rhizomes) and can suffer frost damage in colder areas; lift and store the plants overwinter or in frost-prone areas.

Hardiness Frost-tender ❄ to very frost-tender ❅.

Cultivation Grow cannas in sheltered borders in fertile soil and full sun. In cold areas, plant outside after all threat of frost is past, in early summer. **Water** well during summer and feed monthly with a high-potash fertilizer to encourage flowers. Deadhead regularly to prolong flowering. In cold districts, **lift** the plants in autumn, cut them down, and store the rhizomes in compost in frost-free conditions. **Sow** seed (*see pp.391–393*) in spring or autumn at 21°C (70°F). **Divide** the rhizomes (*see p.395*) in early spring, making sure that each piece has a healthy bud before replanting it.

Canna 'Tropicana'
↕1.2–1.8m (4–6ft) ↔ 60cm (2ft), summer flowers and green foliage striped with pink, gold and orange ❄

Canna 'King Midas'
↕90cm (3ft) ↔ 60cm (2ft), medium height plant flowering late summer and into autumn

Canna 'Carmen'
↕60cm (2ft) ↔ 30cm (1ft), summer and autumn flowers on a dwarf plant

Cardamine

Bittercress

A LARGE GROUP, but not commonly grown, the bittercresses include dainty garden plants, mostly perennial, some annual. Ornamental types are grown for the four-petalled flowers that they bear in late spring and early summer. The flowers are in shades of pale purple, lilac, white, and occasionally pink. The leaves are variable, sometimes made up of smaller leaflets, and may be lance-shaped and toothed in some species, rounded or kidney-shaped in others. The small, compact types are ideal for growing in a rock garden or at the front of a garden with other plants that flower in late spring, such as camassias (*see p.205*).

Hardiness Fully frost-hardy ***.

Cultivation Grow in moist soil that has been enriched with plenty of well-rotted organic matter. Position in full sun or partial shade. **Divide** plants (*see p.395*) in spring or after flowering. **Sow** seed in containers in a cold frame in autumn or spring (*see pp.391–392*).

Cardamine pratensis 'Flore Pleno'
↕20cm (8in) ↔ 30cm (12in), flowers in late spring and has glossy dark green leaves; produces many plantlets at the base

Cardiocrinum

Giant Lily

THESE COVETABLE, STATELY PLANTS grow to around 4m (12ft) in ideal conditions, so need careful siting. Grow a small group as a specimen planting in woodland or in a shady garden. They are bulbous perennials, related to lilies (*Lilium, see pp.274–277*). Trumpet-shaped, scented white flowers, occasionally tinged with maroon-purple or green at the base, are borne in clusters in summer. The stems are strong and stout, and the leaves glossy green and heart-shaped. The bulbs die after flowering, but leave many offsets (*see p.164*) that will flower in four or five years: the spectacular show is well worth the wait.

Hardiness Fully frost-hardy ***; new growth may be damaged by frost.

Cultivation **Plant** bulbs just below the soil surface in autumn, in a moist but well-drained, deep, fertile soil. Site in a sheltered spot in part shade; they will not do well in hot, dry places. **Feed** with a balanced fertilizer two or three times during the growing season to encourage the development of offsets. Top-dress annually with well-rotted organic matter. **Divide** and grow on the bulb offsets (*see p.395*) or sow seed in a deep tray (*see pp.391–392*) in a cool shady place as soon as ripe; seed-raised plants may take seven years to flower. Prone to snail and slug damage (*see p. 398*).

Cardiocrinum giganteum
↕1.5–3m (5–9ft) ↔ 45cm (18in), has up to 20 strongly scented flowers in each cluster, on tall stout stems (*see inset*)

Catananche

Cupid's Dart, Blue Cupidone

GROWN FOR THEIR BRIGHT summer flowers, this is a small group of annuals and perennials. Their flowerheads, up to 5cm (2in) across, are similar to those of cornflowers (*Centaurea, see facing page*) and are good for cutting and drying. Produced from midsummer until autumn, they may be lilac-blue, yellow, or white with purple centres. Grass-like, hairy leaves grow from the base. Grow *Catananche caerulea* with other summer flowering plants like asters (*see pp.192–193*), annual rudbeckias (*see p.317*), and impatiens (*p.263*).

Hardiness Fully frost-hardy ***.

Cultivation Grow in any well-drained soil. **Position** in full sun. **Sow** seed (*see pp.391–393*) in a container in a cold frame in early spring or in drills outside in mid-spring. **Divide** perennials in spring (*see p.395*). **Take** root cuttings in winter (*see p.394*) of plants grown as perennials. If powdery mildew is a problem (*see pp.398–399*), avoid wetting the leaves.

Catananche caerulea 'Bicolor'
↕50–90cm (20–36in) ↔ 30cm (12in), this perennial is sometimes treated as an annual or biennial because it flowers best when young

CELOSIA

Prince of Wales Feathers

SHOWY, UPRIGHT PLUMES of bright flowers are the reason for growing this sunny annual. The flowers come in a range of colours, including yellow, orange, pink, red, and scarlet. These are in feathery clusters above the mid-green lance-shaped leaves in summer and well into autumn. These plants perform best in warmer and even tropical climates, where the flowering period is more extensive. They are useful for summer displays of annuals and can often be seen in public gardens in this role. They also make useful fillers in a garden with other summer flowers, such as gaillardia (*Gaillardia, see p.246*). They can also be grown in containers to brighten a deck or patio.

Hardiness Frost-tender ❄.

Cultivation Grow in full sun in any well-drained soil that is fertile and enriched with plenty of well-rotted organic matter. **Sow** seed (*see p.391*) in spring and thin or transplant to about 20–30cm (8–12in) apart, depending on the cultivar.

Celosia 'New Look'

↕25–40cm (10–16in) ↔ 30cm (12in) long-flowering summer and autumn annual with bronze coloured foliage

CENTAUREA

Cornflower

STRIKING, THISTLE-LIKE FLOWERHEADS, which last for many weeks over summer, are the main attraction of this group of plants, which includes annuals, biennials, and perennials. Characteristically rounded, the flowerheads may be purple, pink, blue, or yellow, and are often deeply and sometimes darkly fringed; they attract bees and butterflies. The leaves, which are not particularly attractive, are sometimes toothed, and occasionally grey-green beneath. Try centaureas in a wild planting, or among other bright herbaceous perennials such as achilleas (*see pp.166–167*), daylilies (*Hemerocallis, see p.258*), phloxes (*see p.306*), or loosestrifes (*Lythrum, see p.283*).

Hardiness Fully frost-hardy ❄❄❄ to frost-hardy ❄❄.

Cultivation Most will tolerate some drought and can be grown in well-drained soil in full sun. Taller varieties may need support in the garden. **Grow** *C. macrocephala* and *C. montana* in moist but well-drained soil; they tolerate some shade. **Divide** perennials (*see p.395*) in spring or autumn. **Sow** seed in containers in a cold frame (*see pp.391–392*) in spring. Powdery mildew may be a problem (*see pp.398–399*) in humid summers; avoid wetting the leaves.

SUPPORTING PLANTS
Once plants are growing, place a ring of short canes around each and tie string securely around these. The foliage will soon hide them completely.

Centaurea hypoleuca 'John Coutts'

↕60cm (24in) ↔ 45cm (18in), clump-forming perennial, flowers are long-lasting and fragrant in summer ❄❄❄

Centaurea dealbata 'Steenbergii'

↕↔ 60cm (24in), easy-to-grow, clump-forming perennial, needs support, flowers in midsummer, excellent for cutting ❄❄❄

Centaurea cyanus (Cornflower)

↕20–80cm (8–32in) ↔ 15cm (6in) upright annual, flowers from late spring to midsummer, white and pink forms exist ❄❄❄

Centranthus ruber

Red Valerian, Kiss Me Quick

THIS IS A RELATIVELY EASY-TO-GROW and trouble-free evergreen perennial. If it does have one downside – and this depends on your perspective – it is that it can self-sow readily. It has a cluster of starry flowers at the tips of the growth throughout spring and summer, and often well into autumn. They come in shades of pink, from pale through to almost red. A white form is also available. The leaves are fleshy, lance-shaped and pale green. This plant is heat- and drought-tolerant and can be used in difficult spots, such as the base of a wall or cracks in steps.

Hardiness Frost-hardy ❄❄.

Cultivation Grow in full sun in free-draining soil. **Cut back** older plants in autumn or winter to almost ground level to encourage new growth (*see pp.391-392*). **Sow** seed (*see pp.382-384*) in autumn or spring in a cold frame. **Divide** mature plants in winter (*see p.395*).

Centranthus ruber
↕↔ 60cm (2 ft), has bright pink flowers for months and will tolerate hot spots and poor, dry soils

Cerastium

Snow-in-Summer

MAINLY CARPET-FORMING, this is a large group of annuals and vigorous perennials; only one is grown in gardens. They produce masses of small, starry flowers, singly or in clusters, and have usually simple and hairy leaves. The species grown in gardens, *Cerastium tomentosum*, make excellent ground-cover plants. They will spread to cover a large area and can become invasive, but are fairly easily to control by simply chopping down with a spade around the edges and uprooting the surplus. These can be used to cover an area such as a dry bank where little else will grow.

Hardiness Fully frost-hardy ❄❄❄.

Cultivation Grow these plants in any well-drained soil, in full sun; *C. tomentosum* tolerates even poor soils. **Divide** established plants (*see p.395*) in early spring. **Sow** seed in a container in a cold frame in autumn (*see pp.391–392*). **Take** stem-tip cuttings (*see p.394*) in early summer.

Cerastium tomentosum **(Snow-in-Summer)**
↕ 5–8cm (2–3in) ↔ indefinite, rampant perennial, usually smothered with flowers during summer

Cerinthe

Honeywort

EXOTIC-LOOKING, these flower from late spring until summer and attract bees. At the tips of the stems, petal-like bracts (modified leaves) that are often sea-blue are packed around small clusters of tubular, nodding flowers, which may be rich purple-blue, dark red, yellow, or white, often combining two colours. The leaves are fleshy and blue-green, and there is often white mottling on the foliage and stems. This small group includes annuals, biennials, and short-lived perennials. Use them in gardens or containers, or with summer annual plants such as China Asters (*see pp.192–193*), begonias (*see pp.196–197*), impatiens (*see p.263*), and marigolds (*Tagetes, see p.329*).

Hardiness Very frost-tender ❀.

Cultivation Grow in any well-drained soil, in full sun. Provide a winter mulch or some other winter protection if grown as perennials; they can also be taken indoors as pot plants. **Sow** seed (*see pp.391–392*) in spring at 20–30°C (65–86°F), and plant out the young plants in early summer when any threat of frost has passed.

Cerinthe major **'Purpurascens'**
↕ to 60cm (24in) ↔ 45cm (18in), most striking bracts and flowers and is the only cerinthe grown in gardens

ꞏHAMAEMELUM
hamomile

ꞏHESE AROMATIC, MAT-FORMING, hairy perennials and nnuals have feathery or thread-like, fresh green leaves nd bear daisy-like white flowerheads with yellow entres in summer. The Lawn or Roman Chamomile, *ꞏhamaemelum nobile,* is the best known and is ttractive in a herb garden, as edging or for growing ı crevices in paving. The scent from the foliage, hich is reminiscent of apples, is released when it is rushed. The non-flowering form 'Treneague' is often sed for making a scented lawn; although it does not eed mowing, it is not hard-wearing, and so is not ıitable for areas that are frequently walked over.

ardiness Fully frost-hardy ❄❄❄.

ultivation Grow in well-drained soil, in full sun, in an open site. **ıt back** plants regularly to maintain a compact habit. **Sow** seed here it is to grow (*see p.393*), or divide plants in spring (*see p.395*). reneague' is always grown from divisions. **Plant** divided sections 3–15cm (5–6in) apart to make a lawn, and weed and water regularly ntil established.

ꞏhamaemelum nobile 'Flore Pleno'
15cm (6in) ↔ 45cm (18in), double flowers, shorter than the ngle-flowered form, ideal for edging

CHIONODOXA
Glory of the Snow

↕10–20cm (4–8in)
↔ 3cm (1½in)

IN EARLY SPRING, these bulbous perennials produce starry, clear blue or pink flowers with white eyes. The glossy green leaves usually curve outwards, showing off the flowers. This is a small group of plants, related to the scillas (*see p.323*). Grow them in a rock garden or raised bed, or naturalized in grass. Like cyclamens (*see p.221*), they make a pool of colour if planted around the base of deciduous shrubs, so can be useful in drawing the eye to an interesting winter silhouette such as that of *Corylus avellana* 'Contorta' (*see p.44*).

Hardiness Fully frost-hardy ❄❄❄.

Cultivation Grow in any well-drained soil in full sun. **Plant** bulbs 8cm (3in) deep in autumn. **Sow** seed (*see pp.391–392*) in containers in a cold frame as soon as it is ripe, or remove offsets from bulbs (*see p.395*) in summer; either of these methods should produce bulbs of flowering size after about three years.

① *Chionodoxa luciliae* 🏆 the species names are sometimes confused on labels, so it may be best to buy it in flower ② **'Pink Giant'** is named for the size of its flowers, rather than its height

CHRYSOCEPHALUM
Everlasting Daisy

THESE EVERGREEN PERENNIALS are probably more familiar to most people as dried flowers. They have narrow, grey-green leaves that are sometimes hairy. The plants are generally very narrow and upright, although there is some natural variability in the species. In spring and summer the plants are topped with daisy-like flowers. These can be white, as in *Chrysocephalum baxteri*, or more commonly golden yellow, as in the other two grown in gardens, *C. semipapposum* and *C. apiculatum.* While naturally suited to native gardens, they are also appropriate for cottage gardens and rockeries as well as for use in containers. All used to be in the *Helichrysum* genus.

Hardiness Frost-hardy ❄❄ to frost-tender ❄.

Cultivation Grow in full sun or in dappled shade, such as under lightly foliaged trees. The soil must not sit wet for too long. **Prune** minimally; flower stems can be removed for drying. Suckering forms can be renewed by hard pruning in spring (*see pp.382–384*). **Sow** seed (*see p.391*) in spring in containers, but only barely cover with mixture. **Take** cuttings in late spring of new growth that is just starting to harden (*see p.394*).

Chrysocephalum apiculatum (Common Everlasting)
↕10–60cm (4–24in) ↔ 0.6–2.4m (2–8ft), very variable perennial with some suckering forms covering a huge area ❄❄(borderline)

Chrysanthemum

POPULAR FOR THEIR BRIGHT SHOWY FLOWERS, this group of upright, bushy annuals and herbaceous perennials are the stars of late summer and autumn. They are grown primarily for cutting and for exhibition. Chrysanthemums come in a range of glowing colours from ivory to pink, crimson, and gold, with blooms that vary vastly in shape, size, and form. Bloom form descriptions include incurved, incurving, reflexed, reflexing, single, anemone or fantasy. Within these bloom forms further classifications occur relating to bloom size and numbers, as well as petal and floret shape. The quality of exhibition blooms can be affected by rain, fog, and dew and serious exhibitors will take steps to reduce these effects. Annual chrysanthemum,s such as *C. carinatum,* put on a long colourful display and mix well with other annuals.

Hardiness Fully frost-hardy ❄❄❄ to very frost-tender ❀.

Cultivation Check the plant label or supplier's catalogue for growing requirements and hardiness when buying. **Plant** from late spring in full sun, in fertile, moist, but well-drained soil. **Support** tall varieties with canes and tie in regularly. Pinch out (*see below*) to improve plant shape and flowering. **Water** freely during dry spells and feed with a balanced fertilizer every 7–10 days from midsummer until the buds begin to show some colour. Watch for snails, aphids, and caterpillars as well as powdery mildew and rust and treat as appropriate.

Pinch pruning chrysanthemums

Pinch pruning a plant – taking out the growing tip or tips – encourages it to produce plenty of sideshoots from the buds in the leaf axils (where leaf stalk joins stem) lower down the stem. This results not only in a bushier, more attractive shape, but also in extra flowers on plants such as chrysanthemums and fuchsias. The more frequently a plant is pinch pruned, the greater the number of sideshoots and flowers it will produce. This is a technique much used by show exhibitors, but it can also be worthwhile in the garden, especially in containers, where you may want to maintain a more compact style of growth. For the greatest success, plants need to be growing strongly, so if necessary feed them with a balanced fertilizer.

Shoot tip only is removed

❶ *When the plant is 15–20cm (6–8in) high, pinch out the tip of the shoot just above a leaf joint, using your finger and thumb. Remove only the small tip to encourage the maximum number of flower-bearing sideshoots (known as breaks).*

Next generation of shoots have all their tips taken out
Stems branch after pinch pinching

❷ *Side buds grow and develop into shoots. When these shoots have developed four leaves, repeat the pinching (called the second stop). Pinch pruning stimulates shoots from the tip and lower down the stem, creating a much bushier plant.*

❸ *Keep pinching out the tips of the shoots until the plant is furnished with plenty of bushy growth. Stop pinching in early autumn to let flowering shoots develop. Here, several plants have been pinch pruned into a spectacular, colourful display.*

① ***Chrysanthemum* 'Alison Kirk'** ↕1.2m (4ft) ↔ 40cm (16in), a popular cultivar with exhibition growers ❄ ② ***carinatum* 'Court Jesters'** 60cm (2ft) ↔ 30cm (1ft) annual ❄ ③ **'Fire Fall'** ↕1m (3ft) ↔ 1m (3ft), very bushy habit, excellent as a bedding plant ❄❄ ④ **'Jolly Roger'** ↕1m (3ft) ↔ 1m (3ft), makes a good garden display plant and hanging basket ❄❄ ⑤ **'Satin Pink Gin'** ↕1.2m (4ft) ↔ 75–100cm (30–39in), good for showing ❄❄ ⑥ **'Shin o Tome'** ↕1m (3ft) ↔ 1m (3ft), excellent for

4

7

8

arden display ✲✲ ⑦ **'Valley Candy'** ↕ 1m (3ft) ↔ 1m (3ft), very bushy growth for garden display and asket planting ✲✲ ⑧ **'Yellow Smile'** ↕ 1m (3ft) ↔ 1m (3ft), good for garden display, baskets and for aining as a cascade ✲✲

CIRSIUM

Plumed Thistle, Creeping Thistle

THE OPULENT, JEWEL-LIKE SHADES sported by the flowers of the cirsium deserve a place in every garden. The hues range from deep crimson-purple to rich reds, yellows, and sometimes white. The flowers, up to 3cm (1¼in) across, are carried singly or in small clusters over dark green, prickly leaves in summer and autumn. Cirsiums belong to a large group of perennials and biennials; some form clumps, others spread by means of underground stems (rhizomes) and can be invasive. Cirsiums look dramatic grown among fine grasses (*see pp.340–355*) or with other summer-flowering perennials such as coreopsis (*see p.217*), phloxes (*see p.306*), and cranesbills (*Geranium, see pp.250–251*). They also blend in well in naturalistic or wildflower gardens.

Hardiness Fully frost-hardy ✲✲✲.

Cultivation Cirsiums need moist but well-drained soil, in full sun. **Deadhead** to avoid self-seeding if growing cirsiums in a formal garden. **Sow** seed (*see pp.391–393*) in a cold frame in spring or divide plants (*see p.395*) in autumn or spring.

Cirsium rivulare 'Atropurpureum'
↕1.2m (4ft) ↔ 60cm (24in), clump-forming perennial, flowers in early and midsummer

CLEMATIS

Old Man's Beard, Virgin's Bower

see also pp.136–139

THERE ARE A FEW CLEMATIS that are herbaceous perennials, forming open, sometimes woody-based plants smothered in delicate, often scented flowers. These appear in summer to late autumn. All the herbaceous clematis have very attractive, dark, mid- or grey-green leaves that vary in shape. Their soft stems require some support to stop them flopping over with the weight of the flowers. Plant these clematis in large containers or towards the centres of herbaceous or mixed borders among other summer-flowering perennials such as achilleas (*see pp.166–167*) and hardy geraniums (*see pp.250–251*).

Hardiness Fully frost-hardy ✲✲✲ to frost-hardy ✲✲.

Cultivation These clematis require full sun in fertile soil that has been enriched with well-rotted organic matter. **Prune** (*see pp.382–383*) the previous year's growth back to two or three buds, about 15–20cm (6–8in) from the base of the plant, before new growth starts in early spring. **Support** the stems with twiggy sticks. **Mulch** with a layer of garden compost or well-rotted manure in late winter. **Divide** in spring (*see p.395*) or take semi-ripe cuttings (*see p.394*) in summer.

Clematis integrifolia
↕↔ 60cm (24in), flowers in summer, followed by silvery brown, silky seedheads ✲✲✲

CLEOME

Spider Flower

THE CURIOUSLY SPIKY FLOWERS and sharply spined stems of the flowers reveal how this plant gained its common name. Of the many species, only the bushy annuals are widely grown. These produce upright stems to 1.5m (5ft) tall, with hairy leaves. They bear dense clusters of white, pink, red, or violet-purple, scented flowers from early summer to early autumn. Cleomes make good gap-fillers in beds and borders where they are useful for extending colour into late summer and autumn. Alternatively, grow in large containers or with other annuals such as rudbeckias (*see p.317*). The long stems of cleomes make them ideal for cutting.

Hardiness Very frost-tender ❀.

Cultivation Grow cleomes in full sun, in light, fertile, free-draining preferably sandy – soil. **Water** freely in dry weather. In containers, use a quality potting mix; water the plants regularly; and feed them with a balanced fertilizer at weekly intervals. **Deadhead** fading flowers regularly to prolong flowering. **Sow** seed at 18°C (64°F) in spring (*see pp.391–393*); harden off and plant out seedlings after the last frosts.

Cleome hassleriana
↕1.2m (4ft) ↔ 45cm (18in), hairy annual, with scented flowers in violet-pink, rose-red, or white to 10cm (4in) across in summer

LIVIA

hese bulbous perennials are particularly useful for owing in deep shade, such as occurs under evergreen ees, where often little else will grow. They have ick, fleshy roots and dark green, strap-like leaves at are evergreen. The orange trumpet flowers are ld in a ball at the top of a short, stocky stem just ove the foliage. They usually occur in late winter to e middle of spring. The plants look a little like ange agapanthus (*see p.170–171*) and, like them, are uth African, but differ in that they are not sun- or ought-tolerant.

ardiness Frost-tender ❄ to very frost-tender ❅.
ltivation Grow in well-drained soil in partial or deep shade as the t sun will scorch the foliage. Give water in summer if the weather is . **Trim off** spent flower stems for neatness if seeds are not required *e p.390).* **Sow** seed (*see p.391*) in containers in spring. **Take** visions from mature clumps in autumn or early winter (*see p.395*).

Clivia nobilis
↕60–75cm (2–2.5ft) ↔ 60cm (2ft), is very similar to *C. miniata*, but the flowers tend to be more pendulous

livia miniata
0–75cm (2–2.5 ft) ↔ 60cm (2ft), is great for filling the deep ady area under trees where few things thrive

Clivia 'Yellow Hybrid'
↕60–75cm (2–2.5ft) ↔ 60cm (2ft), an uncommon yellow flowered form

COLCHICUM

Autumn Crocus

AUTUMN CROCUSES ARE A TREASURE, their flowers emerging seemingly from nowhere in autumn before the leaves appear. A few appear in spring. The flowers are sometimes fragrant and come in delicate shades of lilac-pink or white. The strappy leaves of these bulbous perennials last from winter to spring. Sizes vary from tiny to large cultivars such as 'The Giant' which has a height of 20cm (8in) and spread of 10cm (4in). Colchicums can sprawl untidily after the wind or rain and should be grown in the shelter of deciduous shrubs. Naturalize others such as *C. speciosum* in grass. All are highly toxic.

Hardiness Fully frost-hardy ❄❄❄ to frost-hardy ❄❄.
Cultivation Plant the corms 10cm (4in) deep, in deep, fertile, well-drained, moisture-retentive soil, in summer or early autumn. Choose an open, sunny site, preferably out of strong winds. Small alpine species need gritty, sharply draining soil. **Feed** with a low-nitrogen fertilizer before growth starts. **Divide** large clumps (*see p.395*) in summer.

① ***autumnale*** 'Album' ↕10–15cm (4–6in) ❄❄❄
② ***byzantinum*** 🏆 ↕13cm (5in) ❄❄❄ ③ 'Waterlily' 🏆
↕13cm (5in) ❄❄❄

CONSOLIDA

Larkspur

↕to 1.2m (4ft)
↔to 35cm (14in)

CLOSELY RELATED TO DELPHINIUMS, these slender-stemmed annuals produce daintier versions of the tall flower spikes over a period of many weeks during summer. The flowers may be in shades of blue, lilac-blue, pink, or white. They are good for cutting, especially those of longer-stemmed types, and may also be dried. The foliage is feathery and downy, usually rounded, and mid- to dark green in colour. They are excellent plants for growing with other hardy annuals, such as marigolds (*Calendula, see p.204*) and coneflowers (*Rudbeckia, see p.317*). Larkspurs make charming additions to a cottage garden or annual display.

Hardiness Fully frost-hardy ✻✻✻.

Cultivation Larkspurs grow best in full sun and with their roots in light, fertile, well-drained soil. **Support** may be necessary with canes or twiggy sticks. Pay attention to watering in dry weather, because the soil must not dry out. **Remove** fading flowers to prolong flowering. **Sow** seed (*see pp.391–393*) directly in the garden in spring or autumn, when seedlings benefit from cloche protection over winter.

Consolida **cultivars** (Larkspurs)
Mixed and single colours are available in these summer flowering annuals

CONVALLARIA MAJALIS

Lily-of-the-Valley

FAMED FOR THEIR STRONG FRAGRANCE, the dainty white flowers of this small, creeping perennial are borne on arching stems in late spring to early summer. Lily-of-the-Valley has mid- to dark green leaves, and makes an excellent ground cover in a woodland garden or moist, shady garden. It spreads by means of underground stems (rhizomes) and rapidly forms new colonies in favourable conditions. To show off these plants at their best, grow them under deciduous shrubs so that their bell-shaped flowers stand out against a background of newly opening spring leaves. Forms with pink flowers or variegated leaves are available.

Hardiness Fully frost-hardy ✻✻✻.

Cultivation A shady position in moist, fertile soil that has been enriched with well-rotted organic matter is best for Lily-of-the-Valley. **Lift** some of the rhizomes and pot them up in autumn for a display of fragrant flowers indoors. Replant them outdoors after flowering in the spring. **Sow** seed (*see pp.391–393*) in containers in a cold frame as soon as it is ripe.

Convallaria majalis 🏆
↕23cm (9in) ↔ 30cm (12in), waxy flowers are held in graceful sprays, good for cutting

CONVOLVULUS

Bindweed

DO NOT CONFUSE THESE annuals and perennials with the pernicious, choking weed that shares their common name. These plants produce flowers in several shades, from white, blue, and creamy white, and are suitable for rock gardens and sunny banks. *Convolvulus sabatius* is good in containers, including hanging baskets, and particularly useful for trailing down over unsightly embankments.

Hardiness Fully frost-hardy ✻✻✻ to frost-hardy ✻✻.

Cultivation These trouble-free plants require poor to moderately fertile, well-drained soil and a sunny, sheltered site. **Deadhead** flowers to prolong the flowering period into autumn. **Container-grown** plants require good potting mix and occasional watering in dry weather. **Sow** seed (*see pp.391–393*) directly in the garden in mid-spring, or in autumn with cloche protection over winter. **Divide** (*see p.395*) perennials in spring.

Convolvulus sabatius 🏆
↕15cm (6in) ↔ 50cm (20in), trailing, slender-stemmed perennial, deep lavender flowers from summer to early autumn ✻✻

;OREOPSIS

ickseed

↕to 75cm (30in)
↔ to 60cm (24in)

BOTH THE PERENNIALS AND ANNUALS are grown for their bright, daisy-like, summer-long flowers. Masses of single or double flowers, all in shades of gold, are produced on stems rising above fine foliage. The flowers not only attract bees into the garden, they ılso make successful cut flowers. Many of the perennials are short-lived, however, and are grown as annuals – usually flowering freely in their first year from seed sown in spring. Grow them in a sunny garden bed with perennials such as achilleas (*see pp.166–167*) and phloxes (*see p.307*).

Hardiness Fully frost-hardy ❄❄❄ to very frost-tender ❀.

Cultivation Fertile, well-drained soil and a position in full sun or partial shade are required for this plant. **Remove** fading flowers to prolong flowering. **Stake** taller-growing plants to support the flower stems. **Sow** seed (*see pp.391–393*) in a seedbed outdoors in spring or indoors at 13–16°C (55–61°F) in late winter or early spring; sow n small batches from early spring to early summer for a longer succession of flowers. **Divide** (*see p.395*) perennials in early spring.

Coreopsis 'Sunray'
↕45–90cm (18–36in) ↔ 45cm (18in), flowers late spring to late summer ❄❄❄

CORYDALIS

LOW-GROWING AND CLUMP-FORMING, the numerous perennials, annuals, and biennials are favoured by gardeners for their distinctive flowers. These occur in shades of blue, white, and red, and are borne in clusters above the foliage in the spring, summer, or autumn. The ferny leaves are usually mid- to light green and in a few species, such as *Corydalis lutea* and *C. ochroleuca*, are evergreen. The perennials have tuberous ('George Baker') or rhizomatous roots. Some species will self-seed freely. They are best grown in a border or rock garden, but often survive in soil-filled cracks in walls and paving. Some corydalis require a dry, dormant summer period and protection from winter wet, and are best grown in shallow pots in an unheated greenhouse or cold frame.

Hardiness Fully frost-hardy ❄❄❄ to frost-hardy ❄❄.

Cultivation All need free-draining, moderately fertile soil enriched with well-rotted organic matter. Some Corydalis prefer sun, others like partial shade. **Sow** seed (*see pp.391–393*) in pots in an open frame as soon as it is ripe; germination can be erratic. **Divide** spring-flowering species in autumn, and summer-flowering ones in spring (*see p.395*).

1

2

① *flexuosa* ↕30cm (12in) ↔ 20cm (8in) ② *lutea* ↕40cm (16in) ↔ 30cm (12in)

Cordyalis ochroleuca
↕↔ 30cm (12in)

Cordyalis solida 'George Baker' 🏆
↕25cm (10in) ↔ 20cm (8in) – all ❄❄❄

Cosmos

Cosmos are invaluable plants for informal gardens. They include easy-to-grow tuberous perennials and annuals favoured for their attractive crimson-red, pink, or white, bowl- or saucer-shaped flowers, produced on long, graceful stems in summer. The perennial Chocolate Cosmos (*Cosmos atrosanguineus*), with reddish-brown stems and spoon-shaped, dark green leaves, has velvety, chocolate-scented flowers from midsummer until autumn. Slightly tender, it needs winter protection once the foliage dies back. Grow them with other border plants such as phloxes (*see p.306*) and grey-leaved plants like santolinas (*see p.116*) to contrast with the dark flowers. Sow the annual *C. bipinnatus* in a drift, or plant to fill mid- and late-summer gaps in a garden.

Hardiness Frost-hardy ✻✻ to very frost-tender ❀.

Cultivation Grow in reasonably fertile soil that is moist but well-drained, in full sun. **Deadhead** to prolong flowering. **Lift** and store tubers in autumn in the coldest districts and keep in frost-free conditions. **Sow** annuals where they are to grow in spring or autumn in milder gardens, or in pots (*see pp.391–393*). Thin seedlings to 15cm (6in).

① ***atrosanguineus*** ↕75cm (30in) ↔45cm (18in) ✻✻
② ***bipinnatus*** **'Sea Shells'** ↕to 90cm (3ft) ↔45cm (18in), with ferny foliage, good for cutting ✻

Crambe

Tall, but with an airy presence, these woody-based annuals or perennials are grown for their handsome, wavy-edged leaves and sprays of tiny, often white, sometimes fragrant flowers which attract bees. The flowers appear from late spring to midsummer, carried on strong stems above undulating, dark green or blue-grey foliage. The large leaves are decorative when young, but tend to die down in mid- to late summer. While crambes are magnificent in a mixed border, taller species, such as *Crambe cordifolia,* need lots of space. They are a good choice for coastal sites because the tough foliage withstands sea spray and salt-laden winds. Grow them with old garden roses (*see pp.110–113*) and philadelphus (*see p.93*).

Hardiness Fully frost-hardy ✻✻✻.

Cultivation Grow crambes in deep, fertile, well-drained soil in full sun, although they also tolerate poor soil and partial shade. Shelter from strong winds. **Sow** seed (*see pp.391–393*) in a pot in a cold frame in spring or autumn. **Divide** plants (*see p.395*) in early spring.

EMERGING SHOOTS
The soft, new foliage of crambes shooting from the woody crowns give interest to a garden in spring.

Crambe cordifolia ♀
↕to 2.5m (8ft) ↔1.5m (5ft), perennial, bristly leaves to 35cm (14in) across, flowers from late spring to midsummer ✻✻✻

Crinum

↕50cm–1.5m (20in–5ft)
↔15–30cm (6–12in)

Reminiscent of Lilies, Crinums belong to a large group of stately, deciduous and evergreen bulbous perennials. They are grown for their showy, white and pink flowers that are often scented; these are borne on long, leafless stalks from spring to autumn, depending on the species. The long, strappy leaves are a glossy, light to mid-green. Crinums are best grown outside in a warm, sheltered garden with other perennials like *Anemone hupehensis* and forms of *A.* × *hybrida* (*see p.180*), and border phloxes (*see p.306*).

Hardiness Fully frost-hardy ✻✻✻ (borderline) to very frost-tender ❀

Cultivation Plant in spring with the neck of each bulb just above soil level, in deep, fertile soil that is moist but very well-drained, and enriched with well-rotted organic matter. Choose a position in full sun, preferably by a wall. **Water** generously when crinums are in growth and keep moist after flowering. **Divide** large clumps of the huge bulbs in early spring (*see below and p.395*) to increase your stock.

DIVIDING CRINUMS
Lift a clump of bulbs in spring and shake off the excess soil. Pull or cut it apart and replant well-developed, healthy offsets.

***Crinum* × *powellii* 'Album'** ♀
↕1.5m (5ft) ↔30cm (12in), deciduous, up to ten fragrant flowers per stem from late summer to autumn ✻✻✻ (borderline)

Crinum moorei
↕ 1–1.5m (3–5ft) ↔ 60–100cm (2–3ft), late summer and autumn flowers, each individual up to 12.5cm (5in) wide

Crinum pedunculatum
↕ 1–1.5m (3–5ft) ↔ 1–1.5m (3–5ft), deciduous, up to 25 scented flowers per stem in summer

Crocosmia

Montbretia

PERFECT FOR HOT-COLOURED GARDENS, these eye-catching perennials produce arching sprays of flowers in vivid shades of scarlet, orange, and yellow, as well as bicolors in red and orange. From mid- to late summer, long-lasting flowers are held on wiry stems that may be branched or unbranched – they are good for cutting. Crocosmias are robust, forming clumps of flat, sword-like, often ribbed leaves that stand erect but fan out slightly, making a strong accent in a garden bed. Established clumps spread to around 60cm (2ft). Plant crocosmia corms in a cottage garden or with other late-summer perennials, such as Michaelmas Daisies (*Aster, see pp.192–193*), rudbeckias (*see p.317*), and sedums (*see p.324*). Is an environmental weed in some areas, so grow with caution.

Hardiness Fully frost-hardy ❄❄❄ to frost-hardy ❄❄.

Cultivation Plant corms in spring, 8–10cm (3–4in) deep, in soil enriched with well-rotted organic matter, in sun or partial shade. In frost-prone gardens, plant the corms close to a sheltered wall. **Divide** congested clumps in spring or autumn every three or four years to maintain the vigour of the plants (*see right and p.395*).

DIVIDING A CLUMP
Dig up a clump of corms; prise apart with your hands or a spade. Separate the healthy corms, trim off the top-growth, and replant.

Crocosmia masoniorum 🏆
↕ 1.2m (4ft), pleated leaves and upward-facing flowers on unbranched spikes in midsummer ❄❄❄ (borderline)

Crocosmia 'Lucifer' 🏆
↕ 1–1.2m (3–4ft), flowers 5cm (2in) long in midsummer on sparsely branched spikes ❄❄❄ (borderline)

Crocus

NOT JUST A WELCOME SIGN OF SPRING, some Crocuses also extend the season well into autumn. This is a large group of dwarf perennials that grow from corms, producing flowers at the same time as, or just before, the narrow, grassy foliage. The flowers come in vivid or pastel shades from yellow to lilac, purple, and white and are sometimes striped or shaded. The leaves are mid-green with a central, silver-green stripe. Crocuses are easy to grow and look best planted in drifts at the front of a border or naturalized in short grass for carpets of colour. Grow them with spring-flowering bulbs like Dwarf Narcissi (*see pp.288–289*) or autumn-flowering hardy cyclamens (*see p.221*).

Hardiness Fully frost-hardy ❄❄❄ to frost-hardy ❄❄.

Cultivation Most prefer gritty, not too rich, well-drained soil in full sun or partial shade. **Plant** in situ; spring-flowering types 8–10cm (3–4in) deep in autumn, autumn-flowering ones in late summer. Autumn Crocuses can be planted densely in containers and brought indoors to flower. **Divide** cormlets (*see p.395*) while the plants are dormant and replant them, or leave to self-seed freely.

Crocus chrysanthus 'Gipsy Girl'
↕8cm (3in) ↔ 5cm (2in), flowers in early spring ❄❄❄

Crocus chrysanthus 'Snow Bunting' 🏆
↕8cm (3in) ↔ 5cm (2in), scented flowers in early spring, up to four per plant ❄❄❄

Crocus speciosus 🏆
↕10–15cm (4–6in) ↔ 5cm (2in), autumn-flowering crocus which increases rapidly; flowers produced before the leaves ❄❄❄

ꞆYCLAMEN

-IARDY CYCLAMEN BRING WINTER CHEER to gardens ɪnd windowboxes. The elegant flowers of these uberous perennials are held aloft on leafless flower talks. They are produced, depending on the species, rom autumn until late winter and vary in hue from vhite to pink to carmine-red. The leaves are heart-haped to rounded, attractively marked with silver :ones or patterns; they last through winter to spring. Grow these hardy cyclamens under trees, with early ›ulbs such as snowdrops (*Galanthus, see p.247*) and pring-flowering crocuses (*see facing page*); they also lo well in a rock garden, raised bed, or container. Do ɪot confuse them with winter-flowering cyclamens old as houseplants, which are not hardy.

lardiness Fully frost-hardy ❄❄❄ to frost-hardy ❄❄.
:ultivation Plant the corms 2.5–5cm (1–2in) deep in well-drained, ɪumus-rich, fertile soil. They prefer dryish conditions in summer. **Iulch** (*see p.388*) with leafmould every year after the leaves die lown. **Rodents** can be deterred by placing a layer of chicken wire ›ver the tubers at planting time before replacing the soil.

Cyclamen cilicium ♈
↕5cm (2in) ↔ 8cm (3in), pink or white flowers in autumn, stained carmine-red at the mouth, strongly patterned leaves ❄❄

PLANTING CYCLAMEN
To ensure flowers in the first year, plant tubers in root growth, with the tops just visible at soil level. Fill in with soil and firm gently.

Cyclamen hederifolium ♈
:10–13cm (4–5in) ↔ 15cm (6in), sometimes scented flowers in nid- and late autumn, before the variously patterned leaves ❄❄❄

Cyclamen coum ♈
↕5–8cm (2–3in) ↔ 10cm (4in), compact white, pink, or carmine-red flowers in winter or early spring, plain or marbled leaves ❄❄❄

CYNARA

↕1.5–2m (5–6ft)
↔1.2m (4ft)

THESE IMPOSING, ARCHITECTURAL plants have great presence in a garden. The clump-forming perennials produce tall, thistle-like flowerheads in shades of blue and violet from summer until autumn. The unopened buds of the Globe Artichoke (*Cynara scolymus*) are edible, and the flowers can be dried and used in indoor arrangements. The boldly cut, silver or greyish-green leaves arch elegantly in the manner of a fountain, making this an impressive foliage plant for the back of a mixed garden bed with other perennials such as veronicas (*see p.337*), salvias (*see p.318*), or daylilies (*Hemerocallis, see p.258*). Cynaras also attract bees and other pollinating insects into the garden.

Hardiness Fully frost-hardy ❄❄❄ to frost-hardy ❄❄.
Cultivation Grow in any reasonably fertile soil that is well-drained and in full sun. **Sow** seed (*see pp.391–393*) in a container in a cold frame or divide plants (*see p.395*) in spring. New shoots are vulnerable to slugs and snails.

Cynara cardunculus ♈ (Cardoon)
↕1.5m (5ft) ↔ 1.2m (4ft), spiny leaves, woolly grey stems, flowers early to late summer, blanched leaf-stalks and midribs edible ❄❄❄

DAHLIA

DAHLIAS ARE POPULAR GARDEN PLANTS, putting on a bravura performance from midsummer until the first frosts of autumn, in shades from white to vivid yellow, orange, scarlet, pink, and purple. In addition to bringing welcome colour as summer plants fade, the blooms are good for cutting, and a few cultivars have rich, chocolate-coloured foliage. Dahlias, which grow from tubers, are generally tender perennials. In permanent plantings, reserve spaces for them as tubers cannot be set out until late spring or early summer, except in mild, frost-free areas. The smaller bedding types are often treated as annuals and grown from seed each year; they are superb for edging gardens or growing in containers. Dahlia flowers come in a striking range of shapes, sizes, and forms, which as well as brightening gardens and cut-flower arrangements, have great appeal for show exhibitors. There are several categories, including singles and fully doubles, with collarettes and waterlilies somewhere in between. Cactus types have spiky, quill-shaped petals, while pompoms and balls have a pleasing geometry. The giant decoratives may have flowers the size of a tea plate. Dahlias readily mutate and therefore also appeal to plant breeders, who have produced an extraordinary number of cultivars to choose from.

Hardiness Frost-hardy ❄❄ to frost-tender ❄.

Cultivation Grow in full sun in deep, fertile soil enriched with plenty of well-rotted manure or garden compost. Bedding Dahlias tolerate less rich conditions. In milder areas, tubers can be left in the ground, covered with a dry mulch over winter. **Plant out** young plants in leaf when the threat of frost has passed in late spring or early summer – dormant tubers a little earlier – and lift in mid-autumn (*see below*). **Support** with stout stakes or three canes inserted at planting and tie in new growth regularly. Bedding Dahlias do not need staking. **Water** well in dry periods, and feed regularly during the growing season with nitrogenous fertilizer; from midsummer switch to a high-potash fertilizer to encourage flowering. **Cut** flowers regularly to ensure a succession of blooms; for large flowers restrict the plants to two or three shoots. **Propagate** by starting tubers into growth in spring in a greenhouse or cold frame. Divide the tuber into sections, each with a growing shoot, and pot up each as a new plant. Slugs (*see p.398*) and earwigs (*see p.397*) may eat the leaves and flowers.

Storing Dahlias over winter

❶ *In mid-autumn, ideally after the foliage has been blackened by the first frost, cut the old stems back, taking care to leave about 15cm (6in) of stem attached to each tuber. Loosen the soil and lift the tubers out gently. Clean off any excess soil from the tubers and attach a label to each around one of the stems.*

❷ *Store the tubers upside-down for about three weeks in a frost-free place, to allow moisture to drain from the stems, which are hollow. When the stems have dried out, put the tubers in a cool, frost-free place and cover with a layer of bark chippings. Keep them dry until spring, but inspect them occasionally for disease.*

❸ *In spring, about six weeks before the last frosts are expected, plant out dormant tubers. Before planting tall types, insert a stout 1m (3ft) stake in the planting hole. Add soil around the tuber so that the crown, where the stem and tubers are joined, is 2.5–5cm (1–2in) below soil level. Shoots will show in about six weeks.*

①

⑤

⑥

① *Dahlia* **'Bishop of Llandaff'** 🏆 ↕1.1m (3½ft) ↔ 45cm (18in), chocolate-coloured foliage ② **'Hamari Accord'** 🏆 ↕1.2m (4ft) ↔ 60cm (2ft), large semi-cactus ③ **'Hamari Gold'** 🏆 ↕1.2m (4ft) ↔ 60cm (2ft), giant decorative ④ **'Nina Chester'** ↕1.1m (3½ft) ↔ 60cm (2ft), small decorative

3

4

8

9

) **'Noreen'** ↕ 1m (3ft) ↔ 45cm (18in), pompon ⑥ **'Small World'** ♀ ↕ 1.1m (3½ft) ↔ 60cm (2ft),
mpon ⑦ **'White Alva's'** ♀ ↕ 1.2m (4ft) ↔ 60cm (2ft), giant decorative ⑧ **'Wootton Cupid'** ♀
1.1m (3½ft) ↔ 60cm (2ft), miniature ball ⑨ **'Zorro'** ♀ ↕ 1.2m (4ft) ↔ 60cm (2ft), giant decorative

DAMPIERA

VALUED FOR THEIR BLUE FLOWERS, there is a diverse range of species, with quite a few available through garden centres. Commonly grown types are evergreen perennials, although small shrubs also occur. Some colonise areas with a suckering habit, while others are low and spreading. Flower colours vary from pale blue, to dark blue, lavender and purple. While these are only small, they attract attention as they are vibrant and smother the foliage in spring to early summer. The leaves are small and oval to linear and can be green or grey-green and often hairy. They make excellent ground covers between rocks or along edges in full sun. Some are suitable for containers.

Hardiness Frost-hardy ❄❄ to frost-tender ❄.

Cultivation Grow in any well-drained soil that is enriched with well-rotted organic matter in full sun or partial shade. **Prune** minimally; suckering species such as *Dampiera diversifolia* and *D. linearis* can be renewed by hard trimming once established (*see pp.382–384*). **Take** cuttings of firm new growth in late summer (*see p.394*). **Divide** suckering types at any time of the year. **Watch** for caterpillars and control as necessary (*see p.398*).

Dampiera diversifolia
↕2.5cm (1in) ↔ 1m (3ft), makes a tight, suckering, ground cover with gorgeous blue flowers

DARMERA PELTATA

HANDSOME AND UNUSUAL, this spreading perennial enjoys moisture. In late spring, pink or white flowers are borne in clusters at the tips of sturdy, hairy stems that can grow to 2m (6ft) in height. It is only when the flowers begin to fade that the rounded, long-stemmed leaves, which are up to 60cm (24in) across, begin to unfurl. This impressive foliage turns scarlet in autumn, before dying down over winter. *Darmera peltata* is a large plant that needs plenty of space, and although it will grow in a shady border, darmera prefers sites in bog gardens or by water. Try it with other moisture-loving plants like calla (*see p.204*) or caltha (*see p.205*), or plant a group of them together to emphasize their striking forms.

Hardiness Fully frost-hardy ❄❄❄, although flowers may be damaged by late frosts.

Cultivation This plant prefers moist or boggy soil in sun or shade, but it will tolerate drier soil in shade. **Sow** seed (*see pp.391–392*) in containers in a cold frame in spring or autumn, or divide plants (*see p.395*) in spring.

Darmera peltata 🏆
↕2m (6ft) ↔ 1m (3ft) or more

DELPHINIUM

WITH THEIR TOWERING SPIKES of flowers, Delphiniums are perfect for adding height and form to a garden. The blooms are borne in early and midsummer, in a wide range of colours from creamy whites through to lilac-pinks, sky-blues, and deepest, darkest indigo. The mid-green leaves form clumps around the bases of the flower stems. The garden delphiniums are usually herbaceous perennials. Their flower spikes make the stems top-heavy and prone to snapping in winds, so they need support and a position sheltered from wind. This can often be provided by placing them at the back of a border by a wall or fence. Small species and dwarf varieties are suited to more exposed areas.

Hardiness Fully frost-hardy ❄❄❄.

Cultivation Delphiniums like fertile, moist but well-drained soil in full sun. Provide support with sturdy bamboo canes (*see facing page*). **Deadhead** regularly (*see p.390*) and you may be rewarded with anoth flush of flowers later in the summer, but do not expect them to be as spectacular as the first. **Sow** seed (*see pp.391–393*) at 13°C (55°F) in early spring. **Slugs** and snails (*see p.398*), and powdery mildew (caused by damp leaves) can be troublesome.

***Delphinium* 'Compact Blue'**
↕60–75cm (24–30in) ↔ 30cm (1ft), perennial grown as an annual that also makes a good cut flower

elphinium nudicaule
0–90cm (24–36in) ↔ 20cm (8in), short perennial grown as an
nual, flowers in midsummer only

Delphinium 'Emily Hawkins' 🏆
↕ 1.7m (5½ft) ↔ 60–90cm (24–36in), clump-forming perennial

Dianella

Flax Lilies

THESE ARE RHIZOMATOUS PERENNIALS that at first glance look like a grass because of their metre high tufts of narrow upright foliage. This is sword-like and grey-green, or light to dark green. The flowers appear above the foliage in loose clusters at the ends of thin wiry stems in spring and summer. They are small, star-shaped and blue to purple, or occasionally white. Most have berries, but these are only showy in a few species. They are round, fleshy and blue to purple and in *Dianella tasmanica* up to 2cm (1in) across. Most grow well in shade and damp spots and so blend well with ferns that enjoy similar conditions.

Hardiness Fully frost-hardy ❄❄❄ to frost-hardy ❄❄.

Cultivation Grow in full sun or partial shade in just about any well-drained soil. **Sow** seed (*see p.391*) when it is fresh into containers. **Propagation** is usually done by division of existing clumps in autumn.

SUPPORTING A STEM
Insert a cane as tall as the full height of the plant and begin tying in the stem when it is about 30cm (12in) tall, with a figure-of-eight loop.

Delphinium 'Black Knight'
↕ 1.2–1.5m (4–5ft) ↔ 30–45cm (12–18in), tall perennial with dark blue flowers in summer

Dianella tasmanica
↕ 1.5m (5 ft) ↔ 60cm (2ft), has tufty, grass-like foliage and blue flowers and enjoys similar conditions to many ferns

Dianthus

Carnation, Pink, Sweet William

↕8–90cm (3–36in)
↔20–40cm (8–16in)

THE MAIN GARDEN PLANTS IN THIS GROUP of evergreen perennials and annuals are pinks and carnations. In summer, both bear a profusion of bright flowers, which last well when cut, above narrow, silvery leaves. The flowers are single or double in many shades of pink, white, carmine, salmon, and mauve, often with darker, contrasting markings on the petals. Some are fragrant, particularly the rich, spicy "clove-scented" cultivars. Pinks are smaller than carnations and have fewer petals, but other than this their flowers and growth habits are similar. Smaller pinks, including the alpine types like *Dianthus* 'Little Jock', are excellent in rock gardens and troughs. The perpetual carnations, grown under glass for cut flowers, are by far the tallest in the group. Sweet William (*D. barbatus*) is a short-lived perennial usually grown as a biennial from seed sown in summer; plants flower in the following year.

Hardiness Fully frost-hardy ✳✳✳ to frost-tender ✳.

Cultivation All Dianthus require a well-drained, neutral to alkaline soil enriched with well-rotted manure or garden compost. Position plants in full sun. Alpine cultivars, especially, benefit from sharp drainage in alpine troughs and raised beds. **Plant out** young plants in spring and early summer and feed with a balanced fertilizer in spring. **Support** tall cultivars in spring using thin canes and string. **Deadhead** (remove fading flowers) to encourage plants to produce more flowers and maintain a compact growth habit (*see p.390*). Annuals and biennials are discarded after flowering.

Increasing pinks

***Taking pipings** is an easy way to propagate all kinds of* Dianthus, *but especially Pinks. Choose non-flowering shoots. Hold a shoot near the base and sharply pull out the tip. The shoot should break easily at a leaf joint, giving a cutting or piping about 8–10cm (3–4in) long with three or four pairs of leaves. Remove the lowest pair of leaves and insert the pipings in pots containing equal parts cuttings mix and sharp sand. Place in a shady spot, keep moist, and when they have rooted, after three or four weeks, pot up the young plants separately.*

Layering border carnations

❶ *Loosen the soil around the plant and mix in equal parts sharp sand and sieved compost. Select non-flowering sideshoots and remove all but the top four or five leaves on each shoot. Below a bud, cut into the stem along its length to form a tongue* (see inset). *Wounding the stem in this way encourages roots to form. Dust the cut surface with hormone rooting powder.*

❷ *Push the tongue of each shoot into the prepared soil and pin down with a piece of bent wire. Tie the leafy part of the shoot to a cane so it is held upright and the cut is held open. Water lightly, cover the shoot with soil, and put a stone over it to retain moisture. Check if roots have formed after five or six weeks. Separate and lift the layers from the parent plant and plant out.*

①

⑤

⑥

① **'Doris'** 🏆 ↕45cm (18in) ↔ 40cm (16in), scented pink ② **'Mrs Sinkins'** ↕45cm (18in) ↔ 30cm (1ft), scented pink ③ ***deltoides*** ↕45cm (18in) ↔ 30cm (1ft), pink ④ **'Forest Treasure'** ↕60cm (2ft) ↔ 40cm (16in), carnation ⑤ **'Houndspool Ruby'** 🏆 ↕45cm (18in) ↔ 40cm (16in), pink ⑥ **'La**

ourboule' ↕20cm (8in), ↔ 30cm (1ft), scented alpine pink ⑦ **'Musgrave's Pink'** ↕45cm
8in) ↔ 30cm (1ft), pink ⑧ **'Valda Wyatt'** ♀ ↕45cm (18in) ↔ 40cm (16in), scented pink
'Little Jock' ↕20cm (8in), ↔ 30cm (1ft), scented alpine pink

Diascia

For their length of flowering alone, these annuals and semi-evergreen perennials are worthy of any garden. Loose, densely packed flowerheads bloom from early summer to late autumn above narrowly lance-shaped to heart-shaped, mid-green leaves. The colour range includes shades of apricot, deep pink, rose-pink, purplish-pink, or salmon-pink. Try growing diascias at the front of a garden, under roses, or in a rock garden. Most are creeping or mat-forming, but some diascias have a trailing habit which makes them excellent in containers.

Hardiness Most are frost-hardy to –8°C (18°F) ❄❄.

Cultivation Diascias prefer moist but well-drained, fertile soil, in full sun. Water in dry periods. **Sow** seed (*see pp.391–393*) at 16°C (61°F) as soon as it is ripe, or in spring. Take semi-ripe cuttings in late summer (*see p.394*). Divide perennials in autumn.

① *barberae* 'Blackthorn Apricot' 🏆 ② *fetcaniensis* – all these ↕25cm (10in) ↔ 50cm (20in) ③ *rigescens* 🏆 ↕30cm (12in) ↔ 50cm (20in)

Dicentra

see also p.140

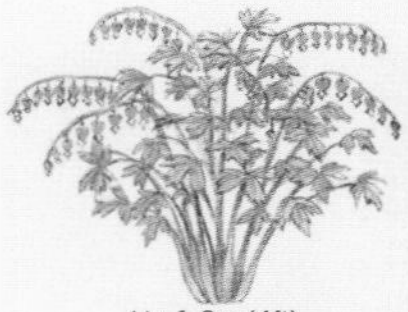

↕to 1.2m (4ft)
↔45cm (18in)

This cottage-garden favourite is grown both for its finely cut foliage and heart-shaped flowers. Most are perennials and form compact clumps with ferny, often greyish leaves and arching stems from which the flowers are suspended. Flowers are produced from spring to early summer in a range of shades from red, purple, and deep pink to white or yellow. Dicentras are also at home in a mixed garden, cottage-garden planting, or in woodland garden. They may die down early in dry summers. Their delicate flowers and foliage contrasts nicely with the broad young foliage of hostas (*see pp.260–261*).

Hardiness Fully frost-hardy ❄❄❄, but frost can damage early growth.

Cultivation Most Dicentras thrive in partial shade and moist, fertile, slightly alkaline (limy) soil enriched with well-rotted organic matter. *D. spectabilis* tolerates sun if in moist soil. **Sow** seed (*see pp. 391–393*) in a container in a cold frame as soon as it is ripe, or in spring. **Divide** the fleshy-rooted plants (*see p.395*) carefully in spring or after the leaves die down.

Dicentra formosa (Wild Bleeding Heart)
↕45cm (18in) ↔ 60–90cm (24–36in), spreading perennial, leaves glaucous below, late spring and early summer flowers fade to white

Dicentra spectabilis 🏆 (Bleeding Heart)
↕to 1.2m (4ft) ↔ 45cm (18in), clumping perennial, light green leaves, flowers in late spring and early summer

Dicentra cucullaria
↕to 20cm (8in) ↔ 25cm (10in), tuberous perennial, compact clumps, white flowers in early spring, needs gritty soil

icentra spectabilis 'Alba' ♡
› 1.2m (4ft) ↔ 45cm (18in), robust, clump-forming perennial,
ht green leaves, flowers from late spring until midsummer

DICTAMNUS ALBUS

Burning Bush, Dittany

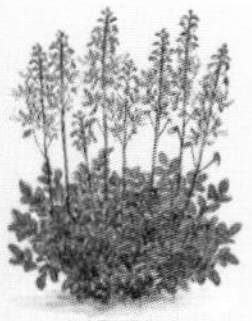

↕40–90cm (16–36in) ↔60cm (24in)

THIS TALL, WOODY-BASED perennial is grown for its dense spikes of fragrant flowers, produced above lemon-scented foliage in summer. The leathery leaves are composed of light green leaflets. Volatile, aromatic oils produced by the flowers and ripening seedpods can be ignited in hot weather, giving rise to the common name of Burning Bush. This clumping plant mixes well in a herbaceous or mixed border with other tall perennials such as achilleas (*see p.166*), phloxes (*see p.306*), daylilies (*Hemerocallis, see p.258*) and loosestrifes (*Lythrum, see p.283*). Contact with the foliage may cause skin irritation aggravated by sunlight (photodermatitis).

Hardiness Fully frost-hardy ✻✻✻.

Cultivation Grow this plant in any well-drained, reasonably fertile soil, in full sun or partial shade. **Sow** seed (*see pp.391–393*) in containers in a cold frame as soon as it is ripe. **Divide** plants (*see p.395*) in autumn or spring; bear in mind that the woody rootstocks may take some time to get established again.

① ***albus*** white or pinkish-white flowers
② ***albus* var. *purpureus*** ♡ purplish-pink flowers

DIERAMA

Fairies' Fishing Rod, Angel's Fishing Rod

ONE OF THE MOST DELICATE-LOOKING and mobile plants in the garden, dieramas carry their flowers on long, gently arching stems, so slender that they move in every breeze. The funnel- or bell-shaped flowers in shades of coral-pink to red, bright pink, or purple-pink and white, are borne in succession and hang from the stems on individual flower spikes. The fine, grassy, green to grey-green leaves of these evergreen perennials grow from tufts at the base and can be up to 90cm (36in) long. Grow dieramas with other summer-flowering perennials such as penstemons (*see p.304*), phloxes (*see p.306*), and salvias (*see p.318*).

Hardiness Frost-hardy ✻✻ to frost-tender ✻; established clumps tolerate temperatures down to –10°C (14°F).

Cultivation Plant the corms 5–8cm (2–3in) deep in spring; site them in well-drained soil enriched with rotted organic matter, in a sheltered site in full sun. Do not let plants dry out in summer. In frost-prone areas, cover them with a protective dry mulch over winter. Young plants take some time to settle, but once established grow freely. **Sow** seed (*see pp.391–393*) in a seedbed or in containers in a cold frame as soon as it is ripe. **Divide** clumps (*see p.395*) in winter or early spring.

Dierama pulcherrimum
↕1–1.5m (3–5ft) ↔ 60cm (24in), flowers pale to deep magenta-pink, occasionally white or purple-red, in summer ✻✻

DIETES

THESE SOUTH AFRICAN NATIVES are useful not only for their beauty, but for their general toughness. They have erect, narrow, permanent, light green leaves in a tight, upright or slightly arching clump. The iris-like flowers are held at the top of the foliage on straight stems emerging from the clumps. These occur in late spring and summer, and open flat with their faces looking roughly skywards. In the commonly grown *Dietes bicolor* the flowers are pale yellow with brown flashes towards the centre, while in *D. grandiflora* they are white with markings of pale orange and mauve at the centre.

Hardiness Frost-hardy ✻✻.

Cultivation Grow in a well-drained soil in full sun for best results. They will tolerate extended dry periods. **Trim** out spent flower stems of *D. bicolor* but leave those of *D. grandiflora* as they will produce more flowers in the future. **Propagate** by dividing existing clumps in autumn.

Dietes bicolor
↕1.2m (4 ft) ↔ 60cm (2ft), grows well in full sun on very little water so is often used in municipal plantings

DIGITALIS

Foxglove

CLASSIC COTTAGE-GARDEN PLANTS, foxgloves form a large group of biennials and short-lived perennials. Their imposing flower spikes come in a variety of shades, from the classic purple of *Digitalis purpurea* to pink, white, and yellow, and appear from spring through to midsummer in the second year. They are striking plants, with one or more leafy rosettes at the base, and flower stems often reaching 1.5m (5ft) or more. Use them to give height to a mixed garden with other early-flowering perennials such as dicentras (*see p.228*) and doronicums (*see facing page*) or in a woodland planting. They self-seed prolifically, adding a natural charm to the garden. All foxgloves are toxic.

Hardiness Fully frost-hardy ✻✻✻ to frost-hardy ✻✻.

Cultivation Grow in almost any soil and situation, except extremely wet or dry conditions. Most prefer soil enriched with well-rotted organic matter in partial shade. **Deadhead** after flowering if you do not want the seedlings springing up everywhere. **Collect** the seed and sow in containers in a cold frame in late spring (*see pp.391–393*). The leaves might be disfigured (*see p.399*) by leaf spot and powdery mildew: avoid splashing the foliage when watering and pick off affected leaves.

Digitalis davisiana
↕to 70cm (28in) ↔ 45cm (18in), perennial with underground stems (rhizomes), flowers in early summer ✻✻

Digitalis × mertonensis 🏆
↕to 90cm (3ft) ↔ 30cm (12in), clump-forming perennial, flowers i late spring and early summer, comes true from seed ✻✻✻

)igitalis grandiflora ♡
to 90cm (3ft) ↔ 45cm (18in), clumping biennial or perennial, veined
aves up to 25cm (10in), flowers in early and midsummer ❄❄❄

SELF-SOWN SEEDLINGS
Check for seedlings at the foot of
each plant in early autumn. Lift
them with a trowel so each retains
a ball of soil around its roots and
replant them 30cm (12in) apart.

)igitalis purpurea Excelsior Group
90cm–2m (3–6ft) ↔ to 60cm (24in), biennial or perennial, at their
est when grown annually from seed, good for cut flowers ❄❄❄

Doronicum

Leopard's Bane

LEOPARD'S BANE ARE GROWN FOR their delightful yellow flowers, which can be single or double. They are held, on their own or in small clusters, on slender stems high above the leaves. These perennials flower for several weeks over spring, but may come into bloom in mid- or late winter if the weather is mild. Some species are bulbous and have tubers or rhizomes (*see p.164*). Leopard's Bane look quite at home in a woodland garden; alternatively, plant them in a garden with daffodils (*Narcissus, see pp.288–289*), pulmonarias (*see p.314*) and primulas (*see pp.312–313*). They are also good for cutting.

Hardiness Fully frost-hardy ❄❄❄.

Cultivation Grow in moist soil enriched with well-rotted organic matter, in part or dappled shade. *D. orientale* and its cultivars are vulnerable to root rot, especially on heavy clay soils that are wet in winter: dig in plenty of coarse sand and gypsum to improve drainage on heavy soils. Raising the soil level by 5–8cm (2–3in) can also help. **Water** well in the growing season and deadhead to prolong flowering. **Sow** seed in containers in a cold frame in spring (*see pp.391–393*). **Divide** plants in early autumn (*see p.395*). Powdery mildew may affect the leaves if the air is damp; avoid splashing leaves when watering.

Doronicum × excelsum
↕60–90cm (2–3ft) ↔ to 60cm (2ft), butter yellow flowers on upright thin stems in spring

Doryanthes

Gymea Lily, Spear Lily

THESE ARE LARGE, CLUMP-FORMING, evergreen herbaceous perennials. Mature plants can form clumps over 1.5m (5ft) high and 3m across (9ft) with their over 1m-long (3ft), sword-like, light green foliage. From the centre of these clumps rise spectacular, straight flower stems up to 3m (9ft) high. The red flowers are 10cm (4in) across and occur in a 30cm (1ft) globe at the top of the stem. In *Doryanthes excelsa* this happens in spring or summer, while in the less commonly grown *D. palmeri* it is restricted to spring. Foliage clumps survive frosts but unfortunately the flowerheads will not.

Hardiness Frost-hardy ❄❄ to frost-tender ❄.

Cultivation Full or part sun or dappled shade and a well-drained soil that is enriched with well-rotted organic matter is best. Shelter from strong winds is also preferable. **Prune** minimally; remove any old or damaged leaves and spent flower stems after seed has been collected (*see p.383*). **Sow** seed (*see p.391*) which germinates readily, as soon as collected in containers. Plants can be propagated by division done in the autumn (*see p.395*).

Doryanthes excelsa
↕↔ 3m (9 ft), is a spectacular plant when in flower

Dracunculus vulgaris

THIS UNUSUAL PLANT is not grown much in gardens, and anyone who has smelt it in flower knows why. It gives off the putrid smell of rancid and rotting meat to attract the flies that will pollinate the flower. The leaves are large and glossy and roughly arrowhead-shaped, although deeply lobed. They are dark green and mottled with silver and the stems are white with black splotches. The flower is like those of Arum Lily (*Arum, see p.190*) and up to 30cm (12in) long. They appear in mid- to late summer and are velvety in look and deep scarlet in colour.

Hardiness Frost-hardy ✲✲.

Cultivation Plant tubers 15cm (6in) deep and 25cm (10in) apart in winter while they are dormant. The soil should be well-drained and enriched with well-rotted organic matter. They can also be grown in large containers of quality potting mix. Full sun or very light shade and shelter from hot, drying winds is best. **Staking** may be necessary in windy areas. **Propagate** by dividing tubers in winter. **Pests** are rarely a problem, but keep a watch out for snails and slugs (*see p.398*).

Dracunculus vulgaris
↕90cm (3 ft) ↔ 60cm (2ft), looks attractive but smells of rotten meat to attract flies

Dryas

Mountain Avens

MATS OF PLEASING, EVERGREEN FOLIAGE distinguish these prostrate, low-growing, woody-based perennials. The oak-like, leathery leaves have a whitish down on their undersides. The plants are also valued for their large, white or yellowish flowers produced from spring to early summer. Upright or nodding, they have a central boss of golden stamens and are borne singly at the tips of slender stems. Pinkish, feathery seedheads follow. An open, sunny site at the front of a garden suits these easy-to-grow, carpeting plants. They will also happily scramble over rocks in a rock garden or even colonize dry-stone walls.

Hardiness Fully frost-hardy ✲✲✲.

Cultivation Grow these plants in well-drained soil enriched with well-rotted organic matter. They will grow in full sun or partial shade. **Add** plenty of sand to maintain good drainage. **Sow** seed (*see pp.391–393*) in a container in a cold frame as soon as they are ripe, or take softwood cuttings (*see p.394*) in early summer. **Lift**, detach, and transplant rooted stems in spring.

Dryas octopetala ♀ (Mountain Avens)
↕10cm (4in) ↔ 1m (36in), mat-forming, flowers in late spring or early summer, suitable for the rock garden

Echeveria

A DIVERSE RANGE OF EVERGREEN, perennial succulents, they do have in common that they are all rosette-forming. The leaves are very fleshy and generally grey and arranged in a tight or slightly loose bowl-shape. Some cultivars have leaves that are tinged with pink, or have black tips, and some even have gently wavy ends. The flowers are pendent, pink tube that droop on the end of long thin stems held well above the foliage and occur at various times of the year depending on the species and the weather. Extremely drought-tolerant, they grow well in containers, as well as making interesting borders to garden beds.

Hardiness Frost-hardy ✲✲ to very frost-tender ❀.

Cultivation They must have free-draining soil and do best in full sun. Container-grown plants can be grown in a quality potting mix tha has hard sharp sand or grit added to improve drainage. **Take** leaf or stem cuttings in spring or summer (*see p.394*). Offsets or divisions planted in spring can also be used for propagation (*see p.395*).

Echeveria glauca
↕10cm (4in) ↔ 30cm (12in), clump forming and extremely drough tolerant, the flower stem rises 30cm (12in) above the foliage

:CHINACEA
oneflower

/ITH THEIR LARGE DAISIES in shades of purple, rose-ink, or white, these tall perennials from dry prairies, pen woodland, and gravelly hillsides make an eye-atching display in the late-summer garden. The large entral cone standing proud of its petals gives rise) the plant's common name and may be brownish-ellow to ochre. Each daisy is up to 15cm (6in) cross and is held on stout, upright stems. The flowers ersist for about two months and they also make ong-lasting cut flowers. The leaves reach up to 20cm 3in) in length. Grow these undemanding plants in garden with other late-flowering perennials, such s rudbeckias (*see p.317*). The seedheads continue ooking good into winter.

ardiness Fully frost-hardy ❄❄❄.

ultivation Coneflowers need deep, fertile, well-drained soil riched with well-rotted organic matter and full sun, although they erate some shade. **Cut back** the stems as the flowers fade for more ooms. **Sow** seed (*see pp.391–393*) in spring. **Divide** in spring or tumn (*see p.395*). **Take** root cuttings (*see p.394*) in late autumn.

Echinacea purpurea
↕1.5m (5ft) ↔ 45cm (18in), stems sometimes red-tinted, flowers are 13cm (5in) across and borne from midsummer to early autumn

***Echinacea* 'White Swan'**
↕60–90cm (2–3ft) ↔ 45cm (18in) , white flowers from midsummer well into autumn

***chinacea purpurea* 'Magnus'**
↕.5m (5ft) ↔ 45cm (18in), extra-large flowers are 18cm (7in) cross and borne from midsummer to early autumn

***Echinacea purpurea* 'Kim's Knee High'**
↕45cm (18in) ↔ 30–60cm (12–24in), unusually compact, dwarf habit, flowers from midsummer to early autumn, drought-tolerant, can be grown in containers

ECHINOPS

Globe Thistle

GROWN FOR THEIR THISTLE-LIKE FLOWERS that appear from midsummer until autumn, these perennials, biennials, and annuals are very undemanding plants. The flowers can be up to 4cm (1½in) across, often have bristly bracts (modified leaves), and are usually blue or white and carried on stout stems. Globe Thistles usually form clumps and often have dissected foliage that is spiny and greyish-white. The flowers are also good for cutting and drying. Plant them in a wild garden, or grow them with other perennials such as echinaceas (*see p.232*), monardas (*see p.286*), and phloxes (*see p.306*).

Hardiness Fully frost-hardy ❄❄❄ to frost-hardy ❄❄.

Cultivation Globe Thistles are best grown in poor, well-drained soil in full sun, but they will tolerate almost any situation. **Remove** fading flowers to prevent self-seeding. **Sow** seed in a seedbed in mid-spring (*see pp.391–393*). **Divide** established plants from autumn to spring or take root cuttings in winter (*see pp.394–395*).

Echinops ritro
↕ to 90cm (3ft) ↔ 45cm (18in), compact perennial, leaves have white, downy undersides, flowers in late summer ❄❄❄

ECHIUM

THIS IS A LARGE GROUP OF ANNUALS, biennials, evergreen perennials, and shrubs, with charming flowers that appear from early to late summer in shades of deep blue, pink, purple, or white. They are carried either on large, impressive spikes, or in dense clusters close to the stems. The bristly, hairy leaves are usually borne in basal rosettes and on the stems. Grow echiums in gardens with echinaceas (*see p.232*), chrysanthemums (*see pp.212–213*), and phloxes (*see p.306*). *Echium wildpretii* is a biennial that dies after flowering, so allow it to set seed before removing. Wear gloves when handling echiums because contact with the bristly foliage may irritate your skin.

Hardiness Fully frost-hardy ❄❄❄ to very frost-tender ❁.

Cultivation Grow these plants in reasonably fertile, well-drained soil, in full sun. **Sow** seed at 13–16°C (55–61°F) in summer and overwinter the seedlings in a frost-free greenhouse or cold frame; annuals can be sown in spring where they are to grow (*see pp.391–393*).

Echium wildpretii
↕ to 60cm (2ft) ↔ 60–90cm (2–3ft), extremely tall biennial flowering mid-spring ❄

:PIMEDIUM

arrenwort, Bishop's Mitre

HE FOLIAGE IS PRIZED AS MUCH AS THE FLOWERS ith these perennials. The mid- to light green leaves 'e lost in autumn in some species or after new leaves ave formed in others. They often develop attractive ›nes in autumn and occasionally bronze tips on the ew leaves in spring. From spring until early summer, ›ose clusters of saucer- to cup-shaped flowers, ften with spurs, are produced in a range of colours ıcluding gold, beige, white, pink, crimson, and urple. They make excellent ground-cover plants, pecially under trees where little else will grow.

ardiness Fully frost-hardy ❄❄❄, although sharp frosts may mage young foliage and flowers.

ultivation Grow epimediums in fertile soil, enriched with well-tted organic matter, in partial shade. Provide shelter from strong, hot nds. **Sow** seed in a container in a cold frame as soon as it is ripe *ee pp.391–393*). **Divide** established plants in autumn or just after wering (*see p.395*).

SPRING PRUNING Use shears to clip old leaves to the ground in late winter or early spring, before the new flower spikes appear, to encourage new growth, except for *E. perralderianum*.

Epimedium × *youngianum* 'Niveum' ♀
↕20–30cm (8–12in) ↔ 30cm (12in), deciduous clump, red-tinted leaf stalks, coloured foliage when young, flowers mid- to late spring

pimedium acuminatum
30cm (12in) ↔ 45cm (18in), clumping evergreen, leaf undersides ave waxy or powdery bloom, flowers in mid-spring to early summer

Epimedium pinnatum subsp. *colchicum* ♀
↕30–40cm (12–16in) ↔ 25cm (10in), slow-growing, clump-forming evergreen, new leaves have white or red hairs, flowers in spring

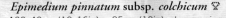

Epimedium 'Versicolor'
↕↔ 30cm (12in), clump-forming evergreen, young leaves copper-red and brown (*inset*) turning mid-green, flowers in mid- and late spring

Eranthis hyemalis

Winter Aconite

Winter Aconites provide a splash of gold to signal the end of winter. Their buttercup-like flowers bloom from late winter to early spring; each appears to sit on an elegant ruff of finely dissected leaves. The leaves at the bases are broader and deeply lobed. These clump-forming perennials grow from knobbly tubers just below soil level in damp, shady places. They look best under deciduous shrubs or trees where, once established, they rapidly spread to form a carpet of colour, especially on alkaline (limy) soils. Winter Aconites also naturalize well in grass and combine well with other winter- and early-spring bulbs, such as snowdrops (*Galanthus, see p.247*). Contact with the sap may aggravate skin allergies.

Hardiness Fully frost-hardy ❄❄❄ to frost-hardy ❄❄.

Cultivation Fertile soil that does not dry out in summer and a position in full sun or light, dappled shade are required here. **Plant** the tubers 5cm (2in) deep in autumn. Dried-out tubers will not thrive. **Sow** seed (*see pp.391–393*) in containers in a cold frame in late spring. Lift and divide large clumps (*see p.395*) in spring after flowering.

Eremurus

Desert Candle, Foxtail Lily

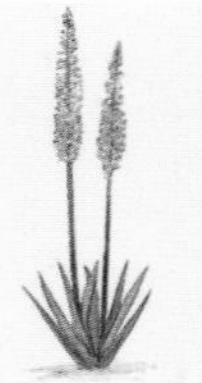

↕1–3m (3–10ft) ↔to 1.2m (4ft)

Majestic flower spikes densely covered in pink, white, or golden, starry flowers soar skywards in spring and early summer. Usually, these clump-forming perennials produce only one flowering stem from each crown. Their long, fleshy, strappy leaves deteriorate quickly, however, so Foxtail Lilies are best positioned toward the middle or back of a garden among shrubs or herbaceous perennials, where the dying foliage will be hidden from view. The flowers are long-lasting when cut. Since grasslands and semi-desserts are the natural home of foxtail lilies, their large, starfish-shaped, fleshy rootstocks are prone to rot in damp conditions.

Hardiness Fully frost-hardy ❄❄❄; although young growth is often damaged by frosts.

Cultivation Plant in well-drained, fertile soil, in full sun with shelter from winds. To improve drainage on heavy clay soils, dig in plenty of gypsum around the planting area; fork extra into the bottom of the planting hole. **Support** in exposed sites. **Sow** seed (*see pp.391–393*) in containers in a cold frame in autumn or late winter. **Divide** plants after flowering (*see p.395*); handle the brittle rootstocks gently.

Eranthis hyemalis 🏆 (Winter Aconite)
↕5–8cm (2–3in) ↔ 5cm (2in), rapid colonizer especially in alkaline (limy) soils, flowers 2–3cm (¾–1¼in) across ❄❄❄

Eremurus himalaicus ↕1.2–2m (4–6ft) ↔ 60cm (24in), green leaves, flowers in late spring to early summer

:RIGIGERON

leabane

ONG-LASTING, SINGLE OR DOUBLE DAISIES are orne over many weeks in summer by the annuals, iennials, and perennials in this group. The flowers re available in a wide range of shades, from white, ink, purple, to yellow or orange. All have a bright ellow eye and are borne singly or in small clusters. 'he leaves are found mostly at the bases of the plants, re sometimes spoon-shaped, and mid- or light green. rigerons range from low-growing alpines to medium-zed clumps, so need a position at the front of a arden. They also stand up well to salt-laden winds, naking them invaluable in coastal gardens. The owers last well if they are cut when fully open.

ardiness Fully frost-hardy ✲✲✲.

ultivation Erigerons prefer fertile, well-drained soil, in full sun. **emove** fading flowers regularly for more flowers; cut down old growth autumn. **Divide** plants every 2–3 years in late spring (*see p.395*). **ake** root cuttings (*see p.394*) in spring or detach new shoots near the ase and treat as softwood cuttings.

Erigeron karvinskianus ♡
↕15–30cm (6–12in) ↔ 1m (3ft) or more, vigorous carpeting species suitable for cracks in walls or paving, white flowers fade to pink

rigeron 'Profusion'

Erigeron 'Quakeress'
↕60cm (24in) ↔ 45cm (18in), vigorous, clump-forming border perennial, clusters of single flowers in early and midsummer

ERINUS

Fairy Foxglove

DAINTY, OPEN FLOWERS in shades of pink, purple, or white are borne in clusters by these trouble-free plants. There are only two species, which are semi-evergreen, short-lived perennials. The leaves are lance- to wedge-shaped, softly textured, and produced in rosettes. Fairy Foxgloves are ideal for alpine or rock gardens, or for growing in crevices in old walls or between gaps in paving. If you let them, they will self-seed themselves around the garden.

Hardiness Fully frost-hardy ***.

Cultivation Grow these plants in light, reasonably fertile soil that is well-drained, in full sun or partial shade. **Sow** seed in the ground where they are to grow or in containers in a cold frame in autumn (*see pp.391–393*). **Take rosettes** as cuttings in spring (*see p.394*).

Erinus alpinus ♀
↕8cm (3in) ↔ 10cm (4in), sticky leaves, pink, purple, or white flowers from late spring to summer

ERODIUM

Heron's Bill, Stork's Bill

THE FOLIAGE AND LONG FLOWERING PERIOD of the annual and perennial erodiums make them valuable plants for the garden. The flowers resemble those of cranesbills (*Geranium, see pp.250–251*) and are produced singly from the joints of leaves and stems or in clusters at the ends of the stems. Flower hues range from pink to purple, and occasionally yellow or white. The curious, pointed seed pods give the plant its common name. Grow the smaller species in a rock garden and the taller ones in a mixed garden with other summer-flowering perennials such as achilleas (*see p.166*), geraniums, phloxes (*see p.306*), or among shrub roses (*see pp.110–113*).

Hardiness Fully frost-hardy *** to frost-hardy **.

Cultivation Grow the plants in well-drained soil that is neutral to alkaline (limy), in full sun. **Protect** the smaller species from excessive winter wet to avoid them rotting off by covering them with an open-sided cloche. **Sow** seed as soon as it is ripe in containers in a cold frame (*see pp.391–393*). **Divide** plants in spring or take stem cuttings in late spring or early summer (*see pp.394–395*).

Erodium manescaui
↕20–45cm (8–18in) ↔ 20cm (8in), clumping perennial, flowers summer to autumn ***

ERYNGIUM

Sea Holly, Eryngo

SEA HOLLIES ARE STRIKING, ARCHITECTURAL plants that lift any garden, while some can be naturalized in a wildflower meadow. Most form basal rosettes of leaves that are often spiny, with attractive silvery whit veins. From midsummer to autumn, they bear thistle like flowers on branched stems. These consist of round to cone-shaped heads of tiny flowers, that are surrounded by conspicuous ruffs, also usually silvery white. Grow smaller Sea Hollies in a rock garden and taller ones in a herbaceous border, where their skeleta forms can be enjoyed through winter. The flowers ca be dried, but cut them before they are fully open for best effect. Eryngiums are a large group of annuals, biennials, and deciduous and evergreen perennials.

Hardiness Fully frost-hardy *** to frost-hardy **.

Cultivation All Sea Hollies prefer well-drained soil in full sun, but some like poor to moderately fertile soil and protection from excessive winter wet whereas others need moist, rich soil. **Sow** seed as soon as they are ripe in containers in a cold frame (*see pp.391–393*). **Divide** plants in spring – they can be slow to re-establish; take root cuttings of perennials in winter (*see pp.394–395*).

Eryngium giganteum
↕1.2m (4ft) ↔ 75cm (2.5ft), striking foliage and blue flowers in late summer ***

yngium × *tripartitum* ♀
‡0–90cm (2–3ft) ↔ 50cm (20in), clump-forming perennial, dark
een toothed leaves, flowers midsummer to early autumn ❄❄❄

Eryngium variifolium
‡30–40cm (12–16in) ↔ 25cm (10in), clump-forming evergreen, flowers in mid- and late summer, protect from winter wet ❄❄❄

ERYSIMUM

Wallflower

THE MOST COMMONLY GROWN WALLFLOWERS are usually grown as biennials or short-lived perennials. The fragrant flowers are produced in pastel and brilliant hues of scarlet, orange, and gold, with some purples. Wallflowers spread to 20–60cm (8–24in), so are ideal for containers, a rock garden, or the front of a mixed garden bed. Use with spring-flowering plants such as forget-me-nots (*Myosotis*, *see p.287*), primulas (*see pp.312–313*), and tulips (*see pp.334–335*).

Hardiness Fully frost-hardy ❄❄❄ to frost-hardy ❄❄.

Cultivation Grow in poor to reasonably fertile, well-drained, slightly alkaline (limy) soil, or potting mix, in full sun or light shade. **Trim** perennials lightly after flowering to keep them compact. **Sow** seed of perennials in a cold frame in spring. Transplant to flowering positions in autumn (*see pp.392–393*). **Take** softwood cuttings from woody-based perennials in summer (*see p.394*).

Erysimum 'Winter Joy'
‡45cm (18in) ↔ 45cm (18in), useful for bringing colour into the garden in winter ❄❄

ERYTHRONIUM

Dog's-Tooth Violet, Trout Lily

THE ELEGANT, DROOPING FLOWERS of these perennials are produced from spring until early summer, singly or in clusters on slender, upright stems. They have distinctive, swept-back petals, in shades of purple, violet, pink, yellow, or white, and conspicuously long stamens. The broad leaves grow from the base and may be glossy or glaucous; some have a strong bronze marbling, as in *Erythronium dens-canis*, or are veined with white. The common name derives from the long-pointed, tooth-like bulbs from which these clump-forming perennials grow. Natives of meadows and woodlands, they thrive in a rock garden or beneath deciduous trees, and also if naturalized with other bulbs such as dwarf narcissi (*see pp.288–289*) and crocuses (*see p.220*).

Hardiness Fully frost-hardy ❄❄❄.

Cultivation These plants like deep, fertile soil that does not dry out, in partial or light, dappled shade. Plant the bulbs at least 10cm (4in) deep in autumn; keep them slightly damp if stored before planting. **Divide** established clumps (*see right and p.395*) after flowering.

***Erythronium* 'Pagoda'** ♕

↕15–35cm (6–14in) ↔ 10cm (4in), very vigorous, leaves are glossy green and marbled bronze, clusters of up to ten flowers in spring

DIVIDING CLUMPS
After the leaves wither, lift the bulbs carefully with a fork; separate the offsets, and replant them.

***Erythronium californicum* 'White Beauty'** ♕

↕15–35cm (6–14in) ↔ 10cm (4in), vigorous, soon forms a large clump, bears clusters of up to three flowers in spring

Erythronium revolutum ♕ (American Trout Lily)

↕20–30cm (8–12in) ↔ 10cm (4in), clusters of up to four flowers in mid-spring, sometimes slow to establish, but can self-sow freely once it is settled, leaves heavily marbled bronze

Erythronium dens-canis ♕ (European Dog's-Tooth Viole

↕10–15cm (4–6in) ↔ 10cm (4in), pink, white, or lilac flowers with blue or purple-blue anthers singly in spring, naturalizes well in gras

:SCHSCHOLZIA

alifornia Poppy

N FIERY SHADES OF ORANGE, gold, and sometimes ream, white, or pink, the tissue-thin, satiny flowers f California Poppies are carried singly on slender :ems. They may be simple and cup-shaped, double, r even ruffled. Although they open fully only in sun, ıe flowers are still colourful when closed and are ood for cutting. The ferny foliage is light to blue- reen. The most commonly grown are the summer- owering hardy annuals – often in a border with ther annuals such as annual phloxes (*see p.306*) or in gravel garden. *Eschscholzia californica* types also do ell in containers and hanging baskets. These oppies' fragile appearance belies their robust nature; ıey self-seed freely, even into cracks in paving or ɔncrete.

ardiness Fully frost-hardy ❄❄❄.

ultivation These poppies thrive in a poor, well-drained soil, in full ın. **Sow** seed (*see pp.391–393*) of annuals where they are to grow in ring or early autumn. Repeat sowings at two or three week intervals provide a succession of flowers. Thin to around 15cm (6in) apart.

'schscholzia californica ♀ (California Poppy)
:o 30cm (12in) ↔ to 15cm (6in), very variable habit, often ɔrawling, flowers orange, red, white, and gold in summer

EUCHARIS GRANDIFLORA

Amazon Lily

As the common name suggests, this bulb is from South America, and it is not surprising to find that it prefers moist, humid conditions. The generally evergreen leaves are long and narrowly oval, somewhat reminiscent of aspidistra. The flowers look like white daffodils and fill the area around them with a sweet fragrance. They usually occur in bunches of two to four per stem. Flowering happens in spring and occasionally in early autumn as well. They can be grown in garden beds outdoors only in the warmest districts and elsewhere are restricted to containers in warm or heated glasshouses.

Hardiness Very frost-tender ❀.

Cultivation Grow in humid areas in any well-drained neutral to acid (lime-free) soil enriched with well-rotted organic matter. Shade from the hot sun is important, along with shelter from hot, drying winds. Place container-grown plants in the same conditions. Water during active growth but reduce in the dormant period. **Divide** overcrowded bulbs in spring only if necessary, as they resent disturbance (*see p.395*).

Eucharis grandiflora
↕60cm (2 ft) ↔ 30cm (1ft), is only for humid areas, but worth it for the strong perfume of the daffodil-like flowers

EUCOMIS

Pineapple Lily, Pineapple Flower

↕15–75cm (6–30in)
↔15–20cm (6–8in)

THESE STRIKING PLANTS are grown for their unusual clusters of flowers in late summer and early autumn. The starry flowers are usually pale greenish-white or white, but what sets them apart is the tuft of green bracts leaves, similar to that on a pineapple, that tops each tight cluster. The flowers are followed by seed pods. In warm districts, grow these bulbous perennials in a sunny spot, where the upright stems and strappy leaves contrast well with the foliage plants such as cerastium (*see p.210*). In very cold districts, grow them in containers so they can be overwintered under cover.

Hardiness Fully frost-hardy ❄❄❄ (borderline) to very frost-tender ❀.

Cultivation Plant the bulbs 15cm (6in) deep in fertile, well-drained soil in full sun. **In pots**, use a quality potting mix, and water freely in summer and sparingly in winter. **Sow** seed (*see pp.391–393*) at 16°C (61°F) in autumn or spring or remove bulb offsets (*see p.395*) in spring.

Eucomis bicolor ♀
↕30–60cm (12–24in) ↔ 20cm (8in), maroon-spotted, light green stems and leaves ❄❄❄ (borderline)

Eupatorium

Joe Pye Weed

ADORED BY BEES AND BUTTERFLIES, the clusters of tiny flowers on upright, leafy stems are the attraction of the hardy eupatoriums. The flowers come in shades of white, pink, violet, or purple and are mostly borne from summer until early autumn. There are many, varied annuals and perennial eupatoriums that are worthy of the garden, with leaves that differ in shape and shade. The large, hardy, herbaceous perennials such as *Eupatorium cannabinum* look lush in large borders, with grasses (*see pp.340–355*) or in a wild or woodland garden. *E. purpureum* is even taller and has similarly strong stems that need no support.

Hardiness Fully frost-hardy ❄❄❄ to very frost-tender ❅.

Cultivation Eupatoriums thrive in any soil, providing it remains moist, in full sun or partial shade. **Deadhead** fading flowers. **Divide** hardy species (*see p.395*) and take softwood cuttings of tender species (*see p.394*) in spring. Sow seed in spring (*see pp.391–393*).

Euphorbia

Milkweed, Spurge

see also p.57

THE FLAMBOYANT, ACID-YELLOW BRACTS characteristic of many garden spurges contrast dramatically with other plants, and ensure that they always catch the eye. The bracts, which are really modified leaves, surround tiny flowers, borne in clusters at the stem tips. As well as acid-yellow, plants with bracts in warm shades of red, orange, purple, or brown are available. The leaves are usually green to blue-green. This huge and incredibly varied group that includes annuals, biennials, evergreen and semi-evergreen perennials, and succulents, and you can find a euphorbia to suit almost any garden situation. Spurges can be short-lived, particularly in wet soils; luckily, many such as *Euphorbia polychroma* self-seed freely about.

Hardiness Fully frost-hardy ❄❄❄ to very frost-tender ❅.

Cultivation Most herbaceous euphorbias like either well-drained, light soils in full sun or moist, humus-rich soils in light, dappled shade. **Sow** seed (*see pp.391–393*) in containers in a cold frame. **Divide** plants in early spring (*see p.395*). Tender and succulent species should be overwintered in a cool greenhouse or conservatory.

Euphorbia schillingii 🏆
↕1m (3ft) ↔ 30cm (12in), clump-forming perennial for moisture and light shade, flowers from midsummer to mid-autumn ❄❄❄

Eupatorium purpureum (Joe Pye Weed)
↕2.2m (7ft) ↔ 1m (3ft), clump-forming perennial, flowers from midsummer to early autumn, prefers alkaline soil ❄❄❄

Euphorbia polychroma 🏆
↕40cm (16in) ↔ 60cm (24in), perennial, likes sun, flowers mid-spring to midsummer, good ground cover, can be invasive ❄❄❄

BEWARE THE SAP
All euphorbias exude a milky sap which irritates the skin, so wear gloves when handling the plants.

Euphorbia griffithii **'Fireglow'**
↕75cm (30in) ↔ 1m (3ft), perennial, for moist, light shade, autumn leaves red and gold, flowers in early summer, can be invasive ❄❄❄

uphorbia dulcis **'Chameleon'**
↔ 30cm, spreading perennial, tolerates dry shade, dark green or
onze leaves colour well in autumn, flowers in summer ✲✲✲

uphorbia myrsinites 🏆
10cm (4in) ↔ 30cm (12in), evergreen succulent, trailing stems,
owers in spring, needs good drainage and sun ✲✲✲

EUSTOMA

Lisianthus, Prairie Gentian

A REMARKABLE CUT FLOWER that lasts for weeks and weeks in a vase, the Prairie Gentian can be difficult to obtain and has to be sought from specialist nurseries and seed suppliers. It is a short-lived perennial, generally treated as an annual or biennial. It has dull green foliage. The flowers occur at the top of the straight rigid stem. They look like rose buds before they open. The full flowers are single, semi-double or double and come in a range of colours from buff apricot through pink to purple. They look a little like a cross between a poppy or a tulip with a rose.

Hardiness Frost-tender ✲ to very frost-tender ❀.

Cultivation Grow in a well-drained soil that is reasonably fertile and enriched with well-rotted organic matter. Full sun or very light shade is best and shelter from hot, drying winds. **Sow** seed (*see p.392*) at 20°C (68°F) in a cold frame or straight where they are to be grown.

Eustoma grandiflorum
↕ 60cm (2 ft) ↔ 30cm (1ft), makes long-lasting cut flowers

FELICIA

Blue Daisy

MASSES OF DAISIES OF PURE BLUE, or occasionally white, mauve, or lilac, smother felicias throughout summer, making the plant a popular choice for bedding and containers, including hanging baskets. Felicias are not entirely hardy, so are generally treated as annuals or tender perennials. In mild, dry winters, they should survive to form substantial, bushy plants with a maximum height and spread of 30–50cm (12–20in). The plentiful, tiny leaves are grey- or mid-green in colour.

Hardiness Frost-hardy ❄❄ to frost-tender ❄.

Cultivation Grow felicias in poor to moderately fertile, well-drained soil, in full sun. They do not thrive in damp conditions. For plants in containers, use a premium quality potting mix; then water them well in summer. **Pinch back** young shoots regularly to encourage a bushy habit. **Sow** seed (*see p.391–393*) at 10–18°C (50–64°F) in spring. Take softwood cuttings (*see p.394*) in late summer and overwinter the young plants in frost-free conditions under glass.

Felicia amelloides (Blue Marguerite)
↕60cm (2ft) ↔ 60–90cm (2–3ft), peak flowering is late spring and summer, although some at other times as well

FILIPENDULA

FROM A DISTANCE, THE FLOWERS of filipendulas look like a cloud of foam floating above a sea of bright green leaves. At closer quarters, their unusual, musky fragrance can be detected. These perennials bear large heads of fluffy white, cream, pink, or red flowers on branching stems in late spring and summer. They thrive in damp soil, so are most at home in woodland plantings in soil that stays moist through summer. Try them with other moisture-loving perennials such as eupatoriums (*see p.242*) or hostas (*see pp.260–261*). *Filipendula vulgaris* tolerates drier conditions, and prefers alkaline (limy) soils in dappled sun; it has dark green, ferny leaves, which look good with lupins (*see p.280*) and poppies (*Papaver, see p.299*).

Hardiness Fully frost-hardy ❄❄❄.

Cultivation Grow filipendulas in moderately fertile, moist but well-drained soil, in sun or partial shade. Planting gold-leaved cultivars in shade results in a stronger colour. **Sow** seed (*see pp.391–393*) in autumn in pots and place them in a cold frame, or sow in spring at 10–13°C (50–55°F). **Divide** plants (*see p.395*) in autumn or spring. Take root cuttings (*see p.394*) from late winter until early spring.

Filipendula vulgaris
↕60cm (2ft) ↔ 60cm (2ft),cream flowers in late summer and interesting foliage

Filipendula palmata
↕1.2m (4ft) ↔ 60cm (2ft), clump-forming, variable leaves to 30cm (12in) long with densely woolly, white undersides, pale to deep pink flowers 20cm (8in) across borne in midsummer

-OENICULUM VULGARE

ennel

.HE LARGE, BILLOWING CLUMPS of green or purple iligree foliage make fennel a star in a garden bed, vhere the finely cut leaves contrast well with broad- eaved plants or blowsy flowers. Try purple fennel with he huge, dusky pink blooms of the oriental poppy, Patty's Plum'. Fennel is perhaps best known as an romatic herb with a strong anise flavour used for lavouring foods, and all parts have the strong aroma f anise. This perennial reaches a height of 2m (6ft) nd spread of 45cm (18in) from large, deep roots.)uring mid- and late summer, flat clusters of tiny, ellow flowers appear, followed by large, aromatic eeds. Herb fennel and ornamental fennels both work vell in mixed beds or in a herb garden. A serious weed ı some districts, so use with extreme caution.

lardiness Fully frost-hardy ✻✻✻, although new shoots may be amaged by frosts.

ultivation Fennels prefer fertile, moist but well-drained soil, in full un. **Deadhead** flowerheads before the seeds form to prevent prolific elf-seeding. **Sow** seed (*see pp.391–393*) in spring at 13–18°C 55–64°F) or outdoors where the plants are to grow.

FENNEL SEEDHEADS
Fennel seedheads should be removed before they are mature to prevent self-sowing beyond the garden.

'oeniculum vulgare 'Purpureum'
2m (6ft) ↔ 45cm (18in), bronze-purple foliage when young, ırning glaucous green with age

FRANCOA

Bridal Wreath

GROWN AS A FLOWER FOR CUTTING, Bridal Wreath has graceful, dainty flower spikes of pink or white that give an airy feel to a garden. The main flowering period of these few evergreen perennials is summer, but often the plants produce a second flush of flowers in autumn. They are 60–90cm (24–36in) tall, and have attractive rosettes of softly hairy leaves with wavy edges that spread to about 45cm (18in). Bridal Wreaths seed themselves about without becoming invasive if conditions are right. Place them in mixed gardens with plants such as persicarias (*see p.305*), phloxes (*see p.306*), or use them in containers or as edging plants.

Hardiness Frost-hardy ✻✻, although may survive to –10°C (14°F).

Cultivation Undemanding, these plants like moist but well-drained soil, that has been enriched with well-rotted organic matter, in full sun or partial shade. **Water** freely in summer and apply a balanced feed every four weeks. **Divide** plants (*see p.395*) in spring. **Sow** seed (*see pp.391–393*) at 15–24°C (59–75°F) in spring.

Francoa sonchifolia
↕60–90cm (24–36in) ↔ 45cm (18in)

FREESIA

THE FREESIAS THAT ARE COMMONLY GROWN can be broadly split into two groups: the old-fashioned cream-flowered and highly perfumed *Freesia alba* and the multi-coloured forms of the florist's freesias *F.* × *hybrida*. The former species has been a garden favourite for decades and sometimes has feint mauve striping or hue on the flowers. The latter are often sold by individual name or colour or in mixed colours, including white, yellow, orange, red, and mauve and tend to be less heavily scented. They are spring-flowering deciduous bulbs with a fan of light green leaves. The species is proving to be a weed in some areas, so plant with caution.

Hardiness Frost-hardy ✻✻.

Cultivation Grow in any well-drained soil that is reasonably fertile that is in full sun or partial shade. **Divide** established clumps in autumn, after all foliage has died down.

Freesia alba
↕30cm (1 ft) ↔ 20cm (8in), beautifully perfumed, this bulb can escape from gardens, so use with caution

FRITILLARIA

Fritillary

ELEGANT, NODDING BELLS are the common feature of this diverse group of perennial bulbs. The flowers come in muted shades, such as soft green, tawny reds, and purples, often with strikingly patterned petals, and are borne in spring and early summer, singly or in clusters. Fritillaries vary from diminutive, delicate types only 8cm (3in) tall to more robust species with stout stems up to 1.5m (5ft). Crown Imperials thrive in mixed gardens. The more demure Snake's Head Fritillary (*Fritillaria meleagris*) can be naturalized in moist meadows or in the dappled shade under trees and shrubs. Alpine species can be tricky to grow and need sharp drainage and usually alpine-house conditions.

Hardiness Fully frost-hardy ❄❄❄ to frost-hardy ❄❄.

Cultivation Plant the bulbs at four times their depth. Fritillarias differ in their needs, but most garden plants need fertile, well-drained, moisture-retentive soil in full sun, or moist, humus-rich soil in light shade. **Divide** large clumps (*see p.395*) in late summer. Smaller species such as *F. acmopetala*, produce numerous but tiny bulblets (called "rice"); treat them like seeds and grow on in a seed tray (*see pp.391–393*).

Fritillaria imperialis (Crown Imperial)
↕1.5m (5ft) ↔ 25–30cm (10–12in), orange, red, or yellow flowers in early summer, needs fertile, well-drained soil in full sun ❄❄❄

Fritillaria meleagris (Snake's Head Fritillary)
↕30cm (12in) ↔ 5–8cm (2–3in), purple or white flowers in spring, needs moist, enriched soil in full sun or light shade ❄❄❄

Fritillaria acmopetala ♀
↕40cm (16in) ↔ 5–8cm (2–3in), robust, flowers in late spring, needs fertile, well-drained soil in full sun ❄❄❄

GAILLARDIA

Blanket Flower

THESE PLANTS HAVE CHEERFUL, LARGE DAISIES that appear for a long period throughout summer and into autumn. The flowers, which are up to 14cm (5½in) across, are yellow, crimson, or orange with contrasting bosses in brown, red, or yellow. Occasionally, single colours are available. These are held on long stems up to 90cm (36in) tall above bushy plants with soft, hairy, long leaves. Cultivars of the perennial *Gaillardia* × *grandiflora* are most commonly grown of the group, which also includes annuals and biennials. They brighten up containers or garden beds; try them with pinks (*Dianthus, see pp.226–227*), Pot Marigolds (*Calendula, see p.204*), and rudbeckias (*see p.317*). Gaillardias are also good for cutting.

Hardiness Fully frost-hardy ❄❄❄ to frost-hardy ❄❄.

Cultivation Gaillardias prefer fertile, well-drained soil in full sun; they will also tolerate poor soils. **Deadhead** regularly to encourage more flowers. **Cut back** perennials to around 15cm (6in) in late summer to encourage fresh growth at the base. **Sow** seed (*see pp.391–393*) at 13–18°C (55–64°F) in early spring. Seed of annuals can also be sown in situ in late spring or early summer. **Divide** perennials (*see p.395*) in spring or take root cuttings (*see p.394*) in winter.

***Gaillardia* 'Dazzler'** ♀
↕60–85cm (24–34in) ↔ 45cm (18in), perennial, mid- to grey-green leaves, flowers from early summer to autumn ❄❄❄

;ALANTHUS

'nowdrop

NOWDROPS ARE A WELCOME SIGHT in late winter and ırly spring, appearing before many other bulbs. here are many different kinds with subtly different etal shapes and green markings. Each snowdrop bulb sually produces a single, white, pendent flower on an ching flower stalk. Some have scented flowers. Most owdrops are vigorous and easily grown in cold imates, often forming large clumps. They look ırticularly good if naturalized in grass. *Galanthus ginae-olgae* flowers in autumn. Contact with the ılbs may cause a rash.

ardiness Fully frost-hardy ❄❄❄ to frost-hardy ❄❄.

ıltivation Soil enriched with well-rotted organic matter, that es not dry out in summer, in sun or partial shade, suits Snowdrops. **vide** clumps of bulbs every 3–4 years to stop the plants becoming ngested and losing vigour; this is done in spring after flowering while e bulbs are "in the green" (*see below*). Snowdrops cross-pollinate ely so may not come true to type from seed.

Galanthus 'Atkinsii' ♡

↕20cm (8in) ↔ 8cm (3in), flowers 3cm (1¼in) long appear in late winter ❄❄❄

DIVIDING SNOWDROPS

nowdrops should be divided "in ne green" while they still have eaves and shortly after the flowers ave faded. Carefully dig up the lumps with a fork, pull apart the ulbs, and replant individually or n small groups where required.

alanthus 'S. Arnott' ♡

'0cm (8in) ↔ 8cm (3in), strongly honey-scented flowers, 5–3.5cm (1–1½in) long, in late winter and early spring ❄❄❄

Galanthus nivalis 'Flore Pleno' ♡

↕↔ 10cm (4in), robust, double-flowered, spreads rapidly from offsets, honey-scented, irregular flowers in winter ❄❄❄

GALAX URCEOLATA

THIS EVERGREEN PERENNIAL IS GROWN for its elegant wands of small, white flowers produced in late spring and summer, followed by rich, red-bronze foliage in autumn. The flower spikes are up to 25cm (10in) tall and the leaves up to 8cm (3in) across. It spreads by creeping roots and makes a useful ground cover under shrubs in a shady bed or in a woodland garden. It is also happy in a large rock garden.

Hardiness Fully frost-hardy ❄❄❄.

Cultivation This plants thrives in moist, acid (lime-free) soil in partial shade; make sure that the roots will not dry out. **Mulch** annually in spring with pine needles or leafmould. **Sow** seed (*see pp.391–393*) in containers of lime-free potting mix in an open frame outdoors in autumn. **Separate** rooted runners in early spring: carefully dig up the rooted stem; trim back the stub; and transplant the divided pieces where required.

Galax urceolata

↕30cm (12in) ↔ 1m (3ft)

Galtonia

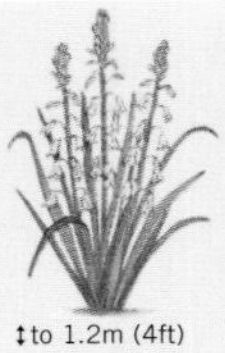

↕ to 1.2m (4ft)
↔ 10cm (4in)

LIKE A LATE-SUMMER HYACINTH, *Galtonia candicans* has tall, elegant spikes of pure white, slightly fragrant flowers. The only commonly grown species, it is particularly useful in the garden, and deserves wider recognition, because few bulbs of this beauty flower at this time of year. The grey-green, strappy leaves are quite fleshy. This trouble-free, bulbous perennial mixes well with grasses and other perennials like dicentras (*see p.228*), monardas (*see p.287*), poppies (*Papaver, see p.299*), and rudbeckias (*see p.317*). *G. viridiflora* has pale green, nodding flowers, but is less hardy to frost.

Hardiness Fully frost-hardy *** to frost-hardy **.

Cultivation Fertile, well-drained soil that is reliably moist in summer, in full sun, suits galtonias. **Lift** the bulbs in late autumn in areas with severe winters, and overwinter in pots in a frost-free greenhouse or conservatory. Alternatively, leave the bulbs in the soil and cover with a deep winter mulch (*see p.388*). **Sow** seed in a container (*see pp.391–393*) in a cold frame as soon as it is ripe. **Divide** large clumps (*see p.395*) and replant in early spring.

Galtonia candicans ♀
↕ 1–1.2m (3–4ft) ↔ 10cm (4in), tubular flowers open from the base of the flower spike in late midsummer ***

Gaura lindheimeri

THE SUMMER AND AUTUMN FLOWERS of this gracious perennial would soften any garden with their light, airy growth. Each bloom nestles inside the leaves and is short-lived, but is soon replaced by another, keeping up a continuous display for several months. This trouble-free plant forms a bushy clump. *Gaura lindheimeri* has several pretty cultivars – 'Corrie's Gold' has gold-edged leaves and 'Siskiyou Pink' has pinkish flowers. 'Whirling Butterflies' is named after the shape of its white flowers; it forms a smaller clump, and is very free-flowering. Gauras contrast well with late-flowering perennials that have large blooms, like chrysanthemums (*see pp.212–213*), and rudbeckias (*see p.317*).

Hardiness Fully frost-hardy ***.

Cultivation Any fertile, moist but well-drained soil, in full sun will do; drought and partial shade are tolerated. **Sow** seed (*see pp.391–393*) in containers in a cold frame from spring until early summer. **Divide** clumps (*see p.395*) in winter to increase stock. Take softwood cuttings in spring or heel cuttings in summer (*see p.394*).

Gaura 'Siskiyou Pink'
↕ 90cm (3ft) ↔ 60cm (2ft), pink flowers for many months over spring, summer and autumn

Gaura lindheimeri ♀
↕ to 1.5m (5ft) ↔ 90cm (36in), pinkish buds open to white flowers that fade to pink, from late spring to early autumn

ĴAZANIA

HE BRIGHT AND CHEERY, sunflower-like blooms of ıese evergreen perennials are most often seen in ınny, even hot districts. The summer flowers come a wide range of bold colours, often with darker ːntres and markings on the petals. They need a ınny site because they close up on dull days. The ırk green, hairy foliage is a good foil to the flowers. azanias grow well in coastal areas. They can be vasive, so check with local gardeners before growing.

ardiness Frost-tender ✲ to very frost-tender ❀, but most can rvive periods at 0°C (32°F).

ltivation Grow gazanias in light, sandy, well-drained soil, in full n. **Remove** dead blooms to prolong flowering. **Sow** seed at 18–20°C 4–68°F) in late winter or early spring (*see pp.391–393*). **Take** new oots from the base and treat as softwood cuttings (*see p.394*) in late mmer or early autumn.

Gazania 'Montezuma'
↕30cm (12in) ↔ to 40cm (16in), flowers from spring right through until autumn on a sterile plant that will not become weedy ✲

azania **Mini Star Series** 🏆
ɔ 20cm (8in) ↔ to 25cm (10in), compact, tuft-forming, evergreen perennial, white silky hairs beneath ıves, summer flowers may be bright yellow, orange, copper, bronze, white, pink, and beige ✲

GENTIANA

Gentian

IT IS THE INTENSE BLUE, trumpet- or bell-shaped flowers that draw gardeners to gentians, but there are also white-, yellow- and rarely, red-flowered forms. Flowering times vary, from late spring (*Gentiana acaulis),* late summer (*G. septemfida),* and autumn (*G. sino-ornata).* Gentians are a large and varied group, but perennials are usually grown; they may be deciduous, evergreen, or semi-evergreen, and range from low mats and trailing types to clumping or upright forms. Many are alpines, needing rock-garden conditions; a few suit herbaceous borders, such as the relatively tall, shade-loving *G. asclepiadea* with late-summer flowers. Some gentians have very specific soil needs, so you may have to grow them in containers. Autumn-flowering gentians have rosettes of leaves.

Hardiness Fully frost-hardy ✲✲✲.

Cultivation Most need light but rich, well-drained but moist soil, in full sun only where summers are cool. Provide partial shade in warmer areas. Autumn-flowering gentians need neutral to acid soil. **Sow** seed (*see pp.391–393*) of species as soon as it is ripe in a cold frame. **Divide** rooted offshoots (*see p.395*) carefully in spring.

① ***acaulis*** 🏆 ↕8cm (3in) ↔ 30cm (12in) ② ***septemfida*** 🏆 ↕15–20cm (6–8in) ↔ 30cm (12in) ③ ***sino-ornata*** 🏆 ↕to 8cm (3in) ↔ 15–30cm (6–12in)

GERANIUM

Cranesbill

EASY-TO-GROW, VERSATILE, AND LONG-FLOWERING, few plants are as useful in the garden as hardy geraniums. The genus contains about 300 annuals, biennials, and herbaceous perennials, some of them semi-evergreen or evergreen. The flowers are delicate and abundant, with colours ranging from white, shades of pink and purple, to blue, often with contrasting veins. Leaves are usually rounded or palm-like (palmate) and are frequently aromatic. Some types have colourful autumn foliage. They are often confused with less frost-hardy *Pelargonium* (*see pp.300–301*), which is popularly called geranium. Cranesbills are found in many habitats, except in very wet areas, and can be grown almost anywhere in the garden, and in pots. There are compact varieties to 15cm (6in) tall, suitable for a rock garden, and plants of 1.4m (4ft) or more for mixed and herbaceous borders. Mat-forming species like *Geranium macrorrhizum* are useful as ground cover, including on slopes, where the dense root system helps to prevent soil erosion.

Hardiness Fully frost-hardy ✻✻✻ to frost-tender ✻.

Cultivation Grow the larger species and hybrids in fertile soil in full sun or partial shade. Small species need a well-drained site in full sun. Avoid soils that are excessively wet in winter. **Water** plants well during dry spells and feed with a liquid fertilizer monthly. **Trim off** the faded blooms and foliage after the first flush of flowers in early or midsummer, to encourage fresh leaves and another show of flowers. **Sow** seed (*see pp.391–393*) of hardy species outdoors in containers as soon as it is ripe or in spring. Seed of half-hardy species is sown at 13–18°C (55–64°F) in spring. **Divide** overgrown clumps in spring (*see p.395*). **Take** basal cuttings (the base of the stem and a small piece of the crown) in spring. Treat them in the same way as soft-tip cuttings (*see p.394*).

Using Geraniums in the garden

◁ ***Woodland planting*** *Loose, spreading shapes and plentiful flowers, even in dappled shade, make geraniums an appropriate choice for the woodland garden. Here, the airy foliage and dainty pink flowers of* G. endressii *make an effective contrast to the solid forms of the tree trunks. This species, together with* G. himalayense *and* G. macrorrhizum *and their cultivars, and* G. nodosum, *all make good cover in any shady site.*

▷ ***Ground cover*** Geranium × magnificum *is used here as ground cover under climbing roses. Roses and geraniums are a classic garden combination. A geranium's vigorous, spreading habit camouflages bare soil and hides dull rose stems – and its small, saucer-shaped flowers are good foils to the showier rose blooms. Their characteristic blue, mauve, and pink hues harmonize with many rose colours. Here, a profusion of rich violet blooms makes an eye-catching contrast to the bright scarlet roses.*

1

2

7

8

13

14

17

18

① ***Geranium*** **'Ann Folkard'** 🏆 ↕60cm (24in) ↔ 1m (3ft) ② ***asphodeloides*** ↕30–45cm (12–18in), ↔ 30cm (12in), evergreen ③ × ***cantabrigiense*** ↕30cm (12in) ↔ 60cm (24in), evergreen, aromatic ④ × ***cantabrigiense*** **'Biokovo'** ↕30cm (12in) ↔ 75–90cm (30–36in), evergreen ⑤ ***cinereum*** **'Ballerin** 🏆 ↕15cm (6in) ↔ 30cm (12in), evergreen, needs good drainage ⑥ ***cinereum*** **var.** ***subcaulescens*** 🏆 ↕15cm (6in) ↔ 30cm (12in), evergreen, needs good drainage ⑦ ***clarkei*** **'Kashmir White'** 🏆 ↕45c

4

5

6

10

11

12

20

16

21

in) ↔ indefinite ⑧ ***dalmaticum*** 🏆 ↕15cm (6in) ↔ 50cm (20in), evergreen ⑨ ***endressii*** 🏆 ↕45cm in) ↔ 60cm (24in), evergreen ⑩ ***erianthum*** ↕45–60cm (18–24in) ↔ 30cm (12in), good autumn leaf our ⑪ ***himalayense*** ↕30–45cm (12–18in) ↔ 60cm (24in) ⑫ ***himalayense* 'Gravetye'** 🏆 ↕30cm in) ↔ 60cm (24in) ⑬ ***ibericum*** ↕50cm (20in) ↔ 60cm (24in) ⑭ ***macrorrhizum*** ↕50cm (20in) ↔ 60cm in), aromatic ⑮ ***macrorrhizum* 'Ingwersen's Variety'** 🏆 ↕50cm (20in) ↔ 60cm (24in), semi-evergreen ⑯ ***maculatum*** ↕60–75cm (24–30in) ↔ 45cm (18in) ⑰ × ***magnificum*** 🏆 ↕↔ 60cm (24in) ⑱ ***nodosum*** ↕30–50cm (12–20in), ↔ 50cm (20in) ⑲ ***orientalitibeticum*** ↕30cm (12in) ↔ 1m (3ft) ⑳ × ***oxonianum*** ↕80cm (32in) ↔ 60cm (24in), evergreen ㉑ ***maderense*** 🏆 ↕↔ 1.2–1.5m (4–5ft), evergreen ☆

Geum

Avens

LOOKING RATHER LIKE BUTTERCUPS or small roses, the bold flowers of geums come in attractive shades of red, orange, and yellow. They appear from late spring into summer and are held above clumps of deep green, wrinkled and divided leaves. The smaller geums are suitable for growing in a rock garden, while the larger ones are almost tailor-made for the front of a sunny garden. Combine them with other herbaceous perennials such as the closely related potentillas (*see p.311*), which have a similar style of flower, and hardy geraniums (*see pp.250–251*).

Hardiness Fully frost-hardy ❄❄❄.

Cultivation Grow most geums in fertile, well-drained soil in full sun. *Geum rivale* and its cultivars, need more moisture and plenty of organic matter, but avoid soil that becomes waterlogged in winter. **Sow** seed in containers in a cold frame in spring or autumn (*see pp.391–393*). 'Lady Stratheden' and 'Mrs J. Bradshaw' generally come true from seed, but the majority of the larger geums cross-pollinate freely and produce unpredictable offspring. **Divide** other named varieties (*see p.395*) to be sure that new plants are true to type.

Geum 'Lady Stratheden' ♡

↕40–60cm (16–24in) ↔ 60cm (24in), a popular geum for a sunny garden, its flowers will be produced all spring and into summer

Geum 'Mrs Bradshaw'

↕60cm (2ft) ↔ 45cm (1.5ft) multitudes of flowers on long wispy stems from spring into summer

Gladiolus

WITH THEIR TALL, STRONGLY UPRIGHT spikes of summer flowers, gladioli can look especially striking in cut-flower displays as well as in the garden. The funnel-shaped flowers open from the bottom of the stem upwards and come in shades of white, red, pink yellow, orange, and some bicolours, sometimes with dainty splotches on the lower petals. Gladioli grow from corms, with long, sword-like leaves arranged in fans. Many are not hardy and need a warm, sheltered spot away from frosts. Partner them with other herbaceous perennials such as daylilies (*Hemerocallis, see p.258*) and grasses. They are sometimes grown in rows in the vegetable garden specifically for cutting.

Hardiness Fully frost-hardy ❄❄❄ to very frost-tender ❀.

Cultivation Grow in fertile, well-drained soil in full sun. **Plant** corm 10–15cm (4–6in) deep in spring. In heavy soil, fork coarse grit into planting area. Large-flowered kinds need staking. **Lift** corms in frost-prone areas once leaves begin to yellow, dry them for a fortnight or s then remove all leafy remains. **Separate** the corms, discarding the ol dried-up, dark brown ones, and store over winter in a cool, frost-free place. Check occasionally and remove any that show signs of mould

Gladiolus 'Elvira'

↕80cm (32in) ↔ 8–10cm (3–4in), each corm produces two or th slender flower spikes in early summer that are ideal for cutting ❄

ladiolus tristis ♀
-5–150cm (1½–5ft) ↔ 5cm (2in), pale yellow or creamy white
wers in spring, strong evening scent ✲

ladiolus communis subsp. *byzantinus* ♀
ɔ 1m (3ft) ↔ 8cm (3in), vigorous, spreading, flowers in early
mmer, mulch over winter in cold areas ✲✲✲ (borderline)

SUPPORTING GLADIOLI
Tall varieties must be tied to stakes from midsummer. Use soft twine every 20cm (8in), taking care not to damage or restrict emerging flowers.

Gladiolus x *colvillei* 'The Bride'
↕45–60cm (1.5–2ft) ↔ 30cm (1ft), spring flowers that are white with a very pale green throat ✲✲

GLORIOSA
Glory Lily

THESE DECIDUOUS CLIMBERS are from the lily family and actually arise from fleshy tubers and climb by means of tendrils. The summer flowers are a remarkable lily-like arrangement with six petals which are crimson-red and feature wavy, yellow edges. The leaves are also lily-like and mid-green. Ideally suited to the tropics and sub-tropical areas of summer rainfall and cool season dry, they can be grown further south if these conditions can be duplicated. They can be grown in containers for this purpose, provided they are large and there is a trellis or frame for them to climb on. They make long-lasting cut flowers.

Hardiness Frost-tender ✲ to very frost-tender ❀.

Cultivation Plant in winter in any well-drained soil that is enriched with well-rotted organic matter. Full sun is best and give plenty of water, including liquid feeds, while they are actively growing. They should be allowed to dry out over their dormant period, which is from early autumn to spring. **Sow** seed (*see p.391*) in spring in containers. **Take** divisions in the spring (*see p.395*) but treat the tubers with care as they are easily damaged.

Gloriosa superba 'Rothschildiana'
↕1.5–2m (5–6ft) ↔ 50cm (6in) has a remarkable long-lasting flower

GUNNERA

THE FOLIAGE OF GUNNERAS is one of gardening's sensations. Although there are diminutive mat-forming gunneras like *Gunnera magellanica*, which is no more than 15cm (6in) tall, it is the Giant Rhubarb, *G. manicata*, for which this group of perennials is famed. This plant reaches a majestic 2.5m (8ft) or more within a season. The undersides of the rhubarb-like leaves and their thick stalks are coarsely spined. The flower spikes are also attractive in some species. Large-leaved specimens make excellent architectural plants for stream- or pondsides, but in large gardens only. They combine well with other moisture-loving plants, such as astilbes (*see p.194*). The small gunneras are best in a rock garden.

Hardiness Fully frost-hardy ❄❄❄ to frost-hardy ❄❄.

Cultivation Grow in deep, permanently moist soil in sun or partial shade in a sheltered position. In frosty areas, protect their crowns in winter with a covering of the old leaves. **Increase** large species by taking cuttings of leafy, basal buds, with a section of root attached, in spring. **Divide** small species in spring (*see p.395*). **Sow** seed (*see pp.391–393*) in containers in a cold frame as soon as it is ripe.

Gunnera tinctoria
↕1.5m (5ft) ↔ 2m (6ft), the enormous leaves and rusty flowerheads are slightly smaller than those of the hardier *G. manicata* ❄❄

GYPSOPHILA

THE DIFFUSE, STARRY SPRAYS of small, white or pink summer flowers of gypsophilas will be familiar to anyone who buys cut flowers. They make a pretty and airy filler for indoor arrangements and the same principle applies to gypsophilas in the garden. Small types are ideal for rock gardens or for tumbling over retaining walls; the annual and larger perennial gypsophilas, such as *Gypsophila paniculata,* suit borders. The clouds of flowers look good with many herbaceous perennials, for example coreopsis (*see p.217*), hardy geraniums (*see p.250–251*), and geums (*see p.252*). Popular cultivars include 'Bristol Fairy', with double white flowers. All are good for cutting.

Hardiness Fully frost-hardy ❄❄❄ to frost-hardy ❄❄.

Cultivation Grow in deep, light, preferably alkaline (limy) soil that is sharply drained and in full sun. **Sow** seed of annuals where they are to flower in spring (*see p.393*), and thin out seedlings to around 15cm (6in) apart. Seed of perennials should be sown at 13–18°C (55–64°F) in spring (*see pp.391–392*). **Take** root cuttings of perennials in winter (*see p.394*) as an alternative way of making new plants.

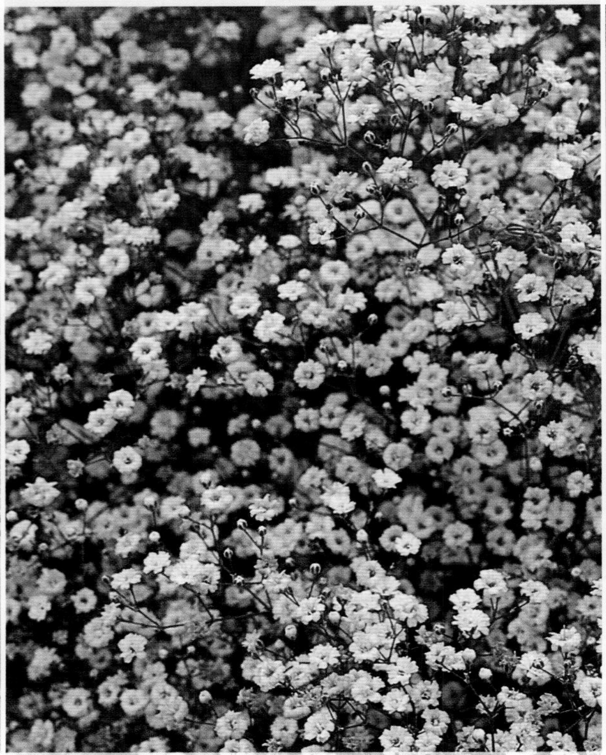

***Gypsophila* 'Rosenschleier'** 🏆
↕40–50cm (16–20in) ↔ 1m (3ft), also known as 'Rosy Veil' for its billowing clusters of pale pink, semi-double flowers ❄❄❄

HACQUETIA EPIPACTIS

THE BRIGHT, EARLY FLOWERS of this species are composed of a central boss of tiny, yellow true flower surrounded by bright green bracts (modified leaves). They are borne in dense clusters from late winter to mid-spring. The plant has glossy, green leaves that only fully develop once the flowers are finished. This is a small clump-forming perennial for a moist, shady site. An ideal position would be a damp rock garden in shade or a woodland area with plants such as snowdrops (*Galanthus, see p.247*), dwarf daffodils (*Narcissus, see pp.288–289*), anemones (*see p.181*), winter aconites (*Caltha, see p.205*), and corydalis (*see p.217*). Other natural companions include hellebore (*see p.256–257*) and epimediums (*see p.235*).

Hardiness Fully frost-hardy ❄❄❄.

Cultivation This plant will thrive in any reliably moist but not waterlogged, neutral to acid (lime-free) soil, that has been enriched with well-rotted organic matter. **Sow** seed in a container in a cold frame as soon as it is ripe or in autumn (*see pp.391–392*). **Divide** plants in spring (*see p.395*) to increase stock and to maintain vigour, or take root cuttings in winter (*see p.394*).

Hacquetia epipactis 🏆
↕5cm (2in) ↔ to 15cm (6in), a fascinating colour combination that will help to light up damp areas in shade

ᑊAEMANTHUS

lood Lily

ᑊHESE UNUSUAL BULBS are for bulb fanciers and those ᵥith a keen sense of the bizarre. The flowers look as if ıey have been made of plastic and feature six waxy, ːd, petal-like bracts holding in a tight clump of ellow-ended pink stamens. These appear in autumn n a short stout stem while the plant is totally devoid f leaves. These add to the strange impression of this lant as they grow along the ground to over 60cm 24in) long and 15cm (6in) wide. There are only two ːaves per bulb and they finish in a curved tip, giving se to the occasional common name of Ox-Tongue Lily.

ardiness Frost-hardy ❄❄ to frost-tender ❄.

ultivation Grow in full sun or partial shade in a free-draining soil at is enriched with well-rotted organic matter. They do well in ontainers of good quality potting mix. Place the containers high on a and so the long leaves can trail down. **Divide** mature clumps in ummer while they are dormant and place with the neck of the bulb at il level (*see p.380*). Snails and slugs can ruin the foliage, so guard gainst them (*see p.398*).

laemanthus coccineus
15cm (6in) ↔ 1.2m (4ft) wax-like autumn flowers before the new aves emerge ❄❄

HELENIUM

Helen's Flower

A TOP CHOICE FOR THE AUTUMN GARDEN, heleniums make a superb late-flowering contribution to the garden. Their daisy flowers, in wonderfully hot colours, appear over a long period from summer to autumn. These relatively tall, clump-forming perennials slowly spread over the years to create bold expanses of colour in shades of yellow, bronze, orange, and red. The flowers are good for cutting and also attract bees and other beneficial insects into the garden. Grow in a herbaceous border with such late-flowering perennials such as sedums (*see p.324*), rudbeckias (*see p.317*), and asters (*see pp.192–193*). Contact with foliage may aggravate skin allergies.

Hardiness Fully frost-hardy ❄❄❄ to frost-hardy ❄❄.

Cultivation Grow in any fertile, moist but well-drained soil in full sun. **Provide** support for tall varieties. **Divide** clumps every few years in autumn, winter or spring (*see p.395*) to increase stock or maintain vigour. **Sow** seed (*see pp.391–392*) of species in containers in a cold frame in spring. **Propagate** cultivars by taking spring shoots from the base of the plant and treating them as softwood cuttings (*see p.394*).

Helenium 'Moerheim Beauty' 🏆
↕ 90cm (36in) ↔ 60cm (24in), flowers from early to late summer ❄❄❄

Helenium 'Crimson Beauty'
↕ 90cm (36in) ↔ 60cm (24in), the shaggy, red flowers take on a brownish tinge with age ❄❄❄

Helenium autumnale (Sneezeweed)
↕ to 1.5m (5ft) ↔ 45cm (18in), flowers from late summer to mid-autumn; use twiggy sticks to support stems ❄❄❄

Helianthus

Sunflower

‡to 5m (15ft)
↔to 1.2m (4ft)

A FAVOURITE FOR CHILDREN'S gardens, these annuals and perennials are grown for their dramatic height and often huge, bright, daisy flowerheads. These appear in summer and autumn in shades of yellow, red, bronze, and mahogany, and are borne singly or in loose clusters. The flowers of some annuals may measure up to 30cm (12in) and more across. Despite their coarse foliage, they make showy plants for the garden; some of the dwarfer annuals also do well in containers. Sunflowers are good for cutting; they attract pollinating insects into the garden, and the seedheads may provide food for birds. Tall types make a good, fast-growing summer screen.

Hardiness Fully frost-hardy *** to frost-hardy **.

Cultivation Grow in reasonably fertile soil that is well-drained, neutral to alkaline (limy) and in full sun. Tall types, especially those with large, heavy heads, will need support. **Sow** seed (*see pp.391–393*) of perennials in containers in a cold frame in spring. Sow annuals at 16°C (61°F) in spring. **Divide** (*see p.394*) and replant perennials every two to four years in spring or autumn to maintain vigour.

Helianthus annus (double form)
‡1.5–2m (5–6ft) ↔ 60–90cm (2–3ft), huge double flowered form of the popular summer flowering annual

Heliopsis

Ox Eye

ORIGINATING IN THE DRY PRAIRIES of North America, these clump-forming perennials are valuable for their long flowering period and for being relatively trouble-free. Their cheerful, golden yellow, daisies, up to 8cm (3in) in diameter, are produced from midsummer through to early autumn. Ox Eyes have stiff, branching stems to 1m (3ft) tall, clothed with mid- or dark green foliage. The flowers may be single or double. These are useful plants in a mixed or an herbaceous border; grow them with other colourful perennials such as achilleas (*see pp.166–167*), rudbeckias (*see p.317*), hardy geraniums (*see pp.250–251*), and campanulas (*see p.206*).

Hardiness Fully frost-hardy ***.

Cultivation Grow in reasonably fertile, well-drained soil enriched with well-rotted organic matter, in full sun. The taller types may need supporting with twiggy sticks or canes. **Divide** plants (*see p.394*) every two to three years to maintain vigour. **Sow** seed (*see pp.391–392*) in a container in a cold frame in spring. **Take** cuttings of new shoots at the base of the plant in spring and treat as softwood cuttings (*see p.394*). Young shoots are prone to slug damage (*see p.398*).

Heliopsis **'Light of Loddon'**
‡90–1.2m (3–4ft) ↔ 60cm (2ft), cheery summer to autumn flowers, plants may require staking in windy areas

Helleborus

Hellebore, Winter Rose

HELLEBORES ARE STARS OF THE WINTER garden. All species in this group of mainly evergreen perennials are grown for their handsome, glossy foliage which sets off the exquisite flowers in subtle shades of purple, pink, green, white, and cream, many with contrasting spots. The flowers are extremely long-lasting; some face outwards, others look gracefully to the ground, and a few are scented. Hellebores are most effective when grown in groups in a mixed or shrub garden or in a natural woodland setting. Grow them with winter-flowering shrubs like Witch Hazels (*Hamamelis, see p.68*) and viburnums (*see pp.126–127*).

Hardiness Fully frost-hardy *** to frost-hardy **.

Cultivation Hellebores tolerate a fairly wide range of soil types and conditions. Most prefer neutral to alkaline (slightly limy) soil in sun or shade. Avoid overly dry or waterlogged soils. **Dig in** plenty of well-rotte organic matter before planting and mulch with a layer of organic matter. **Sow** seed (*see pp.391–392*) in containers in a cold frame as soon as it is ripe; named forms will not come true. Hellebores self-see freely. **Divide** (*see p.394*) in early spring or late summer.

SEEDLINGS
Lift and transplant self-sown seedlings found at the base of a plant in spring, when each has at least one true leaf.

Helleborus foetidus ♀ (Stinking Hellebore)
‡to 80cm (32in) ↔ 45cm (18in), deeply cut foliage, which smells only when crushed, flowers from midwinter to mid-spring ***

Ielleborus × *hybridus* (Lenten Rose)
↔ to 45cm (18in), flowers, in white, purple, yellow, green, or pink, from midwinter to mid-spring, remove d, tattered leaves before the flowerbuds open ❄❄❄

Helleborus argutifolius ♀ (Corsican Hellebore)
↕ to 1.2m (4ft) ↔ 90cm (3ft), overwintering leaves, shallow pale green flowers in late winter and early spring ❄❄❄

Ielleborus niger (Christmas Rose)
to 30cm (12in) ↔ 45cm (18in), overwintering leaves, particularly ırge flowers from early winter to early spring ❄❄❄

***Helleborus* × *hybridus* Ashwood Garden hybrids**
↕↔ 45cm (18in), variously spotted and speckled, some double flowers in midwinter to mid-spring ❄❄❄

Hemerocallis

Daylily

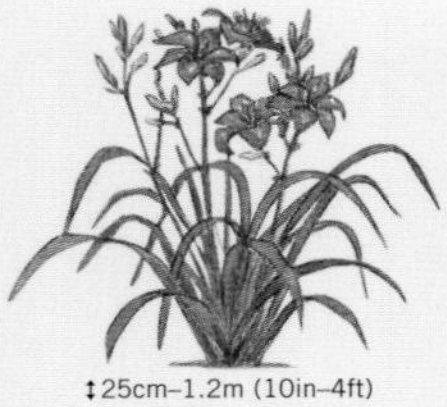

↕25cm–1.2m (10in–4ft)
↔30cm–1.2m (12in–4ft)

The exotic blooms of daylilies last for only one day – hence the name – but more buds open to take their place. Thousands of cultivars are available, with blooms in dazzling hues from near-white, gold, and apricot to orange, red, and blue, that vary in shape from spidery or flat to very full doubles. Deciduous, evergreen, or semi-evergreen, these easy-to-grow, clump-forming perennials flower from spring to late summer, adding height and long-lasting colour to a border. Many flower repeatedly through the season (remontant). They are especially successful in drifts. Dwarf daylilies are good in containers.

Hardiness Fully frost-hardy ❄❄❄; some evergreens are frost-hardy ❄❄.

Cultivation Daylilies like fertile, moist but well-drained soil; most need full sun for best colour but also grow in partial shade. **Divide** plants (*see p.395*) every 2–3 years to maintain vigour; divide or plant evergreens in winter or spring.

Hemerocallis 'Cosmic Caper'
↕60cm (2ft) ↔60cm (2ft), flowers spring to autumn

Hemerocallis 'Gentle Shepherd'
↕75cm (30in) ↔60cm (2ft), flowers spring to autumn

Hemerocallis 'Joan Senior'
↕60cm (2ft) ↔60cm (2ft), flowers spring to autumn

Hepatica

This small group of early-flowering perennials is related to anemones (*see p.180*). Their solitary, bowl- or star-shaped flowers are unusual in that they open from late winter until early spring, before the leaves have fully developed. The flowers come in shades of pale blue to mauve. The leaves are often purple underneath and sometimes marbled in silver or white They form basal rosettes to 13cm (5in) across and las all summer after the flowers fade. Hepaticas do well i moist soil in partial shade, such as in a woodland planting or shady corner of a rock garden. They combine well with small spring bulbs.

Hardiness Fully frost-hardy ❄❄❄.

Cultivation Hepaticas grow well in partial shade, in heavy, neutral to alkaline (slightly limy) soils, but will also thrive in well-drained soils that have been enriched with well-rotted organic matter. **Top-dress** with a layer of leafmould or garden compost around the plants in spring or autumn. Hepaticas do not transplant well since they resent root disturbance. **Sow** seed (*see pp.391–393*) in a cold frame as soon as it is ripe. Divide plants in spring (*see p.395*); divisions are slow to re-establish.

Hepatica nobilis 🏆
↕10cm (4in) ↔15cm (6in), slow-growing, domed, semi-evergreen, blue, or purple flowers in early spring

HESPERIS MATRONALIS

Sweet Rocket, Dame's Violet

↕to 90cm (36in)
↔45cm (18in)

THE SWEET-SCENTED FLOWERS of hesperis are borne on tall, swaying stems above rosettes of hairy, dark green leaves. Only the biennial or the short-lived perennial, *hesperis matronalis*, and its cultivars are usually grown. The blooms are usually lilac or purple, appear in late spring to early summer, and have an intensely spicy fragrance at evening. Some cultivars have double flowers and they are all good for cutting. Hesperis is usually grown as a biennial and freely self-seeds. It works well in a cottage garden, herbaceous border, or wild garden, with other early flowerers, such as poppies (*Papaver, see p.299*).

Hardiness Fully frost-hardy ***.

Cultivation Grow this plant in fertile, moist but well-drained soil that is neutral to alkaline (limy), in sun or partial shade. **Sow** seed (*see pp.391–393*) in spring or early summer, in spare ground, or where the plants are to grow, and plant out in autumn.

Hesperis matronalis var. *albiflora*

Flowers 3–4cm (1¼–1½in) across, attractive to insects, seedlings are white if no other hesperis are grown nearby

HEUCHERA

Coral Flower

Richly coloured foliage is the chief feature of heucheras. Evergreen and semi-evergreen, the lobed, rounded, or scalloped leaves are often tinted bronze or purple, are mottled or marbled, and have bold veins. They form neat mounds, above which rise airy spikes of dainty flowers in shades of pink to almost pure white from early to midsummer. They are good for cutting and drying, and attract bees into the garden. Commonly used as ground cover in gardens and as edging for pathways, heucheras also look good in rock gardens. Contrast the foliage with that of plants like *Stachys byzantina* (*see p.328*) or *Choisya ternata* 'Sundance' (*see p.40*).

Hardiness Fully frost-hardy *** to frost-hardy **.

Cultivation Heucheras prefer a neutral, fertile soil that is moist but well-drained, in sun or partial shade. They tolerate deep shade if the soil is moist. **Sow** seed of species in containers (*see pp.391–393*) in a cold frame in spring. **Divide** all types in autumn (*see below and p.395*) to stop the woody rootstock pushing up from the soil.

DIVIDE CLUMPS of heucheras to prevent them from becoming too woody and sparse at the centre.

Heuchera micrantha 'Palace Purple'

↕↔ 45–60m (18–24in), mound- or clump-forming, leaves to 15cm (6in) long, free-flowering in early summer, pink seed heads ***

HIPPEASTRUM

LARGE, TRUMPET-SHAPED FLOWERS are the hallmark of this popular bulb. Up to half a dozen of these are held on a single fleshy, upright stem from winter well into spring. Hundreds of forms are available and colours are in the white to red range and include single colours but also many striped and hued forms. The flowers often appear before or just as the foliage emerges. This is long and strap-like and tends to arch. In warmer areas these plants are planted in gardens and are used in garden displays instead of, or along side annuals. In colder areas they can be grown in containers.

Hardiness Frost tender * to very frost tender ❄.

Cultivation These need reasonably fertile, well-drained soil that has been enriched with well-rotted organic matter. Grow in full sun or part shade, preferably in a spot protected from strong winds. Plant the bulbs in late summer to early autumn with their necks at or just below the soil surface. Container-grown plants require a rich and moist, yet free-draining potting mix. **Sow** seed (*see p.391*) in containers as soon as it is ripe. These germinate readily at around 15–18°C (60–65°F). **Take** offsets from mature bulbs in autumn (*see p.395*).

Hippeastrum 'Apple Blossom'

↕60cm (2 ft) ↔ 30m (1ft) very large flowers on the top of a stiff, upright stem

Hosta

Plantain Lily

Hostas are among the most impressive of foliage plants, their ribbed, sometimes huge, leaves appearing in shades of green, yellow, blue-green, and blue-grey. In many cultivars, they are edged or banded with white or cream. In summer, spires of trumpet-shaped flowers are held well above the foliage. These herbaceous perennials grow naturally along rocky streamsides, and in woodland and alpine meadows. Most form clumps, but a few spread by underground stems. All make excellent ground-cover plants because the dense, overlapping leaves block out light from the soil surface, preventing weed seeds from germinating. They are ideal, too, for shady sites, but if planted under trees will need plenty of well-rotted organic matter adding to the soil to retain moisture. Hostas also look effective in pots, where they are easier to protect against snail and slug damage. Their lush, rounded foliage looks especially pleasing by ponds or streams, or when contrasted with tall, spiky plants, such as grasses. The neat, small-leaved cultivars are good for growing in rock gardens.

Hardiness Fully frost-hardy ❄❄❄.

Cultivation Grow hostas in fertile, moist but well-drained soil, sheltering them from hot, drying winds. Never let the soil dry out and water plants thoroughly during dry spells. Most hostas prefer a site in full or partial shade, although yellow-leaved and variegated cultivars have better leaf colour if they receive morning sun. Too strong sunshine, however, may cause scorch. **Mulch** (*see p.388*) between plants in spring to help conserve soil moisture. **Propagate** by division in spring (*see p.395*). Hostas are very prone to damage from slugs and snails and protective measures generally need to be taken (*see below*).

Preventing slug and snail damage

The leaves of hostas are stunning, but they also often prove irresistible to slugs and snails, which leave irregular holes and silvery slime trails. It is not uncommon to find some leaves completely shredded after slugs have been feasting at night. There are several ways to control them without resorting to the use of slug pellets, which may harm wildlife and pets (*see p.397*). Slug traps can be purchased, or you can construct a "slug pub" (*see below*) by sinking a container in the ground and filling it with beer to attract slugs and snails. Coarse grit, gravel, crushed eggshells spread around the plants may act as a deterrent as they dislike crossing rough surfaces (put the material in place before the leaves emerge in spring and renew when necessary). Collect slugs and snails at nightfall with the aid of a torch, especially in damp weather.

Band of copper *Containers can offer hostas a degree of protection. As a further barrier, stick adhesive copper tape around the pot rim. The copper produces a natural electric charge to which molluscs are sensitive and they will not cross.*

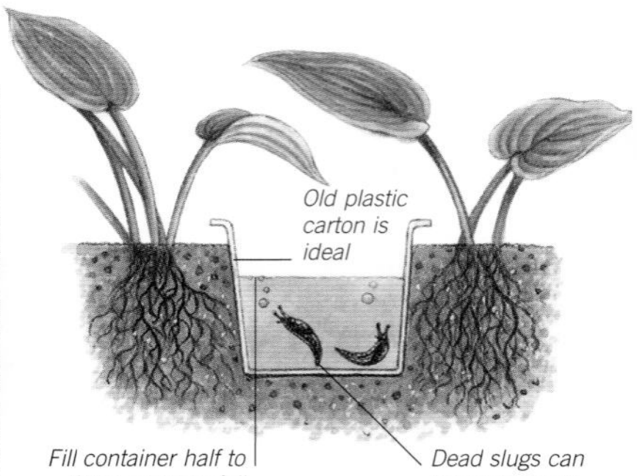
Old plastic carton is ideal
Fill container half to three-quarters full
Dead slugs can be composted

Slug pub *A slug pub is an organic way to catch slugs and snails. Attracted by the smell of the beer, they fall into the container and drown. Sink the container in the ground with the rim about 2.5cm (1in) above soil level to prevent beneficial creatures tumbling in.*

1

5

9

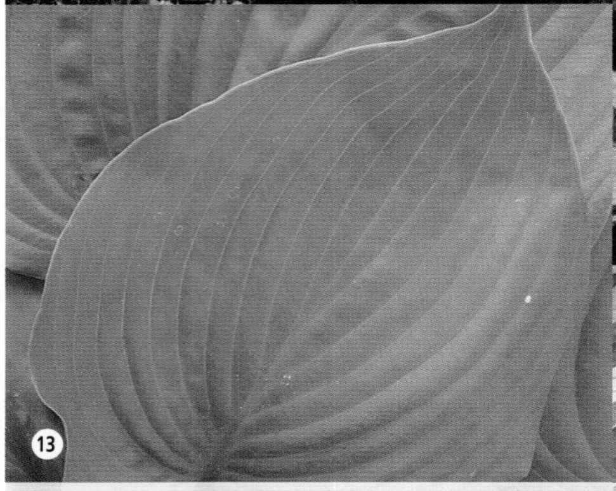
13

14

① ***Hosta* 'Aureomarginata'** ↕50cm (20in) ↔ 1m (3ft), tolerates sun or partial shade ② ***fortune*** **var. *albopicta*** 🏆 ↕55cm (22in) ↔ 1m (3ft) ③ ***fortunei* var. *aureomarginata*** 🏆 ↕55cm (22in) ↔ 1m (3ft), tolerates sun or partial shade ④ **'Francee'** 🏆 ↕55cm (22in) ↔ 1m (3ft) ⑤ **'Golden Prayers'** ↕35cm (14in) ↔ 60cm (24in) ⑥ **'Honeybells'** 🏆 ↕75cm (30in) ↔ 1.2m (4ft), fragrant, whi or lavender-blue-striped flowers ⑦ ***lancifolia*** 🏆 ↕45cm (18in) ↔ 75cm (30in), purple flowers, red-

tted stems ⑧ **'Love Pat'** 🏆 ↕45cm (18in) ↔ 1m (3ft), off-white flowers ⑨ **'Frances Williams'** 60cm (24in) ↔ 1m (3ft), greyish-white flowers ⑩ **'Halcyon'** 🏆 ↕35–40cm (14–16in) ↔ 70cm (28in), vender-grey flowers ⑪ **'Shade Fanfare'** 🏆 ↕45cm (18in) ↔ 60cm (24in) ⑫ ***sieboldiana*** **var.** ***egans*** 🏆 ↕1m (3ft) ↔ 1.2m (4ft) ⑬ **'Sum and Substance'** 🏆 ↕75cm (30in) ↔ 1.2m (4ft), pale lilac owers ⑭ ***undulata*** ↕1m (3ft) ↔ 45cm (18in), mauve flowers ⑮ ***undulata*** **var.** ***univittata*** 🏆 ↕45cm (18in) ↔ 70cm (28in) ⑯ ***ventricosa*** 🏆 ↕50cm (20in) ↔ 1m (3ft) ⑰ ***venusta*** 🏆 ↕5cm (2in) ↔ 25cm (10in) ⑱ **'Wide Brim'** 🏆 ↕45cm (18in) ↔ 1m (3ft)

Hyacinthoides

Bluebell

Bluebells are familiar to us as a shimmering blue carpet of blooms in woodland in late spring. They can become invasive, but are easy to control by digging up unwanted bulbs. The small flowers, usually violet-blue but occasionally white or pink, are held on sturdy stems above strappy, mid-green foliage. Plant the English Bluebell (*Hyacinthoides non-scripta*) in dappled shade *en masse* beneath deciduous trees; the flower colour will seem all the more intense. The larger, more robust Spanish Bluebell (*H. hispanica*) tolerates sun and drier conditions. Bluebells may be naturalized in grass or in a wild garden, or can be used in a garden.

Hardiness Fully frost-hardy ✻✻✻.

Cultivation Plant bulbs 8cm (3in) deep in autumn, in reasonably fertile soil that is well-drained, in partial shade. Remove flowers as they fade to prevent self-seeding, except where planted in woodland. **Sow** seed (*see pp.391–393*) in a container in a cold frame as soon as it is ripe or divide clumps in summer (*see p.395*).

Hyacinthoides hispanica (Spanish Bluebell)
↕40cm (16in) spring flowering, blue and white forms are also available

Hyacinthus

Hyacinth

Possibly the most sweetly scented of all spring-flowering bulbs, hyacinths are grown for their densely packed flowerheads in white, pink, red, yellow, and shades of purple. Each sturdy flower stem rises up above the deep green, strappy leaves. All cultivated forms derive from *Hyacinthus orientalis*, growing 20–30cm (8–12in) tall. Make a virtue of their slightly unnatural appearance by using them in formalized spring bedding displays, with polyanthus (*Primula, see pp.312–313*), winter-flowering pansies (*Viola, see p.338*) and tulips (*see pp.334–335*). Hyacinths can be forced to flower earlier in pots than outdoors.

Hardiness Fully frost-hardy ✻✻✻.

Cultivation **Plant** bulbs 10cm (4in) deep and 8cm (3in) apart in autumn. Grow in well-drained, reasonably fertile soil in sun or partial shade. Protect container-grown bulbs from excessive winter wet.

① ***orientalis*** **'Blue Jacket'** 🏆 flowers in early spring
② ***orientalis*** **'City of Haarlem'** 🏆 flowers in late spring

Hymenocallis

Spider Lily, Sacred Lily of the Incas

These are evergreen or deciduous bulbs mostly from tropical and sub-tropical South America. As such they prefer hot and humid areas of summer rainfall and here they can be grown in the garden. Further south they can be grown in containers. They have white or yellow flowers that look a little like daffodils, but with long, trailing, ribbon-like petals behind the central cup. The flowers occur in most species in spring or summer and at the top of a stron upright stem. In species such as the Sacred Lily of th Incas (*Hymenocallis narcissiflora*) they are sweetly perfumed. The leaves are long and strap-like and die off in late autumn in deciduous species.

Hardiness Frost-tender ✻ to very frost-tender ❀.

Cultivation Grow in well-drained soil that has had plenty of well-rotted organic matter incorporated into it. Let the bulbs dry out in lat autumn and remain dry through winter. Part shade to deep shade ar shelter from hot, drying winds is best. **Sow** seed (*see p.391*) when ri in containers. **Propagate** by offsets in winter (*see p.395*).

Hymenocallis littoralis
↕90cm (3 ft) ↔ 60cm (2ft), has amazing spidery flowers, but is probably best for warm areas or a heated glasshouse

]BERIS

ndytuft

.USTERS OF SMALL, OFTEN SCENTED FLOWERS almost nceal candytuft's low mounds of spoon-shaped, rk green leaves. This group of spreading perennials d bushy annuals flower in shades of white, purple, l, or pink from late spring until early summer. ergreen *Iberis sempervirens*, 30cm (12in) tall, oduces round heads of densely packed, white wers. Perennial forms are good plants for rock rdens and walls, where their growth can spread and mble, hiding hard edges. Grow the annuals as dding, at the front of gardens or in containers; good mpanions include other hardy annuals such as lendula (*see p.204*) and nigellas (*see p.291*).

rdiness Fully frost-hardy ❄❄❄ to frost-hardy ❄❄.

ltivation **Grow** in poor to reasonably fertile soil that is moist well-drained, in sun. After flowering, trim perennials back to tidy. **w** seed of annuals where they are to grow (*see p.393*), in spring autumn. Sow seed of perennials in containers in a cold frame in umn (*see pp.391–392*). **Take** softwood cuttings in late spring, or ni-ripe cuttings in summer (*see p.394*).

***eris umbellata* Fairy Series**

5–30cm (6–12in) ↔ to 23cm (9in), annual, with a mixture of k, lilac-purple, and white, scented flowers ❄❄❄

IMPATIENS

Busy Lizzie

FREE-FLOWERING EVEN IN SHADE, Busy Lizzies are among the most useful plants for long-lived summer colour. They produce a profusion of flowers, in reds, purples, pinks, and white, and many bicolours, from early summer until well into autumn. Most grown in gardens are either annuals, or tender perennials grown as annuals – used as summer plants and discarded at the end of the season. All have brittle, almost succulent stems with fleshy leaves. The New Guinea hybrids and *Impatiens walleriana* varieties are invaluable both in gardens and containers in shady spots; try some of the more unusual types in a windowbox or in pots on a patio to bring their flowers nearer the eye.

Hardiness Fully frost-hardy ❄❄❄ to very frost-tender ❀.

Cultivation Grow in soil enriched with well-rotted organic matter in partial shade, with shelter from cold winds. In pots, use quality potting mix and keep well watered; feed with a liquid fertilizer every month. **Sow** seed (*see pp.391–393*) at 16–18°C (61–64°F) in early spring. **Take** softwood cuttings (*see p.394*) in spring and summer to overwinter.

***Impatiens niamniamensis* 'Congo Cockatoo'**

↕90cm (36in), erect, short-lived perennial ❀

IPHEION

THE STARRY FLOWERS OF THESE PLANTS sit like jewels among their grassy leaves in spring. This is a small group of bulbous perennials whose blue, violet, or white flowers are often honey-scented. Most other parts of the plant, especially the leaves, smell of onions when crushed. The most commonly grown species, *Ipheion uniflorum*, may be small, but is sturdy and quickly clump-forming. These are beautiful plants for a rock garden, or can be used in a garden to underplant herbaceous perennials such as hostas (*see pp.260–261*) and peonies (*see p.298*). They can also be grown in pots and bowls.

Hardiness Frost-hardy ❄❄ to very frost-tender ❀.

Cultivation **Grow** in reasonably fertile, well-drained soil enriched with well-rotted organic matter, or in good potting mix, in full sun. **Plant** the bulbs 8cm (3in) deep, 5cm (2in) apart in autumn. **Divide** (*see p.395*) in summer, when the plants are dormant. **Sow** seed (*see pp.391–393*) in containers in a cold frame when ripe, or in spring.

***Ipheion uniflorum* 'Wisley Blue'** 🏆

↕15–20cm (6–8in), leaves produced in late autumn, scented solitary flowers in spring ❄❄

IRISES PRODUCE THEIR DISTINCTIVE, HANDSOME FLOWERS mainly from midwinter to midsummer on plants that vary greatly in height. Diminutive types such as *Iris danfordiae* and *I. histrioides* unfold their petals when snow may be on the ground. These are bulbous irises, one of the many types included in this wide-ranging genus. Other irises grow from rhizomes, fleshy stems that creep on or below the soil surface. Those with this kind of rootstock include the widely-grown bearded irises, with stiff, sword-like leaves shooting from fat surface rhizomes. They are at their peak in spring to early summer. Beardless irises lack the decorative tuft on the lower petals of the bearded types, but their flowers are often beautifully marked. They include early summer-flowering Siberian Irises (which grow from below-soil rhizomes), and moisture-loving water, or flag, irises. Those classed as crested irises also spread by rhizomes and produce showy but flatter-shaped flowers. There are many more garden-worthy irises besides. All are perennial, and on a few the strappy leaves are evergreen. Taller irises often make typical cottage-garden plants and have a stately presence in mixed or herbaceous borders. Smaller varieties tend to be best suited to a rock garden, raised bed, or container.

Hardiness Fully frost-hardy ✲✲✲ to very frost-tender ❁.

Cultivation Different types of iris require different growing conditions, so check the label carefully when you buy. **Plant** bearded irises in well-drained soil in sun (*see below*). Moisture-loving species need the soil to be damp at all times and suit bog gardens or pond margins. Most types grow well in slightly neutral to slightly acid soil, but a few have special requirements: *I. laevigata* and Pacific Coast Irises, for instance, need acid soil, and winter-flowering *I. unguicularis* needs alkaline soil as well as a sheltered site. **Remove** faded flowers and spent flower stems if unsightly, for example on bearded irises, but leave them if you want the decorative seedheads, as with *I. foetidissima*. **Divide** rhizomes from midsummer until early autumn (*see below*). **Sow** seed in containers in spring or autumn (*see pp.391–393*). Bearded irises are susceptible to rot if the soil is not sufficiently well-drained.

How to divide iris rhizomes

❶ *Lift the iris (here* Iris pseudoacorus*) and wash the soil from the roots. Split the clump apart with your hands or an old knife. Make sure there is one good rhizome with roots and leaves for each new clump.*

❷ *Use a sharp knife to trim the rhizome carefully. Discard any pieces that do not have any new shoots. Trim the roots by up to one-third, then cut down the leaves to 15cm (6in) to prevent wind rock. The leaves can act like sails.*

How to plant irises

***Water irises** should be replanted in a basket if they are destined for a pond, or in damp ground. In baskets, use soil and a top-dressing of gravel to prevent the soil from washing away.*

***Bearded irises** need to be planted with the roots in the soil but the rhizomes set on the surface, 13cm (5in) apart. Firm in and water to settle the soil around the roots. Water regularly until established.*

① ***danfordiae*** ↕8–15cm (3–6in), dwarf bulbous, late winter ② ***Iris* 'Alcazar'** ↕60–90cm (24–36in), bearded ③ ***douglasiana*** 🏆 ↕15–70cm (6–28in), beardless, late spring ④ ***confusa*** 🏆 ↕1m (3ft), crested, mid-spring ⑤ ***decora*** ↕30cm (12in), beardless, best raised from seed, early summer ⑥ ***chrysographes*** 🏆 ↕40–50cm (16–20in), Siberian, early summer ⑦ **Eyebright'** 🏆 ↕30cm (12in),

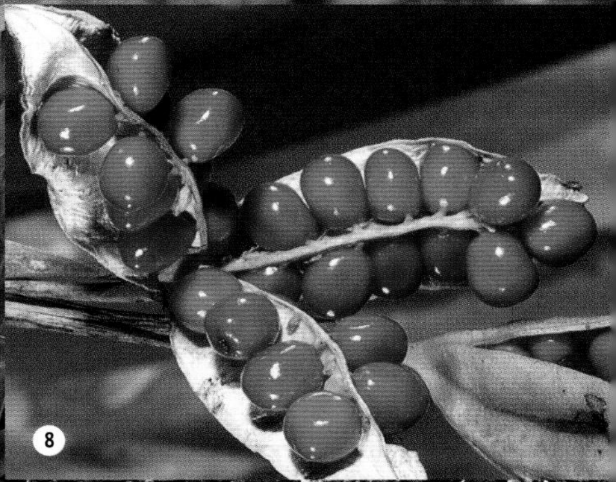

arded, early spring ⑧ ***foetidissima*** ♡ ↕30–90cm (12–36in), beardless, seedheads in autumn, purple
owers tinged yellow in early summer ⑨ ***forrestii*** ♡ ↕35–40cm (14–16in), Siberian, early summer
delavayi ♡ ↕1.5m (5ft), Siberian, summer ⑪ ***graminea*** ♡ ↕20–40cm (8–16in), beardless,
ented, late spring ⑫ ***ensata*** ♡ ↕90cm (36in), bulbous water iris, midsummer ⑬ ***histrioides***
'Major' ↕10–15cm (4–6in), dwarf bulbous, early spring ⑭ ***innominata*** ↕15–25cm (6–10in), beardless, early summer

⑮ ***magnifica*** ♡ ↕30–60cm (12–24in), bulbous, mid-spring ⑯ ***missouriensis*** ♡ ↕20–50cm (8–20in), beardless, early summer ⑰ ***orientalis*** ↕90cm (36in), beardless, late spring ⑱ ***pallida*** **'Variegata'** ♡ ↕1.2m (4ft), bearded, late spring ⑲ ***laevigata*** ♡ ↕80cm (32in), beardless water iris, early summer ⑳ ***laevigata*** **'Variegata'** ♡ ↕80cm (32in), beardless water iris, ea summer ㉑ ***prismatica*** ↕40–80cm (16–32in), beardless, early summer ㉒ ***pseudacorus*** ♡ ↕90cm–1.5m (3–5ft), beardless water iris, midsummer ㉓ ***setosa*** ♡ ↕15–90cm (6–36in), beardless, late

19

20

21

24

25

30

ing ㉔ ***sibirica* 'Anniversary'** ↕75cm (30in), Siberian, mid-spring ㉕ ***sibirica* 'Butter and gar'** 🏆 ↕70cm (28in), Siberian, mid-spring ㉖ ***sibirica* 'Ruffled Velvet'** 🏆 ↕55cm (22in), erian, early summer ㉗ ***sibirica* 'Shirley Pope'** 🏆 ↕85cm (34in), Siberian, early summer

㉘ ***tectorum*** ↕25–40cm (10–16in), crested, early summer ㉙ ***unguicularis*** 🏆 ↕30cm (12in), beardless, fragrant, late winter ㉚ ***unguicularis* 'Mary Barnard'** 🏆 ↕30cm (12in), beardless, midwinter

IXIA

SPRING-FLOWERING BULBS, ixias come in a range of colours from crimson through pink and yellow to white. They are upward-facing, starry to cup-shaped and are held in a cluster along the top of a thin, wiry stem that stands above the foliage. The leaves are narrow and up to 20cm (8in) long. They form a tight and very upright clump of foliage before it dies down in the autumn. This can be disguised by autumn flowering plants such as diascias (*Diascia, see p.228*). Bulbs should be allowed to dry out a little in their late summer and autumn dormancy period or their future success will be affected.

Hardiness Frost-hardy ❄❄ to frost-tender ❄.

Cultivation Full sun is necessary to get the flowers to open. A well-drained soil enriched with well-rotted organic matter also helps. Bulbs are planted in autumn 10–15cm (4–6in) deep. **Sow** seed (*see p.391*) in autumn in containers in a cold frame. **Divide** existing clumps in autumn (*see p.395*).

Ixia viridiflora
↕60cm (2 ft) ↔ 30cm (1ft), the flowers are a pale blue-green, which is an unusual colour to find in garden plants

KNAUTIA

↕1.5m (5ft)
↔45cm (18in)

THESE CHARMING PLANTS are particularly suited to growing in a cottage garden, or a wildflower area, where their exuberant habit lends an air of informality to the planting. Garden Knautias are perennials, but there are annual species. They have basal rosettes of simple, broad leaves that last through the winter and tall, slender stems. From summer to autumn, these bear numerous, long-lasting, bluish-lilac to purple flowers, similar to those of scabious (*see p.322*), that wave gracefully in the breeze and attract bees. If the plants flower profusely for 2–3 years, they may become exhausted and have to be replaced.

Hardiness Fully frost-hardy ❄❄❄.

Cultivation Grow in any moderately fertile, well-drained soil, preferably alkaline (limy), and in full sun. Knautias can be prone to rot in wet soils during winter. **Dig in** plenty of coarse sand and gypsum to improve drainage permanently on heavy clay soils. Raising the level of the soil by 5–8cm (2–3in) can also help to improve drainage. **Sow** seed (*see pp.391–393*) in containers or take cuttings (*see p.394*) from the base of the plant in spring.

Knautia macedonica
↕60–80cm (24–32in) ↔ 45cm (18in), flowers 1.5–3cm (½–1¼in) across in mid- and late summer

KNIPHOFIA

Red Hot Poker

THE SPIKY FLOWERHEADS IN BRAZEN HUES and erect habit of these striking perennials reveal how they became known as red hot pokers. Most form large clumps with arching, strappy, light green or blue-green leaves. During summer, strong stems soar up to 2m (6ft) and bear flower spikes composed of many small, tubular flowers. They may be in shades of scarlet, orange, gold, white, or greenish-white – some flower spikes are bicoloured. Some cultivars and species flower in autumn and winter. There are also dwarf kniphofias that are no more than 50cm (20in) tall. Use these plants in gardens to provide a vertical contrast to plants with broad foliage such as cardoon (*Cynara, see p.221*). They are also bird-attractors.

Hardiness Fully frost-hardy ❄❄❄ to frost-tender ❄.

Cultivation Grow in fertile, well-drained soil with plenty of well-rotted organic matter added to it before planting. Kniphofias prefer fu sun or very light shade. **Sow** seed (*see pp.391–393*) in containers in cold frame in spring. **Divide** (*see p.395*) established clumps of spring and summer flowerers in autumn or winter. Divide autumn and winte flowerers in spring.

Kniphofia 'Ice Queen'
↕to 1.5m (5ft) ↔ 75cm (30in), deciduous, green buds open to pal primrose, then to ivory, in late summer to early autumn ❄❄❄

.ACHENALIA

ɔldier Boy

HESE BULBS ARE WORTHWHILE for bringing some ɔlour to the garden in late winter and early spring. hey have small tubular flowers hanging on the top f a fleshy stem that, along with the foliage, is ɜnerally spotted with purplish-brown splotches. lowers are most often red and yellow with a shade of ·een, but pure yellow, orange-red and lavender blue ·e also available. Each bulb has two fleshy leaves that ·ch up slightly and then trail along the ground. raditionally these plants were grown in rows as an lge for garden beds (thus the common name), though now you are more likely to see them containers.

ardiness Frost-hardy ❄❄ to frost-tender ❄.

ıltivation Grow in well-drained soil that is enriched with well-:ted organic matter. Full sun or very light shade is best. When ɔwing in containers use a good quality potting mix and do not have ɔ wet in the summer and autumn dormant period. **Sow** seed (*see 391*) in autumn into containers. **Divide** established clumps in tumn (*see p.395*).

***achenalia aloides* 'Quadricolor'**
.5–25cm (6–10in) ↔ 10cm (4in), is a fleshy bulb with unusually loured flowers in late winter

LAMIUM

Dead Nettle

THIS GROUP OF ANNUALS AND PERENNIALS are grown mainly for their very decorative foliage, and make good ground-cover plants among shrubs and larger, vigorous perennials. The leaves are roughly textured and, in some plants, are mottled or tinted. Lamiums have the distinctive square stems of plants belonging to the nettle family, but fortunately no stings. From late spring until summer, the two-lipped flowers are borne either singly or in tiers in dense clusters or spikes. Easily grown, the larger species can be invasive in very rich soils, but less so in poorer soils. Lamiums look particularly good at the front of a garden or in light, dappled shade under deciduous trees.

Hardiness Fully frost-hardy ❄❄❄.

Cultivation Grow vigorous species in moist but well-drained soil in shade. Dig out the spreading underground stems (rhizomes) if needed, to keep them away from less robust plants. Less vigorous lamiums prefer sharply drained soil in full sun or partial shade. **Trim** straggly plants with shears in early spring or in summer after flowering. **Sow** seed (*see pp.391–393*) in autumn or spring in pots in a cold frame; take stem-tip cuttings (*see p.394*) in early summer. **Divide** existing clumps in winter.

① ***maculatum*** ↕20cm (8in) ↔ 1m (3ft) ② ***maculatum* 'Album'** ③ ***maculatum* 'Beacon Silver'** both ↕15cm (6in) ↔ 60cm (2ft)

LATHYRUS VERNUS

Spring Vetchling

see also p.145

↔ 45cm (18in)

THIS DENSE, CLUMP-FORMING herbaceous perennial is related to the climbing sweet pea (*Lathyrus odorata*). However, despite the plant's pea-like appearance it does not climb. In spring, it bears one-sided clusters of 3–6 flowers, poised above dark to mid-green pointed leaflets. The plant dies back in summer after flowering. Since the spring vetchling grows only 20–45cm (8–18in) tall and spreads to only 45cm (18in), it is suitable for rock gardens and woodland settings. It can also be grown in herbaceous and mixed borders, but the plants should be placed near the back of the border so that they are hidden when their foliage dies back. There is also a fine pink-flowered form, *L. vernus* f. *roseus.*

Hardiness Fully frost-hardy ❄❄❄.

Cultivation Spring Vetchlings prefer well-drained soil in partial shade. They will tolerate poor soil, but resent being disturbed or transplanted. **Sow** seed (*see pp.391–393*) in pots in spring or directly into the soil where they are to grow.

Lathyrus vernus 🏆
Flowers are 2cm (¾in) across

LAVATERA

Mallow

see also p.81

↕ most to 1.2m (4ft) ↔ 60cm (24in)

THE ANNUAL MALLOWS have very similar flowers to the shrubby types, and like them grow vigorously and flower very profusely in a single season, but once seed is set, they die. They produce masses of showy, open, funnel-shaped flowers in shades from white to pale pink to reddish- or purple-pink. The leaves are mid- to dark green with heart-shaped bases. The flowers are also good for cutting. Mallows grow wild in dry, rocky places and in the garden they thrive in sunny herbaceous gardens or summer bedding displays. For a traditional cottage-garden look, grow them with other annuals, such as calendulas (*see p.204*) and nasturtiums (*Tropaeolum, see p.333*).

Hardiness Fully frost-hardy ❄❄❄ to frost-hardy ❄❄.

Cultivation Grow in ideally light to moderately fertile soil, in full sun.The plants can grow quite tall, and so may need supporting with twiggy sticks in windy gardens. **Sow** seed in containers under glass in mid-spring, or slightly later outside where plants are to grow (*see pp.391–393*).

***Lavatera trimestris* 'Silver Cup'**
↕ 75cm (30in) ↔ 45cm (18in), one of the brightest coloured mallows, with large flowers in summer ❄❄❄

***Lavatera trimestris* 'Mont Blanc'**
↕ 50cm (20in) ↔ 45cm (18in), compact plant that does not need staking, very dark green foliage, flowers in summer ❄❄❄

Lavatera cachemiriana
↕ 2.5m (8ft) ↔ 1.2m (4ft), short-lived, woody perennial grown as an annual, flowers in summer, good at the back of a garden ❄❄❄

***Lavatera trimestris* 'Pink Beauty'**
↕ to 60cm (24in) ↔ to 45cm (18in), soft, hairy leaves, flowers measure 8–10cm (3–4in) across, excellent for cutting, easily raised from seed to flower from early summer until early autumn ❄❄❄

ˌEUCANTHEMUM

ROBUST AND CLUMP-FORMING, these perennials and nnuals bloom for long periods in summer and the lense flowerheads are carried singly at the ends of ɔng stems, well above the foliage. The flowers are xcellent for cutting. The dark green leaves are long nd toothed. *Leucanthemum* × *superbum* cultivars Shasta Daisies) are what used to be called *Chrysanthemum maximum* and are white-flowered, ut usually with fancy petal details. Grow them in a vild or informal area, or in mixed or herbaceous ardens to lighten planting schemes in which richer olours predominate.

Hardiness Fully frost-hardy ❄❄❄ to frost-hardy ❄❄.

Cultivation Grow in reasonably fertile soil that is well-drained, in ıll sun or partial shade. Taller plants may need support with twiggy ticks. **Divide** perennials in autumn or winter (*see p.395*). **Sow** seed of nnuals where plants are to grow, in spring. Sow seed of perennials in ɔntainers in a cold frame in spring or autumn (*see pp.391–393*).

Leucanthemum × *superbum* 'Cobham Gold'
↕60cm (24in) ↔ 75cm (30in), robust perennial, double flowerheads n short stems, dark green leaves ❄❄❄

Leucanthemum × *superbum* 'Wirral Supreme' 🏆
↕90cm (36in) ↔ 75cm (30in), strong-stemmed perennial with glossy leaves and dense, double flowerheads ❄❄❄

LEUCOJUM

Snowflake

SIMILAR TO SNOWDROPS, although some are larger, these bulbous perennials flower in spring or autumn. The flowers have attractive greenish spots on the tips of the petals. The slender, strappy leaves grow direct from the bulbs. The larger species are good in a border or near water, while the smaller species are ideal for a rock garden or alpine trough. *Leucojum vernum* and *L. aestivum*, both spring-flowering, associate well with other bulbs, such as crocuses (*see p.220*) and narcissus (*see pp.288–289*). *L. autumnale* which is small and flowers in autumn, looks good planted with dainty schizostylis (*see p.323*).

Hardiness Fully frost-hardy ❄❄❄ to frost-hardy ❄❄.

Cultivation Plant bulbs 8–10cm (3–4in) deep in autumn, in moist but well-drained soil in full sun. Add plenty of organic matter for *L. aestivum* and *L. vernum*, which need soil that retains moisture reliably. **Sow** seed in a container in a cold frame in autumn (*see pp.391–392*), or remove well-rooted offsets (*see p.395*) once the leaves have died down.

Leucojum aestivum 'Gravetye Giant' 🏆
↕90cm (36in) ↔ 8cm (3in), the largest of the snowflakes, spring flowers are faintly chocolate-scented, likes damp conditions

Lewisia

THESE POPULAR, HARDY ALPINES are grown for the pretty, often bright colours of their flowers. There are both deciduous and evergreen kinds, forming either rosettes or tufts of fleshy leaves. The deciduous species are more commonly native to high meadows or to grassland, and will die down after flowering; the evergreens are found in shady crevices among rocks. Lewisias have many-petalled flowers in shades of pink, peach, magenta, purple, yellow, or white – they are often striped. They bloom for many weeks in spring and summer. Grow them in a rock garden or in crevices in a dry-stone wall, with other rock plants and perhaps aubrietas (*see p.195*).

Hardiness Fully frost-hardy ✲✲✲.

Cultivation Grow in reasonably fertile, sharply drained, neutral to acid (lime-free) soil, in full sun or partial shade. Protect all Lewisias from winter wet. In containers, grow in equal parts loam, leafmould, and sharp sand. **Sow** seed in containers in a cold frame in autumn (*see pp.391–392*). Seed of *L. cotyledon* hybrids produces plants that may look different to their parents. Evergreens may produce plantlets around the main rosette of leaves, which can be removed and potted up in early summer. Prone to attack from slugs and snails (*see p.398*).

***Lewisia cotyledon* hybrids**
↕15–30cm (6–12in) ↔ 20–40cm (8–16in), evergreen perennial, yellow, orange, magenta, or pink flowers in late spring to summer

Liatris

Blazing Star, Gayfeather

THE TALL FLOWER SPIKES OF LIATRIS are unusual in that they open from the top of the spike downwards, instead of from the bottom upwards, giving them a distinctive bottle-brush shape that is emphasized by the thread-like appearance of the tightly packed flowers. These are produced on stiff stems in shades of purple, reddish-purple, blue-purple or white, and are highly attractive to bees. Liatris grow wild on prairies and in open woodland. In the garden, they provide an unusual shape and late-summer colour. The flowers are good for cutting, too. Try growing them with perennials with open-faced flowers, such as erigerons (*see p.237*), coreopsis (*see p.217*), and geums (*see p.252*), to accentuate their striking form.

Hardiness Fully frost-hardy ✲✲✲.

Cultivation Grow in light, reasonably fertile, moist but well-drained soil in full sun. In heavy soils, use gypsum and organic matter to improve drainage, or plants may rot in wet winters. **Divide** in winter (*see p.395*). **Sow** seed in a container in a cold frame in autumn (*see pp.391–392*). Prone to attack by slugs and snails (*see p.398*).

Liatris spicata
↕60cm (2ft) ↔ 30cm (1ft), the upright flower stems appear in summer and open from the top down

***Liatris spicata* 'Alba'**
↕60cm (2ft) ↔ 30cm (1ft), an uncommon white form of this herbaceous perennial

IBERTIA

'ALUED FOR THEIR STRIKING FORMS, libertias have iff, narrow, evergreen leaves that are a feature all year ound. At the base, the leaves are leathery and long; ose on the stem are smaller and more sparse. In late ring and summer, libertias produce slender spires of ucer-shaped, white, yellow-white or blue flowers. hese are followed by shiny, light brown seedheads at are useful in flower arranging. The leaves and eds of *Libertia ixioides* are tinted orange in late itumn and winter. These clump-forming perennials ould be grown towards the front of a garden; they ake perfect partners for the garden tradescantias (*see 331*), and also look good with bronze-tinted grasses.

ardiness Fully frost-hardy ✻✻✻ (borderline) to frost-hardy ✻✻, t with protection, all can survive all but the coldest winters.

ltivation Grow in reasonably fertile soil enriched with well-rotted ganic matter, in full sun. In frost-prone areas, protect with a thick ulch of organic matter in winter. **Divide** in spring (*see p.395*). **Sow** ed in containers outdoors as soon as it is ripe (*see pp.391–393*).

ibertia grandiflora 🏆
o 90cm (36in) ↔ 60cm (24in), forms dense clumps, flowers early ring to early summer ✻✻✻ (borderline)

LIGULARIA

THESE ARCHITECTURAL PLANTS are large, robust, clump-forming perennials grown for their cone-shaped spikes of flowers, produced in shades of yellow and orange from midsummer until early autumn. Each individual flower is daisy-like, often with a contrasting centre. The large, usually rounded or kidney-shaped, mid-green leaves are equally bold. Ligularias look imposing grown in a garden, with other moisture-loving perennials such as astilbes (*see p.194*), daylilies (*Hemerocallis, see p.258*) and border phloxes (*see p.306*). Tall species, such as *Ligularia przewalskii,* need to be at the back of planting schemes. They also look very striking by a stream or pond, where they will enjoy the damp conditions.

Hardiness Fully frost-hardy ✻✻✻.

Cultivation Grow in reasonably fertile, deep and reliably moist soil, in full sun or partial shade. Provide shelter from strong winds, otherwise taller plants may need staking with twiggy sticks. **Divide** in spring or after flowering (*see p.395*). **Sow** seed of species outdoors in autumn or spring (*see pp.391–393*).

Ligularia przewalskii
↕ 1.5–1.8m (5–6ft) ↔ 90cm (3ft), tall summer flowering perennial that prefers damp conditions

***Ligularia* 'The Rocket'** 🏆
↕ 2m (6ft) ↔ 1m (3ft), sturdy black stems, large, boldly toothed leaves with purple veins, tall "candles" of flowers with orange-yellow centres, flowers in early and late summer

LILIUM

Lily

LILIES HAVE LONG GRACED GARDENS, both in the West and in the East, where many originate. Their appeal lies in their extravagant, often fragrant, blooms, which can measure up to 8cm (3in) across and over 10cm (4in) long. There are about 100 species; all are perennial bulbs. Some of the earliest in cultivation are among the most demanding, for instance the Madonna Lily, *Lilium candidum*, which can be disease-prone. Others have definite preferences for acid or alkaline soil. Modern hybrids, however, tend to be vigorous, disease-resistant, and less fussy about soil. Lilies are available in most colours except blue, and the flowers come in four distinct shapes: trumpet, funnel, bowl, and turkscap, with swept-back petals. One of the easiest ways to grow them is in a container on the patio where their perfume is readily appreciated. Most do well in sunny spots; some, such as *L. martagon*, prefer the dappled shade of a woodland garden. A few dwarf species are at home in the rock garden.

Hardiness Fully frost-hardy ❄❄❄ to frost-hardy ❄❄, but young shoots may be damaged by frost.

Cultivation Grow in any well-drained soil enriched with well-rotted organic matter or in containers in good potting mix. On heavy clay soils, improve drainage by digging in plenty of gypsum in the area of the planting hole. Most lilies prefer full sun, but some tolerate partial shade. **Plant** bulbs in autumn or spring at a depth of 2–3 times their height; the distance between should be three times the diameter of the bulb. **Water** regularly during dry spells in summer and feed with a high-potash fertilizer in the growing season. **Stake** tall varieties in exposed sites. **Deadhead** fading flowers before seed sets to maintain the plant's vigour. **Sow** seed (*see pp.391–392*) as soon as it is ripe in pots in a cold frame. **Detach** stem bulbils and bulblets from those cultivars that produce them (*see below*). Plants, including the flowers, may be eaten by slugs and snails (*see p.398*).

Propagating from bulblets

Lilies such as L. auratum, L. longiflorum, *and* L. speciosum *naturally produce bulblets (small rooted bulbs that will grow into flowering plants in 3–4 years). These form below ground at the base of the main stem. Lift the parent plant in autumn, remove the bulblets and replant the mature bulb. Prepare pots of moist, premium quality potting mix. Insert the bulblets to twice their own depth, and cover. Label and keep in a frost-free place before planting out the young lilies in the following autumn.*

Propagating from bulbils

Bulbils are *tiny bulbs which form where the leaf stalks join stems of lilies such as* L. lancifolium *and their hybrids. They ripen in summer, and will produce flowering plants in 3–4 years. Take them only from healthy plants as bulbils can transfer disease. Fill a pot with moist, premium quality potting mix and press the bulbils into the surface. Cover with a 1cm (½in) layer of coarse sand and label. Grow on in a frost-free place until planting out the following autumn.*

1

2

7

① ***Lilium* African Queen Group** 🏆 ↕1.5–2m (5–6ft), scented ❄❄ ② ***auratum* var. *platyphyllum*** ↕1.5m (5ft), scented ❄❄❄ ③ **'Black Beauty'** ↕1.4–2m (4½–6ft), scented ❄❄❄ ④ ***canadense*** ↕1–1.6m (3–5½ft) ❄❄❄ ⑤ ***candidum*** 🏆 ↕1–2m (3–6ft), scented, neutral to alkaline soil ❄❄❄ ⑥ **'Casa Blanca'** 🏆 ↕1–1.2m (3–4ft), scented ❄❄❄ ⑦ ***davidii* var. *willmottiae*** ↕2m (6ft) ❄❄❄ ⑧ ***formosanum* var. *pricei*** ↕10–30cm (4–12in),

3

4

5

6

8

9

10

scented, ❄❄ ⑨ **Golden Splendor Group** 🏆 ↕1.2–2m (4–6ft), scented ❄❄❄
⑩ **'Grand Paradiso'** ↕90cm (36in) ❄❄❄

⑪

⑫

⑬

⑭

⑰

⑱

⑲

⑪ ***henryi*** 🏆 ↕1–3m (3–10ft), neutral to alkaline soil, partial shade, late summer ❄❄❄ ⑫ ***lancifolium*** ↕60cm–1.5m (2–5ft), acid soil but tolerates some lime, late summer and early autumn ❄❄❄ ⑬ ***longiflorum*** 🏆 ↕40–100cm (16–39in), lime-tolerant, partial shade ❄ ⑭ ***mackliniae*** ↕30–60cm (12–24in) ❄❄❄ ⑮ ***martagon*** 🏆 ↕90cm–2m (3–6ft), rank scent, well-drained soil, sun or partial shade ❄❄❄ ⑯ ***martagon* var. *album*** 🏆 ↕90cm–2m (3–6ft), rank scent, well-drained soil, sun or partial shade ❄❄❄ ⑰ ***pardalinum*** 🏆 ↕1.5–2.5m (5–8ft) ❄❄❄ ⑱ **Pink Perfection Group** 🏆 ↕1.5–2m (5–6ft), scented ❄❄❄ ⑲ ***pyrenaicum*** ↕30–100cm (12–39in), rank scent, neutral to alkaline soil ❄❄❄ ⑳ ***regale*** 🏆 ↕60cm–2m (2–6ft), scented, full sun, midsummer ❄❄❄

'Star Gazer' ↕1–1.5m (3–5ft) ✲✲✲ ㉒ ***superbum*** ↕1.5–3m (5–10ft), acid soil, late summer and early
tumn ✲✲✲

LIMONIUM

Statice, Sea Lavender

This is a genus of annuals and evergreen perennials, with some of the latter being shrub-like and some grown as annuals. The predominant colour is purple and all its shades, although the annuals are available in mixed colours including orange, cerise, white, pink, and yellow. The flowers are small papery cups held in large clusters on stems above the foliage. Perennial forms tend to flower in the warmest months, although they can flower continuously if conditions are right. The annuals will flower about five months after the seed is planted. All flowers are used as dried flowers. The leaves are oval and leathery. These plants are adapted well to seaside gardens and to dry conditions.

Hardiness Frost-hardy ❄❄ to very frost-tender ❀.

Cultivation Grow in full sun in well-drained soil. **Cut** quality flower stems when the colour reaches its peak and hang in an airy place to dry if using for dried flowers. **Trim out** flowers that become damaged or bedraggled (*see p.390*). **Sow** seed of annuals in autumn or spring (*see pp.391–392*) and thin to about 25–30cm (10–12in) apart when large enough. **Take** root cuttings in late winter and divide plants at the same time (*see pp.394–395*).

Limonium perezii
↕75cm (30in) ↔ 60cm (24in) is drought hardy and has flowers that can be used in dried flower arrangements ❄❄

LINARIA

Toadflax

THIS IS A LARGE GROUP of annuals, biennials, and herbaceous perennials. Their stems, which can be erect, trailing, or branched, are clothed with clusters of flowers that look like tiny snapdragons. They bloom abundantly from spring to autumn, in hues of white, pink, red, purple, orange, and yellow. The smaller species suit a rock garden, or wall crevice. Taller annuals and perennials, such as *Linaria vulgaris*, are a choice for the foreground of gardens, forming soft masses of colour that act as foils to plants with bolder flowers; they also grow and look well in gravel beds and containers.

Hardiness Fully frost-hardy ❄❄❄ to frost-hardy ❄❄. All shown below are fully frost-hardy ❄❄❄.

Cultivation Grow in reasonably fertile, well-drained soil, in full sun. **Divide** perennials in early spring (*see p.395*). **Sow** seed of annuals where they are to flower in early spring or in autumn in warm districts (*see p.393*). Thin the seedlings to around 15cm (6in). Sow seed of perennials in containers in a cold frame in early spring (*see p.391*). **Take** softwood cuttings of perennials in spring (*see p.394*).

① ***alpina*** ↕ ↔ 15cm (6in) ② ***dalmatica*** ↕ 1m (3ft) ↔ 20cm (8in)
③ ***purpurea* 'Canon Went'** ↕ to 90cm (36in) ↔ 30cm (12in)
④ ***vulgaris*** ↕ to 90cm (36in) ↔ 30cm (12in)

LINUM

Flax

see a
p.

THESE ANNUALS, BIENNIALS, AND PERENNIALS produc clouds of brilliantly coloured, saucer-shaped flowers on graceful, wiry stems. The flowers appear for man weeks from early to late summer, and are mainly in pale primary colours – yellow, blue, or red – or whit The flowers of *Linum perenne* last for only one day, but are replaced by more the next day. The perennia tend to be short-lived, but are easy to raise from seed The smaller flaxes are at home in a rock garden, whi the larger ones make a stunning display *en masse* in gardens; grow them in drifts among other herbaceou plants with soft outlines, such as hardy geraniums (*s pp.250–251*) and monardas (*see p.286*).

Hardiness Fully frost-hardy ❄❄❄ to frost-hardy ❄❄.

Cultivation Grow in light, reasonably fertile soil enriched with wel rotted organic matter in full sun. Smaller alpine species need sharply drained soil and protection from winter wet. **Sow** seed in spring or autumn. Annuals can be sown where they are to grow; sow perennia in containers in a cold frame (*see pp.391–393*). **Take** stem-tip cuttir of perennials in early summer (*see p.394*).

Linum perenne (Perennial Flax)
↕10–60cm (4–24in) ↔ 30cm (12in), relative of the flax used for linseed oil and linen, short-lived perennial, but seeds freely ❄❄❄

.IRIOPE

lyturf

VERGREEN HERBACEOUS PERENNIALS, these have fine ass-like leaves arising from a fleshy rhizome. They ake solid clumps of arching foliage, but also spread pidly and can colonize a large area if the conditions e right. The leaves are narrow and dark green, though a variegated form is available. In late ımmer but mainly autumn, they have small purple owers round the top of a narrow, upright flower em, partly hidden amongst the foliage. A white *iriope muscari* 'Munroe White') and a deep purple ıltivar (*L. muscari* 'Royal Purple') are available, as is larger form, sold as 'Evergreen Giant'. All are ırticularly useful for growing in shade.

ardiness Frost-hardy ❄❄.

ıltivation Free-draining soil that is enriched with well-rotted ganic matter and full or partial shade are the best. **Plants** that have ceeded their allotted space can be removed by cutting down with a arp spade and removing the unwanted pieces (*see pp.382–384*). **w** seed (*see p.392*) in autumn in a cold frame. **Divide** clumps in rly spring (*see p.395*).

***iriope muscari* 'Variegata'**

0cm (1 ft) ↔ indefinite, is often used as an edger in formal rdens but can be used as an informal filler under trees

LOBELIA

ANNUAL BEDDING LOBELIA IS HUGELY POPULAR, producing masses of flowers in the familiar blues, but also pink, purple, and white. Use it in summer gardens, as edging, or trailing from hanging baskets and windowboxes. Planted around the edges of containers, they are perfect partners for fuchsias (*see pp.60–63*) and other summer flowers. There are also hardier, perennial lobelias, from such diverse habitats as the meadow, riverbank, and woodland. They usually bear flowers in erect spikes, in jewel-like shades of azure, violet, carmine-red, and scarlet. The perennials can be grown in borders or, as with *Lobelia cardinalis,* in bog gardens or even shallow water.

Hardiness Fully frost-hardy ❄❄❄ to frost-tender ❄.

Cultivation Grow in deep, fertile, reliably moist soil, in sun or partial shade. *L. cardinalis* can be grown in baskets (*see p.381*) in water 8–10cm (3–4in) deep. Bedding lobelia flowers for longer in shade. In containers, it needs weekly feeding with a balanced fertilizer. **Protect** perennials in frost-prone areas with a thick winter mulch (*see p.388*). **Divide** perennials in winter; aquatics in summer (*see p.395*). **Sow** seed of perennials as soon as ripe; annuals in late winter, at 13–18°C (55–64°F) (*see pp.391–393*). Prone to slug damage (*see p.398*).

***Lobelia* 'Crystal Palace'**

↕10–15cm (4–6in) ↔ 15cm (6in),spring and summer flowering annual used to trail over the edges of garden beds and pots

LOBULARIA

Sweet Alyssum, Sweet Alice

FROM SPRING UNTIL AUTUMN, Sweet Alyssum forms cushions of densely packed, four-petalled flowers in shades of white, pink, rose-pink, mauve- and deep purple. In some cultivars, the flowers are honey-scented, too. There are both annuals and perennials in the group, and their long-flowering season and colourful blooms make them a popular choice in the garden. They originate from maritime areas and thus thrive in similar conditions – light soil and full sun – in gardens. Sweet Alyssum is a useful edging plant for gardens and in raised beds; white-flowered forms are often grown with blue trailing lobelia for a showy display, especially in hanging baskets. Gravel beds and cracks and crevices in paving also suit it well, and it will often self-seed into sunny niches such as this.

Hardiness Fully frost-hardy ❄❄❄.

Cultivation Grow in light, reasonably fertile soil that is well-drained and in full sun. **Trim** the plants after the first flush of blooms has faded to encourage more flowers later on. **Sow** seed where plants are to grow (*see pp.391–393*) in late spring.

***Lobularia* 'Royal Carpet'**

↕10cm (4in) ↔ 30cm (12in), grow in pots or raised beds to appreciate the sweet scent of the flowers

Lunaria

Honesty, Satin Flower

FLOWERS, SEED PODS, AND LEAVES are all decorative in this small group of plants. They bear purple or white flowers in late spring and early summer, followed by flat, silvery or beige seed capsules, the sides of which fall to reveal a satiny inner membrane. The capsules last quite well into autumn, although for use in dried flower arrangements they are usually cut in late summer and dried indoors to avoid any damage from autumn weather. The leaves vary in shape and have toothed edges. Annual, biennial, or perennial, honesty self-seeds easily and naturalizes well in an informal cottage garden. It can also be grown in a shrub garden or with herbaceous perennials like aquilegias (*see p.185*), lupins (*see right*), and poppies (*Papaver, see p.299*).

Hardiness Fully frost-hardy ❄❄❄.

Cultivation Grow in fertile, moist but well-drained soil, in full sun or partial shade. **Divide** *L. rediviva* (*see p.395*) in winter. **Sow** seed (*see pp.391–393*) in a seedbed in spring.

COLLECTING SEED
When the capsules become thin and papery, the seeds will be ripe. Peel the papery sides away and pick the seeds from the central membrane.

***Lunaria annua* 'Alba Variegata'**
↕ to 90cm (36in) ↔ to 30cm (12in), the white flowers will be followed by seed pods that are silvery outside and inside

Lunaria rediviva (Perennial Honesty)
↕ 60–90cm (24–36in) ↔ 30cm (12in), the flowers are fragrant; the seed pods of this species are more fawn-coloured than silvery

***Lunaria annua* 'Variegata'**
↕ to 90cm (36in) ↔ to 30cm (12in), as well as white-edged leaves, this has more deeply coloured flowers than *L. annua*

Lupinus

Lupin

THE ENDURINGLY POPULAR FLOWER SPIKES of Lupins provide some of the brightest colours to be seen in the early-summer garden. There are plenty to choose from, in almost any colour and even bicolours; they last well when cut. The attractive foliage is mid-green with lance-shaped leaflets; a rain shower will leave it starred with small, silvery droplets. Most lupins grown in gardens are stately perennials, to be paired with other classic herbaceous plants such as delphiniums (*see pp.224–225*) and Oriental Poppies (*Papaver orientale, see p.299*). However, there are smaller-flowered, less formal low-growing annuals.

Hardiness Fully frost-hardy ❄❄❄ to frost-tender ❄.

Cultivation Grow in reasonably fertile, well-drained soil in full sun or partial shade. **Deadhead** (*see p.390*) for a second flush of flowers. **Sow** seed, after soaking for 24 hours, in spring or autumn, outside or in containers in a cold frame (*see pp.391–393*). **Take** cuttings of new shoots of named varieties in mid-spring (*see p.394*). Are likely to be attacked by slugs and snails (*see p.398*). It is worth taking precaution against these pests.

***Lupinus* 'The Chatelaine'**
↕ 90cm (36in) ↔ 75cm (30in), this crisp combination is popular and among the brightest of the bicoloured forms

upinus 'Chandelier'
90cm (36in) ↔ 75cm (30in), restrained creamy-yellow spikes like urch candles allow the form and foliage to shine

Lupinus Russell hybrids
↕90cm (36in) ↔ 75cm (30in), among the earliest and most reliable hybrids, these have a wide colour range

Lupinus 'Noble Maiden'
↕90cm (36in) ↔ 75cm (30in), the densely packed flower spikes such as this make a strong impact in the border

Lupinus 'The Page'
↕90cm (36in) ↔ 75cm (30in), more open flower spikes such as these allow some lupins to look at home in an informal scheme

LYCHNIS

Campion, Catchfly

CAMPIONS HAVE BRIGHT SUMMER FLOWERS in shades of vivid scarlet, purple, and pink as well as in white. The flowers are usually tubular or star-shaped and borne singly or in small clusters. The erect flower stems make them ideal for cutting. Butterflies find the flowers attractive, so they are a good choice for a wild garden. The leaves may be hairy. Campions are biennial or perennial. Smaller species are pretty in rock gardens, and the taller ones are best in informal gardens with other perennials including aquilegias (*see p.185*), lupins (*see pp.280–281*), and Oriental Poppies (*Papaver orientale, see p.299*). Some campions, such as *Lychnis chalcedonica*, have brittle stems and need the support of twiggy sticks.

Hardiness Fully frost-hardy ***.

Cultivation Campions thrive in reasonably fertile soil that is well-drained, in full sun or partial shade. Grey-leaved species produce the best leaf colour in well-drained soil in full sun. **Remove** fading flowers regularly. **Sow** seed in containers (*see pp.391–392*) in a cold frame when it is ripe or in spring. **Divide** plants (*see p.395*) or take cuttings (*see p.394*) from new shoots at the base in spring.

Lychnis chalcedonica ♀ (Jerusalem Cross, Maltese Cross)
↕90cm–1.2m (3–4ft) ↔ 30cm (12in), perennial, flowers in early and midsummer, self-seeds freely

Lychnis coronaria ♀ (Rose Campion)
↕60cm (24in) ↔ 45cm (18in), biennial or short-lived perennial, flowers in late summer, self-seeds freely

LYSICHITON

Skunk Cabbage

THESE STRIKINGLY SHAPED, COLOURFUL perennials flower in early spring. Dense spikes of tiny, greenish flowers are surrounded by elegantly sculptural, hooded bracts (modified leaves). These are followed by clusters of large, glossy, mid- to dark green leaves springing directly from the ground. The Yellow Skunk Cabbage, *Lysichiton americanus*, is larger than the white-flowered *L. camtschatcensis*, which has 40cm (16in) hoods and leaves up to 100cm (39in) long; it has a height and spread of 75cm (30in). Both plants have a musky, some would say unpleasant, smell. Their native habitat is beside water, so grow them by a pond or stream along with *Caltha palustris* (*see p.205*) and other moisture-loving marginal plants.

Hardiness Fully frost-hardy ***.

Cultivation Fertile soil enriched with plenty of well-rotted organic matter, at the edge of a stream or pond, in full sun or partial shade will suit these aquatic marginals. Allow sufficient space for the leaves to develop without swamping other plants. **Remove** offsets (*see p.395*) at the bases of the main stems in spring or summer.

Lysichiton americanus ♀ (Yellow Skunk Cabbage)
↕1m (3ft) ↔ 1.2m (4ft), the hooded flowers are up to 40cm (16in) long, leaves up to 120cm (48in) long

.YSIMACHIA
ɔosestrife

·OOSESTRIFES ARE A LARGE AND VARIED GROUP that ıcludes many herbaceous perennials, and some vergreens. Flowers appear from mid- to late summer, nd may be star-, saucer- or cup-shaped; they are sually white or yellow, but sometimes are pink or urple. Larger loosestrifes are suitable for planting in amp herbaceous and mixed gardens along with other ıoisture-loving perennials such as astilbes (*see p.194*), nd border phloxes (*see pp.306–307*). They are happy ı a bog garden or by pool margins and also look at ome when naturalized in a woodland garden. ;reeping Jenny (*Lysmachia nummularia*) makes a ɔod ground-cover plant. Yellow-flowered *L. punctata* ın spread and become a problem, but is less invasive n dryish soil.

ardiness Fully frost-hardy ❄❄❄ to very frost-tender ❄.

ultivation Grow these plants in soil that is well-drained but ıriched with well-rotted organic matter, in full sun or partial shade, ıd in a site that does not dry out in summer. **Support** tall species with in bamboo sticks. **Sow** seed in containers outdoors (*see pp.391–393*) spring or divide plants in spring or autumn (*see p.395*).

Lysimachia nummularia (Creeping Jenny)
↕ to 5cm (2in) ↔ indefinite, mat-forming evergreen, rooting stems spread rapidly, cup-shaped, bright yellow flowers all summer ❄❄❄

ysimachia clethroides 🏆
90cm (36in) ↔ 60cm (24in), spreading, hairy leaves, flowerheads ɔpear mid- to late summer becoming upright as they mature ❄❄❄

Lysimachia ciliata 'Firecracker' 🏆
↕ 1.2m (4ft) ↔ 60cm (24in), flowers in midsummer ❄❄❄

LYTHRUM
Loosestrife

EVEN LONGER-FLOWERING THAN THEIR NAMESAKES (*see left*), these upright annuals and perennials are valued for their slender spikes of pretty flowers in shades of purplish-pink, or occasionally white. Individual flowers are up to 2cm (¾in) wide, with 4–8 petals, and are borne along the ends of tapering, square stems in summer to autumn. The leaves are up to 10cm (4in) long and sometimes add to autumnal displays by turning yellow. Some of these loosestrifes flourish at the margins of streams and ponds. For a colourful, natural display, combine them with other flowering plants such as astilbes (*see p.194*), bergamots (*Monarda, see p.286*), and phloxes (*see pp.306–307*).

Hardiness Fully frost-hardy ❄❄❄.

Cultivation These Loosestrifes thrive in any fertile, moist soil in full sun. **Remove** fading flowers to prevent self-seeding. **Sow** seed at 13–18°C (55–64°F) in spring (*see pp.391–393*) or divide plants in winter or early spring (*see p.395*). Take cuttings from new shoots at the base of the plant (*see p.394*) in spring or early summer.

Lythrum virgatum 'Rose Queen'
↕ 1m (3ft) ↔ 60cm (2ft), summer flowering herbaceous perennial with almost woody stems

Macleaya

Plume Poppy

THESE MAJESTIC HERBACEOUS PERENNIALS are grown for their handsome foliage and graceful plumes of tiny, petalless flowers. The feathery flower plumes, in buff-white, cream, or soft apricot to coral pink, are carried on erect blue- or grey-green stems from early to midsummer, and appear to almost float above the foliage. The fine leaves, in grey-green to olive-green, are deeply lobed and may be up to 25cm (10in) across. Plume Poppies can grow quite tall, up to 2.5m (8ft), so are best planted at the back of a garden, where they have great presence; they can be invasive, however. Grow them in a spacious garden with other summer-flowering perennials; they can also be used to create superbly subtle effects with tall grasses.

Hardiness Fully frost-hardy ❄❄❄, but the new growth may be damaged by late frosts.

Cultivation Grow in any soil that is moist but well-drained, in full sun or partial shade. Provide shelter from hot, drying winds. **Divide** plants in spring or autumn. **Sow** seed (*see pp.391–393*) in containers in a cold frame in spring. **Take** root cuttings in winter (*see p.394*) or separate the rhizomes (*see p.395*).

Macleaya microcarpa
↕2.5m (7ft) ↔ 1m (3ft), grey-green leaves are 5- to 7-lobed, buff to coral-pink flowers in early and midsummer

Malva

Mallow

↕20cm–1.2m (8in–4ft)
↔ 23–60cm (9–24in)

MALLOWS ARE EASY AND REWARDING plants to grow and flourish on the poorest of soils. This colourful group of annuals, biennials, and woody-based perennials produce leafy spikes of pink, purple, blue, or white flowers throughout summer on upright plants. The flowers are bowl- or saucer-shaped and last for many weeks, making mallows useful plants for mixed, annual, and herbaceous gardens alike. Use them as gap-fillers among other summer-flowering plants such as campanulas (*see p.206*), phloxes (*see pp.306–307*), and lilies (*see pp.274–277*), or for a more informal look, with flowering grasses such as *Carex pendula* (*see p.345*).

Hardiness Fully frost-hardy ❄❄❄.

Cultivation Grow in any moist but well-drained soil in full sun. Provide some support especially if growing in very fertile soil. Perennial cultivars and species are often short-lived, but they self-seed freely. **Sow** seed of annuals where the plants are to grow, or in containers, in spring or early summer (*see pp.391–393*). **Take** cuttings of new young shoots from perennials in spring (*see p.394*).

Malva moschata (Musk Mallow) ↕90cm (36in) ↔ 60cm (24in), erect perennial with bright pink summer flowers

Matthiola

Stock, Gillyflower

FOR SWEET FRAGRANCE, few plants can better stocks. They include the dainty, annual, night-scented stock (*Matthiola longipetala* subsp. *bicornis*) and the chunkier gillyflowers (*M. incana*), widely sold as cut flowers. Both are essentials for a cottage-style garden. Gillyflowers, which include the popular Brompton Stocks, although perennial, are grown as biennials or annuals. There are tall and dwarf forms with single or double flowers in bright or pastel shades of purple violet, pink, and white. Dwarf varieties make good container plants. Night-scented stocks come in simila colours and can be grown in pots, but must be direct sown. Grow them in a sunny spot, near a door, seat, or window and enjoy their evening fragrance.

Hardiness Fully frost-hardy ❄❄❄ to frost-hardy ❄❄.

Cultivation Grow in any moist but well-drained soil in full sun; *incana* types tolerate partial shade. Tall forms may need some suppo **Sow** seed (*see pp.391–393*) from mid-summer to autumn; overwinte in a cold frame to plant out the following spring. Sow night-scented stocks in situ and thin to 10–15cm (4–6in) apart.

***Matthiola incana* Cinderella Series**
↕20–25cm (8–10in) ↔ to 25cm (10in), double flowers held in dense spikes 15cm (6in) tall, in late spring to summer ❄❄

/IECONOPSIS

:o 2.5m (8ft)
›to 1m (3ft)

THIS COSMOPOLITAN GROUP of plants includes both the cheerful yellow Welsh Poppy (*Meconopsis cambrica*) and the sapphire-blue Himalayan Poppy (*M. betonicifolia*); despite the must-have appeal of the latter, it must be said that the rmer is much easier to grow. However, if you have e ideal site – a cool, moist woodland garden, or a eltered garden that mimics these conditions, with il rich in humus or leafmould – you can grow any econopsis, in eye-catching shades of turquoise and ded denim, pomegranate-pink, and clear yellows. ıeir silky flowers, with yellow or cream stamens, pear from early to midsummer. The plants may short-lived, but all are worth it; some self-seed.

ırdiness Fully frost-hardy ✻✻✻, but frost may damage young growth.

ıltivation Grow in moist but well-drained, slightly acid (lime-free) ı, in partial shade, with shelter from hot winds. **Divide** established nts after flowering (*see p.395*). **Sow** seed (*see pp.391–393*) in ıtainers in a cold frame as soon as ripe, overwinter seedlings in the ıme, or in spring. Sow thinly, on the surface of the seed raising mix.

betonicifolia ♀ ↕1.2m (4ft) ② *cambrica* ↕45cm (18in), ›ws in all but very dry soils ③ *napaulensis* ↕2.5m (8ft), ›rgreen ④ × *sheldonii* ↕1.2–1.4m (4–5ft)

MELISSA OFFICINALIS

Lemon Balm, Bee Balm

↕to 1.2m (4ft)
↔to 45cm (18in)

THE LEAVES OF THIS HERB give off a clear, fresh lemon aroma when they are crushed or brushed in passing. Apart from their scent, these bushy, upright perennials are grown mainly for their attractive nettle-like foliage, which is hairy and light to bright green, or splashed with golden yellow in variegated forms. The young shoots are popular ingredients in pot-pourri and herb teas. In summer, the plants also produce spikes of small, tubular two-lipped, whitish flowers, which attract bees. Grow balms in a herbaceous or mixed garden or with other herbs in a herb garden. While they enjoy full sun, these plants are also useful for dry shade.

Hardiness Fully frost-hardy ✻✻✻.

Cultivation Grow in any poor soil in full sun, but provide protection from heavy winter rain. **Cut back** hard after flowering to encourage a fresh flush of foliage and to prevent self-seeding. Variegated forms are better trimmed back before flowering to encourage bright foliage (*see below*). **Divide** plants (*see p.395*) as growth starts in spring, or in autumn. **Sow** seed in containers in a cold frame in the spring (*see pp.391–393*) or transplant self-sown seedlings.

TRIMMING LEMON BALM Harvesting shoot tips for pot-pourris will also encourage a new flush of leaves and help to prevent self-seeding.

Melissa officinalis 'Aurea' (Golden Lemon Balm)
Hairy stems, off-white flowers in summer

MENTHA

Mint

MINTS ARE HERBACEOUS PERENNIALS, with many being deciduous and some staying evergreen. They are grown principally for their aromatic foliage, which is used in cooking or in drinks. Even if not used in the kitchen, the foliage can add a sweet scent to the garden. The leaves are oval to lance-shaped or even heart-shaped. Most have pronounced veins and are coarse to the touch, but some are covered in fine hairs that make them quite smooth. Foliage colour is mid- to dark green, with some variegated forms as well. Most species form dense mats of foliage along the ground The small mouth-like flowers are mauve and occur at the top of the stems in spring and summer.

Hardiness Fully frost-hardy ✻✻✻ to frost-hardy ✻✻.

Cultivation Grow in any well-drained soil that can be kept constantly moist. Many will grow in full sun or partial shade, with some species preferring the latter. Most are vigorous and can be weedy and may be best grown in containers of quality potting mix. **Trim out** damaged or poor stems as they are found (*see p.383*). **Propagate** by divisions in winter or spring (*see p.395*).

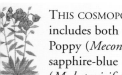

Mentha suaveolens 'Variegata' (Variegated Apple Mint)
↕30–60cm (1–2ft) ↔ 60cm (2ft), has apple-scented foliage and can be grown in containers in the shade

MIMULUS

Monkey Flower

THE NUMEROUS HYBRID MIMULUS are grown as annuals for their bright flowers that bring cheer to containers or gardens from early summer right through to autumn. These resemble snapdragons and are trumpet-shaped or tubular, in a variety of colours and usually heavily freckled with a contrasting hue. The pale to dark green leaves often have silvery hairs. Mimulus often have a creeping habit, but may be upright and bushy; some are perennial. Most prefer moist or even boggy soil; *Mimulus luteus* and *M. ringens* thrive in shallow water at pond edges.

Hardiness Fully frost-hardy ❄❄❄ to very frost-tender ❄.

Cultivation These plants need very moist soil in sun or semi-shade, although *M. cardinalis* will tolerate drier soil; the bedding hybrids require well-drained ground and sun. Mimulus is short-lived, so it is worth propagating regularly. **Sow** seed (*see pp.391–393*) of hardy species in containers in a cold frame in autumn or spring; sow tender annuals at 6–12°C (43–54°F) in spring to early summer. **Root** softwood cuttings in early summer (*see p.394*). **Divide** perennials (*see p.395*) in spring. **Slugs** and snails (*see p.398*) can cause damage.

① ***cardinalis*** ♀ ↕1m (3ft) ↔ 60cm (2ft) ❄❄❄
② ***luteus*** ↕30cm (1ft) ↔ 60cm (2ft) ❄❄❄

MIRABILIS JALAPA

Four O'Clock Flower, Marvel of Peru

These plants look like shrubs, having a much-branched habit and forming a mound of mid-green lance-shaped foliage. They are, in fact, perennials that arise from a tuber. They flower from mid-summer on for several months. The flowers are small tubes that have broad, flat, fused petals at the opening. These come in a range of colours, including yellow, orange, cerise, and red. Flowers are sometimes splotched and striped and all the above colour and pattern combinations can occur on the one plant for an unusual affect. Another unusual aspect is that the perfumed flowers tend to open only later in the day, thus the common name.

Hardiness Frost-tender ❄ to very frost-tender ❄.

Cultivation Grow in any soil that does not sit wet, in full sun or partial shade. **Sow** seed (*see p.391*), which germinates readily, in containers in spring. **Divide** clumps in winter (*see p.394*). In cold areas, the tubers can be treated like dahlias (*see pp.222–223*).

Mirabilis jalapa
↕60cm–1.2m (2–4ft) ↔ 60–90cm (2–3ft), summer flowers tend to open later in the day

MONARDA

Bergamot

↕90cm (3ft)
↔45cm (18in)

WITH SPIDERY FLOWERHEADS and lush foliage, bergamots enhance any garden. Most widely grown are the clump-forming, herbaceous perennials, but there are a few annuals. From midsummer to early autumn, they produce clusters of tubular flowers, in shades of crimson, pink, white, or violet, at the tips of the stems. The leaves are mid- to dark green, with prominent, dark veins, and are often flushed purple. Bergamots are highly aromatic; both the leaves and flowers are used in the fragrance industry. Use these splendid plants in any garden where they will attract bees and other pollinating insects to the garden.

Hardiness Fully frost-hardy ❄❄❄.

Cultivation Any moist but well-drained soil, that does not dry out in summer, is suitable – in full sun or dappled shade. **Sow** seed (*see pp.391–393*) in a container in a cold frame, in spring or autumn. **Divide** plants (*see p.395*) in winter or early spring before new growth begins. **Slugs** may attack in spring. Powdery mildew may become a problem in humid weather (*see p.398*).

① **'Cambridge Scarlet'** ♀ ↕90cm (36in) ↔ 45cm (18in), clump-forming perennial ② **'Croftway Pink'** ♀ ↕90cm (36in) ↔ 45cm (18in), clump-forming perennial

ᛁUSCARI

rape Hyacinth

HESE BULBOUS PLANTS, although rarely more than)cm (8in) in height, are very versatile. In spring, and ccasionally in autumn, they bear tight clusters of tiny owers that are usually blue, but sometimes yellow, hite, purple, or even black. Some species are very agrant. The flowerheads are held above clumps of eshy, mid-, blue- or grey-green leaves. Plant Grape Iyacinths in large groups in a garden, or in carpets eneath deciduous shrubs and trees. They are often own naturalized in grass with other colourful, ring-flowering bulbs such as daffodils (*Narcissus, e pp.288–289*) and tulips (*see pp.334–335*). Some ecies are invasive in favourable conditions; ensure ey do not encroach on other plants.

ardiness Fully frost-hardy ❄❄❄ to frost-hardy ❄❄.

ıltivation Plant the bulbs 10cm (4in) deep in autumn, in any ell-drained soil, in sun or dappled shade. **Lift and divide** (*see p.395*) ımps every five or six years, in summer, to maintain vigour and prove flowering. **Sow** seed in containers in a cold frame in autumn *ee pp.391–393*).

luscari macrocarpum
.0–15cm (4–6in) ↔ 8cm (3in), clumps spread much farther, ring flowers are strongly fragrant, prefers hot, dry summers ❄❄

***Muscari armenicanum* 'Blue Spike'**
↕20cm (8in) ↔ 5cm (2in), may form large clumps, mid-green leaves in autumn, flowers in spring ❄❄❄

MYOSOTIS

Forget-Me-Not

A LARGE GROUP OF ANNUALS, biennials, and short-lived perennials grown for their delightful flowers and hairy leaves. Most forget-me-nots have blooms in shades of blue, with white or golden eyes, but pink, yellow, or white varieties are available. The biennial *Myosotis sylvatica* and its cultivars, widely used in bedding schemes and containers, are also easy to grow in borders. The water forget-me-not (*M. scorpioides*) is happiest in mud or shallow water, and some of the small, mat-forming perennials, like the alpine forget-me-not (*M. alpestris*), prefer very sharply drained conditions. Nearly all self-seed freely, so can be left to create large drifts of colour in wildflower gardens.

Hardiness Fully frost-hardy ❄❄❄.

Cultivation Forget-me-nots thrive in any moist but well-drained, not too fertile, soil, in sun or semi-shade. **Sow** seed (*see pp.391–393*) of all mysotis in situ in spring. Seed of *M. scorpioides* should be sown in pondside mud. **Divide** plants (*see p.395*) when they are dormant. **Mildew** can create white patches on the foliage (*see p.398*) in damp conditions.

Myosotis scorpoides
↕30cm (1ft) ↔ 30cm (1ft), summer flowering perennial for very wet ground

NARCISSUS

Daffodil, Jonquil

DAFFODILS AND NARCISSI ARE THE HERALDS OF SPRING. The flowers, in cheerful yellows, creams, and white, occasionally tinged with pink or a hint of green, are a welcome sight after a long winter. The range of species and cultivars runs into thousands, varying enormously in height and flower shape, with flowers that may be borne singly or several per stem. All are bulbous perennials. The tall, showy varieties look splendid growing among shrubs in garden beds or used as spring colour along with clumps of polyanthus primulas. The smaller types are to be preferred for more naturalistic plantings and are often at their most effective in drifts in grass or in a woodland setting, where they will gradually spread if left undisturbed. Dwarf types are suitable for rock gardens and containers. Some, including many of the jonquil, tazetta, and poeticus narcissi, are fragrant. Grow these where you can catch their delicious scent, such as in a trough by the door, or in a windowbox. Most daffodils also make excellent cut flowers.

Hardiness Fully frost-hardy *** to frost-tender *.

Cultivation Daffodils and narcissi tolerate a wide range of soil types, but most grow best in fertile, well-drained soil that is moist during the growing season. Position them in full sun or partial shade. **Plant** the bulbs to twice their own depth in autumn, slightly deeper in light, sandy soils and when naturalizing them in grass. **Water** late-flowering daffodils during dry spring weather to encourage good blooms. **Deadhead** faded flowerheads before the seedheads form, but leave the foliage to die down naturally. This helps the bulb to build up food reserves for the following year, needed for the formation of flower buds. **Feed** foliage until it dies down with a high-potash fertilizer to encourage subsequent flowering. If daffodils are being grown in grass, delay mowing until the foliage has died down. **Lift and divide** bulbs (*see p.395*) if flowering deteriorates, usually where bulbs become congested after four or five years. The tiny young bulbs can be grown on into new plants, which need three to four years to begin flowering. Poor flowering, or "blindness", may also be due to bulbs not having been planted deeply enough and replanting may be necessary.Flowers and foliage are sometimes attacked by snails and slugs.

Using Daffodils in the garden and the home

❶ *One of the most common ways daffodils are used is in informal drifts in grass under deciduous trees. Plant them randomly and remember to let the foliage die down completely after flowering to promote flowering the following year.*

❷ *Daffodils can be planted with other early spring flowering bulbs and perennials such as here. Plant some summer flowering annuals such as petunias to give colour once the early flowering plants have finished.*

❸ *Most narcissi will do well in containers. The pots can be brought indoors or placed in a high profile spot such as the front door or back porch while flowering. Shift the pots to a less obvious part of the garden after flowering.*

1

2

7

8

12

13

18

19

① ***Narcissus* 'Actaea'** 🏆 ↕45cm (18in), late spring, scented ② **'Baby Moon'** ↕25–30cm (10–12in), late spring ③ ***bulbocodium*** 🏆 ↕10–15cm (4–6in), mid-spring, can be naturalized in grass, suitable for growing in a rock garden ④ **'Cassata'** ↕40cm (16in), mid-spring ⑤ **'Cheerfulness'** 🏆 ↕40cm (16in), early spring, scented ⑥ **'Dove Wings'** 🏆 ↕30cm (12in), early spring ⑦ **'February Gold'** 🏆 ↕30cm (12in), early spring, can be naturalized in grass ⑧ **'Fortune'** ↕45cm (18in), mid-spring

'**Golden Ducat**' ↕35cm (14in), mid-spring ⑩ '**Grand Soleil d'Or**' ↕45cm (18in), mid-spring, ...nted, suitable for forcing ❄❄ ⑪ '**Hawera**' ♀ ↕18cm (7in), late spring ❄❄ ⑫ '**Ice Follies**' ♀ ...0cm (16in), mid-spring, prolific ⑬ '**Jack Snipe**' ♀ ↕20cm (8in), early and mid-spring, increases ...pidly ⑭ '**Jenny**' ♀ ↕30cm (12in), early and mid-spring, can be naturalized in grass ⑮ '**Liberty** ...**ells**' ↕30cm (12in), mid-spring ⑯ '**Little Beauty**' ♀ ↕15cm (6in), dwarf, early spring ⑰ '**Mount Hood**' ♀ ↕45cm (18in), early spring ⑱ '**Pencrebar**' ↕18cm (7in), mid-spring, scented ⑲ ***romieuxii*** ♀ ↕8–10cm (3–4in), early spring ❄❄ ⑳ '**Salome**' ♀ ↕45cm (18in), mid-spring, produces consistently good-quality flowers ㉑ '**Sweetness**' ♀ ↕40cm (16in), mid-spring, vigorous, scented, long-lasting as a cut flower ㉒ '**Thalia**' ↕35cm (14in), mid-spring, scented ㉓ ***triandrus*** ♀ ↕10–25cm (4–10in), mid-spring

NELUMBO

Sacred Lotus

WATER PLANTS OF EXTREME BEAUTY, the lotus is probably best grown in tropical areas, where it occurs naturally. In cooler southern areas the semi-double form (*Nelumbo nucifera* 'Semi-plena') can be successfully grown. The deciduous leaves are large, flat and round, and have a waxy coating that allows them to shed water. They generally stand above the water rather than resting on it, as do those of water lilies (*Nymphaea, see p.292*). The summer flowers can be up to 30cm (1ft) across and are also held above the water on a narrow, but strong stem. They are dark pink, fading to light pink, and the centre features a yellow seedpod that resembles a salt-shaker.

Hardiness Very frost-tender ❄.

Cultivation In warmer climates they can be grown in deep water; in colder areas try them at about 15cm (6in) deep, as this will warm up better. Plant in winter (or late spring in colder areas) so only the tip is showing and hold in place with a brick or rock, without covering the growing tip. Full sun is essential. **Sow** the nut-like seed (*see p.391*) in summer at 25–30°C (77–86 °F) in containers kept wet, after first filing the outer coating to allow water to penetrate. Named varieties should be propagated from divisions taken in early- to mid-spring.

Nelumbo nucifera
↕90cm (3 ft) above the water ↔ 1.2m (4ft), all parts are edible and the roots are prized for certain Chinese dishes

NEMESIA

ANNUAL NEMESIAS ARE POPULARLY used as riotous summer annuals or container plants. They are easy to grow and produce abundant, brightly coloured flowers in an assortment of blues, reds, pinks, yellows, oranges, and whites. Many are bicoloured, too. The perennials are taller and less brash in appearance, flowering mainly in mauve and white; they may not survive cold winters unless grown in pots and brought under cover. Some of the newer named perennials are more reliably hardy, and will withstand being left in a sheltered position outside over winter, especially if given a protective mulch.

Hardiness Frost-hardy ❄❄ to frost-tender ❄.

Cultivation Grow in any moist but well-drained soil in full sun. Nemesias may suffer from root rot in wet soils. **Pinch out** the growing tips of annuals to promote a bushy habit and plenty of flowers. Ensure plants in pots are watered regularly. **Sow** seed at 15°C (59°F) from early to late spring, or in autumn (*see pp.391–393*). **Take** softwood cuttings from perennials in late summer (*see p.394*) and overwinter young plants in frost-free conditions.

***Nemesia strumosa* Carnival Series** ↕17–23cm (7–9in), dwarf annual with large blooms ❄

NEPETA

Catmint

THE CATMINT BEST KNOWN for its strongly aromatic leaves is catnip (*Nepeta cataria*) which cats find hypnotic, but there are other varieties widely grown in gardens that are less appealing to cats. They are perennials with soft, silvery grey foliage and small, erect flower spikes in white and shades of blue, purple, and sometimes yellow. Most have a loose, spreading habit and act as good ground-cover plants since the dense growth suppresses weeds. They can be used to line a broad, sunny path where their scent can be enjoyed whilst walking; some tiny species also suit a rock garden. Taller catmints are best sited in a mixed garden bed.

Hardiness Fully frost-hardy ❄❄❄ to frost-tender ❄.

Cultivation Grow in any well-drained soil in full sun or partial shade. The more loosely growing, taller Nepetas may benefit from staking (*see p.390*). **Trim** the plants after flowering to maintain a compact habit and encourage more flowers. **Divide** plants in autumn or winter (*see p.395*). **Sow** seed in a container in a cold frame in autumn (*see pp.391–392*).

① ***govaniana*** ↕90cm (36in) ↔ 60cm (24in) ② ***sibirica*** ↕90cm (36in) ↔ 45cm (18in) ③ **'Six Hills Giant'** ↕90cm (36in) ↔ 60cm (24in) ④ ***subsessilis*** ↕ to 90cm (36in) ↔ 30cm (12in)

ERINE

HESE BULBOUS PERENNIALS have the most unlikely owers for autumn – delicate, trumpet-shaped clusters bright pink, or occasionally white, crimson or range-red. They cannot help but lend an vigorating, airy feel to the garden at a time when ost other plants are fading. Nerines enjoy well-rained, dry conditions, and usually flourish under a orth- or west-facing wall or in a sheltered garden. In ost, only once the flowers open or even die down, the strappy, mid-green leaves start to emerge, aking the bare-stemmed flowers stand out even ore dramatically; they are stunning seen in isolated oups against dark soil, pale stone, or painted asonry. Alternatively, plant them with other late-owering bulbs, such as schizostylis (*see p.323*) and illa scilloides (*see p.323*).

ardiness Fully frost-hardy ✱✱✱ to frost-tender ✱.

ltivation Plant in well-drained soil in full sun in early spring. to site them carefully, because they are best left undisturbed to m a large clump. May need protection against slugs (*see p.398*).

erine bowdenii ♀
5cm (18in) ↔ 8cm (3in), robust plant, broad leaves to 30cm 2in) long, faintly scented flowers ✱✱✱

NICOTIANA

Tobacco Plant

THE PERFUMED, TRUMPET-SHAPED FLOWERS are the main reason for growing this group of annuals, biennials, and perennials. The flowers, in shades of lime-green, red, pink, apple-green and white, last for many weeks over summer and autumn. They usually open fully only in the evening, when they release their heady scent, but some newer cultivars will open during the day if sited in part-shade. Most Tobacco Plants have sticky, mid-green leaves. Although some are herbaceous perennials, most are usually grown as annuals and are raised from seed every year. Plant in groups for the best effect and site them on a patio or near the house so that their rich evening fragrance can waft across and into doorways. Contact with the foliage can irritate the skin.

Hardiness Frost-hardy ✱✱ to frost-tender ✱.

Cultivation Grow in any moist but well-drained soil in full sun or partial shade. **Stake** tall plants in exposed positions. **Sow** seed at 18°C (64°F) in spring on the surface of the compost (*see pp.391–392*); they need light to germinate.

Nicotiana sylvestris ♀ ↕ to 1.5m (5ft) ↔ to 60cm (24in), perennial in mild areas, strongly perfumed ✱

NIGELLA

Love-in-a-Mist

NIGELLA HAS BEEN GROWN IN GARDENS for centuries, and today is available in several colours – white, mauve, rose-pink, and deep pink – as well as the original blue. Some seed mixtures, such as the popular Persian Jewels, produce flowers in several harmonizing shades. These bushy annuals flourish on rocky slopes and wastelands, and will grow almost anywhere. Their dainty summer flowers sit within a hazy ruff of feathery foliage (the "mist" of the common name), and are followed by inflated seed pods, equally good for cutting. Sky-blue 'Miss Jekyll' with yellow and orange eschscholzias (*see p.241*) makes a fine and fast-growing, summery contrast. Both of these easy plants fill your garden with colour at very little cost since they self-seed freely.

Hardiness Fully frost-hardy ✱✱✱.

Cultivation Grow in any well-drained soil in full sun. **Sow** seed where it is to grow (*see pp.391–393*) in shallow drills about 15cm (6in) apart and thin seedlings to about the same distance. Seed can be sown in spring or autumn, but autumn-sown seedlings benefit from protection, for example with a cloche, over winter.

Nigella damascena 'Miss Jekyll'
↕ to 50cm (20in) ↔ to 23cm (9in), self-seeded offspring may flower in different shades, good for cutting

Nymphaea

Water Lily

With their jewel-like, often fragrant, blooms, water lilies bring an exotic touch to garden ponds and pools. These herbaceous, submerged, aquatic plants grow from tubers or rhizomes (underground stems) that run at or just below the soil surface. There are hardy and non-hardy water lilies, all of which flower in summer. Hardy varieties have mostly white, yellow, or crimson flowers that float on the surface and open during the day (unless overcast). Non-hardy tropical water lilies bloom either in the day or at night and the flowers, which include shades of blue, are held above the water. Water lilies look stunning in large ponds, and there are dwarf varieties to suit small pools, even pools in containers such as half-barrels. Their handsome leaves cover the water and provide shade for fish and also have the effect of reducing algal growth in the water by cutting out sunlight. Hardy water lilies survive even when water is frozen: the old foliage dies and new leaves grow in spring. Tropical water lilies grow as perennials in frost-free areas, but are often treated as annuals in cool climates. Regular attention is needed to keep water lilies flowering freely.

Hardiness Fully frost-hardy ❄❄❄ to very frost-tender ❅.

Cultivation Grow in still water in full sun at the correct depth for the variety; water lilies will not thrive in moving or rippling water. **Plant** hardy types in early summer in ordinary garden topsoil in planting baskets lined in hessian. Insert the rhizomes just under the soil surface and top-dress with gravel to help keep soil in place. **Submerge** the basket so that it sits with 15–25cm (6–10in) of water above it. It can be placed on a stack of bricks if the pond is too deep. Once the plant is established, gradually lower the basket (removing bricks if necessary), allowing the leaves to grow to the surface between each move, until it sits at the right depth. Most water lilies grow at a depth of 30–45cm (12–18in), but a few prefer shallower or deeper planting (*see below*). In a natural pond lined with mud, you can plant directly into the mud. **Remove** fading flowers, if possible, to encourage further flowering. **Cut off** dead or dying foliage to prevent it rotting and giving off poisonous gases that can harm fish. **Divide** established plants after three or four years (*see below*).

How to divide and replant water lilies

Water lilies grow vigorously and will eventually become overcrowded and exhausted. A sure sign of this is when their leaves begin to stand out of the water instead of resting on the surface, and plants start to produce fewer flowers than normal. If this is the case, they need dividing. This is best done in spring when plants are starting into growth, preferably in late spring, when the warmer water and longer daylight hours ensure that the plants will re-establish quickly.

❶ *Lift a mature clump during spring, when the new leaves are beginning to show. Dip the plant in fresh water to remove any soil or algae from the roots.*

❷ *Using a sharp knife, cut the rhizome into several sections, with each having 2–3 buds. Trim off any coarse or damaged roots, and pot each section.*

❸ *Plant in a basket with the crown just below soil level. Top with a layer of gravel. Place the basket in shallow water until the plant is established.*

① ***Nymphaea alba*** ↔ 1.7m (5½ft), water depth 30–90cm (1–3ft) ❄❄❄ ② **'American Star'** ↔ 1.2–1.5m (4–5ft), water depth 45cm–1.2m (1½–4ft) ❄❄❄ ③ **'Attraction'** ↔ 1.2–1.5m (4–5ft), water depth 45cm–1.2m (1½–4ft) ❄❄❄ ④ **'Aurora'** ↔ 90cm–1.5m (3–5ft) ❄❄❄ ⑤ **'Escarboucle'** 🏆 ↔ 1.2–1.5m (4–5ft), flowers 15–18cm (6–7in) across, water depth 30–60cm (1–2ft) ❄❄❄ ⑥ **'Fabiola'** ↔ 1.5cm (5ft), water depth 15–30cm (6–12in) ❄❄❄ ⑦ **'Fire Crest'** ↔ 1.2m (4ft) ❄❄❄

'Froebelii' ↔ 90cm (36in), water depth 15–30cm (6–12in) ✳✳✳ ⑨ 'Gonnère' ♀ ↔ 90cm–1.2m
-4ft), water depth 20–45cm (8–18in) ✳✳✳ ⑩ 'James Brydon' ♀ ↔ 90cm–1.2m (3–4ft) ✳✳✳
'Laydekeri Fulgens' ↔ 1.2–1.5m (4–5ft) ✳✳✳ ⑫ 'Marliacea Albida' ↔ 90cm–1.2m (3–4ft) ✳✳✳
'Marliacea Carnea' ↔ 1.2–1.5m (4–5ft) ✳✳✳ ⑭ 'Marliacea Chromatella' ♀ ↔ 1.2–1.5m (4–5ft)
✳✳ ⑮ 'Norma Gedye' ↔ 1.2–1.5m (4–5ft), water depth 30–90cm (1–3ft) ✳✳✳ ⑯ 'Odorata

Sulphurea Grandiflora' ↔ 90cm–1.2m (3–4ft) ✳✳✳ ⑰ 'Pink Sensation' ↔ 1.2m (4ft)
✳✳✳ ⑱ 'Pygmaea Helvola' ♀ ↔ 25–40cm (10–16in), flowers 5–8cm (2–3in) across, water
depth 8–15cm (3–6in) ✳✳ ⑲ 'René Gérard' ↔ 1.5m (5ft) ✳✳✳ ⑳ 'Rose Arey' ↔ 1.2–1.5m
(4–5ft) ✳✳✳ ㉑ tetragona ↔ 25–40cm (10–16in), water depth 8–15cm (3–6in) ✳✳ ㉒
'Vésuve' ↔ 1.2m (4ft), flowers 18cm (7in) across ✳✳✳ ㉓ 'Virginalis' ↔ 90cm–1.2m (3–4ft)
✳✳✳

OENOTHERA

Evening Primrose

THE DELICATE, PAPERY FLOWERS of evening primrose grace the garden from spring until summer's end. Although individually short-lived, they are borne in such profusion that new flowers constantly unfurl to replace their predecessors. This varied group includes annuals, biennials, and perennials that produce yellow, white, or pink flowers. Some have the additional attraction of decorative, red or coral flower buds that form subtle colour contrasts with the open flowers. Heights range from low-growing species suitable for rock gardens or raised beds, such as *Oenothera macrocarpa*, to plants such as the tall, graceful wands of *O. biennis,* which attains a height of 1–1.5m (3–5ft) and spreads to 60cm (24in). Grow these larger plants in mixed gardens.

Hardiness Fully frost-hardy ❄❄❄ to frost-hardy ❄❄.

Cultivation Grow in well-drained soil in full sun – rock plants in a site not prone to excessive winter wet. **Divide** perennials (*see p.395*) in early spring, or take softwood cuttings (*see p.394*) from late spring to midsummer. **Sow** seed in pots in a cold frame (*see pp.391–392*), of perennials in early spring and of biennials in early summer.

Oenothera macrocarpa ♀
↕15cm (6in) ↔ 50cm (20in), vigorous perennial with hairy, branching, red-tinted stems, flowers in late spring ❄❄❄

OMPHALODES

Navelwort

SPRAYS OF BLUE OR WHITE FLOWERS that are similar to those of forget-me-nots (*Myosotis, see p.287*) are produced in spring and summer. The flowers are held on long, wiry, upright stems, which gives them the look of fairylights, particularly when they shine out in shade. This small group of annuals, biennials, and perennials, some evergreen or semi-evergreen, have a spreading habit that makes good ground cover. Some are suitable for shady borders where the plant choice is limited; companions could include hostas (*see pp.260–261*), carexes (*see p.345*), or *Arum italicum* 'Pictum' (*see p.190*).

Hardiness Fully frost-hardy ❄❄❄.

Cultivation Grow *O. cappadocica* and *O. verna* in moist, fertile soil in partial shade. **Sow** seed (*see pp.391–393*) in spring; annuals where they are to grow, and perennials in pots in a cold frame. **Divide** perennials (*see p.395*) in early spring. Prone to damage by slugs and snails (*see p.398*).

Oenothera speciosa **'Rosea'**
↕↔ 30cm (12in), spreading perennial, a long flowering season from early summer to autumn, can be invasive, dislikes winter wet ❄❄❄

Omphalodes cappadocica **'Cherry Ingram'** ♀
↕25cm (10in) ↔ 40cm (16in), evergreen perennial, flowers that are larger than those of the species, in early spring

)PHIOPOGON

ondo Grass

HE GRASSY LEAVES OF THESE PLANTS range in colour om an unusual shade of near-black to light green ith cream, yellow, or white margins. In summer, ey produce small clusters of bell-shaped, lilac, pink, · white flowers, followed by glossy, round, blue or ack seed pods. Their unusual hues associate well ith many other plants, including small grasses *ee pp.340–355*) such as carexes. Blue Fescue *'estuca*) makes a striking contrast to the dark Iigrescens'. Alternatively, use as a ground-cover ant or as a border to garden beds. All are ergreen perennials.

ardiness Fully frost-hardy ❄❄❄ to frost-tender ❄.

ıltivation Grow in moist, but well-drained soil that is slightly id (lime-free), in full sun or partial shade. **Divide** plants in spring *ee p.395*) as the new growth appears. **Sow** seed in containers a cold frame (*see pp.391–392*) as soon as it is ripe. Slugs and ails (*see p.398*) can damage young leaves.

phiopogon planiscapus **'Nigrescens'** 🏆
20cm (8in) ↔ 15cm (12in), purplish-white flowers borne in mmer, followed by round, dark blue-black fruits ❄❄❄

Ophiopogon **'Vittatus'**
↕60cm (24in) ↔ 30cm (12in), white, sometimes lilac-tinted flowers in late summer and oblong, violet-blue fruits ❄❄

ORIGANUM

Oregano, Marjoram

see also p.91

BEST KNOWN AS CULINARY HERBS, marjorams have eye-catching flowers, aromatic foliage, and varied habits that make them useful and ornamental garden plants. These perennials have tiny flowers that are usually pink, surrounded by bracts (modified leaves) which determine the dominant colour, in shades of purple, pink, or green. *Origanum laevigatum* 'Herrenhausen' has branched stems to 45cm (18in) tall, clothed with leaves that are flushed purple when young, and dense clusters of flowers with red-purple bracts. *O. marjorana, O. onites*, and *O. vulgare*, which has a gold-leaved form, are the well-known culinary herbs. Grow marjorams in a mixed or herbaceous border or herb garden, and smaller species in a rock garden, as edging, or in paving crevices.

Hardiness Fully frost-hardy ❄❄❄ to frost-hardy ❄❄.

Cultivation Grow in full sun in well-drained and, preferably, alkaline soil. **Cut back** flowered stems in autumn. **Divide** (*see p.395*) in winter or take cuttings (*see p.394*) in spring. **Sow** seed (*see pp.391–393*) in pots in autumn or at 10–13°C (50–55°F) in spring.

① ***laevigatum*** 🏆 ↕50–60cm (20–24in) ↔ 45cm (18in) woody-based perennial ❄❄❄ ② ***vulgare*** ↕↔ 30–90cm (12–36in), woody-based perennial ❄❄❄

Ornithogalum

Star-of-Bethlehem

Glistening, silvery white flowers that shine through the dusk of evening are the key charm of these bulbous perennials. The flowers are cup-, star-, or funnel-shaped, occasionally scented, and borne on stout stems in spring and summer. Each thick, long leaf curls attractively to a point and some have a silver stripe down the centre. *Ornithogalum nutans* and *O. umbellatum* can be invasive; they are best naturalized in short grass or at the base of shrubs.

Hardiness Fully frost-hardy ❄❄❄ to very frost-tender ❅.

Cultivation Plant frost-hardy and frost-tender bulbs in autumn, 10cm (4in) deep in reasonably fertile, well-drained soil in full sun; some tolerate partial shade. Tender bulbs are best planted in spring, for summer flowers, in cool climates. On heavy clay soils, plant bulbs on a layer of coarse grit to improve drainage. **Lift** and separate offsets (*see p.395*) when the bulbs are dormant in summer.

Ornithogalum nutans 🏆 ↕20–60cm (8–24in), flowers borne in spring ❄❄❄

Orthrosanthus

Morning Iris, Morning Flags

Clump-forming evergreen perennials, these have narrow, grass or iris-like leaves that are upright. Flowers appear above the foliage in spring along the top of a straight stem and its branches. Colours range from pale mauve through to purple and the flowers are six-petalled. These mostly Australian plants are relatively easy to grow and are ideal for rockeries and the front of gardens. They also do well in containers. *Orthrosanthus multiflorus* is a widely dispersed plant in nature and is the form most commonly grown in gardens, because of this adaptability.

Hardiness Frost-hardy ❄❄ to frost-tender ❄.

Cultivation Grow in a free-draining yet moisture retentive soil, in full sun or partial shade. Older plants can be rejuvenated by cutting foliage to almost ground level in late autumn or very early spring. **Sow** seed (*see p.391*) when ripe in containers. **Divide** clumps in early spring or late autumn (*see p.395*). Snails and slugs may attack young foliage (*see p.398*).

Orthrosanthus multiflorus
↕↔ 30–90cm (1–3ft), has showy flowers over a long period in spring and into summer

Osteospermum

Beguiling daisies with a satin sheen and soft evergreen foliage make these plants worthy of any garden. The petals are sometimes spoon-shaped and either white washed with a delicate shade of violet, pink, lilac, or blue, or saturated with a single hue, from cream or magenta to purple. The central boss of each bloom has a contrasting tint. Osteospermums can flower from late spring until autumn. They include annuals and subshrubs, but perennials are most commonly grown. Osteospermums can become a little straggly after a few years, but are easily increased from cuttings to replace old plants.

Hardiness Fully frost-hardy ❄❄❄ to frost-tender ❄.

Cultivation Grow these in light, moderately fertile, well-drained soil, in a warm, sheltered site in full sun. **Remove** fading flowers regularly. **Take** softwood cuttings in late spring and semi-ripe cuttings in late summer (*see p.394*). **Sow** seed at 18°C (64°F) in spring (*see pp.391–393*).

***Osteospermum* 'Buttermilk'** 🏆
↕↔ 60cm (24in), upright subshrub, toothed mid-green leaves have pale yellow edges, flowers are bronze-yellow beneath ❄❄

steospermum 'Orange Symphony'
0–45cm (12–18in) ↔ 45cm (18in), bright orange flowers for a
nny spot

Oxalis

Soursob

LOW CLUMPS OF PRETTY, CLOVER-LIKE LEAVES provide a fine setting for these plants' small flowers. These appear in spring and summer, and may be funnel-, cup-, or bowl-shaped and tinted in shades of pink, yellow, and reddish-purple. In dull weather, the flowers close up. Some oxalis are spreading weeds, and some of the ornamental types can also be invasive. Bulbous perennials, these plants may spring from tubers, rhizomes, or true bulbs. Many oxalis thrive in the free-draining soil of a rock garden or in a container.

Hardiness Fully frost-hardy ❄❄❄ to very frost-tender ❅.

Cultivation Woodland species need moist, humus-rich, fertile soil in sun or partial shade; hardy species need moderately fertile, humus-rich, well-drained soils in full sun. For plants in containers, use a quality potting mix with extra grit for good drainage. **Sow** seed at 13–18°C (55–64°F) in late winter or early spring (*see pp.391–393*). **Divide** plants (*see p.395*) in spring.

Oxalis hirta
↕↔ 20cm (8in), takes well to growing in containers

Pachysandra

GOOD GROUND-COVER PLANTS, these low, bushy perennials quickly spread to create an evergreen, or semi-evergreen, carpet of dark or grey-green foliage. These leaves are sometimes toothed and cluster at the tips of upright, fleshy stems. *Pachysandra terminalis* 'Variegata' has pleasing white leaf margins. In spring to early summer, pachysandras produce small spikes of greenish-white female, and white male, flowers. These are easy plants to grow and look very much at home in shady areas or at the feet of flowering shrubs, for example rhododendrons (*see pp.104–107*) and camellias (*see pp.32–33*). Pachysandras spread particularly freely where the soil is moist and the conditions are humid.

Hardiness Fully frost-hardy ❄❄❄.

Cultivation Any soil is suitable – except very dry soil – in full sun or partial shade. Soil enriched with plenty of organic matter is best. **Divide** established plants (*see p.395*) in spring or take softwood cuttings (*see p.394*) in early summer.

Pachysandra terminalis
↕ 20cm (8in) ↔ indefinite, evergreen, leaves to 10cm (4in) long, male flowers in early summer

PAEONIA

Peony

see also p.92

↕↔ 34–110cm (14–40in)

WITH THEIR SPECTACULAR BLOOMS and bold, lush foliage, the many herbaceous perennial Peonies remain a classic choice for any garden. The flowers open from large buds, usually in late spring or early summer, and vary from single cups, some with golden stamens, to blowsy doubles. They range in size from 5cm (2in) to an impressive 20cm (8in) or more. The large leaves of these clump-forming plants are usually dark green, and deeply divided. Think carefully before you plant peonies – they are long-lived plants, and suffer if moved once they are established.

Hardiness Fully frost-hardy ❄❄❄ to frost-hardy ❄❄.

Cultivation Grow in fertile, moist but well-drained soil, and dig in well-rotted organic matter before you plant. Choose a position in full sun or partial shade. **Support** stems of peonies with very large flowers. **Take** root cuttings (*see p.394*) in winter or divide the tuberous roots in autumn or early spring (*see p.395*).

RING STAKES provide support for the huge flowers: simply let young stems grow up through the gaps.

Paeonia lactiflora 'Sarah Bernhardt' 🏆
↕↔ 90–100cm (36–39in), vigorous, with mid-green leaves and erect stems, fragrant flowers are over 20cm (8in) across ❄❄❄

Paeonia lactiflora 'Bowl of Beauty'
↕ 1m (3ft) ↔ 60cm (2ft), very large single flowers in late spring

Paeonia lactiflora 'Festiva Maxima' 🏆
↕↔ 90–100cm (36–39in), abundant mid-green leaves, fragrant flowers on strong, erect stems are over 20cm (8in) across ❄❄❄

Paeonia lactiflora 'Shirley Temple'
↕ 1m (3ft) ↔ 60cm (2ft), soft pink double flowers in mid- to late spring

APAVER

ppy

HESE COTTAGE-GARDEN FAVOURITES are beloved by rdeners for their bright, papery, summer blooms. well as classic blood-red, poppies come in glowing anges, and more subtle pinks, yellows, and white; any are smudged black at the bases of their petals. ch flower is short-lived, but is followed by many ore, and later by striking, pepper-pot seedheads. e light to mid-green, often hairy or bristly, ferny ves are very distinctive, even as seedlings. The wers of annuals and biennials are generally more licate than the bold, brash blooms of the perennial iental Poppies, but they all have a place. Large ppies look good in any garden, while annuals thrive d self-seed freely, in gardens with loose soil.

rdiness Fully frost-hardy ❄❄❄ to frost-hardy ❄❄.

ltivation Grow in fertile, well-drained soil in full sun. **Sow** seed *e pp.391–393*) in spring: annuals and biennials in situ; perennials a cold frame. **Cut back** Oriental Poppies after flowering for a second sh later in summer. **Divide** perennials (*see p.395*) in spring, or raise m from root cuttings (*see p.394*) in autumn and winter. **Mildew** *e p.398*) may be troublesome in damp summers.

POPPY SEEDHEADS scatter their tiny seeds like pepperpots; they last well into winter and are excellent for drying.

Papaver orientale **'Cedric Morris'** 🏆
↕45–90cm (18–36in) ↔ 60–90cm (24–36in), clumping perennial, hairy, grey leaves, 16cm (6in) flowers late spring to midsummer ❄❄❄

Papaver rhoeas **'Mother of Pearl'**
↕90cm (36in) ↔ 30cm (12in), annual, downy leaves, summer flowers in soft shades such as dove-grey, pink, and lilac-blue ❄❄❄

paver orientale **'Beauty of Livermere'**
5–90cm (18–36in) ↔ 60–90cm (24–36in), clumping perennial, wers to 20cm (8in) across in late spring to midsummer ❄❄❄

Papaver rhoeas **Shirley Series**
↕90cm (36in) ↔ 30cm (12in), annual, downy leaves, single to double flowers in yellow, pink, orange, and red in summer ❄❄❄

Pelargonium

Pelargonium, Geranium

THESE POPULAR PLANTS ARE WIDELY, but incorrectly, called geraniums. They are related to the hardy geraniums (*see pp.250–251*), but are quite different in many ways, not least in being almost universally frost-tender. Pelargoniums have deservedly been garden favourites for many years. There is a huge range to choose from, with not only beautiful flowers, but attractive, multicoloured, and often fragrant leaves as well. Pelargoniums are generally used in garden beds, or in hanging baskets and other containers, producing dense clusters of bright flowers from summer until autumn. Flower forms vary from the double, heavily frilled 'Apple Blossom Rosebud' to the delicate 'Bird Dancer', and colours range from orange to pink, red or purple, in soft and restrained or bold and vivid shades. Most form upright, bushy plants with rounded or divided leaves, sometimes with darker zones, but there are also trailing forms (details of main types are given below).

Hardiness Almost all are frost-tender ❄ to very frost-tender ❄.

Cultivation Grow in fertile, well-drained soil, or in a quality potting mix. Position most plants in full sun; zonal pelargoniums will tolerate some shade. **Deadhead** regularly. **Feed** with a high-potash fertilizer through the summer to encourage plenty of flowers. In frost-prone areas, place container-grown plants under protection in winter. **Cut back** the top-growth by about one-third and, if necessary, repot the plants in late winter as growth begins. **Cuttings** can be taken in spring, summer, and autumn (*see p.394*), but these will need to be kept in a frost-free place over winter. **Sow** seed (*see pp.391–392*) in spring. Pelargoniums are generally trouble-free, but plants can suffer from grey mould (botrytis) and rust. Cut out all affected parts and treat with a fungicide if necessary.

Ivy-leaved Pelargoniums

***These trailing** perennials make a spectacular show in containers such as windowboxes and hanging baskets, or even as small climbers, if tied into suitable supports. They have clusters of single or double flowers in shades of red, pink, mauve, and purple or white. As their name suggests, they resemble ivy in both their habit and in the shape of their stiff, fleshy, evergreen leaves, 2.5–13cm (1–5in) long, which are lobed and occasionally pointed.*

Scented-leaved Pelargoniums

***Plant these** in containers where you can touch them easily so that the leaves release their scent, or along a path where you will brush against them. Each cultivar has its own delicious perfume, from sweet to spicy or citrus. These pelargoniums are grown mainly for their leaves, which are usually mid-green, occasionally variegated, 1.5–13cm (½–5in) long, and varying in shape. The flowers, in shades of mauve, pink, purple, and white, are usually not very large.*

Regal Pelargoniums

***Bushy and evergreen,** these bear dense clusters of single or double flowers to 4cm (1½in) across, in red, pink, purple, orange, white, or reddish-black, often with more than one shade. The rounded leaves are up to 9cm (3½in) long. Some plants become quite large and should be cut back in spring. Those described as unique types have larger leaves, sometimes divided and often scented; angel types have smaller leaves and flowers.*

Zonal Pelargoniums

***Zonal pelargoniums** are long-established favourites for growing in containers. They are bushy, evergreen perennials with short-jointed stems. The round leaves are marked with zones of dark bronze-green or maroon; those of fancy-leaved cultivars may be tricoloured, with white or green, bronze, silver, and gold. The flowers are single to fully double, in white and many shades of orange, purple, pink, and scarlet.*

① **'Amethyst'** ↕30cm (12in) ↔25cm (10in), ivy-leaved ② **'Ann Hoystead'** 🏆 ↕45cm (18in) ↔25cm (10in), regal ③ **'Apple Blossom Rosebud'** 🏆 ↕40cm (16in) ↔25cm (10in), zonal ④ **'Bi Dancer'** 🏆 ↕20cm (8in) ↔15cm (6in), zonal ⑤ **'Caligula'** ↕13cm (5in) ↔10cm (4in), zonal ⑥ **'Clorinda'** ↕50cm (20in) ↔25cm (10in), cedar-scented leaves ⑦ ***crispum* 'Variegatum'** 🏆 ↕35cm (18in) ↔15cm (6in), lemon-scented leaves ⑧ **'Crystal Palace Gem'** ↕45cm (18in) ↔30cm (12in),

3

4

5

8

9

13

14

17

18

nal ⑨ **'Dolly Varden'** ♀ ↕30cm (12in) ↔ 15cm (6in), zonal ⑩ **'Fair Ellen'** ↕40cm (16in) ↔ 20cm n), spicy-scented leaves ⑪ **'Flower of Spring'** ♀ ↕60cm (24in) ↔ 25cm (10in), zonal ⑫ **Fragrans roup** ↕25cm (10in) ↔ 20cm (8in), pine-scented leaves ⑬ **'Francis Parrett'** ♀ ↕13cm (5in) ↔ 10cm n), zonal ⑭ **'Freckles'** ↕↔ to 30cm (12in), zonal ⑮ **'Graveolens'** ↕60cm (24in) ↔ 40cm (16in), non-rose-scented leaves ⑯ **'Happy Thought'** ♀ ↕45cm (18in) ↔ 25cm (10in), zonal ⑰ **'Irene'** ↕45cm (18in) ↔ 30cm (12in), zonal ⑱**'Lachskönigin'** ↕30cm (12in) ↔ 20cm (8in), ivy-leaved

⑲ *Pelargonium* **'Lady Plymouth'** ♀ ↕40cm (16in) ↔ 20cm (8in), eucalyptus-scented leaves ⑳ **'Mabel Grey'** ♀ ↕35cm (14in) ↔ 15cm (6in), lemon-scented leaves ㉑ **'Mr Everaarts'** ↕20cm (8in) ↔ 13cm (5in), zonal ㉒ **'Mr Henry Cox'** ♀ ↕30cm (12in) ↔ 13cm (5in), zonal ㉓ **'Mrs Pollock'** ↕ 30cm (12in) ↔ 15cm (6in), zonal ㉔ **'Old Spice'** ↕30cm (12in) ↔ 15cm (6in), spicy-scented leaves ㉕ **'Rouletta'** ↕60cm (24in) ↔ 20cm (8in), ivy-leaved ㉖ **'Royal Oak'** ♀ ↕40cm (16in) ↔ 30cm (12in), spicy-scented leaves ㉗ **'Schöne Helena'** ↕40cm (16in) ↔ 25cm (10in), zonal ㉘ ***tomentosum*** ♀ ↕90cm (36in) ↔ 75cm (30in), peppermint-scented leaves

2

23

6

27

28

Penstemon

THESE FLAMBOYANT PLANTS bring colour to the garden from early summer, often lasting into winter. Upright spires produce a continuous succession of tubular flowers, similar to foxgloves (*see p.230*), in rich hues of purple, scarlet, pink, yellow, and white; many are bicoloured. This is a large group of mostly evergreen, bushy but neat perennials. They range from dwarf kinds around 15cm (6in) tall, that are suitable for rock gardens, to taller plants of 60cm (24in) or more; these may need staking (*see below and p.390*). The leaves may be narrow and up to 8cm (3in) long or oval, from 13cm (5in) long.

Hardiness Fully frost-hardy ❄❄❄ to frost-tender ❄.

Cultivation Penstemons like fertile, well-drained soil in full sun or partial shade; dwarf and shrubby species need gritty, sharply drained, poor to moderate soil. **Deadhead** unless seed is needed. **Sow** seed (*see pp.391–393*) in late winter or spring at 13–18°C (55–64°F). **Take** softwood cuttings in early summer or semi-ripe cuttings in midsummer (*see p.394*). **Divide** plants (*see p.395*) in winter.

Penstemon 'Chester Scarlet' ♈
↕60cm (24in) ↔ 45cm (18in), large leaves and flowers 5–8cm (2–3in) long from midsummer to mid-autumn ❄

Penstemon 'Evelyn' ♈
↕45–60cm (18–24in) ↔ 30cm (12in), bushy, narrow leaves, flowers 2.5–3cm (1–1¼in), paler inside, midsummer to mid-autumn ❄❄❄

SUPPORTING CLUMPS
Put cane and twine or metal supports in place before Penstemons grow too tall so that they can develop a natural habit.

Penstemon 'Stapleford Gem' ♈
↕to 60cm (24in) ↔ 45cm (18in), large leaves, flowers 5–8cm (2–3in) long from midsummer to early autumn ❄❄❄

Penstemon 'Pennington Gem' ♕
to 75cm (30in) ↔ 45cm (18in), narrow leaves, flowers 5–8cm
2–3in) long from midsummer to early or mid-autumn ❄❄

Penstemon 'White Bedder' ♕
↕60cm (24in) ↔ 45cm (18in), large leaves, flowers become tinged pink as they age, from midsummer to mid-autumn ❄❄

Persicaria

Short, bottlebrush blooms – made of tiny pink, white, or red, funnel- or bell-shaped flowers that cluster tightly on wiry stems – appear from summer to autumn. Persicarias also have pleasing foliage: with broad, long-stalked leaves at the base and smaller leaves clothing the fleshy stems. Many of these clump-forming perennials and annuals spread by means of creeping stems and can become invasive, but are easily kept under control if necessary. Ranging in height from 5cm (2in) to 1.2m (4ft), most are medium-sized and make an undemanding, weed-suppressing ground cover. Grow persicarias with phygelius (*see p.95*), and perennials like hardy geraniums (*see pp.250–251*) and monardas (*see p.286*).

Hardiness Fully frost-hardy ❄❄❄ to frost-hardy ❄❄.

Cultivation Any moist soil in full sun or partial shade suits this plant; the best flower colour is obtained in full sun. *Persicaria bistorta* tolerates drier soil. **Sow** seed (*see pp.391–393*) in a container in a cold frame in spring. **Divide** perennials in early spring or autumn or winter (*see p.395*).

Persicaria bistorta 'Superba' ♕ (Bistort)
↕to 90cm (36in) ↔ 45cm (18in), semi-evergreen, mat-forming perennial, autumn leaves rich brown, flowers over long period ❄❄❄

Petunia

STAPLE BEDDING DISPLAY AND CONTAINER PLANTS, petunias are prized for their showy, velvety flowers borne from late spring to late autumn. They may be single or double, and often brightly veined or striped with a contrasting colour; the choice of forms increases every year. Use them in annual displays or for filling gaps in garden beds. Container-grown plants will bring summer colour to outdoor eating areas. Trailing petunias are perfect for hanging baskets. Petunia leaves and stems are sticky and hairy. Many petunias are perennial, but most are grown as annuals.

Hardiness Frost-tender ❄.

Cultivation Petunias enjoy light, well-drained soil or potting mix in full sun. Feed plants in containers with a liquid fertilizer every 10–14 days. **Deadhead** regularly (*see p.390*) to keep them in bloom. **Sow** seed (*see pp.391–393*) at 13–18°C (55–64°F) in autumn or mid-spring, or root softwood cuttings (*see p.394*) in summer. Overwinter seedlings under cover; plant out when all danger of frost has passed.

Petunia 'Colour Parade'

↕30–45cm (12–18in) ↔ 30cm (1ft), vibrant mixed colours to bring life to the summer garden

Phlomis

see also p.94

THE HERBACEOUS PERENNIAL phlomis are good year-round plants. Although the silvery or grey-green, sage-like leaves die down in winter, the attractive seedheads remain to provide interest through the barest months. In spring, white-woolly young shoots emerge, to form an erect or spreading clump of foliage. Clusters of hooded flowers, somewhat like the Dead Nettle (*Lamium, see p.269*), are borne on tall stems in summer, and are usually white, dusty pink, or soft yellow. Phlomis is a very good choice of plant for hot, dry areas because their hairy leaves help them to retain moisture. They are also lovely planted in groups to form softly-coloured mounds in a warm, sunny garden. There are also shrubby types of phlomis.

Hardiness Fully frost-hardy ❄❄❄ to frost-hardy ❄❄.

Cultivation Grow in any fertile, well-drained soil in full sun, although *Phlomis russeliana* and *P.* 'Samia' will tolerate some shade. **Sow** seed (*see pp.391–393*) at 13–18°C (55–64°F) in spring. **Divide** (*see p.395*) large clumps, ideally in early spring, but also in autumn.

Phlomis russeliana ♀

↕90cm (36in) ↔ 75cm (30in), upright, hairy leaves up to 20cm (8in) long, flowers from late spring to early autumn ❄❄❄

Phlox

PHLOXES ARE TREASURED for their flat, blue, milky- to bright pink, or red flowers, which are borne in fat clusters at the tips of tall stems. They are a diverse group that include spreading to erect, evergreen and herbaceous perennials, and some annuals. Spring-flowering, dwarf varieties, such as *Phlox subulata*, are perfect in a rock garden. Tall, midsummer-flowering phloxes, such as perennial *P. maculata* or *P. paniculata* make a colourful addition to a sunny garden. Annual bedding phloxes (forms of *P. drummondii*) flower from late spring to autumn and can be used in containers or as borders.

Hardiness Fully frost-hardy ❄❄❄ to frost-tender ❄.

Cultivation Perennial border phloxes prefer well-drained soil in sun or partial shade; annuals and rock garden types need well-drained soil in full sun. **Deadhead** (*see p.390*) *P. maculata* and *P. paniculata* regularly. **Sow** seed (*see pp.391–393*) of annuals at 13–18°C (55–64°F) in spring and summer; that of perennials in containers in a cold frame when ripe, or in spring. **Divide** (*see p.395*) tall plants in autumn or winter, or take root cuttings (*see p.394*) in autumn or winter.

***Phlox paniculata* 'Brigadier'**

↕1.2m (4ft) ↔ 60cm (2ft), lightly fragrant flowers in late summer

hlox subulata 'G.F. Wilson'
0cm (4in ↔ 60cm (2ft), a dwarf summer flowerer for rockeries
d garden edges

THINNING SHOOTS
Pinch out one-third of the shoots at the base to reduce congestion and the chance of powdery mildew, and ensure strong, healthy growth.

hlox paniculata 'Alba'
.2m (4ft) ↔ 60cm (2ft), scented flowers in summer and autumn

Phlox paniculata 'Mia Ruys'
↕60cm (2ft) ↔ 60cm (2ft), flowers in mid- to late summer

Phuopsis stylosa

THIS IS A MAT-FORMING PERENNIAL with slender, branching stems bearing clusters of up to eight narrow, pointed leaves that have a musky fragrance. Over many months in summer, it produces a profusion of round heads of tiny, pink flowers at the tips of the stems. These are delicately scented. Phuopsis spreads by rooting stems and makes a good ground-cover plant at the front of a garden or on a sunny bank. You could also try it in a rock garden with other alpines such as phloxes (*see pp.306–307*) and saponarias (*see p.320*).

Hardiness Fully frost-hardy ❄❄❄.

Cultivation This plant needs reasonably fertile, moist but well-drained soil, in full sun or partial shade. **Cut back** the top-growth after flowering to maintain a compact habit. **Sow** seed (*see pp.391–393*) in a container in an open cold frame in autumn. **Divide** established plants (*see p.395*) or take stem-tip cuttings (*see p.394*) from spring until early summer.

Phuopsis stylosa
↕15cm (6in) ↔ 50cm (20in) or more, individual flowers are 1.5–2cm (½–¾in) long

Physalis

Ground Cherry

↕60–75cm (24–30in) ↔90cm (36in)

WITH THEIR STRIKING SEEDHEADS, this group of upright, bushy annuals and perennials bring welcome colour to the garden in autumn. Clusters of tiny, white or cream flowers appear in the summer, but it is the seedheads that give these plants their impact. Vivid orange or scarlet, papery lanterns, or calyces, enclose bright red, gold, or purple berries. These lanterns retain their colour well when dried for decorative use or they may be left on the plant through winter to decay into skeletons, revealing the berries inside. The leaves often have silvery hairs. The Cape Gooseberry (*Physalis peruviana)* is sometimes grown for its edible fruit.

Hardiness Fully frost-hardy ❄❄❄ to frost-hardy ❄❄.

Cultivation Any well-drained soil in full sun or partial shade will suit these plants. **Cut** stems for drying as the calyces begin to colour. **Sow** seed (*see pp.391–393*) of perennials in containers in a cold frame in spring; sow seed of annuals where they are to grow in mid-spring. **Divide** perennials (*see p.395*) in spring.

Physalis alkekengi 🏆 (Chinese Lantern, Japanese Lantern)
↕60–75cm (24–30in) ↔ 90cm (36in) or more, vigorous perennial, spreads by underground stems, lanterns are 5cm (2in) across ❄❄❄

Physostegia

Gallipoli Heath, Obedient Plant

VALUABLE IN THE LATE-SUMMER GARDEN, the upright herbaceous perennials in this group form dense clumps. Their flower spikes rise up in midsummer, crowded with almost stalkless blooms in shades of pink, lilac-pink, magenta-pink, or white. The flowers usually face in one of two directions; if they are moved on the stalks, the flowers remain in their new position, earning them the name of Obedient Plant. Like Dead Nettles (*Lamium, see p.269*), to which the are related, physostegias have square stems. The variably shaped leaves often have toothed edges. Physostegias spread by underground stems (rhizomes and can be invasive in rich soils, but are well-behaved in poor soils. Combine them with perennials such as phlomis (*see p.306*) and persicarias (*see p.305*). They are also good for cutting.

Hardiness Fully frost-hardy ❄❄❄ to frost-hardy ❄❄.

Cultivation Moderately fertile soil that is reliably moist, in full sun c partial shade, suits these plants. **Sow** seed (*see pp.391–393*) in a container in a cold frame in autumn. **Divide** plants (*see p.395*) in winter or early spring before growth starts.

***Physostegia virginiana* 'Vivid'** 🏆
↕30–60cm (12–24in) ↔ 30cm (12in), toothed leaves to 13cm (5in) long, flowers from midsummer to early autumn ❄❄❄

ᑊLATYCODON GRANDIFLORUS

alloon Flower

ARGE BUDS LIKE MINIATURE BALLOONS give this plant s common name. The several cultivated forms of ɩis perennial are grown for the pretty flowers borne ɩ late summer, in blue, lilac-purple, pale pink, or hite. The Balloon Flower varies in habit, but most ɹrm neat, compact clumps with toothed, blue-green aves. These are lovely plants for a large rock garden : a mixed garden bed, and are also good for cutting. ry them with other herbaceous perennials, such as :hilleas (*see p.167*), physostegias (*see left*), and thrums (*see p.283*). Once they are well-established, ɩe plants should not be moved because they do not cover well if their roots are disturbed.

ardiness Fully frost-hardy ❄❄❄.

ıltivation The Balloon Flower prefers deep, fertile, well-drained ıt reliably moist soil, in full sun or partial shade. **Support** the stems ıecessary in exposed positions (*see p.390*). **Sow** seed (*see ɩ.391–393*) in pots in a cold frame in spring. **Divide** plants (*see 395*) in summer. You can also try removing shoots that have rooted the base in early summer and using them as cuttings (*see p.394*).

latycodon grandiflorus ♕
ɔ 60cm (24in) ↔ 30cm (12in), compact clump, flowers to 5cm in) across

POLEMONIUM

Jacob's Ladder

NAMED FOR THEIR DISTINCTIVE LEAVES, these mostly clump-forming annuals and perennials are excellent for cottage gardens. The leaves are composed of many paired leaflets that resemble the rungs of a ladder, and are produced in rosettes, from which spring erect stems. The cup-, bell-, or saucer-shaped flowers are borne in spring and summer and are either solitary or held in small clusters at the stem tips. Usually blue or white, they can also be purple or pink. Taller species look good in a mixed garden, with other spring- or summer-flowering perennials such as aquilegias (*see p.185*) or tradescantias (*see p.331*) while small ones look best in a rock garden.

Hardiness Fully frost-hardy ❄❄❄.

Cultivation Taller species thrive in any well-drained but moist soil in full sun or partial shade. Small species prefer very gritty, sharply drained soil in full sun. **Deadhead** regularly to prolong flowering. **Sow** seed (*see pp.391–393*) in a container in a cold frame in autumn or spring. **Divide** plants (*see p.395*) in spring.

Polemonium caeruleum (Greek Valerian, Jacob's Ladder)
↕30–90cm (12–36in) ↔ 30cm (12in), leaves 40cm (16in) long, flowers, rarely white, on ends of branching stems in early summer

***Polemonium* 'Lambrook Mauve'** ♕
↕↔ 45cm (18in), also called 'Lambrook Manor', rounded mounds of neat leaves, free-flowering in late spring and early summer

POLIANTHES TUBEROSA

Tuberose

THE TUBEROSE IS A BEAUTIFUL-SMELLING, summer to autumn-flowering rhizome, once popular for wedding bouquets and buttonholes. A group of leaves forms a tuft, like grass, at ground level. Above this rises the flower spike up to 90cm (3ft) high. Individual flowers are white or cream and trumpet-shaped. Rhizomes that have flowered do not flower again, but the plants can be perpetuated, and annual flowering achieved, by continually growing on the side shoots that form. Grow these plants close to a window or door where the sweet fragrance can be enjoyed.

Hardiness Frost-tender ❄ to very frost-tender ❀.

Cultivation Grow in an acid (lime-free), well-drained soil that is enriched with well-rotted organic matter, in full sun. Plant out in spring after the danger of frosts has passed and keep moist. Liquid feeding from late spring on will help flowering and the formation of side shoots. They grow well in warmer areas and can be grown in containers in cooler places where they can be stored for their winter dormancy in a glasshouse or cold frame. **Divide** and plant out side shoots in spring.

Polianthes tuberosa

↕90cm (3 ft) ↔ 15cm (6in), is one of the sweetest-smelling bulbs you can grow

POLYGALA

ALTHOUGH THERE ARE some larger, frost-tender shrubs in this genus, there are tiny rock polygalas, with their rich flower colours. *Polygala chamaebuxus* flowers in a mix of purple and yellow. It is evergreen, with small, leathery leaves, and flowers in late spring and early summer. Grow them in a rock garden, or in containers.

Hardiness Fully frost-hardy ❄❄❄.

Cultivation Grow in moist but well-drained soil in full sun or dappled shade. In containers, use a free-draining potting mix, and top-dress with a layer of grit. **Sow** seed in containers in a cold frame in autumn (*see pp.391–392*). **Take** softwood cuttings in early summer or semi-ripe cuttings in mid- to late summer (*see p.394*).

Polygala chamaebuxus var. *grandiflora* ♡

↕5–15cm (2–6in) ↔ 30cm (12in), spreading evergreen, purple "wings" are plain yellow in the species ❄❄❄

POLYGONATUM

Solomon's Seal

ARCHING, LEAFY STEMS dripping with pendent flowers are the defining characteristic of most Solomon's Seal – vigorous, clump-forming perennials with creeping, fleshy roots that thrive in shade. With their drooping habit, even the tallest ones have a shy look that is perfect for a woodland garden. The bell-shaped flowers that hang from the stems in spring and early summer are creamy-white, with green markings. Plant Solomon's Seal amongst shrubs or beneath trees, or use them in pots on a shady patio to create a lush, textural display together with hostas (*see pp.260–261*) and ferns (*see pp.356–365*).

Hardiness Fully frost-hardy ❄❄❄ to frost-hardy ❄❄.

Cultivation Grow in moist soil enriched with well-rotted organic matter, in deep or partial shade. **Divide** large species (*see p.395*) as growth begins in spring, but take care not to damage brittle young shoots. **Sow** seed in containers in a cold frame in autumn (*see pp.391–393*).

DEEP PLANTING Deep, humus-rich soil suits these plants best; plant them with the top of the rootball a little below the surface

Polygonatum x *hybridum*

↕90cm (3ft) ↔ 60cm (2ft), plants go completely dormant in winter so mark the spot to avoid damaging them

'ORTULACA

ın Plant

HESE LOW, SPREADING PLANTS are grown as summer-
ıd autumn-flowering annuals. They have short,
ırrow leaves that are very fleshy, and plants could be
ınsidered to be succulents because of this. The
›wers are round and open, with conspicuous
ımens at the centre. They are very bright shades of
›t colours such as yellow, white, orange, pink, and
d. They can be single, semi-double and double.
ıese are probably the most heat- and drought-
lerant of all the annuals grown in gardens and as
ch are useful in dry spots such as embankments,
ntainers and under the eaves. They must have full
n if the flowers are to open fully.

ırdiness Frost-tender ✲.

ltivation Plant out seedlings after the danger of frosts has ssed. Grow in full sun, in free-draining soil. **Deadhead** frequently to end flowering duration. **Sow** seed in spring or early summer (*see .391*) in a cold frame in colder areas or straight into the ground in rm districts.

ırtulaca **'Sundial Mixed'**
0cm (8in) ↔ 15cm (6in, cheery summer annuals that will erate even quite dry conditions

POTENTILLA

Cinquefoil

see also p.99

CINQUEFOIL IS A REFERENCE to the five-petalled flowers. The heavily veined foliage of these herbaceous perennials is very reminiscent of the foliage of strawberry plants. These plants are valued both for their brightly coloured flowers and mid- to dark green foliage. Their saucer-shaped, single or double blooms are borne in summer and into early autumn. The smaller types suit a rock garden, while the taller, clump-forming potentillas are popular choices for garden beds and cottage gardens, where together with other late-flowering favourites such as asters (*see pp.392–393*) and chrysanthemums (*see pp.212–213*), they continue to warm up the fading garden into autumn with fiery shades of blood-red, burnt orange, and golden-yellow.

Hardiness Fully frost-hardy ✲✲✲.

Cultivation Grow in full sun and well-drained soil. **Divide** (*see p.395*) in autumn or spring. **Sow** seed in containers in a cold frame in autumn or spring (*see pp.391–392*).

Potentilla **'Gibson's Scarlet'** 🏆
↕45cm (18in) ↔ 60cm (24in), extremely popular, flowers to 3cm (1¼in) across from early to late summer

Potentilla megalantha 🏆
↕15–30cm (6–12in) ↔ 15cm (6in), widely available, hairy leaves, flowers from mid- to late summer

PRIMULA

Primrose

THERE IS A PRIMULA FOR ALMOST EVERY SITUATION in the garden, and the majority are long-flowering and easy to grow. This diverse group of herbaceous perennials grows naturally in a wide range of habitats from boggy marshes to woodland and alpine areas. Most bloom in early spring and early summer, although a few flower from winter onwards. Their delicate clusters of flowers come in an appealing range of colours from deep purple and maroon through to pink, scarlet, and several shades of yellow, cream, and white. Occasionally the flowers, stems, and foliage are covered with a white or yellow meal, or "farina". Garden primulas are divided into three groups: candelabra, auricula and polyanthus (*see below*), although these groups do not include all species. Polyanthus types are easiest to grow. Compact varieties make a bright display in containers, while more robust ones are suitable for the cottage garden. Many primulas enjoy the dappled shade of the woodland edge, and work well planted with other woodland plants, such as lilies (*see pp.274–275*) and trilliums (*see p.332*). Water-loving candelabras thrive in bog gardens or on the banks of streams and ponds. Grow tender species in a cool greenhouse or conservatory.

Hardiness Fully frost-hardy ❄❄❄ to very frost-tender ❀.

Cultivation Grow primulas in full sun or partial shade, for the most part in moisture-retentive soil. **Dig in** plenty of well-rotted organic matter (such as leafmould, manure, or garden compost) before planting. Mix coarse grit into the soil before planting alpine species, since these require excellent drainage. **Water** plants well in dry weather. **Deadhead** the flowers as they fade to prevent unwanted self-seeding, or allow seedheads to develop to collect your own seed. **Sow** seed as soon as it is ripe (*see pp.391–392*). Scatter those of hardy species on the surface in pots or trays and place in a cold frame. **Divide** hybrids and cultivars, which will not come true from seed, between autumn and spring (*see p.395*).

Candelabra Primulas

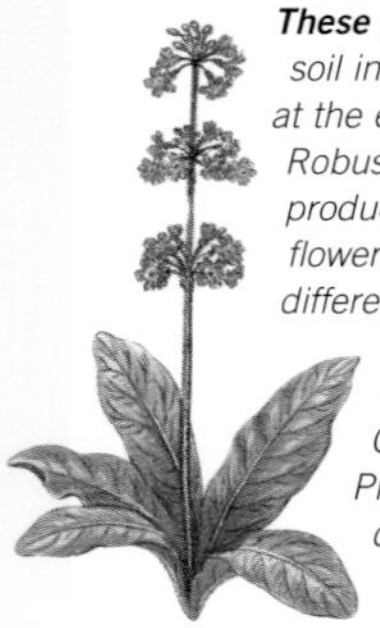

These grow best *in moist soil in a shady glade or at the edge of a pond. Robust perennials, they produce their rings of flowers, in many different colours, all the way up their sturdy stems. Candelabra Primulas are deciduous and die back in autumn. Once established, plants will freely scatter their seed, which germinates quite easily and eventually make a large and colourful colony. Unwanted seedlings are easy to control by weeding, or can be transplanted in spring to other parts of the garden.*

Auricula Primulas

The beautiful markings *and colourings of many auriculas are a result of several hundred years of selection by enthusiasts. Developed originally for showing, these evergreen primulas, with rather leathery leaves, have been highly bred. Show types need the protection of a glasshouse, as do many alpine auriculas, although these will also thrive in rock gardens. Those classed as border auriculas are the ones to choose for general garden cultivation. They particularly suit cottage-style plantings and can look good in troughs.*

Polyanthus group

This group includes *many of the most familiar primulas and the bright- and bold-flowered primulas and polyanthus that are used as biennials in winter and spring bedding. Although perennials, these are usually replaced annually.*

1

6

7

① ***bulleyana*** ♀ ↕↔ 60cm (2ft), candelabra ② ***denticulata* var. *alba*** ↕↔ 45cm (18in), drumstick ③ ***elatior*** ♀ ↕ 30cm (1ft) ↔ 25cm (10in), evergreen, suits woodland ④ ***florindae*** ♀ ↕ 1.2m (4ft) ↔ 90cm (3ft), fragrant cowslip, for bogs and streams ⑤ **'Guinevere'** ♀ ↕ 13cm (5in) ↔ 25cm (10in), polyanthus ⑥ ***malacoides*** ↕ 30cm (1ft) ↔ 20cm (8in), winter flowers ⑦ **x *polyantha*** ↕ 20cm (8in)

3

4

5

9

10

30cm (12in), winter flowers ⑧ ***veris*** 🏆 ↕↔ 25cm (10in), evergreen, fragrant cowslip ⑨ ***vialii*** 🏆
0cm (2ft) ↔ 30cm (1ft), moist shade ⑩ ***vulgaris*** ↕ 20cm (8in) ↔ 30cm (12in), fragrant winter to
ring flowers

Pulmonaria

Lungwort

↕15–45cm (6–18in)
↔45–90cm (18–36in)

OFTEN HANDSOMELY SPOTTED in silver or white, the deciduous or evergreen leaves were said in medieval times to resemble lung tissue and were used in remedies for chest complaints. Today, they make pulmonarias invaluable as ground cover that spreads slowly by underground stems (rhizomes). Pulmonaria flowers are a welcome sight in the late-winter garden, and the display continues until late spring or even early summer. The delicate blooms may be blue, pink, red, or white and are held above the foliage in small clusters; they attract bees into the garden. Show off the flowers beneath deciduous trees and shrubs or with bulbs for a jewelled carpet in spring.

Hardiness Fully frost-hardy ***.

Cultivation Grow in moist, but not wet, humus-rich soil in full or dappled shade; *Pulmonarias officinalis* tolerates some sun. **Cut back** after flowering to promote new foliage. **Divide** (*see p.395*) every 3–5 years to keep plants healthy. **Sow** seed (*see pp.391–393*) when ripe; seedlings will vary. **Powdery mildew** may spoil leaves in humid weather.

① **'Lewis Palmer'** ♀ ↕↔40cm (16in) ② ***saccharata*** ↕30cm (12in) ↔60cm (24in) ③ **'Sissinghurst White'** ♀ ↕40cm (16in) ↔40cm (16in)

Pulsatilla

AMONG THE MOST BEAUTIFUL of perennial alpine plants, pulsatillas have fine, ferny foliage, large, silky flowers, and round, fluffy seedheads. The leaves, buds, and petals are often covered with soft, silvery down. In spring and early summer, blooms appear in white or shades of yellow, pink, and purple – usually with a large, central boss of golden stamens. As the seedheads develop, the flower stems grow even taller. Pulsatillas form clumps in a rock garden or at the front of a garden, if you have well-drained soil, with other spring-flowering plants such as aubrietas (*see p.195*) or scillas (*see p.323*). In areas with heavy soil, it is best to grow pulsatillas in containers so they can enjoy free-draining soil and be moved easily to a position sheltered from the worst of the winter rain.

Hardiness Fully frost-hardy ***.

Cultivation Pulsatillas prefer fertile, very well-drained, gritty soil in full sun. They resent being disturbed; plant them out while they are young and site them carefully so they do not have to be moved. **Sow** seed (*see pp.391–393*) as soon as it is ripe in a cold frame. **Take** root cuttings (*see p.394*) in winter.

Pulsatilla halleri ♀
↕20cm (8in) ↔15cm (6in), violet-purple to lavender-blue flowers that are 9cm (3½in) across in late spring

Pulsatilla vulgaris ♀ (Pasque Flower)
↕10–20cm (4–8in) ↔20cm (8in), young leaves very hairy, pale to deep purple flowers 4–9cm (2½–4½in) across, rarely white, in spring

PUSCHKINIA SCILLOIDES

THIS LITTLE BULB HAS a snowdrop-like flower, with each delicate white, or very pale blue, petal marked with a thin, dark blue stripe. The blooms are borne in thick spikes on arching stems in spring. Each bulb has two leaves. *Puschkinia* var. *libanotica* has smaller, pure white flowers. Puschkinias spread freely in a rock garden, or can be used for a pretty display beneath deciduous trees and shrubs before the leaf cover becomes too dense. In common with other rock-garden or alpine plants, puschkinias can be successfully grown in containers; they enjoy the well-drained conditions, especially while they are dormant.

Hardiness Fully frost-hardy ✲✲✲.

Cultivation This plant likes any well-drained soil in full sun in cold districts or dappled shade. **Sow** seed (*see pp.391–393*) in a container in a cold frame in spring or autumn; seedlings may take 2–3 years to reach flowering size. **Divide** clumps of bulbs (*see p.395*) as leaves die down in summer.

Puschkinia scilloides
↕20cm (8in) ↔ 5cm (2in), although larger clumps will quickly form

RANUNCULUS

Buttercup

THERE ARE HUNDREDS OF TYPES of Buttercup – some are annuals and biennials – but herbaceous perennials are by far the most common; some are evergreen. They are very variable in habit, with widely ranging needs, so there should be one suited to any spot in the garden. Buttercups all bear cupped flowers, with bold central stamens, in spring, summer, or occasionally in autumn. They are mainly golden yellow, but white, pink, orange, or scarlet varieties are available. Most commonly grown is *Ranunculus asiaticus*, a tuber-forming perennial, usually referred to by its generic name. These spring-flowering bulbs are popular for both beds and containers.

Hardiness Fully frost-hardy ✲✲✲; *R. asiaticus* is frost-hardy ✲✲.

Cultivation Buttercups have a range of cultivation requirements. **Most species** are fine in fertile, moist but well-drained soil, in sun or semi-shade. Tuberous ranunculus need well-drained soils or potting mix in full sun. **Woodland** buttercups need rich, moist soil in shade. **Alpine** plants require full sun and sharply drained soil. **Aquatic** or bog plants need wet soil at the edge of a stream or pond. **Sow** seed (*see pp.392–393*) of most buttercups in a container in a cold frame as soon as it is ripe. **Divide** (*see p.395*) all but alpines, in spring or autumn.

***Ranunculus ficaria* 'Brazen Hussy'** (Lesser Celandine)
↕5cm (2in) ↔ 30cm (12in), woodland type, flowers are bronzed underneath and borne in early spring, may spread rapidly

REHMANNIA

THESE ARE RARELY GROWN herbaceous perennials that are worthy of much wider cultivation as they have very showy, foxglove-like flowers over several months in summer. These are pink with a yellow throat and, like foxgloves, are also slightly pendulous at the top of a 90cm (3ft) tall upright stem. The leaves are pointed oblong- to lance-shaped and are toothed along the margin. These and the stems are covered in fine hairs. The plants enjoy sunny or shady conditions, but the soil should be kept moist while they are actively growing. They spread by suckering.

Hardiness Frost-hardy ✲✲.

Cultivation Grow in any well-drained soil enriched with well-rotted organic matter. Partial shade may be necessary in hotter districts, along with shelter from hot, drying winds. In cooler areas grow in full sun or partial shade. **Prune** minimally except to remove spent flower stems if seed is not required (*see p.384*). **Sow** seed (*see p.391*) in autumn in a cold frame. **Take** root cuttings in winter (*see p.394*). **Dig** up and plant out suckers in winter or early spring.

Rehmannia elata
↕90cm (3 ft) ↔ 60cm (2ft), is in the same family as penstemon

Rhodohypoxis baurii

These small, corm-forming deciduous perennials have very narrow, hairy, upright leaves that are grass-like. The flowers are up to 2.5cm (1in) across and are starry, opening out flat and last for many weeks over summer. The species grown has white flowers, but occasionally colour variants of pink and crimson have been available and will still be found in collectors' gardens. These delicate little plants can be grown as an edge to a garden, provided they will not be swamped by more vigorous neighbours. They grow admirably in pots, where a potting mix for acid-loving plants is probably best.

Hardiness Frost-hardy ❄❄.

Cultivation Grow in full sun in any acid (lime-free), well-drained soil that is reasonably fertile. **Sow** seed (*see p.391*) in autumn in containers. **Divide** existing clumps in autumn (*see p.394*).

Rhodohypoxis baurii
↕7.5–10cm (3–4in) ↔ 7.5cm (3in), is a dainty South African bulb that grows well in containers

Rodgersia

↕90cm–2m (3–6ft)
↔ 75cm–2m
(30in–6ft)

A superb choice for moist soil, these vigorous, clump-forming perennials are valued for their fabulous foliage and tall flower spikes. The giant leaves are up to 90cm (36in) across, and are dark green and glossy. They are often boldly veined or wrinkled, especially when young, and occasionally tinged purple or bronze. Some varieties also display rich, reddish-brown autumn tints. The flower stems are often dark purple, and bear fluffy clusters of tiny, sometimes scented, blooms in summer, in shades of pink or white. Grow rodgersias by the edge of a pond or stream, or in a damp border.

Hardiness Fully frost-hardy ❄❄❄, although late frosts may damage young leaves.

Cultivation Reliably moist soil, enriched with well-rotted organic matter, in full sun or partial shade, with shelter from hot, drying winds is required. Drier soil is tolerated in shadier areas. **Mulch** (*see p.388*) with a thick layer of organic matter in spring to help retain soil moisture. **Sow** seed (*see pp.391–393*) in containers in a cold frame in spring. **Divide** (*see p.395*) plants in early spring.

Rodgersia pinnata 'Superba' 🏆
↕1.2m (4ft) ↔ 75cm (30in), new purple foliage (*as shown*) matures to dark green, stalks reddish-green, flowers in mid- and late summer

Romneya coulteri

Californian Tree Poppy

This is a large and, once established, vigorous perennial with grey stems over 1m (3ft) tall. In late spring and all summer, it is topped by showy, single, white flowers with crinkled crepe-paper-like petals and a prominent boss of central stamens. The flowers are up to 15cm (6in) across and look like those of poppies (*Papaver, see pp.299*). The leaves are grey and heavily toothed and lobed, and occur at ground level and occasionally on the stems. Although becoming shrub-like, these plants should be treated as perennial and cut down to almost ground level in autumn. The spread can be controlled by severing unwanted growth with a sharp spade in autumn, similar to the treatment suggested for bamboos.

Hardiness Frost-hardy ❄❄.

Cultivation Grow in full sun in any well-drained soil. This plant is very drought-tolerant and prefers areas with a hot dry climate and little or no summer rainfall. **Cut back** to almost ground level in autumn (*see p.384*). **Sow** seed (*see pp.391*) in autumn in containers. **Take** root cuttings in winter or softwood cuttings of basal shots in spring. **Divide** plants in autumn or winter (*see p.394*). All new material should be treated with caution as young plants hate root disturbance.

Romneya coulteri
↕1.2–1.5m (4–5ft) ↔ 30cm–1.8m (1–6ft), has spectacular flowers but can be invasive once established

ᴚOMULEA

'HESE ARE TINY BULBOUS PERENNIALS with very arrow, upright and slightly arching leaves, that rarely each more than 30cm (12in) in height. The flowers ppear in spring, usually one per stem and are about –7.5cm (2–3in) across. They have six petals which pen right out to look quite starry. Colours range rom pure white, through pink and red to lavender-nauve, some with a yellow throat. A few species are nvironmental weeds, so should not be grown in some reas. The others are probably best grown in ontainers. This not only reduces the risk of them preading, but allows their delicate beauty to be more ntimately enjoyed.

ardiness Frost-hardy ❄❄.

ultivation Grow in any well-drained soil in full sun. Potting mix hould be of premium quality. **Remove** seedheads before they mature reduce the risk of seed spread (*see p.390*). **Propagate** by growing on e offsets of the corms, lifting and dividing these in autumn or winter *ee p.394*).

omulea bulbocodium
10–15cm (4–6in) ↔ 7.5cm (3in), the tiny, early spring flowers are est enjoyed when grown in containers

RUDBECKIA

Coneflower

THIS LARGE GROUP OF ANNUALS, biennials, and perennials are grown for their large, brightly coloured daisies in late summer and autumn. They bloom in many yellow shades from burnt orange to vivid yellow and last for many weeks – seeming to glow in the golden autumn light. The prominent, conical centres may be black, brown, or green and give the plant its common name. Rudbeckias form leafy clumps with the flowers at the tips of sturdy, upright stems. Very easy to grow, rudbeckias provide a wonderful late burst of colour. Try them with sedums (*see p.324*) and Michaelmas Daisies (*Aster, see pp.192–193*). They are also good for cutting.

Hardiness Fully frost-hardy ❄❄❄ to half-hardy ❄.

Cultivation Reliably moist, heavy but well-drained, moderately fertile soil, in full sun or partial shade, is needed. **Sow** seed (*see pp.391–393*) of perennials in containers in a cold frame in early spring. Sow seed of annuals at 16–18ºC (61–64ºF) in spring to early summer and plant out young plants when all threat of frost has passed. **Divide** established plants (*p.395*) in winter, early spring or autumn. Staking may be necessary in windy areas.

Rudbeckia laciniata
↕ 1.5m (5ft) ↔ 1m (3ft), loosely clumping perennial, flowers 8–15cm (3–6in) across in midsummer to early autumn ❄❄❄

***Rudbeckia* 'Herbstsonne'**
↕ 2m (6ft) ↔ 90cm (36in), rhizomatous perennial, flowers 10–13cm (4–5in) across in midsummer to early autumn ❄❄❄

Rudbeckia maxima
↕ 1m (3ft) ↔ 45–60cm (18–24in), perennial, large, waxy, grey-green leaves, flowers from midsummer to autumn ❄❄❄

Salpiglossis

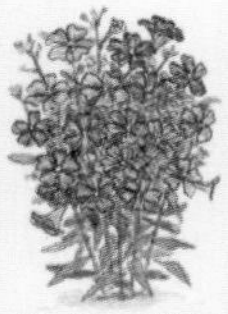

↕to 60cm (24in)
↔to 30cm (12in)

SELECTED FOR THEIR CHEERFUL, funnel-shaped flowers, this small group of annuals brings bold colour to summer beds and containers. The flowers, with heavily veined and strikingly marked petals, come in a variety of bright shades, from rich red to yellow, bronze, violet-blue, and purple. They are produced in the leaf joints of the slender, branching stems and last from summer through to autumn. Grow with other bright summer annuals, such as petunias (*see p.306*) or salvias (*see right*), or use them to fill gaps in garden beds. Salpiglossis are excellent plants for containers.

Hardiness Frost-tender ✲.

Cultivation Grow in reasonably fertile, moist, but well-drained soil in full sun. In containers, use a premium quality potting mix; water freely during summer and feed fortnightly with a balanced fertilizer. **Remove** fading flowers to prevent seeds forming and prolong the flowering period. Provide thin, twiggy sticks for support in open sites. **Sow** seed at 18–24°C (64–75°F) in early spring to early summer (*see pp.391–392*) outdoors where plants are to grow (*see p.393*).

Salpiglossis Casino Series
↕to 60cm (24in) ↔ to 30cm (12in), compact and branching, with flowers to 5cm (2in) across

Salvia

Sage

THE HARDY CULINARY SAGE (*Salvia officinalis*), grown for its pungent leaves, is attractive enough for gardens. The herbaceous perennials are mostly hardy, and will grace a garden with elegant flower spires in clear blues and reds. Salvias grown as annuals and biennials fall into two broad groups: the frost-tender, brightly coloured bedding plants typified by scarlet salvias, and hardy, more bushy plants in subtler colours, such as the clary sages, that look good in an informal or a herb garden. Hairy, woolly, or even white-mealy leaved salvias are more demanding, best grown in rock gardens or raised beds.

Hardiness Fully frost-hardy ✲✲✲ to very frost-tender ❀.

Cultivation Grow in reasonably fertile, well-drained soil, in sun or partial shade. Small species with hairy leaves need sharply drained soil in full sun and protection from winter wet. **Divide** perennials (*see p.395*) in winter. **Take** cuttings from new shoots in spring or early summer (*see p.394*). **Sow** seed of frost-tender annuals at 16–18°C (61–64°F) in spring. Sow hardy annuals in situ in spring.

Salvia argentea ♡
↕90cm (36in) ↔ 60cm (24in), rosette-forming biennial or perennial, woolly-leaved, grown for its foliage ✲✲✲ (borderline)

Salvia coccinea 'Lady in Red'
↕40cm (16in) ↔ to 30cm (12in), erect, bushy annual or short-lived perennial with flowers 2cm (¾in) long from summer to autumn ✲

Salvia patens 'Cambridge Blue' ♡
↕45–60cm (18–24in) ↔ 45cm (18in), erect perennial with blue flowers from midsummer to mid-autumn ✲✲

alvia discolor 🏆
5cm (18in) ↔ 30cm (12in), erect perennial bearing spires of very
rk indigo flowers in late summer and early autumn ✲

Salvia elegans (Pineapple Sage)
↕1.5m (5ft) ↔ 1.5m (5ft), pineapple-scented foliage and summer and autumn flowers ✲

alvia fulgens 🏆
50–100cm (20–39in) ↔ 40–90cm (16–36in), woody-based
rennial with downy leaves and flowers in summer ✲✲

***Salvia involucrata* 'Bethelli'**
↕1.2m (4ft) ↔ 1m (3ft), late summer and autumn flowers ✲

Salvia ulignosa (Bog Sage)
↕1.5m (5ft) ↔ indefinite, prefers moist soils, flowers summer and autumn ✲

Sandersonia aurantiaca

Chinese Lantern Lily

A TUBEROUS PERENNIAL, this has lily-like foliage, with many of the leaves ending in twining tendrils which help the plant to climb. The flowers are orange to golden yellow and appear in summer. They hang from the ends of thin stems, spaced evenly along an upright central stalk growing up from the tuber. The flowers look a little like paper lanterns, but are more like an upside-down goblet cup. The foliage dies down very quickly once the flowers have finished. They need ample moisture as they put on growth in spring and early summer, but need to largely dry out in winter, or at least be in a free-draining growing situation.

Hardiness Frost-tender ❄.

Cultivation Plant tubers in autumn with their prongs downwards and grow in full sun or light shade in any well-drained soil or free-draining potting mix. In heavy frost areas plant the tuber in a container and grow in a protected spot until frosts have passed. **Sow** seed (*see pp.391–392*) when fresh into containers. Seedlings will take two years to flower. **Take** divisions of the tubers in autumn (*see p.395*).

Sandersonia aurantiaca
↕60–90cm (2–3ft) ↔ 25–30cm (10–12in) is an uncommon bulb whose flowers make long lasting cut flowers

Sanguisorba

Burnet

FOR AN UNUSUAL SUMMER HIGHLIGHT in a moist border or corner of a garden, this small group of tall, clump-forming perennials is ideal. The wiry stems clothed with attractive leaves produce bottlebrush-like spires of small, fluffy flowers in red, pink, white, or greenish-white, with prominent stamens. The leaves are composed of toothed leaflets that are heavily veined and sometimes greyish. Burnets are suitable for mixed and herbaceous borders or particularly for naturalizing in a damp meadow or wildflower garden as they form spreading clumps. The flowers and foliage are good for cutting. Grow them with other perennials and with tall ornamental grasses (*see pp.340–355*).

Hardiness Fully frost-hardy ❄❄❄.

Cultivation Grow in any reasonably fertile soil that is moist but well-drained, in sun or partial shade. Taller species may need some support. In ideal conditions, plants may become invasive, but can be controlled by regular division (*see p.395*) in spring or autumn. **Sow** seed in a container in a cold frame in spring or autumn (*see pp.391–392*).

Sanguisorba officinalis
↕30–90cm (1–3ft) ↔ 30–60cm (1–2ft), herbaceous perennial with late summer flowers that prefers damp soil

Saponaria

Soapwort

The sap of soapwort was once used for laundering clothes as well as medicinally, for skin complaints. This group of sprawling and upright perennials is no grown for its profusion of tiny, pink to deep pink flowers in summer and autumn, as well as its ground covering ability. The plants thrive in sunny, dry sites. The low-growing, mat-forming species are excellent for the front of a garden, perhaps spilling over paving or in a rock garden. Grow taller ones with old-fashioned, pastel perennials such as pinks (*Dianthus, see pp.226–227*).

Hardiness Fully frost-hardy ❄❄❄.

Cultivation Grow border perennials in reasonably fertile soil that is well drained and neutral to alkaline (limy), in full sun. Compact species such as *S. caespitosa* require sharply drained soil in a rock garden or between paving. Cut *S. ocymoides* hard back after flowerin to maintain a compact habit. **Divide** border perennials (*see p.395*) in autumn or spring. **Sow** seed in containers in a cold frame in spring or autumn (*see pp.391–392*). **Take** softwood cuttings in early summer (*see p.394*). Saponarias may be damaged by slugs and snails; lay traps or pick them off by hand (*see p.398*).

Saponaria ocymoides ♡ (Tumbling Ted)
↕8cm (3in) ↔ 45cm (18in), mat-forming perennial, flowers in summer, can swamp small plants

ARRACENIA

cher Plant

HESE EVERGREEN HERBACEOUS PERENNIALS are nusual in that they are insectivorous. Originating ostly in boggy areas with poor nutrition they have lapted to take in extra nutrition from the insects at slip into the tubes, which are their modified aves. These are often hooded and feature various lours and patterns that are particularly attractive. he flower stems arise in spring and are taller than e pitchers and feature a five-petalled, nodding ower. These plants must be kept wet at all times and n be grown at the water's edge or even indoors in ass terrariums, which is an option for those wishing try them in frosty areas.

ardiness Frost-tender ❄ to very frost-tender ❀.

ultivation Grow in full sun, part shade or bright light if indoors d keep the root zone permanently wet. They can be grown in ggy ground or in containers of mossy potting mix, with the pots ting in trays of water. **Sow** seed (*see p.391*) in spring in containers at can be kept damp. Established clumps can be divided in spring ee *p.395*).

arracenia purpurea

20cm (8in) ↔ 60cm (24in), a carnivorous plant with an unusual odding flower

SAXIFRAGA

Saxifrage

A STAPLE OF THE ROCK GARDEN, saxifrages are mostly low-growing plants that make dense mounds or mats of foliage, carpeting the ground or cascading down walls. There are more than 400 species, including evergreen, semi-evergreen, or deciduous perennials, biennials, and a few annuals, many of which come from cool, mountain regions. Arising from the foliage are masses of delicate, star- or saucer-shaped flowers in shades from white to lemon, bright yellow to rose, and indigo. In some, the tiny rosettes of leaves are attractive in themselves. Apart from rock gardens, saxifrages are grown in containers.

Hardiness Fully frost-hardy ❄❄❄.

Cultivation Grow in moist, well-drained soil in deep or partial shade or sun. Grow in containers of quality potting mix with a little gritty sand added. **Sow** seed (*see pp.391–392*) in autumn in containers and put in a cold frame. **Divide** herbaceous types in spring (*see p.395*). Single rosettes can be detached and rooted as cuttings (*see p.394*) in late spring and early summer.

***Saxifraga* 'Jenkinsiae'** 🏆

↕5cm (2in) ↔ 20cm (8in), group 3

***Saxifraga* 'Aureopunctata'**

↕30cm (12in) ↔ indefinite, good for hanging baskets, group 3 or 4

***Saxifraga* 'Variegata'**

↕30cm (12in) ↔ indefinite, group 3 or 4

Scabiosa

Pincushion Flower, Scabious

As the common name suggests, the centres of these plants' flowers look like pincushions. Whether you choose to grow the annuals, biennials, or perennials, each bears masses of delicate, solitary, sometimes fragrant flowers in summer to autumn. Shades range from lilac, purple, or white to deep crimson. Most of the leaves cluster at the bases of the stems. All attract bees and other beneficial insects into the garden. The tall-stemmed species, such as *Scabiosa caucasica* which has a height and spread of 60cm (24in), are good for cutting. Scabious blend in well in informal or cottage-garden plantings, or in containers.

Hardiness Fully frost-hardy ✻✻✻ to frost-hardy ✻✻.

Cultivation Scabious prefer well-drained, moderately fertile soil that is neutral to slightly alkaline (limy), in full sun and with protection from excessive winter wet. **Sow** seed (*see pp.391–393*) of annuals at 6–12°C (43–54°F) in early spring or where they are to flower in mid-spring. **Sow** seed of perennials in containers in a cold frame as soon as it is ripe, or in spring. **Deadhead** regularly to encourage more flowers. **Divide** established plants (*see p.395*) or take stem-tip cuttings (*see p.394*) of perennials in spring.

Scabiosa Columbaria var. *ochroleuca*
↕50cm (20in), ↔40cm (16in), has lemon coloured flowers which is unusual for this genus ✻✻✻

Scabiosa 'Butterfly Blue'
↕↔40cm (16in), hairy, herbaceous perennial with branched stems, flowers to 4cm (1½in) across in mid- and late summer ✻✻✻

Scaevola

Unusual, fan-shaped flowers in shades of purple-blue, lilac, or blue are produced by scaevolas in large numbers between spring and autumn. The flowers a[re] borne singly or in clusters on slender stems, above spoon-shaped, mid-green leaves. Most are evergreen perennials. The perennial *Scaevola aemula* and its cultivars are commonly grown in gardens. Grow scaevolas in mixed gardens, in hanging baskets, or in large containers, where they make attractive specime[n] plants that can be moved under cover for winter in the coldest districts.

Hardiness Very frost-tender ❀, but survives to –3°C (27°F) on sharply drained soil.

Cultivation Scaevolas require a well-drained, reasonably fertile soi[l] in full sun or partial shade. Use a quality potting mix for plants grown in containers; water freely in summer; and feed with a balanced fertilizer at monthly intervals. **Sow** seed (*see pp.391–393*) at 19–24° (66–75°F) in spring, or take softwood cuttings (*see p.394*) in late spring or summer.

Scaevola aemula (Fairy Fan Flower)
↕↔ to 50cm (20in), erect or prostrate, hairy stems, purple-blue or blue flowers to 2.5cm (1in) across in summer

CHIZANTHUS

tterfly Flower, Poor Man's Orchid

KOTIC-LOOKING, ORCHID-LIKE FLOWERS that almost nother the entire plant and last for many weeks over mmer and autumn make this an excellent plant. here is a wide range of flower colours to choose from cluding yellows, purples, pinks, reds, and white. The owers also last well when cut. The spreading, bushy liage is attractively fern-like, with leaves made up of eply lobed leaflets. This group of mostly annuals d some biennials thrive with other summer bedding ants such as marigolds (*Calendula, see p.204*), or lvias (*see pp.318–319*), in mixed gardens or ntainers. In a pot it is a good, long-flowering plant r a porch or outdoor entertaining area.

rdiness Very frost-tender ❄.

ltivation Full sun and reasonably fertile soil is needed to grow nizanthus. For plants in containers, use a premium quality potting x; water them well in summer; and feed with a balanced fertilizer at ekly intervals. **Support** flowering stems with twiggy sticks if cessary. **Pinch back** the young shoots to encourage a bushy habit. w seed (*see pp.391–393*) at 16°C (61°F) in spring for summer wers; for spring flowers in containers indoors, sow in late summer d overwinter the seedlings in frost-free conditions.

hizanthus × *wisetonensis* 'Hit Parade'
↔ 23–30cm (9–12in), annual with white, pink, gold, purple, scarlet flowers to 8cm (3in) across from spring to autumn

SCHIZOSTYLIS COCCINEA

Kaffir Lily

TALL SPIKES OF DELICATE, SHIMMERING flowers in hot shades of red, pink, or scarlet make the Kaffir Lily a welcome addition to any garden. They resemble the gladiolus and are borne on stems up to 60cm (24in) in height, in late summer, autumn, or early winter, when there is little else in flower. A native of southern Africa, this vigorous, clump-forming perennial and its cultivars spread by means of underground stems (rhizomes). Try placing it in mixed gardens with other late-flowering plants – for example Michaelmas Daisies (*Aster, see pp.192–193*) or coneflowers (*Rudbeckia, see p.317*) – in containers, in waterside plantings, or by a sunny wall. The flowers are excellent for cutting.

Hardiness Frost-hardy to –10°C (14°F); flower spikes can be damaged by frost ❄❄.

Cutivation Grow in moist but well-drained, fertile soil in full sun. **Support** the flower stems if necessary with twiggy sticks in exposed gardens. **Protect** the plants with a mulch of organic matter in winter when the flowers are finished. **Divide** clumps (*see p.395*) in spring to maintain their vigour. **Sow** seed (*see pp.391–392*) at 13–16°C (55– 61°F) in spring.

Schizostylis coccinea 'Major' 🏆
↕60cm (24in) ↔ 30cm (12in), flowers 5–6cm (2–2½in) across are borne on stiff stems in late summer

SCILLA

Squill

↕8–120cm (3–48in)
↔ 5–10cm (2–4in)

THE DAINTY, DIMINUTIVE FLOWERS of scillas are extremely eye-catching, often with attractive, contrasting markings to the petals. They may be star- or bell-shaped, mostly in shades of blue but sometimes in purple or white, and are borne in loose or tight clusters amid strappy leaves in spring, summer, and autumn. Scillas are bulbous plants that will grow in a wide range of conditions and if left to their own devices, will self-seed freely. Naturalize the bulbs in grass, in rock or gravel gardens, or grow them in mixed gardens, beneath deciduous shrubs and trees where they will receive plenty of light before the woody plants put on leaves. Scillas are also suitable for coastal gardens.

Hardiness Fully frost-hardy ❄❄❄ to frost-hardy ❄❄.

Cultivation Plant bulbs 8–10cm (3–4in) deep in late summer or early autumn, in well-drained, humus-rich, fertile soil that is in full sun or partial shade. **Sow** seed (*see pp.391–392*) in pots and place in a cold frame. **Divide** and pot up offsets (*see p.395*) when the bulbs are dormant in summer.

① *bifolia* 🏆 ↕8–15cm (3–6in) ❄❄❄ ② *peruviana* 'Alba' ↕15–30cm (6–12in) ❄❄ ③ *scilloides* ↕15–20cm (6–8in) ❄❄❄ ④ *siberica* 'Spring Beauty' ↕20cm (8in) ❄❄❄

SEDUM

Stonecrop

SEDUMS BRING A RANGE OF TEXTURES and shapes to a garden; there are hundreds of annuals and perennials, many of which are succulent. There are low, creeping plants with tiny flowers that hug the ground, such as the common Stonecrop (*Sedum acre*). This thrives in a rock or gravel garden, or in the crevices of paving or stone walls. The tall herbaceous perennials usually form architectural clumps, with large, flat heads of pink or white flowers. These provide late-season colour in summer and autumn, attract butterflies, and their tawny seedheads persist through winter. Sedums are often vigorous and very easy to grow.

Hardiness Fully frost-hardy ❄❄❄ to very frost-tender ❅.

Cultivation Sedums like moderately fertile, neutral to alkaline (limy), well-drained soil in full sun, although vigorous plants tolerate light shade. **Trim** spreading species after flowering to keep them neat. Support Sedums with heavy flowerheads early on to stop the stems collapsing outwards. **Divide** (*see p.395 and right*) large herbaceous plants every 3–4 years in spring to improve flowering. **Sow** seed in containers in a cold frame in autumn (*see pp.391–393*). **Take** softwood cuttings of perennials (*see p.394*) in early summer. **Rots** may occur in wet conditions or heavy soils.

LIFT LARGE SEDUMS with care as the fleshy growth is very brittle. Pull a clump into pieces the size of a large hand; discard old, woody growth. Replant.

Sedum 'Ruby Glow' 🏆
↕25cm (10in) ↔ 45cm (18in), low, spreading, deciduous perennial, flowers from midsummer to early autumn ❄❄❄

Sedum spathulifolium 'Cape Blanco' 🏆
↕10cm (4in) ↔ 60cm (24in), mat-forming, evergreen perennial, powdery bloom on leaves, summer flowers, stands light shade ❄❄

Sedum spathulifolium 'Purpureum' 🏆
↕10cm (4in) ↔ 60cm (24in), vigorous, mat-forming, evergreen perennial, golden flowers in summer, tolerates light shade ❄❄❄

Sedum spectabile 'Brilliant' 🏆 (Ice Plant)
↕↔ 45cm (18in), clumping, deciduous perennial, flowerheads 15cm (6in) across in late summer, seedheads persist, needs support ❄❄

·EMPERVIVUM

ɔuseleek

HESE EVERGREEN SUCCULENTS are grown for their ·shy rosettes of leaves, which are often flushed red or ırple, and sometimes thickly covered in hairs. There ɛ numerous varieties with leaves of differing colours, ːes, and shapes. Although each plant is small, they read across the soil by rooting stems, or runners, at produce new plantlets to form large mats of ·nsely packed rosettes. In summer, starry, white, llow, red, or purple flowers cluster on sturdy, fleshy ·ms. After a rosette flowers, it dies, but the gap is ıickly filled by a new offset. Houseleeks need only allow soil, so thrive in rock or gravel gardens or ntainers, with other alpines such as Saxifrages (*see ·.320–321*) or Pinks (*Dianthus, see pp.226–227*). ıey are even used to clothe tops of walls or roofs.

ırdiness Fully frost-hardy ✻✻✻.

ıltivation Houseleeks grow in full sun, in poor, sharply drained l and add plenty of grit or gritty compost. Shield hairy Houseleeks m winter rain to avoid rots. **Sow** seed (*see pp.391–393*) in pots in old frame in spring. **Rooted offsets** can be detached in spring or ·ly summer, they establish more quickly if kept out of direct sun.

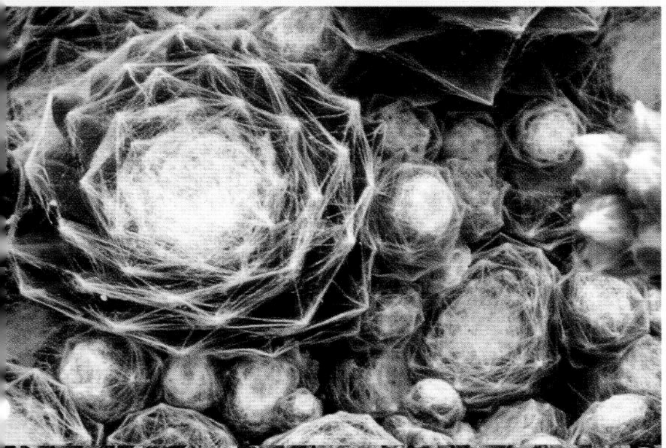

arachnoideum 🏆 (Cobweb Houseleek) ↕8cm (3in) 30cm (12in), pink flowers ② ***tectorum*** 🏆 (Common ouseleek) ↕15cm (6in) ↔ 50cm (20in), red-purple flowers

SENECIO

see also p.116

THERE ARE HUNDREDS OF SENECIOS, including annuals and biennials, succulents, shrubs, trees, and climbers. The shrubs are often grown in the garden for their foliage, but the clump-forming annuals and perennials are mostly valued for their daisies. They bloom from early summer until late autumn in shades of white, yellow, blue, crimson, and purple; usually with a golden yellow centre. Check the plant label or with the nursery about each plant's specific needs before you buy. Generally, annuals are used as summer display or in containers; small perennials and succulents in rock or gravel gardens, and larger varieties in borders or areas devoted to wild flowers. Some Senecios are quite tender, but can be grown in containers and moved under cover in winter.

Hardiness Fully frost-hardy ✻✻✻ to very frost-tender ❀.

Cultivation Senecios may need gritty or moist, poor or moderately fertile, well-drained soil, in full sun or partial shade. **Sow** seed (*see pp.391–393*) in spring at 19–24°C (66–75°F); seed of bog plants and alpines can be sown in a cold frame. **Take** softwood cuttings (*see p.394*) of perennials in early summer.

Senecio rowleyanus
↕↔ 1m (3ft), pendulous, narrow, wiry stems with round bead-like leaves make this plant ideal for hanging baskets

SIDALCEA

False Mallow, Prairie Mallow

FROM EARLY TO MIDSUMMER, these annuals and perennials produce tall spires of long-lasting flowers, rather like those of hollyhocks. The petals are thin and silky, sometimes fringed round the edges, and in clear shades of pink, purple-pink, or white. They are good value because they often produce a second flush of blooms in autumn if the fading flowers are cut back before seeds develop. Another bonus is that the dense clumps of attractive, lobed or serrated, round leaves cover the soil and suppress weeds. Use Sidalceas to add some height to a garden bed; they also are excellent for cutting.

Hardiness Fully frost-hardy ✻✻✻.

Cultivation A site in full sun, with moderately fertile, neutral to acid, moist but well-drained soil, enriched with well-rotted organic matter, is best. Sidalceas tolerate a range of soils, but do not like to be too wet, especially in winter. **Mulch** (*see p.388*) with straw or bracken where winters are cold. **Cut back** stems hard after the first flowering. **Sow** seed (*see pp.391–393*) in a container in a cold frame in spring or autumn. **Divide** (*see p.395*) in spring or autumn. **Remove** leaves affected by rust (orange-brown pustules); thin the foliage to improve air circulation and help prevent a recurrence.

***Sidalcea* 'Monarch'**
↕1.2m (4ft) ↔ 60cm (2ft), flowers throughout summer can be extended by removing spent flower stems

Silene

Campion, Catchfly

THERE ARE HUNDREDS of these annuals, biennials, and deciduous and evergreen perennials. They are grown for their pretty flowers which have delicately notched or split petals. In summer, erect stems bear blooms, singly or in clusters, in shades from dark pink to pure white. Most campions are easy to grow; many are prolific self-seeders. This makes them an excellent choice for a cottage garden. If they are regularly deadheaded, smaller perennials can be used in a rock or gravel garden; place taller varieties in beds and borders. Some catchflies have sticky hairs on their leaves that trap insects – hence the common name.

Hardiness Fully frost-hardy ✻✻✻ to frost-tender ✻.

Cultivation Grow these plants in moderately fertile, neutral to alkaline (limy), well-drained soil, in full sun or dappled shade. Smaller alpine species need gritty, sharply drained soil. **Sow** seed (*see pp.391–393*) of perennials in a cold frame in autumn. **Take** new shoots from the base in spring and treat as softwood cuttings (*see p.394*).

Silene schafta 🏆
↕25cm (10in) ↔ 30cm (12in), clumping, semi-evergreen perennial, flowers in late summer and autumn, good for rock gardens ✻✻✻

Sisyrinchium

PRETTY, STAR- OR CUP-SHAPED FLOWERS are produced by these annuals and perennials in profusion over many weeks in spring or summer. They bloom in rich blues and mauves, or subtle yellows and whites, singly at the tips of stems or in tall flower spikes. The long leaves, sometimes variegated with creamy white stripes, form grassy clumps or large, iris-like fans. The spiky foliage complements that of ornamental grasses (*see pp.340–355*) or provides a textural contrast to plants with feathery or broad leaves. Smaller varieties are best in a rock or gravel garden where they can be left to self-seed, for a pleasing natural effect, and will not be swamped by large, vigorous plants; the tall sisyrinchiums are able to hold their own in a garden.

Hardiness Fully frost-hardy ✻✻✻ to frost-tender ✻.

Cultivation Poor to moderately fertile, neutral to alkaline (limy), well-drained soil in full sun, is required, with protection from extreme winter wet which encourages root rot. Some small or frost-tender plants are best grown in pots and moved under cover in damp winters. **Sow** seed (*see pp.391–393*) in a container in a cold frame in spring or autumn. **Divide** clumps (*see p.395*) in early spring.

PLANT SISYRINCHIUMS with their crowns slightly above soil level. This allows water to drain away quickly in wet weather and reduce the risk of rot in the crowns.

***Sisyrinchium striatum* 'Aunt May'**
↕50cm (20in) ↔ 25cm (10in), clumping perennial, flowers 2.5cm (1in) across, borne in early and midsummer ✻✻✻

Sisyrinchium striatum
↕60cm (2ft) ↔ 30cm (1ft), tolerates light shade, summer flowers ✻✻✻

OLIDAGO

olden Rod, Aaron's Rod

HE WARM YELLOW FLOWERS of these vigorous, oody-based perennials glow in the golden light of te summer and autumn. They are borne in spikes clusters, densely packed with tiny blooms, on stiff, pright stems. The leaves are usually mid-green. ecies Golden Rods can be invasive, and although ey can be controlled by digging them out, they are st reserved for larger gardens. Happily, less unruly brids, with larger flowerheads, are available. They ld late colour to the garden, and to the house cause they are excellent for cutting. Use them with her autumn flowers such as rudbeckias (*see p.317*) d asters (*see pp.192–193*) among earlier-flowering ants for a prolonged seasonal display.

ardiness Fully frost-hardy ✲✲✲.

ltivation Golden Rods thrive in poor to moderately fertile, eferably sandy, well-drained soil, in full sun. **Deadhead** regularly to event self-seeding. **Divide** (*see p.395*) plants every three or four ars in autumn or spring to keep them healthy: discard the old, ody centres. **Powdery mildew** may be disfiguring in humid summers.

olidago canadensis
.2–1.5m (4–5ft) ↔ indefinite, tall herbaceous perennial with lden autumn flowers

x SOLIDASTER LUTEUS

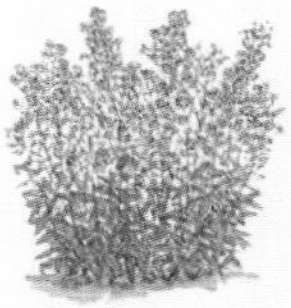

↕90cm (36in)
↔80cm (32in)

THIS HYBRID IS A CROSS between a solidago and an aster: as you might expect, it combines elements of both plants. Much like Golden Rod (*see left*), it bears a profusion of tiny blooms in dense clusters from midsummer through to autumn. The flowers themselves are daisy-like, and similar to those of an aster (*see pp.192–193*). They open a pale, creamy yellow with a darker centre, then fade as they age. The plant forms a clump with erect stems. Like both its parents, this perennial is a splendid choice for adding late-summer colour to a border, and makes an excellent cut flower.

Hardiness Fully frost-hardy ✲✲✲.

Cultivation Moderately fertile, well-drained soil, in full sun or dappled shade, suits this plant. Take care not to over-fertilize the soil, because this encourages foliage at the expense of flowers. **Divide** clumps in autumn or spring (*see p.395*) every three or four years to maintain vigour and discard the congested, woody centres. Take new shoots from the base in spring and treat as softwood cuttings (*see p.394*). **Powdery mildew** may be disfiguring in humid summers.

x *Solidaster luteus* 'Lemore' 🏆
↕↔80cm (32in), more spreading habit and a paler yellow than the species

SPREKELIA FORMOSISSIMA

Jacobean Lily

THIS DECIDUOUS BULB has narrow, strap-like leaves that are dark green, up to 30cm (1ft) long and occur from spring to autumn. The flower is quite remarkable and looks somewhat like an orchid. It is a deep red, with a velvety sheen to it, adding to its attractions. Flowering time varies a little depending on the climate. In northern Australia it may flower as early as late spring, while in southern parts it may not until midsummer. In any case, it can be widely grown and is best left undisturbed for many years once established. They are effective in garden beds, but also grow well in containers and rock gardens.

Hardiness Frost-hardy ✲✲.

Cultivation Plant the bulb in full sun or partial shade in late autumn to mid-winter, about 5–10cm (2–4in) deep in a well-drained soil that is enriched with well-rotted organic matter. **Plant** divisions in winter.

Sprekelia formosissima
↕30cm (1ft) ↔ 20cm (8in), is a late spring-flowering bulb that is not commonly grown yet is widely available

STACHYS

Betony, Hedge Nettle, Woundwort

CARPETS OF LARGE, FELTED OR VELVETY LEAVES are the main attraction of these plants. Held on square stems, the leaves are usually covered in fine hairs; in some species, they are aromatic. Stachys include many spreading perennials that make excellent ground-cover plants, for example *Stachys byzantina* of which 'Silver Carpet' is a non-flowering form ideal for edging. Their silvery foliage will complement many border plants: try penstemons (*see pp.304–305*), and shrub roses (*see pp.110–113*). The flower spikes, in white or shades of pink, purple, or gold, appear in summer and attract bees, butterflies, and other beneficial insects into the garden. Low-growing species, like *S. byzantina*, are good for dry banks or gravel gardens.

Hardiness Fully frost-hardy ❄❄❄ to frost-hardy ❄❄.

Cultivation Grow in well-drained, reasonably fertile soil in full sun. Smaller rock garden species need very sharply drained soil. **Sow** seed (*see pp.391–392*) in a container in a cold frame in autumn or spring. **Lift and divide** entire plants (*see p.395*) in spring, as growth starts, or cut off and replant rooted sections from the outside of large clumps.

Stachys byzantina (Lambs' Ears, Lambs' Tongues)
↕45cm (18in) ↔ 60cm (24in)

Stachys macrantha **'Superba'** ↕60cm (24in) ↔ 30cm (12in), ❄❄❄

STERNBERGIA LUTEA

Yellow Autumn Crocus

THIS IS A VERY SMALL, autumn-flowering bulb, sometimes referred to as the Yellow Autumn Crocus because of its similarity to that plant (*Colchicum, see p.395*). Indeed, it is similar in many ways except for flower colour. It has very fine, narrow leaves that emerge with, or just after, the flower in autumn. The flowers are egg-to cup-shaped, never opening fully. They are a bright canary yellow, and while there is only one flower per bulb, in an established planting flowering can last for many weeks. Overall the plant never reaches more than 15cm (6in) in height. They are fairly adaptable and can be grown in containers.

Hardiness Frost-hardy ❄❄.

Cultivation Plant bulbs in late summer while dormant, in full sun or light shade, in free-draining soil or quality potting mix. Winter moisture and summer dryness is ideal. **Divide** existing clumps in late summer before they start into their autumn growth (*see p.395*).

Sternbergia lutea
↕15cm (6in) ↔ 10cm (4in), delightful yellow flowers in autumn

STRELITZIA

Bird of Paradise

EVERGREEN HERBACEOUS PERENNIALS that become quite large, the most commonly grown is *Strelitzia reginae*. This has flowers that look like the head of a bird, with a bright orange 'cocky's crest' of feather-like petals at the top. These appear year-round in most gardens on the end of long stiff stems and are excellent as cut flowers. The leaves are grey-green and oval and held at the end of a metre-long (3ft) stem. This plant has a giant cousin, S. nicolai, which has foliage more like a banana palm and up to 5m (15ft) tall! The flowers are also very large, and although the same arrangement, have a cream 'crest' out of a dark blue 'head'.

Hardiness Frost-tender ❄ to very frost-tender ❀.

Cultivation Grow both in any well-drained soil that is enriched with well-rotted organic matter. *S. nicolai* prefers some shade, while *S. reginae* should be grown in full sun. Both should be grown out of the wind, which can damage the foliage. **Trim** out dead flowers and damaged foliage as they occur (*see p.390*). **Propagate** by dividing existing clumps in spring or by separating off and growing on the suckers that appear at the base. Watch for scale and control as necessary (*see p.395*).

Strelitzia reginae
↕1.5m (5ft) ↔ 2.1m (7ft), the flowers are long-lasting as cut flowers for indoors

ΣYMPHYTUM

omfrey

→ 30cm–2m (1–6ft) or more

PRIZED FOR THEIR SHADE tolerance, these hairy, clump-forming perennials make useful ground cover in a shady garden. Although essentially coarse plants, they have decorative, crinkly foliage and pretty, long-lasting flowers. hese are tubular or bell-shaped, in shades of bright lue, pale blue, cream, pale yellow, purple-violet, or hite, and are borne in clusters amid the foliage from te spring to late summer. The leaves may be plain reen, cream- or gold-variegated. Pick a site carefully ecause all but the variegated species can be invasive. hey thrive under trees where little else will grow.

ardiness Fully frost-hardy ✲✲✲.

ultivation Grow in moist soil in sun or shade, or in dry shade. **vide** plants (*see p.395*) in spring; Comfrey spreads by underground ems (rhizomes) and will reshoot from a tiny bit of stem left in the soil. omfrey leaves make a rich, if smelly, liquid feed: one-third fill a ucket with leaves and top up with water. Cover and leave for 2–3 eeks, then use diluted one part Comfrey liquid with two parts water.

***ymphytum* 'Hidcote Blue'**
→ 45cm (18in), hairy, erect then lax stems, red buds, flowers to 5cm (½in) long in mid- and late spring that fade with age

TAGETES

Marigold

FOR LENGTH OF FLOWERING AND SHOW of colour, marigolds have few rivals, and make excellent subjects for formal annual displays. The many annuals and perennials are usually treated as annuals and sown in spring. Germination is swift and they start flowering just a few weeks after sowing. The flowers, in a range of shades from deep orange to bright yellow, are produced from early summer until the first frosts of autumn. In some forms, they are single, often with contrasting darker markings on the petals; in others they are like carnations. The ferny foliage is usually strongly aromatic. Taller African Marigolds, with pompom flowers, can be grown in a border, but others, including French Marigolds, are equally at home in containers or garden beds.

Hardiness Frost-tender ✲.

Cultivation Any reasonably well-drained soil in full sun will suit marigolds. **Deadhead** regularly to prolong the flowering period and water freely in dry weather. If growing marigolds in containers, water them well, and feed with a balanced fertilizer at weekly intervals. **Sow** seed (*see pp.391–393*) at 21°C (70°F) in spring.

***Tagetes* 'Lemon Gem'**
↕23cm (9in) ↔ to 40cm (16in), Signet Marigold, flowers to 2.5cm (1in) across from late spring to early autumn

TANACETUM

Pyrethrum, Tansy

MOST SPECIES IN THIS LARGE, DIVERSE GROUP of annuals and perennials have finely cut, pungently aromatic leaves and daisy flowers in early and midsummer. Some flowerheads have a prominent central disc and others have small, double pompoms. The ferny leaves are very decorative. *Tanacetum balsamita* smells minty and is an ingredient of pot pourri. Some species, such as *T. haradjanii*, are suitable for a rock garden, while others, such as forms of *T. parthenium*, can be grown in a herb garden or as an edging to gardens. Pyrethrums also make interesting plants for raised beds and containers.

Hardiness Fully frost-hardy ✲✲✲ to frost-tender ✲.

Cultivation Grow these plants in any well-drained soil in full sun. Dwarf and silver-leaved species prefer sharply drained soil. **Cut back** the flowers of *T. coccineum* after flowering to encourage a further flush of blooms. Feverfew *(T. parthenium)* self-seeds prolifically. **Sow** seed at 10–13°C (50–55°F) in early spring (*see pp.391–393*). **Divide** perennials (*see p.395*) or take new shoots from the base and treat as cuttings (*see p.394*) in spring.

① ***haradjanii*** ↕to 15cm (6in), mat-forming evergreen, tiny yellow daisies in late summer ✲✲✲ ② ***parthenium*** (Feverfew) ↕45–60cm (18–24in), bushy perennial, flowers in summer ✲✲✲

Thalictrum

Meadow Rue

↕2.5m (8ft)
↔60cm (24in)

THALICTRUMS ARE A LARGE GROUP of moisture-loving perennials with delicate, grey-green foliage and airy clouds of tiny flowers from early to late summer. The numerous flowers may be coloured white, pink, and purple to yellow, often with showy central stamens, which create a fluffy effect from a distance. The leaves are composed of many fine-textured leaflets. They are mostly upright plants, although some, such as *Thalictrum kiusianum*, are mat-forming. Taller species are excellent in mixed gardens with perennials like achilleas (*see p.166*), sidalceas (*see p.325*), and Golden Rod (*Solidago, see p.327*), or in a woodland planting. Small ones add grace to a shady rock garden.

Hardiness Fully frost-hardy ❄❄❄ to frost–tender ❀.

Cultivation Grow in partial shade, in moist soil enriched with well-rotted organic matter. Small species like well-drained soil in cool, partial shade. **Stake** taller plants. **Sow** seed (*see pp.391–393*) in a container when ripe or in early spring. **Divide** plants (*see p.395*) as growth begins in spring. Powdery mildew can be a problem in humid areas.

***Thalictrum delavayi* 'Album'**
↕1.2m (4ft) or more ↔ 60cm (24in), erect clumps, leaves up to 35cm (14in) long, flowers from midsummer to early autumn ❄❄❄

Thalictrum aquilegiifolium
↕to 1m (3ft) ↔ 45cm (18in), erect clumps, leaves up to 30cm (12in) long, flowers in early summer ❄❄❄

***Thalictrum delavayi* 'Hewitt's Double' 🏆**
↕1.2m (4ft) or more ↔ 60cm (24in), leaves up to 35cm (14in) long, long-lasting flowers from midsummer to early summer ❄❄❄

Tiarella

Foam Flower

FROTHY SPIRES OF TINY FLOWERS appear to float above the foliage of these herbaceous perennials. The white or pinkish-white flowers are borne over a long period from late spring to midsummer. The foliage is also a valuable feature of these plants, being oval to heart-shaped and pale to mid-green with bristly hairs. In autumn, the leaves turn reddish-copper. Since the foliage is so dense, and some species have a spreading habit, foam flowers make attractive and effective ground-cover plants, particularly in a shady area or a woodland garden. They combine well with other shade- or moisture-loving perennials such as coral flowers (*Heuchera, see p.259*), hostas (*see pp.260–261*) and speedwells (*Veronica, see p.337*).

Hardiness Fully frost-hardy ❄❄❄.

Cultivation Foam flowers thrive in any moist soil that has been enriched with well-rotted organic matter, in deep or partial shade. **Protect** the crowns from winter wet if necessary. **Sow** seed in a container (*see pp.391–393*) in a cold frame as soon as they are ripe. **Divide** plants (*see p.395*) in spring.

***Tiarella cordifolia* 🏆 (Foam Flower)**
↕10–30cm (4–12in) ↔ to 30cm (12in), hairy leaves bronze-red in autumn, flower spikes 10–30cm (4–12in) long in autumn

ᛁIGRIDIA PAVONIA

ɔckey's Cap, Tiger Flower

beautiful, if little unusual, flower is the key reason ɪr growing this bulb. The flower is made up of three etals arranged to form a central bowl with three ·parate petal extensions beyond this. Remove two of ɪese and it really does look like an upside down ·ckey's cap! The centre of the bowl is usually marked ith splotches while the rest is in a single colour. The owers appear in summer, and while each one lasts a ngle day, there are usually large numbers, giving owering over weeks and even months. Colours vary ıd include white, cream, yellow, orange, red, and ːrise. The leaves are upright, mid-green and ıstinctly ribbed.

ardiness Frost-hardy ❄❄ to frost-tender ❄.

ultivation Grow in well-drained soil that is enriched with well-rotted ganic matter in a sunny spot. In areas of particularly wet winters ow the bulbs to dry out by lifting and storing, then replanting in ·ring or by growing in a free-draining medium.
w seed (*see pp.391–393*) in spring in containers. These often reach ·wering size in one or two years.

igridia pavonia
30–60cm (1–2ft) ↔ 15cm (6in), unfortunately the flowers do not st if picked, so enjoy them in the garden or containers

TRADESCANTIA

THE HARDY TRADESCANTIAS are very useful, clump-forming perennials, and although each flower is short-lived, they are produced in profusion in summer and much of autumn. The blue, purple, rose-pink, rose-red, or white blooms stud the mounds of matt-green, or occasionally purple-tinged, grassy foliage. Grow these easy-going plants in a mixed garden, perhaps married with ornamental grasses such as hakonechloas (*see p.348*), or with other herbaceous perennials. Some tradescantias are used as indoor plants with trailing stems and evergreen, often stripy or purple leaves. The garden weed Wandering Jew is also a tradescantia.

Hardiness Fully hardy ❄❄❄ to frost-tender ❄.

Cultivation Hardy species prefer moist, fertile soil, in full sun or partial shade. **Cut back** hard after flowering to prevent seed setting and for a further flush of flower. **Divide** hardy tradescantias in spring or autumn (*see p.395*).

① **'J.C. Weguelin'** 🏆 ↕40–60cm (16–24in) ↔ 45–60cm (18–24in) ❄❄❄ ② **'Purewell Giant'** ↕↔ 45cm (18in) ❄❄❄ – both flower from early summer to early autumn

TRICYRTIS

Toad Lily

TOAD LILIES HAVE SPECTACULAR FLOWERS, produced in white, shades of pinkish-white, or green flushed white or yellow, and frequently spotted with contrasting markings in pink or purple. They are star- or funnel-shaped and borne singly or in small clusters during summer and autumn. The leaves are often glossy, dark green to pale green, and usually clasp erect or arching stems. Some foliage is spotted or has prominent veins. Toad lilies are herbaceous perennials and particularly suitable for woodland gardens and shady spots. Try combining them with other perennials that enjoy moist, shady situations such as Solomon's Seal (*Polygonatum, see p.310*).

Hardiness Fully frost-hardy ❄❄❄.

Cultivation Toad lilies prefer moist but well-drained soil, that is humus-rich, in partial shade. **Sow** seed as soon as it is ripe in a cold frame and overwinter seedling plants in frost-free conditions (*see pp.391–393*). **Divide** plants (*see p.395*) in early spring while they are still dormant.

① ***formosana*** 🏆 ↕to 80cm (32in) ② ***hirta* 'Alba'** ↕to 80cm (32in)

Trillium

Wood Lily, Trinity Flower, Wake Robin

These spring-flowering plants of the woodland floor are prized for their curious three-petalled flowers held above the foliage, also grouped in threes. A small group of deciduous perennials, they are clump-forming once established. The flowers, in white and shades of pink, dark red, and yellow, are held at the tips of slender stems in spring and summer. The rich or dark green leaves are sometimes mottled or marbled with silver or purple. Trilliums can be slow to get going, but once established resent being disturbed, so site them carefully. They are suitable for moist, shady spots or woodland gardens, in the company of plants such as hostas (*see pp.260–261*).

Hardiness Fully frost-hardy ❄❄❄.

Cultivation Grow in moist soil, preferably slightly acid (lime-free), in deep or partial shade. **Divide** plants (*see p.395*) after flowering, preferably by lifting small, rooted sections; try to keep the central clump undisturbed. **Sow** seed as soon as it is ripe in containers in a cold frame (*see pp.391–393*). Plants may take up to seven years to reach flowering size from seed. Young leaves can be damaged by slugs and snails, so lay traps or pick off by hand (*see p.398*).

Trillium chloropetalum 🏆
↕ to 40cm (16in) ↔ to 20cm (8in), with thick red-green stems and fragrant flowers in spring

Trillium luteum 🏆
↕ to 40cm (16in) ↔ to 30cm (12in), leaves palely mottled, with stalkless, sweet-scented flowers in spring

Trillium rivale 🏆
↕ to 13cm (5in) ↔ to 15cm (6in), dwarf species with leaves only 3cm (1¼in) long, flowers in spring

Trillium sessile (Toad Shade)
↕ to 30cm (12in) ↔ to 20cm (8in), patterned leaves and dark, stalkless flowers in late spring

RITELEIA

hese deciduous bulbs generally flower in late spring r early summer. They occur in a loose open ball rangement at the top of an erect but thin stem. ndividually the small flowers are funnel-like, with a arry opening. Flowers are generally mauve-blue at ne tips and white in the centre, although in *Tritelia ioides* the flowers are yellow, while in *T. hyacintha* ey are white. *T.* 'Queen Fabiola' is the most ommonly grown of the triteleias and has darker blue owers. The leaves are narrow and arching. These die ff just before or at flowering, so it is advisable to ow these bulbs with low groundcovers to disguise is fact.

ardiness Frost-hardy ✲✲

ultivation Plant out corms to a depth of 5–8cm (2–3in) and 5–8cm –3in) apart. **Plant** in full sun and prefer a well-drained soil that is asonably fertile. They benefit from good moisture while in active owth, but watering can be reduced for their dormant period of late mmer and autumn. **Propagate** by dividing mature clumps in autumn ee *p.394*) or **sow** see in autumn (*see p.391*).

riteleia laxa
20–30cm (8–12in) ↔ 15cm (6in), a bulb flowering in early mmer as the leaves die down

TROPAEOLUM

see also p.154

NASTURTIUMS ARE THE MOST FAMILIAR of these vigorous, scrambling annuals and frost-tender perennials, grown for their cheerful, spurred flowers from summer until the first frosts of autumn. The trumpet-shaped flowers are borne in a variety of warm colours from red to orange and yellow, many bicoloured or with contrasting markings on the petals. The round or lobed, light to mid-green leaves are held on long stalks. The bushy plants are best with other annuals or as gap-fillers. Those with trailing stems scramble over the ground or climb; use them to clothe new structures quickly over the summer. Semi-trailing types are ideal for hanging baskets. Tender perennials grown in pots may be overwintered under glass.

Hardiness Frost-hardy ✲✲ to very frost-tender ❀.

Cultivation Grow in moist but well-drained soil, in sun or partial shade. Water plants in pots freely in summer. **Sow** seed (*see pp.391–393*) of annuals where they are to grow, in mid-spring; sow seed of perennials in a container in a cold frame as soon as ripe.

Tropaeolum majus **Alaska Series A (Nasturtium)**
↕to 30cm (12in), annual, variegated leaves ✲

TULBAGHIA

Society Garlic, Sweet Garlic

MOSTLY EVERGREEN FLOWERING BULBS, some are deciduous in areas with extremely cold winters. The leaves are narrow and grey-green and generally in the 30–45cm (12–18in) range. Flowers are small and starry and in a balled cluster at the top of a straight stem. Two species and their cultivars are grown. The most common of these is the Society Garlic (*Tulbaghia. violacea*) which has pinky-mauve flowers from spring well into summer and even into autumn in some districts. The foliage gives off a distinct garlicky smell when crushed. Sweet Garlic (*T. fragrans*) has similar flowers, but from winter to summer, and these are sweetly scented, while the foliage does not have the garlic smell. Both have white-flowered forms and the former also has variegated leaf cultivars.

Hardiness Frost-hardy ✲✲ to frost-tender ✲.

Cultivation These will grow in both full sun and relatively heavy shade. The soil should be well drained and kept moist in summer. **Propagate** by dividing existing clumps in winter (*see p.394*).

Tulbaghia violacea **(Society Garlic)**
↕45cm (18in) ↔ 15cm (6in), these long-flowering evergreen bulbs make useful edgers in light and shade ✲✲

TULIPA

Tulip

↕min. 10cm (4in)
↕max. 75cm (30in)

TULIPS HAVE BEEN PRIZED FOR CENTURIES for their brilliantly coloured spring blooms. They were one of the first of the many bulbous perennials to be introduced into western gardens from the eastern Mediterranean. Here, in the parched summer earth of their native lands, the sun "ripens" the bulbs, helping to form the buds that produce the following season's flowers. Single or double, these come in a dazzling array of colours, often fascinatingly flushed or streaked with other shades. Petals may be frilled, fringed, pointed, waisted, or tinged with green, as in the viridiflora types such as 'Spring Green'. The species tulips, for instance *Tulipa sprengeri* and *T. saxatalis*, are often the smallest and among the easiest to grow. They suit gardens, rock gardens, and areas of naturalistic planting. The taller, more highly bred hybrids put on an eye-catching display, but flowers can diminish over the years and are best lifted (*see below*) or treated as annuals. All are excellent in pots.

Hardiness Fully frost-hardy ❄❄❄.

Cultivation Grow in well-drained, fertile soil in full sun. All tulips dislike heavy damp soil. Plant at twice the bulb's own depth in late autumn. **Deadhead** to prevent seedheads forming, thereby concentrating the plant's energy into developing the bulb and next year's flower bud within. **Apply** a balanced liquid fertilizer once a fortnight after flowering until the foliage withers, to build up the bulb. **Lift** bulbs (except for small species tulips) once the foliage has died down (*see below*), and discard or separate small offsets. **Plant** large bulbs in late autumn. If you want, grow on offsets in a spare corner until they reach flowering size (up to seven years).

Planting Tulip bulbs for easy lifting

Most tall, hybrid tulip bulbs are best lifted once the foliage withers, then dried (if possible in a greenhouse or cold frame), and stored until autumn. This, to some extent, mimics their natural ripening process in the wild and helps bulbs perform well for years, especially on heavy soils. Species tulips, including the Greigii and Kaufmanniana types, need not be lifted.

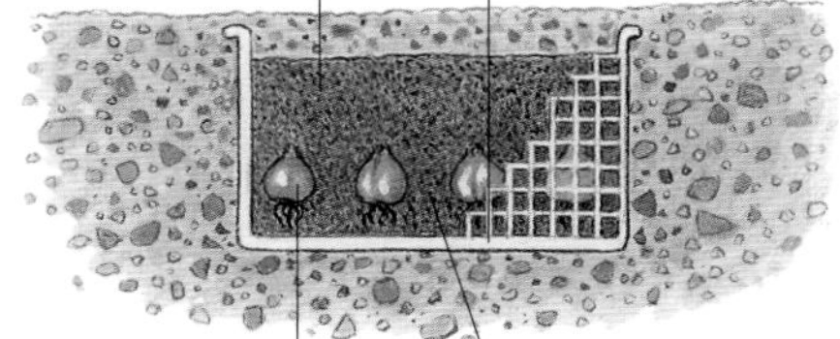
Proprietary potting mix is used for planting
Basket must measure at least 15cm (6in) deep
Bulbs are planted at twice their own depth
Gap between bulbs equals one bulb's width

◁ ❶ *Planting tulips in a basket means that they can be easily lifted after flowering and stored when not in season. Use a container with plenty of drainage holes in the bottom – a lattice basket for pond plants is ideal. Lift carefully, so as not to damage roots that have grown through the basket. Bury the basket in a resting place in the garden so the top of it is just below the soil surface. Remember to label the basket and water it in well.*

▷ ❷ *Tulips planted directly in the soil can be gently lifted with a fork. Shake off any soil and leave them in a dry place, such as a garden shed, to dry off. Once dry, remove any old soil, withered leaves and flaking skin. Any bulbs showing signs of disease with soft spots on them should be thrown away. Keep the bulbs in a cool, dark and dry place. Check them at intervals to prevent disease spreading. Replant in autumn for flowering the following spring.*

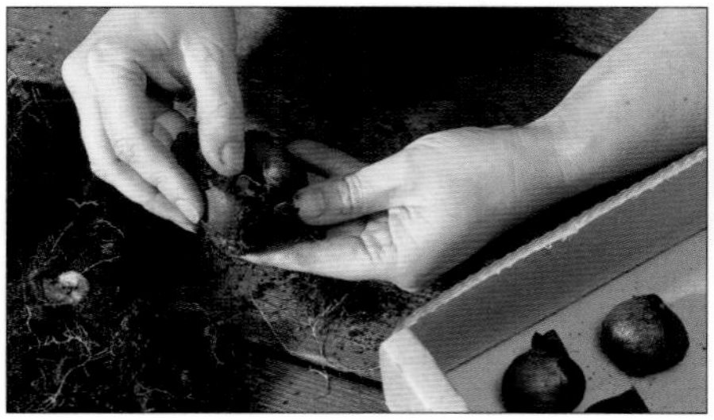

1

2

8

12

① *Tulipa acuminata* ↕50cm (20in), early and mid-spring ② **'Ancilla'** 🏆 ↕15cm (6in), mid-spring, good for rock gardens ③ **'Angélique'** 🏆 ↕30cm (12in), mid-spring, suitable for bedding or borders ④ **'Apeldoorn'** ↕60cm (24in), mid-spring ⑤ **'Carnaval de Nice'** 🏆 ↕40cm (16in), late spring ⑥ ***linifolia* Batalinii Group** 🏆 ↕35cm (14in), late winter to late spring ⑦ **'Madame Lefeber'** ↕35cm (14in), early spring, large blooms, may need staking ⑧ ***clusiana* var. *chrysantha*** 🏆 ↕30cm (12in),

rly and mid-spring ⑨ **'Prinses Irene'** ♕ ↕35cm (14in), mid-spring, good for cut flowers
'Purissima' ♕ ↕35cm (14in), mid-spring ⑪ **'Queen of Night'** ↕60cm (24in), late spring
sprengeri ♕ ↕50cm (20in), early summer, will self-seed in sun or partial shade ⑬ **'Spring Green'**
↕40cm (16in), late spring ⑭ ***turkestanica*** ♕ ↕30cm (12in), early and mid-spring, unpleasant
agrance ⑮ **'White Parrot'** ↕55cm (22in), late spring

VALERIANA OFFICINALIS

Common Valerian

THIS IS A HERBACEOUS PERENNIAL that forms a tight clump of foliage at ground level. This is made up of mid-green leaves, each of which consists of pairs of toothed, lance-shaped leaflets. In spring flower stems rise well above the foliage. By summer these are topped with fragrant, white to pink small, tubular flowers. These are in loose spheres on the ends of the many branchlets that come from the main flowering stem. This plant is more often grown by people interested in herbs at it is the source of Valerian, a popular medicinal herb for thousands of years. This plant is also said to attract cats.

Hardiness Fully frost-hardy ❄❄❄.

Cultivation Grow in any well-drained soil in full sun and shelter from hot, drying winds. It prefers a moist position. **Trim** back the spent flower stems unless the seeds are required (*see pp.382-384*). **Sow** seed (*see pp.391-393*) in a cold frame in spring and only lightly cover. **Divide** clumps in autumn (*see p.395*).

Valeriana officinalis
↕1.2m (4ft) ↔ 90cm (3ft), this attractive plant is also the source of the herbal medicine, Valerian

VELTHEIMIA

THESE UNCOMMON EVERGREEN OR DECIDUOUS BULBS are from South Africa and, unfortunately, are very susceptible to frosts. The wavy-edged, light green leaves are quite broad and long, and look a little like larger versions of those of the Pineapple Lily (*Eucomis, see p.241*). The flowers occur on upright stems in late winter and into spring and are somewhat reminiscent of Red Hot Pokers (*Kniphofia, see p.268*). They are most often a dusky pink, but paler forms do occur. The species most commonly seen is *Veltheimia bracteata* and it comes from areas of summer rainfall and does best in gardens with similar conditions. Its rarer cousin, *V. capensis*, conversely comes from areas of summer dry.

Hardiness Very frost-tender ❄.

Cultivation The bulbs are planted in autumn with only about one-third below the soil surface. They will grow in full sun or quite dark shade. **Sow** seed (*see p.391*) in a cold frame as soon as it is ripe and these will be flowering size by about the third year. **Bulb** offsets can also be taken in autumn (*see p.395*).

Veltheimia bracteata
↕45cm (18in) ↔ 30cm (1ft), is an uncommon South African bulb

VERBASCUM

Mullein

THESE STATELY PLANTS are grown for their tall flower spikes, densely set with saucer-shaped blooms from summer to autumn. The short-stemmed flowers occu usually in shades of yellow, but are occasionally purple, scarlet, brownish-red, or white. While the individual flowers are short-lived, there are always more opening to sustain the display. Most garden mulleins are vigorous, rosette-forming plants that are useful in any garden, particularly in gravel and cottag gardens. The often woolly, silvery rosettes of leaves remain attractive into winter. They generally are not long-lived, being biennials, short-lived perennials, an some annuals. Mulleins self-seed prolifically if allowe to do so, although the seedlings may not come true.

Hardiness Fully frost-hardy ❄❄❄ to frost-hardy ❄❄.

Cultivation Grow in well-drained, alkaline (limy) soil in full sun. Tall plants may require support, especially in rich soil. **Sow** seed (*see pp.391–393*) of perennials in containers in a cold frame in late spring or early summer. Sow seed of biennials in early summer to flower the following year. **Divide** perennials (*see p.395*) in spring. **Take** root cuttings (*see p.394*) in winter.

Verbascum chaixii 'Album' 🏆
↕90cm (36in) ↔ 45cm (18in), rosette-forming, semi-evergreen perennial, flower spikes to 40cm (16in) mid- to late summer ❄❄❄

/ERBENA

HIS LARGE GROUP OF ANNUALS AND PERENNIALS are valuable in a summer garden, with dense clusters ' small flowers in shades of red, blue, pink, lilac, ıd violet borne on stiff, square stems. All are long- ›wering, but only a few are reliably frost-hardy. ›rbenas fall into two main groups: the hardy ›rennials will grow quite tall and bring height and an ›y feel to a garden, while the many shorter-growing, ›st-tender perennials tend to sprawl. Grown as ınual bedding they will add colour to containers and ınging baskets as well as the edges of gardens. Grow ›rennials with tall plants like *Cynara cardunculus* (*see* *221*) and annuals with plants such as pelargoniums *›e pp.300–303*).

ırdiness Fully frost-hardy ❄❄❄ to very frost-tender ❀.

ıltivation Moist but well-drained soil in full sun is best for ›benas. In containers, use a quality potting mix – water well in ımmer, and feed with a balanced fertilizer at weekly intervals. **Sow** ›d (*see pp.391–393*) at 18–21°C (64–70°F) in early spring. **Divide** ›rennials (*see p.395*) in spring and take stem-tip cuttings ›e *p.394*) in late summer. Powdery mildew can be a problem.

›rbena 'Peaches and Cream' ♀ ↕to 45cm (18in), sprawling ›rennial grown as annual ❄

VERONICA

Speedwell

THE SLENDER, GRACEFUL SPIRES of veronica carry small, outward-facing flowers in intense or pastel shades of blue, pink, purple, or white. The numerous annuals and perennials in this group are mostly mat- or cushion-forming, but sometimes upright and branching. Their long or rounded leaves have toothed edges and are mid- to dark green, sometimes felted. Speedwells flower over a long period, from spring to autumn, and are excellent garden plants, especially for the front of a sunny garden. They make good partners for shrubby or perennial plants such as lavenders (*see p.80*) and hardy geraniums (*see pp.250–251*). The smaller types are best grown in a rock garden.

Hardiness Fully frost-hardy ❄❄❄ to frost-hardy ❄❄.

Cultivation Alpine Speedwells require sharply drained, poor to moderate soil, in full sun and protection from winter wet for those with felted leaves. Others like any fertile soil in full sun or partial shade. **Sow** seed (*see pp.391–393*) in a container in a cold frame in autumn. **Divide** perennials (*see p.395*) in spring or autumn. Veronicas may suffer from powdery mildew in dry weather; remove affected parts.

Veronica gentianoides ♀

↕↔ to 45cm (18in), mat-forming perennial, dark green leaves, pale blue (*see inset*) or, more rarely, white flowers in early summer ❄❄❄

VINCA

Periwinkle

THESE ARE EVERGREEN PERENNIALS that are most often used as ground covers, particularly in very shady positions. They have glossy, dark green, pointed oval leaves that appear in pairs opposite each other along an upright wiry stem. The flowers appear at the top of these stems in spring and summer and are from pale to deep purple in colour. They are a short narrow tube that ends with five flattened out petals. *Vinca major* is most commonly found in gardens, while its sibling *V. minor* is similar, but as the botanical name suggests, is a scaled down version. Both can be particularly invasive and should be used in gardens with extreme caution.

Hardiness Frost-hardy ❄❄.

Cultivation Grow in any well-drained soil in a shady spot. Old plants can be sheared down to ground level in spring to rejuvenate them every few years (*see p.384*). **Propagate** by division from existing clumps in winter (*see p.395*).

Vinca minor

↕20cm (8in) ↔ indefinite, is a vigorous colonizer of shady areas and should be used with caution lest it escape

VIOLA

Pansy, Violet

THE RICHLY-COLOURED AND OPEN "FACES" of these well-loved flowers bring cheer to the garden all year around. Hundreds of forms are available, with flowers in hues of gold, orange, crimson, purple, black, blue, lilac, and white; many are bicoloured and or even tricoloured. Traditional violas are compact, tufted perennials, with dainty, often scented flowers, such as the classic English Violet, *Viola odorata*. This is an evergreen perennial with a strong, sweet scent and is a good ground cover for a shady spot. Garden pansies include the brasher, large-flowered hybrids, mostly unscented; they are biennials or short-lived perennials, and include winter-flowering forms. There are also annual violas. Violas look pretty as garden edging or in hanging baskets and other containers.

Hardiness Fully frost-hardy ❄❄❄ to frost-tender ❄.

Cultivation Violas like fertile, humus-rich, moist but well-drained soil, in full sun or partial shade. Violas can be short-lived, so it is best to raise new plants regularly. **Sow** seed (*see pp.391–393*) in late winter for summer flowers, or in summer for winter or spring flowers. **Take** softwood cuttings of perennials (*see p.394*) in spring or late summer.

***Viola* 'Nellie Britton'** 🏆
↕15cm (30cm) ↔ 30cm (12in), clump-forming, evergreen perennial, abundant flowers, 2.5cm (1in) across, all summer ❄❄❄

***Viola* 'Jackanapes'** 🏆
↕13cm (5in) ↔ 30cm (12in), clump-forming, short-lived, evergreen perennial, 2cm (¾in) flowers in late spring and summer ❄❄❄

DEADHEAD regularly to prolong flowering. Cut out faded flowers near the base of the stalks to encourage new shoots to grow.

***Viola* 'Rebecca'**
↕10cm (4in) ↔ 25cm (10in), spreading perennial, heavily scented flowers – tinged blue in cold conditions – borne in summer ❄❄❄

Viola tricolor (Heartsease, Johnny Jump-Ups, Wild Pans
↕8–13cm (3–5in) ↔ 10–15cm (4–6in), annual, biennial, or short-lived evergreen perennial, flowers from spring to autumn ❄❄❄

?ANTEDESCHIA

rum Lily

'HESE IMPOSING, ARCHITECTURAL PERENNIALS have ısh foliage and elegant, funnel-shaped blooms. The owers are borne in spring and summer on stems p to 90cm (36in) tall and are usually clear yellow, though white, pink, lilac, or dark purple forms re available. The large, mid- to dark green leaves are rrow-shaped and sometimes spotted. *Zantesdeschia ethiopica* can be grown in moist gardens, where it an form large clumps, or as a marginal aquatic in ater up to 30cm (12in) deep, in a 25–30cm 10–12in) aquatic basket filled with heavy loam but nsure it does not escape.

ardiness Fully frost-hardy ❄❄❄ to very frost-tender ❀.

ıltivation *Z. aethiopica* needs moist soil, enriched with organic atter, in full sun. In frost-prone areas, protect the crowns with a deep nter mulch. *Z. elliotiana* is best raised in pots under frost-free glass d stood outside for summer display. Use a soil-based compost and ed weekly at flowering time with a balanced fertilizer. **Divide** (*see* *395*) in spring. **Sow** seed (*see pp.391–393*) at 21–27°C (70–81°F).

antedeschia aethiopica **'Green Goddess'** 🏆
0cm (36in) ↔ 60cm (24in), clumping, evergreen in mild areas, –20cm (6–8in) flowers from late spring to midsummer ❄❄

Zantedeschia elliottiana 🏆 (Golden Arum)
↕60–90cm (24–36in) ↔ 20cm (8in), erect habit, leaves to 45cm (18in) long, flowers 15cm (6in) long in summer ❀

ZINNIA

THESE RELIABLE AND RELATIVELY TOUGH ANNUALS can be used to bring summer and autumn colour to the garden. They have mid-green leaves that have a fine sandpaper texture to them. Plants are fairly narrow and upright and are topped with a multitude of daisy-type flowers. These are in numerous forms from semi-double through to ones that are so multi-petalled that they look like pompoms! Colours too, are diverse, but are usually in the yellow, orange, and pink range, but all sorts of bicolours and variations can be found. Heights also vary among those available and gardeners in windy districts should seek out lower-growing forms as these will be less prone to damage.

Hardiness Frost-hardy ❄❄ to frost-tender ❄.

Cultivation Grow in full sun in well-drained soil that is enriched with well-rotted organic matter. Protection from strong winds may be necessary for taller cultivars. **Deadheading** frequently should prolong flowering (*see p.390*). **Sow** seed (*see pp.391-393*) from spring to early summer in a cold frame in colder districts or straight into the garden in warmer districts. From seed to flower takes about 12 weeks.

Zinnia elegans
↕75cm (30in) ↔ 30cm (1ft), summer and autumn flowering annuals ❄

Bamboos and Grasses

using grasses in the garden

Most gardeners have a grass lawn or an area of turf in their gardens, but there is also a wonderful array of ornamental grasses that can be used in the gardens. They are very architectural plants, with arching or upright stems, feathery or tufted flowerheads, and subtly shaded seedheads. Ornamental grasses are easy to grow and bring constant movement and grace to the garden, as well as soothing sounds as they rustle in the wind. Many grasses will also remain attractive well into autumn and winter.

What is a grassy plant?

Ornamental grasses include several groups of grass-like plants. True grasses include lawn grasses; they may be annual or perennial and most have flowerheads formed of many tiny flowers in clusters or spikes. Bamboos are very large, handsome, evergreen grasses. Many are vigorous, and once established can spread over a large area. The grass-like sedges and rushes are usually much smaller, often with coloured or variegated foliage.

Many grassy plants thrive in most situations. True grasses often tolerate very dry conditions, whereas rushes and sedges prefer moister soils. Before planting, however, it is a good idea to incorporate plenty of well-rotted organic matter in dry soils to ensure moisture retention. Heavier clay soils need gypsum dug in to improve the drainage. Grasses require little further attention apart from cutting down old foliage, where needed, in early spring.

True grasses, like this *Miscanthus sinensis* 'Silberfeder' vary in colour and habit, but are grown for their flower spikes and seedheads, and sometimes for their coloured stems.

Bamboos, such as this *Bambusa multiplex*, are true grasses but have attractive, segmented woody stems or canes, and up to 20 pairs of long, thin, delicate, divided leaves.

Rushes have tightly packed, upright leaves arising straight out of the soil. They prefer moist or wet soil, like this flowering rush, *Butomus umbellatus*, which grows in pond margins.

Sedges are low-growing, usually perennial and evergreen. They are valued for their foliage, such as this carex. Sedge stems are triangular and feel distinctly ridged.

Planting ideas

)rnamental grasses, bamboos, and edges can be used in a wide variety of 'ays. Larger grasses such as *Stipa igantea* (*see p.354*), are excellent as pecimens planted on their own in a wn or in a hot, gravel garden.

If you have the space, you could ave an entire garden dedicated to rasses. It is possible to create many 'onderful contrasts of foliage colour, hape, and height, by planting drifts of rasses to form a garden that shimmers nd changes with every passing breeze. 'ary the pace by placing tall, bold rasses next to fine-leaved ones.

Grasses and sedges also look good ı mixed gardens. They provide the erfect foil to the broad leaves of ostas or the bright colours of owering annuals and perennials, such s cirsiums (*see p.214*).

The slender stems of grasses make ıem semi-transparent so that you are ble to glimpse other flowering plants ırough them. They give a light, airy el to the planting.

Taller grasses can be planted in umps at intervals to act as focal oints in a bed, or grown as a pecimen or a screen – bamboos with oloured stems are a handsome choice.

In a container Many grasses thrive in containers. Choose one that tones with or complements the colour of the foliage – here the bronze of an old coal scuttle highlights the same tint in a carex.

In a raised bed Smaller grasses look particularly good in a raised bed. Here festucas, and acorus, in greys and blues, along with astilbes and stachys, echo the hue of the wood.

In a mixed garden Grasses can look particularly good grown amongst herbaceous perennials in a mixed ɔed or garden. The finer foliage of the grasses contrasts well with the more static shapes and bolder colours of 'lowering perennials and shrubs. Dwarf grasses, such as festucas, also make an elegant edging for a garden bed.

Extending the display

One of the advantages of growing grasses in the garden is that many of them are late-flowering, and so extend the season of interest into autumn with their fluffy or feathery flowerheads silhouetted against clear autumn skies. Some also provide autumn colour when their architectural foliage turns brown or bronze and holds these russet tones right through the winter, giving the garden some structure during the bleakest months of the year.

The flowerheads also are long-lasting, and look just as graceful when they go to seed. They can look stunning when encrusted with frost. Most grasses are then cut down in spring, so you could cover the gap until they grow back by planting spring-flowering bulbs.

Leaving grasses uncut during winter provides a much-needed food source – the seeds – for birds. Beneficial insects such as beetles also like to shelter in the bases of the plants until spring.

Winter interest *Miscanthus sinensis* 'Zebrinus' is a great specimen plant that looks as good in winter as it does in summer. The dark green and yellow, banded leaves turn a subtle brown-bronze, the maroon flowerheads fade to silver, and the lax stems remain unbroken despite winter winds.

Keeping bamboos within bounds

Unless you have a large garden, you should choose bamboos with care. Some have fibrous root systems that form compact clumps. Others will colonize the soil using underground stems, or rhizomes. As these spread through the soil, they push new canes up at intervals to form new clumps and can overwhelm other plants in a garden. Spreading bamboos are best grown as specimen plants in an island bed so that their rhizomes be kept in check by the mowing of the lawn around them. You could also confine them by sinking a continuous barrier, made from concrete or flexible plastic, into the ground, but it may be easier to chop the roots back (*see right*).

Controlling spreading roots with a spade Dig a 30cm (12in) deep trench around the base of the plant to uncover the roots. Using a spade with a sharpened blade, chop through the roots on the inside wall of the trench and remove them. Fill in the trench with sand so that it will be easier to do this again next year. Alternatively, chop through the roots of unwanted offshoots and dig them out.

Acorus

Two species of Acorus, are grown in gardens and both are evergreen or semi-evergreen water lovers. *Acorus calamus* is the taller of the two, reaching 75cm (30in), and has iris-like foliage that gives off a citrus smell when crushed. A variegated form with yellow striping is also available. This form needs to be grown in shallow water. *A. gramineus* grows to approximately 10cm (4in) in height, has grassy foliage and can be grown in shallow water. It can be grown out of the water provided the soil is kept permanently moist. There are two variegated forms of *A. gramineus*: *A. gramineus* 'Ogon' with yellow stripes; and *A. gramineus* 'Variegatus', with creamy stripes, which is taller than the species.

Hardiness Frost-hardy ❄❄.

Cultivation Grow in a a site that is permanently wet and in full sun. **Divide** in spring every few years as clumps become overcrowded. **Propagation** is also by division.

Acorus gramineus **'Variegatus'**
↕to 25cm (10in) ↔ 15cm (6in), grows happily along the water's edge

Bambusa

Bamboo

This is a large genus of a diverse range of evergreen bamboos, including many ornamental cultivars. They are generally clump-forming and some species, such as *Bambusa oldhamii* can reach as much as 15m (50ft) tall. They have mid-green leaves on very narrow stems growing from the nodes of the vertical canes. The familiar canes are hollow and generally green, although there are a number of colour variations. These include *B. multiplex* 'Alphonse Karr', which has yellow stems striped green, and *B. multiplex* 'Golden Goddess' which has yellowish canes. Bamboos have a number of garden uses, as hedging and as decorative container plants. Many also have a large number of practical uses as well as producing edible shoots.

Hardiness Frost-hardy ❄❄ to very frost tender ❄.

Cultivation Grow in any well-drained soil in full sun or partial shade. **Prune** out older shoots altogether at any time of the year. (*see p.382*). **Propagate** by dividing existing clumps in late winter (*see p.395*). **Control** of some rampant forms may be necessary (*see p.389*).

Bambusa multiplex (Hedging Bamboo)
↕10m (30ft) ↔ 3m (10ft), is a clumping bamboo

Calamagrostis

Reed Grass

The most widely grown reed grasses are cultivars of *Calamagrostis* × *acutiflora*. These are perennial grasses that are generally slow-spreading and clump-forming, with particularly soft and elegant plumes of flowers in subtle shades. Their upright, architectural forms add height to garden beds, while their open habits allow you to see through to other plants growing behind them. They give excellent value through the year, coming into growth quite early and bearing open clusters of summer flowers. The flowers slowly compress to become narrow seedheads that are retained through the autumn. 'Karl Foerster' has pink-bronze flowers fading to buff, and 'Overdam' has purplish summer flowers that fade to greyish-pink.

Hardiness Fully frost-hardy ❄❄❄.

Cultivation Grow in moist soil, ideally enriched with plenty of well-rotted organic matter, but all except the poorest soils are tolerated. Position in sun or partial shade. **Leave** the season's growth uncut for winter effect, then cut down in early spring, before new growth starts. **Divide** overgrown clumps in spring (*see p.395*).

Calamagrostis × *acutiflora* **'Overdam'**
↕to 1.2m (4ft) ↔ 60cm (24in), pale yellow edges and stripes on the leaves, which fade to pink-flushed white as they age

CAREX

edge

'HESE GRASSY, TUFTED perennials are grown mainly ɔr their form, and the colours or markings on their ɔng, narrow leaves. There are many sedges in shades f copper or russet, and others striped with gold or lvery white. Mixed groups – for example, rich yellow *Carex elata* 'Aurea' next to the red-brown *C. flagellifera* create unusual colour contrasts. Some also have ttractive clusters of flowers, such as *C. pendula.* Most re evergreen, some deciduous, and while some prefer damp spot, others are very unfussy.

ardiness All sedges described here are fully frost-hardy ***. thers from New Zealand, such as *C. morrowii*, are frost-hardy **, nd benefit from a winter mulch.

ultivation Sedges can be grouped by their differing cultivation equirements. **Group 1** will thrive in any soil in sun or partial shade. **roup 2** needs a moist, fertile, but well-drained alkaline soil and a osition in sun or partial shade. **Group 3** includes *C. flagellifera* and *. siderosticha* 'Variegata' and requires fertile, moist or wet soil in un or partial shade. **Cut back** deciduous species in spring. Trim ut any dead leaves on evergreen species in summer. **Divide** plants *ee p.395*) between mid-spring and early summer. Aphids *ee p.398*) occasionally attack the bases of the stems.

Carex oshimensis 'Evergold' 🏆
↕30cm (12in) ↔ 35cm (14in), group 2, evergreen

Carex pendula (Weeping Sedge)
↕to 1.4m (4½ft) ↔ to 1.5m (5ft), group 3, evergreen, self-seeds freely

MULCHING CAREX with gravel or bark gives a decorative finish and will help protect frost-hardy varieties in winter. Spread the mulch over the root area during mild, moist autumn weather.

Carex elata 'Aurea' 🏆 (Bowles' Golden Sedge)
to 70cm (28in) ↔ 45cm (18in), group 3, deciduous

Carex testacea
↕to 1.5m (5ft) ↔ 60cm (24in), group 1, evergreen

Chimonobambusa

THESE EVERGREENS are running forms of bamboo. The canes are upright, but tend to arch out a bit, particularly those on the outside edge of the clumps. The dark green leaves and branchlets also tend to arch forward, giving the whole plant an elegant weeping appearance. Only two are grown, along with some of their cultivars. They are the Marble Bamboo (*Chimonobambusa marmorea*), which only grows to around 2m (6ft) and has very dark stems. The other is the Square Bamboo (*C. quadrangularis*), which has stems that are square in section. Although elegant looking, it is a vigorous giant, and must be contained.

Hardiness Fully frost hardy ❄❄❄ to frost-tender ❄.

Cultivation Grow in a shady site where it will be protected from hot, drying winds. A well-drained soil that is reasonably fertile is also important. **Remove** old canes as necessary. Control will be essential if it grows beyond where it is wanted (*see p.389*). **Propagate** by dividing offsets from the main clump.

Chimonobambusa quadrangularis
↕ to 7m (21ft) ↔ indefinite, has unusual square stems and an elegant, weeping habit

Cymbopogon

Lemon Grass

THIS IS AN EVERGREEN perennial grass. It forms a tuft of leaves that can reach 1.5m (5ft) long. These tend to grow upright, slightly arching out from the base. The leaves are pale green and have a strong and distinct lemon scent when crushed. The plant rarely produces flowers. The leaves and the leaf bases are used in flavouring Asian dishes and in some drinks. It can be grown in herb or vegetable gardens as well as in containers, provided these are quite large. It has attractive foliage and there is no reason it shouldn't be grown among other ornamental plants in a mixed garden bed.

Hardiness Very frost-tender ❄.

Cultivation Grow in well-drained soil that is reasonably fertile and enriched with well-rotted organic matter. **Position** in full sun or very light shade and shelter from hot, drying winds. **Propagate** by divisions of existing clumps in winter (*see p.395*).

***Cymbopogon citratus* (Lemon Grass)**
↕ 1–1.5m (3–5ft) ↔ to 1m (3ft), although best known for its culinary properties, this grass is also ornamental

Cyperus

THIS IS A VERY LARGE GENUS of plants with representatives from most parts of the world, including Australia. Generally referred to as sedges, they are evergreen perennials. Plants range from a few centimetres to over 3m (10ft) tall. They have shiny, mid- to dark green, grass-like leaves. These sometimes emerge from tufts at ground level, or more individually, spreading over a large area. The seedheads are often a globose ball of grass seeds at the end of thin, arching stems, all radiating out from one point at the end of an upright stem above the foliage. A number are in cultivation, particularly as plants for the water's edge. Unfortunately, several of the genus are also weeds, notably Nut Grass (*Cyperus rotundus*).

Hardiness Frost hardy ❄❄ to frost-tender ❄.

Cultivation Grow in full sun in soil that can be kept moist at all times. Some actually grow best in shallow water. **Divide** large clumps in spring every few years to reduce overcrowding. (*see p.395*). **Sow** seed (*see p.391*) in spring under glass and keep the seed moist. **Propagation** can also be carried out by division of existing clumps in spring. (*see p.395*).

Cyperus papyrus
↕ to 3m (10ft) ↔ indefinite, grows in warm shallow water and was the raw material of paper-making in ancient Egypt

Danthonia

Wallaby Grass

These grasses are native to Australia, and while perennial, most have a distinctive dormant period when the foliage and seeds have dried off and gone a pale straw colour. This is usually in late summer and autumn. For the rest of the year the foliage is mid-green and arises from a tussock at ground level. The seedheads appear from late spring and through summer, often remaining for months afterwards. Plants vary from 10cm (4in) to over 1m (3ft) tall.

Hardiness Fully frost-hardy *** to frost-tender *.

Cultivation Requirements vary among the species, but generally they will grow in any well-drained soil in full sun or very light shade. **Rejuvenate** old clumps every few years by lifting and dividing in spring. An alternative is to burn off the old foliage in spring and follow up with some extra waterings to promote new growth. **Propagate** by divisions in spring. **Sow** seed (*see p.391*) in spring after storing it for a year first. **Sow** seed into containers and only barely cover the seed with mixture.

)anthonia setacea
15–60cm (6–24ft) ↔ 30cm (12in), flower spikes, often flushed pink purple, from late summer ***

Fargesia

These clump-forming bamboos have slender, arching stems and lance-shaped leaves growing from purplish sheaths. The large, striking *Fargesia murielae* makes a fine focal point or a hardy hedging or screening plant. The stems are white-powdery when young, maturing to yellow-green and then yellow. They arch under the weight of the leaves, which are up to 15cm (6in) long, with drawn-out tips. The leaf sheaths age to pale brown. For wonderful foliage contrast, grow it next to the bold gunnera (*see p.254*), although you will need a fair amount of space to accommodate both plants. The similarly large *F. nitida* has very slender, purplish canes and long, narrow leaves, which give it a more airy, delicate appearance, despite its hardiness.

Hardiness Fully frost-hardy *** to frost-tender *.

Cultivation Grow in fertile, moisture-retentive soil. Position *F. nitida* in dappled shade with shelter; *F. murielae* will tolerate full sun and windy sites. **Divide** established clumps (*see p.395*). Take root cuttings (*see p.394*) of lengths of underground stem (rhizomes) in spring.

Fargesia murielae ♀ (Umbrella Bamboo)
↕ to 4m (12ft) ↔ to 1.5m (5ft) ***

Festuca

Fescue

Fescues are a large, varied group, deciduous and evergreen, mostly suited to sunny positions. They are grown mainly for the narrow, arching, smooth leaves, but also bear flowerheads that fade to golden shades. The densely tufted evergreen perennial *Festuca glauca* is very popular. Grow fescues as edging or to provide a contrast to other smallish plants with bolder leaves: most are too small to make specimen plants. Blue flowers, like those of felicias (*see p.244*), complement the steely blue of *F. glauca*, while silver foliage plants, such as *Stachys byzantina* (*see p.328*), make a wonderful contrast. A mulch of dark, even dyed woodchips would complete a striking, urban look.

Hardiness Fully frost hardy ***.

Cultivation Grow fescues in poor to moderately fertile, well-drained soil, in full sun. **Sow** seed (*see pp.391–392*) from autumn until spring in containers in a cold frame. **Divide** and replant (*see p.395*) in spring every 2–3 years to maintain good foliage colour and keep plants vigorous.

Festuca glauca (Blue Fescue)
↕ to 30cm (12in) ↔ 25cm (10in) evergreen, violet to blue-green flowerheads in early and midsummer

Gahnia

Saw Sedge

THESE ARE CLUMP-FORMING GRASSES, ranging from dwarfs to the more commonly cultivated tall forms. The leaves are dark green and very narrow and tend to arch out from the tight base. The most commonly available is *Gahnia sieberiana*, and this has large, spreading, creamy flowerheads in spring, followed by small but shiny, red-brown nuts. These stems can be used in floral decorations, either at flower or seed stage. Handle with care as many have sharply serrated leaf edges, which has given rise to the common name.

Hardiness Frost-hardy ❄❄.

Cultivation Grow in full sun or part shade, with *G. sieberiana* even tolerating deep shade. Most are moisture-loving plants and need damp, but not waterlogged, soils. **Cut** out old stems in spring or summer and divide in spring if overcrowded. (*see p.395*). **Sow** seed (*see p.391*) in a cold frame in spring, although germination can be haphazard. **Propagate** by division of existing clumps but ensure plenty of roots are taken with the divisions (*see p.395*). Care should be taken when handling these plants because of the sharp edges to the leaves.

Gahnia sieberiana (Red-fruit Saw Sedge)
↕1.5–3m (5–10ft) ↔ 1.5–3m (5–10ft), is a native alternative to the weedy Pampas Grass

Hakonechloa macra

Hakone Grass

THIS BRIGHTLY COLOURED GRASS brings warmth and light to low-level plantings or the front of a garden, forming a dense mound of narrow, arching, pale green leaves and producing reddish-brown flower spikes in summer. It is a deciduous perennial, flushed with orange and rust in autumn, and slowly spreading to form mats. The leaves remain on the plant well into winter and often keep their colour, forming a bright splash in winter. This is one of the most attractive ornamental grasses to grow in containers on a patio, forming a neat, bushy mop of gently arching foliage that will almost completely cover its pot. There is only one species and a cultivar with variegation is available.

Hardiness Fully frost hardy ❄❄❄.

Cultivation Grow in fertile soil enriched with well-rotted organic matter, or loam-based potting compost, in full sun or partial shade. **Cut off** the old foliage in autumn if its winter show is not wanted, or in spring. **Divide** plants (*see p.395*) in spring.

Hakonechloa macra 'Aureola' 🏆
↕35cm (14in) ↔ 40cm (16in), leaves flushed red in autumn, is best grown in partial shade

Helictotrichon

Barley

FORMING TUSSOCKS OF LEAVES in shades of blue-grey or mid- to light green, these grasses come from open sites, often with poor soils. They are particularly suited to the conditions offered by rock gardens or gravel plantings, but are also happy in gardens with well-drained soil. There is one species that is commonly grown, and it is an evergreen perennial. In summer, upright or nodding clusters of flowers glister in the light; these age to a straw colour. Blue Oat Grass, *Helictotrichon sempervirens*, forms a dense, fine clump of tightly rolled leaves. Its flattened spikes of flowers, tinged with purple, have a graceful, nodding habit. These grasses make good specimens and associate well with purple or silver foliage plants.

Hardiness Fully frost-hardy ❄❄❄.

Cultivation Grow in well-drained, poor to moderately fertile soil, preferably alkaline (limy), in full sun. **Cut** back dead foliage and flowers in spring. **Sow** seed (*see pp.391–392*) in spring in containers a cold frame or on a windowsill. **Divide** (*see p.395*) in spring.

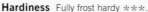

Helictotrichon sempervirens 🏆 (Blue Oat Grass)
↕to 1.4m (4ft) ↔ 60cm (24in), evergeen, grey-blue leaves fade in autumn (*see above*), flower spikes in early and midsummer

MPERATA

lood Grass, Japanese Blood Grass

HIS GRASS COMES FROM HIGH RAINFALL AREAS of ustralia and New Guinea, despite what is implied y one of its common names. It is a slender, upright erennial, which spreads by an underground rhizome. he leaves are narrow and erect and can be rolled r opened out flat. The most sought after form is *nperata cylindrica* 'Rubra' which has blood-red liage for most of the upper portion of the foliage. his looks particularly effective if seen with sunlight ehind it. Alternatively, use it as an erect highlight nerging from a grey ground cover such as Lamb's ars (*Stachys, see p.328*).

ardiness Frost-hardy ❄❄ to frost tender ❄.

ultivation Grow in a moist spot in a well-drained soil that is asonably fertile. **Plant** in full sun or partial shade and shelter om hot, drying winds. **Cut** back hard in spring every few years to courage rejuvenation of large clumps. Alternatively, lift and divide e clumps (*see p.395*). **Propagation** is by division of the clumps by lifting suckers beyond the main clump. Propagation is done in ring by division of the clumps or by lifting suckers beyond the main ump (*see p.395*).

mperata cylindrica **'Rubra'**
30–90cm (1–3ft) ↔ 30cm (1ft), is one of the few ornamental rasses with red foliage ❄

MICROLAENA STIPOIDES

Weeping Grass

THIS IS A SLENDER, PERENNIAL GRASS that spreads by way of a rhizome. The foliage is mid- to dark green and faintly hairy. The summer flowering stems are long and arching and have a distinct pendulous habit to the tips, giving rise to the common name. This Australian grass is sometimes used as an alternative to traditional grasses in lawns. Unfortunately, it will not withstand heavy foot traffic, nor regular mowing and does best in shady areas. It is an excellent colonising ground cover, however, and can be used as such. Here it can be mowed two or three times a year to keep it low and tidy.

Hardiness Frost hardy ❄❄.

Cultivation Grow in well-drained soil in partial shade. **Trim** with hedge clippers or mow at least annually to help keep it tidy (*see p.390*). **Sow** seed (*see pp.391–393*) in spring in containers. Take divisions or runners in spring (*see p.395*).

Microlaena stipoides
↕10–60cm (4in–2ft) ↔ 20cm–1m (8in–3ft), makes a thick, grassy groundcover in shade

MILIUM

Wood Millet

MAINLY WOODLAND GRASSES, these are a small group of annuals and perennials. The leaves are sometimes quite broad, and yellow-green to light green. Open, delicate flower clusters appear from spring to midsummer. Milium adds a bright splash of colour to herbaceous borders or the dappled shade at the edge of a garden bed. Plants with dark green leaves, such as astilbes (*see p.194*) or some hostas (*see pp.206–261*), will highlight the leaf colour. *Milium effusum* 'Aureum', is named for E. A. Bowles – a famous gardener and writer – with smooth, flat, arching, golden leaves, at their best in early spring, fading slightly as summer goes on. Miliums associate well with other grasses such as pennisetums (*see p.351*).

Hardiness Fully frost-hardy ❄❄❄.

Cultivation Grow in fertile, moist but well-drained soil with plenty of organic matter. Position in partial shade; may be grown in sun if the soil remains moist at all times. **Sow** seed (*see pp.391–393*) outdoors in spring. **Divide** plants (*see p.395*) in early spring and early summer.

Milium effusum **'Aureum'** ♀ (Bowles' Golden Grass)
↕to 60cm (24in) ↔ 30cm (12in), perennial with slender, nodding, golden flower spikes from late spring to midsummer

Miscanthus

GRACEFUL SPECIMEN PLANTS in gardens, these wonderful grasses add height without overpowering other plants. They bring movement and a rustling sound in the lightest breeze, and although they look delicate, the flowering stems stand up well to wind; this and their often fine autumn colour gives them added value late in the season. Miscanthus form large clumps of arching, narrow, light green foliage. Many cultivars of *Miscanthus sinensis* are widely grown. During late summer and autumn, they produce large, distinctive tassels of silky, hairy flowers, some red-tinted, others silvery. These grasses are deciduous, but the dying foliage of many develops russet or golden tints in autumn.

Hardiness Fully frost-hardy *** to frost-hardy **.

Cultivation Tolerant of most conditions, but they grow best in fertile, moist but well-drained soil in full sun. May be slow to settle in. **Protect** from excessive winter rains. **Cut** old foliage to the ground in early spring before growth starts. **Sow** seed (*see pp.391–392*) in spring in a cold frame or on the windowsill. **Divide** plants (*see p.395*) as new growth emerges in spring.

Miscanthus sinensis 'Zebrinus' (Zebra Grass)
↕↔ to 1.2m (4ft), the most spreading of several striped cultivars, lighter bands on leaves in summer ***

DIVIDING A LARGE CLUMP
Cutting up the rootball and replanting will both rejuvenate the centre of the clump and help to control its spread. A saw may be needed for tough roots.

Miscanthus sinensis 'Gracillimus' (Maiden Grass)
↕ 1.3m (4½ft) ↔ 1.2m (4ft), dense, fine leaves with good bronze tints in autumn, may not flower in cooler summers ***

Miscanthus sinensis 'Silberfeder'
↕ to 2.5m (8ft) ↔ 1.2m (4ft), abundant flowerheads that age to silver and are retained into winter, particularly dislikes wet soil ***

Molinia caerulea

Purple Moor Grass

ONLY THIS SPECIES is grown in gardens, but there are a number of different varieties. These are tall and slender grasses, making excellent structural plants for mixed and herbaceous gardens, or for the far edges of informal ponds. They are grown for their attractive habits, forming clumps of narrow, dark green leaves, and for dense, purple flower spikes, which are held on graceful, arching, golden stems over a long period from spring to autumn. The flowerheads and leaves in some cultivars turn glorious shades of golden yellow in autumn, but the flowering stems do not usually last into winter. A beautiful way to highlight the purple flowers and yellow-tinted stems is by growing tall, pale blue delphiniums (*see pp.238–239*) behind it.

Hardiness Fully frost-hardy ***.

Cultivation Grow in any moist but well-drained soil, preferably acid to neutral (lime-free), in full sun or partial shade. **Sow** seed (*see pp.391–393*) in spring in containers in a cold frame or on the windowsill. **Divide** plants (*see p.395*) in spring and pot up until they become established and then replant in the garden.

Molinia caerulea* subsp. *arundinacea
↕ to 1.5m (5ft) ↔ 40cm (16in), a variegated leaf form of this grass is available

ᴾENNISETUM

ountain Grass

HESE ORNAMENTAL GRASSES are grown for their ·athery clusters of flowers or overarching stems, roduced in summer and autumn and popular in esh and dried flower arrangements. Several types f these clump-forming perennials and annuals are rown. The evergreen fountain grass, *Pennisetum lopecuroides*, up to 1.2m (4ft) tall, has flat, dark reen leaves, with bottlebrush-shaped, bristly owerheads in yellowish-green to dark purple. The naller, deciduous fountain grass, *P. orientale*, has istinctive, pink flowerheads and combines well with Mediterranean plants such as lavenders (*Lavandula, e p.80*). Care should be taken about where these rasses are planted as they can self-sow.

ardiness Fully frost-hardy *** to very frost-tender ❄.

ultivation Grow in light, reasonably fertile soil in full sun. **Cut** back ead growth in spring. **Sow** seed (*see pp.391–392*) in heat in early pring. **Divide** plants (*see p.395*) in late spring or early summer.

ennisetum alopecuroides 'Hameln'

→ 50cm (20in), compact and early flowering, dark green leaves turn olden yellow in autumn, may not survive cold, wet winters **

PHALARIS ARUNDINACEA

Reed Canary Grass, Ribbon Grass

THIS SPREADING PERENNIAL and its cultivars are widely grown. It is an erect, evergreen grass with flat leaves. From early to midsummer, it bears narrow clusters of silky, pale green flowers that age to buff. It makes highly effective ground cover, crowding out weeds, and looks at home planted by a pond or stream. This grass can be invasive, so needs plenty of space or firm control: it requires lifting and dividing regularly when grown in small gardens. There are several variegated cultivars. *Platycodon grandiflorus* (*see p.309*) is a striking plant to grow alongside these grasses – its blue flowers will be highlighted by the bright white stripes on the foliage.

Hardiness Fully frost-hardy ***.

Cultivation Tolerates any soil in full sun or partial shade. Contain its spread if necessary by planting it in a sunken, bottomless half-barrel. **Cut** back the dead foliage in spring. Variegated types may revert to plain green foliage in midsummer; cut down all but young shoots in early summer to encourage new, variegated foliage. **Divide** plants (*see p.395*) from mid-spring to midsummer.

Phalaris arundinacea var. *picta*

↕ to 1m (3ft) ↔ indefinite, variable, white-striped leaves, classic pond- and stream-side plant where space is not a problem **

PHRAGMITES AUSTRALIS

Common Reed

THIS IS AN EVERGREEN, perennial grass that can reach as much as 3m (10ft) tall. It is bamboo-like, having erect stems with long, thin, narrowly pointed foliage emerging regularly along the stem. The flower clusters are carried at the top of each stem in summer and into autumn. These are quite large and showy and the creamy plumes wave in the breeze. Stems usually die after flowering, although there are always plenty of young shoots coming on to replace them. This plant is adapted to wet conditions and grows in water up to about 2m (6ft) deep.

Hardiness Frost hardy **

Cultivation Grow in full sun in a permanently wet spot from low-lying ground to below water line inside a pond or dam. **Prune** this grass minimally; remove any damaged or dead shoots at any time of year (*see p.382*). **Divide** in late autumn to late winter (*see p.395*).

Phragmites australis

↕ 2–3m (6–10ft) ↔ 2–5m (6–15ft), makes great wildlife habitat, but is probably best for very large water features only

Phyllostachys

Black, Golden, or Zigzag Bamboo

Valued for their graceful forms, fine stems, and rustling foliage, these medium to large, evergreen bamboos can be included in almost any garden. They spread by underground stems (rhizomes) to form expanding clumps, but can become invasive. Phyllostachys can be grown in garden beds or in containers outdoors. They have been used as an elegant alternative to traditional hedging plants. These bamboos are particularly noted for their grooved, beautifully coloured stems: brilliant yellow in *Phyllostachys aureosulcata* 'Aureocaulis' or black in *P. nigra*. They often grow in a zig-zag fashion and have a branching habit, bearing fairly small leaves.

Hardiness Fully frost hardy ✻✻✻.

Cultivation Grow in well-drained soil enriched with well-rotted organic matter. Position in full sun or dappled shade. In containers, use a quality potting mix and feed with a liquid fertilizer monthly. **Shelter** from hot, drying winds that can scorch leaf edges. **Cut out** some of the old canes each year. **Divide** clumps (*see p.395*) in spring.

Phyllostachys aurea ♀ (Golden, or Fishpole Bamboo)
↕2–10m (6–30ft) ↔ indefinite, stiffly upright young canes are bright to mid-green, maturing to brownish-yellow

Phyllostachys nigra ♀ (Black Bamboo)
↕3–5m (10–15ft) ↔ 2–3m (6–10ft), arching, slender young canes are green, turning to shiny black over two years

Pleioblastus

Most pleioblastus are dwarf only in relation to other bamboos, most being 1–1.5m (3–5ft) in height although the pygmy bamboo, *Pleioblastus pygmaeus*, grows to only 40cm (16in) tall. This generally reduce stature, however, makes them ideal bamboos for containers, as they will not appear top-heavy. Growin them in large pots also has the advantage of restraining their vigorously spreading habit, the pygmy bamboo being a particular offender in this respect. *P. auricomis* and *P. variegatus* are naturally more restrained, especially in cooler climates. They make dense thickets of erect, leafy canes, and while they will thrive in the dappled shade of deciduous trees, they should be used cautiously in gardens.

Hardiness Fully frost-hardy ✻✻✻.

Cultivation Grow in moist, well-drained soil enriched with well-rotte organic matter. Position in full sun or partial shade, sheltered from ho drying winds that may scorch leaf edges. **Restrain** their spread by confining the roots if necessary (*see p.343*). **Take** root cuttings in spring and plant out widely spaced, keeping the soil reliably moist unt plants are established.

① ***auricomus*** ♀ ↕↔ to 1.5m (5ft), leaves edged with fine bristles ② ***variegatus*** ♀ ↕75cm (30in) ↔ 1.2m (4ft), leaves hairy, pale green canes

ᴾOA

ʼHIS LARGE GENUS OF GRASSES is represented in nearly l parts of the world. They can be annual or perennial nd are most often tufted or tussocky. Some species ave rhizomes, while others are stoloniferous, meaning ıey have runners. Foliage is very narrow and upright to ghtly arching. Flat or rolled, the leaves are green to lue-green. The flowers appear above the foliage in ›ring or summer. Many species have a dormant period ı autumn and winter where the dried, straw-coloured ›liage remains above ground. While many are quite nall, a number are tall and showy and are used in rivate and public gardens.

ardiness Fully frost-hardy ✻✻✻ to frost tender ✻.

ultivation Grow in any well-drained soil in full sun or partial shade. ost can withstand periods of dryness. **Rejuvenate** old clumps by cutting near ground level in spring (*see p.382*). Alternatively, clumps can be ırnt in autumn or early winter. Another technique is to pull all the dead aterial out by hand. **Sow** seed (*see p.391*) in spring in containers or ıto a seedbed and prick out when large enough. **Divide** clumps in early ›ring, retaining as much root with the divisions as possible (*see p.391*).

ᴾoa labillardieri
↔ 60cm–1.2m (2–4ft),forms a large tussock of green to blue-reen foliage

PSEUDOSASA

GROWN FOR THEIR ERECT, WOODY CANES, this small group of robust, thicket-forming bamboos require quite a bit of space, such as in a large garden. They do have features that strongly recommend them in spite of this, making excellent screening plants to hide ugly structures, such as sheds or compost heaps. Cooler climates help to keep them clump-forming rather than invasive, but *Pseudosasa amabilis* may look ragged if not sheltered. The leaf sheaths tend to remain on the stems for some time, giving a striped appearance. The leaves are generally large, lance-shaped, and mid- or dark green. Rarely, lax clusters of small spike-like green flowers are produced.

Hardiness Fully frost-hardy ✻✻✻.

Cultivation Grow in moist but well-drained, fertile soil; *P. japonica* tolerates poor, dry, or wet soils. Position in sun or partial shade. **Divide** the clumps (*see p.395*) in spring and keep the divisions moist until they are well established. **Cut** back plants if they flower, and apply fertilizer and a deep organic mulch.

Pseudosasa japonica 🏆 (Arrow Bamboo)
↕6m (20ft) ↔ indeterminate, canes are olive green when young and mature to pale beige, stands up well to winds

SASA

↕to 2m (6ft)
↔ indefinite

THESE THICKET-FORMING bamboos are small to medium in height, and grown as much for their handsome foliage as for their canes. The leaves are large and turn white and dry around the edges from late autumn onwards, giving a variegated appearance. Sasas are useful ground-cover plants, or as a hedge if you have the space. The moderately spreading *Sasa veitchii* is invaluable under trees, tolerating deep shade: its natural habitat is in damp hollows in woodland.

Hardiness Fully frost-hardy ✻✻✻.

Cultivation Tolerant of most sites and soils, except for dry soils in full sun. Dig in well-rotted organic matter before planting. **Contain** its spread by growing in a large tub sunk in the soil. **Divide** plants (*see p.395*) in spring, or cut off pieces of rhizomes (underground stems).

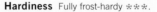

Sasa veitchii
↕90cm–1.5m (3–5ft) ↔ indefinite, slender, purple canes are round and smooth with a fine bloom, bristly sheaths protect new leaves

Schoenoplectus

Bullrush, Club-rush

THIS GROUP OF SEDGES includes both annuals and evergreen perennials, suitable for a bog garden or as aquatic plants in still or gently moving water. They are valued mainly for their stems and for their grassy leaves. Growing in planting baskets around the edges of a pond, the narrow foliage makes an interesting textural contrast to the broader leaves of water irises (*see pp.264–267*). The brown flowers, which are borne from early to late summer in clusters, are a fairly low-key display. Among those grown is the variegated club-rush *Schoenoplectus lacustris* 'Zebrinus': striking stems are reminiscent of tiny tide-marker poles rising from the water.

Hardiness Fully frost-hardy ❄❄❄.

Cultivation Grow in fertile, wet soil or in water to a depth of up to 30cm (12in), in a position in full sun. **Restrict** growth in small ponds by cutting back the roots every year. **Cut** out any plain green stems to the ground on variegated rushes. **Propagate** by uprooting and planting out sections of underground stem (rhizome) from mid-spring to midsummer.

Schoenoplectus lacustris 'Zebrinus'
↕1m (3ft) ↔ 60cm (24in), perennial, almost leafless stems arise at intervals from rhizomes

Semiarundinaria

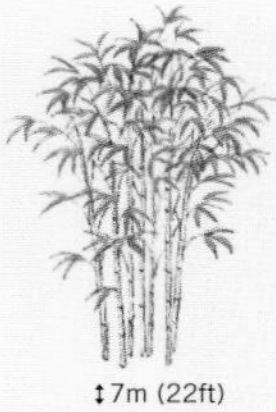

↕7m (22ft)
↔2m (6ft)

THESE ARE TALL, UPRIGHT bamboos, forming thickets in warmer climates, but clumps in cooler climates. These bamboos are at home in a woodland garden, making elegant companions to slender, small-leaved trees such as birches (*Betula, see p.28*). Their strongly vertical forms also make fine informal screens if you have the space. The leaf sheaths often hang onto the canes by the bases for some time before falling. With *Semiarundinaria fastuosa*, the lower levels of its canes are bare of leaves, making it ideal to position among lower plants in a garden. The glossy, mid-green canes have purple-brown stripes that are most prominent when the leaves are young.

Hardiness Fully frost-hardy ❄❄❄ to frost-hardy ❄❄.

Cultivation Grow in well-drained, reasonably fertile soil, adding plenty of well-rotted organic matter. Position in full sun or light shade. **Divide** clumps (*see p.395*), or uproot and plant out sections of underground stem (rhizome) in spring.

Semiarundinaria fastuosa ♀ (Narihira Bamboo)
↕to 7m (22ft) ↔ 2m (6ft) or more, glossy, mid-green leaves, sheaths reveal a polished, deep-red interior when they open ❄❄❄

Stipa

Feather Grass, Needle Grass, Spear Grass

THIS LARGE GROUP OF PERENNIAL GRASSES includes evergreen and deciduous types that form lax tufts of narrow foliage, above which tall flower stems rustle and wave. The growth habit alone is appealing; the flowering display in summer and early autumn is spectacular, ranging from the ethereal, drooping flowers of *Stipa arundinacea* to the towering stems of *S. gigantea*. Elegant in dried flower arrangements, many age to rich golden yellow and russet, keeping their colours into winter. There is a range of shapes and sizes suitable for use in most situations. Plant *S. gigantea* in a garden with the tall eupatorium (*see p.242*) to give height to the planting scheme.

Hardiness Fully frost-hardy ❄❄❄ to frost-hardy ❄❄.

Cultivation Grow in any reasonably fertile soil that is well-drained, in full sun. Dig in some gypsum on heavier soils to improve drainage. **Cut** back deciduous species in early winter or spring. **Sow** seed in containers in spring (*see pp.391–392*). **Divide** plants (*see p.395*) from mid-spring to early summer.

Stipa calamagrostis
↕1m (3ft) ↔ 1.2m (4ft), deciduous, blue-green leaves, summer flowerheads are silvery and buff to purplish-tinted ❄❄❄

tipa gigantea ♀ (Giant Feather Grass, Golden Oats)
:o 2m (6ft) ↔ 1.2m (4ft), evergeen or semi-evergreen, purple-
een flowers are gold when ripe in summer ✽✽✽

THEMEDA

Kangaroo Grass

TUFT-FORMING PERENNIAL GRASSES, these have long, arching mid- to dark green leaves. The leaves can have a purple hue to them in spring or autumn. The flower stems rise above the foliage in late spring to flower in summer. These stems, too, tend to arch, giving the plants a layered appearance, with arching flower stems above arching foliage. The seedheads are rusty-coloured and often hold a large number of seeds. These plants can be grown in rock gardens or in containers. They also look good in mixed garden beds, especially with smaller Australian plants such as Everlasting Daisy (*Chrysocephalum, see p.211*) and Flax Lilies (*Dianella, see p.225*).

Hardiness Frost-hardy ✽✽

Cultivation Grow in any well-drained soil in full sun. Tolerates dryness, especially in summer. **Rejuvenate** old tussocks by cutting back really hard in autumn or winter (*see p.382*). **Sow** seed (*see p.391*) in spring in containers. **Divide** clumps in spring (*see p.395*).

Themeda triandra
↕60cm–1.2m (2–4ft) ↔ 60–90cm (2–3ft), a tussock-forming grass for rockeries and containers

UNCINIA

Hook Sedge

GENERALLY GROWN FOR THEIR shiny, richly coloured, grassy leaves, these evergreen sedges are small perennials with a loosely tufted habit, at home in damp places. Upright, triangular to cylindrical stems bear flowers in narrow spikes, with male flowers at the top and female flowers beneath them, followed by the hooked, nut-like fruits that give the plants their common name. The most widely grown hook sedge is the russet-leaved *Uncinia rubra* which resembles the New Zealand species of carex (*see p.345*) in many ways and is also a New Zealand native. Uncinias look very attractive surrounded by a gravel mulch, although the soil below must be moisture-retentive.

Hardiness Frost-hardy ✽✽.

Cultivation Grow in reasonably fertile, but well-drained soil, containing plenty of well-rotted organic matter. Position in full sun or dappled shade. **Sow** seed (*see pp.391–392*) in heat in spring. **Divide** well-grown plants (*see p.395*) between spring and midsummer.

Uncinia rubra
↕30cm (12in) ↔ 35cm (14in), greenish-red or reddish brown foliage, russet, then dark brown to black flowers in mid- to late summer

Ferns

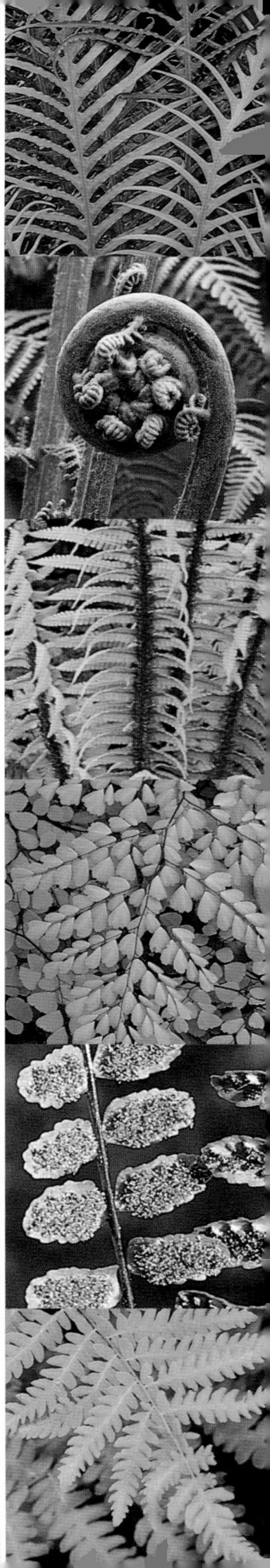

using ferns in the garden

Ferns are frequently underrated as foliage plants. They can create an impact on both a large and small scale: their outlines are bold and architectural whether used singly or *en masse*, and their leaves, or fronds, can be crimped, curled, or lacy, and provide attractive contrasts when combined with other plants. In an area of deep or dappled shade, or by the side of a pond or stream, ferns bring atmosphere to the garden and, in some cases, year-round colour.

How to use ferns in the garden

The mood that you want to create in the garden will determine where you plant ferns and how you combine them with other plants. You can create interesting effects by interspersing the fine foliage of ferns with other leafy plants, such as irises (*see pp.264–267*) or hostas (*see pp.260–261*).

In a formal setting, plant Japanese Holly Fern (*Cyrtomium falcatum, see p.362*) behind a low hedge of trimmed box (*Buxus, see p.30*); the clean, horizontal lines of the hedge create a contrast with the open, toothed and crinkly fronds.

For informality, group ferns by a pool or in a bog garden, where the delicate fronds contrast strikingly with the coarser foliage of other moisture-loving plants such as rodgersias (*see p.316*) and gunneras (*see p.254*).

Ferns can make lush ground cover in a shady or semi-shady spot under trees and shrubs, providing an interesting understorey. Choose tall, arching ferns, for example the Male Fern (*Dryopteris filix-mas see p.363*) or the Soft Shield Fern (*Polystichum setiferum, see p.365*), to screen bare or leggy stems of shrubs. Once the fronds open in spring, they create dense shade to suppress weeds.

A touch of mystery The ferns planted alongside and in-between these steps help to soften the hard lines of the stone and blend well with the mossy surfaces. They thrive in the cool, shady conditions below the walls, giving a quiet and natural feel to this obscure corner. Many ferns thrive in crevices in walls and stonework and this planting exploits that natural tendency.

Another option is to create a fernery, dedicated to ferns of different types. Choose a shady corner backed by a wall or mossy bank where few other plants grow and plant it thickly with ferns, in the ground and wall crevices.

Ferns also flatter flowering plants, particularly woodland plants that prefer similarly damp and shady conditions. Try mixing them with early-flowering lungworts (*Pulmonaria, see p.314*) in dappled shade.

Fascinating foliage

he foliage of ferns displays a striking riety of shapes and habits, from stiff ıd upright to gracefully arching. ›me have fronds that are quite athery and glossy, while others are ore fragile, for example adiantums *ee p.360*).

Ferns also possess foliage in a range ' different shades of green and with btle hues of silver and bronze. ›me have coloured spring foliage, such as Wallich's Wood Fern (*Dryopteris wallichiana, see p.363*). Clumps of several types of fern can be combined to create stunning contrasts of form and texture.

Many ferns are very attractive in spring as their new fronds begin to unfurl; they often have a brown, furry coating which glows in the spring sunshine, and makes them excellent companions for bulbous plants.

vided frond This ropean Chain Fern *'oodwardia radicans*) an example of a highly vided, classically aped fern frond.

Broad frond Strappy, undivided leaves characterize some ferns, such as this Glossy Hart's Tongue Fern (*Asplenium scolopendrium*).

Leafy frond Some ferns, like this Japanese Holly Fern (*Cyrtomium falcatum*) have fronds that are shaped more like conventional leaves.

Coloured frond Colour variation in ferns may be subtle, as with the silvery white undersides of the fronds of this Lip Fern (*Cheilanthes argentea*).

What is a fern?

Ferns are perennial foliage plants – some are evergreen and others are deciduous. Unlike most other plants, which flower and then set seed, ferns reproduce by means of tiny spores. Spore cases form on the undersides of the fronds and, when ripe, the spores fall to the soil, where they eventually germinate if the soil is moist.

Propagating ferns from spores is not straightforward. It is easier to increase most ferns, by lifting and dividing clumps (*see p.395*). Some ferns, such as *Asplenium bulbiferum* (*see p.360*) and some polystichums (*see p.365*), form bulbils on the fronds. Detach a frond of bulbils and peg it on to a tray of compost. Keep it watered and in warmth and light until plantlets form and have rooted, then detach them and pot up the plantlets as soon as they are large enough to handle.

Fern spores The spore cases that may appear on the undersides of fronds vary in colour and pattern. The ripening spores shown here are on *Polypodium vulgare*. When spore clusters are ripe, they darken. After the spores have been shed, the underside of the frond will feel rough to the touch.

Choosing a suitable planting site

:ardy ferns are generally easy to grow . moist, shady areas. As they are quite ›ugh, their needs are minimal and ıey need very little maintenance once ıey are established. Most ferns need a ːe in dappled, partial, or full shade – rong sunlight can scorch the thin onds. The hot winds that blow over ːposed sites can also cause scorching. :hoose a sheltered position. The few ːceptions to this include Lip Ferns *Cheilanthes*) and some polypodiums *ee p.364*), which tolerate some sun ıd drier conditions. Some ferns will :ow in rock crevices on a shady wall.

Good garden soil that is rich in organic matter is best for most ferns. Before planting, dig in as much well-rotted organic matter as you can to help the soil retain plenty of moisture. Most ferns require neutral to alkaline soils although there are some, such as the Hard Ferns (*Blechnum, see p.361*) that prefer acid conditions.

Humidity is also important for ferns to thrive, which is why damp corners, bog gardens, and pond-side areas, with sheltered, still air, often provide the optimum conditions for encouraging lush foliage growth.

Woodland native Many ferns, such as this Hard Fern (*Blechnum spicant*), naturally grow in established woodland where the shady conditions retain moisture in the soil. You can create a similar effect in your garden.

Select a place shaded by trees and shrubs and arrange rocks, old branches and stumps to give a natural effect. Plant ferns in crannies and pockets of soil between the rocks and stumps.

Once the ferns become established, the fernery will give the romantic illusion of an area of ancient bush.

Adiantum

Maidenhair Fern

Graceful, often finely divided foliage is the most desirable characteristic of this large group of evergreen, semi-evergreen, and deciduous ferns often grown as house plants. The fronds are usually mid-green, but may be paler green or even bronze-pink when young. They have black or brown-black stems which stand out well against the foliage. These ferns spread by underground stems (rhizomes). They require shady areas, such as under trees or large shrubs, and also flourish beside water. Show off the delicate foliage by contrasting it with the bold foliage of plants such as hostas (*see pp.260–261*). They also grow well in containers.

Hardiness Fully frost-hardy ❄❄❄ to very frost-tender ⊛.

Cultivation Grow hardy ferns in moist but well-drained, reasonably fertile soil in partial or deep shade. **Cut** old foliage from deciduous species in late winter or early spring. **Divide** rhizomes in early spring every three or four years. Pull apart the rhizomes to obtain about three new ferns and replant, or grow them on in a pot of premium potting mix with added copra peat or wetting agents (*see also p.395*).

Asplenium

Spleenwort, Bird's Nest Fern

This huge and varied group of ferns includes evergreens and semi-evergreens. The green fronds range in shape and texture from fine and feathery to long, pointed, and glossy. The hen-and-chicken fern (*Asplenium bulbiferum*) is one of many with fronds composed of tiny leaflets. Spleenworts grow from erect, sometimes creeping, rhizomes. Plant small species in wall crevices, or in a rock garden. Grow larger species among shrubs in a shady garden.

Hardiness Fully frost-hardy ❄❄❄ to very frost-tender ⊛.

Cultivation These ferns need partial shade and moist but well-drained soil, enriched with plenty of well-rotted organic matter. Most need an acid (lime-free) soil, but *A. scolopendrium,* and *A. trichomanes* prefer alkaline (limy) soils. **Divide** hardy species (*see p.395*) in spring every four or five years to obtain new plants with at least two leaves; replant them or pot up in premium potting mix.

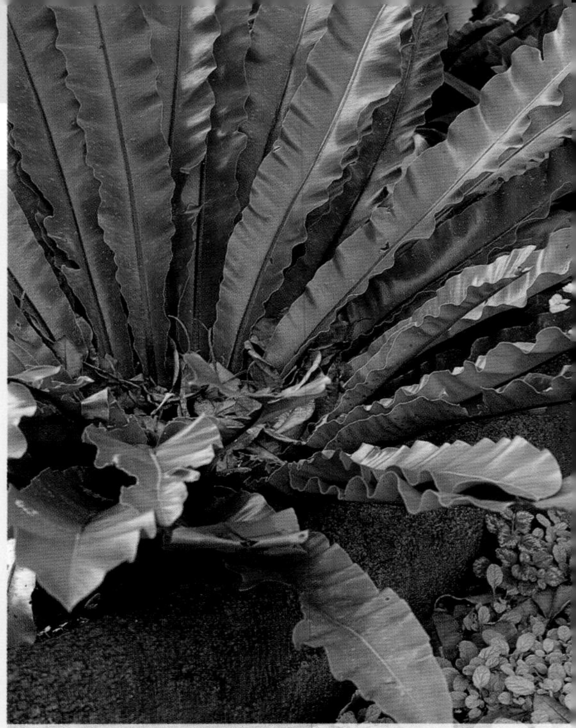

Asplenium australasicum (Bird's Nest Fern)
↕1.2m (4ft) ↔ 1.2m (4ft), evergreen fronds radiate out from a central base ❄

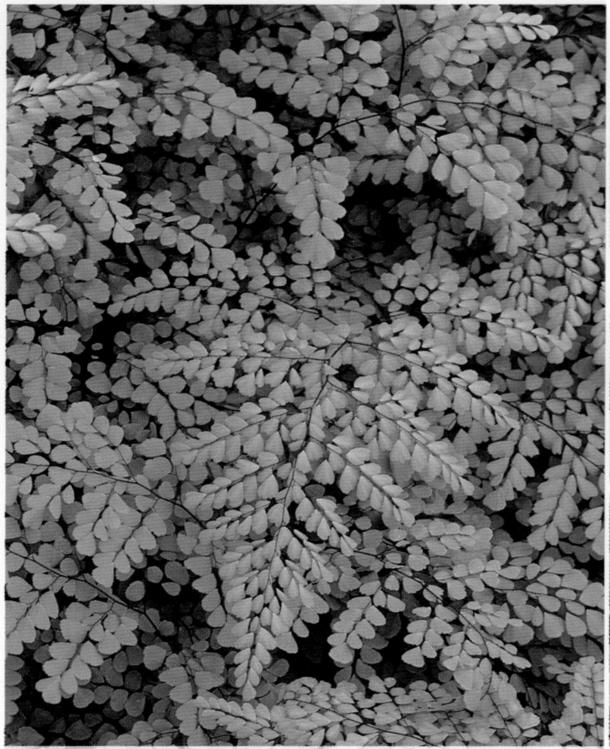

Adiantum venustum ♀ (Himalayan Maidenhair Fern)
↕15cm (6in) ↔ indefinite, evergreen fronds 15–30cm (6–12in) long, bright bronze-pink in late winter and early spring ❄❄❄

Asplenium scolopendrium ♀ (Hart's Tongue Fern)
↕45–70cm (18–28in) ↔ 60cm (24in), evergreen, fronds 40cm (16in) or more long, prefers alkaline (limy) soils ❄❄❄

Asplenium trichomanes ♀ (Maidenhair Spleenwort)
↕15cm (6in) ↔ 20cm (8in), evergreen or semi-evergreen, fronds 10–20cm (4–8in) long, rusty-red spores on undersides ❄❄❄

ATHYRIUM

ıdy Fern

HE LACY-LEAVED FRONDS of *Athyrium filix-femina* ıd its cultivars, and the silvery green, deeply divided onds of *A. niponicum* mean that these deciduous dy ferns are decorative plants for shady areas. The idribs are reddish in colour, contrasting sharply with e foliage. The ferns are found growing wild in moist oodlands or forests, and they also look best grown a woodland setting in the garden. You can create natural-looking habitat for them by placing old logs a shady garden and planting the lady ferns among em as if they were growing among fallen trees.

ardiness Fully frost-hardy ❄❄❄ to very frost-tender ❀; *A. filix-mina* is hardy to -30°C (-22°F).

ıltivation Grow lady ferns in moist, fertile soil that is neutral to id and enriched with plenty of well-rotted organic matter. Choose a e that is both shaded and sheltered. Lady ferns will tolerate all but e driest sites. **Divide** hardy species in spring every four or five years. se a spade to cut up larger clumps, obtaining several new plants with o or three leaves each. Replant the new pieces in prepared ground.

thyrium filix-femina 'Frizelliae' 🏆 (Mrs. Frizell's Lady rn, Tatting Fern)

⁰cm (8in) ↔ 30cm (12in), fronds 10–20cm (4–8in) long ❄❄❄

BLECHNUM

Hard Fern

SOME SPECIES OF HARD FERNS have spectacular foliage, which bursts upwards and outwards in a fountain shape, sometimes from a small "trunk". This trunk is in fact an upright rhizome, up to 90cm (36in) tall, and covered in black scales; the fronds grow out from the top. Other species, such as *Blechnum penna-marina* have creeping rhizomes and are more suitable as ground-cover plants. Hard ferns are generally evergreen, with tough fronds standing through the winter. They flourish in moist soil under trees or in shady gardens. The smaller species are also suitable for a shady corner in a rock garden.

Hardiness Fully frost-hardy ❄❄❄ to very frost-tender ❀.

Cultivation Hard ferns like moist soil, preferably acid, enriched with well-rotted organic matter to retain moisture. Grow hard ferns in pots of bark-based compost or ericaceous (lime-free) potting mix with plenty of added sharp sand or grit. Hard ferns need partial to deep shade. Grow tender species in large pots and keep them in frost-free conditions over winter; in mild areas, they may survive winter outdoors if protected with straw held in place with netting. **Divide** *B. penna-marina* and *B. spicant* in spring (*see p.395*); other species can be divided, but take longer to re-establish.

Blechnum penna-marina 🏆

↕10–20cm (4–8in) ↔ indefinite, creeping, fronds are 10–20cm (4–8in) long and glossy or matt, depending on the form ❄❄❄

Blechnum nudum (Fishbone Water Fern)

↕30–90cm (1–2ft) ↔ 1.2m (4ft), can be grown in most soils in light or heavy shade and in containers

Blechnum gibbum

↕↔ to 90cm (36in), trunk-like rhizomes, fronds 90cm (36in) or more long, spectacular conservatory plant ❀ (minimum 18°C/64°F)

CYATHEA

Tree Fern

THIS IS A LARGE GENUS OF EVERGREEN FERNS, with a number of commonly grown ones native to Australia and New Zealand. They develop a single, straight trunk. In some species, such as the Rough Tree Fern (*Cyathea australis*), this can be up to 1m (3ft) thick while in others, such as the Slender Tree Fern (*C. cunninghamii*) it may be less than 10cm (4in) wide on a plant 6m (20ft) tall. At the top of this emerges a broad crown of fronds that are up to 4m (12ft) long. These are mid- to dark green and very finely divided. They unfurl from the stem apex out, often in a radiating pattern.

Hardiness Frost-hardy ❄❄ very frost-tender ❀.

Cultivation These prefer shady to semi-shady positions in well-drained soils enriched with plenty of well-rotted organic matter. **Shelter** from hot, drying winds and consistent moisture, particularly in the summer months. **Remove** dead fronds from species that do not shed them naturally. **Propagation** is rather difficult with this species of fern.

Cyathea cooperi
↕↔ 6–10m (20–30ft), the Scaly or Straw Tree Fern grows well in moist, shaded areas without frosts

CYRTOMIUM

Holly Fern

THESE GROUND-GROWING RHIZOMATOUS FERNS have upright fronds made up of a long central stem and up to fifteen pairs of leaflets on either side of this. These are toothed along the margins and are quite glossy, and their passing resemblance to the leaves of hollies (*Ilex* sp. *see p.75*) has given rise to the common name. The foliage is mid- to very dark green and has a leathery feel to it. The Japanese Holly Fern (*Cyrtomium falcatum*) is the most commonly grown and will withstand even the deepest shade, although it will not tolerate frosts. It reaches up to 1m (3ft) tall. It has been known to escape from gardens into the bush if the conditions are right, so plant with caution.

Hardiness Frost-tender ❄ to very frost-tender ❀.

Cultivation Grow in well-drained soil that is enriched with well-rotted organic matter, in full or partial shade and shelter from hot, drying winds. **Remove** dead fronds that spoil the look of plants (*see p.390*). **Divide** plants (*see p.394*) in spring.

Cyrtomium falcatum
↕↔ 20cm (8in), clump-forming with upright rhizomes, fronds are 15–45cm (6–18in) long

DAVALLIA

Hare's Foot Fern

IN NATURE THESE FERNS ARE OFTEN FOUND growing over rocks or trees, while in gardens they make excellent specimens for hanging baskets. They have long, creeping rhizomes that are covered in a fine "fur" making them look like the paws of an animal and these look particularly attractive as they wrap over the edges of the container. From these rhizomes very finely divided light green fronds rise up to 45cm (18in).

Hardiness Frost-tender❄ to very frost-tender ❀.

Cultivation Grow in a shaded position out of hot, drying winds, such as a shady verandah, pergola or bush house. When growing in containers an open, friable potting mixture such as is used for orchids is ideal. **Divide** overgrown plants every few years (*see p.394*). **Use** the excess divisions to start new plants (*see p.394*).

Davallia pyxidata (Hare's Foot Fern)
↕30–60cm (1–2 ft) ↔ 1.2m (4ft), makes an interesting hanging basket specimen ❄

)ICKSONIA

oft Tree Fern

PECTACULAR, TREE-LIKE FORMS and dramatic foliage istinguish these very large, evergreen ferns. They have nick, furry "trunks" formed from a mass of old stems nd leaf bases. Each stem can be up to 60cm (24in) in iameter and has only a few roots – much of its utrients are derived in the wild from decaying matter nat collects in the fronds. The large, leathery fronds row to 3m (10ft) and sprout from the top of the em. The new fronds have a furry protective coating they unfurl in spring (*see inset, below*). Dicksonias row to their full height only in favourable conditions. hey are extremely slow-growing plants. If you invest one, take good care of it. Show it to its best dvantage as a specimen or with other ferns a shady garden.

ardiness Frost-hardy ❄❄ to frost-tender ❀.

ultivation Dicksonias need fertile soil in partial or full shade. **Hose** e trunk with water daily in spells of hot, dry weather. **Cut** off old fronds early spring. These ferns are difficult to propagate.

)icksonia antarctica ♈ (Soft Tree Fern)

:o 10m (30ft), usually much less ↔ 4m (12ft), flourishes in a ild, damp climate sheltered from wind and sun ❄❄

DRYOPTERIS

Wood Fern, Buckler Fern

THIS LARGE GROUP OF FERNS produce long, elegant fronds, often in a shuttlecock shape. Many retain their leaves over winter in mild, sheltered conditions, although they die down in less favourable climates. The evergreen fronds of the golden male fern (*Dryopteris affinis*) are pale green when young, contrasting with golden brown midribs. *D. erythrosora* has copper foliage in spring, turning dark green, with green midribs. The midribs of *D. wallichiana* are covered with dark brown or black scales, and they are particularly striking in spring against the new yellow-green fronds; these age to dark green. With their distinctive shapes, they add height to a fern garden or look good as foliage plants in a shady, mixed garden bed.

Hardiness Most fully frost-hardy ❄❄❄; a few are frost-hardy ❄❄ and very frost-tender ❀.

Cultivation Grow these ferns in partial shade in soil with plenty of well-rotted organic matter to retain moisture. **Shelter** from hot, drying winds. **Divide** mature plants (*see p.395*) in spring or autumn every five or six years; use a spade for older clumps.

Dryopteris wallichiana ♈ (Wallich's Wood Fern)

↕90cm (36in), sometimes to 2m (6ft) ↔ 75cm (30in), upright rhizome, deciduous fronds 90cm (36in) or more long ❄❄❄

NEPHROLEPIS

Fishbone Fern, Sword Fern

THESE FERNS HAVE UNDERGROUND RUNNERS that allow them to spread quite rapidly, colonizing shady areas of a garden thickly. They can also invade surrounding areas, so plant with caution if near areas of natural vegetation. The fronds have one wiry, central stem and pairs of leaflets opposite each other along this. The popular container-grown plant, sword fern (*Nephrolepis exaltata*), has cultivars with ruffled and/or divided fronds. The leaves are mid-green and generally tend to be upright or slightly arching. As suggested by its name, the Weeping Sword Fern (*N. falcata*) has weeping fronds. This, and most others, are well adapted to growing in containers.

Hardiness Frost-hardy ❄❄ to very frost-tender ❀.

Cultivation Grow in well-drained soil that is enriched with well-rotted organic matter. Partial shade to dark shade is best, although some, such as *N. cordifolia,* can withstand some sun. **Shelter** from hot, drying winds and keep the soil consistently moist. Remove any damaged or dying fronds (*see p.390*). **Divide** clumps in spring. (*see p.394*).

Nephrolepis exalta

↕1m (3ft) ↔ indefinite, will rapidly colonize a damp, shady area ❄

PELLAEA

THESE EVERGREEN FERNS GROW from an underground rhizome. Depending on the species, the rhizome can be much-branched and far-spreading, giving rise to large areas of the one plant, or short-spreading, creating tufts of fronds. These too, are variable, with some being very symmetrical, with leaflets in pairs opposite each other, while others are much-branched and divided and asymmetrical in shape and arrangement. The commonly grown sickle fern (*Pellaea falcata*) looks very similar to the sword fern (*Nephrolepis exaltata*), although the former is somewhat stiffer and has thicker leaflets.

Hardiness Frost hardy ❄❄ to very frost -ender ❅.

Cultivation The soil must be kept moist in dry periods and should not sit wet. **Grow** in full sun or partial shade and shelter from hot, drying winds. **Remove** dead or damaged fronds to keep the plant neat (*see p.390*). **Divide** clumps in spring (*see p.394*).

Pellaea falcata (Sickle Fern)
↕30–60cm (1–2ft) ↔ 1.2–2.4m (2–8ft), is an Australian fern that is not too demanding ❄

PLATYCERIUM

Elkhorn Fern, Staghorn Fern

THESE ARE UNUSUAL EPIPHYTIC EVERGREEN FERNS, with two distinct types of fronds. The sterile fronds – also referred to as nest fronds – grow more or less vertically at the back of the plant and are part of the mechanism that allows the plant to cling to trees, rocks and other surfaces. These fronds are often wavy and lobed along the top and with the bottom half curved in to form a cup or 'nest'. The fertile fronds emerge from the centre of the cluster of sterile ones. These are much divided and do resemble the horns of an elk, stag or moose. Plants are pale green and covered in a pale grey bloom.

Hardiness Frost-tender ❄.

Cultivation As epiphytes, these will need a surface to cling to. This can be timber or a slab of tree fern or the like. The young plant will need to be wired or tied to this until it has clung on by its own fronds and roots. The "nest" can be filled with sphagnum moss to assist in keeping the plant moist. **Grow** in a shady, frost-free spot, preferably one that is humid. Keep it moist and shelter from hot, drying winds. **Propagate** by division for most species (*see p.394*). The staghorn fern (*P. superbum*) is reproduced from spores, which is difficult.

Platycerium bifurcatum (Elkhorn Fern)
↕60–90cm (2–3ft) ↔ 30–60cm (1–2ft), mature clumps can be several metres across and made up of many individual plants

POLYPODIUM

THESE ADAPTABLE FERNS make excellent ground cover with their spreading habit and beautiful, sculptural fronds. Many produce relatively long, arching fronds randomly from the creeping stems, or rhizomes. Some have spores on the undersides of the fronds in contrasting colours. The mostly evergreen ferns in thi group look particularly good growing in mixed gardens or on a bank where ground cover is required. Their spreading habit helps to suppress weeds.

Hardiness Fully frost-hardy ❄❄❄ to very frost-tender ❅.

Cultivation Grow polypodiums in well-drained, moderately fertile soil, with plenty of well-rotted organic matter added. On heavy clay soils, dig in gypsum to improve drainage. **Site** in morning sun or partial shade and provide shelter from hot, drying winds. **Divide** in spring or early summer (*see p.395*) when the plants are four or five years old.

Polypodium vulgare (Common polypody)
↕30cm (12in) ↔ indefinite, thin to leathery fronds are 40cm (16in) long ❄❄❄

ᴾOLYSTICHUM

ₛhield Fern

ᵀHE FINE FOLIAGE OF THESE FERNS is usually arranged ı shapely "shuttlecocks", forming exuberant bursts of ›ften dark green fronds. The fronds tend to be highly ntricate, especially in the soft shield fern (*Polystichum etiferum*) and its cultivars, and the leaflets may end in sharp bristle. This large group of mostly evergreen erns includes plants that are 40cm–1.2m (16in–4ft) all. These all combine well with other ferns, or with ›ther shade-loving plants such as hydrangeas (*see ›p.72–73*) in a well-drained shady planting. The ›maller shield ferns are best displayed in a shady rock ;arden or in containers.

ardiness Fully frost-hardy ✲✲✲ to very frost-tender ❀.

ultivation Shield ferns prefer fertile soil enriched with ›ell-rotted organic matter, in deep or partial shade. **Protect** the lants from excessive winter wet by ensuring good drainage. In early ›pring, remove any dead fronds. **Divide** the rhizomes in spring. In ate summer or early autumn, detach fronds with bulbils for ›ropagation (*see p.359*). Once they have rooted, transfer to 8cm 3in) pots of soilless compost with added grit; keep frost-free; and ›lant out in spring.

Polystichum setiferum (Soft Shield Fern)
↕60cm (2ft) ↔ 1.2m (4ft), needs shade and ample moisture ✲✲✲

PTERIS

Brakes

THESE EVERGREEN FERNS ARE TERRESTRIAL, with a few being also naturally found in semi-aquatic environments. They have short-spreading rhizomes, resulting in most species being clump-forming. The fronds have an upright to arching, wiry main stem. The leaflets are arranged in opposite pairs along this stem. These can be few and simply linear, with smooth leaf margins. On some species they are much-divided and look particularly delicate. Most are mid- to dark green, although there are a number of variegated cultivars available where the variegation is generally silver. Many of these are valued as indoor plants. The common name is derived from the similarity of some species to the common bracken (*Pteridium* sp.).

Hardiness Frost-hardy ✲✲ to very frost tender ❀.

Cultivation Grow in partial shade or morning sun only, in a free-draining soil enriched with well-rotted organic matter and that can be kept moist year round. Little pruning is needed except to remove dead or damaged fronds (*see p.390*). **Propagate** by division in spring or early summer (*see p.394*).

Pteris tremula (Tender Brake)
↕30cm–1.5m (1–5ft) ↔ 60cm–1.2m (2–4ft), does best in filtered light or morning sun only with moist soil ✲✲

WOODWARDIA

Chain fern

LARGE, SPREADING, AND ARCHING plants, the chain ferns are so-called because the spores are arranged on the undersides of the fronds in a chain-like formation. This small group of ferns includes evergreen and deciduous species. The intricate fronds are particularly attractive as they unfurl in spring. On their upper surfaces, small bulbils may be produced over the summer near the tips. The chain fern is ideal for covering a shady bank that has moist soil. It looks particularly natural near water, and it combines well with bold foliage plants, such as gunneras (*see p.254*), that also like moist soil.

Hardiness Fully frost-hardy ✲✲✲ to frost-hardy ✲✲.

Cultivation Chain ferns like neutral, reasonably fertile, damp soil in partial shade. In warm areas, shelter the ferns from hot, drying winds. **Divide** the plants in spring using a spade (*see p.395*) or sharp knife; replant the pieces in a similar site. Alternatively, propagate from bulbils in late summer or early autumn (*see p.359*). Once they have rooted, pot the new ferns into 8cm (3in) pots of potting mix; keep them frost-free over winter, and plant them out in spring.

Woodwardia radicans 🏆 (European Chain Fern)
↕2m (6ft) ↔ 3m (10ft), evergreen, each leaflet to 30cm (12in) long ✲✲

CARING FOR PLANTS

If you choose plants for your garden wisely, you can reduce the amount of work you have to do to maintain them, but they will perform at their peak only if you give them a certain amount of attention, particularly in the growing season. In this chapter, you are guided through the basic principles of caring for garden plants, from assessing where to plant them and what to look for when you buy them, to all aspects of caring for them once they are in the ground. There are also guidelines on easy ways to increase stocks of your favourite plants.

planning your garden

Whether adapting an existing garden or designing one from scratch, there are many things to consider before rushing out and buying lots of plants. Taking time at the planning stage will help you to avoid making costly mistakes and ensure that you end up with your ideal garden.

First, make a rough sketch of your garden, preferably to scale on graph paper. Then list the things you want to include, how you want it to look, how you intend using it (*see box, right*). With this information in mind, take another look at your sketch and see what changes need to be made.

Moving into a new house and then creating a garden completely from scratch can seem daunting. It does however have the great advantage of giving you complete freedom to develop your own design. Unlike an established garden that may be full of plants, a bare plot of freshly laid turf gives few clues as to what plants can be grown successfully. So it is essential to take into account the garden's location, effect of the local climate (*see p.371*), and soil type (*see pp.376–377*) before buying any plants.

If you are redesigning an existing garden, don't be too hasty in your initial assessment of the site, as you may inadvertently remove some useful plants and features. Make changes gradually, over a full year if possible, adapting existing features to your plan.

Flowers and foliage come in an infinite palette of shades, providing the opportunity to experiment with colour schemes and moods in the borders. Do your homework before buying trees, shrubs, climbers, and perennials since these can be expensive and will form the permanent structure of the garden. By comparison, annuals and biennials – including bedding plants – last for one or two growing seasons and are much cheaper, so you can ring the changes from year to year, if you wish.

When organizing the layout of your garden, try to show each plant to its best advantage. It is important not to place new plants too close together: allow room for them to reach their full size, even if it leaves a few gaps at first.

Good planning ensures a long season of colour.

Assessing your priorities in the garden

- How will you use your garden?
- Do you enjoy gardening or just want a place in which to relax?
- Do you want to maximize your planting space or increase the amount of hard landscaping for a low-maintenance option?
- Is an outdoor entertaining or dining area required?
- Informal or formal? Which garden style do you prefer?
- What should the mood of the garden be – restful or vibrant?
- If children use the garden, do they need their own play area?
- Are new paths or steps needed?
- Are you happy to grow fruit and vegetables among other plants, or do you want a separate garden?
- Is there space for a utility area for a shed and compost bins? (Hide them behind hedges or trellis.)
- Do you want a pond or some sort of water feature ?

Night lights Carefully positioned lighting allows you to continue using and enjoying the garden during the evening. Here, gentle spotlights create a pool of light that picks out the colours and textures of the plants and rocks in this naturalistic pond.

Fruit and vegetables can be combined with ornamental plants to create some stunning planting effects. Also, by growing the plants together in a garden, they will be less susceptible to attack from pests and diseases.

Quiet corners After a busy day, enjoy the peace and quiet of a secluded corner filled with scented plants. An old railway sleeper resting on a stone boulder and a brick pillar makes a simple but comfortable bench.

Choosing a style of planting

The plants are the most important element in a garden. No matter how many ornamental features you may include, the space will still look bare until the plants are in place, bringing movement and life into the garden.

There are many styles of planting to choose from and thousands of plants with which to plan a scheme. If you are looking for inspiration, one of the best ways to discover what style or theme would suit your garden is to visit gardens that are open to the public. Looking at other people's gardens will give you a good idea of different layouts and of which plants are most happy growing in the local soil and climate.

Extending the visual interest over several seasons is the key to getting the most out of a small garden. Ideally, each plant that you choose should remain attractive over many months, for example displaying spring blossom and autumn leaf colour as well as flowers, if possible.

△ **Formality and order** Large areas of hard landscaping are often a feature of formal gardens, but although it allows for easy maintenance it can look clinical. A balance can be struck with planting. Here, bricks have been set into a sweep of stone slabs to warm up the colour and to add texture, while the hard edges of the paving are softened by the large drifts of restrained planting that spill over onto the stone.

▷ **Informal charm** The free-flowing charms of the cottage garden call for an unforced naturalness and spontaneity, created by intermingling plants so that they appear to jostle for space. The plants take centre stage and are allowed to self-seed where they will. Given a free rein, they will grow together to create gardens of great charm.

Ponds and water features

Informal pond Unlike formal ponds which are regular in shape, an informal pond is designed to look as natural as possible. To help it blend into the rest of the garden, the edges may be lined with rocks, pebbles, slate, or wood. Plants that grow in the shallow water around the edge (called "marginals") conceal the outline of the pond completely, creating a lush appearance.

A water feature always adds an extra dimension to a garden, whether it is a formal or natural pond, or a half-barrel of water. It is also a magnet for wildlife – birds will bathe in the shallows, while frogs, which help to control slugs and snails, will become regular visitors.

Consider the style of pond you prefer and how it relates to the overall plan of your garden. Ponds are not easy to move once installed. To help visualize it in detail, mark the outline on the ground using rope or a length of hose. Avoid siting the pond under a tree because falling leaves will foul the water.

If you want to keep fish, ask your aquatic supplier to recommend numbers for your size of pond.

A bubble fountain is a safe option if you have young children. A pump circulates water from a shallow tank to splash over a tray of pebbles so you can enjoy the tranquil sound of water without any danger.

Using containers

Bring colour right up to the windows of your house by planting containers with an ever-changing selection of plants, from annuals and spring bulbs, to shrubs and even small trees. Choose planters, pots, and window boxes in materials that enhance, not compete with, the planting. Roots will quickly become restricted within the confines of a container, so replenish the nutrients in the potting mix and water regularly.

Bulbs in containers Most bulbs can be grown successfully in containers. These pink tulips, top-dressed with moss, can be enjoyed near the house while in flower.

Using colour in the garden

Garden flowers come in an infinitely varied and dazzling array of colours and shades. However, foliage, bark, stems, berries, and seedheads can be colourful, too, and foliage and bark often have a longer season of interest than flowers. How you combine colour is a matter of personal preference, but there are a few ways to ensure successful planting schemes. Many designers use a colour wheel for inspiration. This is simply a circle divided into six wedges, coloured in this order: yellow, green, blue, purple, red, and orange. Colours adjacent to each other on the wheel create harmonious effects, while colours opposing each other on the wheel make for lively contrasts. Yellows through to reds are warm and stimulating; while greens to purples are restful and cool.

Restricting the colour palette can produce a more pleasing effect than using very many colours, which often looks rather fussy. Strong colours attract the eye and could be used for specimen plants. Colour can be used to set a mood – reds, golds, and oranges, typical of a hot scheme, are exciting and dominant; while blues, soft pinks, and whites are soothing and subtle.

Hot reds and yellows *Kniphofia caulescens*

Cool blues *Agapanthus* 'Blue Giant'

Foliage and form

Contrasting leaves With so many colours, shapes, and textures available, it is possible to make dramatic planting schemes with foliage alone. Here, luxuriant hostas and feathery ferns combine to great effect with colourful shrubs.

Growing beautiful flowers is one of gardening's obvious pleasures, but you can have great fun designing with plants grown specifically for their attractive growth habits and strikingly shaped or coloured foliage. Unlike a brief burst of flower colour, a foliage plant will offer a long season of interest. Plants with different types of foliage can be used to build up three-dimensional layers of texture, giving even a narrow garden a feeling of depth and movement.

Create a collage of leaf shapes and sizes by planting spiky specimens, such as grasses and yuccas, next to round-leaved cultivars, such as hostas (*see pp.260–261*) and bergenias (*see p.198*). Look for subtle contrasts in leaf texture, such as glossy or hairy leaves, as well as striking variegation and complementary colours, from silver and cream to purple and gold.

Seasonal interest

The huge choice of herbaceous and annual plants available makes planning a beautiful summer garden relatively easy. Colourful gardens need not be a transient pleasure – there are many plants that provide interest over a longer period. As well as creating a permanent framework, trees and shrubs are often blessed with attractive spring blossom, followed in autumn by good leaf colour or berries and hips. There may also be attractive stems or bark to enjoy in winter. Keep the colour coming through the year with spring bulbs, commencing in late winter with snowdrops (*Galanthus, see p.247*).

Spring Blossoms (here of *Prunus* 'Kanzan') announce spring has arrived

Summer Rose blooms and perfume are a feature of the summer garden

Autumn Glorious leaf colours bring life to the autumn garden (*Acer palmatum* 'Sango-kaku')

Winter Even in winter there are many plants that flower, such as *Erysimum* 'Winter Joy'

climate and location

Jot only does the weather dictate when certain jobs can be ackled in the garden, but the local climate will determine he types of plants that will thrive in your garden. Although nany plants are adaptable, choosing ones that are most suited to your locality and particular aspects in the garden is fundamental to success. Providing suitable conditions for all the plants and matching as closely as possible their natural habitats, is both challenging and satisfying.

'he weather – temperature, frost, rain, umidity, sun, and wind – affects how lants grow and will dictate the length f the growing season. Only when the reather turns warmer can we plant out ost tender plants or start sowing seed utdoors. Colder areas tend to have ter springs, sometimes weeks later ian warmer areas farther north, as well s shorter growing seasons. Inland regions are often drier than areas by the coast. Although plants have to contend with salt spray and strong winds, coastal areas are also generally much milder.

You don't have to travel far, however, to discover significant variations in climate. There is a huge difference between the growing conditions on a sheltered valley floor compared to the exposed slopes of the surrounding hills. In the same way, while most of your garden may be warm and sunny, it may contain a range of different microclimates, where the growing conditions are modified by factors such as the shelter of a warm wall or the heavy shade cast by an evergreen tree. Such areas in the garden will need to be treated and planted differently.

Since the local climate will dictate which kinds of plants you can grow successfully, it is worth taking some time to find out what weather patterns you can expect over the course of the year. Consider joining a gardening club – gardeners are always willing to share their experiences with like-minded people and they will be a valuable source of information.

Assessing your garden

Before making any changes it is worth assessing your garden to give yourself an idea of the plants you can grow.

- How high above sea level are you? The higher you are, the colder it generally is.
- Does the garden face north or south? This will have a bearing on how much sun the garden gets.
- How shady is the garden? Is there heavy shade cast by established trees and shrubs or by the house?
- Is the garden on a slope? Cold air will gather at the bottom of a slope to cause a frost pocket (*see p.372*).
- Does it get very cold in the winter or very hot in summer? Temperature extremes can stress plants and you may have to take extra care of them.

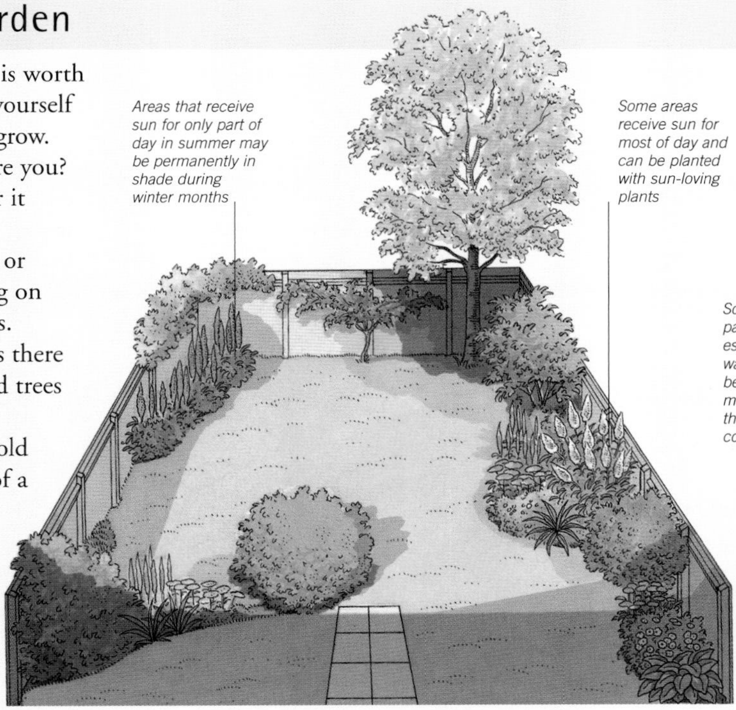

Areas that receive sun for only part of day in summer may be permanently in shade during winter months
Some areas receive sun for most of day and can be planted with sun-loving plants

South-facing garden The shade cast by the house keeps the air cool and the soil moist.

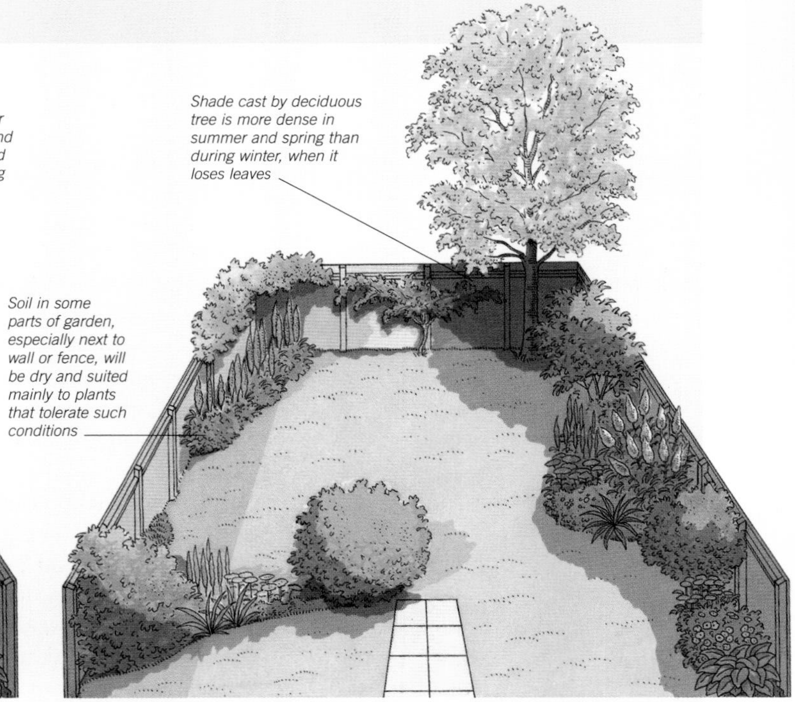

Shade cast by deciduous tree is more dense in summer and spring than during winter, when it loses leaves
Soil in some parts of garden, especially next to wall or fence, will be dry and suited mainly to plants that tolerate such conditions

North-facing garden is warm and sunny, but the soil may dry out in summer.

The dangers of frost

One of the greatest hazards that a gardener has to contend with is frost, especially in spring and autumn. An unexpected spring frost can destroy flower buds, ruining the display for the year. Tender, new shoots are also susceptible. Still, clear nights often signal that a frost is on the way, and quick action can protect vulnerable plants. If you cannot bring them under cover, loosely wrap them in some hessian, newspapers or a similar insulating material.

The incidence of late spring frosts in your area will determine the time at which it is safe to plant out frost tender plants, such as annuals. The onset of autumnal frosts determines the end of their growing season.

Where there are low points in the garden, frost pockets (*see below*) may form. If there is a frosty hollow in the garden, avoid growing fruit there and choose plants that are fully hardy (*see right*) and will not suffer in low temperatures.

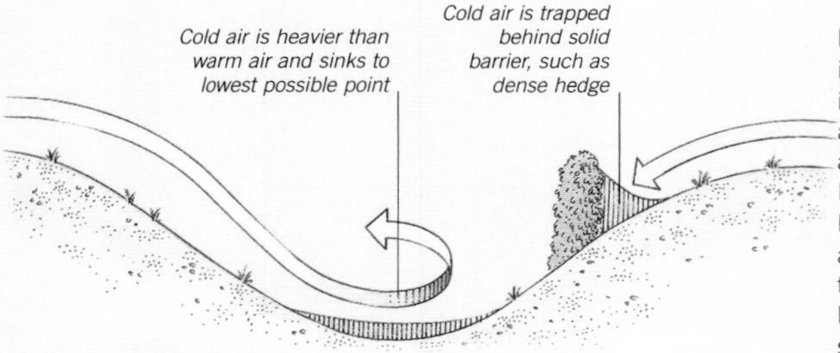

Cold air is heavier than warm air and sinks to lowest possible point
Cold air is trapped behind solid barrier, such as dense hedge

Frost pocket Cold air is denser than warm air; it always flows downhill and becomes trapped in any slight dip or hollow. Frost also collects at the bases of fences, walls, and closely planted, thick hedges, or even large objects such as a statue or solid seat.

Hardiness of plants

The hardiness of a plant refers to its ability to withstand year-round climatic conditions, including frost, without any protection. Fully frost-hardy plants withstand temperatures down to -15°C (5°F). Frost-hardy plants are happy in temperatures down to -5°C (23°F), whereas frost-tender ones prefer temperatures above 0°C (32°F) and are damaged by frost. Very frost-tender plants need shelter in conditions cooler than 5°C (41°F).

Hardier plants need less nurturing because they survive without harm in the garden all winter. The more tender plants, on the other hand, have to be brought under cover before the first frost in autumn and can be relocated or planted out only when all danger of frost has passed, in spring. This varies from one area to another, but is generally around late spring to early summer.

Snowy shrub Although it looks pretty, heavy snow can weigh down branches, causing them to break. After a fall of snow, go out with a broom and knock it off the plant. If more falls are forecast, tie vulnerable branches into the main stem – this works well with conifers.

Helping plants to survive the winter

Young or slightly tender plants need protection to help them survive a severe winter. Protect top-growth by covering plants with hessian sacking, plastic bubble wrap, or some layers of newspaper.

A thick mulch of garden compost spread over the crowns of plants, such as herbaceous perennials that have died down over winter, will give the plants protection from several degrees of frost.

Cloches, usually made of glass or plastic, are excellent for keeping a few degrees of frost off plants.

Where the site is exposed, protect plants from winds with a shadecloth supported on stout stakes.

Frost-tender plants (*see above, right*) must be taken over winter into an unheated glasshouse in a higher part of the garden. The plants can then be brought out during the day and moved into the garden permanently when frosts have passed.

Very frost-tender plants (*see above, right*) are probably best grown only in the warmer districts. An alternative option is to shift them over winter into a greenhouse or a conservatory where gentle heating will help to keep the temperature well above freezing.

Plastic cloche This cloche is made of heavy plastic and wire and protects seedllings from frosts. It can be removed during the day to maximise sunlight to the young plants. Ventilation holes allow air circulation to reduce risk of fungus diseases.

Corrugated cloche Clear corrugated sheeting is used here to protect young plants from frosts, as well as acting as a miniature glasshouse. Held in place with curved metal stakes, this style could be made by any handy person. The open ends allow good air movement.

Wind and its effect on your garden

Strong winds can have positive benefits, helping to disperse pollen and seeds. However, they can be a destructive force causing damage to plants, especially young ones that have yet to become established. They can also discourage beneficial insects that help to control pests. Although they have a cooling effect on plants, strong winds increase the rate at which water vapour is lost from plants' leaves (called desiccation), causing browning and leaf drop.

When some woody plants are exposed to strong winds, their top-growth becomes unbalanced, making the plants appear one-sided. The tips of shoots and leaves are also at risk of being damaged, or scorched. The higher the wind speed, the more damage is done, with stems being broken and, in severe cases, entire plants being uprooted.

Protect vulnerable plants with a windbreak. Choose a material that will allow about 50 per cent of the wind to pass through, because a solid structure will create problems of its own (*see above*). Hedging plants are ideal, or choose open-weave fencing or shadecloth netting. For best protection, a windbreak should be 4m (12ft) tall, but a lower one would work well for smaller plants.

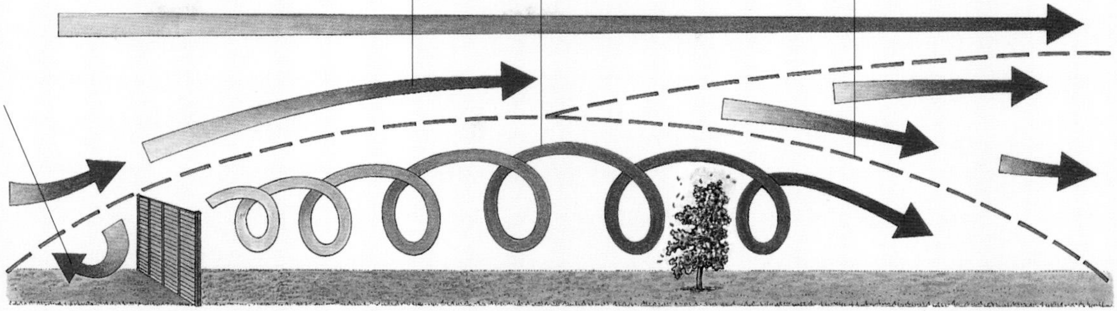
Stream of air passing over barrier whips up turbulence beneath it
Air remains disturbed for distance of twice height of barrier
Effects may extend over entire garden
As wind hits fence, air is forced up, causing turbulence

Action of wind In the same way that your washing dries quicker on a blustery day, wind rushing over your plants causes rapid water loss from the leaves. Strong winds will rock any tall, unstaked plants until their roots become loosened in the soil, while greenhouses and other garden structures may be damaged. On light, sandy soil, there is a risk of the topsoil being blown away.

The effects of shade

Shady areas of the garden can have dryish soil and plants have to cope with very low light levels.
The ground under trees poses a real challenge to gardeners, because some types of tree and hedging plant, such as conifers and other evergreens, cast deep shadow and take lots of water and nutrients from the soil. The soil at the base of walls and fences can also be shady and dry. However, if the soil is enriched by digging in plenty of well-rotted manure or garden compost (*see p.377*), and any overhanging plants are judiciously pruned, a number of beautiful plants that can be grown, for example *Cyclamen hederifolium* (*see p.221*). You may also have areas of cool, moist, dappled shade – often under deciduous trees. In such conditions, there are plenty of plants that will thrive.

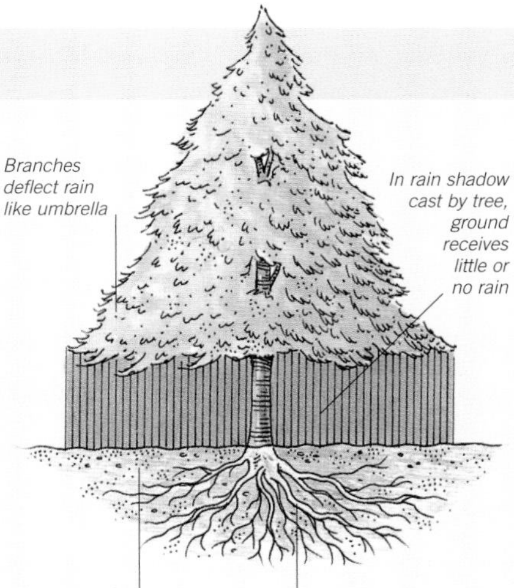
Branches deflect rain like umbrella
In rain shadow cast by tree, ground receives little or no rain
Ground under dense tree canopy receives little rain
Roots suck up moisture from area usually extending farther than spread of branches

Providing shelter

If you are planting on an exposed site, most young plants, especially evergreen shrubs and perennials, will require protection from strong winds and fierce sun until their root systems become established. If the garden does not enjoy the natural shelter of trees and hedging plants (*see above*), there are several temporary measures you can take.

Open-weave fencing provides a suitable solution, as does planting fast-growing climbers to cover trellis panels. For an instant and economical fix, make a small windbreak using mesh and canes (*see right*). For best results, erect the shelter on the windward side of the plant or, if fierce sun is the problem, on the sunny side.

Temporary shelter Staple a length of fine mesh shadecloth or hessian sacking to two long canes. Push the canes firmly into the ground around the plant. If the site is very windy, you may need to insert extra canes to stabilize the structure. Remove the shade or windbreak as soon as the plant becomes established.

buying plants

The old saying, "You get what you pay for", is never truer than when buying plants. Young plants do not have the resources to survive too many shocks and so it is essential they get a good start in life. Buying quality plants from a reputable nursery is always money well spent. You may be tempted by trays of plant 'bargains' but they may have been on the shelf for ages, starved of light, food and water and sc they will never grow as vigorously as good-quality stock.

When selecting a plant, look for one that is well-balanced, with plenty of healthy growth and, where appropriate, lots of flower buds. If the plant shows any signs of pests or disease, choose another one. Yellowing leaves may signify a lack of nutrients, a sign that the plant has not been looked after very well. Wilting leaves are caused by a lack of water; if the potting mix dries out too often the plant becomes stressed and vulnerable to pests and diseases. Gently knock the plant out of its pot and take a look at the root system. Do not buy it if the roots are tangled and crammed tight – it has become pot-bound (*see facing page*) and probably will not grow properly.

Bare-root plants

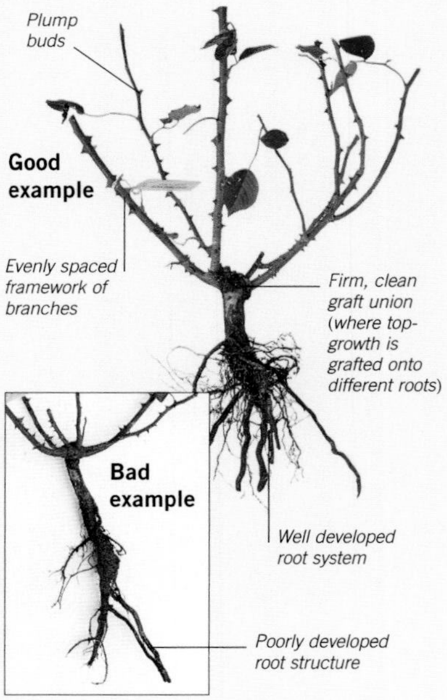

Bareroot plants, like this rose, should have a good root system to support the plant. To encourage fibrous, feeding roots to form, trim the longest of the thick roots back hard.

Woody plants, including deciduous trees, shrubs, and roses, are often sold as bare-root plants. Grown in the ground rather than in pots, they are cheaper to produce in bulk and the nurseries can pass on their savings to their customers. The plants also tend to be bigger and stronger than similarly priced container plants. Bare-root plants are available in nurseries, but they are generally sold by mail order.

The plants are dug up in their dormant season, cleaned of soil, wrapped for posting and dispatched in time for planting in winter. Unwrap and plant as soon as they arrive to prevent the roots drying out – they should then be well established before the spring. If you cannot plant immediately, store them for a few days wrapped in damp newspaper in a cool shed.

Container-grown plants

Most plants are available in containers, from annuals in punnets to large shrubs and trees in pots. The big advantage to buying plants grown in this way is that they are available all year round.

Most hardy container-grown plants can be planted out at any time of year. The exception is frost-tender annuals, which often go on sale in spring.

If you cannot resist buying, grow the plants on under cover, and move them outdoors after the last frost, usually in late spring or early summer. In hot, dry seasons it may be best to postpone planting until cooler and moister times.

When choosing a container-grown plant beware of neglect – signs include algal growth on the potting mix, pests and disease, a stunted appearance, dry potting mix, and yellowing leaves. If you can, gently knock the plant out of its container and inspect the root system. If it looks pot-bound (*see facing page*), don't buy it.

Healthy shrub Look for strong, bushy growth.

Sickly pot plant

Healthy annuals have lots of flower buds.

Pot-bound plants

Pot-bound roots may be visible on surface of potting mix

Pot-bound root ball The tangled mass of roots indicates this plant has been in its pot for too long. Such severe constriction may inhibit the plant's ability to take up water and nutrients.

Before buying a plant, do not be shy about gently knocking it out of its pot to check the root system. If lots of roots are growing through the drainage holes, or you find a solid mass of roots growing round the outside of the root ball, then the plant is pot-bound. In this state, the plant's growth will have been severely stunted and it may never fully recover and thrive.

If you find you have purchased a pot-bound plant, then tease out the roots carefully and cut off some of the thicker sections. This will encourage new roots to venture out into the surrounding soil. Before planting it, soak the root ball in a bucket of water for a couple of hours and water the planting hole.

Water-garden plants

Always take care to introduce only healthy plants into a pond, otherwise the delicate ecosystem may be disturbed by pests or diseases carried in on the plants. Choose those with clean, green leaves and a good crown (the point where the leaves and roots meet) with several buds. If leaves are slimy or yellow, or if the water the plants are growing in is murky, then select another plant.

The best time to buy water-garden, or aquatic, plants is in late spring and early summer so that they have a chance to become established before winter sets in. Most aquatic plants tolerate being out of the water for only a short time. Take them home in a plastic bag and put them into the pond as soon as possible.

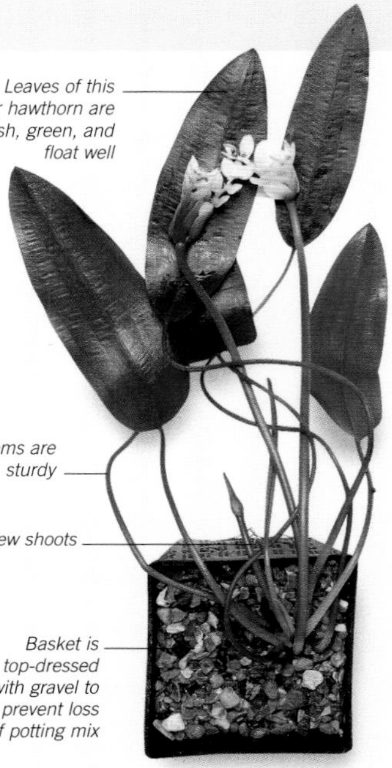
Leaves of this water hawthorn are lush, green, and float well
Stems are sturdy
New shoots
Basket is top-dressed with gravel to prevent loss of potting mix

Aquatic plants help to keep the pond healthy.

Root-balled plants

Netting stops roots drying out

Evergreens, like this conifer, are often sold root-balled

Root-balled plants are grown in open ground rather than in pots. They are lifted with a ball of roots and soil which is wrapped in net or hessian. Some trees are sold in this way in winter by specialist nurseries, often by mail order. Check that the root ball feels firm and that the net is intact or the roots may dry out. Soak the netted root ball in water for an hour, then unwrap and plant it immediately.

Bulbous plants

Spring-flowering bulbs, corms, and tubers are sold in autumn, whereas summer-flowering cultivars will be available in spring. Always buy bulbs as soon as they go on sale, when they will be in prime condition (firm, plump, and blemish- and rot-free). The longer you delay, the more dried out they will become, and the plants will not perform as well. Inspect the bulbs and reject any that show signs of disease, such as soft patches.

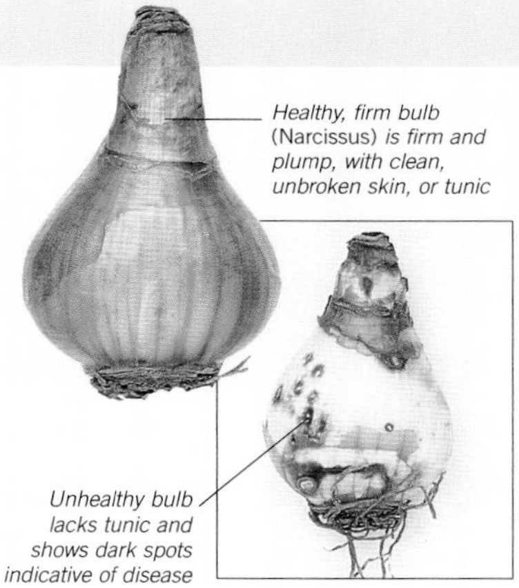
Healthy, firm bulb (Narcissus) is firm and plump, with clean, unbroken skin, or tunic
Unhealthy bulb lacks tunic and shows dark spots indicative of disease

Mail-order plants

If buying plants by mail order, always deal with a reputable supplier, placing your order early to get the ones you want. The plants will be despatched in special packs, such as moulded, snap-shut containers, designed to keep them moist. When they arrive, open the package and check them, making sure they are healthy and the ones you ordered. Plant immediately or pot them up in potting mix and grow on for later planting.

Plants are kept moist in sealed plastic bag
Healthy plants with no sign of pests and diseases, ready to grow on

soils and compost

Soils are made from minute particles of rock and organic matter that has been weathered and broken down over time. Fertile soil is essential for healthy plant growth and success in the garden. The soil supports the plant, supplying it with water, air, and nutrients. Not every type of soil is suitable for the widest range of plants, but almost any soil can be improved over the years, especially if good garden compost is worked into it on a regular basis.

Treat the soil well and you should be able to grow a wide range of plants successfully.

It is important to know what type of soil you have in your garden so that you can grow plants that thrive in it. It is relatively easy to determine your soil type (*see right*) and its pH (*see facing page*). The soil within the garden, however, can vary so you may have to choose different plants to suit each site.

To ensure that your plants get off to a good start, it is always a worthwhile investment to condition the soil (*see facing page*) before planting with plenty of well-rotted organic matter, such as home-made garden compost (*see p.378*) or commercial soil conditioners.

Types of garden soil

The soil type you have largely dictates the plants you can grow. Soils in different sites, or even in different parts of a garden, vary in terms of their fertility, ease of cultivation, and how easy it is for plant roots to penetrate. There are several basic kinds of garden soil.

Clay soil is often very fertile, but slow-draining. Heavy clay soil can be difficult to work and will often form a crust on the surface which can make it quite difficult for water to penetrate. If you open up the structure of the soil by digging in gypsum and organic matter, clay soils can support vigorous plant growth. A mulch on the soil surface (*see p.388*) will help prevent the crust from reforming. Clay soils tend to hold nutrients well.

Sandy soil feels gritty and light, is easy to work, and warms up quickly in spring. Very free-draining, it dries out fast; nutrients can be washed out easily by rain and by watering, so it needs regular additions of organic matter and fertilizer. Mulching will help to reduce evaporation and will also add organic matter to sandy soil as it breaks down.

Loam has an ideal balance of clay and sand particles. It is the perfect growing medium – rich in nutrients and with a friable, crumbly texture that allows good drainage and water-retention.

Intermediate soil types such as clay-loam and sandy-loam are also commonly found.

Sandy soil is very light and easy to work. When it is dry it runs easily between the fingers and will not form a ball, even when wet. It feels coarse and gritty to the touch.

Clay soil is heavy, cold, and sticky when wet. In dry conditions, it sets like concrete and then cracks. Clay has a very fine texture (*inset*) and rolls into a soft ball that is shiny if smoothed.

Loam soil has a mixture of particle sizes and textures, and often a lot of organic matter. It holds water well, yet allows excess water to drain away. It will only form a crumbly ball that breaks up quite easily.

What is soil pH?

Before buying any plants, check the pH of your soil to ensure that they will thrive in it. The pH reflects the level of lime in the soil. Soils lying over limestone are rich in lime and known as alkaline, but soils over sands often become acid. Soil pH is measured on a scale of 1–14. Neutral soil, in which most plants thrive, has a pH of 7; soils of more than pH7 are alkaline (limy) while those of less than pH7 are acid (lime-free). Soil testing kits, which indicate pH by reacting with soil and changing colour (*see right*), are available from garden centres.

Soil pH affects the solubility of vital nutrients in the soil and their availability to plants. Acid and alkaline soils vary in the amounts of nutrients they contain. Plants like or tolerate different levels of lime, so some, such as azaleas and many ericas, thrive only on acid (called lime-free) soils and others, such as clematis and pinks, are happy in limy soils. The optimum soil pH for plant growth is within pH5.5–7.5.

pH scale and soil testing kits

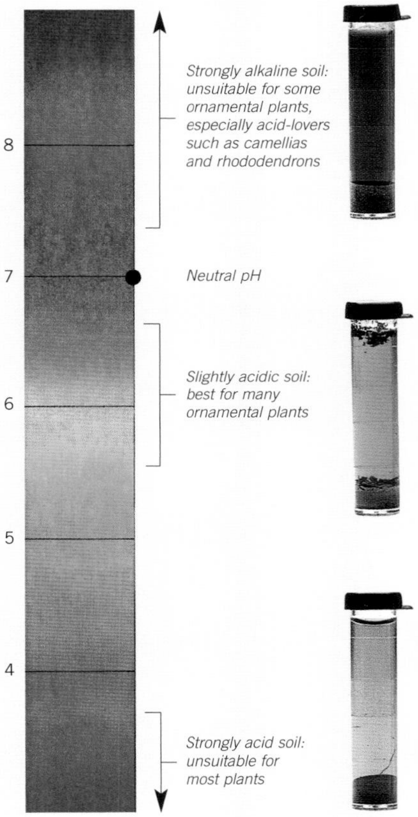

Conditioning the soil

There are many soil-conditioning materials available from garden centres. The best are bulky organic materials, like manures, composted bark, or garden compost, which improve the soil structure so that it drains freely but retains moisture in dry weather. Manures and compost also replace some of the nutrients taken up by plants or washed out of the soil. Organic matter must be well-rotted; if not, it will deplete the soil of nutrients as it rots.

The more organic matter you add to the soil, the more organisms such as bacteria and worms will populate the soil, help to work it, and improve its structure.

Well-rotted horse manure is one of the best soil conditioners, but can be hard to obtain. Making garden compost is easy and costs nothing (*see p.378*). Spent mushroom compost contains rotted manure and peat. It also has some lime, so do not use it where acid-loving plants are grown. Seaweed is an excellent conditioner because it makes the soil more friable and is rich in trace elements. Composted straw and leafmould use otherwise wasted resources, but they take a long time to rot. Pelleted chicken manure adds vital nutrients, but has no conditioning value since the pellets have little bulk.

Incorporating manure or other well-rotted organic matter into the soil is most effectively done by digging it in during late winter. Scatter a thick layer all over the bed and fork it in (*see right*). Alternatively, leave it as a surface mulch. This will help to reduce evaporation in summer and in the course of the year, the material will be incorporated into the soil by worms and other beneficial soil organisms.

The importance of good soil drainage

The amount of water available to plants through their roots depends on the type of soil (*see facing page*) and how free-draining it is. In well structured soils, like loam, sufficient water and air is held in the spaces, or pores, between the soil particles to supply most plants with adequate water. A soil with poor structure may dry out very quickly or become waterlogged.

For example, finely textured clay soils hold most moisture, but it is bound up in such a way that it is unavailable to plants. As a result clay soils are often poorly drained. The large pores of sandy soils make water easily available to plant roots, but it drains away quickly.

Digging in well-rotted organic matter (*see above, right*) will improve the structure of both clay and sandy soils. Drainage can also be improved by adding gypsum (*see right*).

Improving soil drainage with gypsum
You can greatly improve the drainage of heavy clay soils by incorporating gypsum and organic matter into the soil. Digging it in will open up the structure and facilitate the flow of water through the soil. Spread a good 5–8cm (2–3in) layer of organic matter and about one kilogram per square metre of gypsum over the area and dig it in with a fork. Any smaller amount will be ineffective. This should make an instant and permanent improvement to the soil aeration and drainage, making it easier for plant roots to penetrate and extract the moisture and nutrients that they need.

Making garden compost

Rotted compost is dark, friable, and odourless.

Even in the smallest garden, it is worth making your own compost – it enables you to recycle waste and return it to the garden in a form which is unsurpassed for improving soil structure and fertility. It also saves you the expense of buying proprietory soil conditioners.

To make good garden compost, you first need a suitable container. There are many compost bins on the market, but you can make one easily at home, for example from builder's pallets or old wood. The main thing to bear in mind is that the bin should be 1–1.5m (3–5ft) square, with fairly solid sides to retain heat and moisture.

The best compost is made from mixing fast-rotting, succulent material, such as grass clippings and vegetable trimmings, with drier material, such as straw and shredded newspaper, which is slower to decompose. Try to add materials in well-mixed layers.

Compost takes about a year to rot down, but the process can be speeded up if the heap is turned at least once to mix the contents thoroughly. The easiest way to do this, if space allows, is to have two bins, so you can turn the contents of one bin into the other. If the compost is slimy and smelly, mix in more "dry" material such as twigs and hay. If it is dry and not rotting, add sappy stuff or try watering it.

Garden compost ingredients

Almost any materials of organic origin can be recycled into compost. You can add any plant waste from the garden into the heap, except perennial weeds. Seedheads must be removed because seeds will survive and cause problems in future; any diseased material should be binned. Shred woody prunings, thick, fibrous stems, newspapers, cardboard, and old clothing. Vegetable kitchen waste can also be used, but meat, fish, and cooked foods will attract vermin. Litter from small pets such as rabbits, guinea pigs, or birds is suitable, but not from cats and dogs. You can also add manure and autumn leaves.

Grass clippings need to be mixed with coarser material like straw or paper.

Woody prunings are slow to rot and must first be shredded into small pieces.

Annual weeds with the seedheads removed are usable.

Kitchen waste of vegetable material only – or put in a vermin-proof bin.

Natural fibres, such as 100 per cent wool or cotton, rot quickly if cut into small pieces.

Woollen carpet must be cut into pieces and mixed with green stuff to break it down.

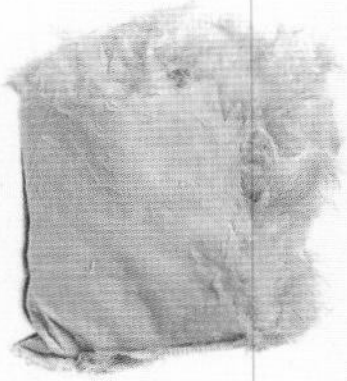

Feathers rot better if they are taken out of the pillow and mixed with other waste.

Newspapers, torn into strips, are good for mixing with soft grass clippings.

How to make leafmould

Autumn leaves rot slowly and if you have large quantities, you can compost them separately in an open bin made from a timber frame and wire netting (*see right*) or in sealed plastic sacks with a few holes punched in them. The resulting leafmould takes about two years to form. It is very crumbly and makes an excellent mulch (*see p.388*) and soil conditioner.

Leafmould bin is open to the elements.

Using a worm bin

Worms feed on organic matter and eject the waste in the form of worm casts. This process can create a fine, crumbly, nutrient-rich compost that can be used in potting mixes and as a top-dressing or plant feed.

You can buy a kit complete with worms, or make your own wormery from a dustbin. Drill drainage holes in the base and stand the bin on some bricks. Put a 15cm (6in) layer of garden soil in the bottom and add a large potful of compost worms, not garden earthworms. Top with a small layer of garden or kitchen waste, allowing the worms to digest each layer before adding more. Worms don't like citrus fruits or onions, but do like lime, such as crushed egg shells. When the bin is full, sieve out the worms and start again.

planting basics

iive your plants a good start in life and there is every hance that they will grow strong and healthy. The first and nost important step is to create a welcoming environment or their roots, encouraging them to spread out into the urrounding soil where they will take up water and nutrients.

ood planting practice results in healthy plants.

ll plants appreciate being planted ı a suitable and well prepared site. ienerally, the better the soil, the uicker they will become established. It best to choose plants that are suited ı the conditions you can offer. For xample, if the soil in your garden is ery light and dries out quickly, you an do much to improve its condition y enriching it with well-rotted organic natter, such as farmyard manure or arden compost (*see p.377*). However, you then opt for plants that require ch, moist soil, they will struggle and ower indifferently. You will have far etter results with plants that need free-rainage and tolerate dry conditions.

Before planting, clear the garden of weeds that could compete with your plants for water and nutrients.

Take care to ensure that each plant has room to grow to its full size. Check the mature height and spread on the plant label and mark it out around each planting hole. Fill the gaps with annual plants until they mature. If it outgrows its space, transplant it in autumn, winter or spring: dig it up, saving as much of the root mass as possible, and replant it in a previously prepared site.

Plants always look more natural in a garden when grouped in odd numbers because the brain automatically sorts even numbers into pairs.

Many trees and shrubs are planted in the same way as those grown in containers (*see right*), but bare-root and root-balled plants (*see pp.374–375*) require slightly different treatment.

Plant bare-root plants in winter so they can establish before summer. Even with careful handling, they may suffer some root damage. To encourage new growth, cut damaged or dry roots back; to compensate for the loss of roots, trim the top-growth back also.

Root-balled plants are best planted in autumn or winter. After soaking the root ball, remove the netting and tease out the roots. Both root-balled and bare-root plants should be planted with the old soil mark level with the surface.

Planting container-grown trees and shrubs

Container-grown plants can be planted (*see below*) at any time, so long as the soil is not waterlogged, but the best results are from autumn, winter or spring planting. If you plant in summer you must keep the roots watered while the plant establishes itself. Before planting, prune out dead or diseased growth and awkwardly placed shoots. Scrape away the top layer of potting mix from the pot to remove any weed seeds, then stand it in its pot in a bucket of water for two hours to soak the root ball thoroughly.

Dig a good-sized planting hole. Fill the hole with water and allow it to seep away. Next, fork a thick layer of well-rotted manure or garden compost into the bottom of the hole to give the plant a good start. Shrubs also appreciate the addition of some slow-release fertilizer. If the soil gets very wet in winter, improve the drainage by forking in gypsum. Gently knock off the pot, tease out the roots and place the plant in the prepared hole.

Planting at the correct depth is crucial to avoid a check in growth. With a few exceptions, you should keep the plant at the same depth as it was in its container.

It also helps to enrich the removed soil by mixing it with well-rotted organic matter. If the plant needs support, insert canes or stakes, taking care not to damage the root ball, and tie it to the stake with soft, broad, slightly flexible ties.

How to plant a container-grown tree or shrub

❶ *Soak the plant's root ball in a bucket of water for 1–2 hours before planting. Dig a hole that is at least twice as wide and one-and-a-half times deeper than the root ball. Fork in plenty of well-rotted organic matter and, if it is needed for improved drainage, some gypsum.*

❷ *Set the plant at the same depth as it was in its original pot. Use a cane to check that the root ball is level with the soil surface.*

❸ *Fill in the hole with soil. Use your heel to firm the soil around the plant to remove air pockets.*

❹ *Water the plant well to settle the soil, even if it is raining. Apply a 5cm (2in) layer of well-rotted compost or bark as a mulch over the root area to help retain moisture and suppress weeds.*

Planting non-woody plants

The principles of planting are much the same for perennials, annuals, and other plants as for shrubs (*see p.379*). However, these plants are more prone to drying out, so should be planted without delay. Some plants are sold in pots (*see below*), but annuals are usually sold in punnets, with one seedling per module to stop the roots being disturbed during planting. As soon as you buy annuals, give them a good soaking and plant them or, if there is still a risk of frost, pot them up separately to grow on under cover until it is safe to plant them out.

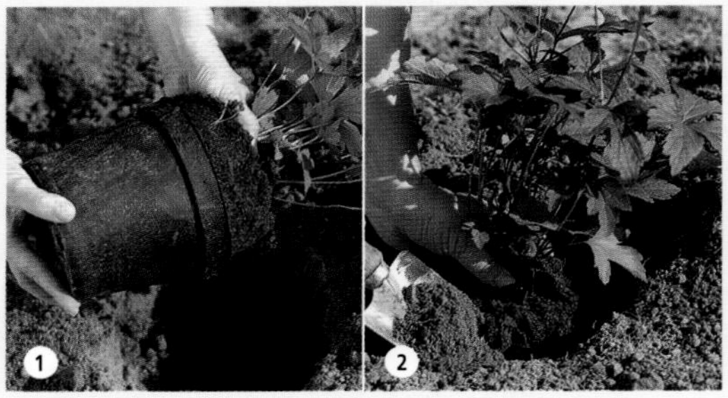

Planting a perennial
❶ *Dig a planting hole and loosen the soil around the edges. Mix some well-rotted organic matter or general fertilizer into the removed soil. Gently knock out the plant while holding the crown in one hand.*
❷ *Tease out the roots and hold the root ball level with the surface. Fill in the hole, and firm with your fingers. Water well and mulch; keep watered until plant is established.*

Planting climbers

The soil at the base of a wall or fence can be extremely dry because it is in a rain shadow, where rain rarely reaches the soil. When planting a climber, you should first improve the soil's moisture-retention by digging in plenty of well-rotted organic matter (such as garden compost). Follow the technique for planting a container-grown shrub (*see p.379*), but make sure that the planting hole is at least 15–20cm (12–18in) away from the wall. Also don't forget to angle the top of the root ball towards the wall, while keeping the crown of the plant level with the soil surface.

Before planting, fix up a support. An easy system is horizontal wires threaded through galvanized screw eyes in the wall, or trellis panels (*see p.390*) attached to battens.

Training a climber Once the climber has been planted, separate out the shoots and tie them into the supports, using garden twine. Canes pushed into the ground and angled towards the wall will encourage the shoots to grow towards it.

Planting bulbs

There are a couple of important points to remember when planting bulbs. Firstly, most should be planted at a depth equivalent to three times their size. For example, if a bulb stands 5cm (2in) tall, then there should be 10cm (4in) of soil on top of it, and the planting hole should therefore be 15cm (6in) deep. Check the label because some bulbs, such as nerines and some lilies, prefer to have their tops level with the soil surface.

If bulbs are planted at the wrong depth, they may fail to flower (a condition referred to as "blindness"). Blindness can also occur when the bulbs become crowded; lifting and replanting bulbs every three to four years should prevent this problem.

The second point to bear in mind is to check that the bulb is the right way up. This is easily done with true bulbs, like narcissi, but on corms and tubers (*see p.164*) the buds are not always very distinct.

The most natural way to grow bulbs is in large drifts in grass. There are two ways to do this – but first, cut the grass as short as possible, leaving it uncut until the bulb foliage dies down in early summer.

Using a bulb planter This tool takes out a neat plug of soil just big enough for one bulb. Push it vertically into the ground, giving it a firm twist before lifting out the plug of soil. If the planter doesn't have depth markings on its side, use a ruler to measure the hole. If it is too deep, top up the level with soil, compost or grit.

With large bulbs, such as daffodils, scatter them over the chosen area. Check they are all at least 10cm (4in) apart, then plant each bulb where it fell. Use a bulb planter (*see above*) or trowel to dig a hole, insert the bulb, and replace the soil.

To plant a large number of small bulbs, such as crocuses, make an "H"-shaped cut in the lawn using a half-moon edger or spade. Turn back the turf flaps. Take out the soil to the correct depth if necessary; plant the bulbs about 2.5cm (1in) apart; then fold back and firm the turf.

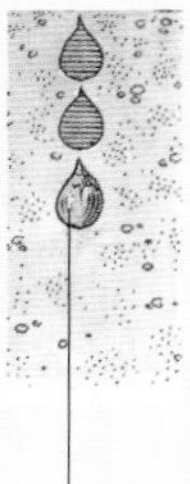
Bulb is planted at three times its height

Planting depths The correct planting depth for each type of bulb depends on its size. As a rough guide, plant each bulb at a depth equal to three times the bulb's height. In light soils, bulbs should be planted slightly deeper.

Wet conditions In soil with poor drainage, it is a good idea to fork gypsum and grit into the soil and also to sit each bulb on a thick bed of grit. This will help to prevent the bulb from rotting.

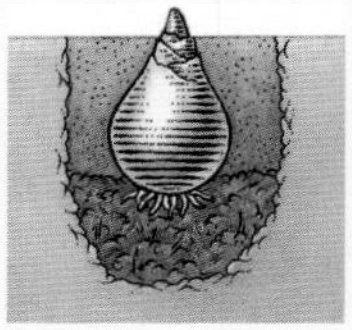

Dry conditions Light soils dry out very quickly, especially in hot conditions. To stop the roots of bulbs drying out, sit each one on a layer of well-rotted organic matter such as garden compost.

Preparing containers

Most plants grow happily in containers but they will demand more attention than if they had been planted in the garden.

Terracotta pots are very attractive but, once planted up, they can be heavy to move around. They are also porous and dry out more quickly than plastic ones. Line the base with nylon flywire or broken crocks to stop potting mix running out the large hole. Plastic containers may not look as elegant, but they are cheap, light, and good at retaining moisture. They also don't need crocks because they usually have several smaller drainage holes.

Choose a premium potting mix for containers. Mix the water-retaining granules and slow-release fertilizer into it (if they are not already in the mix) to cut down on watering and feeding later.

Potting mixtures
These are available in a range of formulations and qualities. Look for ones that have been made to a particular standard. Some also contain water-retaining granules and fertilizers.

Planting a hanging basket

A hanging basket packed full with colourful plants is a spectacular sight, yet it is not that difficult to achieve.

There are many types of basket but the most popular ones are wire mesh. These need lining to hold the compost in place. Sphagnum moss should be conserved, so is no longer recommended, but there are alternatives, including liners made from coconut fibre, plastic, or wool.

The number of plants you will need to plant up a basket depends on its size, but you can pack them in quite tightly. The plants and potting mix will be very heavy, especially when watered, so it is best to use a lighter, soilless potting mix. Don't forget to add a slow-release fertilizer to avoid having to feed the basket.

Planting a basket
❶ *Steady the basket by standing it on an upturned pot. Insert the liner and place a saucer or piece of plastic in the base. Cover with potting mix. Cut slits in the sides and push through trailing plants from the outside, holding them by their roots. Fill with potting mix.*
❷ *Plant tall plants in the centre and more trailing plants around the edge. Fill any gaps with potting mix. Firm and water.*

You can also improve moisture retention by mixing in water-retaining granules.

The baskets should be planted thickly so that the plants will grow to conceal the sides. Work from the base of the basket upwards, cutting slit holes in the liner and feeding the plant roots through. Protect the foliage of the plants by rolling them in a tube of paper first if necessary.

Plant baskets of summer annuals in mid-spring, and keep under cover until after the last frost. Baskets of hardier perennials, planted in spring, winter or autumn, can stay outdoors.

Planting water-garden plants

Late spring or early summer are the best planting times. The majority of aquatic plants benefit from being planted in a basket. There are different planting baskets to choose from – the most common ones are made of plastic mesh and require lining with a piece of hessian to contain the soil. The mesh allows water to penetrate to the roots, while helping to contain the growth of more rampant plants.

Aquatic plants are generally easy to grow. Use ordinary garden soil, but only if no fertilizer has been added to it (as too much nitrogen in water will cause a green algae to grow in the pond).

Correct planting depth is vital: marginal plants will need shallow water, while deep-water aquatics, such as water lilies, need deep water to thrive. Always check the label on the plant.

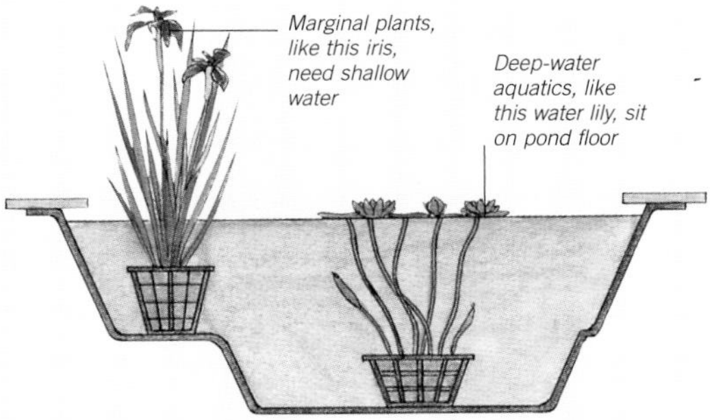

Correct planting depth is vital to plant survival.

Planting in an aquatic basket
Line the basket with hessian so the soil does not escape. Partly fill the basket with soil. Sit the plant (here a water lily) so its crown is level with the top of the basket. Fill in soil around the roots and firm. Top-dress with a thin layer of gravel, so the growing points are exposed, to hold the soil in place. Soak the compost well before setting the basket in shallow water. Move into deeper water as the stems grow.

pruning

If you grow woody plants, sooner or later you will have to prune them to keep them looking good. Pruning is often regarded with dread by gardeners, but it really is just a matter of common sense and learning a few fundamental rules. Also, good-quality tools make the job easier.

Pruning encourages new, strong growth and increases the number of flowers, maintains a well-balanced shape, and keeps a plant to the desired size. The methods vary depending on the type of plant. It is most important in a plant's early years because early pruning affects the shape of the established plant. However, renovation pruning (*see p.384*) can also breathe new life into an old plant. By pruning out dead and diseased growth, you can also improve the health of an ailing plant.

It may seem contrary, but by cutting back a plant you encourage it to grow bigger and stronger, because it reacts by sending out new shoots from below the cuts. You can also persuade a plant to grow in a particular direction and regulate the quantity and vigour of that growth. Conifers do not need much pruning, except when grown as hedging (*see p.384*) or topiary.

When pruning, make a clean cut just above a bud or leaf joint (*see below*). The cut should not be too close or you may cause the bud to die, but if you cut too wide, the stub will die back and may become diseased.

Before you start pruning, take a good look at the plant. Give some thought to the cuts you are about to make. If you rush in with the secateurs, you could end up with a badly shaped plant or lose a season of flowering because you have cut out the wrong stems.

Basic tools for pruning

If you invest in a few good-quality pruning tools, it will make your job much easier. Using good cutting tools will also ensure that the pruning cuts are clean and heal quickly without becoming vulnerable to disease. For most pruning tasks, you need only a pair of secateurs, a pruning saw, and perhaps some loppers. Use a tool suited to the stem size – if you try to cut a large stem with secateurs, you will damage it and make a blunt cut. Keep blades clean and sharp: blunt blades tear rather than cut, allowing disease to take hold.

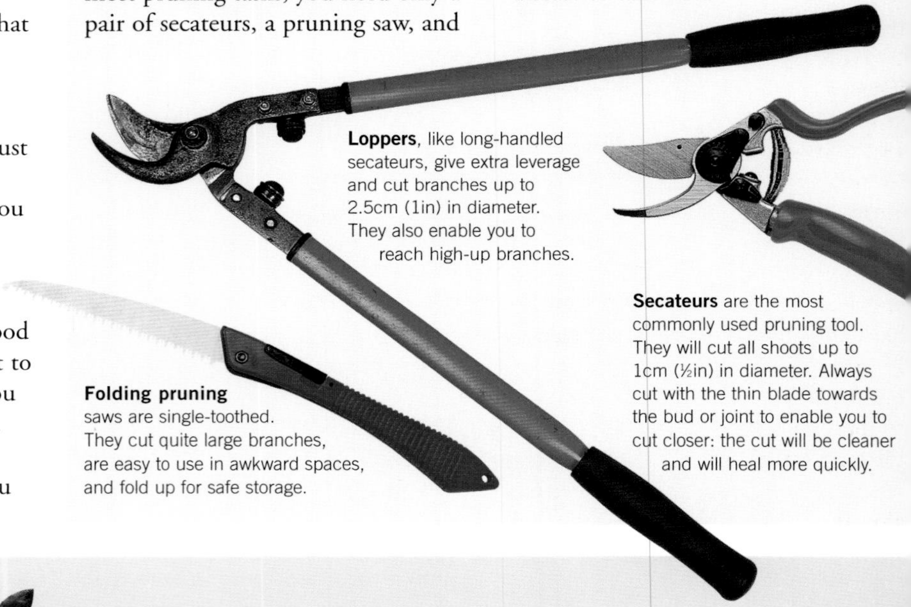

Loppers, like long-handled secateurs, give extra leverage and cut branches up to 2.5cm (1in) in diameter. They also enable you to reach high-up branches.

Secateurs are the most commonly used pruning tool. They will cut all shoots up to 1cm (½in) in diameter. Always cut with the thin blade towards the bud or joint to enable you to cut closer: the cut will be cleaner and will heal more quickly.

Folding pruning saws are single-toothed. They cut quite large branches, are easy to use in awkward spaces, and fold up for safe storage.

Basic principles of pruning

Prune above outward-facing bud for new growth away from heart of plant

Single bud Make your cut at a 45° angle, 5mm (¼in) above the bud so any moisture runs off.

Remove dead wood to stop disease spreading. Cut back to a strong bud or healthy, new shoot.

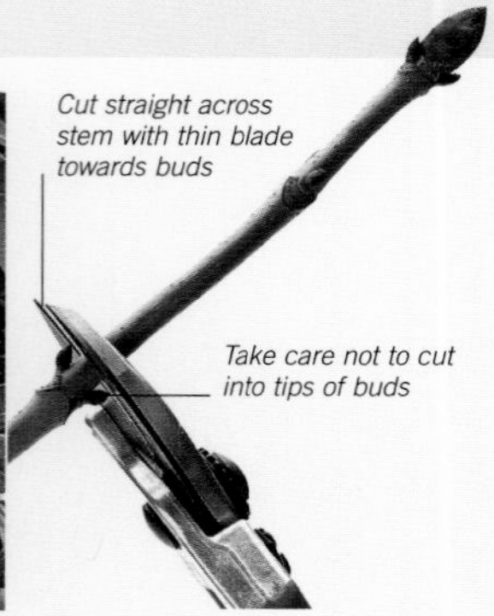
Cut straight across stem with thin blade towards buds
Take care not to cut into tips of buds

Opposite buds Cut straight across the stem as close as possible to the tips of the buds.

No matter what type of plant you are pruning, certain basic principles apply. Fast-growing plants that put on more than 30cm (12in) growth in a year respond well to hard pruning. Slow-growing plants usually do not respond well to being pruned back hard, so avoid it unless absolutely necessary.

When pruning dead or diseased wood, wipe the blades between cuts with a proprietory disinfectant to avoid spreading spores or infection to the next plant that you prune.

Crossing stems rub together causing chafing damage to bark, creating a wound where disease can enter. Overcrowded stems are weak, block out light, and trap damp air which encourages disease. Thinning out such stems restores a plant's vigour.

After hard pruning, always give the plant a good feed and mulch, and water it if necessary. Inspect your plants regularly and take out any broken or damaged stems without delay to minimize the risk of disease.

Pruning a spring-flowering plant

Spring- or early flowering plants are best pruned after they flower and before they start to put on new growth. This is because their flowers develop from buds growing on the previous year's stems. If pruning is left too late in the season, you might remove next year's flowering shoots.

Start by thinning out any old, damaged, and diseased wood. Then cut some older stems right back to the ground. Next, cut shoots with buds back to five or six buds, even if they have started to put on new growth at the tips. The following year's flowering shoots will develop from these buds.

Many spring-flowering shrubs can be trained flat against a wall. On planting, tie in all the main stems and sideshoots into a support. Cut back any shoots that cannot be tied in to one or two buds and pinch out the tips of forward-facing shoots so that they branch sideways. Shorten the longest sideshoots, especially where growth is sparse. In later years, after flowering, tie in new growth and cut back badly placed or overly long shoots. Take out any diseased or dead wood; check ties are not too tight. Cut back the flowered shoots to 5–6 buds.

Unpruned sideshoots flower sparsely
Sideshoots pruned to 2–3 buds produce more flowers

Results of pruning Unpruned stems (*see left*) of flowering quince produce few flowers; pruning stimulates profuse flowering (*see right*).

Pruning a late-summer flowering plant

In the first spring, aim to form a base of strong, woody stems from which spring-flowering shoots will grow each year. Cut out any weak or diseased stems and shorten the remainder to 15–45cm (6–18in), or if a large plant is required to 1.2m (4ft). Prune in subsequent early springs before growth starts. Restore the original framework by pruning all the old flowering stems to leave two or three pairs of fat, healthy buds from the previous year's growth. At the same time, if it is necessary, thin out dense congested stems.

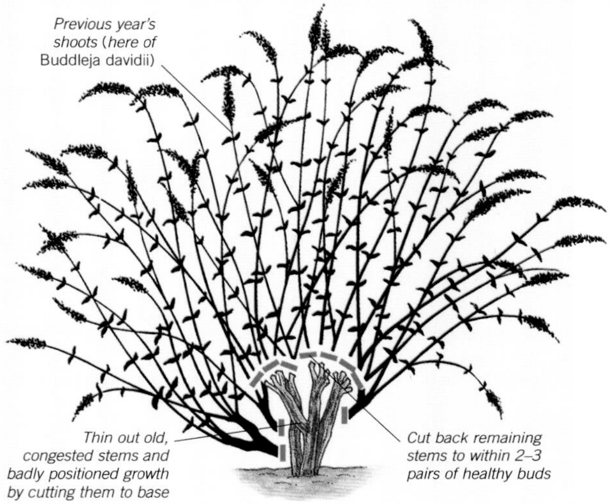
Previous year's shoots (here of Buddleja davidii)
Thin out old, congested stems and badly positioned growth by cutting them to base
Cut back remaining stems to within 2–3 pairs of healthy buds

Late-summer flowering plants produce flowers on growth made in the current growing season. Early spring is the best time to prune them, because it diverts each plant's energy to existing buds rather than to developing more, and gives it sufficient time to produce new flowering shoots from the buds.

Hard annual pruning suits many deciduous shrubs and climbers, such as caryopteris, *Hydrangea*, and phygelius – as well as many grey-leaved evergreens, for example lavenders. It produces the best-quality flowers and prevents the plant from becoming too big. Old or neglected late-summer flowering shrubs respond well to hard pruning.

On windy sites, shorten tall growth by about one half in autumn to prevent the winds from rocking the plant and loosening the roots.

Pruning an early summer-flowering plant

Early summer-flowering shrubs, for example philadelphus (*see p.93*) and weigelas (*see p.128*), and many climbing plants are generally pruned in late summer, immediately after flowering has finished. You should aim to open up the plant to allow light and air to reach the centre while retaining an uncluttered, balanced shape.

In the first year after planting, remove all weak and crossing shoots by cutting each out just above an outward-facing bud or at the base. Trim back any overlong shoots to within the overall outline, again cutting each to an outward-facing bud.

In subsequent years, thin out the plant by removing about one in four of the oldest stems, cutting them back to the ground. This makes room for new stems to grow from the base. Shorten younger stems to encourage flowering sideshoots. Wayward stems should be pruned back to maintain a good shape.

Pruning a mature shrub after flowering Using loppers, cut out one in four of the old stems (here of philadelphus) just above the base. Take care to leave a few strong buds on each. Shorten any younger shoots by a quarter to one-third. This will open up the shrub and encourage new, vigorous growth to flower next year. Any dead, damaged, diseased, or crossing shoots on the remaining stems should be pruned out at the same time.

Renovation pruning

When trees, shrubs, and climbers become overgrown or neglected, their growth weakens and flowering declines. Provided that the plants are basically healthy, renovation pruning can give them a new lease of life, spurring strong growth and flower production. Many deciduous plants, like lilacs (*Syringa*) and buddlejas, respond well to renovation pruning.

The best time is in late winter or spring because the plants have a chance to put on new growth before the next winter. Many plants, though, tolerate drastic pruning at their usual pruning time, for example early summer-flowering philadelphus can be tackled in late summer after flowering.

The stems of some shrubs, like berberis, become so tangled that they need cutting right back to ground level. Less vigorous woody plants, particularly evergreens such as rhododendrons, must be cut back in stages over 2–3 years, to give them a chance to recover.

Unfortunately, not all old shrubs survive such drastic pruning, so be prepared for some losses.

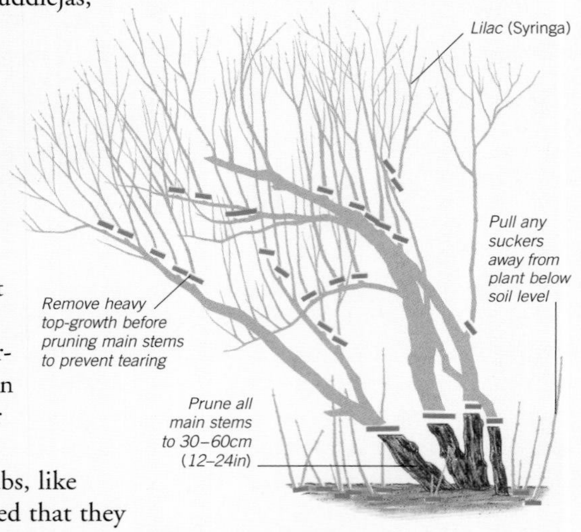
Lilac (Syringa)
Pull any suckers away from plant below soil level
Remove heavy top-growth before pruning main stems to prevent tearing
Prune all main stems to 30–60cm (12–24in)

Drastic renovation involves pruning all growth.

Rhododendron
Each year, prune half of remaining old stems that have not yet been pruned, cutting them to ground level
Thin out new growth arising from last year's cuts to 2–3 strong stems

Staged renovation is done over three years; this is the second year.

Pruning hedges

Regular trimming not only keeps a hedge looking neat, it also promotes strong, dense growth and longevity. Trim established evergreen hedges, for example privet and fast-growing conifers, in late spring or early summer and again in late summer or in early autumn, while they are in growth.

Deciduous hedges, such as berberis, are best trimmed in summer. A second tidy up can be given in autumn. If the hedge is particularly fast growing it may be necessary to do three trims annually. In this case a third trim can be done in early winter. Time the pruning of flowering hedges to suit their flowering periods (*see p.383*).

It is especially important to prune evergreen and coniferous hedges regularly, because very few will reshoot from old wood. When training an evergreen or conifer hedge, keep the sides trimmed, but allow the main stem to reach the desired height before pruning it.

As with shears, keep the blade parallel to the hedge for an even cut. Always wear eye and ear protectors and gloves. Sweep the blade away from your body and the cable.

Keeping a climbing plant within bounds

Many climbers, such as *Clematis montana* and rambling roses, make a lot of growth in one season. Prune spring-flowering climbers after flowering; summer-flowering plants in spring. Remove overlong shoots and unhealthy growth. However, do not over-prune them because it will encourage leafy growth rather than flowering shoots. You can thin out congested climbers (*see below*), but only once every three years or so.

Prune crowded shoots by cutting back to pair of healthy buds or to base of stems
Trim overlong stems to healthy buds
Cut damaged or weak stems to 2 buds or to base

Pruning a congested climber

routine tasks

little time spent regularly on maintenance, such as feeding, vatering, weeding, mulching, and deadheading, will keep our plants in top condition so that they perform at their est. Enjoy the chance these simple tasks give you to enjoy our garden, and take in all its scents and colours.

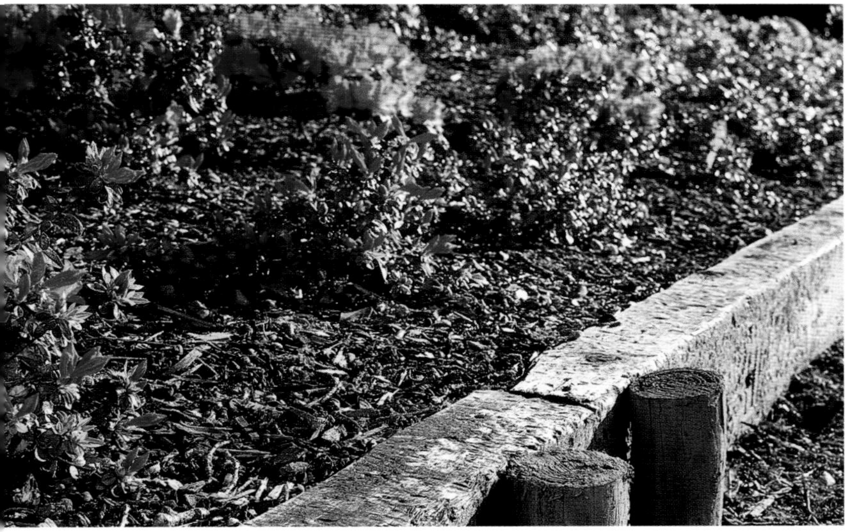

ulching a raised bed keeps down the weeds and keeps the soil moist for the plants (here azaleas).

ny job in the garden is easier if you se the correct tools. Essentials include spade, a fork, a hand trowel and hand ork, and a hoe and short-tined rake for oil cultivation and weeding. Secateurs re needed to deadhead and prune lants and if you have trees, shrubs, or oody climbers, loppers and a pruning aw are useful. If you have a lawn, a ood lawnmower and a long-tined awn rake will help you to keep it ooking good. Add to those a watering an and a wheelbarrow and you can ndertake most routine tasks in the arden. Always buy the best-quality ools you can afford since cheap ones nay last only one or two seasons.

Routine tasks can be minimized by making sure that plants are growing in a position with a soil and conditions that suit them (*see Climate and location, pp.371–373, and Soils and compost, pp.376–378*). If you grow a plant in an unsuitable site, it is unlikely to flourish and will need much more attention. It is also essential that plants have space to grow to maturity; you may be tempted to cram them in for immediate effect, but this will make them weak and more prone to attack from pests and diseases.

Above all, it is more effective and easier to care for your plants by doing a little quite often, rather than leaving tasks until the garden becomes neglected.

What to do when

Spring

- Cut back any old growth left over winter
- Begin mowing lawns, as grass begins to grow; tidy up edges
- Feed and mulch all woody and herbaceous perennial plants as soon as soil starts to warm up
- Repot or top-dress plants grown in containers
- After they flower, prune spring-flowering deciduous shrubs and climbers; also prune late-flowering shrubs and climbers,
- Prune or trim evergreens if needed
- Divide clump-forming perennials, bamboos, and grasses
- Plant new plants and autumn-flowering bulbs, and sow seed
- Provide support now for perennials and biennials that will need it when fully grown
- In late spring, start to bring frost-sensitive container-grown plants that have been overwintered under cover out into the garden
- Keep young and newly planted varieties watered regularly if it's dry
- Keep on top of routine tasks such as deadheading, and weeding; start to feed plants in containers
- Layer shrubs and climbers
- Plant, thin, and divide oxygenating plants in ponds

Summer

- Mow lawns regularly with the blades set high
- Clip hedges
- After they flower, finish pruning spring-flowering deciduous shrubs and climbers
- Continue routine tasks such as feeding, deadheading, and weeding
- Prune apricot and cherry trees in midsummer to avoid infection by gummosis and other diseases
- Take soft and semi-ripe cuttings
- In late summer, prune early summer-flowering deciduous shrubs and climbers

Autumn

- Keep up with routine tasks such as weeding and deadheading; stop feeding plants
- Prune flowering hedges
- Clear dying growth of perennials and grasses, but leave it in cold regions to act as winter insulation
- Lift tender rootstocks, such as dahlias, and store over winter
- Mow lawns regularly
- Move tender plants under cover
- Plant hardy trees, shrubs, climbers, perennials, and spring-flowering bulbs; sow seed of hardy plants
- Take hardwood cuttings
- Clear out any leaves and dead material from ponds

Winter

- Plant hardy trees, shrubs, hedges, climbers, and perennials
- Plan what seeds and plants you wish to order
- Take root cuttings
- Prune roses and deciduous fruit trees

feeding

Using fertilizers

Plants need nutrients to encourage strong, healthy growth and plentiful flowers. Whether you use organic or non-organic fertilizers is down to personal choice. Organic feeds tend to release nutrients over a longer period; chemicals give a fast, but short-lived, boost to growth. Both are available as granules, powders, or liquids. Powdered or granular feeds, such as poultry pellets, can be scattered over the entire planting area or around individual plants. Dry fertilizers, such as blood and bone should be watered into the soil. Liquid feeds are quick-acting and easy to apply, using a special hose-end applicator or watering can.

Apply fertilizers from mid-spring to midsummer, when the plants are growing rapidly and will benefit from extra nutrients. Take care when applying a concentrated fertilizer because it may scorch the stems and the foliage. Always take heed of the manufacturer's instructions, and avoid the temptation to overfeed the plants; it is wasteful and will result in weak, sappy growth and fewer flowers.

Slow release fertilizers are a safe alternative if you are unsure of using fertilizers. These release the nutrients over a long period of time, meaning it is almost impossible to overfeed with them.

Forking in fertilizer Fertilizer granules should be worked into the soil surface around the plant, taking care not to fork too deeply and damage the roots. Unless heavy rain is expected, water the area well to release the nutrients into the soil.

Foliar feeding Liquid feed can be sprayed onto plants as a fast, effective pick-me-up if they are not doing well. Most is absorbed through the leaves, and any excess is taken up by the roots. To avoid scorch, apply in the evening or on dull days.

Applying a top-dressing

Potting mix in containers becomes less fertile over time as its nutrients are taken up and used by the plant, and leached out by rain and watering. If the plant has not outgrown the pot and become root-bound, you can apply an annual top-dressing at the beginning of the growing season to replenish the nutrients. Remove the top layer of old soil, and replace it with fresh potting mix (*see right*).

Alternatively, for shrubs and trees, you could use garden compost or composted bark. A mulch (*see p.388*) of bark chips or gravel will conserve moisture and give a decorative finish. Rock-garden plants, especially alpine species, like well-drained soil; a top-dressing of gravel or pebbles, avoids water puddling around the plants and causing rot. Top-dressing will mix with the soil or get washed away, so in spring, scrape it off, fertilize the soil, and top with a fresh layer of grit.

Gently scrape soil away using trowel

Top-dressing a container Carefully remove the top 5–8cm (2–3in) of old soil, taking care not to go too deep and damage the roots (*see inset*). Then fill the container back up to the original level, using fresh potting mix of the same type mixed with slow-release fertilizer. Finally, water it in well.

watering

Why water?

Watering is essential for healthy, growing plants. Moisture is taken up from the soil and used by the plant to make and transport vital nutrients for survival. Water keeps every plant cell turgid, so the first visible sign of thirst is the wilting of leaves and stems.

Dry conditions can cause a check in growth and leave plants more vulnerable to attack by diseases or pests. Although you should expect some watering to be necessary after planting and during very hot spells, it can be reduced by choosing plants that tolerate such conditions.

Drought-tolerant plants, such as lavender and stachys, naturally prefer a well-drained, or sunny area. Their leaves are often small and silvery or are protected by a hairy or waxy layer. Thirsty plants usually have large, thin leaves, for example trollius or primulas, and thrive in damp, sheltered spots.

To reduce water loss from the soil surface, apply a mulch (*see p.388*); avoid leaving large areas unplanted; and if needed provide a windbreak. Wind draws moisture from leaves in the same way as it dries your washing.

Although drought is damaging, waterlogging is also harmful. The soil becomes saturated so plant roots cannot breathe and begin to rot. It occurs after very wet periods, or on heavy soils with poor drainage. Plant moisture-loving plants in these situations.

When to water

How often you need to water will depend on the local conditions. Frequent rain should supply enough moisture, but in dry spells you may have to water beds, lawns, and containers frequently. Some plants require moist soil and will soon die if the ground starts to dry out, but others will be able to cope once they become established. New plantings are also at risk from drought until they form a strong root system.

Try basin watering (*see right*) to direct water to the roots. Another option is pot watering: sink a deep pot into the soil next to a plant; fill it with water and allow it to drain into the soil. Seedlings especially need constant attention – too much water and they will rot off, too little and they will quickly die.

In summer, water in the evening or early morning. The heat of the day increases evaporation so your efforts will be wasted and water droplets act like lenses to scorch the foliage.

Basin watering Surround the plant with a raised dam of soil. Water into this basin so that all the water is directed straight to the roots, saving time and conserving water.

Watering cans

Every gardener needs a watering can for small areas of the garden and for containers. When buying one, go for the best you can afford because you will find yourself using it often.

Choose a watering can that is well balanced, and not too heavy for you to lift when it is full. Other useful features include an opening large enough to make it easy to fill by a tap or hose, and a strainer at the bottom of the spout so that it does not become clogged by debris. A long spout is useful for reaching to the back of a garden.

Watering seedlings Seedlings require only a gentle shower since their tiny roots are easily dislodged. Attach a fine, metal rose to your can so that it points upwards. Start watering to the side of the tray to establish an even spray, then pass it smoothly over the seedlings.

Most watering cans are fitted with a removable rose. A fine rose is perfect for delicate plants (*see left*). A coarse rose will give a spray that is better for watering larger, more established plantings quickly.

Keep a separate watering can for pesticides or weedkillers to avoid cross-contamination; buy a plastic one because some chemicals can corrode metal.

Hoses and sprinklers

Watering can be a time-consuming task, so consider investing in a hose that will carry water to where it is needed, without having to fill and refill a watering can. Reinforced hoses are less likely to kink than cheaper ones. Hoses that neatly wind onto their own reels are easy to store. All should be fitted with a nozzle that can adjust the flow of water from a stream to a fine spray, so you can water appropriately (*see right*). Sprinklers on the end of a hose can be used for large areas. Their fine sprays soak the soil evenly, but they are wasteful, and have to be moved often to stop puddles forming. Some types of hose are laid around the garden as a permanent irrigation system controlled by a tap or a timer. Seep hoses let water ooze out along their entire length; drip hoses deliver water through holes to individual plants in containers or beds, microsprays give a fine spray to larger areas. All types are good for garden beds, but can be unsightly, so it is best to disguise them (*see below*).

Using a hose Watering plants with a hose requires some care. A strong stream of water can erode soil from around the plant roots, leaving them exposed and prone to dry out (*see above*). Alternatively, if the ground is hard, it may not penetrate the soil at all and run over the surface away from where it is needed. Always use a spray nozzle on the hose, unless you are watering into a pot placed as a reservoir by the plant.

Installing a seep hose

❶ *To lay a seep hose, wind it in loops around the plants in your garden, allowing for it to moisten the soil for a distance of about 10cm (4in) on each side of the hose. This will be more in clay soils and less in sandy ones. If you find the hose will not lie flat, peg it down at intervals with hoops of strong, galvanized wire.*

❷ *With the hose in place, rake a 8cm (3in) thick layer of mulch, such as bark chips or gravel, between the plants. Cover the bare soil and the hose. The mulch gives a neat, decorative finish, suppresses weeds, and will help prevent moisture from evaporating from the soil. The finished bed is low-maintenance, especially if the seep hose is controlled by a timer.*

mulching

Why do you need to mulch?

A mulch is a layer of material applied as a skin over the soil, and has many advantages over leaving the surface bare. Loose mulches maintain a more even soil temperature, that is warmer in winter and cooler in summer than naked ground. The need for watering is reduced, because moisture cannot evaporate from the soil so readily.

Gravel mulch *provides a good foil for grasses.*

Mulches also help to suppress weeds. The weeds are prevented from germinating by the lack of light, although some persistent perennial weeds such as couch grass may grow through a loose mulch unless the soil has been throughly weeded beforehand (*see p.389*). Any weeds that appear after the mulch is laid will be easier to spot and remove. As well as being useful, mulches can also be very ornamental, especially if you use materials such as chipped bark, pebbles, or coloured wood chips.

These are many types of organic and synthetic mulch available, but to be effective it should be long-lasting and not easily dislodged by rain or blown away. Organic mulches such as compost will, in time, be carried down into the soil by worms, improving the soil structure and replenishing nutrients, filling the role of mulch and fertilizer in one. If you are using an organic material, make sure it has a loose texture that will allow moisture to pass through easily. If using sheet mulch make sure it is a woven one so air and water can reach the soil. To be really effective mulch should be 5–8cm (2–3in) thick.

Types of mulch

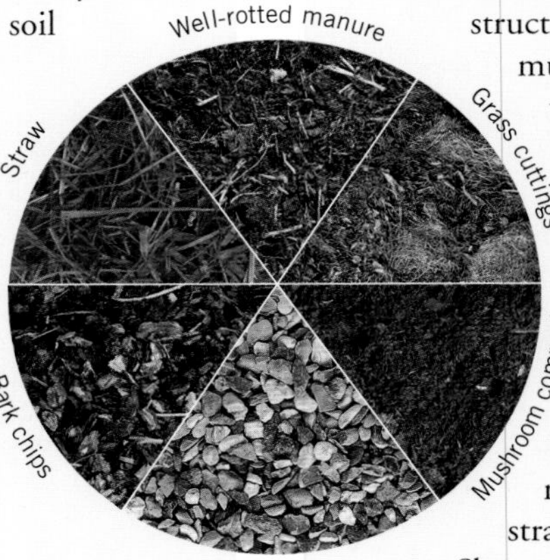

Organic mulches, such as well-rotted manure, improve soil structure, but do not use mushroom compost with acid-loving plants. Grass cuttings are free, but may turn slimy or spread weed seeds. Bark chips look good and use an otherwise wasted resource, as do pea straw and lucerne hay. Sheet mulches are effective, but need disguising (*see below*). Gravel makes a handsome mulch.

Applying and using mulches

A mulch will have the effect of stabilizing and maintaining soil conditions, so the best time to apply one is in autumn or spring. At these times of year, the soil should be reasonably warm, not too wet or too dry, and free from weeds – in other words, perfect for plant growth.

A loose mulch, such as gravel, well-rotted manure, and chipped bark, can be applied by spreading it liberally around plants with a shovel and raking it level (*see right*).

Sheet mulches of woven weed mat are easy to use if laid over a bed before planting. Cut the sheet so that it is at least 15cm (6in) larger on all sides than the area to be covered. Secure the sheet at the edges with pegs, or push the edges into the ground with the edge of a spade, making sure that it is taut. The plants can then be inserted through planting holes (*see below*).

Applying organic mulch Spread loose mulches directly onto the soil to a depth of 5–8cm (2–3in) to control weeds and reduce evaporation. Tuck the mulch under each plant but, if using an organic mulch, leave a 10cm (4in) gap to avoid rot setting in. Top up the mulch as needed.

Using a sheet mulch

1. *Rake the soil level and, if needed, water it well. Lay a sheet mulch (here of woven weed mat) over the bed. To plant, make two cuts, 15cm (6–8in) long and at right angles, in the sheet. Fold the flaps back and dig a planting hole.*
2. *Insert the plant, firm, water, and replace the flaps. Add a 5cm (2in) layer of organic or mineral mulch to hide as well as hold down the sheet mulch.*

weeding

Types of weed

Any plant growing where it is not wanted can be called a weed. In favourable conditions, some garden plants can become invasive. Weeds are a nuisance because they grow very fast, taking water, nutrients, and light from less vigorous, cultivated plants.

There are two types of weed: annual and perennial. Annual weeds, such as chickweed, have thin, shallow roots and complete their life cycle within one year. When they are left to grow they will self-seed prolifically and grow rapidly, producing up to three generations in a season. If you don't allow them to seed, they are fairly easy to control.

Perennial weeds usually have deep, fleshy, or spreading roots, such as oxalis, or creeping underground stems, for example couch grass. They are difficult to remove completely, and return year after year even if only a small piece of root is left in the soil after weeding.

Annual weeds

Common chickweed

Fat hen

Capeweed

Perennial weeds

Couch grass

Creeping Buttercup

Oxalis

Controlling weeds

The method of control you choose for your garden will depend on the types of weed, the scale of the invasion, and whether you are prepared to use chemicals.

If you want to avoid weedkillers, then mulching (*see facing page*) as well as using ground-cover plants will prevent weeds taking hold. If a few annual weeds do appear, they are simple to deal with. Cut them down with a hoe, or pull them up by hand, before they set seed.

Small patches of perennial weeds can be dug out with a fork, but they may reappear unless you remove every last bit of root. If there is a very bad infestation, then a drastic solution may be needed. A sheet mulch (*see facing page*), covered with a 8cm (3in) layer of mulch will kill most weeds if it is left in place over two seasons.

Chemical weedkillers save time and effort. Many are effective only when the plants are actively growing. Some weedkillers are selective and kill only certain types of plants, so first identify the problem weed. Several applications may be necessary to clear persistent perennial weeds. Always follow carefully the manufacturer's instructions when using chemicals.

If an area has more weeds than desirable plants, consider digging up the ornamental plants and treating the entire area. Before replanting the ornamentals, wash the soil off the root balls, check, and remove any perennial weed fragments.

Using a hoe Walk backwards, pushing and pulling the blade along the surface as you go, aiming to slice off the tops of annual weeds without digging into the soil. This will be easiest to achieve when the soil is fairly dry. Either leave the hoed weeds to wither if it is hot, or if it is damp remove them and add them to the compost bin.

Chemical weedkiller Ready-mixed weedkillers are less hazardous than concentrates that need dilution. A small hand-sprayer like this is the safest method of application, but it is wise to shield nearby ornamental plants with plastic. Wash your hands throughly after use.

Weeding rows by hand Sowing seed in rows makes it easier to distinguish weed seedlings from the ornamental seedlings. Anything out of line can be pulled out by hand. Hand weeding is easiest to do when the soil is slightly moist.

supporting plants

Providing temporary supports

Many herbaceous plants need some support as they grow to prevent them from being snapped by wind or being flattened by heavy rain, so they look their best throughout the season. Push supports into the soil when the plant is no more than 30cm (12in) tall, so that it has time to grow through and disguise the support. If you delay staking the plant until it begins to flop, the supports will look obvious and unnatural.

Traditionally, bamboo canes are used – either singly, for tall plants such as gladioli, or in a circle with twine for clumping plants. A more natural alternative is sticks – twiggy branches usually discarded from pruned shrubs. You could use large plastic or wire mesh stretched between canes; the plant stems grow through the mesh and obscure it. There are also many metal and plastic staking systems available which are re-usable and versatile. Small climbers, like sweet peas (*Lathyrus, see p.145*), can be grown over a wigwam of canes, tied at the top with raffia, or over a wooden or metal obelisk.

Link stakes These come in varying heights and slot together easily (*see inset*). You can position them around any shape of clump. Insert to a depth of 10cm (4in) to keep them steady.

Using trellis

Train climbers and wall shrubs on trellis used as a freestanding screen, fixed to battens on a wall, or to extend the height of a fence. Make sure that the wood has been treated with preservative before it is covered by the plant. Most plants grown on trellis need to be tied regularly into the support; a loose figure-of-eight loop of twine will allow for stems to grow. Once plants are established, check the ties at least once a year and loosen any that are too tight.

Fixing a trellis kit to a drainpipe This is a good way to conceal an unsightly feature. Use two or three narrow, 2m (6ft) trellis panels and place them around the drainpipe. Secure at 45cm (18in) intervals with plastic ties or wire.

keeping plants neat

Deadheading and pinch pruning

Deadheading woody plants Using secateurs, regularly remove withered flowers, cutting back to a strong, outward-facing bud to encourage open growth.

Deadheading by hand Grasp each fading flower of a herbaceous plant between thumb and forefinger, and bend it over so it snaps off.

Pinching out leafy shoots The tips of soft shoots (here of purple sage) are nipped out just above healthy buds or sideshoots to encourage denser growth.

During the growing season, you can prolong each plant's flowering period by deadheading. This directs energy that would have gone into producing seed into forming more flowers. Try to get into the habit of deadheading whenever you go into the garden, and you will be rewarded with a constant and tidy display of flowers.

Removing the spent flowers of most herbaceous plants can be done by hand. Some perennials, for example delphiniums and lupins, can have their spent flower stems removed to encourage a prolonged or second flowering later in the season. Other plants, such as catmint, cranesbills, and pulmonarias can simply be sheared over.

To deadhead shrubs and woody climbers, use secateurs and cut back the flowered shoot to a healthy, outward-facing bud. The new shoot should grow in a direction that will enhance the shape of the plant.

Remember that many plants, including some roses and grasses, should not be deadheaded if you wish to enjoy their decorative seedheads in late autumn and winter.

If you want to save the seed of any annuals or biennials, you can still remove most of the spent flowers because each seedhead produces a large quantity of seeds.

You can also keep the foliage of plants, for example herbs, looking neat by pinch pruning. This is a similar process to deadheading, but involves removing the growing tips of shoots before flowering to encourage lots of new sideshoots and a dense, bushy habit. It is a technique often used with fuchsias and annual plants early in the season; if you stop pinch pruning after about a month, the plants will burst into bloom, producing a continuous mass of flowers.

raising your own

)ne of the great joys of gardening is propagating your own ·lants by taking cuttings, dividing, layering, and sowing seed. Jot only are these techniques fun to learn, they will also ave you a great deal of money – when compared with ursery plants the price of a packet of seed is negligible.

potting tray stops seed-raising mixture spilling everywhere when sowing seed or potting up cuttings.

: is not necessary to purchase much quipment to raise your own plants, or do you need a great deal of space – sunny windowsill will do – but you o need clean containers, good-quality, esh potting mix (not salvaged from ther pots) and, if taking cuttings, lean, sharp secateurs. Poor hygiene is ıe prime enemy of young seedlings and uttings, as it allows diseases such as rots ɔ attack the vulnerable young plants.

New seedlings and cuttings need the orrect balance of nutrients, a good upply of oxygen and moisture, and appropriate light and temperature levels. All you have to do is provide suitable growing conditions and nature will do the rest for you. Seed and all cuttings, except hardwood ones, succeed in the protected environment of a propagator. Create a similar conditions by covering a pot with a clear plastic bag. Warming the potting mix gently will also help.

Division and layering are even easier ways of raising new plants, because they are undertaken outdoors, but these methods produce only one or a few new plants at a time.

growing plants from seed

Sowing seed in containers

Most plants are easy to raise from seed, including annuals, perennials, and even trees. If you have never sown seed before, it is best to buy packeted seed because it is quality controlled and comes with full instructions for each type of seed.

The most natural way to grow seed is, of course, outdoors but by sowing indoors you have more control over the environment and each seed has a better chance of survival. Indoor sowings can also be made earlier than outdoor ones, getting the plants off to a good start.

Sow seed thinly to avoid problems with overcrowding. Fine seed will be easier to sow if mixed with sand.

Whether you use a full- or half-sized seed tray will depend on the amount of seed that you are sowing. Many gardeners use modular trays or coir or peat seed blocks – if sown one per module or block, each seedling can grow to a good size before being disturbed. Biodegradable pots also avoid root disturbance because each seedling is planted out together with its pot. Seedlings that develop long roots, such as sweet peas, are best grown in tall tube pots.

You can use recycled containers: yoghurt tubs and foil trays work well (just make drainage holes), while cardboard egg boxes and toilet roll tubes make biodegradable modules.

How to sow seed in a tray

❶ *Fill the tray with good-quality, fresh seed-raising mixture. Tap the tray firmly on the bench two or three times to settle the mixture and scrape off the excess with a flat stick. Press another tray on the surface to firm the mixture to 1cm (½in) below the rim. Stand the tray in a reservoir of water until the surface is just moist.*

❷ *Sprinkle seed thinly on the surface of the mixture, then cover with a fine layer of the mixture. Press large seeds into the mixture at a depth of twice their diameter; fill in the holes.*

❸ *Water the surface with a fine spray. Cover the tray to prevent moisture loss and maintain an even temperature – use a sheet of glass, clear kitchen film, or a purpose-made plastic lid.*

Germinating seed successfully

A seed contains a plant in embryo and to kickstart it into life, it needs the correct balance of warmth, air, and moisture. In most cases, you can achieve these conditions by placing pots or trays of seed in a propagator (*see right*). Electric propagators and heated trays provide what is called "bottom heat", gently warming the soil to encourage germination. Alternatively, cover the container with kitchen film or a sheet of glass.

Some seed needs special treatment to trigger it into germination, for example, low light levels. A period of cold, to mimic winter, can be created by placing the seed container in the refrigerator for a time. Some thick seed coatings need to be soaked before sowing. These details will be listed on the seed packet.

As soon as the seedlings emerge, increase ventilation or remove any film, but keep them out of the sun. If left covered, they may fall prey to damping off, a fungal disease that spreads fast in damp, still air. Seeing the affected seedlings blacken and die is disheartening, but you can protect them by observing good hygiene.

Propagator The cover of the propagator allows light through, while keeping the air moist. Open the vent to get rid of heavy condensation, but don't let the air dry out completely.

Caring for seedlings

Seedlings should never be allowed to dry out, nor should they sit in wet potting mix, which is a breeding ground for diseases such as damping off (*see above*). Watering from overhead can wash seedlings out of the potting mix. Instead, stand pots and trays in clean tap water and lift them out as soon as the surface of the potting mix starts to moisten. Allow excess water to drain away.

Seedlings sown indoors can tend to be taller and weaker than those sown outside. Ensure that they get plenty of light and relocate outside as soon as possible *(see* Hardening Off *opposite).*

Overcrowded seedlings compete for light, water, and space. They may grow leggy and more vulnerable to disease. They should therefore be transplanted, or pricked out, as soon as they have formed two true leaves above the first pair of seed leaves, to give them space.

Select the healthiest, strongest seedlings to grow on and discard the rest. You can thin them out, by pulling out unwanted seedlings with tweezers, or transplant them into new containers of fresh potting mix (*see below*). Insert them about 5cm (2in) apart with the seed leaves just above the potting mix. Pop them in a ventilated propagator and shade from bright sun until they get established.

Etiolated seedlings are weak and spindly as a result of growing in poor light and may never thrive. Bright, diffuse light is best for seedlings – strong sun can burn tender shoots.

Hold seedlings by the leaves.

Chopstick makes good dibber

Pricking out Use a dibber to ease the seedlings out of the old potting mix. Try not to damage any roots. Make a hole for each seedling, lower its roots into the hole, and firm gently by pushing in the potting mix from the sides.

Hardening off

Hardening off acclimatizes young plants that have been indoors to the dryer and cooler conditions of the open garden. If this is not done, the young plants will be knocked back and suffer a check to their growth. It is best not to rush this final stage, so allow a week or two for the process.

Wait until all danger of frost has passed before moving young susceptible plants outdoors. Choose a warm, dry, but dull day to commence hardening off. In the early stages, cover the plants with a layer of shade cloth to protect them from windchill if necessary, and keep them out of heavy rain or strong sun. Bring them back under cover at night for the first few days. If the weather stays mild, leave them out overnight under a thin layer of glass or plastic. When plants look healthy, remove it altogether. Your plants will be fully hardened off and ready for planting out.

A cold frame is the ideal halfway house for hardening off. For the first few days, open the lid for 2–3 hours, but keep it shut at night. Increase the time the lid is left open during the day, and eventually, leave it open at night.

Making use of punnet and bloomer

Raising plants from seed is very satisfying and it is still the only way you can obtain some of the more unusual plant cultivars. There is no denying, however, that it can be time- and space-consuming.

Plants in punnets are a speedy alternative. These are young plants that have been grown in small trays or modules so that they have a well-developed root system. This helps to form an easy-to-handle plant. You can still enjoy the process of potting up the plants, growing them on to maturity, and hardening the plants off.

These plants are widely available, especially of annuals and perennials. They can be bought from nurseries and garden centres that sell them individually in trays. Pot up or plant out these plants (*see p.380*) as soon as possible, and water them well.

Bloomer pots are generally more expensive than standard punnets; however, they are larger plants, and they are likely to establish and flower more quickly. In fact, with bloomers, as the name suggests, many are already in flower when you purchase them. They are particularly useful for bringing instant colour to a garden.

Plants in punnets can be grown in small flat trays or in individual modules within the punnet as shown here. This latter system makes them easy to separate for planting out individual plants.

Bloomer pots give you larger seedlings in individual small pots. These are particularly useful when you want a quick result. Remember to tickle the roots gently before planting out.

Sowing an annual display

You can create a colourful border full of annuals by sowing seed directly outdoors. The sheer volume of seed sown (packets are still fairly cheap) will more than compensate for any seedlings you lose to pests and harsh conditions. Also, you do not have to worry about pricking out, growing on, and hardening off the seedlings. Start sowing outdoors as soon as the soil has started to warm up in early spring.

Give plants a good start in life by preparing the area thoroughly. Remove any weeds (which could compete for water, light, and nutrients) and large stones, then roughly level the surface. Do this several weeks prior to sowing, so the soil has time to settle and any germinating weeds can be removed. Before sowing, rake the soil until it resembles fine breadcrumbs (known as a "fine tilth") and the surface is level. Water the plot well if it is dry, otherwise the freshly sown seed might dry out and die.

Fill a bottle with sand and use it to trickle out a line delineating the shape of each sowing area; make these plots irregularly shaped so that the different plants will form drifts.

You can either sow seed in rows, or drills, within each area (*see below*) or broadcast sow. The latter is done simply by scattering seed as evenly as possible to fill each sowing area, then lightly raking over the plot to mix the seed into the soil. Rake the soil in two directions to ensure that the seed is evenly distributed. Broadcast sowing is quicker, but it is more difficult to spot weeds among the seedlings later.

Once they have appeared, cover the seedlings with horticultural fleece to protect them from frost or heavy rain and from pests such as mice, birds, and cats.

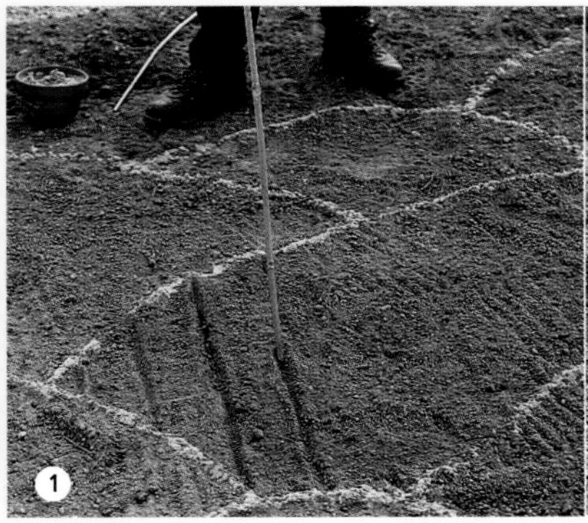

Sowing seed in drifts

1. *Mark out the sowing areas for each plant. Within each area, use a stick or a hoe to draw out drills (shallow trenches) for sowing the seed. Check the seed packets for the correct spacings of drills for each plant.*
2. *Water the drills if the soil is dry, then sprinkle fine seed thinly along each row. Space sow large seed in twos and threes. Pull a thin layer of soil gently over the seed with a rake.*
3. *When seedlings appear, thin them to leave the strongest ones at the correct spacings. Place your fingers around the base of each chosen seedling's stem to keep its roots firm as you pull out unwanted seedlings around it.*

cuttings

Softwood, semi-ripe, and heel cuttings

Cuttings are the quickest and most successful way of propagating many perennials, shrubs, biennials, and alpines. It may be of soft or semi-ripe wood. A softwood, or slightly more mature greenwood, cutting is taken from the actively growing tip of a shoot in early summer. Look for strong, young growth. It will be a lighter green than older growth or wood. Later in the summer when the shoots begin to ripen or become woody and stiff, semi-ripe cuttings can be taken. Test stems by bending them – if they split they are still soft, if they spring back they are semi-ripe.

When taking a stem-ripe cutting (*see below*), cut off a shoot about 10cm (4in) long. Handle it carefully: the tissues are soft and easily damaged. Cuttings wilt swiftly – keep them moist and prepare them as soon as possible so they have the best chance of rooting. You can dip the cuttings in fungicide to protect against rot, and the ends in a hormone rooting compound to encourage rooting. You can also take cuttings of woody plants with a heel (*see below, right*).

Cover a pot of cuttings with a plastic bag to retain moisture, or in a propagator, in a warm, light place.

Taking stem-tip cuttings

❶ *Cut just above a leaf joint using a clean, sharp knife, or secateurs and place cuttings in a bucket of water or plastic bag to stop them wilting.*

❷ *Trim all but the top 2–4 leaves off each cutting and cut the end just below a leaf joint. Insert the cuttings in pots of moist, gritty potting mix, so that their leaves are not touching.*

Cuttings inserted so that leaves are just above surface

Heel cuttings Select a new sideshoot that is about 10cm (4in) long and semi-ripe. Gently pull it from the main stem (*see inset*) so that it retains a small sliver of bark. Trim the bark, using a clean, sharp knife, to leave a small "heel" on the cutting. The heel contains high levels of growth hormone that promotes rooting. Useful for rooting evergreens.

Hardwood cuttings

Hardwood cuttings are normally taken from the mature wood of deciduous and evergreen trees and shrubs at the end of the growing season (from late autumn until the end of winter). Hardwood in this context, does not mean woody and old, it refers to shoots of the current season that have started to toughen up.

Look for stems that are the same thickness as a pencil. Cut them off just above a bud or leaf joint on the parent plant. Trim the cuttings to length and insert in a trench (*see below*) in a cool, sheltered spot in the garden. Hardwood cuttings tend not to dry out as quickly as other types of cuttings, but you should still keep them watered in dry spells. Instead of planting the cuttings in a trench, you could root them in deep pots of coarse sand in a cold frame.

Leave the cuttings undisturbed for a year, watering and weeding them during the growing season. By the following autumn, they should have rooted and be ready to transplant.

Taking hardwood cuttings

❶ *Trim the cuttings to 20–23cm (8–9in) long. Use clean, secateurs to cut the bottom off just below a leaf joint. Trim off any soft wood at the top to just above a leaf joint.*

❷ *Use a spade to sink a shallow (slit) trench about 15cm (6in) deep. Line it with coarse sand. Dip the bases of the cuttings in hormone-rooting compound (see inset). Stand them in the trench, 10cm (4in) apart, firm and water.*

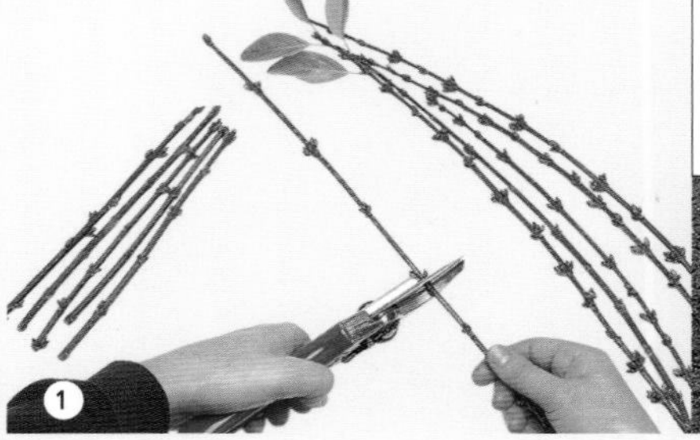

Root cuttings

Fleshy-rooted perennials, such as eryngiums, can be grown from root cuttings. Dig round a plant in autumn or winter to expose some roots. Cut off a few healthy, medium-thickness roots close to the crown. Wash off the soil and cut the roots in 5–10cm (2–4in) pieces. Dust with fungicide. Lay the pieces flat in a tray of gritty potting mix and cover over.

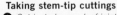

Root cuttings root faster with bottom heat.

division

Methods of dividing plants

This is the easiest and quickest way of propagating herbaceous perennials, grasses, ferns, and many alpine and aquatic plants. Most of these plants form mats or clumps, and as they grow the centre of the plant becomes congested and can die.

The practice of lifting and dividing a plant every three or four years, in autumn, winter or early spring when it is dormant, restores its vigour and gives the plant a new lease of life.

When dividing a clump, always look for the natural divisions between the shoots; some plants will have distinct crowns or offsets. Replant only healthy growth from the clump, or in the case of fleshy crowns, sections with healthy buds or roots.

There are various ways to divide a plant and which one you follow depends on the plant and the type of root system it has (*see below*). First shake or wash off as much soil as possible so that you can see the roots. Pull apart large clumps using forks; small plants with your hands. Cut fleshy crowns into sections.

Plant out the clumps as soon as you have divided them. If you cannot plant immediately, pot them up or heal them in somewhere and prevent them from drying out.

Dividing with forks Large clumps are best divided with two forks. Push the forks back to back into the root mass and pull the handles apart to split the clump. Alternatively, cut the roots with a sharp kitchen knife or pruning saw.

Dividing by hand Small fibrous-rooted plants are easy to pull apart by hand; cut tough or tangled roots with secateurs.

Dividing rhizomes Use a clean, sharp knife or secateurs to cut off young pieces with healthy buds, shoots, and roots from old, woody rhizomes. Replant the divided pieces (here of bearded iris). To avoid wind rock, trim the leaves to 15cm (6in). Discard the old rhizomes.

Dividing bulbous plants

Many bulbs, corms, and tubers, of plants such as alliums, crocosmias, crocuses, daffodils (*Narcissus*), and gladioli, increase by producing offsets around the parent bulb or corm. These types of bulbous plant can quickly form congested clumps. Unless they are lifted every three or four years and divided, the plants will lose vigour and can stop flowering.

After lifting, remove the offsets by pulling them away from the parent bulb. Many offsets will be small and may take three or four years to mature and reach flowering size, so grow them on in pots of potting mix in a sheltered spot – a cold frame is ideal.

Replant large bulbs immediately, or if still in leaf temporarily plant them in a corner of a garden until they are needed. Insert a label so you don't forget where they are. Alternatively, clean off soil and store the bulbs in a cool, dark place for replanting at the appropriate time.

Pull offsets from the main parent bulb.

layering

Rooted stems

Some climbers, such as ivies, and woody plants, like heathers, spread by rooting from their stems wherever they touch the soil. Layering takes advantage of this natural tendency. It is a useful technique particularly for evergreens – their cuttings tend to dehydrate before they root.

Select a low-growing stem, and wound it, preferably near a bud, by scratching or twisting it. Bury the wounded part of the stem in the soil. Support the exposed shoot, which will receive nourishment from the parent plant while it develops roots.

After six months to two years, once there are signs of new growth, dig up the layered shoot, detach it and plant it out.

Layering a stem Strip the middle stem (here of rosemary) of leaves. Dig a hole beneath the stem, bend and wound it, then peg it to hold it in place. Fill in with soil and grit and keep watered. After 4–6 weeks, dig up the rooted shoot, cut off and plant out.

avoiding problems

If plants are given the best possible growing conditions so that they are healthy and strong, they will be able to survive most pests and diseases. Some problems in the garden are almost inevitable, but the majority are easily kept under control, or cured and prevented from returning.

Raking up leaves makes the garden neat and deprives pests and diseases of a place to overwinter.

If you notice symptoms such as discoloured or distorted growth, or holes in leaves and flowers, they are usually caused by pests, diseases, or nutrient deficiencies. The best way to deal with these problems is to use an integrated approach, where cultural and organic methods are used to keep plants healthy, and chemicals are used only as a last resort.

Prevention is always better than cure; if given good growing conditions, plants will be strong enough to survive attacks without any lasting damage. Check plants thoroughly before you buy them for any sign of damage or disease, to avoid bringing problems into the garden. Keep cutting tools clean so they do not spread infection. Promptly remove yellowing leaves and faded flowers, and clear plant debris that could harbour insects and spores.

Be vigilant, squashing pests and cutting out diseased parts as soon as you notice them. Some pests and diseases are persistent on certain plants, such as blackspot on roses. If you find the same problem is returning year after year, it is worth obtaining a resistant cultivar. For example, *Rosa* 'The Fairy' withstands many common rose problems. If you have to resort to chemicals, use a specific remedy if possible, and spray the entire plant thoroughly. If all else fails, remove the plant before the problem spreads.

Keeping a healthy garden

Thriving plants are better able to resist problems, so it is important to maintain a healthy garden. There are several ways in which you can ensure your plants remain in top condition.

Plants that are growing in sites or conditions that do not meet their needs become stressed and more prone to problems. To avoid this, take care to choose plants that are suited to each aspect in your garden and to the local conditions (*see Climate and location, pp.371–373*). It is rare to find perfect soil; before planting, prepare it well (*see Soils and compost, pp.376–378*).

Pay attention also to watering and feeding your plants appropriately so they do not suffer from insufficient or excessive water or nutrients (*see pp.386–387*). It is essential to weed regularly so that your plants do not have to compete with fast-growing invaders for vital light, water, and nutrients (*see p.389*).

Diseases such as bacteria, fungi, and viruses are opportunists, and some infect a weak plant through an existing wound. Avoid giving them easy access by cutting cleanly when pruning (*see p.382*) and removing crossing branches that might chafe as they rub together.

Plants that are overgrown or are planted too closely often become weak and sickly, with elongated shoots as they fight for light. Fresh air cannot circulate freely around the stems and leaves, and the still, stagnant air encourages rots, moulds, and mildews. To avoid this, prune out congested growth (*see p.382*), divide herbaceous perennials (*see p.395*), and allow room for growth when planting any type of plant (*see p.379*).

Nutrient deficiency symptoms are usually first seen on leaves. A lack of iron, shown here, can be identified by yellowing between leaf veins. Nitrogen, phosphates and magnesium are also commonly deficient.

Waterlogged soils often develop mottling on the surface and a bad smell. Plant roots will "drown" through lack of air, rot, and die. The solution is to improve the soil drainage, or to grow plants that are adapted to cope in such wet conditions.

Encouraging beneficial wildlife

The only good aspect of insect pests is that they attract lots of wildlife in search of a meal. If you encourage a range of beneficial wildlife into the garden, the pests will be kept down to acceptable levels. Do not be alarmed if you see a few pests about, but allow their natural predators to take action before you think about resorting to chemical means.

Water attracts lots of animals, including frogs, which eat many pests that crawl on the ground. Lizards such as Blue Tongues are also a valuable friend, and a pile of logs or leaves, or a thick hedge, can provide a home so it stays to eat your slugs. Ladybird larvae and adults feed eagerly on the scourge of almost every garden: aphids (*see p.398*). The larvae of hoverflies also feed on aphids, as well as other soft-shelled pests such as thrips and mealybugs. Using chemicals to control the pests is likely to also kill these beneficial insects, so be very careful.

Birds can damage some seedlings or edible crops, but this is more than made up for by the number of insect pests they eat. Attract birds to the garden by planting trees and shrubs that provide cover or bear bird-attracting flowers or seeds.

Blue Tongue lizards are beneficial animals to have in the garden. They eat small pests, in particular the troublesome snails and slugs. Encourage them by giving them places to hide and keeping your pets under control.

Ladybirds and their larvae feed on aphids, one of the most common garden pests. Using chemicals to control garden pests also eliminates beneficial insects such as these, so keep their use to an absolute minimum.

How to control problems

By keeping a close watch on plants you can stop problems getting out of hand. If you see any pests, pick them off immediately. When you do spot symptoms of disease, remove the affected parts and burn or throw them in the rubbish bin.

Some plants are irresistible to aphids – if you notice that a plant is particularly affected, consider planting French marigolds (*Tagetes, see p.329*) nearby; they will attract hoverflies, the larvae of which feed on aphids and other pests such as mealybugs and thrips. Aromatic plants such as catmint (*Nepeta, see p.290*), and garlic may repel or confuse pests.

Predators or parasites of some pests can be introduced into the garden as a form of biological control. For example, a predatory mite can be introduced into the soil to control two-spotted mites.

If you do use chemicals, follow the manufacturer's instructions. Fertilizers cure deficiency diseases – if you can identify the missing nutrient, it is better to use a specific cure than an all-purpose feed. Organic pesticides, such as pyrethrum, made from plant extracts are available. Use them with the same care as any other chemical. A few inorganic pesticides are toxic to some ornamental plants. There is usually a list on the packaging; if in doubt, test the chemical on a plant.

Spray pesticides in the evening, when butterflies and bees and beneficial insects such as hoverflies and ladybirds are not around, and in still weather so the wind does not carry spray where it is not wanted. Any chemicals past their use-by date should be disposed of safely; contact the local authority for advice.

French Marigold have a scent that is believed to repel some pests and yet encourages hoverflies, whose larvae then feed on aphids.

Earwig traps can be constructed by placing upside-down flower pots on top of canes among susceptible plants. Loosely fill the pots with hay or straw and the earwigs will crawl in overnight. In the morning, empty the pots and destroy the earwigs. These pests affect many plants including chrysanthemums, clematis, and dahlias, appearing after dark to feed and leaving large holes in petals or young leaves.

Number one pests

The most common garden pests crop up regularly from year to year. Slugs and snails attack a wide range of plants. They prefer seedlings and young or fleshy plants, and will eat large holes in leaves or stems or even the entire plant. Curl grubs cause considerable damage to container-grown plants and lawns by eating the roots. The adults, which are beetles, graze on foliage, leaving large holes.

Aphids attack the soft shoots and buds of most plants, and introduce diseases through their piercing mouthparts. Deal with these pests by either picking them off or using an organic control or specific biological or chemical control.

Slugs can be very destructive, grazing through stems at soil level and returning to the same plant night after night. They will even strip the soft bark off shrubs. You can hunt and destroy them under cover of darkness, make traps, or lay barriers (*see p. 260*).

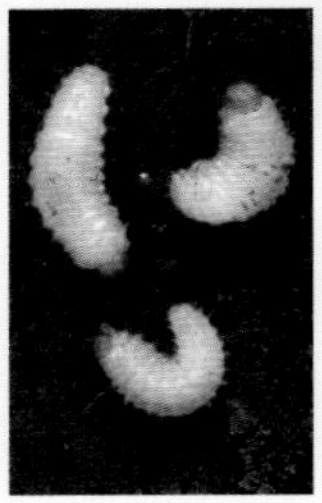

Curl grubs are, creamy white, and devour pot-plant roots. The first symptom of these pests is sudden wilting. Biological control is available.

Whole-plant problems

Occasionally you may notice that a plant is looking sick. The usual causes are incorrect watering, pests, disease, or nutrient deficiencies.

Newly planted and container-grown plants often wilt because of drought or overwatering (*see p.386*). Check the soil or potting mix and either give it a good soak or allow it to dry out. Wilting can also be caused by disease, for example fusarium wilt of carnations or pests such as curl grubs (*see left*). Lack of nutrients can make a plant sickly and yellow, but it should perk up after a liquid feed (*see p.386*). Some clumping plants lose vigour (*see below*) unless they are divided regularly.

Wilted leaves due to poor watering
Old, woody, congested growth

Neglected plants are vulnerable to a range of problems. This heuchera has produced ugly, woody growth at its base and sparse foliage because it has not been regularly divided.

Stem problems

The stems of a plant support the leaves and flowers and contain veins that transport water and food to and from the deepest roots and the tallest shoots. Because they are so important, damage to them may result in the loss of an affected plant. Pests that attack plant stems may eat the skin or bark, suck sap by piercing the veins, or in some cases tunnel right through, or live in, the stem. The wounds that they leave then provide doorways for diseases that can spread through the plant and quickly kill it. Bad pruning and extremely cold, hot, or windy weather can also damage stems. Look out for dead, diseased, or damaged parts and quickly cut out and dispose of them so problems cannot spread to other plants.

***Spittle** is the foamy, protective coating made by small, jumping insects; it does little harm other than looking unsightly*
***Frost damage** can kill, but if only new shoots are affected they often grow back. If frost is forecast, move tender plants under cover and drape early blossom and new shoots of hardy plants with hessian*
***Mildew** is a white, powdery, fungal infection; it attacks if plants are already weak or congested so air cannot move around stems freely*
***Dieback** can occur if pruning cuts are made too far from buds*
***Aphids** are very common; they suck sap from veins, leaving sticky honeydew behind on which sooty mould can develop*
***Canker** first appears as zone of flattened, discoloured bark which later splits, forming ring of flaky bark that kills shoot. Canker affects many plants at any time of the year, and should be cut out*

Possible stem problems These pests, disorders, and diseases are very common and you will certainly see them at some point. Although they can be severe enough to kill, most will cause little long-term damage – especially if they are dealt with quickly – and some can be easily prevented.

Leaf problems

Leaf problems can take the form of discoloured, distorted, or damaged growth, or premature leaf fall. This spoils the plant's appearance and reduces its ability to thrive.

Fungi can cause moulds, mildews, rusts, or spots. They attack weak plants and are unsightly, but rarely deadly, although some, for example phytophthora rootrot can be fatal. Bacteria can cause black spots on leaves; they are not raised or patchy like fungal spots, but appear more like dark shadows. Foliage with pale flecks, streaks, or mottling often has a viral infection.

Some pests, such as caterpillars, eat leaves and others, like leaf miners, burrow into them. Most plants can withstand an attack, but may become weak, providing an easy target for disease. Nutrient deficiencies – the usual cause of yellowing, or chlorosis – also compromise plant defences. With all leaf problems, the first thing to do is to try and identify the cause, then take appropriate action. Pest control or removal of affected foliage is often required. Never put diseased material on the compost heap because that will often spread infection.

Lack of water, nutrients, light, and space all favour disease; and often pampering a plant by thinning stems, watering, and feeding, will make it strong enough to fight off infection. If all else fails, chemical controls are often effective. Use one specific to the problem if possible, following the manufacturer's instructions carefully.

Weevils are slow-moving and eat irregular holes or notches in leaves near ground; they should be destroyed before they lay eggs
Rose blackspot causes dark blotches and early leaf fall
Peach leaf curl results in distorted leaves, which may be flushed red
Fuchsia rust forms tiny, orange spots underneath leaves and is encouraged by damp air
Fungal leaf spot appears as rounded, brown or grey patches containing raised, dark spots
Pelargonium rust develops as dark brown blisters, often arranged in rings, on lower leaf surfaces
Geranium downy mildew shows as pale patches with white fungus on undersides

Possible leaf problems
Some common disorders are shown here. Many of them occur on the undersides of the leaves. Be vigilant and occasionally check under leaves to make sure that there is no problem developing. If you use a contact fungicide or pesticide, spray the whole plant and make sure you include the undersides of the leaves where disease or infestation is usually concentrated.

Flower problems

Discoloured flowerheads may be a sign of pests such as thrips – tiny insects that suck sap from flower buds in hot, dry summers, causing petals with white flecks.

Most plants in the garden are grown for their flowers, but a few problems, including pests, diseases, and the weather, can affect them and spoil the show. If the first blooms are ruined, all is not lost; if you can cure the problem you may be able to encourage another, second flush of healthy flowers by regular deadheading and feeding.

Sap-sucking insects, such as aphids and thrips can distort or discolour blooms (*see left*); keep a watch for them and squash or spray them off. Other insects, for example earwigs, and budworms may eat petals or buds before they open. Diseases can also be a problem, and those affecting flowers are particularly bad if the weather is cool and damp. Symptoms to look out for include white spots, often edged with a darker ring, on the petals; these indicate the presence of grey mould (botrytis). Streaks or flecks, or deformed flowers, usually indicate a viral infection.

Weather damage is also a common problem for delicate blooms. The flowers of roses and other plants often fail to open if wet spells are followed by hot sun because of a condition known as balling. The damp bud is scorched by the sun and cannot open, causing the inner petals to rot. Flowers that open in early spring are often prone to frost damage, made worse by the morning sun. Hot, drying winds can scorch petals, turning them brown, so position sensitive plants with care.

Remain observant so any problems can be overcome before they get a firm hold. If you fail to cure a disease, then it is best to admit defeat and throw away the affected plant before it contaminates others.

plant selections

Every garden presents you with a different challenge. Some have heavy, seemingly unworkable soil; others excessive amounts of shade. The lists in this section are intended to help you identify plants for particular uses, such as herb and bog gardens, and for some of the most common problem areas, such as shaded and dry sites.

Exposed sites

Gardens on hillsides or in flat, open areas regularly experience high winds. Create a shelterbelt using hedges and trees to filter the worst of the wind, and choose hardy plants that are able to withstand a battering.

Acacia howittii
Acacia pravissima
Acer pseudoplatanus and cultivars
Achillea
Acmena smithii
Agonis flexuosa
Ajuga reptans and cultivars
Allocasuarina verticillata
Alnus glutinosa 'Imperialis' 🏆
Anaphalis triplinervis 🏆
Antirrhinum majus and cultivars
Araucaria heterophylla
Arbutus unedo 🏆
Arctostaphylos
Artemisia abrotanum 🏆
Artemisia 'Powis Castle' 🏆
Banksia integrifolia
Banksia serrata
Berberis
Bergenia
Bupleurum fruticosum
Calendula officinalis and cultivars
Callistemon citrinus
Callistemon viminalis
Callitris rhomboidea
Calothamnus quadrificus
Carpinus betulus 'Fastigiata' 🏆
Casuarina glauca
Chaenomeles
Chamaecyparis obtusa 'Nana Aurea' 🏆
Chamaecyparis pisifera 'Filifera Aurea' 🏆
Clethra arborea
Coreopsis 'Sunray'
Cornus
Correa
Corylus avellana 'Contorta'
Cotoneaster horizontalis 🏆
Crataegus laevigata 'Paul's Scarlet' 🏆
Cryptomeria japonica 'Elegans Compacta' 🏆
× *Cupressocyparis leylandii* 🏆
Cupressus macrocarpa and cultivars
Deutzia
Dryas octopetala 🏆
Echinacea purpurea 'Kim's Knee High'
Echinops ritro 'Veitch's Blue'
Elaeagnus
Erigeron karvinskianus 🏆
Eryngium × *tripartitum* 🏆
Escallonia 'Apple Blossom' 🏆
Eschscholzia californica 🏆
Eucalyptus
Euonymus alatus 🏆
Euonymus fortunei and cultivars
Fagus sylvatica 'Dawyck Purple' 🏆
Felicia amelloides
Ficus carica
Forsythia × *intermedia* and cultivars
Fraxinus excelsior
Fuchsia magellanica
Gaultheria
Genista aetnensis 🏆
Ginkgo biloba 🏆
Gleditsia triacanthos 'Sunburst' 🏆
Grevillea
Hakea
Hamamelis
Hebe
Helleborus niger 🏆 and cultivars
Hydrangea paniculata 'Grandiflora' 🏆
Hypericum calycinum
Ilex aquifolium 🏆
Iris sibirica 🏆 and cultivars
Jasminum nudiflorum 🏆
Juniperus
Kalmia angustifolia 🏆
Kerria japonica and cultivars
Kunzea ambigua
Lagunaria patersonii
Laurus nobilis 🏆
Lavatera
Leptospermum
Leucothoe fontanesiana 'Rainbow'
Melaleuca
Metrosideros excelsa
Miscanthus
Nepeta 'Six Hills Giant'
Nerium oleander
Phalaris arundinacea var. picta
Picea abies
Pieris
Pinus nigra 🏆
Poa labillardieri
Populus × *canadensis* and cultivars
Potentilla
Primula
Prunus spinosa
Pulmonaria saccharata
Quercus
Rosmarinus officinalis
Salix alba
Sempervivum arachnoideum 🏆
Sempervivum tectorum 🏆
Senecio cineraria 'Silver Dust' 🏆
Senna artemisiodes
Sorbus aria
Sorbus aucuparia and cultivars
Spiraea
Tamarix
Tanacetum parthenium and cultivars
Taxus
Thuja plicata
Tilia
Tsuga canadensis and cultivars
Viburnum × *bodnantense* 'Dawn' 🏆
Viburnum × *burkwoodii*
Viburnum opulus 'Compactum' 🏆
Viburnum rhytidophyllum
Westringia fruticosa

Seaside gardens

Coastal areas suffer from winter gales and the scorching salt spray that they bring. Create shelterbelts by planting trees around the perimeter, and go for tough plants that conserve moisture.

Achillea
Agonis flexuosa
Allium
Allocasuarina verticillata
Alstroemeria
Anaphalis triplinervis 🏆
Anthemis
Antirrhinum majus and cultivars
Araucaria heterophylla
Arbutus unedo 🏆
Arcotis
Argyranthemum frutescens and cultivars
Armeria

Artemisia abrotanum ♕
Artemisia 'Powis Castle' ♕
Aster
Aucuba
Banksia integrifolia
Banksia serrata
Bergenia
Bougainvillea
Buddleja davidii and cultivars
Bupleurum fruticosum
Callitris rhomboidea
Campanula
Cerastium tomentosum
Choisya ternata SUNDANCE ♕ ('Lich)
Cistus
Cordyline australis
Correa alba
Correa reflexa
Cupressus macrocarpa
Dahlia
Dianthus
Dierama pulcherrimum
Dodonaea viscosa 'Purpurea'
Echinacea purpurea
Echinops ritro 'Veitch's Blue'
Elaeagnus × *ebbingei* 'Gilt Edge' ♕
Erica arborea var. *alpina* ♕
Erigeron karvinskianus ♕
Erigeron 'Quakeress'
Erodium manescaui
Escallonia 'Apple Blossom' ♕
Eucalyptus
Euonymous fortunei and cultivars
Euphorbia
Euryops pectinatus
Felicia amelloides
Ficus carica
Forsythia × *intermedia* and cultivars
Fuchsia magellanica
Garrya elliptica
Gaultheria
Genista aetnensis ♕
Geranium
Gleditsia triacanthos 'Sunburst' ♕
Gypsophila 'Rosenschleier' ♕
Halimium 'Susan' ♕
Hebe
Hemerocallis
Heuchera
Hibbertia scandens
Hibiscus syriacus
Impatiens
Iris
Juniperus
Kennedia prostrata
Kennedia rubicuna
Kunzea baxteri
Lagunaria patersonii
Laurus nobilis ♕
Lavandula
Lavatera
Leptospermum laevigatum
Leucophyta brownii
Limonium perezii
Lobularia maritima
Lonicera nitida
Lychnis coronaria ♕
Melissa officinalis 'Aurea'
Metrosideros excelsa
Monarda
Oenothera
Olearia
Origanum
Osmanthus delavayi ♕
Pachysandra terminalis
Penstemon
Phormium tenax ♕
Phygelius
Pinus nigra ♕
Pittosporum
Potentilla
Pulsatilla
Quercus ilex ♕
Rosa (some)
Rosmarinus officinalis
Salvia
Sambucus racemosa 'Plumosa Aurea'
Santolina
Sisyrinchium
Stachys
Tamarix
Viburnum
Westringia fruticosa
Yucca gloriosa ♕

Dry sun

Situations prone to drought include steeply sloping sunny banks with rapid drainage; the base of a warm north- or west-facing wall; and shallow, sandy, or stony soils in full sun.

Abelia
Acacia baileyana ♕
Achillea
Agapanthus
Agonis flexuosa
Allium
Allocasuarina verticillata
Alstroemeria
Alyogyne huegeli
Anaphalis triplinervis ♕
Anigozanthos
Anthemis
Arctotis
Armeria pseudarmeria
Artemisia
Asphodeline lutea
Banksia
Betula
Brachyscome
Buddleja
Buxus
Callistemon citrinus
Callistemon viminalis
Callitris
Calothamnus quadrificus
Caryopteris × *clandonensis* 'Kew Blue'
Casuarina cunninghamia
Casuarina glauca
Catananche caerulea 'Bicolor'
Ceanothus
Centaurea
Cerastium tomentosum
Ceratostigma willmottianum ♕
Chamaemelum nobile 'Flore Pleno'
Cirsium rivulare 'Atropurpureum'
Cistus
Cleome hassleriana
Correa
Correa reflexa
Corymbia
Crambe cordifolia ♕
× *Cupressocyparis leylandii* ♕
Cynara cardunculus ♕
Danthonia
Dianthus
Diascia
Dictamnus albus
Echinops ritro 'Veitch's Blue'
Erodium manescaui
Erysimum
Escallonia
Eucalyptus
Euonymus
Euryops pectinatus
Euphorbia
Foeniculum vulgare 'Purpureum'
Fuchsia magellanica
Gaillardia
Gaura lindheimeri ♕
Gazania
Genista aetnensis ♕
Genista lydia ♕
Geranium
Gleditisia triacanthos
Grevillea
Gypsophila 'Rosenschleier' ♕
Hakea
Hebe
Helianthemum
Hemerocallis
Hypericum
Impatiens
Ipheion uniflorum 'Wisley Blue' ♕
Iris foetidissima ♕
Iris pallida 'Variegata' ♕
Juniperus
Kniphofia
Kunzea ambigua
Lagunaria patersonii
Lavandula
Leptospermum
Liatris spicata
Limonium perezii
Linaria alpina
Linum perenne
Lobularia 'Royal Carpet'
Lychnis coronaria ♕
Melaleuca
Melissa officinalis 'Aurea'

Nepeta
Nerine bowdenii 🏆
Nerium oleander
Oenothera
Origanum laevigatum 🏆
Osteospermum
Pelargonium
Penstemon
Perovskia 'Bue Spire' 🏆
Phlomis fruticosa 🏆
Phormium
Phygelius aequalis 'Yellow Trumpet' 🏆
Pinus mugo 'Mops' 🏆
Poa labillardieri
Potentilla
Quercus ilex 🏆
Ribes
Rosmarinus officinalis and cultivars
Salvia patens 'Cambridge Blue' 🏆
Sambucus racemosa 'Plumosa Aurea'
Santolina
Schizanthus × *wisetonensis* 'Hit Parade'
Sedum
Sempervivum arachnoideum 🏆
Sempervivum tectorum 🏆
Senna artemisiodes
Solanum
Spiraea
Stachys byzantina
Stachys macrantha 'Superba'
Stipa
Tagetes
Tamarix
Teucrium
Themeda
Thymus
Tulipa
Verbascum
Westringia fruticosa
Yucca gloriosa 🏆

Damp shade

A cool, humid woodland environment where the soil is reliably moist all year.
Acer cappadocicum
Acer griseum 🏆
Acer negundo 'Variegatum'
Acer palmatum f. *atropurpureum*
Acer saccharinum
Alchemilla mollis 🏆
Alnus
Alocasia macrorrhiza
Arisaema flavum
Arisarum vulgare
Aruncus dioicus 🏆
Asplenium australasicum
Asplenium scolopendrium 🏆
Astilbe
Athyrium filix-femina 'Frizelliae' 🏆
Aucuba japonica
Betula pendula 'Youngii'
Blandifordia punicea
Bulbine bulbosa
Buxus sempervirens 🏆
Caltha palustris 🏆
Caltha palustris 'Flore Pleno' 🏆
Camellia japonica and cultivars
Cercidiphyllum japonicum 🏆
Clethra arborea
Convallaria majalis 🏆
Cornus canadensis 🏆
Daphne
Darmera peltata 🏆
Dicentra
Dicksonia antarctica
Dryopteris wallichiana 🏆
Elaeagnus
Epacris impressa
Erythronium
Euonymus fortunei
Fatsia japonica 🏆
Fothergilla major 🏆
Gahnia sieberiana
Gaultheria
Hamamelis
Helleborus
Hibbertia scandens
Hosta
Hydrangea
Hypericum calycinum
Ilex aquifolium 🏆
Ligularia 'The Rocket' 🏆
Lilium martagon 🏆
Mahonia aquifolium
Metasequoia glyptostroboides 🏆
Monarda
Orthosanthus multiflorus
Osmanthus × *burkwoodii* 🏆
Osmanthus delavayi 🏆
Pachysandra terminalis
Picea
Pieris
Polystichum setiferum 🏆
Populus
Primula (candelabra types)
Prunus padus 'Watereri' 🏆
Quercus
Rhododendron
Rodgersia pinnata 'Superba' 🏆
Salix
Sambucus racemosa 'Plumosa Aurea'
Sasa veitchii
Sorbus
Spiraea
Stachyurus praecox 🏆
Symphoricarpos
Symphytum
Taxus baccata 🏆 and cultivars
Viburnum davidii 🏆
Viburnum opulus
Viburnum rhytidophyllum

Dry shade

The combined problems of shade and drought are often found by walls, and beneath thirsty, shallow-rooting trees.
Acanthus spinosus 🏆
Ajuga reptans and cultivars
Alchemilla mollis 🏆
Aquilegia
Arum italicum 'Marmoratum' 🏆
Astrantia
Aucuba
Berberis
Bergenia
Betula
Buxus sempervirens 🏆
Cornus canadensis 🏆
Correa reflexa
Cotoneaster
Dampiera diversifolia
Daphne
Dianella tasmanica
Dicentra formosa
Digitalis
Epimedium
Euonymus fortunei
Fatsia japonica 🏆
Garrya elliptica
Geranium himalayense
Geranium macrorrhizum
Geranium nodosum
Hardenbergia violacea 'Happy Wanderer'
Hedera
Heuchera
Ilex aquifolium 🏆
Indigofera australis
Iris foetidissima 🏆
Juniperus × *pfitzeriana*
Kennedia
Lamium
Lunaria annua and cultivars
Mahonia
Meconopsis cambrica
Melissa officinalis 'Aurea'
Milium effusum 'Aureum' 🏆
Pachysandra terminalis
Pandorea jasminoides and cultivars
Philotheca myoporoides
Pittosporum tenuifolium 🏆
Poa labillardieri
Polygonatum
Polypodium vulgare
Prunus laurocerasus 🏆
Santolina
Symphoricarpos
Taxus baccata 🏆 and cultivars
Teucrium

Deep shade

Permanently shaded positions may be beneath evergreen trees, by high walls, and between tall buildings. Use plants and structures in light colours to help brighten these areas.
Acer cappadocicum
Acer griseum 🏆
Adiantum venustum 🏆

Ajuga reptans and cultivars
Alchemilla mollis ♀
Aruncus dioicus ♀
Asplenium scolopendrium ♀
Astilbe
Athyrium filix-femina 'Frizelliae' ♀
Aucuba japonica
Bergenia
Betula nigra
Blechnum
Buxus
Camellia
Cercidiphyllum japonicum ♀
Clivia
Cyathea
Daphne
Dicentra
Dicksonia antarctica ♀
Digitalis
Dryopteris wallichiana ♀
Epimedium
Erythronium
Fatsia japonica ♀
Fothergilla major ♀
Gaultheria
Helleborus
Hosta
Hydrangea
Ilex
Iris foetidissima ♀
Iris sibirica ♀
Mahonia
Mysotis sylvatica
Osmanthus × *burkwoodii* ♀
Pachysandra terminalis
Pieris
Polypodium vulgare
Polystichum setiferum ♀
Primula (candelabra types)
Prunus laurocerasus ♀
Pulmonaria
Rhododendron
Rodgersia pinnata 'Superba' ♀
Salix
Symphoricarpos
Symphytum
Taxus baccata ♀ and cultivars
Viburnum davidii ♀
Viburnum rhytidophyllum
Viola odorata
Woodwardia radicans ♀

Heavy soils

Heavy clay soils can be hard to work, but are often rich in nutrients. Select hardy plants, avoid alpines, and persist in digging in organic matter and gypsum to improve fertility and drainage.

Abelia
Acer
Acmena smithii
Aconitum
Aesculus
Agapanthus
Ajuga reptans and cultivars
Alnus
Anemone × *hybrida* and cultivars
Aster
Aucuba japonica
Banksia ericifolia
Berberis
Betula
Campanula
Carpinus betulus 'Fastigiata' ♀
Chaenomeles
Choisya ternata
Cornus
Correa reflexa
Corylus avellana 'Contorta'
Cotinus 'Grace'
Cotoneaster
Crataegus
Crocosmia
Cytisus
Darmera peltata ♀
Dietes bicolor
Digitalis
Echinops
Erigeron
Escallonia
Eucalyptus
Forsythia × *intermedia* and cultivars
Fraxinus excelsior 'Jaspidea' ♀
Geranium
Gleditsia triacanthos 'Sunburst'
Hamamelis
Hardenbergia violacea 'Happy Wanderer'
Helenium
Helleborus
Hemerocallis
Hibbertia scandens
Hibiscus syriacus
Hosta
Hypericum
Ilex
Kerria japonica and cultivars
Lysimachia clethroides ♀
Magnolia
Mahonia
Malus
Monarda
Osmanthus × *burkwoodii* ♀
Persicaria bistorta 'Superba' ♀
Philadelphus
Pieris japonica 'Flamingo'
Populus
Potentilla
Prunus
Pyrus salicifolia 'Pendula' ♀
Quercus
Ranunculus
Rhododendron
Rodgersia
Rosa
Rudbeckia
Salix
Sasa veitchii
Sidalcea
Solidago
Sorbus
Syringa
Tilia
Tradescantia
Weigela florida
Westringia fruticosa
Wisteria

Acid (lime-free) soils

Acid soils are typically very fertile, nutrient-rich, and moist with good drainage. You can create the right conditions for some acid-loving plants in containers of acid-loving potting mix.

Acer rubrum 'October Glory' ♀
Banksia ericifolia
Betula
Boronia megastigma
Camellia
Cercidiphyllum japonicum ♀
Corylopsis glabrescens
Cryptomeria japonica 'Elegans Compacta' ♀
Daboecia cantabrica and cultivars
Daphne
Gaultheria
Gordonia axillaris
Ilex aquifolium ♀
Kalmia angustifolia ♀
Leucothoe fontanesiana 'Rainbow'
Liquidambar styraciflua 'Golden Treasure'
Magnolia
Meconopsis betonicifolia ♀
Pinus nigra ♀
Rhododendron
Telopea speciosissima
Tibouchina urvilleana
Trillium

Alkaline soil

Soils in some areas can be quite alkaline (limy). It is generally fairly fertile, but does not suit all types of plants, particularly ones that require an acid soil.

Acanthus spinosus ♀
Acer cappadocicum
Acer griseum ♀
Allocasuarina verticillata
Alyogyne huegelii
Angophora costata
Anthemis
Arbutus unedo ♀
Berberis
Buddleja davidii
Carpinus betulus ♀

'atalpa bignonioides 🏆
'eanothus
'lematis
'orrea alba
'orylus avellana 'Contorta'
)aphne
)ianthus
'remophila maculata
'agus sylvatica 'Dawyck Purple' 🏆
'raxinus excelsior 'Jaspidea' 🏆
'leditsia triacanthos 'Sunburst' 🏆
lebe
aurus nobilis 🏆
iriodendron tulipifera 🏆
lalus
lyoporum parvifolium
'aeonia
'apaver orientale and cultivars
'imelea ferruginea
'ulsatilla vulgaris 🏆
'yrus salicifolia 'Pendula' 🏆
'obinia pseudoacacia 'Frisia' 🏆
edum spectabile 🏆 and cultivars
yringa
'radescantia
'erbascum

Ornamental herbs

;ood-looking culinary plants that are
qually at home in the herb garden or
ie shrub garden.
nethum graveolens
ngelica archangelica
rtemisia abrotanum 🏆
'orago officinalis
'alendula officinalis
'hamaemelum nobile 'Flore Pleno'
'ymbopogon citratus
'oeniculum vulgare 'Purpureum'
aurus nobilis 🏆
avandula angustifolia 'Hidcote' 🏆
lelissa officinalis and cultivars
'osmarinus officinalis
alvia officinalis
'hymus

Rock-garden plants

Rock gardens and raised beds provide good drainage and make an ideal showcase for small plants and alpines.

Ajuga reptans and cultivars
Anchusa cespitosa
Arenaria balearica
Arenaria montana 🏆
Armeria pseudarmeria
Aubrieta
Brachyscome
Bulbine bulbosa
Campanula carpatica 'Weisse Clips'
Chrysocaphalum apiculatum
Daboecia cantabrica and cultivars
Dampiera
Daphne cneorum
Dianthus
Echeveria
Erigeron karvinskianus 🏆
Erinus alpinus 🏆
Eryngium
Euphorbia myrsinites 🏆
Helianthemum
Juniperus communis 'Compressa' 🏆
Lamium maculatum
Linaria alpina
Oxalis hirta
Rhodohypoxis baurii
Romulea bulbocodium
Saponaria ocymoides 🏆
Saxifraga
Sedum
Sempervivum
Thymus

Fragrant plants

To maximize your enjoyment of the wonderful aromas of scented plants, grow them near the house, or by paths.

Akebia quinata
Asphodeline lutea
Azara microphylla
Boronia
Buddleja
Chimonanthus praecox
Choisya ternata
Clematis armandii
Clematis flammula
Clematis rehderiana 🏆
Convallaria majalis 🏆
Cosmos atrosanguineus
Daphne
Dianthus
Eucalyptus
Genista aetnensis 🏆
Hamamelis
Hymenosporum flavum
Iris unguicularis 🏆
Lavandula
Lonicera fragrantissima
Lunaria rediviva
Mahonia
Malus floribunda 🏆
Malus hupehensis 🏆
Monarda
Osmanthus × *burkwoodii* 🏆
Phlox paniculata and cultivars
Rosa
Syringa
Tilia platyphyllos
Viburnum × *burkwoodii*
Wisteria floribunda

Bog-garden plants

All these plants like permanently moist soil. Some will even grow in very shallow water at the edge of a pond.

Alnus incana
Allocasuarina lehmanniana
Aruncus dioicus 🏆
Astilbe
Blechnum nudum
Caltha palustris 🏆
Cardamine pratensis 'Flore Pleno'
Cornus alba and cultivars
Cyperus papyrus
Darmera peltata 🏆
Filipendula
Gunnera
Hemerocallis
Iris ensata 🏆
Iris sibirica 🏆 and cultivars
Ligularia
Lobelia
Nelumbo nucifera
Phragmites australis
Primula bulleyana 🏆
Primula denticulata 🏆
Primula florindae 🏆
Rodgersia pinnata 'Superba' 🏆
Salix alba and cultivars
Saracenia

Sloping sites

Ground-cover plants are ideal for slopes because they help to bind the soil, preventing erosion.

Ajuga reptans and cultivars
Arcotis
Bergenia
Cistus
Cotoneaster horizontalis 🏆
Dampiera
Davallia pyxidata
Epimedium
Euonymus fortunei 'Emerald 'n' Gold' 🏆
Gahnia sieberiana
Gaultheria
Hardenbergia violacea 'Happy Wanderer'
Hypericum calycinum
Juniperus × *pfitzeriana* and cultivars
Juniperus squamata 'Blue Star' 🏆
Kennedia
Lamium
Lavandula
Lysimachia nummularia
Myoporum parvifolium
Potentilla
Rosmarinus officinalis and cultivars
Symphytum caucasicum 🏆
Tiarella
Thymus

index

a

b

c

d

m

n

q

r

S

t

u

v

w

y

z

picture credits

e publisher would like to thank the following for their kind permission
reproduce their photographs; (Abbreviations key; t=top, b=below,
right, l=left, c=centre, f=far, a=above)

Lorna Rose; **2**: Photographer: Steven Wooster; Garden for
helsea Flower Show 2002 by Tamsin Partridge; **3**: Lorna Rose;
Roger Smith/DK; **6**: Photographer: Steven Wooster; The Stonemarket
tio Garden by Geoffrey Whiten for Chelsea Flower Show 2002 (bl);
9: Photographer: Steven Wooster; "The West Midlands-Shizoka
oodwill" garden for Chelsea Flower Show 2002 by Julian Dowle
rtnership; **10-11**: Roger Smith/DK; **11**: Roger Smith/DK (tr, cra,
, cfra); **12**: Eric Crichton Photos/Mrs B. Sterndale-Bennett/White
indows (br); **13**: Peter Anderson (tr, cr); Roger Smith/DK (bc, br);
: Garden Picture Library/Jerry Pavia (bc); **16**: Bob Rundle (bc);
: Lorna Rose (tc), Ivy Hansen (bl, br); **18**: Roger Smith/DK (tl, bcl);
: Andrew Butler (tr), Roger Smith/DK (bcr, cbr); **20**: Roger Smith/DK
ra), Ivy Hansen (l); **21**: Lorna Rose (bl), Roger Smith/DK (bcl); **22**: Ivy
ansen (bl); **23**: Ivy Hansen (l), Lorna Rose (bl), Roger Smith/DK (bcl);
: Leigh Clapp (bc, br); **25**: Australian National Botanical Gardens (br),
oger Smith/DK (crb); **26**: Lorna Rose
c, br), Garden Picture Library/Neil Holmes (bl), Roger Smith/DK
cl); **28**: Roger Smith/DK (clb, bc); **29**: Ivy Hansen (bc), C. Andrew
enley (bfr), Roger Smith/DK (bcr); **30**: Roger Smith/DK (bc); **32**:
oger Smith/DK (br); **33**: Global Book Publishing (lac), Ivy Hansen
cr, tr, lbc), Lorna Rose (tcl), Roger Smith/DK (cla, crb, car, cbl); **34**: Ivy
ansen (br) **35**: Global Book Publishing (lac), Ivy Hansen (tl), Roger
nith/DK (cra, bc); **37**: Roger Smith/DK (crb, bc); **38**: Juliette Wade (br,
a), Roger Smith/DK (tr, cb, bl); **39**: Juliette Wade (cbl), Roger
nith/DK (clb); **40**: Lorna Rose (br), Juliette Wade (bl); **41**: Ivy Hansen
c), Dave Watts (bl); **42**: Andrew Butler (crb), Bob Rundle (car), Roger
nith/DK (cbr); **43**: Andrew Butler (cal); **44**: Leigh
app (bl), Ivy Hansen (br), Roger Smith/DK (crb); **45**: Australian
ational Botanical Gardens (bl), Roger Smith/DK (cra, bcr); **47**: Leigh
app (bc), Roger Smith/DK (bl); **48**: Roger Smith/DK (bc); **49**: Juliette
ade (bcr); **50**: Global Book Publishing (bc), Lorna Rose (br); **51**:
liette Wade (bl); **52**: Leigh Clapp (tr, br), Lorna Rose (bl);
: Ivy Hansen (bl); **54**: Garden World Images (clb); **55**: Leigh Clapp
), Ivy Hansen (bl), Roger Smith/DK (car); **57**: Andrew Butler (br, bcr);
: Roger Smith/DK (bc); **60**: Sunniva Harte (bl), Garden World Images
cr); **61**: Juliette Wade (cra); Sunniva Harte (cla, bcl, cal), Photos
orticultural (crb, cbr), Roger Smith/DK (cbl); **62**: Sunniva Harte (clb),
arden and Wildlife Matters (car), Roger Smith/DK (cra), Sunniva Harte
al, car); **63**: Photos Horticultural (cbr), Roger
nith/DK (cla, clb); **64**: Global Book Publishing (br), Roger Smith/DK
l); **65**: Andrew Butler (bl), Roger Smith/DK (br); **66**: Ivy Hansen (br);
: Leigh Clapp (br), Ivy Hansen (tl, bl, c); **68**: Roger Smith/DK (br); **69**:
y Hansen (tl, bc, tr), Lorna Rose (br); **70**: Lorna Rose (br), Roger
nith/DK (bl); **74**: Ivy Hansen (bl, br); **75**: Ivy Hansen (bc); **78**: Ivy
ansen (br); **79**: Ivy Hansen (bc), Holt Studios International/Rosemary
ayer (bcr); **80**: Roger Smith/DK (tr, br);
: C. Andrew Henley (br); **82**: Jennifer Wilkinson (bc); **83**: Andrew
utler (cb); **84**: Roger Smith/DK (bl); **85**: Ivy Hansen (bl);
: Garden Picture Library/Howard Rice (bl), Photos Horticultural (clb);
87: Ivy Hansen (bl), Lorna Rose (br); **88**: Roger Smith/DK (bc);
89: Ivy Hansen (bc); **90**: Andrew Butler (br), Roger Smith/DK (bl);
91: Ivy Hansen (bl), Roger Smith/DK (crb, bc); **92**: Roger Smith/DK (bc,
bcr); **93**: Andrew Butler (bcr), Annelise Evans (bl), Roger Smith/DK (cbr);
94 Leigh Clapp (bl), Lorna Rose (bc); **95**: Roger Smith/DK (cbr); **96**:
Roger Smith/DK (bcr, cbl); **97**: Roger Smith/DK (bc); **98**: John Fielding
(bcl), Roger Smith/DK (cbl); **99**: Andrew Butler (bl, br, bcr); **100**:
Andrew Butler (cbl), Garden World Images (clb), Ivy Hansen (bl); **101**:
Andrew Lawson (clb), Photos Horticultural (bcr);
102: Global Book Publishing (bl); **103**: Andrew Butler (tr, tcr), Roger
Smith/DK (bc); **105**: Roger Smith/DK (cra, clb, cal); **106**: Roger
Smith/DK (cra); **107**: John Fielding (cbr), Roger Smith/DK (cbl);
108: Garden World Images (bc), Australian National Botanical Gardens
(bl); **109**: Global Book Publishing (bl), Melbourne Botanical Gardens
(br), Kate McLeod (tr), Roger Smith/DK (cb); **111**: Roger Smith/DK
(bcr); **112**: R.N.R.S. St Albans (br); **113**: C. Andrew Henley (clb); **114**:
Garden World Images (bl), Roger Smith/DK (bc); **115**: Roger Smith/DK
(cfr); **116**: Lorna Rose (bc), Roger Smith/DK (br);
117: Ivy Hansen (bl); **118**: Andrew Butler (bcl), Roger Smith/DK (bl,
cbl); **119**: Garden World Images (crb, br); **120**: Andrew Butler (bc),
Lorna Rose (br), Roger Smith/DK (bl); **121**: Leigh Clapp (br), Roger
Smith/DK (tc, tr); **122**: Ivy Hansen (br), Juliette Wade (cra), Roger
Smith/DK (bc); **123**: Ivy Hansen (bl), Juliette Wade (bcr);
125: Lorna Rose (bc); **126**: Roger Smith/DK (tr, car); **127**: Andrew
Butler (bcl), Dave Watts (cbl), Photos Horticultural (bl), Roger
Smith/DK (tcl); **128**: Andrew Butler (bc); **129**: Eric Crichton Photos
(bc), Cambridge Botanic Gardens (br); **130-131**: Roger Smith/DK; **131**:
Bob Rundle (cfra), Roger Smith/DK (cfrb); **132**: Trish Gant (c); **134**:
Roger Smith/DK (blc); **135** Ivy Hansen (bc); **136**: Raymond Evison (cbr);
137: Roger Smith/DK (cra); **138**: Raymond Evison
(tr, lbc), Roseland House Garden & Nursery, Truro, Cornwall (cla, car),
Roger Smith/DK (cbl); **139**: Jill Cowley (car); **140**: Ivy Hansen (bl),
Suttons Seeds (br); **141**: Roger Smith/DK (bl); **142**: Ivy Hansen (bl),
Roger Smith/DK (bc); **143**: Roger Smith/DK (bc); **144**: Mr Fothergill's
Seeds (bcl), Lorna Rose (bc); **147**: Jennifer Wilkinson (br); **148**: Ivy
Hansen (bl), Roger Smith/DK (clb, cbl); **149**: Ivy Hansen (bl);
151: Roger Smith/DK (bcr); **155**: Roger Smith/DK (bl); **157**: Roger
Smith/DK (tr, cra, br); **159**: Roger Smith/DK (tr), Photographer: Steve
Wooster; The Inside-out Garden', Chelsea Flower Show 2002; Garden
Design; Marshall-Lacrox Partnership (cl); **160**: Roger Smith/DK (ca);
161: Roger Smith/DK (cla, ca, cra, cl, br), Steve Wooster; Chelsea Flower
Show 2002, The West Midlands Shizhoka Goodwill Garden (bl);
163: Steve Wooster (bc), Chelsea Flower Show 2002, Careless Rapture
by RHS Diploma Class at Otley College (cl); **164**: Lee Griffiths (br);
166: Global Book Publishing (bl), Roger Smith/DK (br, cbl);
168: Photos Horticultural (c), Roger Smith/DK (bl); **169**: Photos
Horticultural (bc), Roger Smith/DK (tc); **170**: Roger Smith/DK (cb);
171: Photos Horticultural (tc); **172**: Oasis Australia (bl), Roger Smith/DK
(br); **174**: Garden World Images (bc), Roger Smith/DK (tc, bl); **175**:
Roger Smith/DK (tl, br); **176**: Global Book Publishing (bl); **177**: Garden
World Images (l), Roger Smith/DK (br); **178**: Jennifer Wilkinson (bc),
Roger Smith/DK (bl); **179** Suttons Seeds (tc);
180: Roger Smith/DK (br); **182**: Andrew Lawson (l), Photos
Horticultural (bl), Roger Smith/DK (bc); **184**: Roger Smith/DK (bl),
Thompson & Morgan (c, br) Oasis Australia (tr); **185**: Eric Crichton
Photos (br); **186**: Roger Smith/DK (cal), Lorna Rose (ar, bc); **188**: Lorna
Rose (lb), Roger Smith/DK (bc); **189**: Garden World Images
(br), Roger Smith/DK (tc); **190**: Roger Smith/DK (bl, bc, br, bcl); **191**:
Roger Smith/DK (bc); **192** Roger Smith/DK (bl); **193**: Roger Smith/DK
(cb), Jennifer Wilkinson (tr), Lorna Rose (br), Leigh Clapp (bc); **194**:
Juliette Wade (c); **195**: Roger Smith/DK (tc, bc), Ivy Hansen (br); **197**:
Roger Smith/DK (bl); **198**: Lorna Rose (br); **199**: John Fielding (br),
Roger Smith/DK (bl, bc); **200**: Garden World Images (bc), Lorna Rose
(bl); **201**: Roger Smith/DK (tc, bl), Jennifer Wilkinson (br); **202**: Lorna
Rose (bl), Ivy Hansen (br); **203**: Global Book Publishing (tc), Garden
World Images (br); **204**: Mr Fothergill's Seeds (tc, tc), Garden World
Images (bl); **205**: Roger Smith/DK (clb, cb), Global Book Publishing (bl);
207: Ivy Hansen (tr, br); **208**: Roger Smith/DK (bcr); **210**: Roger
Smith/DK (br); **211**: Andrew Lawson (bl) Australian National Botanical
Gardens (br); **215**: Roger Smith/DK (crb, br), Leigh Clapp (cb); **216**:
Roger Smith/DK (cbl); **217**: Roger Smith/DK (crb, bcr); **218**: Roger
Smith/DK (clb, cbl); **219**: Roger Smith/DK (tr, bc), Lorna Rose (tl, bl);
220: Roger Smith/DK (tr, bl); **221**: Roger Smith/DK (bl, bc); **224**: Ivy
Hansen (bl), Oasis Australia (br);
225: Oasis Australia (bl); **226**: Roger Smith/DK (cra); **227**: Roger
Smith/DK (cla, br, tcl); **228**: Roger Smith/DK (bl, bcr); **230**: Roger
Smith/DK (r); **231**: Eric Crichton Photos (bl), Lorna Rose (cb, rb); **232**:
Lorna Rose (br), Roger Smith/DK (bc); **233**: Roger Smith/DK (tc, bl, br);
234: Lorna Rose (br); **236**: Global Book Publishing (bl), Photos
Horticultural (bl), Roger Smith/DK (bc); **237**: Roger Smith/DK (tr);
238: Roger Smith/DK (bc); **239**: Lorna Rose (br), Roger Smith/DK (l, c);
240: Roger Smith/DK (br); **241**: Roger Smith/DK (br); **242**: Roger
Smith/DK (bl); **243**: Lorna Rose (br); **244**: Garden World Images (br);
245: Garden and Wildlife Matters (bl), Roger Smith/DK (bcl), Lorna Rose
(br); **246**: Roger Smith/DK (tc, bl);
247: Roger Smith/DK (bc); **248**: Lorna Rose (r); **249**: Lorna Rose (tc);
250: Eric Crichton Photos (clb), Andrew Lawson (bcl), Garden World
Images (clb), Roger Smith/DK (tr, cla, bcr); **251**: Hidcote Manor (car),
Juliette Wade (cal), Andrew Lawson (crb), Photos Horticultural (tcl), Roger
Smith/DK (cra); **252**: Ivy Hansen (c); Roger Smith/DK (br); **253**: Roger
Smith/DK (bl), Lorna Rose (c); **254**: Roger Smith/DK (c, bl); **255**: Roger
Smith/DK (c, br); **257**: Roger Smith/DK (cl, br); **258**: Leigh Clapp (tc),
Lorna Rose (bc); **259**: Roger Smith/DK (bl); **260**: Andrew Lawson (br);
262: Roger Smith/DK (bl), Lorna Rose (br); **264**: Eric Crichton (tr);
265: Eric Crichton (bl, br, car, cbl), Garden and Wildlife Matters (crb),
Andrew Lawson (bcr); **266**: Eric Crichton (cal), RHS Garden Wisley (tcl),
Garden Picture Library/Densey Clyne (clb), Roger Smith/DK (bcl, cbl);
267: Andrew Butler (bcr), Eric Crichton (cbl), Garden Picture Library/JS
Sira (cal), John Glover (tcl), Roger Smith/DK (bcl); **270**: Roger Smith/DK
(tr, bl); **271**: Roger Smith/DK (tc, br); **273**: Peter Anderson (br);
274: Roger Smith/DK (tcr); **275**: Garden and Wildlife Matters (cbl),
Roger Smith/DK (cra, br); **276**: Roger Smith/DK (bl); **277**: Garden
World Images (cb); **278**: Lorna Rose (br), Roger Smith/DK (bl);
279: Ivy Hansen (bl), Mr Fothergill's Seeds (br), Oasis Australia (bc);

280: Roger Smith/DK (tc); **281**: Roger Smith/DK (tr, c, br); **282:** Beth Chatto (br), Roger Smith/DK (c, bl); **283**: Lorna Rose (br), Roger Smith/DK (bc); **285**: Roger Smith/DK (c, bcl, cbl); **286**: Roger Smith/DK (bcl, bcr, cbl); **287**: Lorna Rose (br); **289**: Roger Smith/DK (cl); **290**: Roger Smith/DK (br, bcr); **291**: Roger Smith/DK (bl); **292**: Merebrook Online (www.pondplants.co.uk)/Roger Kings (crb); **293**: C. Andrew Henley (bcr, cal, tcl), Merebrook Online (www.pondplants.co.uk)/Roger Kings (tl, tr, clb); **294**: C. Andrew Henley (bc), Juliette Wade (br), Roger Smith/DK (tc); **295**: Dave Watts (br); **296**: Andrew Lawson (bcl); **297**: Global Book Publishing (l)Roger Smith/DK (bc); **298**: Roger Smith/DK (tr, c, bl); **299**: Roger Smith/DK (tc, car); **301**: Garden World Images (br), Roger Smith/DK (clb, cal); **302**: Garden and Wildlife Matters (tl), Roger Smith/DK (bc); **303**: Roger Smith/DK (tr); **305**: Garden World Images (l), Roger Smith/DK (c); **306**: Oasis Australia (bl), Roger Smith/DK (bl, bcl); **307**: Jennifer Wilkinson (bl); **309**: Roger Smith/DK (bc); **310**: Roger Smith/DK (bc); **311**: Oasis Australia (bl); **312**: Oasis Australia (bl), Ivy Hansen (br); **313**: Barnsley House, Nr Cirencester (clb), Juliette Wade (tr), Roger Smith/DK (tl); **314**: Roger Smith/DK (br); **315**: Roger Smith/DK (br); **316**: Roger Smith/DK (bc); **317**: Roger Smith/DK (tr, bc, br); **318**: Roger Smith/DK (tr); **319**: Roger Smith/DK (tl, bl); **320**: Lorna Rose (bl); **321**: Lorna Rose (bl), Roger Smith/DK (bc, br); **322**: C. Andrew Henley (bl), Garden World Images (br); **323**: Garden World Images (bcr), Roger Smith/DK (bc); **324**: Roger Smith/DK (tr, br); **325**: Roger Smith/DK (bl); **327**: Lorna Rose (bl); **328**: Roger Smith/DK (bl); **329**: Mr Fothergill's Seeds (bc), Photos Horticultural (bl), Roger Smith/DK (crb, br); **330**: John Fielding (tc), Roger Smith/DK (bc); **331**: Photos Horticultural (bcr); **332**: Roger Smith/DK (tc, r); **333**: Roger Smith/DK (br); **335**: Photos Horticultural (tl), Roger Smith/DK (ctl, tr, tcr); **337**: Oasis Australia (br), Roger Smith/DK (bcr); **338**: Roger Smith/DK (tr, bc); **339**: Oasis Australia (br), Roger Smith/DK (c); **341**: Roger Smith/DK (tr, br); **343**: Roger Smith/DK (cr); **344**: Lorna Rose (bl); **345**: Roger Smith/DK (bc); **347**: Lorna Rose (bl), Roger Smith/DK (bc); **348**: Lorna Rose (bl) **349**: Australian National Botanical Gardens (bc), Roger Smith (br); **350**: Roger Smith/DK (tr, bl, bc, br); **351**: Roger Smith/DK (bl); **352**: Roger Smith/DK (bl, tc); **353**: Lorna Rose (br), Roger Smith/DK (r); **354**: Roger Smith/DK (bc, br); **355**: Lorna Rose (bc); **356-357**: Roger Smith/DK; **358**: Clive Nichols/Preen Manor, Shropshire (c); **359**: Christine M. Douglas (cl, c), Roger Smith/DK (cr, b); **360**: Roger Smith/DK (tr); **361**: Lorna Rose (tr), John Fielding (br); **362**: Ivy Hansen (br); **363**: Leigh Clapp (br), Roger Smith/DK (bl, bc, br); **364**: Global Book Publishing (bl), Roger Smith/DK (bl); **365**: Australian National Botanical Gardens (bc), Christine M. Douglas (br), Roger Smith/DK (bl); **368**: Steve Wooster (br); **369**: Trish Gant (cl), Roger Smith/DK (bc); **370**: Lorna Rose (br), Roger Smith/DK (tc, bl); **376**: Fran Malley (cl, br); **377**: Gary Ombler (cr); **385**: Trish Gant; **393**: Oasis Australia (tr); **397**: Global Book Publishing (ctr) **398**: Peter Anderson (tc); **400**: Photographer: Steven Wooster; "Flow Glow" garden for Chelsea Flower Show 2002 by Rebecca Phillips, Maria Ornberg and Rebecca Heard; **Endpapers**: Roger Smith/DK.

acknowledgments

Author's acknowledgments
Although my name sits on the cover of this book, writing a book is very much a team effort, and I wish to express my heartfelt thanks to all of the people involved. Firstly, I must thank David Lamb, Annelise Evans, Anna Kruger, Lee Griffiths, Alison Donovan, Letitia Luff, Louise Abbott and Pamela Brown. I thank all of them for their professionalism and patience, and for keeping me on the right track.

I also wish to thank the editorial team of Joanna Chisholm, Helen Fewster, Candida Frith-Macdonald, Diana Galligan, Gail Griffiths, Jonathan Hilton, Andrea Loom, Carole McGlynn, Simon Maughan, Christine Morley, Jane Simmonds, Victoria Willan. Also special thanks to the RHS editorial team.

May I also thank the botanists at the RHS Garden, Wisley, for their generous help in providing information on some plants. I am sure they got tired of my incessant phone calls. And my thanks also to all the nurseries which I contacted for information on plants.

Finally, to anyone not mentioned, my apologies and sincere thanks.

Publishers' acknowledgments
Dorling Kindersley would like to thank Susanne Mitchell, Barbara Haynes, and Simon Maughan at the Royal Horticultural Society, Vincent Square for their time and assistance.

Editor for the RHS
Barbara Haynes

Illustrations
Karin Gavin and Gill Tomblin

Editorial assistance
Joanna Chisholm, Helen Fewster, Kate Daniel, Diana Galligan, Gail Griffiths, Jonathan Hilton, Jean Kinget, Andrea Loom, Carole McGlynn, Simon Maughan, Christine Morley, Jane Simmonds, Naomi Stallard, Andy Whyte, Victoria Willan

Additional picture research
Neale Chamberlain, Archie Clapton, Romaine Werblow